CEDAR MILL COMM LIBRARY
12505 NW CORNELL RD
PORTLAND, OR 97229
(503) 644-0043

D0497808

WITHDRAWN
CEDAR MILL LIBRARY

THE DIARIES OF
SOFIA TOLSTOY

THE DIARIES OF
SOFIA TOLSTOY

Translated by Cathy Porter

HARPER PERENNIAL

NEW YORK • LONDON • TORONTO • SYDNEY • NEW DELHI • AUCKLAND

HARPER ● PERENNIAL

All the pictures in this volume are reprinted with permission or presumed to be in the public domain. Every effort has been made to ascertain and acknowledge their copyright status, but should there have been any unwitting oversight on our part, we would be happy to rectify the error in subsequent printings.

Originally published in a different form in Russian in 1978 by Khudozhestvennaya Literatura, Moscow.

First published in a different form in the United Kingdom in 1985 by Jonathan Cape Ltd.

First published in this revised and abridged edition in the United Kingdom in 2009 by Alma Books.

THE DIARIES OF SOFIA TOLSTOY. Copyright © The State Museum of Leo Tolstoy. English language translation and Introduction © 1985, 2009 by Cathy Porter. Foreword © 2009 by Doris Lessing. All rights reserved. Printed in the United States of America. No part of this book may be used or reproduced in any manner whatsoever without written permission except in the case of brief quotations embodied in critical articles and reviews. For information address HarperCollins Publishers, 10 East 53rd Street, New York, NY 10022.

HarperCollins books may be purchased for educational, business, or sales promotional use. For information please write: Special Markets Department, HarperCollins Publishers, 10 East 53rd Street, New York, NY 10022.

FIRST U.S. EDITION

Library of Congress Cataloging-in-Publication Data is available upon request.

ISBN 978-0-06-199741-9

10 11 12 13 14 RRD 10 9 8 7 6 5 4 3 2 1

Contents

Foreword

by Doris Lessing

It makes me laugh to read my diary. What a lot of contradictions – as though I were the unhappiest of women! But who could be happier? Could any marriage be more happy and harmonious than ours? When I am alone in my room I sometimes laugh for joy and cross myself and pray to God for many, many more years of happiness. I always write my diary when we quarrel...

Sofia Tolstoy wrote the above in 1868, after six years of marriage. Many of her later diary entries also seem to have been written after quarrels.

This collection of Sofia's diary entries is witness not only to her thoughts, but also to public events and to Lev Tolstoy's work – in the period covered by the collection, he wrote *War and Peace*, *Anna Karenina* and many other books. At the same time, we see the hard work of Sofia: she is an involved mother, though there are nursemaids and all kinds of help. She copies, and copies again, her husband's work.

...why am I not happy? Is it my fault? I know all the reasons for my spiritual suffering: firstly it grieves me that my children are not as happy as I would wish. And then I am actually very lonely. My husband is not my friend: he has been my passionate lover at times, especially as he grows older, but all my life I have felt lonely with him. He doesn't go for walks with me, he prefers to ponder in solitude over his writing. He has never taken any interest in my children, for he finds this difficult and dull.

Sofia longs for new landscapes, intellectual development, art, contact with people: "To each his fate. Mine was to be the auxiliary to my husband..."

When the Tolstoys were first married, they read each other's diaries, as a part of their plan to preserve perfect intimacy between them, but later they might easily create two diaries, one for the other to read, one to remain private.

Sofia had thirteen children with Lev. Some of them died while still babies – one little boy in particular, Vanechka, who was adored by both parents. In *War and Peace,* Tolstoy writes painfully about the sufferings of parents who know how easily some small illness may snatch away their children.

Like most women at the time, Sofia was at the mercy of her reproductive system – the advent of the pill was still almost a century away.

There is an interesting episode in *Anna Karenina* relating to this predicament of nineteenth-century women. Anna is in exile from society due to her adultery, so she is staying in the country. She is visited by Dolly, her sister-in-law. Anna tells Dolly about the birth-control methods of the time. Dolly reacts to the information not with delight, as Anna had expected, but with revulsion – the idea of women refusing to bear children, their traditional role in life, is simply unacceptable to her. On her way back from Anna, Dolly hears a peasant woman giving thanks to God, who has rescued her by "taking" one of her children, leaving more food for the rest. Dolly is sorry for the peasant, but not shocked. This episode illustrates women's views towards contraception at the time – Anna, the one person who accepts its use, is placed outside spheres of acceptable social behaviour, while Dolly, representing social norms, is shocked at the very idea; however, she is not shocked by the peasant woman's more traditional means of birth control. In another episode in the novel, Dolly waits for a visit from her husband Stepan, which is likely to leave her pregnant, and even more worried about money than she already is. "What a scamp," she muses about Stepan. In this, we see how accepted the burdens of childbirth were for women at the time.

Another factor in the Tolstoys' marital circumstances which proved difficult for Sofia – as it emerges from her diaries – was Lev's relationship with Vladimir Grigorevich Chertkov. Chertkov was Lev's secretary. He became one of Lev's closest friends and confidants, and the founder of "Tolstoyanism" – the school of thought of those who followed Tolstoy's religious views. He was also a singularly unpleasant version of Lev himself. Lev became in thrall to Chertkov. Chertkov loathed Sofia, intriguing against her in every way he could.

Tolstoy once said that he had been more in love with men than he had ever been with women. *The Kreutzer Sonata*, which poor Sofia had to copy, though she hated it, seems to me a classic description of male homosexuality. There was a great scandal over this novel, which describes the murder of a supposed lover by the husband.

In defending this novel, which he did in another treatise, Tolstoy returned to his ways of describing real women as being like doves, pure and innocent. Had he ever met any real women? When it comes to the figure of Tolstoy himself, he is a sea of contradictions. He was an ideologue, he preached at people, he was always in the right, and yet he took his stand on a number of different and sometimes opposing platforms.

He was also a bad husband, inconsiderate sexually, and in other ways. For instance, he insisted on his poor wife breastfeeding the infants, though her nipples cracked and it was painful for her. She wanted to use wet nurses. The truth was, the great Tolstoy was a bit of a monster.

Sofia Tolstoy must have divided her later years into "before Chertkov" and "after Chertkov". We have had plenty of opportunities to study the activities of ideologues, but Vladimir Chertkov was a newish phenomenon, and probably Sofia's inability to cope with this man was partly because of the difficulty in categorizing him: was he religious? – oh yes, dedicated to the good, a fanatic in fact. But Chertkov wanted just one thing – to dominate Tolstoy, and in this he succeeded. And there was not only Chertkov, but all the fans who turned up from everywhere in the world, expecting to be housed, fed and advised by the Master. They turned servants out of their beds, slept in the corridors, were under everyone's feet.

Sofia was not well: it was said then, and is still said now, that she was demented. I am not surprised if she was. Tolstoy was threatening to leave her, leave the family, which meant to be with Chertkov. Sofia rushed out, distraught, into a pond. They saved her. "I want to leave the dreadful agony of this life... I can see no hope, even if L.N. does at some point return..."

In the end the whole world watched as Tolstoy fled his home for the little house near the railway where he died. Sofia was forbidden to go to her dying husband by Chertkov until the very last moment.

Sofia Tolstoy lived for many long years as Tolstoy's widow. She sometimes went to visit his grave, where she begged forgiveness from him for her failings.

The diary entries in these pages bear witness to a remarkable life: the life of an exceptional woman, married to one of the most exceptional men of the time, with all her passions and difficulties laid bare. This is a book which is interesting for what it says about the predicament of women in the past, and how that compares to their present circumstances. While reading it, I was so enthralled that

I found myself dreaming about Sofia, about speaking to her myself, desperately wanting to reach out to her and offer her words of comfort for her pain. Perhaps, hopefully, this record of her struggles will be a comfort and inspiration to present and future generations.

Introduction

by Cathy Porter

Sofia Andreevna Tolstoy started keeping a diary at the age of sixteen. But it was two years later, in 1862, shortly before her marriage to the great writer, that she embarked in earnest on the diaries she would keep until just a month before her death in 1919, at the age of seventy-five. In this new edited version of their first complete English translation, she gives us a candid and detailed chronicle of the daily events of family life: conversations and card games, walks and picnics, musical evenings and readings aloud, birthdays and Christmases; the births, deaths, marriages, illnesses and love affairs of her thirteen children, her numerous grandchildren and her many relatives and friends; friendships and quarrels with some of Russia's best-known writers, musicians and politicians; and the comings and goings of the countless Tolstoyan "disciples" who frequented the Tolstoys' homes in Yasnaya Polyana and Moscow. She records the state of the writer's stomach and the progress of his work, and she describes the fierce and painful arguments that would eventually divide the couple for ever. All this is in the foreground. In the distant and muted background are some of the most turbulent events of Russian history; the social and political upheavals that marked the transition from feudal to industrial Russia; three major international wars, three revolutions and the post-1917 Civil War.

But it is as Countess Tolstoy's own life story, the story of one woman's private experience, that these diaries are so valuable and so very moving. Half a million words long, they are her best friend, her life's work and the counterpart to her life and marriage.

Indeed throughout the Tolstoys' forty-eight-year marriage diaries were the very currency of their relationship, and they wrote them in order that the other should read them. In the early days she tried desperately to hide her troubled moods from him, recording them instead in her diary. When he expected her to merge with him and become his shadow, she stood out for her independence – in her diary. When he insisted on revealing to her all the ghosts of his past, demanding "truth" and confessions from her at every turn, she would keep silent and record her wretchedness in her diary, and communicate it to him in this way. And as time went on, and communication between them became more difficult, it was increasingly to her diary that she confided her worst fears, her deepest anxieties and her tormented desires for revenge – in the hope that he might see them there. The happy periods – and there were many of them – were rarely recorded.

In 1847, at the age of nineteen, Count Lev Nikolaevich Tolstoy became master of the 4,000-acre estate of Yasnaya Polyana and the 330 serfs living on it. He was a restless and changeable young man. An enthusiastic maker and breaker of good resolutions, he dreamt of social equality while enjoying to the full his aristocratic privileges ("serfdom is an evil, but a very pleasant one!"). Yearning for purity yet craving fame and women, he was constantly lured from his peaceful country existence with his beloved Aunt Tatyana to the brothels and gypsy cabarets of Moscow and Tula, where he would drink, gamble and sow his wild oats.

At the age of twenty-three he decided it was time he brought some order to this aimless life and, kissing his aunt goodbye, he moved to Moscow. His purpose there, spelt out in his diary, was: 1) to gamble, 2) to find a position and 3) to marry. The first two resolutions he pursued enthusiastically enough. As for the third, although he did for a while entertain dreams of the woman he would marry, and fell rapidly in and out of love in search of a wife, his hunger for gypsy and peasant women soon got the better of him and after a few months he gave up Moscow as a bad job and left with the army for the Caucasus.

There it was that he started to write. By the time he left to serve in the Crimean War, his *Childhood*, *Boyhood* and *Youth* had been published, and his reputation as a writer was assured. His experiences as a cavalry officer during the bloody siege of Sevastopol provided yet more inspiration, and by the time he returned to Moscow in 1856 his name as the author of the *Sevastopol Tales* had preceded him.

But now it was the simple peasant life he wanted. On his return to Yasnaya Polyana he wore a peasant shirt, let his beard grow, abandoned writing for the plough and opened a school for peasant children based on Rousseauesque principles. He also fell deeply in love with a peasant woman named Axinya, who in the summer of 1858 gave birth to their son, Timofei. He longed increasingly now for a respectable wife to save him from sin. "I must get married this year or never!" he wrote in his diary on New Year's Day, 1859. "A wife! A wife at any price! A family and children!" he wrote the following year. But he was still a bachelor when in the summer of 1862 he fled to Moscow.

By then he was thirty-four. His books had made him famous, he had travelled widely in Russia and Europe and he was more than ready to settle down. He had no one particularly in mind, but he was determined to marry someone of his own aristocratic class, and to choose a young girl. Property-owner, womanizer, hunter and gambler, he was a rake ready to be reformed.

Sofia Behrs was eighteen at the time, the daughter of his old childhood friend Lyubov Behrs, in whose crowded, hospitable apartment in the Kremlin Tolstoy was a regular visitor. Lyubov was the daughter of an illegal marriage, and though she was of an ancient aristocratic family her name had been changed at birth. At the age of sixteen she had married Andrei Evstafovich Behrs, a distinguished doctor eighteen years her senior, who was attached to the court. (Although as the grandson of a German military instructor who had settled in Russia in the eighteenth century, he was definitely not of the aristocracy, and the Russian aristocracy tended anyway to look down on the medical profession.)

Between 1843 and 1861 Lyubov Behrs bore eight children, three of them girls: Liza, her eldest child, clever and rather distant, Sofia, a year younger, poetic and graceful, and Tanya, a lively laughing tomboy. The Behrs watched strictly over their daughters, but they had fairly progressive ideas on girls' education, and they arranged for them to take lessons in foreign languages and literature, music, painting and dancing, so that by the time she was seventeen Sofia had received her teacher's certificate. She and her sisters were also taught to keep accounts, make dresses and sew and cook, in preparation for marriage – for it was on this that all three girls' thoughts were focused. And in 1862 all three of them were of marriageable age.

Tolstoy, who had never had any proper family life of his own, was drawn again and again to the Behrses' warm and unaffected family circle, and he would later use them as his model for the Rostovs in *War and Peace*. As for the girls, he found them all enchanting. But by the time he left Moscow that summer for his estate he knew that Sofia was the one he wanted. They were in many ways very similar: impetuous, changeable, wildly jealous, romantic, high-minded and passionate. And they both idealized family life. When Tolstoy met Sofia again later that summer, he had become the centre of her thoughts, and – though she was barely old enough to know what she wanted – the wedding was fixed for 23rd September.

But not before he had insisted (with her parents' permission) on showing her his bachelor diaries (and insisting that she keep one too). Sofia was a very childish eighteen-year-old who, although her family had had its share of scandals, had led an extremely sheltered life, and what she read shattered her. For his diaries were one long catalogue of lurid, guilt-racked confessions: of casual flirtations with society women, loveless copulations with peasants, his passionate affair with Axinya, who now lived on his estate with their son, professions of homosexual love, disgusted diatribes against women, himself and the world in general – not to mention a desperate round of gambling sessions and drunken orgies. Sofia had dreamt of the man she would love as "completely whole, new, *pure*". She never forgave him for thus shattering her dreams and assaulting her innocence, and forty-seven years later she was still referring bitterly to Axinya.

Youthful promiscuity and gambling were not in fact so uncommon amongst young Russian aristocrats, but even so Tolstoy and his family had a reputation for fast living. His brother Dmitry had bought a prostitute from a brothel and died in her arms at the age of twenty-nine. His brother Sergei lived with a gypsy woman by whom he had eleven children. And his sister Maria left her despotic husband and lived in sin with a Swedish count, by whom she had a daughter. Sofia's family did not live this way – and Tolstoy would always apply a double standard when dealing with his wife and with the world at large (including his own family). She could never really forget his sordid, loveless past, and was deeply scarred by the episode, to which she would refer again and again in her diaries.

At their magnificent wedding in the Kremlin, she couldn't stop weeping for the family she was leaving. She wept all the way to her new home. And she wept when, crushed and terrified by Tolstoy's clumsy attempts to embrace her, they finally arrived at Yasnaya Polyana, where she would spend the next fifty-seven years of her life.

Waiting for them on the steps of the large white-painted wooden house were Tolstoy's old aunt, Tatyana Ergolskaya, holding an icon of the Holy Virgin, and his brother Sergei, bearing the traditional welcome of bread and salt. Sofia bowed to the ground, embraced her relatives and kissed the icon. (She would be guided to the end of her life by the simple rituals of the Russian Orthodox Church.) Then Aunt Tatyana handed her new mistress the keys of the house, and these she hung on her waist and carried there until the day she died.

The house, cold, spartanly furnished and infested with rats and mice, had been Tolstoy's home all his life. There was a large farm, with cattle, sheep, pigs and bees, and until the 1880s Tolstoy took a keen interest in its management. But he was not a successful farmer. The pigs kept dying of hunger, the sheep proved unprofitable and the cows were thin and didn't give enough milk. The only profit came from the apple orchards, but even so the estate was always running at a loss. Yasnaya Polyana's greatest asset was its forests ("my daughters' dowry", Sofia would call them), but these too were neglected. Tolstoy's other estate, in Nikolskoe, was even more dilapidated and even more forested, and in these forests, inhabited only by wolves and birds, Tolstoy loved to hunt, for until the 1880s he was a passionate sportsman.

Sofia was determined to like her new home and to be a good wife. She took over the accounts, organized the housekeeping and marshalled the small army of dependants and domestics living there who comprised her new family. There was Aunt Tatyana, with her personal maid and companion Natalya Petrovna; there was Maria Arbuzova, Tolstoy's old nanny, with her two sons, one of whom was Tolstoy's personal servant; there was Agafya Mikhailovna, who had been Tolstoy's grandmother's maid and was now the "dog's governess". There was Nikolai the cook, Pelageya the laundress, and many, many others who came and went, and lived either in the house or in the village of Yasnaya Polyana.

Tolstoy's young bride was a stern mistress. Tolstoy never lost his temper with the servants; she was constantly doing so, for she lacked his authority. She was also desperately worried he would resume his old passion for teaching the peasants. She thought it improper for a count to associate so closely with the common people, and feared they might take him from her. Had his diaries not revealed to her just how ruthlessly he had exercised his power over the women on his estate?

But of course she didn't talk to him of such things, and remained for many weeks very much in awe of her new husband, always addressing him in the formal "you". She supervised all the domestic work. She sewed everything, including his trousers and jackets. She attended to all the peasants' medical needs (for which she had quite a talent). She was supported, to be sure, by a large staff of servants, but her upbringing had taught her to be self-reliant, and she washed, boiled, gardened, pickled and sewed all day in the eager desire to serve her husband.

The revelations in his diaries had badly shaken her sexual confidence. She yearned for tenderness and was shocked by his coarseness, hurt by his outbursts of passion followed by coldness and withdrawal. But she submitted uncomplainingly to his fierce embraces. Since he believed sexual intercourse should be for purely procreative purposes, they used no form of contraception. She became pregnant almost immediately, and her diary for this first year of their marriage established the regular cycle of pregnancies and births that would fill her life. (She bore thirteen children in all, of whom nine lived.) Lev Tolstoy, who held that sex during pregnancy was "both swinish and unnatural", kept out of her way as much as possible at these times, and she grew increasingly desperate.

Her mother, uncomplainingly bearing her eight children and tending her home, had provided her with an excellent model of the selfless role women were traditionally expected to play in marriage. Orthodox religion had for centuries endowed women with this special capacity for self-sacrifice, and Sofia would throughout her life look to the Church, with its emphasis on suffering, selflessness and humility, to give dignity to her wifely role. But by the mid-1860s attitudes to women and the family were already undergoing a profound change, and Sofia too in this first year of marriage felt the stirrings of change in her.

Alexander II's emancipation of the serfs in 1861 had spelt the end of the old feudal Russia and the orthodox religious values underpinning it, and the start of a process that would affect every area of people's lives. Thousands of women, forced to make themselves financially independent of husbands and fathers, left their families for good to find work and education in the cities. Conservative men jeered at them as "nihilists", but among the men of the intelligentsia there was now a new and serious commitment to treat women as equals and support their desire for education and autonomy. Debates raged about women's social role and the future of marriage and the family. More radical women would go so far as to reject love and marriage altogether, since to them marriage meant inevitably being trapped in endless domestic chores, while sexual relations, in the absence of reliable contraception, led to endless pregnancies. But even respectably married women were now claiming that husband and children were no longer enough to fill their lives, and that only through work could they find the emotional and economic independence they longed for. The "woman" question was the burning issue of the day, and for Sofia it meant the discovery of a wholly unexpected dissatisfaction with her new life. Despite her endless labours for Tolstoy, toiling in the house and caring for him body and soul, she felt she was merely his toy. "If I don't interest him, if he sees me as a doll, merely his *wife*, not a human being, then I will not and cannot live like that," she writes in her diary. "I am to gratify his pleasure and nurse his child, I am a piece of household furniture, I am a *woman*." She longed to find her own interests outside the house and, feeling increasingly inadequate, she alternately toyed with thoughts of suicide and nursed murderous feelings for Axinya and her son. Pregnant and wretched, she was even jealous of Tolstoy's feelings for her beloved younger sister Tanya.

But he, for all his extraordinary sensitivity to the women in his novels, had no apparent desire to understand his wife's suffering. And for all his optimistic faith in the virtues of equality, simplicity and hard work, he would to the end of his days use his enormous moral authority in Russia to preach a particularly savage kind of Christian asceticism, which equated sexuality with godlessness and proclaimed that women existed merely to arouse the beast in men and frustrate it. In countless interviews, articles and plays he would make abundantly clear his view of women's weakness, their inferiority and moral subordination to men, and would indulge in countless ironic, contemptuous or frivolous comments on the "woman question". These anti-feminist views, many of which Sofia records in her diary, became more violently and lengthily argued as time went on, and help to explain the early tensions between the couple, which would remain remarkably constant throughout their long life together.

On 28th June 1863, Sofia gave birth prematurely to their son Sergei, a sickly baby who had difficulty feeding. Her nipples grew inflamed and she longed to hire a wet nurse, but Tolstoy, who held advanced views on the matter, wouldn't hear of it: not to breastfeed was disgusting and unnatural, to hire a wet nurse to do so was obscene. Besides, a woman who abandoned her maternal duties so lightly would surely have no qualms about abandoning her wifely duties. Terrified of losing his love, she struggled in agony until eventually ordered by the doctor to stop, and Fillip the coachman's wife was asked to help out. (The woman's son, Sergei's "milk brother", was to be his lifelong friend.)

Tolstoy angrily withdrew from her and wrote a five-act comedy called *The Infected Family*, about a woman who couldn't breastfeed her baby because she was an "unnatural, emancipated woman" and a "nihilist". (Thankfully, he couldn't persuade the Maly Theatre in Moscow to put it on, and soon dropped it.) He grew increasingly possessive towards Sofia, and obsessed by the idea of marital chastity. He was terrified by the new egalitarian attitudes to women – taken by some to their logical conclusion of demanding for women an equal right to commit adultery. He thought of the great writer Alexander Herzen, whose wife had claimed her right to fall in love with a poet, and he concluded that Herzen's tragedy was that he had lightheartedly betrayed his wife with housemaids and prostitutes, and the more liberated sexual attitudes of the 1860s had caught up with him.

Tolstoy's past too was haunting him, and he became wildly jealous. Not that he had any reason to be, of course: Sofia had dedicated her life to him, and needed him as much as he needed her to care for him and create the family he had never had. But perhaps more importantly, she represented for him a moral purity he felt he had long ago lost, or had never had, which he desperately needed for his own moral regeneration. And despite everything, relations between them began to improve. For that autumn he started writing *War and Peace*, and she was able to devote herself entirely to him.

She assumed responsibility for everything that concerned his everyday life, supervising his diet, ensuring he wasn't disturbed while he sat hour after hour in his study, gladly going without sleep or food to care for him whenever he was ill. She assumed all responsibility for the servants, the housekeeping and the accounts, and she arranged and catalogued the books in their large library.

These were just some of her responsibilities over the next forty-five years. But the task she cherished most throughout these years (helped later by her daughters and Tolstoy's secretaries) was copying out his voluminous writings. Every night after the baby had been put to bed, she would sit at her desk until the small hours, copying out his day's writing in her fine hand, telepathically deciphering (sometimes with the aid of a magnifying glass) the scribble that only she could read, straining her eyes to the point of damaging her sight. Every morning she would place the fair copy, along with fresh sheets of writing paper, on Tolstoy's desk. And back they would come to her every evening to be recopied, black with corrections, swarming with marginal notes, a chaos of crossings-out, balloons and footnotes. In the six years he was writing *War and Peace* she would copy some passages over and over again. (Her son Ilya later wrote that she had copied parts of it seven times.) Yet she rarely knocked at his door to ask for help, and never complained of fatigue.

They were happy together. The quarrels between them became less frequent, her diary entries rare. She felt she was not just his secretary but his colleague and confidante, for he always asked her advice and deeply respected her judgement. Even when he was away a couple of days he would write her daily letters, and only when he was writing his fiction did he forget her. As for her, his writing captured her childhood experiences, her own thoughts and words, and as she copied she relived her past. "Nothing touches me so deeply as his ideas, his genius," she wrote in her diary. And when their friend the writer Vladimir Sollogub praised her as the "nursemaid of [Tolstoy's] talent", she was humbly grateful for the compliment.

In the spring of 1864 she became pregnant again. She was twenty years old, strong, healthy (she thought nothing of falling out of a carriage when four months pregnant), and by all accounts extremely attractive. And when her second child Tanya was born that October she was delighted to be able to feed her herself.

Between 1866 and 1869 she gave birth to two more children: Ilya and Lyova, healthy boys, and a sickly girl called Maria (Masha) in 1871. In those years family life was very happy. Everyone commented on what an exceptionally united couple they were. "Sonya couldn't look for greater happiness," wrote Tolstoy's niece Varya in her diary in 1864. "Sonya and Lyova were an exemplary couple. Such couples were rare; all one ever hears about these days is husbands leaving their wives or wives divorcing their husbands." And Sofia's brother Stepan wrote in his memoirs: "The mutual love and understanding between them has always been my ideal and model of marital happiness." Their relationship was charged with passion. And although his was a passion of the flesh, while hers was a passion of the spirit, and for babies, the strength of their feelings for each other remained undiminished (though often horribly distorted) throughout their marriage.

This was surely the source of her remarkable energy. She organized everything, often ignoring his instructions. Gardening, painting, bottling, upholstering, playing the piano, copying – she was always busy. Her son Sergei later recalled a certain lack of spontaneous gaiety about her: she had always found it hard to be happy, even as a young girl. "For me 'aimer' never meant playing with feelings," she wrote before her marriage. "Both then and later on it was something closer to suffering." And shortly after her marriage she wrote: "Love is hard – when you love it takes your breath away, you lay down your life and soul for it, and it's with you as long as you live." She rarely laughed or enjoyed jokes, and as a deeply religious woman she tended to see the business of loving and caring for her husband and children as bound up with inevitable sacrifice. Perhaps this explains why the children always addressed her in the formal "you", even though she was always there to scold or reassure them, whereas their father, who was much more distant and inaccessible, was always the informal "thou".

She made herself responsible for their education too, teaching them Russian grammar, French, history, geography, painting and music. (There was an English governess to teach them English, while their father taught them Russian literature and arithmetic.)

To escape from the demands on her she would withdraw into the "private inner world" of her diary. And when they quarrelled, writing it would open up for her a "peaceful, poetic existence, free of excitements and the material things of the so-called physical world; a life of prayer, holy thoughts, dreams of self-perfection, and a quiet love that has been trampled underfoot".

The year 1871 was not a good one. The couple's second daughter Maria was born prematurely on 12th February, and she almost died of puerperal fever. (She never really felt much warmth for her daughter, and throughout Maria's life there was constant tension between her and her mother.) As Sofia, weak and thin, her head shaved, struggled back to life, Tolstoy was haunted increasingly by fears of death. Two years earlier he had finished *War and Peace*, and after this mighty labour he felt dazed and drained. Fearing he might have consumption, he gave up all idea of writing, and in the summer of 1871 he set off south to Samara (now Kuibyshev) with Sofia's younger brother Stepan. There they lived a simple life on the steppes in a felt Bashkiri tent, and drank health-giving fermented mare's milk (koumiss). Tolstoy worshipped the romantic nomadic Bashkirs, he loved the vast open steppes, and he decided on impulse to buy an estate there. In the summer of 1873 he persuaded Sofia to travel south with the children to stay in their new property. First they travelled 300 miles to Nizhny Novgorod (now Gorky), then another 500 to Samara, and thence another 120 miles by carriage to their new property.

Sofia had just given birth to her sixth child, Petya, and was still feeding him. She and the younger children settled into the main house, which was more like a large peasant hut, with a leaking roof, smoking fireplace and swarming flies, while Tolstoy and Stepan camped out in the felt tent they had bought, and the boys and their tutor lived in the shed. Tolstoy loved this primitive life, and his depression melted away, but Sofia didn't enjoy herself, and was resentful that he had bought the estate without asking her.

Between 1873 and 1876 she gave birth to three babies who died.

In November 1873, one-year-old Petya was carried off by the croup. "The darling, I loved him too much!" wrote Sofia, wild with grief. "He was buried yesterday. What emptiness!" Tolstoy's grief was more restrained, and his main desire seemed to be to escape from his wife and her weeping. In April 1874, the couple's sixth baby, Nikolai, was born, but ten months later he died in agony of meningitis. In 1875, the children all fell ill with whooping cough, and Sofia, pregnant yet again, came down with peritonitis, was prescribed quinine and gave birth prematurely in November to a baby girl called Valya, who died immediately afterwards. Her diary entries dwindle to almost nothing.

Tolstoy had just started work on a new novel, *Anna Karenina*, and she was able to bury her grief in devotedly copying out his day's writing for him again. It was in 1877, as *Anna Karenina* was nearing completion, that his depressions became more frequent and alarming. He was prone to violent rages against her and the world, pursued by fears of death and feelings of guilt, racked by a sense of his own worthlessness. Surrounded by poverty and wretchedness on all sides, he continued to be served and pampered by the peasants (and, of course, his wife). The only solution, he decided, was to find some link, through religion, to the peasants, to accept everything, rites, miracles and all that his reason repudiated, and humbly to abide by the Church's teachings.

The consequences of his long and painful "conversion" were both deeply impressive and utterly intolerable; for Sofia it was a disaster. He became increasingly doctrinaire in his religious views, railing against those who smoked, hunted and ate meat (though continuing to do so himself), and preaching the virtues of living by one's own labour (though still waited on hand and foot by his wife and servants). His philosophy was changing – and he was requiring Sofia to change too – yet his life remained very much the same, and his inability to live by his principles made him acutely depressed, while his inability to impose these principles on his wife and children spelt tragedy to his family.

He was unable to give her any advice as to how she might adapt to his change of course. And when he finally renounced property, sexuality and worldly affairs, his publishers, his children and the estate, he merely made her take responsibility for it all. She was at first genuinely puzzled by his change of heart, and demanded guidance as to how far she should simplify the housekeeping and limit expenses. What about the children's education? And the servants? And his copyright money? But he gave her no clear answers, merely demanding repeatedly that she follow his example, give away his money and abandon material concerns. His disregard for her feelings threw her into despair: "I have been discarded like a useless object. Impossible, undefined sacrifices are demanded of me, in my life and in my family, and I am expected to renounce everything..."

But perhaps the greatest blow was when he renounced the creative writing she had so loved, and turned instead to moral tracts, pamphlets and articles attacking the hypocrisy of the Church and preaching against those who lived in luxury off the labour of the peasants. In the late 1870s, as revolutionaries urged the peasants to rise against their masters, Tolstoy was claimed as their spokesman, and several of his more outspoken works, banned by the Tsar and circulated underground, aroused enormous interest. Increasing numbers of his visitors were uncompromising opponents of tsarist society – Yuriev, a left-wing slavophile, Fyodorov, an ascetic and mystic, Syutaev, a self-educated peasant who refused to pay his taxes, and many, many more. Bohemians, pacifists and revolutionaries, visionaries, students and eccentrics, peasants, artisans and factory workers, the disaffected and the disinherited, they arrived in their hundreds to meet the great writer and prophet; and they stayed and stayed. Sofia hated these "dark ones", as she called them, who took him away from her and filled the house day and night, creating extra work and worries for her; they had to be entertained, reassured, paid or thrown out; they surrounded Tolstoy with an unpleasantly worshipful atmosphere; and they brought the whole family to the unwelcome attention of the police. She was outraged, shocked to her conservative soul and deeply frightened.

But mainly she hated what she saw as the hypocrisy of this conversion of her husband's. He now rose early, tidied his own room, pumped his own water from the well and took it home in a barrel; he chopped wood, made his own boots and worked in the fields with the peasants. But for all his proclamations of universal love and brotherhood, she had to endure his calculated slights and insults. He refused to help her with the education of their children or the management of the estate (at which she was no more successful than he was, being opposed to any sort of technical innovation in farming, and unable to tell a good steward from a bad one). And when he gave up hunting, drinking and eating meat, this merely involved her in preparing two menus every day.

Her diaries are merciless; again and again she refers unforgivingly to his old diaries, accusing him of merely seeking fame and fortune under another name: "He would like the eyes of the world to see him on the pedestal he took such pains to erect for himself. But his diaries cast him into the filth in which he once lived, and that infuriates him."

When terrorists assassinated Tsar Alexander II in 1881, Tolstoy wrote to his heir begging him not to hang them. She was distraught, terrified that the whole family would be thrown into jail. We read her diaries now with an increasing sense that the social order supporting her hasn't long to run, and at this point she appears so tragically blind, yet so powerfully sympathetic that we long to step in, alter the course of history and save her.

In the years that followed, the discord between the two became more acute. He wrote in his diaries (which of course she read) about his loneliness in his family and his domineering wife, with her sharp tongue and her hostility to his changed philosophy of life. Sofia, tired, bewildered and pregnant yet again, retorted in hers that she could no longer do both a man's *and* a woman's work. After nineteen years in the country she was also beginning to chafe at her solitary life, and longed to visit Moscow, to be with Sergei during his first term at the university and Tanya, who was about to start an art course in the capital and had to be introduced to the social life, as well as Ilya and Lyova, now aged fifteen and twelve, who were old enough to go to secondary school. But she also wanted to enjoy herself a little, meet friends and attend some concerts. All this would cost money. And there were also now new children to consider – Andrei (born in 1877), Mikhail (in 1879) and Alexei (in 1881). And so in the autumn of 1881 a house was bought in Moscow, and thereafter the family spent the winters there.

This was the source of yet more bitter arguments. There existed for Tolstoy three types of woman: "*femme du temple*", "*femme du foyer*" and "*femme de la rue*". His wife had moved swiftly through the first two categories, and her outrageous worldly desires now clearly placed her in the third. The girl he had married had been an angel of modesty and obedience. Now that she was beginning to assert herself against him and claim her own needs, for privacy, music, her own friends – even her own sexual needs, for she was now apparently discovering some of the tormenting desires of the flesh – he turned her into the devil, everything he hated in himself, and withdrew from her, devoting himself more and more to the endless visitors who came to see him in Yasnaya Polyana and Moscow with all their religious, personal and political problems. It was to them that he complained of his tyrannical wife. But it was in his story, *The Kreutzer Sonata*, that these complaints were spelt out with their greatest cruelty and clarity, for all the world to read. Yet when the story was banned as obscene, it was Sofia who went in person to the Tsar and pleaded successfully for the ban to be revoked.

When in 1884, at the age of forty, she became pregnant for the fifteenth time, in spite of all Tolstoy's vows of chastity, her shame was so intense she tried to have the baby aborted. (The abortionist refused in horror to proceed on learning who she was.) And when she finally went into labour with the unfortunate Alexandra (Sasha), Tolstoy packed his bag after a petty quarrel and announced he was off to make a new life in America. (He returned to finish the quarrel shortly before the baby was born.) One more child followed in 1888.

Sofia was exhausted. Her diaries record her endless labours: managing the estate and the family's increasingly complicated financial affairs, copying all Tolstoy's voluminous writings, worrying constantly about his every little cough and always fearing the worst, tending him tirelessly through his frequent illnesses (she never allowed anyone else to care for him when he was ill, and only then did she forget her bitterness).

Endless domestic tasks and suffocating confinement breed a boredom as vast as the steppes, a narcotic depression for which there is no cure or release but the madness which gradually and terrifyingly comes over her.

From 1891 there is more and more talk in her diaries of nervous troubles – headaches, sleeplessness, "evil spirits". She is prey to physical symptoms – neuralgia, eye strain, stomach aches, fevers and asthma attacks. Quickened pulse-rates and heightened temperatures are obsessively recorded. And these problems are complicated by the onset of the menopause, with its hot flushes and unspecified "gynaecological problems", for which she consults specialists. She talks of suicide, and makes numerous attempts to kill herself – throwing herself in the pond, poisoning herself with opium, lying in the snow to freeze, refusing to eat.

She writes constantly in her diaries now of Tolstoy's ill-treatment of her. He writes of her too in his diaries, with some anger, but also with pity and despair, and long periods of estrangement between them alternate bewilderingly with periods of passion. Now, in her fifties, with the fear of pregnancy behind her, her physical passion awakens. Yet it is all so late, and makes her feel sad, incomplete and unworthy. "His passion dominates me too but... my whole moral being cried out against it... All my life I have dreamt spiritual dreams, aspired to a perfect union, a *spiritual* communion, not *that*."

There was still some tenderness and friendship left too, and during the disastrous harvest of 1891 the two worked together in the countryside opening canteens for the peasant victims of the famine. Yet amid the last flickerings of their love there is always the sensation of fast approaching death. Indeed fears of illness and death are always present in an atmosphere almost completely ignorant of "scientific" medicine. Her daughter Maria has seven babies die before birth, her beloved eldest daughter Tanya gives birth to three dead babies, and four of her own infants die before the age of seven. These children are frail, spiritual creatures, cherished intensely and mourned inconsolably. It is when her adored youngest son Vanechka dies in 1895 just before his seventh birthday that her spirit is finally broken and, dazed by despair, she longs only to join her dead children in the other world.

Music becomes the focus of her life. It is with its help that she regains her sanity, and through her friendship with the composer Sergei Taneev that she finds peace of mind and the strength to survive. All her thoughts and feelings become focused on her dead Vanechka and the gentle undemanding bachelor Taneev ("the man... at the centre of my disgraceful untimely madness"). Yet the relationship could never conceivably be consummated: "How much spent passion, how many tragic feelings of love pass between decent people and are *never* expressed! And these feelings are the most important of all!" Tolstoy tries furiously and helplessly to intervene against Taneev, as do her friends and her children, but she refuses to be ruled. She visits Moscow to attend concerts and meet him and his friends, she invites musicians back to the house to play, and spends hours herself at the piano.

Away from music and Taneev, despair breaks through. Her diaries, fragmented, confused, charged with emotion, turn now into a sad catalogue of female complaints – of loneliness and powerlessness, jealousy and self-pity, love rejected and work unappreciated, fears of confinement, illness and madness. Endless outpourings of emotions, moods, descriptions and reflections are all jumbled up, the poetic and the prosaic flung recklessly together with a breathless and desperate incoherence, often without so much as an "and" or "but" to help us interpret them.

While Tolstoy soars above the world she remains chained to earth by all the problems he leaves there for her to deal with – and thus she comes to represent to him everything he is trying to rid himself of: "If he is protesting against humanity as a whole, the entire existing social order, he can hardly be expected not to protest against me, a mere weak woman."

The old Tolstoy had died in 1881, he explained, leaving his property to his wife and children, and a new Tolstoy had been born. He had hoped that his family would change with him then – that was why he stayed with them – but they hadn't. So all he asked now was that the copyright on all his post-1881 works be given away. She refused. She had the estate to run and nine children to support, and no wish to line the pockets of his publishers merely for the privilege of finding work as a laundress. Yet his words always carried so much more weight than hers. ("If one were to say which of us caused the other more pain, it would be him: his weapons are so much more powerful and authoritative.")

Her diaries melt into self-pity at every turn. Her labours for him, once performed so gladly, now turn into drudgery. "Everything wears out in the end, even a mother's love." Her endless responsibilities bring her no freedom, and the lack of it becomes increasingly oppressive to her: "I am not free to *think* as I please, to *love* whom I choose, to come and go according to my own interests and intellectual pleasures... to pursue my music..." Meanwhile Tolstoy is writing in his diary: "A woman can be free only if she is a Christian. An emancipated woman who is not a Christian is a wild beast." Again, to his son Lyova, he warns: "A sound healthy woman is a wild beast." And to all three of his elder sons: "The most intelligent woman is less intelligent than the most stupid man."

Meanwhile Sofia muses on her wasted talents: "I was wondering today why there were no women writers, artists or composers of genius," she writes in 1898. "It's because all the passion... of an energetic woman is consumed by her family, love, her husband – and especially her children... When she has finished bearing and educating her children, her artistic needs awaken, but by then it's too late, for by then it's impossible to develop anything." She does not mention the main obstacle to her self-fulfilment – perhaps because even at the age of fifty-four, she still admits to feeling afraid of her husband. But Tolstoy's views on women are all too painfully familiar to her – and all too typical in tsarist Russia: "He announced... that he was against women's emancipation and so-called 'equal rights', and... that no matter what a woman did – teaching, medicine, art – she had only one real purpose in life, and that was sexual love. So whatever she might strive to achieve, all her strivings will merely crumble to ashes." Women shouldn't raise the issue of their own emancipation, he goes on, this would be unwomanly and impertinent. They shouldn't talk of women's inequality at all, in fact, but of people's inequality in general. Sofia agrees: "It's not freedom we women need, but *help*... mainly in educating our sons."

Her cries for help become more frequent, but are unheard. She is bitterly angry about his cynical views on women, which have made her suffer, and which she feels he has come by simply because he hadn't met a decent woman until he married *her*. And in her powerlessness she clings to Taneev.

Tolstoy's disciples all dislike her – particularly Vladimir Chertkov, the most persistent, unimaginative and dogmatic of them all. And it is while the conflict between the couple is at its most intense that Chertkov enters their lives again to set them against each other in earnest. His purpose is to gain Tolstoy's confidence, his copyright and his soul, and he is utterly unscrupulous. Humourless, uninventive and rude, pathologically attached to Tolstoy and pathologically hostile to his wife, his purpose has always been to divide them. As long ago as 1887 Sofia read a letter he wrote to Tolstoy "describing in joyful tones his deep spiritual communion with his wife, and commiserating with L.N. for being deprived of this joy". While Tolstoy enjoins Chertkov: "Let everyone try not to marry, and if he does, to live with his wife as brother and sister... You will object that this would mean the end of the human race?... What a great misfortune! The antediluvian animals are gone from the earth, human animals will disappear too... I have no more pity for these two-footed beasts than for the ichthyosaurus."

Chertkov manages to wheedle his diaries out of the old man, which have until then belonged unquestioningly to Sofia. Then he prevails on him to alter his will in his favour. From 1910 onwards her diaries are dominated by Chertkov's evil genius. (The more normal everyday events of her life for this year are reserved for her Daily Diaries.) Her condition worsens with every moment. Sleepless nights are followed by days blurred by opium and anxious depression, and her obsessional prying and spying drives Tolstoy yet further from her. While he weeps and suffers and rails against her, Chertkov seizes on this discord to exacerbate it: "The shadow of this crazy woman, mad with greed and wrath, hovers over our friendship," he writes to a friend. "Lev Nikolaevich has merely proved by his fortitude that it is possible to carry in one's heart a truly indestructible love: he evidently needs a cruel and ruthless warder to bind him hand and foot."

Chertkov does all he can to encourage Tolstoy to leave his wife and make a new life for himself elsewhere. And in 1910, at the age of eighty-two, this is what he does: on 28th October he leaves Yasnaya Polyana with his doctor and his youngest daughter Sasha, and boards a train heading south. When she finds him gone, Sofia throws herself into the pond. She is dragged out and taken to her bed, where she lies semi-delirious, refusing to eat. By the time she learns he is lying ill at the stationmaster's hut at the station of Astapovo, it is too late. She manages to see him only ten minutes before he dies, and there is no time for them to speak.

She lies for many months after his death in a fever, and when she resumes her Daily Diaries the entries are short and matter-of-fact. With Tolstoy's death she regains her clarity, but loses all her old wild, mad energy. She works hard to the end, copying his writings, dashing off endless articles, supervising the estate, tending and visiting the grave, entertaining the hordes of visitors who come to pay their respects to Tolstoy's widow. And to the end she resents this household drudgery, which takes her from her *real* work – of the intellect and the spirit.

In the last nine years of her life she sees the outbreak of world war, two revolutions and a civil war. Yet her life and her preoccupations remain much as before. She greets the revolution of 1917 with bewilderment, but is grateful to the Bolsheviks for providing her with everything she needs and not expropriating the estate. And when Bolshevik soldiers and commissars are billeted in the village during the Civil War, she finds them unexpectedly sympathetic. She remains as indomitable as ever into her seventies, making little of her own discomforts and going off to the fields to pick potatoes when the shops empty. As her strength declines her diary entries dwindle, and she leaves us in October 1919 with the unforgettable image of civil-war refugees trailing down the highway on their way from Oryol to Tula.

Sofia Tolstoy was a complex woman, a human dynamo with an iron constitution and a poetic soul. The "dark ones" who fill her house see her as a tedious, self-centred, complaining woman, who threatens to drag her husband down with her. And this is the judgement that has been passed down to us. True, one's sympathies are often strained by her exasperating snobbishness, her anti-Semitism, her sentimentality and her conservatism. But her diaries reveal her as someone of immense subtlety, intelligence, dignity and courage. She refuses to be resigned when all are against her, refuses to accept decisions taken over her head, refuses to be mocked, exploited or silenced. Her diaries are the writings of a confused psyche, battered but indomitable, clinging desperately to her self-esteem and the better things of life. She longs to improve herself (though she dreads change), and her writing is informed by her search for clarity, balance and goodness, through love, pain and, increasingly, death.

Like Anna Karenina, she asserts the finer feelings in a barbaric society hostile to enlightenment. Her struggle too is against sexual hypocrisy, but it is also against herself, against her own split psyche and her unloving husband. "If personal salvation and the spiritual *life* means *killing* one's closest friend, then Lyovochka's salvation is assured," she writes. "But isn't this the death of us both?" Her diaries are a terrible reminder of the price of genius and the sacrifices made in its name.

The translation of these immense diaries has given me an all too uncomfortably close understanding of Sofia Tolstoy's despair. The burden has been lightened by help and encouragement from many people too numerous to mention, but I am especially grateful to Professor Reginald Christian, of St Andrews University, for his invaluable suggestions and corrections; to Della Couling, for her patient and sensitive editing; to Barbara Alpern Engel, of the University of Colorado, for her inspiring work on women in nineteenth-century Russia; to Lily Feiler, for sharing with me her enthusiasm for Sofia Tolstoy, and to Dr Faith Wigzell, of the School of Slavonic Studies, London University, for her help with the translation.

In a work of this length, problems of accuracy seem to multiply exponentially, and all such errors are my responsibility. However, because I have opted whenever possible for a literal translation, I have tried not to alter Sofia's own inconsistencies and inaccuracies, particularly when these are clarified in the notes, so that when a name, date or book title in the text does not correspond with that given in the notes, it is the note version which should be taken as correct.

Unless otherwise stated, dates given in the diaries correspond to the old (Julian) calendar, twelve days behind the Western (Gregorian) calendar in the nineteenth century, and thirteen days behind in the twentieth. Russia didn't adopt the Gregorian calendar until 1918, a year before her death.

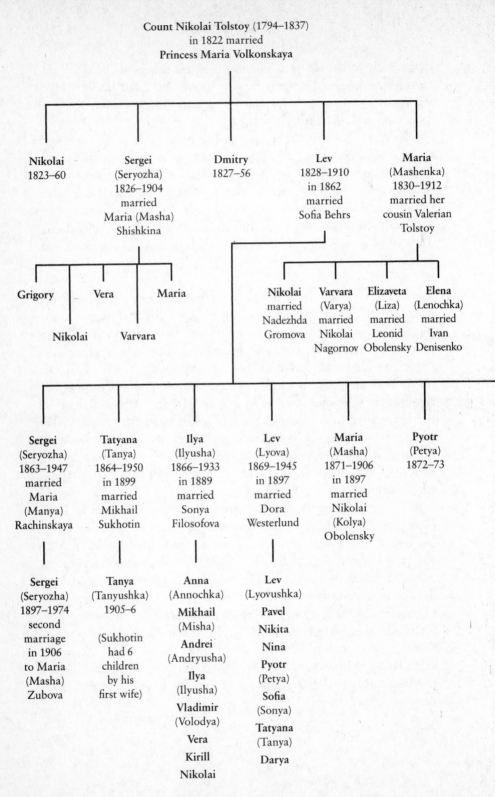

Count Nikolai Tolstoy (1794–1837)
in 1822 married
Princess Maria Volkonskaya

Nikolai
1823–60

Sergei
(Seryozha)
1826–1904
married
Maria (Masha)
Shishkina

Dmitry
1827–56

Lev
1828–1910
in 1862
married
Sofia Behrs

Maria
(Mashenka)
1830–1912
married her
cousin Valerian
Tolstoy

Grigory   **Vera**   **Maria**

Nikolai   **Varvara**

Nikolai
married
Nadezhda
Gromova

Varvara
(Varya)
married
Nikolai
Nagornov

Elizaveta
(Liza)
married
Leonid
Obolensky

Elena
(Lenochka)
married
Ivan
Denisenko

Sergei
(Seryozha)
1863–1947
married
Maria
(Manya)
Rachinskaya

Tatyana
(Tanya)
1864–1950
in 1899
married
Mikhail
Sukhotin

Ilya
(Ilyusha)
1866–1933
in 1889
married
Sonya
Filosofova

Lev
(Lyova)
1869–1945
in 1897
married
Dora
Westerlund

Maria
(Masha)
1871–1906
in 1897
married
Nikolai
(Kolya)
Obolensky

Pyotr
(Petya)
1872–73

Sergei
(Seryozha)
1897–1974
second
marriage
in 1906
to Maria
(Masha)
Zubova

Tanya
(Tanyushka)
1905–6

(Sukhotin
had 6
children
by his
first wife)

Anna
(Annochka)
Mikhail
(Misha)
Andrei
(Andryusha)
Ilya
(Ilyusha)
Vladimir
(Volodya)
Vera
Kirill
Nikolai

Lev
(Lyovushka)
Pavel
Nikita
Nina
Pyotr
(Petya)
Sofia
(Sonya)
Tatyana
(Tanya)
Darya

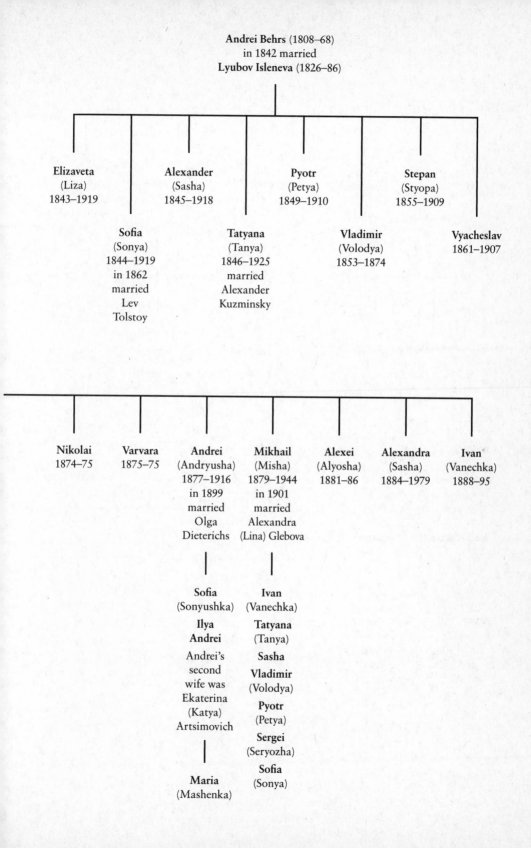

Andrei Behrs (1808–68)
in 1842 married
Lyubov Isleneva (1826–86)

Elizaveta
(Liza)
1843–1919

Sofia
(Sonya)
1844–1919
in 1862
married
Lev
Tolstoy

Alexander
(Sasha)
1845–1918

Tatyana
(Tanya)
1846–1925
married
Alexander
Kuzminsky

Pyotr
(Petya)
1849–1910

Vladimir
(Volodya)
1853–1874

Stepan
(Styopa)
1855–1909

Vyacheslav
1861–1907

Nikolai
1874–75

Varvara
1875–75

Andrei
(Andryusha)
1877–1916
in 1899
married
Olga
Dieterichs

Mikhail
(Misha)
1879–1944
in 1901
married
Alexandra
(Lina) Glebova

Alexei
(Alyosha)
1881–86

Alexandra
(Sasha)
1884–1979

Ivan
(Vanechka)
1888–95

Sofia
(Sonyushka)
Ilya
Andrei

Andrei's
second
wife was
Ekaterina
(Katya)
Artsimovich

Maria
(Mashenka)

Ivan
(Vanechka)
Tatyana
(Tanya)
Sasha
Vladimir
(Volodya)
Pyotr
(Petya)
Sergei
(Seryozha)
Sofia
(Sonya)

I
Diaries
1862–1910

1862

Tsar Alexander II's emancipation of the serfs the previous year ushers in the "era of great reforms" – of law courts, the army and local government.

On 23rd September, Lev Nikolaevich Tolstoy and Sofia Behrs are married in Moscow, and move immediately to Tolstoy's estate at Yasnaya Polyana, near Tula. December to February 1863, the Tolstoys visit Moscow to see his novel The Cossacks *published.*

8th October. My diary again. It's sad to be going back to old habits I gave up since I got married. I used to write when I felt depressed – now I suppose it's for the same reason.

Relations with my husband have been so simple these past two weeks and I felt so happy with him; he was my diary and I had nothing to hide from him.

But ever since yesterday, when he told me he didn't trust my love, I have been feeling terrible. I know why he doesn't trust me, but I don't think I shall ever be able to say or write what I really think. I always dreamt of the man I would love as a completely whole, new, *pure* person. In these childish dreams, which I find hard to give up, I imagined that this man would always be with me, that I would know his slightest thought and feeling, that he would love nobody but me as long as he lived, and that he, like me and unlike others, would not have to sow his wild oats before becoming a respectable person.

Since I married I have had to recognize how foolish these dreams were, yet I cannot renounce them. The whole of my husband's past is so ghastly that I don't think I shall ever be able to accept it. Unless I can discover other interests in my life, like the children I long for, since they will give me a firm future and show me what real purity is, without all the abominations of his past and everything else that makes me so bitter towards my husband. He cannot understand that his past is another world to me, with thousands of different feelings, good and bad, which can never belong to me, just as his youth, squandered on God knows what or whom, can never be mine either. I am giving him everything; not one part of me has been wasted elsewhere. Even my childhood belonged to him. My fondest memories are of my first childish love for him, and it is not my fault if this love was destroyed. He had to fritter away his life and strength, he had to experience so much evil before he could feel anything noble; now his love for me seems to him something strong and good – but only because it's such a long, long time since he lived a good life as I do. There are bad things in my past too, but not so many as in his.

He loves to torment me and see me weep because he doesn't trust me. He wishes I had lived as evil a life as him, so that I might more fully appreciate goodness. It irritates him that happiness has come so easily to me, and that I accepted him without hesitation or remorse. But I have too much self-respect to cry. I don't want him to see me suffer; let him think it's easy for me. Yesterday while Grandfather was here I went downstairs especially to see him and was suddenly overwhelmed by an extraordinary feeling of love and strength. At that moment I loved him so much I longed to go up to him; but then I felt the moment I touched him I shouldn't feel so happy – almost like a sacrilege. But I never shall or can let him know what is going on within me. I have so much foolish pride – the slightest hint that he misunderstands or mistrusts me throws me into despair. What is he doing to me? Little by little I shall withdraw completely from him and poison his life. Yet I feel so sorry for him at those times when he doesn't trust me; his eyes fill with tears and his face is so gentle and sad. I could smother him with love at those moments, and yet the thought haunts me: "He doesn't *trust* me, he doesn't *trust* me." Today I began to feel we were drifting further and further apart. I am creating my own world for myself and he is making himself a practical life filled with distrust. And I thought how vulgar this kind of relation was. And I began to distrust his love too. When he kisses me I am always thinking, "I am not the first woman he has loved." It hurts me so much that my love for him – the dearest thing in the world to me because it is my first and last love – should not be enough for him. I too have loved other men, but only in my imagination – whereas he has loved and admired so many women, all so pretty and lively, all with different faces, characters and souls, just as he now loves and admires me. I know these thoughts are petty and vulgar but I can't help it, it is his past that is to blame. I can't forgive God for making men *sow their wild oats* before they can become decent people. And I can't help feeling hurt that my husband should come into this common category of person. And then he thinks I don't love him. Why would I care so much about him if I didn't love him? Why else would I try to understand his past and his present, and what may interest him in the future? It's hopeless – how can a wife prove her love to a husband who tells her he married her only because he *had* to, even though she never loved him? As if I had ever, for one moment, regretted my past, or could dream of not loving him. Does he enjoy seeing me cry when I realize how difficult our relations are, and how we shall gradually drift further apart spiritually? Toys for the cat are tears for the mouse. But this toy is fragile, and if he breaks it, it will be he who cries. I cannot bear the way he is wearing me down. Yet he is a wonderful, good person. He too loathes everything evil, he cannot bear it. I used to love everything beautiful, my soul knew the meaning of ecstasy – now all that has died in me. No sooner am I happy than he crushes me.

9th October. Yesterday we opened our hearts and I feel much better. We went horse riding today, which was splendid, but I feel downcast all the same. I had a depressing dream last night and it is weighing on me, although I don't remember it in detail. I thought of Maman today and grew dreadfully sad, but I don't regret my past, I shall always bless it, for I have known great happiness. My husband seems much calmer now and I think he trusts me again, God willing. It's true, I realize I do not make him very happy. I seem to be asleep all the time and unable to wake up. If I did, I am sure I would be a completely different person, but I don't know how. *Then* he would realize how much I love him, for I should be able to *tell* him of my love. I should be able to see into his soul as I used to, and know how to make him happy again. I must wake up at once, I must. I am frightened of being on my own. He won't let me into his room, which makes me very sad. All physical things disgust him.

11th October. I am terribly sad, and am withdrawing further and further into myself. My husband is ill and out of sorts and doesn't love me. I expected this, but never imagined it would be so terrible. He grows colder and colder every day, while I love him more and more. His coldness will soon be unbearable to me. Of course, he is much too honest to deceive me. If he doesn't love me he would never pretend to do so, but when he does love me I can see it in his every movement. Lyovochka is a wonderful man, and I feel everything is my fault, yet I am afraid to show him how sad I am for I know how bored men are by foolish melancholy. I used to console myself that it would pass and everything would be all right again, but now I feel things will never get better and will become a great deal worse. Papa writes to me: "Your husband loves you passionately." It's true, he did love me *passionately*, but passion passes, and what nobody realized is that he was attracted to me without loving me. Why have I ruined this dear man whom everybody loves so much?

"You'll be happy, you'll see," people used to tease me. "Don't worry so much!" Now I have lost everything, all my energy for work, life and household tasks has been wasted, and I want only to sit in silence all day, thinking bitter thoughts. I wanted to do some work, but couldn't; why should I dress up in that stupid bonnet which makes my head ache? I long to play the piano but it's so awkward; upstairs you can be heard all over the house and downstairs the piano is too bad to play. I can hear him now playing a piano duet upstairs with Olga. Poor man, he is always looking for something to divert him and take him away from me. What is the point of living?

13th November. An unlucky date. But I have spoken to him, and like a true egoist, I always feel much better after I have had him in my room and set my mind at rest.

It is true, I cannot find anything to occupy me. He is fortunate because he is talented and clever. I am neither. One cannot live by love alone, but I am too stupid to do anything but sit and think about him. He has only to feel slightly under the weather and I think, "What if he dies?" and these hideous thoughts make me wretched for the next three hours. When he is cheerful, I worry only that this mood will pass and can think of nothing else. Whenever he is away or busy I think of him constantly, listening out for him or watching the expression on his face. It's probably because I am pregnant that I am in such an abnormal state; it affects him too I know. It's not hard to find work, there's plenty to do, but first you have to enjoy breeding hens, tinkling on the piano, reading a lot of fourth-rate books and precious few good ones and pickling cucumbers. I am sure all this will come once I've forgotten my idle girlhood ways and grown used to living in the country. I am waiting for that bright day when things run as smoothly as a machine and I can start to live an active life. I am asleep now, nothing brings me excitement or joy – neither the trip to Moscow, nor the thought of the baby. I wish I could take some remedy to wake me up.

I haven't prayed for a long time. Before, I used to love the external aspects of religious ritual. When nobody was looking I would light a wax candle before the icon, put some flowers there, lock the door, kneel on the floor and pray for hours. It seems silly and ridiculous, but I love remembering it. My life is so serious now. Over the next few years I shall make myself a serious *female* world, and love it even more than the old one because it will contain my husband and my children, whom one loves more than one's parents and brothers and sisters. But I haven't settled down yet. I still swing between my past and my future. My husband loves me too much to tell me how to live my life; besides, it's difficult, it's something I must work out for myself. He too feels I have changed. With patience I shall be as I used to be, although no longer a young girl but a woman; I shall wake up then, and both of us will be happy.

23rd November. He disgusts me with his talk of the "people". I feel it's either me, representing his family, or the people, whom he loves so passionately. If this is selfish, so be it. I live through him and want him to live for me, otherwise I feel suffocated in this place. Today I ran out of the house because everyone and everything disgusted me – Auntie,* his peasant students, the walls, life. I slipped out and ran off alone, and wanted to laugh and shout for joy. L. no longer disgusted me, but I suddenly realized how far apart we were: his "people" could never absorb all my attention, and I could never fully absorb his as he does mine. If I don't interest him, if he sees me as a doll, merely his *wife*, not a human being, then I will not and cannot live like that.* Of course I am idle at present, but I am not so by nature; I simply haven't discovered anything I can do. He gets angry. Let him, I feel happy and free today because I am on my own, and although he has been very morose he has left me alone, thank God. I know he has a brilliant mind, he is poetic and intelligent and has many talents, but it makes me angry that he sees only the gloomy side of things. He has been so gloomy these days I could have wept. He won't talk to me. It's terrible to live with him – he'll get carried away by his love for the common people again and I shall be done for, because he loves me merely as he used to love his school, nature, the people, maybe his writing, all of which he loved a little, one after the other, until it was time for something new. Aunt came in and asked why I had run out and where I had been, and I wanted to needle her and said I was escaping from the students, for she always defends them. But it wasn't true. I'm not the least bit angry with the students, it's only old habit that makes me grumble and complain like this. I went out simply because I was bored with doing nothing. I shall go and play the piano now. He is in the bath. He is a stranger to me today.

16th December. One of these days I think I shall kill myself with jealousy. "In love as never before!" he writes. With that fat, pale peasant woman – how frightful!* I looked at the dagger and the guns with such joy. One blow, I thought, how easy it would be – if only it weren't for the baby. Yet to think she is there, just a few steps away. I feel demented. I shall go for a drive. I may even see her. So he really did love her! I should like to burn his diary and the whole of his past.

I have returned and am feeling worse; my head aches, I am distraught, my heart is heavy. I felt free outside in the open air – if only I could always breathe as freely as that. But life is so petty. Love is hard – when you love it takes your breath away, you lay down your life and soul for it and it's with you as long as you live. It would be narrow and mean, this little world of mine, if it weren't for him. Yet it's impossible for us to join together our two worlds. He is so intelligent, he has such energy, and then there is that dreadful, endless past of his. And mine is so small and insignificant. I felt terrified today by the thought of our journey to Moscow, for I shall become even more insignificant there. I have been reading the openings of some of his works, and the very mention of love or women makes me feel so disgusted and depressed I would gladly burn everything.

If I could kill him and create a new person exactly the same as he is now, I would do so happily.

1863

28th June – birth of the couple's son, Sergei. Shortly afterwards Tolstoy talks of going to war (possibly to put down the Polish uprising against Russian domination). But instead he starts on War and Peace. *Summer – Sofia's seventeen-year-old sister Tanya Behrs visits Yasnaya Polyana and embarks on a romance with Tolstoy's brother Sergei, twenty years her senior.*

9th January. Never in my life have I felt so wretched with remorse.* Never did I imagine I could be so much to blame. I have been choked with tears all day, and am afraid to talk to him or look at him. I love him deeply, he has never been so precious to me, and I feel so worthless and loathsome. Yet he is not even angry and still loves me, and his face is so gentle and saintly. A man like this could make one die of humility. Mental pain has made me physically ill. I thought I would miscarry, I was in such pain. I have been praying all day, trying to lighten my crime and undo what I have done. I feel a little easier when he isn't here, for then I can cry and love him. When he is here my conscience tortures me; it's agony to see his sweet face, which I have avoided looking at since yesterday evening. How could I have treated him so badly? I have racked my brains for some way of making amends for that stupid word – or not so much make amends as make myself a better person for him. I cannot love him any more than I already do. I already love him to such excess, with all my heart and soul, that there is nothing in my mind but my love for him, nothing. There is absolutely no evil in him, nothing I could ever dream of reproaching him for.

11th January. I am calmer now because he is being a little kinder to me. But my unhappiness is still so fresh that every memory of it brings on a terrible physical pain in my head and body – I feel it passing through my veins and nerves.

He saw this diary but hasn't referred to it, I don't know if he has read it. It was vile and I have no desire to reread it.

I am alone and afraid, which is why I wanted to write sincerely and at length, but fear has confused my thoughts. I am afraid of being frightened now that I'm pregnant. My jealousy is a congenital illness, or maybe in loving him I have nothing else to love; I've given myself so completely to him that my only happiness is with him and I am afraid of losing him, as old men fear to lose an only child on whom their whole life depends. People always told me I wasn't egotistical, although this is really the most complete egotism. But I love him so much that this too will pass. Only I shall need a lot of patience and strength of will, otherwise it will be no good. There are days when I am morbidly in love with him, and this is one of those days. It is always so when I have done something wrong. It hurts me to look at him, listen to him or be with him, like a devil in the presence of a saint.

*14th January (Moscow).** I am alone again and sad. Yet we have managed to make peace. I don't know what reconciled him to me or me to him, it happened of itself. All I know is that I have my happiness back. I want to go home. I have so many dreams of how I will live in Yasnaya with *him*. I feel sad to have broken so completely from the Kremlin crowd. I see terribly clearly how much my world has changed, yet I love my family more than ever, especially Maman, and it saddens me that I'm no longer part of their lives. I live completely through him and for him, and it's often painful for me to realize that I am not *everything* to him and that if I were suddenly to die he would be able to console himself somehow, for he has so many *resources*, whereas I have such a weak nature. I have given myself to one man and would never be able to find another world for myself.

Life in this hotel depresses me. I am happy only when I am sitting with my family, and with *Lyovochka*, of course. I could leave for home at once I know, it's largely up to me, but I haven't the heart to say goodbye to my family so soon after arriving, and I'm too lazy to move. I had such a bad dream last night. Our Yasnaya peasant girls and women were visiting us in a huge garden, all dressed up as ladies, then started going off somewhere, one after the other. A.* came last, wearing a black silk dress. I began speaking to her and was seized with such violent rage that I picked up her child and began tearing him to pieces. I tore off his head and legs – I was like a madwoman. Then Lyovochka came up and I told him they would send me to Siberia, but he picked up the legs and arms and all the other bits and told me it was only a doll. I looked down and saw that it was indeed, with just cloth and stuffing for a body. And that made me furious.

I often torture myself thinking about her, even here in Moscow. Maman was right when she said I had become sillier than ever – rather, I think my mind is lazier. It's an unpleasant feeling, this physical lethargy. And physical lethargy produces mental lethargy too.

I regret my former liveliness. But I think it will return. I feel it would have as good an effect on Lyovochka as it once had on the Kremlin crowd.

17th January. I've been feeling angry that he loves everything and everyone, when I want him to love only me. Now that I'm alone in my room I realize I was just being wilful again; it's his kindness and the wealth of his feelings that make him good. The cause of all my whims and miseries is this wretched egotism of mine, which makes me want to possess his life, his thoughts, his love, everything he has. This has become a sort of rule with me. The moment I think fondly of someone I tell myself no, I love only Lyovochka. But I absolutely *must* learn to love something else as he loves his *work*, so I can turn to it when he grows cold towards me. These times will become more frequent. I see this clearly now – why should Lyovochka study all the subtleties of our relations as I do, for want of anything else to occupy me? From this I also learn how I should behave with him, and I do this not as a duty but quite involuntarily. I can't yet put this knowledge into practice, but everything comes in time. We must get back to Yasnaya very soon; there he devotes himself more to me, for there is nobody else but Aunt and me. I know I can make the house a happier place, as long as he doesn't want visitors, for I don't know where I would find the right people to ask, and besides I don't like them. But if he wants me to I'll entertain whomever he cares to invite; anything to keep him happy and not bored, for then he'll love me and there's nothing else I want.

I waited and waited for him and have now sat down again to write. Some people live in solitude, but it's terrible to be alone. I don't suppose we shall go to that lecture now. Perhaps I annoyed him. This thought often torments me. I have grown terribly close to Maman and it frightens me, for we can never live together now.

29th January. Kremlin life is oppressive; it evokes the lazy, aimless life I led here as a girl. All my illusions about the aims and duties of marriage vanished into thin air when Lyovochka let me know that one can't be satisfied merely with one's family, one's husband or wife, but needs something more, a larger cause. (*"I need nothing but you. Lyovochka talks a lot of nonsense sometimes.*" [L.N. Tolstoy's note])

3rd March (Yasnaya Polyana). Still the same old story – writing on my own. But I'm not lonely now, I'm used to it. And happy in the knowledge that he loves me, and loves me constantly. When he gets home he comes up to me so kindly and asks me or tells me something. My life is cheerful and easy now. I read *his* diary and it made me happy.* There is me and his work – nothing else matters to him. Yesterday and today he has been preoccupied. I am afraid to disturb him when he is writing, and that he'll get angry and my presence will be unbearable to him. I'm glad he's writing. I wanted to go to church this morning, but instead I stayed at home and prayed here. Since my marriage every form of ceremony has become loathsome to me. I long with all my heart to manage the household and *do* something. But I haven't yet learnt how, I don't know how to go about it. It will come in time.

1st April. I am unwell and in low spirits. Lyova has gone off again. My misfortune is that I have no inner resources to draw on, and this is indeed necessary and important in life. The weather is wonderful, it's almost summer, and my mood is like the summer – sad. It's bleak and lonely here. He has his work and the estate to think about while I have nothing... What am I good for? I can't go on living like this. I would like to *do* more, something *real*. At this wonderful time of year I always used to long for things, aspire to things, dream about God knows what. But I no longer have these foolish aspirations, for I know I have all I need now and there's nothing left to strive for. So much happiness and so little to do.

6th April. We have started attending to the estate together, he and I, him taking it all very seriously, me so far pretending to. But it interests me greatly. He seems preoccupied and unwell, and this makes me anxious. I'm afraid to let him know how much these blood rushes of his worry me. It's a terrible thought, but I can't help worrying that this life of ours and our happiness together is not real happiness at all but just a trick of fate, and will suddenly be snatched away. I'm afraid... It's stupid, but I cannot write it down. I wish this fear would pass quickly, for it poisons my life. He has bought some bees, which pleases me very much; managing the estate is interesting, but hard work. He certainly has something on his mind; he's being so unstraightfoward and secretive. Or is it just a headache? What's the matter with him? What does he want? I would do anything he wanted if only I could. He is out now, but I fear when he comes back he'll be in a bad temper and will find something to irritate him. I love him desperately, I feel I could endure anything for his sake if I had to.

10th April. He has gone to meet Papa in Tula and I already feel miserable. I have been rereading his letters to V.A.* They seem so youthful. It wasn't her he loved but love itself and family life. I recognize him well – his moral precepts, his splendid strivings for all that is noble and *good*. What a wonderful man he is! And reading through these letters I almost stopped feeling jealous, as if it wasn't V. at all but *me*, the woman he *had* to love. I put myself into their world. She was apparently rather a pretty girl, essentially empty-headed, morally good and lovable only because she was so young, while he was just as he is now, not really in love with V. so much as with his love of life and goodness. Poor man, he was still too young to realize that you can never plan happiness in advance, and will inevitably be unhappy if you try. But what noble, splendid dreams these were.

24th April. Lyova is either old or unhappy. He seems to think of nothing but money, the estate and the distillery – nothing else interests him.* If he isn't eating, sleeping or sitting in silence he is roaming about the estate alone the whole day. And I am wretched and alone, always alone. He shows his love for me merely by kissing my hands in a mechanical fashion, and by being kind to me and not cruel.

25th April. The same wretchedness all morning, the same premonition of something terrible. I still feel very shy with him. I cried as if demented and afterwards couldn't understand why this was always happening – I knew only that I had good reason to cry, and even possibly to die, if he had stopped loving me as he used to. I didn't mean to write today, but I am all alone downstairs and have given in to my old habit of scribbling. I've been interrupted—

29th April, evening. I get annoyed about trifles – some parcels, for instance. I make great efforts not to be irritable, and shall soon achieve this. Towards Lyovochka I feel terribly affectionate and rather shy – a result of my petty moods. Towards myself I feel a disgust such as I haven't felt for a long time. I want to go out and look at the bees and the apple trees and work on the estate.* I want to be active, but I am heavy and tired, and my infirmity tells me to sit still and look after my stomach. It's infuriating. It distresses me that it should make him so unkind to me, as if it's my fault I am pregnant. I'm no help to him at present. And there is another thing which makes me disgusted with myself. (One must above all speak the truth in a diary.) It made me happy to recall the time when V.V.* was in love with me. I wonder if it could make me happy if someone fell in love with me now? Oh, how loathsome. I always laughed at him then and never felt anything for him but contempt. Lyova ignores me more and more. The physical side of love is very important for him. This is terrible. For me it's quite the opposite.

8th May. My pregnancy is to blame for everything – I'm in an unbearable state, physically and mentally. Physically I'm always ill, mentally there is this awful emptiness and boredom. As far as Lyova is concerned I don't exist. I feel I am hateful to him, and want only to leave him in peace and cut myself out of his life as far as possible. I can do nothing to make him happy, because I'm pregnant. It's a cruel truth that a wife only discovers whether her husband really loves her when she is pregnant. He has gone to his beehives and I would give anything to go too but shan't, because I have been having palpitations and it's difficult to sit down there, and there'll be a thunderstorm any moment, and my head aches and I'm bored – I feel like weeping, and I don't want him to see me in this state, especially as he is ill too. I feel awkward with him most of the time. If he is occasionally kind to me it's more a matter of habit, and he still feels obliged to continue the old relations even though he doesn't love me any more. I'm sure it would be terrible for him to confess that he did once love me – not so long ago either – but all this is over now. If only he knew how much he has changed, if only he could step into my shoes for a while, he would understand how hard life is for me. But there's no help for it. He will wake up again after the baby is born, I suppose, for this is what always happens.

9th May. He promised to be here at twelve o'clock and now it's two. Has something happened? How can he take such pleasure in torment-ing me? You don't drive out a dog that licks your hand. Maman en-dured a similar fate to mine in the first year of her marriage, only it was worse for her, for Papa was always travelling around visiting patients and playing cards, whereas Lyova merely walks around the estate. But

I am also lonely and bored, also pregnant and ill. You learn so much more from experience than from the intellect. Youth is a misfortune, not a blessing, if you are married. You simply cannot be happy sitting there sewing or playing the piano alone, completely *alone*, and gradually becoming convinced that even though your husband may not love you, you are stuck there for ever and there you must sit. Maman told me her life got happier as she grew older; when her youth passed and her children arrived and she found something to focus her life on. That is how it will be with me too. I am moody and bad-tempered only because I'm bored with waiting for him since twelve o'clock alone. It is wicked of him not to have pity on me, as any moderately decent person would have for another suffering fellow creature.

6th June. My brother Alexander and sister Tatyana have arrived to disturb our life and I'm sorry. They don't seem very cheerful. Or maybe it's just the chilly atmosphere here. They haven't cheered me up a bit, they've merely made me more anxious. I love Lyovochka intensely but it angers me that I should be in a relationship in which we're not equals. I am entirely dependent on him, and God knows I treasure his love. But he either takes mine for granted or doesn't need it, he seems to be alone in everything. I keep reminding myself that autumn will soon be here and all this will soon be over. I don't know what I mean by "all this", though. And what sort of winter we shall have – or whether there will be a winter at all – I cannot imagine. It's terribly depressing that I should wish for nothing and nothing makes me happy, like an old woman, and how unbearable it would be to be old. I didn't want to go for a drive with them after he said: "You and I are old folk, let's stay put." And it seemed such fun to stay at home with him, just the two of us, as though I had fallen in love with him against my parents' wishes. Now the others have driven off and he has gone out, and I am alone with my melancholy thoughts. I am angry with him for not giving me a carriage, which means I can never go out for a drive. It's much simpler for him to leave me on the sofa with a book and not bother his head about me. If I can stop being angry for a moment though, I realize he has a mountain of work which has nothing to do with me, and that running the estate is a gruelling labour; then there are the peasants visiting him all the time and never giving him a moment's peace. And there are those people who cheated him over the carriage, and it wasn't *his* fault – no, he is a *wonderful* man, I love him with all my heart.

7th June. I love him madly. This feeling has taken a hold over me and overwhelms me. He is on the estate all the time, but I am not moping now and I feel happy. And he loves me, I think I can sense that. I fear this means I shall die – how terrible it would be to leave him. The more I get to know him the dearer he becomes to me. I think each day that I have never loved him so much – and next day I love him even more. Nothing exists for me but him and everything that concerns him.

14th July. It's all over, the baby* has been born and my ordeal is over. I have risen from my bed and am gradually entering into life again, but with a constant feeling of dread about my baby and especially my husband. Something in me seems to have collapsed, and I sense that whatever it is it will always be there to torment me; it's probably the fear of not doing my duty towards *my family*. I feel terribly timid with my husband, as if I had wronged him in some way. I feel I am a burden, a foolish person (the same old theme!), even rather vulgar. I am frightened by the womb's love for its offspring, and frightened by my somewhat unnatural love for my husband. All this I try to hide, out of a feeling of shame I know to be stupid and false. I sometimes comfort myself with the thought that most people see this love of one's husband and children as a virtue. I shall never go any further than this I fear, although I should like to be a bit better educated – my education was so bad – again if only for my husband's sake and that of my children. But how strong these maternal feelings are! It strikes me as quite natural and not at all strange that I am now a mother. He is Lyovochka's child, that's why I love him. His present state of mind makes me very anxious. He has such a wealth of ideas and feelings and it is all being wasted. I truly appreciate his great qualities. God knows I would give anything to make him happy.

23rd July. I have been married for ten months and my spirits are flagging. I automatically seek support as my baby seeks the breast, and I am in agonizing pain. Lyova is murderous. He cannot run the estate – I'm not cut out for it, he says. He is restless.* Nothing here satisfies him; I know what he wants and I cannot give it to him. Nothing is sweet to me. Like a dog I have grown used to his caresses, but he has grown cold. I console myself that there are bound to be days like this. But they are all too frequent. *Patience.* I shall now go and sacrifice myself to my son...

31st July. What he says is so *banal.* I know things are terrible, but why should he be so angry?* Whose fault is it? Our relations are frightful, and at such a painful time as this too. He has become so unpleasant that I try all day to avoid him. When he says, "I'm going to bed," or "I'm going to have a bath," I think, thank God. It breaks my heart to sit with my little son. God has taken both my husband and my son from me – to think how devoutly we used to pray to Him. Now I feel everything is over. Patience, I keep telling myself. We were at least blessed with a happy past. I have loved him so much and am grateful to him for everything. I have just been reading his diary. At that wonderful poetic moment everything seemed vile to him. "These past nine months have been practically the worst in my life," he wrote – to say nothing of the tenth. How often he must secretly have asked himself why he got married. And how often he has said aloud to me, "What has become of my old self?"*

2nd August. It was not written for me to read. Why am I idling my life away? You'd do well to pull yourself together, Sofia Andreevna. Grief like this can wear you down. I have sternly forbidden myself ever to mention his name again. Maybe it will pass.

3rd August. It has started raining and I'm afraid he'll catch cold. I am not angry any more. I love him. God bless him.

> *Sonya, forgive me, I have only just realized that I am to blame and have wronged you greatly. There are days when one seems guided not by one's will but by some irresistible external law. That was why I treated you like that then – to think I could have done such a thing. I have always recognized that I have many failings and very little generosity of spirit. And now I have acted so cruelly, so rudely, and to whom? To the person who has given me the finest happiness of my whole life and who alone loves me. I know this can never be forgotten or forgiven, Sonya, but I know you better now and realize how meanly I treat you. Sonya darling, I know I have been vile – somewhere inside me there is a fine person, but at times he seems to be asleep. Love him, Sonya, and do not reproach him too much.* [L.N. Tolstoy's note]

Lyovochka wrote that, begging my forgiveness, but then he lost his temper and crossed it out. He was talking of that terrible time when I had mastitis and my breasts hurt so much I was *unable* to feed

Seryozha, and this made him angry. It wasn't that I didn't *want* to – I longed to, it was what I wanted more than anything. I deserved those few lines of tenderness and remorse from him, but in a moment of rage with me he crossed them out as soon as I had read them.

17th August. I have been daydreaming, recalling those "mad" nights last year, and other mad nights too, when I was utterly free and in such a splendid state of mind. If ever I have known complete happiness it was then. I loved and experienced and understood everything, my mind and my being were completely in tune, and the world seemed so fresh. And then there was the dear poetic *Comte*,* with his wonderful deep bright gaze. It was a heavenly time. I felt pampered by his love. I certainly must have felt it, otherwise I wouldn't have been so happy. I remember he was rude to me one evening when Popov* was here and I was terribly hurt, but I pretended I didn't care and went out and sat on the porch with Popov, straining to hear what the *Comte* was talking about inside, while all the time pretending to be fascinated by everything Popov was saying. I grew even fonder of the *Comte* after that, and made a point of never dissembling to him again. I was just thinking about all this when I suddenly realized with incredulous joy that the *Comte* is now my husband. When he doubts my love for him I feel so stunned I lose my head. How can I prove it when I love him so *honestly*, so steadfastly?

22nd September. It will be a year tomorrow. Then I had hopes of happiness, now only of unhappiness. Before I thought it was all a joke, but now I realize he means it. So he is off to war.* What sort of behaviour is that? Is he unbalanced? No, I think not, merely erratic. I don't know whether it's intentional, but he seems to do all he can to make me unhappy. He has put me in a position where I have to worry from one day to the next that he'll go off, and I'll be abandoned with my baby, maybe more than just one. It's all a joke to them, a fleeting fancy. One day they decide to get married, enjoy it and produce some children – next day it's time to leave them and go off to war. I only hope now that my child will die, for I shall not survive without him. I have no faith in his love for the "fatherland", this *enthousiasme* in a man of thirty-five. Aren't his children also the fatherland, aren't they also Russian? But no, he wants to abandon them so he can enjoy himself galloping about on his horse, revelling in the beauties of battle and listening to the bullets fly. His inconsistency and cowardice have made me respect him less. But his talent is more important to him than his family. If only he would explain to me the true motives of his desire. Why did I marry him? Valerian Petrovich* would have been better, as I wouldn't have minded so much if he left me. What did he need my love for? It was just an infatuation. And I know he's blaming me, for now he is sulking. He blames me for loving him and not wanting him to die or leave me. Let him sulk. I only wish I had been able to prepare myself for it in advance, i.e. stop loving him, for the parting would have been easier. I love him, that's the worst of it, and when I see him he looks so depressed, forever morosely searching his soul.

7th October. What gloom. At least my son gives me some joy. But why is Nurse always fussing over baby clothes and distracting me? Of course he can see how low I feel, it's no use trying to conceal it, but he'll soon find it insufferable. I want to go to the ball, but that isn't the reason I feel low. I shan't go, but it irritates me that I still want to. And this irritation would have spoilt the fun, which I doubt it would have been anyway. He keeps saying, "I am being reborn." What *does* he mean? He can have everything he had before we were married, if only he can be rid of his terrible anxieties and restless strivings. "Reborn"? He says I'll soon understand. But I get flustered and cannot understand a word he is talking about. He is undergoing some great change. And we are becoming more estranged. My illness and the baby have taken me away from him, this is why I don't understand him. What else do I need? Am I not lucky to be close to these inexhaustible ideas, talents and virtues, all embodied in my husband? But it can be depressing too. It's my *youth*.*

17th October. I wish I could understand him fully so he might treat me as he treats Alexandrine,* but I know this is impossible, so I mustn't be offended and must accept that I am too young and silly and not poetic enough. To be like Alexandrine, quite apart from any innate gifts, one would need to be older anyway, childless, and even unmarried. I wouldn't mind at all if they took up their old correspondence, but it would sadden me if she thought his wife was fit for nothing but the nursery and humdrum superficial relationships. I know that however jealous I may be of her soul, I mustn't cut her out of his life, for she has played an important part in it for which I should have been useless. He shouldn't have sent her that letter.* I cried because he didn't tell me everything he had written in it, and because he said, "Something which I alone know about myself. And I'll tell you too, only my wife doesn't know anything about it..." I should like to know her better. Would she consider me worthy of him? She understands and appreciates him so well. I found some letters from her in his desk and they gave me a clear impression of what she was like, and of her relations with Lyova. One was particularly fine. Once or twice it has occurred to me to write to her without telling him, but I can't bring myself to. She interests me greatly and I like her a lot. Ever since I read his letters to her I have been thinking about her constantly. I think I could love her. I'm not pregnant, judging by my state of mind, and long may this continue. I love him to distraction, and it worries me to think I shall love him even more in the future.

28th October. My love cannot be very strong if I am so weak. But no, I love him terribly, there can be no doubt about it. If only I could raise myself up. My husband is so good, so wonderfully good. Where is he? Probably working on *The History of 1812.** He used to tell me about his writing, but now he thinks I'm not worthy of his confidence. In the past he shared all his thoughts with me, and we had such blissful, happy times together. Now they are all gone. "We shall always be happy, Sonya," he said. I feel so sad that he has had none of the happiness he expected and deserved.

13th November. I feel sorry for Aunt – she won't last much longer. She is always sick, her cough keeps her awake at night, her hands are thin and dry. I think about her all day.

He says, let's live in Moscow for a while. Just what I expected. It makes me jealous when he finds his ideal in the first pretty woman he meets. Such love is terrible because it is blind and virtually incurable. There has never been anything of this in me, and there never will be. I am left alone morning, afternoon and night. I am to gratify his pleasure and nurse his child, I am a piece of household furniture, I am a *woman*. I try to suppress all human feelings. When the machine is working properly it heats the milk, knits a blanket, makes little requests and bustles about trying not to think – and life is tolerable. But the moment I am alone and allow myself to think, everything seems insufferable. He doesn't love me, I couldn't keep his love. In a moment of grief, which I now regret, when nothing seemed to matter but the fact that I had lost his love, I thought even his writing was pointless. What did I care what Countess So-and-So in his novel said to Princess So-and-So? Afterwards I despised myself. My life is so mundane. But he has such a rich internal life, talent and immortality. I have become afraid of him, and at times he is a complete stranger.

19th December. I've lit two candles, sat down at the table and I feel perfectly happy. Everything seems funny and unimportant. I feel like flirting, even with someone like Alyosha Gorshkoi,* or losing my temper with a chair. I played cards with Aunt for four hours, which made him furious, but I didn't care. It hurts me to think of Tanya, she's a thorn in my flesh.* But I have put even this out of my mind today. The baby is better, maybe *that's* why I am so happy. At this moment I should love to go to a *dance* or do something amusing. He is old and self-absorbed, and I am young and long to do something wild. I'd like to turn somersaults instead of going to bed. But with whom?

24th December. Old age hovers over me; everything here is old. I try to suppress all youthful feelings, for they seem out of place in this sombre environment. The only one who is younger in spirit than the others is his brother Seryozha,* which is why I like it when he comes. I am gradually coming to the conclusion that Lyova wants only to restrain me; this is why he is so reserved, and why he constantly frustrates my spontaneous outbursts of love. How *can* I love him in this sober, sedate atmosphere? It's so monotonous here, so lacking in love. But I won't do anything. I complain as if I was really unhappy – but then I *am* really unhappy, for he doesn't love me so much. He actually told me so, but I knew it already. As for myself I'm not sure. I see so little of him and am in such awe of him that I can't be sure how much I love him. I dearly want to marry Tanya off to Seryozha, but it frightens me. What about Masha?* All Lyova's pronouncements on the compartments of the heart are nothing but fanciful idealism and are no comfort to me.

1864

In London, Marx's International Workingmen's Association (the First International) formed.

4th October – the Tolstoys' daughter, Tatyana (Tanya, Tanechka) is born. At the end of the year Tolstoy visits Moscow for an operation on his broken arm.

2nd January. My sister Tanya is all I can think about. I am worn out with grieving and planning and wrestling with it. Lyova, Aunt and I are in God's hands. Yet I desperately, passionately, want them both to be happy. I am in a dismal mood. Tula was so cheerless today, it exhausted me. I wanted to buy up the whole town, how pathetic, but I soon came to my senses. Lyova is being sweet; there was an almost childlike expression on his face when he was playing the piano. I thought of Alexandrine and understood her perfectly; I realized how much she must adore him. "Grandmother",* he calls her. He annoyed me just now when he said, "When you're cross you talk to your diary." What does he care? I'm not cross at the moment. Yet the slightest sarcastic remark from him hurts me terribly; he should cherish my love for him more. I am afraid of being ugly, morally and physically.

27th March. My diary is covered in dust, it's so long since I opened it, and today I decided to creep off while nobody was watching and write whatever came into my head. I wanted desperately to love everyone and enjoy everything, but someone only has to brush against me when I'm in this state and it goes away. I feel a sudden trust and tenderness for my husband, perhaps because it occurred to me yesterday how easily I might lose him. Today I resolved never to think of it again, come what may. I shall refuse to listen if anybody, even he, so much as mentions it. I love my sister Tanya so much, why are they trying to ruin her? Although they needn't bother, for she'll never be spoilt. I can give her emotional support but can do almost nothing about the situation she is in. At any rate, I shall do my best to distract her. I think I am less selfish than I was a year ago. Then I moped around pregnant, depressed because I couldn't have fun with the others. Now I have my own joy and am happier than anyone else.

22nd April. I am all alone. There's nothing to write about, there's no life in this place. I can control myself when I am looking after Seryozha, but in the evening, when he is asleep, I bustle about frantically as if I had a million little tasks to do, when in fact I am simply trying to avoid thinking and worrying. I keep imagining he has just gone out hunting or to look at the estate or see to the bees, and will return at any moment, for I am so used to waiting, and he always seems to return when my patience is about to give out. I am always trying to think of something unpleasant in our life together so as not to feel sorry for him, but I cannot, for the moment I think of him I realize how deeply I love him and I want to weep. The moment I catch myself thinking I am *not* sad, it's as if I deliberately make myself so. Tonight for the first time in my life I am going to bed alone. They said I should put Tanya's bed in my room but I didn't want to – I want no one but him beside me, ever. I keep thinking Tanya will hear me crying from the sitting room and I shall feel ashamed, and I haven't been so sensible all day.*

3rd November. It's odd that in these happy surroundings I should be feeling so disconsolate, so filled with dread about him. Last night, and every other night too, I was stricken with such fear and grief that while I was sitting with my little girl* I cried, for I could picture his death so clearly. It started when he dislocated his arm* and I suddenly realized the possibility of losing him; ever since then I have thought of nothing else. I almost live in the nursery now, and looking after the babies sometimes distracts me. I often think he must find this female world of ours insufferably dull, and that I cannot possibly make him happy. I am a good nursemaid, nothing more. No intelligence, education or talent, nothing. I wish something would happen soon. Looking after the children and playing with Seryozha can be delightful, but deep in my heart I sense that my old happiness has fled for good and nothing can give me joy any more. I often have premonitions of his bad moods; now he secretly hates me.

1865

6th April – "Provisional Rules" for the press (in force for the next forty years). Most books and journals exempt from preliminary censorship, but punitive censorship continues, under the control of the Ministry of the Interior. The excitement over the "great reforms" is over, and is followed by intense disillusionment. Some Land and Liberty members favour violence and form a secret society, the Organization, bent on assassinating particularly hated officials.

June – Tanya Behrs betrothed to Sergei Tolstoy, who deserts her at the last moment for the gypsy woman with whom he has been living for many years. July – first fragment of War and Peace *(called* The Year 1805*) published.*

25th February. I am so often alone with my thoughts that the need to write my diary comes quite naturally. Today it feels wonderfully pleasant to sit alone with my thoughts, not having to reveal them to a soul. Yesterday Lyovochka said he felt very young and I understood exactly what he meant. Now I am well again and not pregnant – it terrifies me how often I have been in that state. He said that for him being young means "*I can achieve anything*". For me it means *I want and can do anything.* When the feeling passes, reason tells me there is nothing I want or can do beyond nursing, eating, drinking, sleeping and loving and caring for my husband and babies, all of which I know is a happiness of a kind, but why do I feel so woeful all the time, and weep as I did yesterday? I am writing this now with the pleasantly exciting sense that nobody will ever read it, so I can be quite frank with myself and not write for Lyovochka. He is away at the moment; he spends so little time with me now anyway. But when I feel *young* I prefer not to be with him, for I am afraid he will find me stupid and irritating. Dunyasha* says, "The Count has grown old." Is this true? I often annoy him, he is absorbed in his writing, but it gives him no pleasure. Can it be that he has lost his capacity for enjoyment and fun? He talks of spending next winter in Moscow. I am sure he will be happier there, and I shall try to make the best of it. I have never admitted this, but even with Lyovochka, I am sometimes unconsciously a bit devious in order that he won't see me in a bad light. I have never admitted to him just how vain and envious I am. When we are in Moscow I shall feel ashamed if I don't have a carriage and horses with a liveried footman in attendance, a nice dress to wear, a fine apartment to live in and all the rest of it. Lyovochka is an extraordinary man; he cares nothing for any of this. That is true wisdom and virtue.

The children are my greatest joy. When I am alone I disgust myself, but they awaken the possibility of better feelings in me. Yesterday I prayed over Tanya, but I forget why. With the children I don't feel *young*, but calm and happy.

6th March. Seryozha is ill. I am in a dream. Nothing is real. Better or worse, that's all I understand. Lyovochka is energetic and independent, with the strength of mind to carry on writing. I feel he is strength and life itself, and I am a worm crawling over him and feeding off him. I am afraid of being weak. My nerves have been bad and I feel ashamed. I have such reverence for him, but I realize I have fallen so low as to sometimes pounce on his weaknesses. He has gone for a walk, I am alone and everything is silent. The children are fast asleep, the big stove is burning; upstairs it's so clean and bare that the vivid scented orange blossoms seem out of place and even the sound of my own breathing frightens me. Lyovochka came in for a moment and I felt brighter. He is like a breath of fresh air.

8th March. I am feeling much gayer. Seryozha is better and the illness has passed. Lyova too is better, and is in thoroughly good spirits, but to me he is cold and indifferent. I am afraid to say he *doesn't love me*. Yet the thought torments me, and that is why I feel so hesitant and bashful in my relations with him. I was in a frightful state during those sad days when Seryozha was ill. Suffering doesn't subdue me, and that is bad. I was pursued by ghastly thoughts I am frightened and ashamed to admit. As Lyovochka was treating me so coldly and was forever going out of the house, I got it into my head that he was going off to see A.* This thought has been tormenting me all day, but now Seryozha has taken my mind off it, and I feel terribly ashamed. I should know him better by now. If it were true, how could he be so open and natural with me? It must be said, however, that as long as she and I live in close proximity every bad mood or cold word from him will reduce me to an agony of jealousy. What if he were suddenly to return and tell me?... Oh, what a lot of nonsense, I ought to be ashamed. I just felt obliged to confess this terrible thought that hovers in my mind.

10th March. Lyovochka has a headache; he has ridden off to Yasenki. I am not well either, and both the children have coughs and colds. For his brother's mistress Masha I nurse a "silent hatred", as he puts it, although for her children I have a special and genuine love (not without a tinge of condescension). Lyovochka has been much more affectionate today. He actually kissed me for the first time in days. I am doing a lot of copying and am glad to be of some use.

14th March. Lyovochka is playing some Chopin Preludes. He is in fine spirits, although with me he is distant and wary. The children absorb me completely. They both have diarrhoea; it's driving me frantic. Our friend Dyakov* came, still the same irrepressible "nightingale", as Tanya calls him. I am very fond of him, and find him sympathetic and easy to talk to. I long for spring, but it's late this year. Lyovochka has been feeling the urge to visit Tula, as he apparently needs to see more people. I do too, but not people in general, just Tanya, the Zefirots,* Mother and Father.

15th March. Lyovochka has gone off to Tula and I'm glad. His brother's son is dying* and I feel desperately sad. My headache is better today and I feel full of energy. The children aren't completely well yet but they're a bit better. The sun came out for a moment and its effect on me was like a waltz on a sixteen-year-old girl. I long for spring, for country walks, for summer. It's such ages since I heard from my family. What can my lovely poetic Tanya be doing? Lyovochka and I are happy and straightforward with each other again. He told me he had felt very dissatisfied with himself recently… I love him terribly, I could never become a wicked person with him. His confession, and his knowledge of himself makes me feel very humble, and forces me to search out every single one of my faults.

20th March. For the past two days I have had a fever in the morning and a frightful headache. I was reading a review of *The Cossacks* when I suddenly realized it was *I* who stood in his way, and that his youth and his love were all spent, wasted on Cossack girls and other women. My children cling to me, I have given myself to them, and it is a great joy to know I am indispensable to them. When Tanya lies at my breast, or Seryozha hugs me with his little arms, I feel no jealousy, no grief, no regrets, no desires, nothing. The weather is wonderful, spring is here, but I am not destined to enjoy it. I admire Lyovochka, happy and strong in mind and body. It's a terrible thing to feel so inferior. My only resources, my only weapons to match his, are my children, my energy, my youth, and that I am a fine healthy wife. Now I am just his mangy dog.

23rd March. Lyovochka is very busy with the dairy yard, and is writing his novel* with much enthusiasm. He is bursting with ideas, but will he ever write them all down? He sometimes talks to me about his plans and ideas, which is a tremendous joy. I always understand him too.

26th March. In a sudden fit of domesticity I tidied everything up – I always feel like this when I've put Seryozha and Tanya to bed. They are almost well now. Lyovochka is in a bilious mood. Today a terrible thought occurred to me: what would he do if, after taking my love and devotion for granted for so long and caring so little for my feelings, I were suddenly to grow cold towards him? It's not possible, of course, which is why I can speak of it so lightly, and why he will continue to disregard me. His brother Seryozha has spent the past few days with us. He is very unhappy at present, and I am growing extremely fond of him. It's dull and cloudy outside, but I am in a state of childish excitement and in a holiday mood. Tomorrow is Palm Saturday, a day I used to love at home. After that it will be Easter, which nowadays is just the same as any other weekday in Lent. In the past I used to cry so much, but now I am much calmer. Yesterday Seryozha said: "The only good things in life are love, music, nightingales and the moon," and we had a long talk in which I didn't feel at all shy with him. When I talk to Lyovochka he always looks at me as if to say, "What right do you have to discuss such things? You can't *feel* it."

1st April. Lyovochka is in Tula and I am depressed and beset by morbid thoughts. He keeps complaining of blood rushes, poor digestion and buzzing ears; all this scares me dreadfully, and I am even more a prey to these fears when I'm on my own, especially on such a lovely bright spring day. The children are almost well and I have been taking them for walks, one at a time; Tanya has now seen God's world for the first time in her six-month existence. I have done nothing all day, just tried to escape my gloomy thoughts. He says bad health has shortened his life by a half. And his life is so precious. I love him intensely and it upsets me that I can't do more to make him happy. I feel no bitterness towards him, just the most total and terrifying love.

3rd May. It's a terrible spring. My sister Tanya has come, and the hunting, riding and snipe-shooting have all started again. Everyone has been in good health and I was getting on well with them all, but today everything went wrong and I quarrelled with Lyova; I am a spiteful, wilful person and must mend my ways. The children are ill. I am angry with Tanya for meddling in Lyovochka's life. They go to Nikolskoe, or go off hunting, riding or walking. I actually made a jealous scene for the first time in my life yesterday. I am now bitterly regretting it. I shall let her have my horse, which I think is very nice of me. He is much too self-indulgent, though. The two of them have gone off to the woods alone to shoot snipe and I am imagining God knows what.

9th June. The day before yesterday everything was settled: Tanya and his brother Seryozha are to be married. They are a joy to see. Her happiness gives me more pleasure than my own ever did. I play chaperone as they stroll about the garden together, a role that both amuses and irritates me. Because of Tanya I now love Seryozha too – it's all quite splendid. The wedding will be in twenty days or so.* I wonder how things will work out. She has loved him for a long time, she is a lovely person and has such a splendid character, and I am glad we'll be even closer friends now.

12th July (Nikolskoe). Nothing has come of it. Seryozha has betrayed Tanya. He behaved like a swine.* It has been almost a month of constant grief – it breaks my heart to look at Tanya. To think that such a sweet, poetic, talented person should be ruined. And there are symptoms of consumption, which worry me terribly. I shall never be able to write the whole sad story in my diary. But my anger with Seryozha knows no bounds. I shall do everything in my power to have my revenge on him. Tanya has behaved extraordinarily well. She loved him very much, and he deceived her into believing he loved her too. Whereas of course he loved the gypsy woman more. Masha is a good woman, and I feel sorry for her and have nothing against her. But he is loathsome. Wait a bit, wait a bit, he kept saying, and all the time he was merely toying with her emotions and mocking her feelings for him. In the end she also began to feel sorry for Masha and the children; she could stand being made a fool of no longer and she loved and pitied *him* so much – and she broke it off. And that was twelve days after they had become engaged and had kissed, and he promised her the usual silly things and made all sorts of plans. What a brute. I shall tell everyone about it, including my children, in the hope that it will teach them never to behave like that.* My own family life is wonderfully calm and happy. What did I do to deserve such happiness? The children and Lyova have been well and he and I are on the best of terms, and outside it is gloriously warm. Summer is here, and everyone and everything is perfect. If only this vile business with Seryozha hadn't disturbed our peaceful, honest life. We have been here in Nikolskoe since 28th June, our son Seryozha's birthday. This morning a neighbour of ours called Volkov paid his first visit. He is a shy, agreeable, fair-haired, snub-nosed man, and I liked him. Life here is a series of impressions – swimming, the river, the hills, the heat, contentment of soul, red berries, Tanya's grief. I am consoled by my children and my darling Lyovochka, who is in a wonderfully poetic mood. I am happy – who knows for how long?

16th July. I have quarrelled with Nurse* and feel desperately ashamed of myself, for she is a good woman. I tried to make it up and apologized to her, but one mustn't get too deeply involved with these people for they wouldn't understand. The poet Fet and his wife are here. They are pleasant people, although he is a little pompous; she is rather plain, but good-natured. Poor Tanya troubles me terribly. She is still in a daze and we fear consumption. Little Tanya too has been ill, and I have been worried about her; she is better now. She is a sweet, lively baby, and her eyes and smile are adorable. Seryozha has been naughty recently, probably because he was ill; he is generally the sweetest, most good-natured child. I was terrified by the thunderstorm today. Lyova is reading the war scenes in his novel; I don't care for these parts at all.

Why did I quarrel with Nurse? I am just like Maman. I have recently discovered an alarming number of things about myself which are like her and which I disliked in her, mainly my habit of announcing to the world what a good woman I am and expecting all my faults to be forgiven.

1866

4th April – a former student, Dmitry Karakozov, makes an attempt on the Tsar's life. Hundreds of people rounded up and arrested. 3rd October – Karakozov publicly hanged. The end of the "era of reforms" and the start of a period of repression.

22nd May – the Tolstoys' second son, Ilya (Ilyusha), is born.

12th March. We spent 6 weeks in Moscow and returned here on the 7th,* and in Yasnaya I immediately felt the old security; slightly melancholy, but imperturbably happy nonetheless. I enjoyed myself in Moscow. I loved seeing my family, and they loved seeing my children. Tanya is a clever, healthy, affectionate little girl. Seryozha is much stronger now; he is a reasonable child, less amenable than he used to be, but very sweet-natured. I am afraid I overindulge them, but I am delighted by them. Lyova and I have been cold and awkward together ever since P. behaved so rudely in Moscow in response to my inept treatment of him. It has put a great strain on our relations.* I now feel horribly ashamed, but it's not as if there was the slightest blot on my conscience, now or at any moment in my marriage. Lyova has judged me too harshly. Yet even so it pleases me, for it proves he cares for me, and in future I shall be a hundred times more careful, and shall enjoy being so. Yet it's terrible to think this incident is another "cut" in our relationship. I now feel even more contemptible, even more liable to abase myself, which means that I make even fewer claims on the happiness and self-esteem I need to survive.

We spent most of our time in Moscow with my parents in the Kremlin. In the morning the carriage would come for the children and we would go and see them for the whole day. Lyova would go off to his sculpture classes and his gymnastics. The friends of ours I saw most of were the Perfilevs, the Bashilovs and Princess Gorchakova; we also developed an acquaintance with Princess Obolenskaya. I went to some concerts and very much enjoyed the classical music. It was a nice life and I loved everything in Moscow, even our hotel on Dmitrovka Street, and our stuffy bed-sitting room and study, where Lyova modelled his red clay horse and the two of us sat talking in the evenings. My brother Petya* is a dear creature and I love him. I often think of them still, and it breaks my heart that I cannot see them now.

9th June. On 22nd May I was unexpectedly delivered of my second son, Ilya. I was expecting him in the middle of June.

19th June. We have a new bailiff here with his wife.* She is an attractive young woman and a "nihilist". She and Lyova have endless lively discussions about literature and politics. This is quite improper in my opinion; their conversations go on far too long, and they may be flattering for her but for me they are complete torture. He was the one who preached against admitting any outsider, especially a young and attractive person, into the *intimité* of our family circle, yet now he is the first to do so. I haven't let him know how much I hate it of course, but I haven't a moment's peace of mind. We have been sleeping in separate rooms since Ilya's birth, which is wrong, for if we were together I would have it out with him this evening and blurt out all my resentment, whereas I shan't go into his room now, and he won't come in to see me. The children are the joy of my life. Having experienced the happiness they give me it would be a sin to ask for anything more. Yet it still grieves me that Lyovochka doesn't observe his own rules. And why was he saying only today that a man always worries he might accuse his wife of something she didn't do – as if one suffered only when one's husband actually *did* something wrong. For even the most momentary private doubts about his love for his wife can be just as disastrous. It's very wrong of him to honour Maria Ivanovna with these ardent speeches. It's almost one o'clock in the morning but I can't sleep. I have a horrible premonition that this nihilist woman will be my *bête noire*.

22nd July. Lyovochka invented some excuse for visiting *that* house earlier today. Maria Ivanovna told me so herself, and that he stood under her balcony talking to her. What reason can he have had for going there in the rain? It's obvious: because he likes her. The thought is driving me insane. I wish her every conceivable ill, although I'm always especially nice to her for some reason. I wonder if her husband will turn out to be unfit for the job so they'll have to leave? At the moment I am wild with jealousy. He treats me with the utmost coldness. My breasts ache, and it's agony for me to feed the baby. Today I had to call in Mavrusha to give him some extra milk to allow my breasts to heal. These ailments of mine always make him treat me cruelly.

24th July. Lyovochka visited her house again today and came back saying how he pitied the poor woman and her dull life. Then he asked me why I hadn't invited them to dinner. If I had had my way I would never have had her here in the first place. Oh Lyovochka, can't you see you've been caught! My aching breasts rob me of so much time and happiness. And the worst thing is I have completely withdrawn from him and he has withdrawn even further from me. It disturbs him that I have Mavrusha to help me feed Ilyusha, and it grieves me to see him suckling another woman's milk as well as my own. God only knows when my breasts will heal. Everything is going wrong. My heart rejoices whenever Lyova expresses his dissatisfaction with the way the farm is being run. Maybe he'll dismiss the bailiff, and I shall be rid of my tormenting jealousy for Maria Ivanovna. I would be sorry for his sake, but her I hate.

10th August. There are days when you feel so happy and light-hearted that you long to do something to astonish people and make them love you. When I hear of others' misfortune I count myself very fortunate. Yesterday Bibikov told us the dreadful story of the regimental clerk here in Yasenki who has just been shot for hitting his company commander in the face. Lyovochka was a defence witness at the open court martial, but of course the defence was unfortunately a mere formality.*

We had a lot of visitors all on the same day: the two Princesses Gorchakova, nice Prince Lvov and fat Sollogub with his two adolescent sons. He told me I was the perfect wife for a writer, and that a wife should be "the nursemaid of her husband's talent". I appreciate that, and shall try to be an even better nursemaid of Lyovochka's talent from now on. All my jealousy of Maria Ivanovna has vanished – it was virtually groundless anyway – and our relations are much simpler and happier, if still somewhat reserved.

12th November. Lyova is in Moscow and has taken my sister Tanya with him. She is very poorly and I am desperately worried about her. The more hopeless her health is, the more I love her. She will probably visit Italy with the Dyakovs.* I am afraid I failed to realize how ill she was this autumn. We were having such a good time here in the first three weeks of September that I instinctively repressed all sad thoughts. When I don't open my diary for a long time I always think what a pity it is I don't record the happy times. The Dyakovs spent those weeks with us, with Lyova's sister Mashenka and her little girls and Tanya, and there was so much friendship between us, so much simple affection; it's not often one enjoys such happiness with friends. I shall always remember my name day, 17th September, with special joy.* To my surprise and delight, a band struck up a tune for me as we were eating dinner, and there was dearest Lyova gazing at me so tenderly. That evening we sat out on the veranda, which was lit by lanterns and candles. I shall never forget the young ladies darting about in their white muslin dresses, and good-natured little Kolokoltsev; but it's Lyovochka's sweet cheerful face I remember most clearly, as he rushed here, there and everywhere, doing everything he could to ensure we all enjoyed ourselves. I quite surprised myself, dancing with such abandon. The weather was perfect and everyone had a wonderful time. I now spend most of my time copying out his novel (which I am reading for the first time).* It gives me great pleasure. As I copy I experience a whole new world of emotions, thoughts and impressions. Nothing touches me so deeply as his ideas, his genius. This has only been so recently. Whether it's because I have changed or because this novel really is extraordinarily good, I don't know. I write very quickly, so I can follow the story and catch the mood, but slowly enough to be able to stop, reflect on each new idea and discuss it with him later. He and I often talk about the novel together, and for some reason he listens to what I have to say (which makes me very proud) and trusts my opinions.

1867

May – a Polish émigré attempts to kill the Tsar in Paris. Summer – a small group of populists travel to the villages to teach the peasants.

July – Tanya Behrs marries Alexander Kuzminsky, a young magistrate. December – first three volumes of War and Peace *published.*

12th January. I am in a terrible state of agitation, as though something was coming to an end. There are indeed many things that must soon come to an end, and that terrifies me. The children have been continuously ill, and I still find the Englishwoman awkward and gloomy.* I don't warm to her. They say one becomes very anxious when one is about to die. Well, I feel extremely anxious and keep rushing about and have so much to do. Lyovochka has been writing all winter, irritable and excited, often with tears in his eyes.* I feel this novel of his will be superb. All the parts he has read to me have moved me to tears too; whether this is because as his wife I feel so much for him, or because it really *is* very good I cannot say for certain – although I think the second. His family generally gets nothing but his *fatigues de travail*; with me he is often impatient and bad-tempered, and I am beginning to feel very lonely.

15th March. At ten o'clock last night, when I was already asleep, a fire broke out in the greenhouses and everything was burnt to ashes. Lyova woke me up and I stood and watched the blaze from the window. He dragged the gardener's children and their possessions from the building, while I ran to the village to fetch some peasants. But there was nothing they could do: everything was burnt, all those plants Grandfather had so lovingly cultivated all those years ago, which had given pleasure to three generations; the little that is left is probably frozen and charred too. I wasn't so upset about it last night, but today I had to struggle to control my feelings, otherwise I would have been in floods of tears. What a blow. I feel desperately sorry for Lyovochka; he looks so crushed, and every little tribulation of his weighs heavily upon me. He had lavished so much love on those plants, and everything he planted was just beginning to flourish. But nothing can bring them back now, only time will ease the pain.

16th September. Tomorrow is my name day. All day I have been unable to stop thinking of 17th September last year.* God knows I don't need parties or music or dancing – all I need is for him to want me and love giving me pleasure as he used to; if only he knew how much I appreciated his kindness to me last year – I shall remember it as long as I live. Then I felt so sure of myself, so happy and strong and beautiful. Now I feel equally sure I am worthless, weak and ugly.

This morning we had a friendly discussion about the estate and agreed about everything and were such good friends, just as though we were *one* again, yet we seldom talk to each other about anything these days. I think of nothing but my children and my own trivial preoccupations. Seryozha came up to me just now and said, "What's that you're writing in your little book?" And I told him he could read it when he grew up. What will he make of it? Will he think badly of me? Will the children stop loving me too? It's because I am so demanding that I can never make people love me.

1868

Universities of St Petersburg and Moscow in ferment. September – first issue of Mikhail Bakunin's periodical, the People's Cause, *published in exile in Switzerland.*

Tolstoy immersed in the last part of War and Peace. *Sofia assumes most of the responsibility for the household and estate. Autumn – entire Tolstoy family travels to Moscow, where Sofia's father is dying.*

31st July. It makes me laugh to read my diary. What a lot of contradictions – as though I were the unhappiest of women! But who could be happier? Could any marriage be more happy and harmonious than ours? When I am alone in my room I sometimes laugh for joy and cross myself and pray to God for many, many more years of happiness. I always write my diary when we quarrel. There are still days when we quarrel, but this is because of various subtle emotional reasons, and we wouldn't quarrel if we didn't love each other. I have been married for six years now, but I love him more and more. He often says it isn't really *love*, but we have grown so used to each other we cannot be separated. But I still love him with the same poetic, fevered, jealous love, and his composure occasionally irritates me.

He has gone off hunting with my brother Petya. It's hard for him to write in the summer. Afterwards they'll go to Nikolskoe. I am unwell and have stayed indoors almost all day. The children go out for long walks and come back only to eat their meals on the veranda. Ilya is a perfect darling. Tanya's husband Kuzminsky is neither flesh nor fowl.

1869

20th May – Sofia Tolstoy gives birth to her third son, Lev (Lyova, Lyolya). Tolstoy finishes War and Peace. *4th December – the entire novel is published.*

1870

First strikes in St Petersburg, followed by similar disturbances elsewhere. Numerous people arrested and imprisoned.

Tolstoy starts work on a novel about Peter the Great, writes a series of readers for peasants and learns Greek. Sofia writes a short story called 'Sparrows', and Russian and French grammars for her children.

5th June. I have been weaning Lyova for four days now.* I am almost sadder with him than I was with the others. I blessed him, and cried and prayed for him. It's very hard, this first separation from one's baby. I think I must be pregnant again. With each new child one sacrifices a little more of one's life and accepts an even heavier burden of anxieties and illnesses.

1871

12th February – premature birth of the Tolstoys' second daughter, Maria (Masha). Sofia nearly dies of puerperal fever. Shortly after the birth, Tolstoy leaves for a health cure in Samara, 500 miles east of Moscow, and buys a 67,000-acre estate near Buzuluk.

18th August. I saw my sister Tanya and her children off to the Caucasus yesterday evening. My soul is empty and sad at the prospect of losing my dearest friend. We have never been parted before. I feel as if part of my soul had been torn out, and nothing can comfort me. There is no one else in the whole world who could make me smile, comfort me when I am sad, and lift my spirits when I feel low. I look at nature and at my life stretching ahead of me, dismal and desolate, for everything seems dead without her. I cannot find words to express what I feel. Something has died in me. It's not a grief one can forget through tears, it will make my heart ache for years to come.* I worry constantly about Lyovochka's health. For two months he has been on a koumiss* diet, which has done him no good at all.*

1872

Marx's Capital *(first published 1867) appears in Russian, its first foreign translation.*

Tolstoy, disillusioned with fiction, opens a school for peasant children in the house and writes his peasant ABC. He is increasingly haunted by fears of death. Spring – he abandons his peasant school and turns to teaching his own children. 13th June – Sofia gives birth to her fourth son, Pyotr (Petya).

It has been a happy winter; our souls have been in harmony again, and Lyovochka's health hasn't been bad.

1st April. Lyovochka returned from Moscow on 30th March.* The children have brought yellow and purple flowers in from the garden.

I fasted, returned from Tula by train, then took the carriage. There's snow only in the gullies and it's terribly muddy, but warm and sunny. Lyovochka hunted woodsnipe this evening; he shot one and Mitrofan* sent us another.

3rd April. Still warm. He shot two woodsnipe. We sat up until almost four a.m. getting the proofs of the *ABC** ready to send off.

6th April. A bright windy morning followed by thunder and a violent hailstorm. Lyovochka has had a chill for the past three nights and is still unwell.

8th April. There was a terrific thunderstorm in the night, followed by a downpour of rain. Lyovochka still has a chill in his back and feels unwell but is in good spirits, and says he has enough work to last him a lifetime. Everything is green. The leaves are bursting out, the lungwort is in flower, and the grass is already tall.

19th April. Lyovochka looked at the stars all night until dawn.

20th April. Drove out with his niece Varya and the children to pick violets. Everything is very fresh. I feel slightly feverish. Lyovochka is well.

21st April. I drove out to pick morels with Varya, and her fiancé Nagornov* and the children. We got a whole basketful. It is still cool. Lyovochka, Varya and Nagornov went off to shoot snipe. The sun set like a blazing ball of fire. It is a warm, still evening, 11° above zero. The lime tree is almost in leaf, and all the other trees apart from the oak have opened up. This morning Lyovochka brought in a huge bunch of flowers and branches he had picked from various trees.

27th–28th April. Lyovochka left for Moscow last night. Masha* is very sick.

30th April. Unbearable heat, thunderstorms night and day.

13th May. Lyovochka brought in a bunch of sweet briar covered in flowers.

15th May. We had a swim, made coffee, then picked mushrooms for our basket. Very hot.

18th May. Hannah has gone to Tula to buy toys for the children. We went out to pick mushrooms and were caught in a shower – we got chilled through. Lyovochka is very upset that they haven't yet seen the proofs, and wrote yesterday to Moscow telling them to return the original which is with Ries.* There are huge pods on the acacias. Dry, windy and cold.

20th May. Terrible heat. Lyovochka and Ilyusha went to Tula in the train and I took the other children swimming. The sweet briar has lost its blossom. Yesterday they sold the hay from the orchard.

1873

Summer – young revolutionaries flock "to the people", travelling to the villages dressed as artisans and peasants to teach literacy classes, give medical help and spread socialist ideas. Hundreds arrested.

Spring – Tolstoy gives up work on his Peter the Great novel and starts work on Anna Karenina. *A bull on the estate gores a peasant to death. Shortly afterwards, the whole family travels south to Samara to stay on their new estate. November – publication of the third edition of the* Complete Works of L.N. Tolstoy, *in eight volumes. 9th November – Petya dies of croup. Tolstoy haunted by fears of death.*

13th February. Lyovochka has gone to Moscow* and all day I have been sitting alone here staring into space, a prey to sickening anxieties. I sometimes search my heart and ask myself what I really want. And to my horror, the answer is that I want gaiety, smart clothes and chatter. I want people to admire me and say how pretty I am, and I want him to see and hear them too; I long for him occasionally to emerge from his rapt inner existence that demands so much of him; I wish he could briefly lead a normal life with me, like a normal person. But then my heart cries out against the Devil's temptations of Eve, and I think even worse of myself. I hate people to tell me I am beautiful. I never believed them, and now it would be too late anyway – what would be the point? My darling little Petya* loves his old mother as much as he would love a great beauty. And Lyovochka could get used to the plainest wife, so long as she was docile and quiet and lived the sort of life that suited him. I want to turn my character inside out and demolish everything that is mean and false in me. I am having my hair curled today, and have been happily imagining how nice it will look, even though nobody will see me and it's quite unnecessary. I adore ribbons, I would like a new leather belt – and now I have written this I feel like crying…

The children are waiting upstairs for their music lesson, and here I am in the study writing all this stupid nonsense.

We went skating today. The boys kept bumping into their tutor Fyodor Fyodorovich* and I had trouble pacifying him and trying to comfort them. I don't take to the new Englishwoman* who arrived here the other morning; she is too lethargic and *commune* for my liking. But it's too early to tell.

11th November. On 9th November at nine in the morning, my little Petyushka died of a throat infection.* He died peacefully, after two days' illness. He was born on 13th June, 1872, and I had fed him for fourteen and a half months, and he lived just another three afterwards. What a bright, happy little boy – I loved my darling too much and now there is nothing. He was buried yesterday. I cannot reconcile the two Petyas, the living and the dead; they are both precious to me, but what does the living Petya, so bright and affectionate, have in common with the dead one, so cold and still and serious? He loved me very much – I wonder if it hurt him too to leave me.

1874

Revolutionaries of the Land and Liberty organization continue to go "to the people". By the end of the year some 800 are rounded up and arrested, and Land and Liberty is virtually wiped out.

22nd April – Sofia gives birth to a son, Nikolai. 20th June – Tolstoy's Aunt Tatyana dies after living for fifty years at Yasnaya Polyana. Her companion, Natalya Petrovna, becomes deranged and is moved to an old people's home. Tolstoy's Aunt Pelageya moves in. Tolstoy's spiritual crisis deepens and his religious doubts multiply.

17th February. When I think of the future I see a blank. I am haunted by the premonition that as soon as the grass grows over Petya's grave they will have to plough it up for me.

1875

Two large strikes in Odessa. Peasants near Kiev start to redistribute the land amongst themselves and dispatch one of their number to St Petersburg to petition the Tsar.

January – chapters 1–14 of Anna Karenina *appear in the* Russian Herald. *2nd February – ten-month-old Nikolai dies in agony of meningitis. 1st November – Sofia gives birth to a baby girl, Varvara, who dies immediately afterwards. December – Aunt Pelageya dies after a fall. Tolstoy prone to ever more severe doubts and depressions.*

12th October. This isolated country life is becoming intolerable. Dismal apathy, indifference to everything, day after day, month after month, year after year – nothing changes. I wake up in the morning and lie there wondering who will get me up, who is waiting for me. The cook is bound to come in, then Nurse, complaining that the servants are grumbling about the food and there's no sugar, which means we must send for more. So then I get up, my shoulder aching, and sit silently darning holes, and then it's time for the children's grammar and piano lessons, which I do with pleasure, although with the sad realization that I'm not doing it as well as I should. Then in the evening more darning, with Auntie* and Lyovochka playing endless horrible games of patience together. I get some brief pleasure from reading, but how many good books are there? On days like today I feel I'm living in a dream. But no, this is life, not a dream. Surely it can't go on much longer. My hope is that God will light the spark of life in Lyovochka and he will be the person he used to be.*

1876

Troops put down the rebellious peasants. December – Land and Liberty organizes its first demonstration in St Petersburg.

Summer – Tolstoy visits Samara again to buy horses for a stud farm he plans to start. October – Sofia starts work on a biography of Tolstoy, on which she works until 1878. He resolves his religious doubts by strict observance of the religious rituals.

15th September. We live in such isolation, and here I am again with my silent friend, my diary. I intend to write it every day without fail from now on. Lyovochka went off to Samara,* and from there to Orenburg, a town he had always wanted to visit. I got a telegram from him there. I miss him and worry even more. I try to tell myself I am pleased he is enjoying himself, but it isn't true. I am hurt that he has torn himself away from me when we were getting on so well and were such good friends, and has sentenced me to two anxious weeks without him.

I have decided to make the best of it and am throwing myself into the children's lessons. But goodness, how impatient I am! I keep losing my temper and shouting at them – today I became annoyed beyond endurance by Ilya's laziness and the spelling mistakes in Seryozha's essay on the Volga, and I burst into tears as the lesson was ending. The children were dismayed, but Seryozha was sorry for me and I found that very touching; afterwards he kept following me around and was so quiet and attentive. Tanya and I aren't getting on. How sad to have this endless battle with one's children.

17th September. My name day. One more day has passed without Lyovochka or so much as a word from him. This morning I got up feeling lazy and unwell, plagued by minor worries. The children went off with my brother Styopa* to fly their kite and ran back red-faced and excited to beg me to watch. But I didn't go, for I had ordered all Lyovochka's papers to be fetched from the gun closet and was immersed in the world of his novels and diaries. I was very excited and experienced a wealth of impressions. But I realized I could never write that biography of him as I intended, for I could never be impartial; I avidly search his diaries for any reference to love, and am so tormented by jealousy that I can no longer see anything clearly. I shall try to do it, though.*

18th September. I had a telegram from him in Syzran today saying he will be home the day after tomorrow in the morning. I suddenly felt more cheerful, and the house was all happiness and light; the children's lessons went well and they were adorable. But I have a pain in my chest – I wonder if I'm going to be ill. It reduced me to tears today and I feared for our peaceful life together. Talking and explaining things to the children during lessons was agony. I keep catching my breath. They were in a bad mood when they came upstairs after M. Rey's class.* Apparently they had misbehaved and had been given "twos" for bad conduct. I told Seryozha that as he had been naughty he couldn't go hunting. I hoped this punishment would teach him a lesson, but he just lost his temper and shouted, "*Au contraire!*" which I found very hurtful. But later, when he was saying goodnight, he asked if I was still angry with him, and I was very pleased and forgave him.

1877

March – great public trial opens of those (mainly women) arrested for propagandizing in the factories of Moscow (Trial of the 50). April – Russia declares war on Turkey. Hundreds of revolutionaries volunteer to fight with the Bulgarian partisans in the Balkans. October–January 1878 – second great public trial (Trial of the 193), of those arrested for propagandizing in the villages.

Final chapters of Anna Karenina *published in the* Russian Herald, *earning Tolstoy huge royalties. July – he makes a pilgrimage on foot to Optyna Pustyn monastery. The discord between the couple increases. Sofia assumes yet more of the burdens of running the farm and the house. 6th December – Andrei Tolstoy (Andryusha) born.*

27th February. As I was reading through some of Lyovochka's old diaries today, I realized I would never be able to write those 'Notes for a Biography', as I had intended to. His inner life is so complicated and his diaries disturb me so much that I grow confused, and cannot see things clearly. The other day, when I asked him to tell me about something from his past, he said: "Please don't ask about these things; it disturbs me to think of my past and I'm much too old now to relive my whole life in memories."

1878

*24th January – a young revolutionary called Vera Zasulich attempts
to kill General Trepov, governor-general of St Petersburg. February–
March – student demonstration in Kiev. 31st March – Zasulich tried
and acquitted, and a warrant issued for her rearrest, but by then she
has fled to Switzerland. November – student riots in St Petersburg.*

*April – Tolstoy visits Samara and buys more land. He starts work
on a novel on the uprising of Russia's first revolutionaries, the
Decembrists (never published). Sofia Tolstoy finishes her biography
of him.*

24th September, Sunday. I got up late. Lyovochka attended the liturgy*
and the three of us, Lyovochka, his sister Mashenka and I, drank
coffee together. After lunch the children walked over to Yasenki, and
Mashenka drove to Tula with Seryozha's Classics tutor, the high-
school teacher Ulyaninsky. Lyovochka and Seryozha took their guns
and the hounds and went hunting, and I stayed at home cutting out
jackets for the boys. Then Mashenka, Annie* and I all went off in the
carriage to Yasenki to look for the children. Just before I left, Prince
Urusov* appeared with his gun and went off to look for our huntsmen.
I found the children in the shop at Yasenki buying sweets. We all
met for dinner, then played a game of croquet in the twilight, with
Lyovochka, Ilyusha and I playing M. Nief, Lyova and Urusov; they
beat us. After that Lyovochka and Urusov played chess, the children
ate their sweets and were rather rowdy, and I read Octave Feuillet's
Journal d'une femme. It is all very fine and idealistic, although the
ending is a bit forced. But the whole thing seems to be written in
deliberate contrast to the excessive realism of some contemporary
literature. It is midnight. Lyovochka is having supper, after that we
shall go to bed.

25th September. I taught the children this morning, then Mashenka
came to dinner bringing Anton, Rossa and Nadya Delvig with her.
The children were in ecstasies. After dinner we danced a quadrille
and I partnered little Lyova to make a third couple. Lyovochka and
Alexander Grigorevich* played for us. Then Masha and Alexander

played a piano and violin duet, which was quite successful (the delightful Mozart sonata with the andante that always moves me to tears). Then Lyovochka played some Weber sonatas. But for me Alexander Grigorevich's violin-playing compared badly with Nagornov's. Finally they did Beethoven's *Kreutzer Sonata* – badly; now that should be truly something when played properly!

26th September. Lyovochka and Auntie went to church, while the rest of us played a jolly game of croquet. Then Lyovochka persuaded the children to walk the borzois across the fields. They each took a dog on the lead, one of the huntsmen rode along beside them, also with a dog on the lead, and Annie, Mlle Gachet and M. Nief all followed behind. It made a very pretty picture. After we had finished our game of croquet the others joined them and I went to visit Vasily Ivanovich.* After dinner the children crowded into Lyovochka's sitting room, laughing and chattering and pushing one another. They went to bed early.

27th September. It's still clear and dry. I did a lot of cutting and sewing, gave Liza* a French lesson, and Masha and Tanya a German lesson.

3rd October. I have been indoors all day despite the marvellous weather. I gave the children their lessons, and had to scold Tanya for refusing to take a walk and running away from Mlle Gachet. Lyovochka's sister Mashenka came and sat with me and was in a very good mood. He went hunting and shot five hares. His horse fell under him, although he only hurt his arm, thank God, but it was at full gallop and he flew over its head, and the horse twisted its neck and lay there for a long time unable to get up. Lyovochka has put a plaster on his right side – I am still anxious about him. Andryusha is an adorable child; he feeds himself now on bread and milk. The children played croquet after their lessons. While Lyovochka was having supper after the hunt, a letter arrived from my sister Tanya; I was so happy, and when I read it to the others, I couldn't stop smiling with delight. We all burst out laughing at the part where she sent her regards to "our kind, gentle, devout, fair-skinned papa", which was how our little fortune-telling book *The Oracle* described him, and what we jokingly call him when we play croquet.

4th October. My daughter Tanya's fourteenth birthday. As soon as I got up I walked to the little plantation where the children were having a picnic. M. Nief was there with his sleeves rolled up, making them *une omelette* and some hot chocolate. There were four bonfires, and Seryozha was roasting *shashlyk*. We had enormous fun and ate a lot, and we had magnificent weather. We got home and were just starting a game of croquet when what should we see but a procession of horses and donkeys filing along our "prospect" on their way from Samara. The children were tremendously excited and immediately rushed over, leapt on the donkeys and started riding about on them. Nikolenka came to dinner with Baroness Delvig and Rossa, and we drank Tanya's health in champagne; she blushed but was very pleased. Later that evening Tanya and I drove our guests back to Kozlovka in the carriage, so we didn't get to bed until late. On our way home we met Lyovochka, who had come out to meet us on foot.

6th October. I went downstairs this morning to see Lyovochka, busily writing at his desk. He told me this was his tenth attempt to start his new novel. It's to open with a cross-examination in a trial involving some peasants and a landlord. He got the details of the trial from actual recorded documents, and is even leaving in the relevant dates. The trial, like a fountain, will precipitate events – for the peasants and for the landowner, in St Petersburg, and in all the other places where the various characters will play their part.* I very much like this *entrée en matière*. The children are studying, but they are in a lazy mood and keep thinking up different games.

9th October. Bibikov has just returned from Samara* with bad news: there's practically no money from the estate again. I was terribly angry when I found out they had bought some land there without telling me. They bought some cattle too, and the harvest wasn't good. I had a frightful argument with Lyovochka. I think I have been very ill used, and I still don't think I've done anything wrong. I hate everything: myself, my life, my so-called "happiness"; it's all dreary and disgusting.

15th October. When I went into the drawing room for my morning tea, I found Lyovochka, his brother Seryozha, and the children all sitting there with the two teachers, the hunchbacked drawing master and Ulyaninsky the tutor. One feels slightly constrained by the teachers' presence. Lyovochka then drove to church.

Preparations started for the hunt. Seven horses were saddled up, and Lyovochka, the two Seryozhas, Ilyusha, a couple of servants and

M. Nief rode off with the hounds, while Tanya, Masha, Lyova, Mlle Gachet and Liza rode the donkeys to Kozlovka. I stayed behind on my own and played with Andryusha for a while, but when he fell asleep I grew restless, and ordered them to harness the cart for me to go and meet the children. I found them at the boundary of the estate and managed to persuade Mlle Gachet to drive home with me. There we ordered some grated horseradish and sour milk; we decided not to have dinner until our hunters were back. It was almost seven when they returned, looking very pleased with themselves and triumphantly bearing six hares strung on a stick which they gave us.

18th October. Andryusha has been ill, shivering and feverish, with an upset stomach. I got up late. The children have gone out: the boys took the dogs to the fields to catch mice, and Lyova and the girls went out on the donkeys. Dinner was frightful: the pie was dry, the potato soup greasy, the *levashniki** like shoe-leather, and hare I never eat. I just had a salad, and afterwards gave the cook a piece of my mind. Just then Lyovochka returned, with four hares and a fox. He is lethargic, silent and lost in thought; he does nothing but read.

21st October. Andryusha was very sick indeed yesterday: his little hands and feet grew cold, and he ran a high fever and tossed and sobbed in his sleep; his lips twitched and his eyelids fluttered. This morning the fever passed, but now he has diarrhoea, his sleep is still disturbed and I feel terribly worried. A certain Navrotsky, editor of a new journal called *Russian Speech*, came from Petersburg to visit us. He read us his poems and some extracts from his play – it wasn't bad. He also told us all the Petersburg news, which was quite interesting. The tutors came again today (Saturday). We had pancakes. I had a serious talk with Seryozha. Yesterday I had scolded him for making fun of people and told him how much it distressed me; today I explained that I scolded my children only because I loved them and wanted them to be happy, and our happiness, I said, depended chiefly on being loved by others.

I was thinking what a pity it is that tsars are embalmed. Everyone should be buried in the earth immediately after they die – "dust to dust". All these embalming rituals and burial vaults are disgusting.

22nd October, Sunday. This morning the hunchbacked drawing master told us the interesting story of how he started his career, as a draughtsman in a silk factory. Lyovochka attended the liturgy, then went hunting with Seryozha, but they had no luck. Nurse is in Tula, and I have been with Andryusha since seven this morning and am exhausted.

23rd October. After drinking his morning coffee with me, Lyovochka took the borzois off to Zaseka to hunt. I gave Masha a Russian lesson, Liza a French lesson, and Lyova a German lesson. Lyovochka was back for dinner with three hares, and afterwards Seryozha played a Haydn sonata – quite well – with Alexander Grigorevich accompanying him on the violin. Then this evening Lyovochka played some sonatas by Weber and Schubert, also with a violin accompaniment; I embroidered Andryusha's white cashmere robe in red silk while enjoying the music. The weather is windy and unpleasant. Lyovochka was saying he had read his fill of history and was going to start on Dickens's *Martin Chuzzlewit* for a rest. I happen to know, however, that when he turns to English novels he is about to start writing himself.

25th October. I gave Lyolya a music lesson and searched Haydn's symphonies for an easy minuet for him to play. I read with Masha, helped Liza with her lesson, and worked on a white piqué gown for Andryusha. Lyovochka took the borzois hunting. He returned with a hare and a tiny white creature rather like a weasel. Later the two of us went over Lyovochka's entire life for his biography, and I took notes while he talked. We worked cheerfully and well, and I'm glad we did it. The children are studying hard. The wind is howling and it's pouring with rain. We read more Dumas this evening.

28th October. I drank tea alone, then Tanya came in complaining of a sore throat. I was very alarmed and made her gargle with Bertholet salts, one teaspoonful dissolved in a glass of hot water. Aside from this though, she seems quite well, so I don't feel so anxious now. I went to the woods to watch them making barrels. We took the forest path and it was enchanting – clear, frosty and silent. Then I went for a walk with Masha, Mlle Gachet and Annie, and the boys went back to the threshing floor to play in the straw. The teachers again arrived while we were having dinner. Tanya did a rather good charcoal drawing of a woman's head. I sewed a christening gown for Parasha's* baby boy and gave Andryusha his first bath since his vaccination. Lyovochka went out with the hounds and killed a hare.

29th October. It snowed today, then it became warm and the snow turned to mud. The children played hide-and-seek and made a great noise, but they enjoyed themselves. Everyone stayed indoors all day because of the weather.

1st November. Lyovochka read me the beginning of his new book, *The Decembrists*, yesterday morning. It is an immense, interesting and serious undertaking. It begins with a case of some peasants and a landowner who are in dispute over a piece of land, the arrival in Moscow of Prince Chernyshev and his family, the laying of the foundation stone of the Cathedral of the Holy Saviour, a woman pilgrim, a peasant's wife, an old lady, etc. I went to Tula this morning with Dmitry Alexeevich, Seryozha and Tanya: it was fine and frosty. We bought some fur to make a coat for Tanya and a sheepskin jacket for Seryozha (costing 12 silver rubles); Seryozha was then measured for a winter overcoat (65 silver rubles), and we ordered some boots for Tanya, a fox jacket for me (to be made from our own furs) and various other things. Lyovochka had been working at home all day, and as we were nearing the house he came out to meet us. It's always a joy to return home and see his grey overcoat in the distance. Andryusha hadn't been at all sick or fretful. I had bought some tops for the boys (costing 10 kopecks each), a thimble for Masha, some beads, earrings and a brooch for the dolls, warm gloves and various other little things for the rest of them. I was terribly tired by then, for we had had nothing to eat all day but some sweet cakes and a piece of soft bread.

4th November. I gave the children their lessons and had an argument with Lyovochka about Seryozha's French; I maintain that he should be taught literature but he doesn't agree. Andryusha's nurse pierced Masha's ears so she can now wear her earrings.

6th November. Fog, air oppressive. I read some German, first with Lyova then this evening with Ilyusha. I gave Masha a Russian lesson, and she recited Pushkin's poem 'The snow has veiled the sky in mist...' quite nicely. Her written work was atrocious though, and I tore the page out of her exercise book. Alexander Grigorevich came; he isn't teaching Ilya and Lyolya a thing. Lyovochka went hunting and brought back two hares. He is fretful because he cannot write; this evening, while he was reading Dickens's *Dombey and Son*, he suddenly announced to me, "Aha! I've got it!" When I asked what he meant he wouldn't tell me at first, but eventually he said: "Well, I've been imagining this old woman – her appearance, her manner, her thoughts – but I haven't been able to find the right *feelings* for her. And I suddenly realized: it's the constant awareness that her husband, old Gerasimovich, is languishing in prison with his head shaven for a crime he didn't commit." Then he sat down at the piano and started improvising. I read an article on art and artists in the *Revue des Deux Mondes*, and quilted an eiderdown for Andryusha. This evening the children had a discussion about affectation, and they all criticized Tanya for putting on airs when they were at the Delvigs'. Everyone here is well.

7th November. I cut out shirts for Lyovochka and helped Liza with her studies. There was an unpleasant incident: I thought someone had cut a piece off my length of linen, but in fact I was wrong. Lyovochka went to the bathhouse with Ilyusha and Lyolya this evening; he is much more cheerful now and clearer in his mind about his writing.

11th November. It's a pity that I always write in my diary at the end of the day when I'm worn out. Andryusha woke up wheezing and coughing at four this morning and went on until eight. I was at my wits' end. He is slightly better now, but still has diarrhoea and a harsh rasping cough. I gave him three drops of antimony, and bandaged his neck with a piece of flannel soaked in oil, lard, soap and camphor. Today Lyovochka said all his characters were coming to life, and he saw it all much more clearly. He is cheerful and working again, now that he *believes* in it.

The drawing master and Ulyaninsky the high-school teacher came again today. Tanya is doing quite a good drawing of a shepherd boy's head, while Ilya and Lyolya merely play at it. I have done a lot of sewing and have finished a flannel vest for Andryusha, as well as a pillow and two pillowcases for him. I had a letter from Mother.

14th November. Yesterday evening Lyovochka and Alexander Grigorevich played piano and violin duets together. This morning, after a night filled with the most frightful dreams and nightmares, I had tea with Lyovochka (a rare event nowadays) and we had a long philosophical discussion about death, religion, the meaning of life and so on. These discussions have such a soothing effect on me. I interpret his wisdom on these matters in a very personal way, and can always pick out things he says that lay my doubts to rest. I should set his ideas down on paper but I can't, especially now, when I have a headache and am tired.

16th November. Lyovochka said: "All the characters and events and ideas are here in my head." But he is still unwell and unable to write. He started eating Lenten fare yesterday; I strongly opposed this as I was sure it would do his health no good. This evening the six children, Lyovochka and I all gathered in the balcony room and I suddenly felt how sad it was that the time would come when we would all have gone our separate ways and would look back on this moment.

19th November. Lyovochka went hunting again and caught 4 hares and a fox. Seryozha, Ilyusha and M. Nief rode to Yasenki to watch the Tsar travel past,* but all they saw was the train *"et le marmiton"*,* as M. Nief jokingly put it.

21st November. Various disasters. First Nurse is pregnant and will have to leave in two months, so I shall have to find another nurse for poor little Andryusha. Then Grigory the butler has given his notice. Lyovochka went hunting with Ilyusha today and caught 6 hares. Seryozha has a cough and played waltzes on the piano with Tanya all day; he played Beethoven's *Sonata Fantasia* too. This evening the children danced quadrilles and various other dances. Andryusha has diarrhoea, and in one day has become frightfully weak. It's warm outside – the children have brought in some willow branches still in leaf.

24th November. Tonight I sat feeding Andryusha in the silence, with only the icon-lamp lighting the darkness. The nurse had gone off to hang up the swaddling clothes when I heard Annie shouting from the nursery next door: "Serosha, dare not!* Serosha!" I was terribly alarmed, laid Andryusha in his cradle and hurried into the nursery, to find Annie shouting in her sleep. I tucked up Tanya and Masha, who had kicked off the blankets in their sleep, and went to bed. I was shivering and feverish all night and didn't sleep a wink. Tanya's fur coat arrived from Tula today, as well as my hat and my fox jacket. The jacket is too narrow at the back and the sleeves are too short.

Lyovochka has stayed at home the last two days; on Wednesday he had dinner with the Samarins in Tula. I finished the second version of my biographical essay today, but it's too long, so once more it won't do.

1879

9th February – Grigory Goldenburg's assassination of Prince Kropot-kin, Governor of Kharkov. 13th March – Leon Mirsky's unsuccessful attempt to kill the chief of security police, General Drenteln. 2nd April – Alexander Solovyov fires five shots at the Tsar. The new People's Will party formed in October, dedicated to the assassination of Tsar Alexander II. 18th and 19th November – two more attempts to kill the Tsar.

Tolstoy abandons work on the Decembrists for a series of articles on religious faith, including 'What I Believe' and 'An Investigation of Dogmatic Theology'. Sofia Tolstoy prepares the fourth edition of Tolstoy's Complete Works. *At the end of the year her biography of him is published in the Russian Library series. 20th December – Mikhail Tolstoy (Misha) born.*

18th December. More than a year has passed. I sit waiting for my confinement, which may start at any moment and is overdue. The thought of this new baby fills me with gloom; my horizons have become so narrow and my world is such a small and dismal place. Everyone here, including the children, is in a tense state, with the approach of the holidays and the suspense about my confinement. It has been terribly cold, more than twenty degrees below zero. Masha has had a sore throat and a fever for the past week. She got up today. Lyovochka has gone to Tula to authorize Bibikov to go to Moscow and deal with the new edition,* and has promised to buy something for the Christmas tree. He is writing a lot about religion. Andryusha is the light of my life and a delight.

Two days after writing this, at 6 in the morning on 20th December, 1879, Misha* was born.

1881

1st March – revolutionaries assassinate Tsar Alexander II. A state of emergency is declared, the power of military tribunals is extended, and administrative officials are granted wide powers. A huge round-up starts, and on 5th April five assassins, one of them a woman, are publicly hanged. The reign of the new Tsar, Alexander III (1881–94), sees the reassertion of absolutism, bureaucracy, orthodoxy and nationalism. Extreme reactionaries are appointed to government. There is a wave of pogroms.

Tolstoy writes to the new Tsar begging him not to hang the assassins. His popularity protects him from the consequences of his plain speaking, but in official circles feeling against him is growing. June – Tolstoy makes a second pilgrimage to the Optyna Pustyn monastery. He gives up hunting and smoking and criticizes his family's worldly aspirations. September – the Tolstoys rent a flat in Moscow, and until 1901 they spent their winters in the city, where Sergei attends the university, Tanya attends art school, and Ilya and Lev go to secondary school. Tolstoy becomes increasingly distant from his family, and the discord between husband and wife is at its most intense when he meets Syutaev, a peasant, Christian and socialist, who has a great influence on him. 31st October – Sofia gives birth to Alexei (Alyosha).

1882

In the summer, the Tolstoys buy a house in Dolgo-Khamovniki Street in Moscow. August – Ilya Tolstoy seriously ill with typhus. Arguments between the couple intensify and Tolstoy threatens to leave. He starts writing 'What Must We Do?' and continues 'What I Believe'.

28th February. We have been in Moscow since 15th September 1881.*
We are staying in Prince Volkonsky's house on Denezhny Lane, near Prechistenka. Seryozha goes to the university, and Tanya attends the art school on Myasnitskaya Street, while Ilya and Lyolya go to Polivanov's secondary school, which is virtually next door to us.*
Our life in Moscow would be quite delightful if only it didn't make Lyovochka so unhappy.* He is too sensitive to survive the city, and his Christian disposition cannot reconcile all this idle luxury with people's struggling lives here. He went back to Yasnaya with Ilya yesterday to have a break and do some work.

26th August, Yasnaya Polyana. It was twenty years ago, when I was young and happy, that I started writing the story of my love for Lyovochka in these diaries: there is virtually nothing *but* love in them in fact. Twenty years later, here I am sitting up all night on my own, reading and mourning its loss. For the first time in my life he has run off to sleep alone in the study. We were quarrelling about such silly things – I accused him of taking no interest in the children and not helping me look after Ilya, who is sick. Today he shouted at the top of his voice that his dearest wish was to leave his family. I shall carry the memory of that heartfelt, heart-rending cry of his to my grave. I pray for death, for without his love I cannot survive; I knew this the moment his love for me died. I cannot prove to him how deeply I love him – as deeply as I loved him 20 years ago – for this love oppresses *me* and irritates *him*. He is filled with Christian notions of self-perfection and I envy him... Ilyusha has typhus and is lying in the drawing room with a fever. I have to make sure he is given his quinine at the prescribed intervals, which are very short, so I worry in case I miss a dose. I cannot sleep in the bed my husband has abandoned. Lord help me! I long to take my life, my thoughts are so confused. The clock is striking four.*

I have decided if he doesn't come in to see me it must mean he loves another woman. He has not come. I used to know what my duty was – but what now?

He did come in, but it was the next day before we made up. We both cried, and I realized to my joy that his love for me, which I had mourned all through that terrible night, wasn't dead. I shall never forget the heavenly cool, clear morning, the silvery dew sparkling in the grass, as I walked through the woods after a sleepless night to the bathhouse. Rarely have I seen such a miracle of natural beauty. I sat for a long time in the icy water, hoping to catch a chill and die. But to no avail. I returned home to feed Alyosha,* who smiled with joy at seeing me.

10th September. Lyovochka has taken Lyova to Moscow.* Today was the last warm day of summer. I went for a swim.

1883

Summer – Alexander III's coronation in Moscow. All members of the People's Will behind bars or in exile. Small groups of students and intellectuals form Marxist discussion groups in the cities.

Spring – large fire in the village of Yasnaya Polyana. 21st May – Tolstoy gives Sofia power of attorney to conduct all matters concerning the property. Hordes of "disciples" start to visit Tolstoy – including Vladimir Grigorevich Chertkov.

5th March (Moscow). The spring sun always has a bracing effect on me. It's shining into my little study upstairs, where I sit and look back, in the calm of this first week of Lent, on the events of last winter. I went out into society a bit, enjoying both Tanya's successes and my own; I felt youthful and gay, and enjoyed everything about this sociable life. Yet no one would believe me if I said that the moments of despair outweighed the happiness – moments when I would say to myself, "It's not right, I shouldn't be doing this." But I was *unable* to stop. I simply couldn't. It's clear to me that I am not free to act and live as I want, but am guided by the will of God, or fate – whatever one chooses to call the supreme will that controls even our smallest affairs.

It was three days ago, 2nd March, that I weaned Alyosha, and I am again suffering the pangs of separation. It comes on me again and again, and there is no way I can be rid of it.

Our life at home, away from the crowded city, is much easier and happier than it was last year. Lyovochka is calmer and more cheerful; he does sometimes get in a rage and blame me for everything, but it doesn't last so long now and doesn't happen so often. He is becoming nicer every day in fact.

He continues with his religious writings.* They are never-ending because they can never be published; but he must do it, it is God's will, and they may even serve His great purpose.

1884

Tolstoy starts making boots, chopping wood and drawing his own water from the well, and spends more and more time with his disciple Chertkov. Arguments with Sofia become increasingly ugly, and he talks of leaving her to lead an ascetic life. Sofia, pregnant again, is beside herself with shame and misery. 18th June – Alexandra (Sasha) born. Soon afterwards, Sofia gains Tolstoy's permission to borrow money to bring out new editions of his novels. Tolstoy finishes 'What I Believe', and all copies of the first edition are seized by the police at the printer's.

1885

Spring – huge strikes in two textile factories near Moscow. June – law prohibiting night work in textile mills for women and children.

Sofia converts an empty shed near the Moscow house into a warehouse and publishing office, and assumes responsibility of all the proofreading and publishing of Tolstoy's works. Chertkov sets up his own publishing house, the Intermediary, to offset Sofia's by publishing cheap books for the masses. As Chertkov moves into the role of Tolstoy's executor, secretary and confidant, Tolstoy describes his relationship with his wife as "a struggle to the death". In December, he again threatens divorce after a terrible argument, then leaves with his daughter Tanya to stay with friends.

24th March. Holy Easter Sunday, Lyovochka returned yesterday from the Crimea, where he went with Prince Urusov,* who is ill. The Crimea brought back his old memories of Sevastopol and the war, and he spent a lot of time walking in the mountains and gazing at the sea. On the road to Simeiz, he and Urusov passed the place where he had been stationed with his cannon during the war. He had fired it, just once, in that very spot. That was thirty years ago.* He and Urusov were travelling along, and he suddenly jumped out of the carriage and started searching for something. It turned out he had seen a cannonball lying near the road. Could it really be the same one he had fired during the siege of Sevastopol?

1886

March – law forbidding peasant households to break up unless approved by a two-thirds majority of the village. 6th June – law tightening up labour contracts, while stiffening up penalties for striking.

18th January – four-year-old Alexei Tolstoy dies of quinsy. Tolstoy writing 'Walk in the Light', 'The Death of Ivan Ilich' and a very long essay called 'On Life and Death', and finishes 'What Then Must We Do?' He also dictates to Sofia his play, The Power of Darkness. *Sofia preparing eighth edition of his works (which Chertkov hopes to produce more cheaply). November – Sofia's mother dies in the Crimea. The Archbishop of Kherson and Odessa denounces Tolstoy as a heretic.*

25th October (Yasnaya Polyana). Everybody in this house – especially Lev Nikolaevich, whom the children follow like a herd of sheep – has foisted on me the role of *scourge*. Having loaded me with all the responsibilities for the children and their education, the finances, the estate, the housekeeping, indeed the entire material side of life – from which they derive a great deal more benefit than I do – they then come up to me with a cold, calculating, hypocritical expression masked in virtue, and beseech me in ingratiating tones to give a peasant a horse, some money, a bit of flour and heaven knows what else. It is *not* my job to manage the farm – I have neither time nor aptitude for it. How can I simply give the peasant a horse if I don't know if it will be needed at the farm at a particular moment? All these tedious requests, when I know so little about the state of affairs here, irritate and confuse me.

My God, how often I long to abandon it all and take my life. I am so tired of struggling and suffering. The egotism and unconscious malice of the people one loves most is very great indeed! Why do I carry on despite all this? I don't know; I suppose because I must. I can't do what my husband wants (so he says), without breaking all the practical and emotional chains that have bound me to my family. Day and night I think only of how to leave this house, leave this life, leave this cruelty, all these excessive demands on me. I have grown to love the dark. The moment it is dark I feel happier, for then I can conjure up the things I used to love, all the ghosts from my past. Last night I caught myself thinking aloud, and was terrified that I might be going mad. Surely if I crave the dark I must crave death too?

Although the last two months when Lev Nikolaevich was ill* were an agonizing time for me, strangely enough they were also very happy. I nursed him day and night and what I had to do was so natural, so simple. It is really the only thing I can do well – making a *personal* sacrifice for the man I love. The harder the work, the happier I was. Now that he is on his feet again and almost well, he has given me to understand that he no longer needs me. So on the one hand I have been discarded like a useless object, and on the other, impossible, undefined sacrifices are demanded of me, in my life and in my family, and I am expected to renounce everything, all my property, all my beliefs, the education and well-being of my children – things which not only I, a fairly determined woman, but thousands of others who *believe* in these precepts, are incapable of doing.*

It's a grey and miserable autumn. Andryusha and Misha have been skating on the Lower Pond. Both Tanya and Masha have toothaches. Lev Nikolaevich is starting on a new play, about peasant life.* I pray to God that he may take up this kind of work again. He has rheumatism in his arm. Mme Seuron* is a pleasant, cheerful woman, very good with the children.

The boys, Seryozha, Ilya and Lyova, live mysterious lives in Moscow and it worries me. They have such strange views about human passions and their own weaknesses: according to them these things are completely natural, and if they *do* manage to resist them they consider themselves very fine fellows indeed. But why are people *bound* to have these weaknesses? Naturally one struggles to overcome one's failings, but this is something that happens once in a lifetime, not every day of one's life. And it is well worth the struggle too, even though it often destroys one's life and breaks one's heart. But it has nothing to do with nasty, commonplace little passions like cards or wine.

I am reading the lives of the philosophers.* It is terribly interesting, but difficult to read calmly and sensibly. One always searches for the philosophical teachings that approximate to one's own convictions, and ignores anything incompatible with them. As a result it is difficult to learn anything new. But I try not to be prejudiced.

26th October. Lyovochka has written the first act of his play and I am going to copy it out. I wonder why I no longer blindly believe in him as a writer.

Andryusha and Misha are playing with the peasant boys Mitrosha and Ilyukha, which I dislike for some reason – I suppose because it will teach them to dominate and coerce these children, which is immoral.

I think a lot about the older boys – it grieves me that they have grown so distant. Why do fathers not grieve for their children? Why is it only women whose lives are burdened in this way? Life is so confusing.

27th October. I have copied the 1st act of Lyovochka's new play. It is very good. The characters are wonderfully portrayed and the plot is full and interesting; there will be more too. A letter came from Ilya mentioning marriage.* Surely this is just an infatuation, the first awakening of physical feelings for the first woman with whom he has been in close relations? I do not know whether to welcome this marriage or not – I cannot approve of it quite frankly, but I trust in God. I gave Andryusha and Misha their lessons today without much enthusiasm for success – they are both so dear to me. I have been correcting proofs and am very tired. Meanwhile Masha runs about and does no lessons, the boys harass me and things are in a bad way.

30th October. Act 2 is now finished. I got up early to start copying it out, and recopied it this evening. It is good, but rather *flat* – it needs more theatrical effects, and I told Lyovochka so. I gave Andryusha and Misha their lessons, corrected proofs, and the whole day was taken up by work. Just as I was sitting down to dinner the girls asked me for some money, on Lyovochka's behalf, for some old woman and for Ganya the thief. I wanted to eat my dinner and was annoyed with everyone for being late, and I had no desire to give any money to that Ganya woman. So I lied and said I didn't have any – although I did in fact have a few rubles left. But later I felt ashamed, and after I had had my soup I went and got the money. I said nothing, just sat and pondered: can one *really* find it in one's heart to love everyone and everything, as Lyovochka demands? Even that woman Ganya the thief, who has systematically robbed every person in the village, has a hideous disease and is a thoroughly vile person.

1887

February – The Power of Darkness *forbidden to be staged in Russia, but produced as a pamphlet. Tolstoy receives hundreds of visitors from all over the world. Sofia takes up photography.*

3rd March. We have heard some shocking news: four students in Petersburg have been discovered with some bombs that they planned to throw at the Tsar while he was returning from his father's funeral service.* It agitated me so badly it has driven everything else from my mind. This evil will beget many others. And *any* sort of evil distresses me so much at present! Lyovochka heard the news in despondent silence. He had so often imagined it happening.

The play is a huge success,* and both Lyovochka and I are quite satisfied with it. I was writing in my diary when he first started on it, but I soon had to do so much copying of the play that I had to break it off. On 11th November my mother died in Yalta and was buried there. On the 21st I travelled to Moscow with the family. Lyovochka has written a story about the early Christians,* and is now working on an article entitled 'On Life and Death'.* He keeps complaining of stomach pains. We had a peaceful and happy winter. The new cheap edition has come out,* but I have completely lost interest in it. The money brought me no joy – I never thought it would. Miss Fewson, the new English governess, has arrived. Masha is ill and I have been reading *King Lear* to her. I love Shakespeare, even though he sometimes doesn't know where to draw the line – all those brutal murders and deaths.

6th March. I have finished copying out 'On Life and Death', and have read it through carefully. I tried hard to discover some new ideas in it, but, although I found many apt expressions and beautiful similes, the fundamental idea seemed to me the same unquestionable eternal truth as before: that one should forswear the material personal life for the life of the spirit. One thing I find intolerably unjust, however, is the idea that one should have to renounce one's personal life in the name of universal love. I believe there are obligations which are ordained by God that no one has the right to deny, and that these obligations actually promote spiritual life rather than hinder it.

My soul is oppressed. It grieves me to think of Ilya and his nasty mysterious life full of idleness, lies, vodka and bad company – and more importantly, the complete lack of any spiritual dimension. Seryozha has gone off to Tula again to attend tomorrow's meeting of the peasant bank.* Tanya and Lyova irritate me by playing vint.* I seem to have lost all ability to *educate* the younger children – I always feel so *sorry* for them, and fear I may be spoiling them. I have an old woman's anxiety for them and an old woman's tenderness for them. Yet I still take their education very seriously. I have quite lost my bearings, yet there are some beautiful moments in my life when I contemplate death in solitude, moments when I clearly perceive the duality of the spiritual and the material consciousness, and know both are immortal.

We had a letter from Chertkov.* I don't like him – he is sly, malicious, obtuse and narrow-minded. L.N. warms to him only because he is so obsequious. As for Chertkov's work on popular reading, however, inspired by L.N., that I do respect; I must give him credit for that.* Feinerman* is in Yasnaya. He has left his pregnant wife and his child somewhere and has come to us, without a penny to his name. Now I support the principle of the family, so for me he isn't a person and is lower than an animal. However fanatical his beliefs may be and however beautifully he may express them, the fact is that he has left his family to eat at others' expense, and that is grotesque.

9th March. Lyovochka is writing a new article, 'On Life and Death', which he is to read to the University Psychological Society.* He has been on a vegetarian diet* for the past week, and his present state of mind is ample evidence of this. He deliberately started talking about the evils of money and property in my presence today, hinting that I wanted to hold on to it for the children's sake. At first I kept quiet, but then I lost my temper: "I sell 12 volumes for 8 rubles and you sell *War and Peace* for 10!" I shouted. This made him very angry, but he said nothing. All these so-called friends of his, these "new Christians", are trying desperately to set him against me – not always unsuccessfully either. I read Chertkov's letter describing in joyful tones his deep spiritual communion with his wife, and commiserating with L.N. for being deprived of this joy: what a sad thing it was, he wrote, that L.N., of all people, should be denied this sort of communion* – it was so obviously referring to me I felt quite ill when I read it. To think that this sly, devious, stupid man has fooled L.N. with his flattery and now wants (like a "good Christian", I dare say) to destroy all the things that have kept us together for nearly 25 years!

He must end this relationship with Chertkov, for it involves nothing but lies and rancour; we must get as far away from him as possible.

We had guests today, all young. We ate dinner together, after which they played vint. What a sorry thing this passion for vint is! Cold. 14° below freezing at nights.

14th March (Moscow). I am sitting here on my own, the house is quiet and I am enjoying myself. The three little ones are asleep, Tanya, Masha and young Lyova are out visiting the Tatishchevs, Ilya has been confined to barracks for three days for being late for drill,* and Lev Nikolaevich has gone off to a meeting of the University Psychological Society with Nikolai Gué to read his new article 'On Life and Death'. Gué and I had to copy it in a great rush and I was busy writing it all day. L.N. is unwell; he has bad indigestion and stomach aches, yet he eats such a senseless diet; first it's rich food, then vegetarian, then rum and water, and so on and so on. He is gloomy but kind. We had a visit from the gentleman sent from Petersburg to Yasnaya Polyana for the costumes for our play.* I took the children skating but did not skate myself. All the pleasures of youth are gradually forsaking me. Lyovochka worked very hard on his article and I like it a lot. He is now beginning to bend some of his more eccentric rules: Grigory* often cleans his room for him nowadays; when he is ill he sometimes eats meat, and when we play vint he occasionally sits down for a game. He is no longer angry about the sale of his books either, and is pleased that the collected edition is selling for eight rubles.

30th March. Lyovochka is still in bad health – for three months he has had pains in the pit of his stomach. Doctor Zakharin diagnosed catarrh of the stomach and prescribed the following, which I am jotting down from memory:

1) To wear warm clothes
2) To wear a piece of unbleached flannel around the stomach
3) To avoid all butter
4) To eat little and often
5) To drink half (½) a glass of fresh Ems Kranchen or Kesselbrunn water, heated up, three or four times a day i) on an empty stomach, and ii) an hour before and a quarter of an hour after

lunch – and the third an hour before dinner. He should follow this regime for three consecutive weeks, then stop, and repeat again if necessary. It should be as hot as he can drink it without burning himself, hotter than fresh milk.

6)   To fight his fondness for smoking.

18th June. Lyovochka walked to Yasenki with his two daughters and my sister Tanya's two. It started raining, so I sent the carriage and some warm clothes after them. Now that he is no longer surrounded by Chertkov, Feinerman and the rest of his apostles, he is just as he used to be before, a sweet, happy family man. The other evening he played the piano accompaniment to some violin sonatas by Mozart, Weber and Haydn; he played with such feeling and clearly enjoyed himself immensely. The violinist was the young man I have hired to teach young Lyova. He is called Lyassota; he is only eighteen and is from the Moscow Conservatoire.

When we got back from Moscow on 11th May I firmly insisted that Lyovochka should drink the waters as Zakharin had ordered him to; he consented, and I now silently hand him a glass of heated Ems, which he silently drinks. When he is out of sorts though he says: "They tell you to pour this stuff down me and you believe them. I'm only doing it because I don't suppose it can do me much harm." But he has been taking the waters for three weeks now and has not resumed his vegetarian diet. In my view his health has improved considerably; he walks about, is much stronger, and the only problem now is that he gets a mere seven hours' sleep a night, which is not enough. I suppose it's because his work is so intellectual and sedentary.

He is delighted by his success, or rather by the favourable response to him in America – although fame and success generally have very little effect on him. He looks radiantly happy and keeps saying "How good life is!"

I miss Ilyusha and am sorry I haven't visited him yet.* But he has had so little time for his family this past year and has been so distant from us that it must be supposed he has no need of us. The poor fellow is drifting and has deteriorated mentally; this is why he seems so despondent and sick at heart. I must visit him very soon.

Hordes of sick people visit me every day. I try, with the help of Florinsky's book,* to treat them all, but what torture it is when I cannot recognize what is wrong and don't know what to do! It happens so often that I sometimes feel like abandoning the whole business, then I go out and the sight of their sick pleading eyes and their touching trust makes me feel so sorry for them that although I dread to think I may be doing the wrong thing, I hand the poor dears their medicine then try to put them out of my mind. The other day I didn't have the medicine I needed and had to give the poor woman a note and some money to take to the chemist. She burst into tears, returned the money and said: "I know I'm dying, take back your money and give it to someone worse off than me. Thank you all the same, but I don't need it."

2nd July. I went to Moscow to see Ilya – I was so happy to see his friendly face, and could see he was overjoyed to see me too. He lives in squalor; his landlord and landlady are very fond of him, yet he leads such a disorderly life. As his mother, who can remember feeding him at her breast, I felt sad he should be spending all the money I send him to repay his debts. And he never has a proper dinner, just buys snacks and sweets on credit. But it doesn't bother him. All he can think about is Sofia Filosofova, and he lives on memories, letters and hopes. He is here at the moment – he has just been hunting and has killed three snipe – but he is leaving tomorrow. This makes me very sad; I must accept that the fledglings have flown the nest.

Lyovochka is busy with the mowing, and spends three hours a day writing his article.* It is almost finished now. The other evening he came into the room where Seryozha was playing a waltz on the piano and said: "Shall we take a turn around the floor?" And away we danced, to the delight of the young folk. He is very lively and cheerful, although he's not as strong as he used to be and tires more quickly when moving or walking. I have bought a camera and intend to do landscapes and family portraits. My daughter Tanya is in Pirogovo.

3rd July. Seryozha is playing Beethoven's *Kreutzer Sonata*, with Lyassota on the violin. What power! It expresses every conceivable human emotion. There's a bunch of roses and mignonettes on my table, we are just sitting down to a splendid dinner, the storm has passed and it is mild and calm outside, and my dear children are with me. Andryusha has been hard at work upholstering the chairs in the nursery, sweet gentle Lyovochka will soon be back – this is my life and I revel in it and thank God for it, for in it I have found true *goodness* and *happiness*. And when I copy out Lyovochka's article 'On Life and Death' I realize he has given me a completely different kind of happiness. I remember when I was very young, long before I was married, I longed to live for others: I yearned with all my soul for the joys of renunciation, even asceticism. But fate granted me a family, so I lived for them – only sometimes I am forced to admit that this *wasn't* what I had longed for, that this wasn't *life*. Shall I ever be able to see it as such?

Yesterday Seryozha and I made some experiments with my new camera.

19th July. For the past few days we have been in turmoil. Seryozha was in Samara but hasn't settled anything.* We had a visit from Pavel Golokhvastov, an extreme Orthodox and Slavophile, and he and Lev Nikolaevich had a discussion about religion and the Church, and it was most unpleasant. Golokhvastov described with great pathos the magnificent cathedral in New Jerusalem (Voskresensk), with its beautiful construction and 10,000 worshippers. After listening to him talk on, L.N. said: "And they go there to mock God." He was being ironic, not to say malicious, and I then spoke up and said it was arrogant to say that 10,000 people would go merely to mock, and to assume that he alone professed the true faith, and that he must admit that such vast numbers of people must have a more honourable reason for attending the cathedral. After dinner Golokhvastov started talking about the Patriarch Nikon and his fascinating life and personality. Lev Nikolaevich read his newspaper throughout, then suddenly burst out in the same tone as before: "He was a Mordvinian peasant, and if he did once have something to say he certainly didn't say it." At this Golokhvastov flushed crimson and said: "Either you are laughing at me, or – since I am accustomed to respecting what other people say – I should ponder upon that remark." All in all a very difficult evening.

We also had a visit from Butkevich, a former revolutionary who has twice been in prison, once for political activities, the second time under suspicion. He stayed for two days, in which time I grew to dislike him intensely. He is very dark and silent, has a squint and a fixed expression on his face and wears blue-tinted spectacles. From the few words he utters there is no way of knowing what he believes in. And now he is a "Tolstoyan". What unattractive types Lev Nikolaevich's followers are! There is not one among them who is normal. And most of the women are hysterics. Like Maria Schmidt for example, who has just left. In the old days she would have been a nun – now she is an ecstatic admirer of Lev Nikolaevich's ideas. She used to be a schoolmistress at the Nikolaevsky Institute, but left because she lost her faith in the Church, and now she lives in the village, supporting herself by copying out Lev Nikolaevich's banned works, and bursting into hysterical sobs every time she greets him. Lyovochka's friend and biographer Posha Biryukov is also staying: he is an excellent man – serene, clever and also a proponent of "Tolstoyism".

All very noisy, difficult and tedious. I long to be alone with my family and for life to resume a more sensible leisurely course. These guests take up all my time.

The days are hot, the nights are cool. We go swimming. There is an abundance of fruit.

19th August. The painter Repin* visited on the 9th, and left on the night of the 16th. He did two portraits of Lev Nikolaevich; the first he started painting in the study downstairs, but he wasn't satisfied with it and started on another in the drawing room upstairs, against a bright background. It's extraordinarily good, and is still drying. The first he finished in a rough-and-ready fashion and gave to me. Lyovochka's "dark ones"* are here: Butkevich, Rakhmanov and a student from Kiev. What peculiar and disagreeable people they are, and what a strain they put on our family life. And what a lot of them there are! This is the price we must pay for Lyovochka's fame and the originality of his ideas.

He has been reading Gogol's *Dead Souls* aloud to us in the evening. I have neuralgia.

25th August. I spent the day sorting out Lyovochka's manuscripts, setting aside the ones I want to take to the Rumyantsev Museum for safekeeping. I had a terrible job trying to put in order this jumble of papers, which I am *sure* will never be properly sorted and read.

Lev Nikolaevich started taking Ems Kesselbrunn water on 17th June, 1888. He drank these waters for four weeks starting in June 1889, and for four weeks starting on 8th May, 1890, and he drank mare's milk all summer.

He brought me this flower in October 1890, at Yasnaya Polyana.*

28th February, 1888 – Ilya Tolstoy marries Sofia Filosofova. 31st March – Sofia Tolstoy gives birth to Ivan (Vanechka), her last child and her ninth son. Tolstoy starts writing The Kreutzer Sonata. The Power of Darkness *produced in the Théâtre Antoine in Paris.*

Autumn 1889 – Tolstoy finishes The Kreutzer Sonata. *November – 800 copies secretly lithographed in the Intermediary offices and circulated in St Petersburg before being passed by the censor. This (and the story's contents) provokes furious arguments between the Tolstoys. Sofia's eleventh edition of Tolstoy's* Complete Works *published, Volume 12 separately, and Volume 13, containing* The Kreutzer Sonata, *still not passed by the censors.*

1890

Sofia Tolstoy involved in litigation with priest from nearby village of Ovsyannikovo over some disputed land. Tolstoy working on The Kingdom of God Is within You. *November –* The Kreutzer Sonata *published. Sofia writes her story 'Who Is to Blame?', her riposte to* The Kreutzer Sonata. *Vanechka becomes the centre of her attention.*

20th November (Yasnaya Polyana). I have been copying Lyovochka's diaries, which cover his whole life, so I decided I would start writing mine again, because I've never been more lonely within my family than I am now. My sons are all over the place: Seryozha in Nikolskoe, Ilya and his family in Grinevka and Lyova in Moscow. Tanya too has just gone for a visit there. I stay here with the little ones and give them their lessons. Masha and I have never been close; I don't know whose fault it is,* mine most likely. And now Lyovochka has broken off all relations with me. Why? What can the reason be? I simply cannot understand. When he is ill he lets me nurse him, but only in the most rude and grudging manner, and only so long as he needs his poultices and so on. I have done everything in my power to achieve a deeper, more spiritual intimacy with him – it's what I want more than anything in the world. I secretly read his diaries too, in the hope of discovering how I could help him, and myself, understand how we might be reunited. But these diaries have reduced me to even greater despair; and he must have discovered I was reading them, for he has started hiding them away. He hasn't mentioned it though.

I used to copy everything he wrote, and loved doing it. Now he conceals everything from me and gives it to his daughters instead. He is systematically destroying me by driving me out of his life in this way, and it is unbearably painful. There are times in this useless life of mine when I am overwhelmed with despair and long to kill myself, run away, fall in love with someone else – anything not to have to live with this man who for some reason I have always loved, despite everything. I now see just how I have idealized him, how long I refused to realize that there was nothing in him but sensuality. Now my eyes have been opened, and I see that my life is destroyed. I envy people like the Nagornovs, for they are *together*, and have things in common besides the physical bond. And plenty of other people live like them. As for us – my God, he is always so unfriendly, so querulous and so artificial when he speaks to me! How can he treat me like this when I am so open and cheerful with him, so eager for his affection!

Tomorrow I am going to Moscow on business. I generally find such expeditions hard work and nerve-racking, but this time I am glad to be going. They ebb and flow like waves, these difficult times when I realize how lonely I am and want only to cry, and know that I must somehow put a stop to it, make it easier. I pray for a long time every night now and find this a good way to end the day.

5th December. I am going on with my diary. I went to Moscow, saw a lot of people and enjoyed a lot of hospitality, for which I thank my good fortune. My daughter Tanya was there too; I am always so happy to see her, and I value her company. Lyova is still very jumpy; whenever I go near him he recoils from me, which I find very hurtful. Yet he always senses when he is doing it, which is some consolation. I am sure he will manage to put this anxious, pessimistic state behind him somehow. When I got back, Lyovochka was just leaving for Krapivna with Masha, Vera Tolstaya and Vera Kuzminskaya to attend a trial. It was cold outside and there was a blizzard, but I hadn't the strength to stop them. Thanks to Lyovochka's influence the murderers received a very light sentence – deportation instead of penal servitude – so they all returned well pleased.* Misha was ill for five days with a high fever and an upset stomach. I spent all my time looking after him, which exhausted me, and I haven't rested properly after my visit to Moscow. We have guests at the moment. Today I played Beethoven's *Una Fantasia* and *Adelaide*, and sight-read some Schubert.

6th December. Today is a holiday, Andryusha's 13th birthday. We all walked up the hill and went skating. The girls and boys all looked so smart and cheerful; they had a marvellous time. I dragged myself around on the ice, I don't enjoy it any more. Tanya went off to Tula for a name-day party given by the Zinovievs and the Davydovs. I did almost no work, just copied out a little of Lev Nikolaevich's diary, then entertained our guests and played with the children. I spend all my time with Vanechka.*

9th December. Once more I am ending the day with a heavy heart. Everything makes me anxious. I have been copying out Lyovochka's youthful diaries. Today I went for a walk. It was a marvellous day,

14° below zero, frosty and clear, and every tree, bush and blade of grass was covered in thick snow. I passed the threshing floor and took the path into the plantation. On my left the sun was already low in the sky, and on my right the moon was rising. The white treetops gleamed, the sky was blue, everything was bathed in a rosy light, and in the distant clearing the fluffy snow was dazzling white. What *purity*. And what a fine beautiful thing this whiteness and purity is, whether in nature, in one's heart, morals and conscience, or in one's material life. I have tried so hard to preserve it in myself – and all for what? Wouldn't the mere memory of love – however sinful – be preferable to the emptiness of an immaculate conscience?

I played a Mozart symphony on the piano today, first with Tanya then with Lyovochka. We didn't get it right at first, and he went for me peevishly; it was all very brief and insignificant, but I found it so hurtful that I lost all enthusiasm for playing and felt terribly sad. Then Biryukov came and we had to stop. I do hope he leaves soon, and that Masha will settle down. Now this silly business has started it won't be easily laid to rest.* I read a novel in the *Revue des Deux Mondes* which describes a young girl's joy at staying in the house of the man she loves, surrounded by all *his* furniture, *his* things, *his* life. How true that is! But what if these things are boots, boot-making tools, chamber pots and mud,* what then? No, I shall never grow used to it.

10th December. I have to endure a sad time in my old age. Lyovochka has surrounded himself with the most peculiar circle of friends, who call themselves his disciples. One of them arrived this morning. This man, Butkevich, has been in Siberia for his revolutionary ideas, wears dark glasses and is a dark and mysterious person, and has brought his Jewish mistress with him, whom he refers to as his wife because she lives with him. As Biryukov was here too, Masha went downstairs to prance around and make herself agreeable to this Jewess. It made my blood boil – to think that my daughter, a respectable girl, should associate with such rabble, apparently with her father's approval. I shouted at him in a rage: "You may be used to spending your life with riff-raff but I'm not, and I don't wish my daughters to associate with them!" He sighed of course, and was furious, but said nothing and walked away. Biryukov's presence is also oppressive; I can't wait for him to leave. Masha was lingering in the drawing room this evening after we had left, and I thought I saw him kiss her hand. When I mentioned it to her though she angrily denied it. I suppose she is right, but how is one to know what is right in all the secrecy, lies and artificiality? They have worn me down. Sometimes I feel like letting Masha go. "Why hold on to her?" I think. "Let her go with Biryukov, then I can take her place beside Lyovochka. I shall do his copying, put his affairs and his correspondence in order, and gradually, without him noticing, send this whole hateful crowd of 'dark ones' packing."

Lyova still hasn't come; I wonder how his health is. Andryusha, Misha and I thought that for our Christmas play we might put on a translation from a Japanese story. I knitted Misha a blanket, did some copying, gave the children two hours of religious instruction and shall now do some reading.

11th December. At the dinner table Lyovochka told me that the peasants who had been arrested for felling thirty trees in our birch wood were waiting outside to see me.* Whenever I am told that someone is waiting to see *me*, and that I have to take some decision, I am seized with terror and want to cry. Being expected to manage the estate and the household "in a *Christian spirit*" is like being gripped in a vice, with no possible escape; it is a heavy cross to bear. If personal salvation and the spiritual *life* means *killing* one's closest friend, then Lyovochka's salvation is assured. But is this not the death of us both?

13th December. I didn't write my diary yesterday – I was too distressed all day by thoughts of the peasants who were found guilty, although I didn't know this until the evening. Biryukov left and an Englishman named Dillon arrived; he has translated 'Walk in the Light', etc. I copied Lyovochka's diaries all day yesterday, and there were moments when I felt quite sorry for him – how lonely and helpless he was! But he has always, throughout his life, followed the same path, that of the intellect. Today I learnt that the peasants had been sentenced to 6 weeks in jail and a 27-ruble fine. Once again a sob rose in my throat, and I've felt like weeping all day. I am sorry mainly for *myself*: why should people be punished in *my* name, when I have nothing against them and would never wish anyone any harm? Even from a practical point of view, it is not my property, yet I have become a sort of scourge! I taught the children for three hours without a break and was patient with them. Lyova and I had a talk about Tanya and Masha yesterday; we both want them to get married, though not Masha to Biryukov of course.*

14th December. I copied Lyovochka's diaries up to the part where he wrote: "There is no such thing as love, *only the physical need for intercourse and the practical need for a life companion.*" I only wish I had read that 29 years ago, then I would never have married him. I gave Misha his lesson, played with Vanechka. I taught Sasha* her "Our Father", and did a little copying. I had a talk with Masha about Biryukov. She assured me that if I didn't let her marry him she wouldn't marry anyone. Then she added: "But there's no need to worry. Anything might happen!" And I felt she actually wanted to be released from this entanglement with him. Tanya was deep in some long mysterious discussion with her today and they seemed to be having a good time.

17th December. Lyovochka is beginning to worry about me copying out his diary. He would like to destroy his old diaries, as he wants to appear before his children and the public as a saintly patriarchal figure. Still the same old vanity!

Some "dark ones" have arrived: silly Popov, some weak, lazy Oriental, and stupid fat Khokhlov, who is of merchant origin. To think that these people are the great man's disciples – these wretched specimens of human society, windbags with nothing to do, wastrels with no education. Tanya and young Lyova went off to see Ilya last night. The children's lessons were interrupted by the arrival of Eduard Kern, who used to be a forester on the Zaseka estate and is now a landowner; he gave me some useful tips on the forests and orchards.

19th December. I had an unpleasant scene with Andryusha: he often *deliberately* misunderstands, and simply *refuses* to make the slightest effort to think or remember. This evening I shall entertain our guests, then take a bath.

20th December. This evening I copied part of Lyovochka's article on the Church.*

The Church as an idea, as the true religion, which guards the gathering of the faithful, cannot be denied. But the existing Church with all its rituals is unacceptable. Why should one have to poke a stick in a piece of bread instead of simply reading the Bible story about the soldier who pierced the rib of Christ? There is such a profusion of these primitive rituals and they have killed the Church. It is 10 o'clock. We shall have some tea, then read. I haven't copied

Lyovochka's diaries today, and consequently feel much calmer and fresher.

23rd December. A lot has happened these past few days. The day before yesterday we were woken up at 6 a.m. by two telegrams, the first saying that Sonya was ill, the second announcing that she had had a son.* I was excited and delighted by the news, but not for long, for I soon started thinking what an unreliable father Ilya will be, despite being so sweet and kind. I always feel a special tenderness for Sonya, mainly because unlike all of us, who are restless, nervous, hot-tempered and forever picking quarrels, she is gentle and even-tempered. Ilya, Tanya and Natasha Filosofova came back from Kursk on the train. I had the usual unpleasant discussion with Ilya about money and property, and he left this evening. I spent all yesterday in Tula, dined at the Davydovs' and wearily bought some things for the Christmas tree. Christmas used to be fun, but now I am tired of it. We made flowers for the tree and gilded nuts, and the whole day passed in a rather dreary, futile manner. I received a very flattering letter from Fet which was almost a love letter. I felt terribly pleased, although I've never loved him in the slightest – I have always found him rather unattractive, in fact.*

24th December. I got up late; Vanechka came into my room and I played with him for an hour. Then I went downstairs. Seryozha arrived and played the piano. He is being very affable and kind, like a man who has *achieved* something and can now take a rest. My Masha is pathetically thin and wretched. We had a cheerful dinner and afterwards Lyovochka read the Bible, much of which made us laugh. I cut out cardboard puppets for the children's play I am putting on – what foolishness.

25th December. Christmas Day. Everyone has been in a festive mood all day, and I have been busy decorating the Christmas tree. Lyova and Lyovochka started a heated discussion over morning coffee about happiness and the meaning of life, which all began when Lyova commented on the change of mealtimes here and his general dissatisfaction with the formalities in *our* life. Lyovochka replied in a reasonable and friendly manner that it all depended on the individual, on a person's *inner* needs rather than *external* appearances. All this was very true, but when he points to his disciples as examples it makes me angry.

We had a cheerful party round the Christmas tree, to which about eighty peasant children came; we gave them a wonderful time, and our children enjoyed themselves too.

27th December. In the evening the servants all came in dressed as mummers, and danced to the harmonica and piano. It was Tanya who had arranged this, for she wanted some *silly* fun. She and Masha dressed up too, and when Masha walked through the door Lyovochka and I gasped: she was dressed as a boy, in a pair of tight trousers which showed her behind, and she showed not an ounce of shame. What a strange, foolish, inscrutable creature.

These rowdy parties always make me depressed. I went off to my room, opened the window, gazed out at the bright, frosty, starry sky, and suddenly remembered poor U.* And I felt so unbearably sad that he had died, and I was robbed for ever of that refined, pure, discrete friendship, which was much more than friendship yet left nothing on my conscience, and filled so many years of my life with happiness. Who needs me now? Where will I ever find such affection and consideration? There is only Vanechka, I thank God for that joy.

29th December. A heavenly bright, frosty day. Blue sky, hoarfrost on the trees, utter silence. We spent almost the whole day outside. The little ones and the girls turned the benches into toboggans, and Erdeli, Masha K., Lyova and I all went skating. I am a clumsy, timid skater, but I loved the heady soothing movement. The Zinovievs came for dinner, with Mme Giuliani* and her son. The Zinovievs are pleasant, straightforward people. Lyuba played the piano nicely enough, although too much like a beginner to give real pleasure. Mme Giuliani sang a duet with Nadya, then a solo. Her voice has great passion – her nature too I expect.

30th December. I played with Vanechka all day until dinner time, as Nurse was visiting her mother. Lyova has gone to a party in the village.

31st December. I am so used to living for Lyovochka and the children that I feel empty and uneasy if a day passes when I don't do something for them. I have started copying Lyovochka's diaries again and putting the accounts in order, but still cannot balance our total income over the past twenty months with our expenditure. It doesn't surprise me, I keep the accounts so badly. A telegram arrived from Ilya asking me to be the baby's godmother. Sofia Alexeevna* refused, so did Tanya, so now it's my turn, *faute de mieux*. But I don't care. It's my little grandson I care about, not the others, and I am delighted to be his godmother. I shall leave tonight, or rather at 5 a.m., on New Year's Day.

1891

Trans-Siberian railway line starts construction, opening up vastness of Siberia to colonization. Harvest, followed by famine in which thousands die.

25th February – Volume 13 of the Complete Works *(published separately containing* The Kreutzer Sonata*) seized and banned. March – Sofia successfully petitions the Tsar against the ban. (The volume is published in June, with many textual changes.) April – Tolstoy's property redistributed amongst his family. Spring – Lyova Tolstoy forced to leave the university by a nervous illness. Autumn – Tolstoy works in the countryside, setting up canteens for victims of famine. Sofia joins him. Tolstoy denounced as "impious infidel" by the Archbishop of Kharkov.*

2nd January. I have just returned from seeing Ilyusha and christening the baby. The ceremony, renouncing Satan and so on, was as dull as usual. But the baby, his eyes tightly closed, had such a touchingly contented expression on his red little face, and I was deeply moved by the mystery of his soul and his new life as I prayed for him. There were crowds of Filosofovs in Grinevka, all very large and stout, but astonishingly sweet-natured, both in their manners and the way they live their lives. There is so much genuine unassuming simplicity about them, and they are so completely without malice. And that is splendid. Ilya was somewhat distracted, and seemed almost deliberately inattentive, rushing about on small errands. It was sad to get home, for it was obvious nobody was interested to see me back. I often wonder why they do not love me when I love all of them so dearly. I suppose it's because of my outbursts of temper, when I get carried away and speak too sharply. Then everyone gathered round me, although they hadn't bothered to make me anything to eat. Only Vanechka and Sasha were glad to see me – he with noisy delight, she with quiet pleasure.

Masha and I had another angry argument this evening about Biryukov. She is doing all she can to re-establish contact with him, but I cannot alter my views on the matter: if she marries him she is lost. I was harsh and unreasonable with her, but I cannot discuss it calmly,

and Masha really is the most terrible cross God has sent me to bear.
She has given me nothing but pain from the moment she was born.
She is a stranger to her family and to God, and her love for Biryukov
is incomprehensible.

3rd January. I worked all day on the puppet theatre. The drawing room
was packed with children but it wasn't a success. How disappointing
that they liked Punch best when he was fighting. What nasty coarse
values! I am tired and bored. We have guests and Lyovochka is cheerful;
he did a lot of writing this morning on the subject of the Church. I
am not very fond of these religious and philosophical articles of his
– I love him best as an artist, and always shall. There is a blizzard. 7°
below freezing.

4th January. Terrible snowstorm all day, 10° below freezing. The
wind is howling in the stoves, outside everything is buried in snow.
We had some unpleasant news this morning: Roman the head forester
got drunk last night and rode down to the marshes, where he and
his horse fell into the lake. He got soaked through, but a Yasnaya
peasant called Yakov Kurnosenkov managed to drag him out. The
horse was drowned, however. It's most annoying and a great pity, for
it was a young horse. Roman himself ran home in a terrible state.
Our steward Berger can't be found either. I am very displeased with
him, for he is frightfully lazy and a liar. Masha has bought a washtub
and scrubs her own underwear. I angrily told her she was ruining her
health and would be the death of me, but she answered me with calm
indifference. All four of the young ones have coughs and colds, but
they are up and about and in good spirits. Where can Seryozha be in
this blizzard? He was visiting the Olsufievs – I only hope he didn't
leave. Lyovochka has been complaining that he cannot write.
    Lyova and Berger went to look for the drowned horse, but they
got lost and returned without finding it. My son Lyova is so precious
to me. I only wish he wasn't so distressingly thin and melancholy –
although at present he is looking happier, which is a relief.

5th January. I am feeling ill, my back aches, my nose keeps bleeding,
my front tooth is aching, and I am terrified of losing it, for a false
one would be horrible. I copied Lyovochka's diary all morning, then
tidied his clothes and underwear and cleaned his study until it was
spotless; then I darned his socks, which he had mentioned were all in
holes, and this kept me busy until dinner time. Afterwards I played

with Vanechka. This evening I was angry with Misha for hitting
Sasha. I was much too hard on him and pushed him in the back and
made him kneel in front of everyone. He cried and ran off to his
room, and I felt sorry for him and for our friendship. But we soon
made up.

6th January. I haven't stirred all day, just sat dumbly darning Lyovochka's socks. I was sent some Spinoza but cannot read it: I shall wait
for my head and the black spots in front of my eyes to clear. We had
guests – Bulygin and Kolechka Gué.* Seryozha returned by express
train and is kind and genial. We chatted about frivolous matters, his
visit to the Olsufievs and business. He is going to Nikolskoe tonight.

Andryusha and Misha went to the village to look in on a party.
They evidently didn't have a good time, for the village lads were shy
and wouldn't play. I'm sorry they didn't enjoy themselves. It's all very
difficult with Masha. She goes out on her own with a village girl to
visit typhus patients. I am worried about her and the risk of infection,
and have told her so. This desire of hers to help the sick is all very well
– I do so myself frequently – but she always goes too far. But today I
reasoned gently with her and began to feel so sorry for her, so sorry
too that we are estranged.

7th January. Masha's words to me yesterday have been in my mind all
day: she is going to marry Biryukov next spring, she says. "I shall go
and grow potatoes," were her words. I have now adopted the habit
of waiting until the next day to respond. So today I wrote Biryukov a
letter, enclosing the money for a book he had sent her. I said I didn't
want Masha marrying him, and asked him to stop writing her letters
and coming to see her. Masha overheard me telling Lyovochka about
the letter and was furious with me, saying she took back all the
promises she had made to me. I was upset and in tears too. Masha
really is a torment, everything about her, her deviousness and now
her imaginary love for B.

Lyova left for Pirogovo with his servant Mitrokha this morning.
Tanya went to Tula where she had her money stolen. And last night
two cartloads of firewood were stolen from the shed. I copied L.'s
diaries this morning, then taught the children, darned some socks,
and now I can't do another thing. What infernal drudgery! This
evening I read aloud two tedious and horrible stories which that
stupid, insensitive Chertkov sent.

Today I was thinking that nine tenths of all that happens in this world is caused by love, in all its various aspects, yet people are always anxious to conceal this, since otherwise all their most private emotions, thoughts and passions would be revealed: it would be like appearing naked in public. There is no mention of *love* in Lyovochka's diaries, not as I understand it anyway – he seems to have had no experience of it.

8th January. Overwhelmed with work all day. I went through the accounts for Yasnaya Polyana and the timber sales and checked them and read the proofs for Volume 13 of the new *Collected Works.* Then I gave Andryusha and Misha a music lesson that lasted two hours, and after dinner I wrote down some chords for the children. Then I worked out our expenses on butter and eggs, and wrote yet more rough drafts of my legal petition regarding the division of the estate to the Ovsyannikovo priest and the transfer of the Grinevka estate. So now I have put everything in perfect order – as if before death? I really should pay a visit to Moscow about Volume 13, but I have no desire to go. My heart is heavy, though it shouldn't be: everyone is well and happy, thank God. Sasha, Vanechka and I all said our prayers together. Lyovochka spends all his time downstairs reading and writing, and comes out only to eat and sleep. He is happy and well.

9th January. Tanya and I played the *Kreutzer Sonata* as a piano duet – badly; it's a very difficult piece to play without practising beforehand. This evening Andryusha had a toothache, and I carried Vanechka about in my arms as he had lost his voice. What a gentle, affectionate, sensitive, clever little boy he is! I love him more than anything in the world and am terrified he will not live long. I dream constantly that I have given birth to another son.

10th January. It was almost ten when I got up, so I didn't go to Tula; there's a terrible wind. This morning I cut out some underwear for Sasha and did some copying, gave the children a music lesson and gave Andryusha religious instruction. I took great pains with them and it went very well. Andryusha is stubborn and absent-minded and seems deliberately not to listen or understand. The more I put my heart into the lesson the more inattentive and rude he is. How he distresses me! He will have a hard life with that character, poor boy! Lyovochka and Nikolai Nikolaevich* played chess with Alexei Mitrofanovich,* who played without looking at the board, to our great amazement.

We talked about the ways in which censorship prevents writers from saying what is most important to them, and I argued that there *were* free works, works of pure literature that the censors were unable to silence – like *War and Peace* for instance. Lyovochka angrily replied that he had renounced all such works.* It was obviously the banning of *The Kreutzer Sonata* that was making him so bitter.

12th January. Yesterday I went to Tula, traded in the coupons, submitted my application for the transfer of Grinevka property, settled the bills and wore myself out discussing the division of the Ovsyannikovo estate with the priest's wife, who shares the rights to the land with us. Four times I walked from the district court to the provincial offices and back, as each place sent me to the other, saying the matter was not under their jurisdiction. So I left without accomplishing a thing. It is a long time since I felt so depressed, waiting in Davydov* the magistrate's office for the barrister who was late. These *business* matters are so tedious and difficult – it's much easier to say: "I'm a Christian, it's against my rules!" I must hire a proper businessman to see to it for I cannot be continually going to Tula. At three this morning Vanechka started coughing and running a high fever. I dragged myself out of bed, went to his room and tried to soothe him. I got up late this morning. Today is Tanya's name day, but we both gave the children their lessons; Andryusha played the piano quite nicely, but Misha scowled. Vanechka still has a cough and a temperature but he doesn't complain. The post brought a letter from L.N.'s niece Varya Nagornova, as well as the proofs for *The Kreutzer Sonata*. The affair has now reached some sort of denouement – what *will* happen? Will it be banned? What should I do?

Tomorrow I must read the proofs and cut out underwear. My soul is empty and lonely.

13th January. Vanechka is ill. He didn't get up at midday, and by two he had a temperature of 39.4 – and the same at 9 this evening. Last night he was running a fever and choking on a thick phlegmy cough. He has a bad cold, and this morning he had an earache. I feel so sorry for him, and so exhausted. In my free time I managed to correct a lot of the proofs for Volume 13, which includes *The Kreutzer Sonata*. When Vanechka was choking last night I ran into Masha's room to ask her for an emetic. She was asleep but she woke at once and jumped out of bed with alacrity to get some ipecacuanha. When she turned to me her face looked so touchingly thin and sweet that I had a sudden impulse to hug and kiss her. That *would* have surprised her! She has had a sweet expression on her face all day and I love her. If only I could always feel like this towards her, how happy I would be! I must try.

14th January. Vanechka is better. His cough improved and he grew more cheerful. Lyova went to Moscow. Klopsky arrived. He is utterly repulsive, and a dark one.* I wrote to Misha Stakhovich and Varya Nagornova and did a little copying. I taught Andryusha the liturgy and Misha the Holy Communion. After dinner I sat with Vanechka for a while, copied Lyovochka's diary and reached 1854, then sat downstairs with the girls. My mind is asleep. This evening we saw Mitrokha off to Moscow; Andryusha and Misha both helped him to get ready and gave him an overcoat and 50 kopecks of their own money. There is a hard frost. Lyovochka is irritable and unkind. I am terrified of his sarcasm – it cuts me to the quick.

15th January. It is a hard struggle at times. This morning the children were downstairs doing their lessons and Klopsky was there. "Why are you doing your lessons?" he asked Andryusha. "Do you want to destroy your soul? Surely your father wouldn't want that!" The girls then piped up and asked him if they could shake his noble hand for saying so and the boys ran up to tell me about it. I then had earnestly to assure them that since we did no real, *peasant* labour, without intellectual labour there would be nothing for us but total idleness; that this intellectual work was the justification for the grand life we led. I told them that I had to educate them all on my own, that if they turned into bad people all the shame would be mine, and that I would be very hurt if all my labours were in vain.

16th January. I went to Tula on business again, ran all over the place, saw a lot of people and did a lot of talking.

On my way home I thought of my enemies and prayed for them, and decided to write a friendly letter to Biryukov. I have decided to send Masha to help the families of those peasants who are in jail for stealing the wood.

17th January. I was feeling lazy this morning and got up late. Over dinner we had a frivolous discussion about what would happen if the masters and servants changed places for a week. Lyovochka scowled and went downstairs; I went and asked him what the matter was and he said: "That was a stupid discussion about a sacred matter. It's agony for me to be surrounded by servants, and very painful that this should be turned into a joke, especially in front of the children."

18th January. I had a dreadful scene with Nurse. She was very rude to me yesterday and has been neglecting the baby. She is driving me desperate. I was feeling ill and told her I wouldn't be insulted by a hussy. At that she said something so appallingly vulgar that were I not so besotted with Vanechka I would have sacked her on the spot. The poor little boy, sensing an argument, clung to her skirt and wouldn't leave her, saying, "Maman good, Maman good!" If only we were all little children! I gave Misha a lesson and did some copying. I didn't go to bed, although I was groaning with pain and could eat nothing. This part of Lyovochka's diaries, about the Crimean War and Sevastopol, is so interesting. One page, which had been torn out, struck me particularly. A woman wants *marriage* and a man wants *lechery*, and the two can never be reconciled. No *marriage* can be happy if the husband has led a debauched life. It is astonishing that ours has survived at all. It was my childish ignorance that made it possible for us to be happy. Instinctively I closed my eyes to his past, and deliberately, in my own interests, didn't read all his diaries and asked no questions. If I had, it would have destroyed both of us. He doesn't know this, or that it was my purity that saved us, but I know now that this is true. Those scenes from his past, that casual debauchery, and his casual attitude to it, is poisonous, and would have a terrible effect on a woman who hadn't enough to keep her busy. After reading these diaries a woman might feel: "So this is what you were like! Your past has defiled me – *this* is what you get for that!"

19th January. I am still ill; I have a stomach ache and a temperature. I have observed a connecting thread between Lyovochka's old diaries and his *Kreutzer Sonata.* I am a buzzing fly entangled in this web, sucked of its blood by the spider.

25th January. I got up early this morning, despite being unwell and having a bad cold, and drove to Tula. It was a warm day. At the footbridge I met Lyovochka, bright and cheerful, already returning from his walk. I love meeting him, especially unexpectedly. I had various things to attend to in Tula. I collected the payment for the timber, came to an understanding with the Ovsyannikovo priest, acceding to all his claims and virtually agreeing to the division of the land. I visited the Raevskys, the Sverbeevs and Maria Zinovieva, at whose house I met Arsenev, the local marshal of the nobility. For two years now I have noticed people treating me like an *old woman*. It feels strange, but doesn't greatly bother me. What a powerful habit it becomes, feeling one has the power to make people treat one with a certain sympathy – if not admiration. And I need even more respect and affection from people these days.

It occurred to me this evening as I was correcting the proofs for *The Kreutzer Sonata** that when a woman is young she loves with her whole heart, and gladly gives herself to the man she loves because she sees what pleasure it gives him. Later in her life she looks back, and suddenly realizes that this man loved her only when he needed her. And she remembers all the times his affection turned to harshness or disgust the moment he was satisfied.

And when the woman, having closed her eyes to all this, also begins to experience these needs, then the old sentimental, passionate love passes away and she becomes like him – i.e. passionate with her husband at certain times, and demanding that he satisfy her. She is to be pitied if he no longer loves her by then; and he is to be pitied if he can no longer satisfy her. This is the reason for all those family crises and separations, so unexpected and so ugly, which happen in later life. Happiness comes only when will and spirit prevail over the body and the passions. *The Kreutzer Sonata* is untrue in everything relating to a young woman's experiences. A younger woman has none of that sexual passion, especially when she is busy bearing and feeding her children. Only once in every two years is she a real woman! Her passion awakes only in her thirties.

I returned from Tula at about six and dined alone. Lyovochka came out to meet me but we missed each other, which was sad. He has been more affectionate lately, but I have deceived myself time and again about this, and I cannot help feeling it's for the same old reasons: his health is better and the usual passions are aroused.

I worked hard all evening correcting the proofs for *The Kreutzer Sonata* and the postscript, then did the accounts. I made a list of everything I had to do in Moscow: seeds, shopping, business.

26th January. I got up at ten. Save me Lord, from the sinful dreams that woke me.

4th February. A lot has happened recently. On the night of the 27th

I left for Moscow. My adventures there were of no great interest. On my first day I dined with our friends the Mamonovs. The following morning I paid 7,600 rubles into the Moscow Bank and redeemed the Grinevka estate, then delivered the mortgage papers to the Bank of the Nobility. I dined with Fet and prattled on far too long, stupidly complaining that Lyovochka didn't love me enough. I returned home that evening, and Tanya, Lyova, Vera Petrovna and Lily Obolenskaya visited. I visited the Servertsevs; Uncle Kostya and the Meshcherinovs were there too, and we had a discussion about love and marriage. But my main preoccupation is Lyova, his complicated inner existence, his attempts to write, and his completely joyless attitude to life. He read me a short story he has written called 'Montecristo', which was very touching and affected me deeply – more of a children's story really* – and it suddenly occurred to me what a wonderful thing it was that if I should survive Lyovochka, all the things I had lived for, the artistic world that has always surrounded me, would not be lost. I shall still be involved through my son with all the fascinating things that have filled my life. But it is all God's will!

I was disturbed on my return home to find Misha Stakhovich there, and he confessed to me, much to my amazement, his longstanding love for Tanya: "*J'ai longtemps tâché de mériter Tatyana Lvovna, mais elle ne m'a jamais donné aucun espoir.*"* We had always imagined he wanted to marry Masha, and when I told Tanya I could see she was deeply upset. I would be so happy if Tanya married him though, as I like him more than any other young man I know.

We are all very cheerful these days. Kern and his wife visited, as well as the Raevsky boys, Dunaev and Almazov. The children went tobogganing all over the countryside on upturned benches, and I called on blind Evlania, the mother of Lyova's servant Mitrokha, and told her all about him.

I taught the children today: Andryusha had done no work while I was away, and I lost my temper and sent him out of the room. Lord, how he torments me! Lyovochka is not very well, but he rode to Yasenki today, and after dinner he played some Chopin. Nobody else moves me so much on the piano; he always plays with such extraordinary feeling and perfect phrasing. Masha suddenly made up her mind to go to Pirogovo, but I am not letting her go because she has a sore throat and it's cold – 15° below freezing. I wonder if she was distressed to hear that Stakhovich loves Tanya; for so long everyone believed it was her he loved.

Tanya went to Tula with Miss Lydia to have another photograph taken; Stakhovich had asked for her picture and she eagerly agreed. She is very excited, but once again it is in God's hands...

6th February. I got up at 10. I had been dreaming of my little son Petya who died; Masha had brought him from somewhere, and he was all torn and mutilated. He was already as big as Misha, and bore a great resemblance to him. We were overjoyed to see each other, and all day I have been seeing him as he was when he was ill, lying in the darkness. I cut out and sewed some trousers for Andryusha and Misha, and had finished both pairs by evening. Later on Lyovochka read us Schiller's *Don Carlos** while I knitted. It is now 11 and he has ridden to Kozlovka to collect the post. The girls have gone to bed; both of them are upset and slightly unhappy about Mikhail Stakhovich's declaration of love. I am reading *La Physiologie de l'amour moderne.** I haven't fully grasped what it's about yet, as I have only just started it, but I don't like it.

Lyovochka adores Vanechka and plays with him. This evening he put first him then Sasha into an empty basket, shut the lid and carted it around the house with Andryusha and Misha. He *plays* with all the children, but he never *looks after* them.

7th February. Lyovochka is being stiff, sullen and unpleasant again. I was silently angry with him last night. He kept me up until two in the morning and spent such a long time washing downstairs that I thought he must be ill, for washing is quite an event for him. I try to see his spiritual side, but I can do this only when he is being good to me.

9th February. Yesterday evening my wish was granted and I drove to Kozlovka by sledge in the moonlight. There were just the two of us, Lyovochka and I. Tanya seems a little better, although she still has a temperature of 38.6. My darling little Vanechka has been ill too with a temperature. I made him a sailor suit, gave the children a two-hour music lesson and read Beketov's pamphlet *On Man's Present and Future Nourishment.** He predicts universal vegetarianism and I think he is right. Vanechka is coughing and it distresses me to hear him.

10th February. Tanya was groaning from morning to dinner time with a terrible headache, then her temperature went up to 38.5 again. Vanechka too had a temperature this morning, it was 39.3. What a strange mysterious sickness! I can't say I'm *too* anxious about my patients, but I do feel sorry for them. I don't feel very well either, and couldn't sleep last night. Today I copied out Lyovochka's Sevastopol diaries,* which are very interesting, then took my knitting and sat with the two invalids. I examined Andryusha on this week's lesson, which he hadn't learnt. Masha has opened a school for the riff-raff in "that house",* and the children have been flocking there for lessons. Sasha has been going there for her lessons too while Tanya is ill. Misha has a new watch and is terribly pleased with it. I see almost nothing of Lyovochka. He is writing about art and science again.* He showed me an article today in *Open Court* which accused him of living at variance with his teachings and handing over his property to his *wife*. "And we all know how people in general, and Russians in particular, treat their wives," they wrote. "A wife has no mind of her own." Lyovochka is very upset, but it's all the same to me – I'm used to this sniping.

12th February. All the children were ill today, with various ailments: Tanya and Masha have stomach aches, Misha has a toothache, Vanechka has a rash and Andryusha has a fever and has been vomiting. Only Sasha is happy and well. I have been copying Lyovochka's diary. He has told me several times that he didn't like me copying them, but I thought to myself, "Well, you'll just have to put up with it since you've lived such a disgusting life." Today he brought it up again, and said I didn't realize how much I was hurting him, he wanted to destroy the diaries – how would *I* like to be constantly reminded of everything that tormented me, every bad deed? To which I replied that I wasn't a bit sorry for him, and if he wanted to burn them, let him – I put no value on my own labours. But if one were to say which of us caused the other more pain, then it was he, for he hurt me *so* deeply when he published his latest story* to the entire world that it would be hard for us ever to be quits. His weapons are so much more powerful. He wants the world to see him on the pedestal he has built for himself, but his diaries cast him down into the filth of his past, and that infuriates him.*

I don't know why people connect *The Kreutzer Sonata* with our married life, but this is what has happened, and now everyone, from the Tsar himself down to Lev Nikolaevich's brother and his best friend Dyakov, feels sorry for me. And it isn't just other people – I too know in my heart that this story is directed against me, and that it has done me a great wrong, humiliated me in the eyes of the world and destroyed the last vestiges of love between us. All this when not once in my whole married life have I ever wronged my husband, with so much as a gesture or glance at another man! Whether or not I ever had it in my heart to love another man – and whether or not this was a struggle for me – is a different matter, and that is *my* business. No one in the world has the right to pry into my secrets so long as I have remained pure.

I don't know why, but today I decided to let Lev Nikolaevich know my feelings about *The Kreutzer Sonata*. He wrote it so long ago, but he would have had to know sooner or later what I thought about it, and it was after he had reproached me for "causing him so much suffering" that I decided to speak up about *my* suffering.

Masha's birthday. What a dreadful day it was, and it's still just as dreadful twenty years later.*

13th February. Yesterday's discussion distressed me deeply. But it ended with a reconciliation, and we agreed to try to live the rest of our lives as amicably as we could.

Tanya is in a strange hysterical mood. This mundane life, and all my cares about the children and their illnesses, have once again paralysed my spiritual life and my soul is asleep. It is a hateful feeling.

15th February. Lyovochka has virtually forbidden me to copy out his diaries, and I am furious, for I have already copied so much that there's almost nothing left of the book I'm working on now. I shall go on with it while he is not looking, for I *must* finish: I made up my mind long ago that it *had* to be done. We had a letter from Misha Stakhovich who again urged me to go to St Petersburg for an audience with the Tsar, to discuss with him the censors' attitude to Lyovochka. He puts great faith in this visit. If only I liked *The Kreutzer Sonata*, if only I believed in the future of Lyovochka's *literary* work – then I would go. But now I don't know where I'll find the energy and enthusiasm I would need to exert my influence on the Tsar and his rather inflexible view of the world. I used to have a great sense of power over others, but no longer.

We went to Kozlovka to collect the mail, Lyovochka on horseback and Tanya, Masha, Ivan Alexandrovich and I by sledge.

A heavenly moonlit night, the gleaming snow, the smooth road, frost, silence. On the way home I thought with horror of life in the city. How could I ever live without this natural beauty, and the vast space and freedom of the country?

16th February. I keep dreaming of the Tsar and Tsarina and think constantly about visiting St Petersburg. Vanity plays a major part in all this – I shall not give in to it and won't go.

I have been busy all day, cutting out underwear and sewing on my machine. I am still reading *La Physiologie de l'amour moderne*, and am interested by this analysis of sexual love. I gave the children a music lesson. Andryusha is playing a Beethoven sonata and Misha one of Haydn's. Masha, Andryusha and Alexei Mitrofanovich taught the peasant girls and the housemaids in the "little house" this evening. Tanya is distracted and on edge, waiting for something to happen with Stakhovich.

17th February. We had a letter from Lyova in Moscow saying he has been ill, apparently with the same thing the children had here in Yasnaya. I feel very worried, even though he writes matter-of-factly and says it's not serious. Ilya is also in Moscow, selling clover. Lyovochka is cheerful, but in an agitated state. First he goes to Pirogovo, then to Tula; one moment he refuses meat broth, next he demands oat coffee – being healthy evidently bores him. I personally find his fussiness worrying and a nuisance. He keeps saying he cannot write. Masha gave another evening class today; she was the only teacher there, and was exhausted.

20th February. This evening Lyovochka, the two Gués and I had a painful discussion about our marriages and how much husbands suffer when their wives don't understand them. Lyovochka said: "You conceive a new idea, give birth with all the agony of childbirth to an entirely new spiritual philosophy, and all they do is resent your suffering and refuse to understand!" I said that while they were giving birth in their imagination to all these spiritual children, we were giving birth, in real pain, to real live children, who had to be fed and educated and needed someone to protect their property and their interests; one's life was much too full and complicated to give it all up for the sake of one's husband's spiritual vagaries, which one would never keep up with anyway and could only regret. We both said much more in the same reproachful vein, yet in our hearts we both wanted the same thing – at least I always do: to stop opening up old wounds and try to live together as friends. Any person – not only one's husband whom one loves – will be treated kindly if they are truly good, in word and deed. It may be a slow business and take time, but it cannot be otherwise if a person really means well.

23rd February. Lyovochka was making boots this evening and complaining of a chill. There is a terrible wind outside, a real gale. I spent the day looking after Sasha and playing with Vanechka. I gave Andryusha and Misha a two-hour music lesson and worked on my blanket. I am persecuted by sinful thoughts; I have the strange sensation that they have nothing to do with my life or soul – all my life I have felt they were something quite independent of me, without the power to touch or harm me.

I was pleased with Misha today, who played the piano very well. We started practising the serenade from *Don Giovanni* arranged for four hands, and he beamed with pleasure at the melody.

He and Andryusha are always whispering *secrets*, which I find dreadfully upsetting. Borel* has perhaps corrupted them – goodness knows! Purity, sublime purity, this is what I value more highly than anything in the world.

25th February. Vanechka woke me at 4 in the morning with a rasping cough. Masha and I both leapt out of bed and gave him some heated seltzer water to drink, then we boiled up some water and turpentine, poured it in a basin, covered all our heads in a sheet and made him inhale the steam. This relieved the choking, but his temperature shot up to 40° and he started coughing again. I thought it would be a long illness but it was all over in twenty-four hours, and today he was singing 'The Lyre' in the drawing room. Sasha is much better too and has got up.

I gave the children a scripture lesson and spent a long time explaining the notion of God to Misha. He has heard so many ideas denied, particularly concerning the Church, that he is now thoroughly confused. But I tried my best to explain the true meaning of the Church as I understand it: an *assembly of the faithful*, a *repository* of holiness, contemplation and faith, not a mere ritual. Lyovochka is happy, calm and well. Our relations are friendly and straightforward – superficially: it doesn't go very deep. But it's certainly much better than at the beginning of the winter. The wind is still howling. Olga Ershova's little girl has died in the village. She was her mother's favourite, seven years old and such a darling. I feel dreadfully sorry for her; Lyovochka and Annenkova went to see her but I couldn't go.

2nd March. Yesterday was a lazy holiday. The children and the Raevskys went to the Rovsky Barracks* for tea. They took their things with them and played games after dinner. Vanechka was utterly adorable and tried to understand all the games and join in the fun. The dear, pale, clever little mite is particularly touching when he is with grown-ups, especially the Raevskys. Seryozha and Ilya arrived here today with Tsurikov, Seryozha's colleague and their neighbour. Ilya invariably asks me for money, which is most unpleasant. He has such a frivolous attitude to it and lives such an extravagant life. Lyovochka is wretched; when I asked him why, he said his writing isn't going well. And what is he writing about? About non-resistance.* So it doesn't surprise me in the least! Everybody, including him, is sick of the subject – it has been examined and discussed from every conceivable viewpoint. He wants to work on some *fictional* subject but doesn't know how. That would demand a lot of *philosophizing*. Once he let his true creative powers pour forth he wouldn't be able to stop the flow, and he would then find all this non-resistance most awkward – he's terrified to let it go, yet his soul yearns for it.

My son Lyova took great offence when Seryozha and I told him we thought he was looking unwell. I felt sorry for him, but hurt his feelings instead.

Today I finished Bourget's *Physiologie de l'amour moderne*, in French. It's clever but it bored me; it all centres on one thing and a life that is alien to me.

6th March. Seryozha went to Nikolskoe and Masha took a sick peasant woman to Tula, and Sashka the village girl went too to keep her company. Life has resumed its normal course. It was lovely to see my nine children all sit down at the table with us old folk on Saturday and Sunday. I have been at home all day doing various tasks. As I wanted some exercise after dinner I joined Lyovochka who was playing with the little ones, Sasha, Vanechka and Kuzka. Every evening after dinner he puts them one at a time into an empty basket, closes it and drags it around the house. Then he stops and makes the one in the basket guess which room he is in. Lyova is all skin and bones and my heart aches for him.

I read some Spinoza on my own. His interest in the Jewish people doesn't particularly excite me; we shall see what happens in the part which contains his *éthique*.

Over tea we had a talk about food, luxury and the vegetarian diet Lyovochka is always preaching. He said he had seen one in some German magazine that recommends a dinner of bread and almonds. I am quite sure the man who wrote this keeps to it in the same way Lyovochka practises the chastity he preaches in *The Kreutzer Sonata*.

10th March. Lyovochka was having his breakfast today when the letters and papers were delivered from Kozlovka. "Still no news about Volume 13," I said. "What are you fussing about?" he said. "No doubt I shall be forced to renounce the copyright on all the works in Volume 13." "Just wait until it comes out," I said. "Yes, of course," he said, and left the room. I was seething at the thought that he was intending to deprive me of badly-needed money for my children, and tried to think of a spiteful reply. So as he was going out for his walk, I said to him: "Go ahead, publish your renunciation. But I shall publish a statement immediately below it saying I hope the publisher is sufficiently sensitive not to exploit the copyright that belongs to your children." He then told me *I* was being insensitive, but he spoke gently and I made no answer. If I really loved him, he went on, I myself would publish a statement that he had surrendered the copyright on his new works. He then left the room and I felt so sorry for him: all these material considerations seem so paltry compared to the pain of our estrangement. After dinner I apologized to him for speaking maliciously, and said I wouldn't publish anything; the idea of distressing him was unbearable to me. We both cried, and Vanechka who was standing there looked frightened. "What's the matter, what's the matter?" he kept asking. "Maman hurt Papa," I told him, "and now we're making up." This satisfied him and he said, "Ah!"

A cold windy day. The drawing master came; he asked me to lend him money and I refused, for he is a very bad teacher.

I read an extraordinarily sensitive, intelligent article on *The Kreutzer Sonata* by M. de Vogué. He says, among other things, that Tolstoy had taken his analysis to extremes (*"analyse creusante"*), and that this had killed all the personal and literary life of the work.

Lyovochka is correcting and rewriting his piece 'On Non-resistance', and Masha is copying it for him. It is hard for him as an *artist* to write these weighty articles, but he cannot do his artistic work now.

12th March. We had a visit from an American from New York who edits a paper called the *New York Herald*. Also a "dark one" named Nikiforov. Nothing but talk, endless talk. I have been informed by the Moscow censors that Volume 13 has been irrevocably banned. I shall go to St Petersburg to appeal. I dread the thought of it. I am sure I shall achieve nothing, and feel all my faith, strength and happiness are being wasted. But maybe the good Lord will come to my rescue. Snowing, wind and frost – just the weather for a ride in the sledge.

13th March. I went to Tula. More negotiations with the priest. This evening I had a talk with the American. He needs information about Lyovochka for his newspaper, and I was able to help him, although I've learnt my lesson and didn't tell him too much. I had a letter from Countess Alexandra Tolstaya, Alexandrine, who said the Tsar didn't normally receive ladies, but that I should wait a week or ten days for him to reply.*

I am going to Moscow. I shall bring out the 12 volumes with an announcement that Volume 13 has been delayed.* I wish I did not have to move, what a worry this business is! But who else can do it?

Cold, wind, some snow. We all went out in the sledge again.

20th March. I spent the 15th and 16th in Moscow with Lyova, and heard that Volume 13 had been banned in St Petersburg. (In Moscow only *The Kreutzer Sonata* was censored.) I shall have to go to St Petersburg and do all I can to see the Tsar and vindicate Volume 13. In my mind I keep composing speeches and letters to him, thinking endlessly about what I should say. I am only waiting now for Alexandrine's letter telling me whether or not he'll agree to receive me, and if so when. Lyovochka says his mind is asleep and his writing is going badly.

21st March. I have been reading Spinoza and was deeply impressed by two of his arguments, the first about authority and laws: people should respect authority not out of fear of punishment, but because it represents an ideal, something to aspire to and inspire virtue, not just for the individual but for society as a whole. The other argument is about miracles. The uneducated (*"le vulgaire"*) see the hand of God only in what lies *beyond* the laws of nature and probability, and simply don't see God in the whole of Nature and Creation. This is why they expect miracles – i.e. something that lies beyond nature.

Lyovochka is in an extraordinarily sweet, affectionate mood at the moment – for the usual reason, alas. If only the people who read *The Kreutzer Sonata* so reverently had an inkling of the voluptuous life he leads, and realized it was only this that made him happy and good-natured, then they would cast this deity from the pedestal where they have placed him! Yet I love him when he is kind and normal and full of human weaknesses. One shouldn't be an animal, but nor should one preach virtues one doesn't have.

22nd March. I was busy all day measuring and sewing new clothes for the children. Lyovochka and I played duets after dinner; later on, instead of playing patience he wound some balls of cotton for me, which he found highly entertaining. I wrote a letter to Ilya's wife Sonya. I am ill and tired.

23rd March. I felt spring in the air for the first time today. Although it's still freezing there was a bright sunset, the birds sang and the trunks of the young birch trees at Chepyzh looked particularly beautiful and spring-like. After dinner I took Andryusha and Sasha out and we cleared the snow from the stone terrace in front of the house. Lyovochka rode to Tula.

Still no news from St Petersburg. I am sick with uncertainty.

27th March. On the 25th I went to Tula with Misha and Andryusha and we visited the Wanderers' art exhibition.* I love looking at paintings, but there were few good ones, apart from some lovely landscapes by Volkov and Shishkin. Afterwards we visited the pastry-cook's, the educational suppliers and the Raevskys.

Next morning I got up early and went to town to attend to my business. As I was walking down Kievskaya Street who should I meet but Ilyusha. I was very surprised to see him and asked if he would come with me to inspect a barouche that was for sale. It was a long, tedious business. Afterwards I visited the senior notary to collect the mortgage documents, then went home with Ilya. He had come to find out about the auction of the estate and to ask me for 35,000 rubles, which I refused him. It caused a nasty scene, but it didn't last long. I had gone to Tanya's room to sit with the children after dinner, when he suddenly shouted: "Well I shan't give you that koumiss mare then!" I lost my temper. "I shan't ask you for it anyway – I'll ask the bailiff!" At that he too lost his temper. "But I'm the bailiff here!" he says. "Well, I'm the estate manager," say I. I don't know whether it was because I was tired or if he had driven me to exasperation with his talk of money and property, but I became furious with him. "You've got to the point where you even grudge your father a koumiss mare – I can't think why you came! You can go to the devil – you torment me!" And I slammed the door and went out. I felt so sick and ashamed, and so angry with my son – it was quite horrible.

Then for the first time we had a serious discussion about it all and agreed things couldn't go on like this, and that we would have to divide up the property among all of us. I am delighted by the idea, but agree only on condition that the children draw lots; I don't expect Ilya will accept this, as he wants to hold on to Nikolskoe and Grinevka, but I won't deprive my defenceless little ones. It's really only Ilya who is being so difficult. He is terribly selfish and greedy, maybe because he already has a family of his own. The other children are all very sensitive and will agree to anything. Lyovochka has always had a special fondness for Ilya and will never see his faults, and this time too he was agreeing to all his demands. I am afraid there'll be no end of unpleasantness. Fortunately, though, Grinevka is in my name, and if the others won't agree to draw lots I shall refuse to hand over Grinevka and Ovsyannikovo. I simply won't allow my little ones to be slighted. Lyovochka finds all these discussions a great trial, but they are ten times worse for me, as it is I who have to defend the younger children against the older ones. Then Tanya always takes Ilya's side, which distresses me. Tomorrow I am going to St Petersburg. I am dreading it, for I know I shall not succeed. The very thought terrifies me. It's warmer now, although windy. Today it was 7° above freezing.

22nd April. I haven't written in my diary for almost a month. It has been a particularly interesting and eventful month, but it's always the same: I had so little free time, my nerves were strained and I had to write so many letters home that I didn't manage to write my diary.

Today is the second day of Easter, and the second warm, summery day of the year. In just two days all the bushes and trees have changed from brown to a soft green, and for the first time this morning I heard a nightingale singing at the top of its voice. Yesterday evening it was just tuning up.

I got back from St Petersburg early on Palm Sunday. I wasn't well, and for the first days of Holy Week I rested in bed in the peace of our family circle, and gave the children a few lessons. Then we resumed our discussions about dividing the property, with the children, especially Ilya, all grabbing for the biggest bits. This is how we eventually decided to divide it: Ilya will have Grinevka and part of Nikolskoe, Seryozha will have another part of Nikolskoe, and either Tanya or Masha will have the third and largest part, with responsibility for paying off its debts. Lyova will have the house in Moscow and the Bobrov estate in Samara; either Tanya or Masha will have Ovsyannikovo and 40,000 rubles, and Andryusha, Misha and Sasha will each have 4,000 acres in Samara. Vanechka and I will have Yasnaya Polyana. At first I insisted we draw lots for everything, but Lev Nikolaevich and the children protested so I had to agree with them. The Samara land is good for the children since it will gain in value, and there is nothing to steal, chop down or damage there and it is all run by the same hands. Vanechka and I were given Yasnaya because his father must not be moved, and where Lev Nikolaevich is I must be, and Vanechka too.*

Over Holy Week I made Andryusha and Misha fast, although I couldn't do so myself. They were calm and natural about it, like the common people. We had a service performed here on Saturday, at the request of the servants. Lyovochka was out. When I asked him that morning if he would find it unpleasant if we held a service in the drawing room, he said, "Not a bit."

Yesterday after breakfast I ordered the new carriage to be brought round and gathered up the children. Then we all drove off down the road to pick morels at Zaseka. I was with Vanechka and Sasha all the time. Although I saw almost no morels because I'm so short-sighted, I love the forest, the wild profusion of nature in spring and the silence in the depths of the trees, and I enjoyed myself enormously. Lyova and Andryusha went fishing but didn't even get so much as a bite, and Lyova broke his rod. Today and yesterday the children were playing *pas de géant* in the meadow in front of the house, and romping in front of the byre.

Yesterday evening our boys played games with the village children. It's strange the way these lads of 11 and 13 already treat the peasant girls as *girls*, no longer friends. How sad and hateful it is!

Quite apart from all this, the children are growing up without any religious training. Children need *forms*, as do the common people, to express and contain their relationship with God. This is what the Church is for. And only those with the most lofty and abstract of faiths can separate themselves from it, for without it we feel nothing but the most hopeless emptiness.

Now I shall try to recollect and faithfully record my visit to St Petersburg in connection with the banned Volume 13 of the *Complete Collected Works*, and the audience I had with the Tsar on 13th April 1891.

My Visit to St Petersburg

I left Yasnaya Polyana on the night of 28th–29th March, and arrived in Moscow the following morning. I sat and talked to Lyova for a while, then went to the State Bank to convert my 5 per cent bonds to 4 per cent ones. By 4 that afternoon I was at Nikolaev Station. I found myself a comfortable second-class compartment which I shared with one other lady, a landowner from Mogilyov, whose husband was marshal of the local nobility. We had a very pleasant journey together. When I arrived at my sister's house they were just getting up. My brother-in-law Sasha was away on a tour of inspection in the Baltic provinces, Tanya was getting dressed, and the children were receiving the Eucharist. Tanya and I were overjoyed to see each other, and she put me in her bedroom. We sat down at once and wrote a note to Misha Stakhovich. When he arrived he told me he had already written asking me to attend an audience with the Tsar, since Elena Grigorevna Sheremeteva (née Stroganova), the Tsar's cousin and daughter of Maria Nikolaevna (Lichtenburgskaya), had managed to persuade him to receive me. The reason she gave for my petition to see him was that I wanted to be personally responsible for censoring Lev Nikolaevich's works. Stakhovich showed me a letter to the Tsar he had sketched out. I didn't like it, but took it all the same. The morning after my arrival I called on Nikolai Strakhov* in his apartment, which is filled with his marvellous library. He was surprised and delighted to see me, and we sat down to discuss my letter and my forthcoming discussion with the Tsar. He didn't like Stakhovich's letter any more than I did and drafted another, which was delivered to me at 5 that evening. I didn't like this one any better, so I decided to write a third version myself, based on the other two. My brother Vyacheslav arrived and made the final corrections, and it was this version we sent, on 31st March:

Your Imperial Majesty,
I make so bold as to enquire very humbly about the audience Your Majesty has so graciously granted me in order that I may bring to Your Majesty's notice my personal petition on behalf of my husband, Count L.N. Tolstoy. Your Majesty's gracious attention gives me the opportunity to specify the conditions under which my husband would be able to return to his former artistic and literary endeavours, and to point out that some of the very grave accusations made against his work have been unfounded, and have

stolen the last ounce of spiritual strength from a Russian writer
who is already losing his health, but who might possibly still bring
some glory to his country with his writings.

Your Imperial Majesty's faithful subject,
Countess Sofia Tolstoy

31st March, 1891

As I wasn't sure how to send this letter, Tanya made enquiries on the telephone to a good friend of hers called Skalkovsky, who occupies a senior position in the Post Office, and the following morning Skalkovsky sent his messenger round with a note assuring me that my letter would be delivered to the Tsar that evening at his palace in Gatchina. The letter arrived there on 1st April. On the same day Grand Duchess Olga Fyodorovna, who was in Kharkov on her way to the Crimea, died of pleurisy and a heart attack. Her death, together with the marriage of her son Mikhail Mikhailovich to Countess Merenberg without permission from the Tsar or his parents, was the talk of St Petersburg. People could think of nothing else. Tradition and etiquette demanded a complete cessation of activity at the court for nine days, and the entire royal family went into full mourning. We stood at the window of the Kuzminskys' apartment and watched as the Grand Duchess's coffin was borne along the Nevsky Prospect on its way from the station to the Peter and Paul fortress. The Tsar and Mikhail Mikhailovich went straight to the graveside. The priests and soldiers were inseparable (there was a particularly large number of the latter) and, when they stopped in front of the Church of the Annunciation to read the litany and the prayer, they *beat the drum*, and played a strange sort of whistling music. I have never heard anything like it, it reminded me of a pagan ceremony.

As I wanted to find out how best to address the Tsar and plead with him for Volume 13, I decided to visit Feoktistov, on the censorship committee, to find out why it had been suppressed. My sister accompanied me there. We went in, and when we had greeted Feoktistov (whom I had first met in Moscow as a young man, just after he deceived his mother and eloped with his beautiful wife), I asked him why the *whole* of Volume 13 had been banned. He responded in a cold mechanical fashion by opening a book and reading from it in a monotonous voice: "The book *On Life* is banned by the Church censors on the orders of the Holy Synod. The article 'What

Then Must We Do?' is banned by the Police Department, and *The Kreutzer Sonata* is banned on the orders of the Tsar." I then pointed out indignantly that I had already had several chapters from *On Life* published in the *Week*, and there were no complaints from the censors then. And it was they themselves who had passed some chapters of 'What Then Must We Do?', which were published in Volume 12. That left only *The Kreutzer Sonata*, and I was hoping to obtain the Tsar's permission to publish it.

Feoktistov was very embarrassed to discover that *On Life* and 'What Then Must We Do?' had already been published in abridged forms. He called for his secretary, ordered him to look into the matter and promised me a reply in two days' time. I then complained about the careless and contemptuous way in which a great writer like Lev Nikolaevich Tolstoy had been treated by the censors. They obviously didn't even bother to read the *contents* page, and had brought both the author and me a great deal of trouble and grief. Feoktistov realized he had done something stupid, and on 3rd April he brought me Volume 13 in person and told me it had been passed for publication.

Meanwhile the *New Times* newspaper published the repertoire of the plays being performed that season at the imperial theatres, and these included *The Fruits of Enlightenment* by L.N. Tolstoy. Knowing that the play had been banned from imperial theatres, I visited the Theatre Committee to find out what was happening. It turned out to be true. I asked them if they had been in communication with the author about it, or asked him what his wishes were, and they said they hadn't. I was furious, and told the official there that this was a tactless, discourteous way to treat an author. I also asked him among other things if he would kindly negotiate with *me* in future, not with the author. The following day I had a visit from the producer, who handed me a piece of paper listing various conditions. There were a vast number of obligations I was to take on: I was to *guarantee* that his plays wouldn't be performed at private theatres, *indemnify* them with a fine of 2,000 rubles if one was, and so on and so forth. I was outraged by these conditions, and next morning I set off again to the Theatre Committee and told the official I wasn't prepared to accept *any* of their terms – they could stop the production, nothing would make me sign. He told me I should say this to the director, so I ordered them to announce me to the director, Vsevolozhsky. He refused to see me. "Well, this is a peculiar state of affairs – one can see the Tsar, but the director, whose *job* it is to receive people, refuses to see me." He was disconcerted by my high-and-mighty manner and went off to announce me. "You boors," I kept saying to myself. "One has to shout at people like you."

Vsevolozhsky received me in a somewhat overfamiliar manner and introduced me to his assistant, a person named Pogozhev. "So you don't want to give us your plays, eh Countess?" he said. "I merely don't want to take on a lot of obligations I can't fulfil," I replied. "But all that's just a formality!" he said. "It may be a formality for you," I said. "But for me it's a matter of principle and I shall sign nothing." At that point Pogozhev intervened: "If you don't sign these conditions you'll receive only 5 per cent of the gross takings instead of 10 per cent." At that I turned on him in a fury: "I don't live on Merchants' Row and am not accustomed to haggling with shopkeepers, so kindly leave aside all questions of money since they do not interest me, or, more importantly, the Count. And I shall not give you that play." I then turned to Vsevolozhsky and said: "What is this? How is it that a person of our circle like you doesn't understand that one can't treat Lev Nikolaevich like a vaudeville writer? We must all take his wishes into account, especially I, as his wife and a respectable woman, and that is why I can't sign your conditions or undertake that his plays will *never* be performed on a private stage. It's Lev Nikolaevich's greatest joy that he hasn't made a single kopeck out of the play, and this undertaking would deprive people of the right to perform it at charity benefits..." I became so heated that Vsevolozhsky eventually suggested deleting several of the conditions. But I wouldn't agree to that either, so he proposed that I write an unofficial letter instead, giving the Imperial Theatre the right to perform the play against 10 per cent of the gross takings. This I did.

My son Seryozha suggested that this money be donated to the Empress Maria's Charitable Institutions. I should have been delighted to do this, but I had to think of my 9 children who need the money so badly – where else would I find it for them?

I profited from my free time in the capital to visit two art exhibitions, the Wanderers' and the Academy.* I don't know if I was in a bad mood or just tired, but neither of them impressed me. Afterwards I went shopping with Tanya, sewed my dress and sat with her family and their guests. The rest of the time I stayed at home. They tried to tempt me to go to the theatre and see Duse, the celebrated Italian actress, but my nerves were shattered, and besides I couldn't afford it. All the time I was there I never slept more than five hours a night.

Eventually, on Friday the 12th, I could wait no longer for my audience with the Tsar. Holy Week was approaching, I was feeling homesick, and my nervous condition was growing worse: I decided to return home on Sunday.

At eleven that night I had just gone to bed when a note arrived from Zosya informing me that the Tsar had sent me an invitation, through Sheremeteva, to see him at 11.30 the following morning at the Anichkov Palace.

Early that morning I checked that I had paid all my bills, asked Tanya to settle the rest for me, got dressed and sat waiting for the time when I had to leave. I had on a black mourning dress I had made myself, a veil and a black-lace hat. At a quarter to eleven I set off. My heart was pounding as we approached the Anichkov Palace. I was saluted at the gates, then at the porch, and I bowed back. I entered the antechamber and asked the doorkeeper whether the Tsar had instructed him to receive Countess Tolstoy. No, he said. He then asked someone else, and got the same reply. My heart sank. Then they summoned the Tsar's footman. A handsome young man appeared, wearing a crimson-and-gold uniform and a huge three-cornered hat. "Do you have instructions from the Tsar to receive Countess Tolstoy?" I asked him. "I should think so, Your Excellency!" he said. "The Tsar has just returned from church and has been asking about you." (The Tsar had apparently been at the christening of Grand Duchess Elizaveta Fyodorovna, who has just converted to Orthodoxy.) The footman then ran up a steep stairway covered in an ugly bright-green carpet, and I followed him up. I hadn't realized how fast I was running, and when he left me with a deep bow at the reception room, my heart was pounding so wildly I thought I should die. I was in a terrible state. The first thought that came into my head was that this business wasn't worth dying for. I imagined the footman coming back to summon me to the Tsar and finding my lifeless body. I should be unable to say a word, at any rate. My heart was beating so violently it was literally impossible for me to breathe, speak or cry out. I sat down and longed to ask for a glass of water, but couldn't. Then I remembered that the thing to do when a horse has been driven too hard is to lead it about quietly for a while until it recovers. So I got up from the sofa and took a few paces around the room. That didn't make it any better though, so I discreetly loosened my stays and sat down again, massaging my chest and thinking of the children. How would they take the news of my death, I wondered. Fortunately the Tsar hadn't been informed of my arrival and had received someone else before me. So I had time to rest and get my breath back, and had fully recovered by the time the footman returned and said: "His Majesty begs Her Excellency the Countess Tolstoy to enter." I followed him to the Tsar's study and he bowed and left. The Tsar came to the door to meet me and shook my hand, and I curtseyed slightly.

"Do forgive me, Countess, for keeping you waiting for so long," he said. "It was impossible for me to receive you earlier."

I replied: "I am deeply grateful to Your Majesty for doing me the honour of receiving me."

Then the Tsar began to talk about my husband (I don't remember his exact words), and asked me the nature of my request. I spoke in a quiet but firm voice:

"Your Majesty, I have recently observed that my husband seems disposed to resume his literary endeavours. Only the other day he was saying to me: 'I have moved so far beyond these philosophical and religious works now that I think I might start on some literary work – I have in mind something similar to *War and Peace*, in form and content.' Yet with every day that passes the prejudice against him grows stronger. Volume 13 was banned for instance, although it has now been decided to pass it. His play *The Fruits of Enlightenment* was banned, then the order was given for it to be performed on the Imperial stage. *The Kreutzer Sonata* was banned..."

"Surely though you wouldn't give a book like that to your children to read?" the Tsar said.

I said: "The story has unfortunately taken a rather extreme form, but the fundamental idea is that the ideal is always unattainable if the ideal is total chastity."

I also recall that when I told the Tsar that Lev Nikolaevich seemed disposed to write *literary* works again, he said: "Ah, how good that would be! What a very great writer he is!"

After defining what I took to be the main point of *The Kreutzer Sonata*, I went on to say: "It would make me happy if the ban was lifted from *The Kreutzer Sonata* in the *Complete Collected Works*. That would be clear evidence of a gracious attitude to Lev Nikolaevich. And who knows, it might even encourage his work."

To this the Tsar replied: "Yes I think it might very well be included in the *Complete Works*. Not everyone can afford to buy it after all, it won't have a very wide circulation."

On two separate occasions in the conversation (I don't remember exactly when), the Tsar regretted that Lev Nikolaevich had left the Church. "There are so many heresies springing up among the simple people that are having a very harmful effect on them," he said.

To this I replied: "I can assure Your Majesty that my husband has never preached any philosophy either to the people or to anyone else. He has never mentioned his beliefs to the peasants, and not only does he not distribute the texts of his manuscripts to people, he is actually in despair when others do so."

The Tsar was astounded. "Why that's disgraceful, absolutely disgraceful! It's a wicked thing to do, to steal someone's manuscripts!"

The Tsar is rather shy and speaks in a pleasant, melodious voice. His eyes are warm and kind, and he has a friendly bashful smile. He is very tall and somewhat stout, but he is sturdily built and looks strong. He is almost completely bald, and his head is very narrow at the temples, as though it had been squeezed in at the top. He reminded me a little of Vladimir Chertkov, especially his voice and manner of speaking.

The Tsar then asked me how the children felt about their father's teachings. I replied that they couldn't but feel the greatest respect for the lofty moral standards he preached, but that I considered it important for them to be educated in the faith of the Church. I had fasted with them over August, I said, but in Tula, not in the village, as several of our priests, far from being our spiritual fathers, were in fact police spies who had been sending in false reports about us.

"Yes, I have heard about that," the Tsar said. Then I told him my eldest son was a leading *zemstvo* official, my second was married and had his own home, my third was a student, and the others still lived at home. Oh, and I forgot to note that when we were discussing *The Kreutzer Sonata*, the Tsar said, "Could your husband not alter it a little?"

I said: "No, Your Majesty. He can never make any corrections to his works, and besides, he says that he has grown to hate this story and cannot bear it to be mentioned."

The Tsar then asked: "And do you see much of Chertkov, the son of Grigory Ivanovich and Elizaveta Ivanovna? It seems your husband has completely converted him."

I was quite unprepared for this question and for a moment I was at a loss for words. But I soon regained my composure. "We haven't seen Chertkov for over two years now," I said. "He has a sick wife he cannot leave. His relations with my husband weren't initially based on religion but on other matters. Seeing how many stupid and immoral books were being published for popular consumption, my husband gave him the idea of transforming this popular literature and giving it a moral and educational direction. My husband wrote several stories for the people which sold millions of copies, but were then suddenly found to be harmful and not sufficiently pious, and were also banned. Besides this they published a number of scientific, philosophical and historical books. It was a successful venture and doing very well – but this too has been persecuted by the authorities."*

The Tsar said nothing to this, and finally I made so bold as to add: "Your Majesty, if my husband *should* start writing works of fiction again and I should publish them, it would be a great pleasure for me to know that the final verdict on his work rested with Your Majesty in person."

To this the Tsar replied: "I should be most happy to do so. Send his works directly to me for my perusal."

I cannot remember if anything more was said. I do remember though that at the end he said: "Rest assured, everything will be for the best. I am very happy to have met you." And he stood up and gave me his hand.

I curtseyed again, and said: "I am sorry I didn't ask to be presented to the Empress, I was told she was unwell."

"No, the Empress is quite well today and will receive you. I shall give orders for you to be announced," he said.

I then turned to go. The Tsar stood in the doorway leading to the little room next to his study and took his leave of me. "Will you be staying in St Petersburg for a while?" he asked.

"No Your Majesty, I am leaving today."

"So soon? Why is that?"

"One of my children is sick."

'Really? What's the matter?"

"Chickenpox."

"Well, that's not dangerous, so long as he doesn't catch a chill."

"Yes Your Majesty, I'm afraid they might let him catch a chill in this cold weather if I'm not there."

The Tsar shook my hand very warmly, then I bowed again and went out.

I went back to the reception room, which was upholstered in red satin, with a statue of a woman in the middle, two statues of boys at the sides and two pier glasses in the arches separating this room from the main hall. Everywhere was a profusion of plants and flowers. I shall never forget the mass of bright-red azaleas I had looked at when I thought I was dying. Outside the window was a desolate view of a cobbled courtyard with two waiting carriages and some soldiers on parade.

An elderly footman, who looked and spoke like a foreigner, was standing at the door of the Tsarina's reception room. On the other side stood a Negro in national costume. There were also more Negroes, three I believe, standing by the door of the Tsar's study. I asked the footman to announce me to the Tsarina, telling them the Tsar himself had authorized it. He told me the Empress was with another lady at the moment, but he would announce me the moment she left.

I waited for fifteen to twenty minutes. The lady came out, the footman told me the Tsar had spoken to the Empress and informed her I wanted to be presented to her, and I went in.

The Empress, a slim woman, quick and light on her feet, came to meet me. She had a lovely complexion, and her beautiful chestnut-coloured hair was wonderfully neatly arranged, as though glued to her head. She was neither very tall nor very short, and was wearing a high-necked, narrow-waisted black woollen dress, very narrow in the arms. She gave me her hand, and like the Emperor immediately invited me to sit down. Her voice was loud and rather guttural, and we spoke in French.

"We have already met once before, I believe?" she said.

"I had the pleasure of being presented to Your Majesty several years ago at the Institute of St Nicholas in Mme Shostak's house."

"Ah yes, of course, and your daughter too. Now do tell me, is it really true that people have stolen manuscripts from the Count and published them without his permission? But that is horrifying – what a frightful thing to do!"

"It is indeed true, Your Majesty, and it is very sad. But what can we do?"

Then she asked me how many children I had and what they all did. I said I was happy to hear that her son, Georgy Alexandrovich, was better, and told her I had suffered for her, knowing how hard it must have been for her to be separated from her two sons when one of them was so ill. She said he was fully recovered now; he had pneumonia, the illness had been neglected, he hadn't looked after himself properly and she had been extremely worried. I expressed my regret that I had never met any of her children, and the Empress replied that they were all in Gatchina at present.

She stood up, gave me her hand and warmly took her leave of me.

Tanya and the younger children welcomed me home. Lyovochka had gone to Chepyzh and then out to the park to wait for me. I got back before him though, and it was a long time before he returned. He was displeased about my adventure and my meeting with the Tsar.

He said we had now taken on all sorts of responsibilities we couldn't possibly fulfil. He and the Tsar had managed to ignore each other up to now, he said; all this could do us a lot of damage, and might well have disagreeable consequences.*

23rd April. Why is one's *own* family so much more severe on one than others? How sad it is, how sad that they should spoil one's life and relationships like this. It was a cold fine day. Tanya has just gone past my door and told me Lyovochka asked her to tell me he had lain down and put out the candle.

24th April. I went out for a little walk in the garden with the children, and, just by the lower pond, on the very spot where yesterday I planted all the oaks and firs, I saw a whole herd of village cows. Some village woman and girls were calmly tending them, until I let out a loud scream. I was furious about my little trees and my wasted labours. I then went to Vasily and told him to drive away any cows that got into the estate. The village people are very hard to deal with, for they have been spoilt by Lyovochka. When we got home I ran a bath for Vanechka, bathed him myself and put him to bed. Then I copied out Lyovochka's diaries. It is now 11 o'clock. The wind is howling outside and I am afraid for anyone out in it. I sent the carriage to Kozlovka to fetch Lyovochka, but he will barely make it to Tula and catch the train. It was so cold he was glad of his fur jacket.

29th April. I haven't written my diary for several days. The evening before last I had another asthma attack. I felt as though something was blocking my chest, and had dreadful palpitations and giddiness. I threw myself at Nurse and said: "I am dying!" Then I kissed Vanechka and ran downstairs to Lyovochka to take leave of him before I died. Physically I was terrified, but not mentally. Lyovochka wasn't there, so I crossed myself and waited for death to come, unable to breathe. Then I went back to my room. On the way I managed to ask for some mustard for my chest and a pulverizer, and when I lay down and inhaled the steam I began to feel better. But even now my chest feels heavy, and I don't think I have long to live. I have overstrained myself and broken something; I've used up my allotted share of energy – it's all too much for me at my age.

The day before yesterday I wrote a letter to the Minister of Internal Affairs, asking him to remind the Tsar that he had given me his personal permission to publish *The Kreutzer Sonata* in the *Complete*

Collected Works. We had a wretched letter from Lyova, saying he didn't want to take his exams and was leaving the university.* Both Lyovochka and I wrote advising him not to abandon his university studies until he has clearly decided what he wants to do when he leaves. I don't expect he will take any notice though. Let him do what he thinks is best, the main thing is for us to support him. Tanya is going to Moscow the day after tomorrow. I have been sitting at home ill for the past three days, but outside it is already quite green. The grass and the leaves are coming out, and the nightingales are singing.

1st May. Tanya left for Moscow this morning. Ilya arrived and went to Tula to see about the division of the property. Davydov came for dinner with his daughter and Prince Lvov. I find them both very pleasant, and the day would have passed most enjoyably had I not been unwell. I have catarrh in my respiratory passages, am feverish at night and feel very sluggish.

I copied Lyovochka's diary. After dinner we all went for a walk, and afterwards I played Mendelssohn's *Lieder ohne Worte* and a Beethoven sonata for two hours. It annoys me that I play so badly, I wish I could take lessons and learn properly. Over tea we had a discussion about education. I don't want to send my children to the gymnasium, yet I see no alternative. I don't know what to do for the best. I cannot educate them on my own, and Lyovochka is very good at *talking*, but when it comes to *acting* he never does a thing. It is warmer, and everyone keeps bringing bright fresh violets into the house. We have been eating morels, the nightingale is singing and everything is slowly coming into leaf.

15th May. Again, I haven't written my diary for a long time, and again a lot has happened. On the 2nd or 3rd of May, we had a visit from Princess Urusova (née Maltseva) with her two elder daughters, Mary and Ira. Their presence reminded me painfully of the late Prince himself and I couldn't get him out of my mind. Mary is strikingly like him, and played a Beethoven sonata so well as to leave us in no doubt about her exceptional musical ability. The Princess has changed very much for the better, is more resigned, and full of remorse. I don't know why she is always telling me of the exceptional love her husband felt for me. This time she told me in grave and earnest tones that he had loved me even more than he loved Lyovochka, and that it was I who had given him all the things that she, his wife, should have given him

– true family happiness, sympathy, friendship, affection and concern. I told her she was quite wrong to imagine her husband had loved me, he had never told me so, and we had never been anything more than very good friends.

We spent three happy days together and parted on friendly terms.

They left for the Crimea, and I got a letter from my daughter Tanya summoning me to Moscow to make arrangements for Andryusha and Misha to take their exams. On the 6th the boys, their tutor Alexei Mitrofanovich and I set off for Moscow by express train. It was very hot, and I sat knitting while the children went into the other compartments making friends with the passengers, who gave them things to eat. We arrived at Khamovniki Street that evening, and I went off immediately to see Polivanov and make enquiries about the exams. Andryusha was so nervous he couldn't sleep, but Misha, unperturbed, went to sleep at once. The first exam, on religious knowledge, went well – at any rate they became less nervous. We stayed five days in the apartment, and spent every moment of our free time in our wonderful garden. The boys did badly in their exams. I am not sure of the reason for this – whether it's bad teachers or their poor abilities. Andryusha was accepted into the 3rd form and Misha into the 2nd. But I still cannot decide whether to send them to the gymnasium. I feel so sorry for them and so afraid of what will happen to them there – yet I see no alternative. I am leaving it for fate to decide. How different the two boys are! Andryusha is nervous, shy and cautious. Misha is excitable, talkative and loves the good things of life.

We went to a French exhibition, but it wasn't ready, and apart from a dazzling fountain the only things we saw were some bronzes and porcelain.

Driving past the Kremlin, I saw an enormous number of carriages at the Small Palace. Grand Duke Sergei Alexandrovich has just been appointed Governor General of Moscow and has been receiving the whole city.

The censors are still refusing to release Volume 13 and are cavilling at three passages, which go approximately: "From the Eiffel Tower to universal conscription...", "When all the European nations were busy teaching their young people how to murder..." and "Everything is managed by people who are half drunk." But these phrases had already appeared in the same article, which was published in the form of a prologue to Alexeev's book *On Drunkenness*.* I wrote to the Moscow censor informing him of this, and also to Feoktistov in

St Petersburg. A letter arrived for me in Yasnaya from the Minister while I was away, announcing that he had given permission for *The Kreutzer Sonata* and the 'Epilogue' to be published in the *Complete Works*. In Moscow I learnt of this at the press where it was printed. I cannot help secretly exulting in my success in overcoming all the obstacles, that I managed to obtain an interview with the Tsar, and that I, a woman, have achieved something nobody else could have done! It was undoubtedly my own personal influence that played a major part in this. As I was telling people before, I needed just one moment of inspiration to sway the Tsar's judgement as a human being and capture his sympathy, and the inspiration came, and I did influence his will – although he is a kind man anyway, and obviously quite capable of yielding to the correct influence. Anybody who read this and thought I was boasting would be wrong and unjust.

Volume 13 will come out any day now, and I should dearly love to send the Tsar a copy, enclosing a group photograph of my family, in whom he showed so much interest. Both he and the Tsarina asked in great detail after all my children.

Spring fills the air. The apple trees are covered in flowers – there is something mad and magical about these blossoms, I've never seen anything like it. Every time one looks out of the window one sees an amazing airy cloud of white, pink-fringed flowers, set against a bright green background.

The weather is hot and dry. Bunches of lilies of the valley fill the room with their intoxicating scent.

Poor Lyovochka has inflamed eyelids and has been sitting alone in a darkened room for the past two days. He was a bit better today. Yesterday I sent for Doctor Rudnyov, and he prescribed bathing the eyes in Goulard water, which he sent us. Yesterday Lyovochka dictated to Masha a letter on religious matters for Alekhin (a dark one), and I was amazed by how good it was and how totally it corresponded to my own feelings. It dealt with questions of immortality and the after-life: we should not worry about such things, he said, once we had placed ourselves in God's hands and said, "Thy Will Be Done!" We can never answer these questions anyway, however much we may worry about them.

22nd May. Another busy week has passed. The Kuzminskys came, and Masha's fiancé, Erdeli. The usual summer activities – swimming, lounging in the heat, admiring the beauty of the countryside, crowds of noisy, jostling children with nothing to do. Fet was here with his wife and read us some of his poems – nothing but love, love, love. He was in raptures over everything here at Yasnaya Polyana, and seemed well pleased with his visit and with Lyovochka and me. He is 70 years old, but his lyrics are ageless, lively and melodious, and they always arouse in me suspiciously youthful poetic feelings. Yet they are so good and innocent and always remain in the realms of abstraction – what if these feelings *are* inappropriate?

My Masha went off with the Filosofov girls to stay with them at Paniki. Let her enjoy herself, poor girl, she's only 20 but so serious and old for her age. We went out for a walk, but it started to rain and one by one we all made our way back to the house. Instead of reading, we spent a most interesting evening talking about novels, love, art and painting. Lyovochka said there was nothing more horrible than those paintings that depict lust in everyday situations, like the one of the monk looking at the woman, or the Tartar and the lady riding off on horseback together to the Crimea, or the father-in-law casting lascivious glances at the young bride. All this is bad enough in real life, he said, but in a painting you have to look at this filth *all the time*. I completely agree with him. I only like paintings that depict beauty, nature and lofty ideals.

Today is Ilya's birthday. The poor fellow lives in such a muddled and senseless fashion, preoccupied with his household, his family and his doubts, and permanently dissatisfied with his fate. It is sad that these disagreements over property have put a strain on our relations.

27th May. Very cold and cloudy. There has been a strong north wind for the past three days so we all stayed indoors. Vasya Kuzminsky fired at Sasha's eye with his toy pistol and left a red bruise. Vanechka had a stomach ache last night and didn't sleep. I got up at 3 a.m. to be with him and didn't get back to sleep myself until 5. The lilacs and lilies of the valley are over now. Vanechka and Nurse brought some night violets into the house, and the white mushrooms are out. It's very dry and the grass is withering. Raevsky was saying there was a drought in the Epifania district. We had a letter from Masha. She is evidently enjoying herself at the Filosofovs, which I am happy about.

1st June. Endless guests. First our friend Annenkova's husband, a landowner, much preoccupied with legal affairs, and an odd, vulgar sort of man, although said to be infinitely kind and sensitive. He brought with him a man called Nelyubov, a thin dark idealist full of ecstasy and gloom, and the magistrate of Lgov, their county capital. Then Suvorin, editor of *New Times*, came for the evening. He struck me as a shy man, interested in everything. He asked whether he might bring with him or send along a Jewish sculptor from Paris,* to do a full-length sculpture of Lev Nikolaevich. I begged him to send him here, although Lyovochka said nothing as usual. I am sure he would like it. Yesterday P.F. Samarin was here, as well as Davydov and General Bestuzhev. Lyovochka walked to Tula to inspect the abattoir, but they weren't slaughtering anything so he just looked round. Everybody is terribly interested to hear about my visit to the Tsar. Yet nobody knows my real motive for visiting St Petersburg. It was all because of *The Kreutzer Sonata*. That story cast a shadow over my life. Some people suspected it was based on me, others felt sorry for me. Even the Tsar said: "I feel sorry for his poor wife." Uncle Kostya told me when I was in Moscow that I had become "*une victime*", and everyone pitied me. So I wanted to show that I wasn't a victim at all; I wanted people to say my visit to St Petersburg was something I had done instinctively. I knew in advance that I would be successful and prevail upon the Emperor, for I haven't yet lost my powers of winning people's sympathy; and I certainly made an impression on him, with my words and my demeanour. But it was also for the sake of the public that I had to vindicate the story. Everyone now knows that I *pleaded with the Tsar* for it. If that story had been about me and my relations with Lyovochka, I would hardly have begged him to let it be published. Everyone will see this now. I have had various reports of the Tsar's flattering comments about me. He told Countess Sheremeteva he was sorry he had had urgent work to attend to that day and was unable to spend longer with me, as he found our discussion so interesting and enjoyable, and he hadn't realized I was still so young and pretty. All this flatters my female vanity, and avenges me for all the years in which my husband not only failed to promote me in society, but actually did his utmost to drag me down. I can never understand why.

It has been raining all day and it's cold and windy. About three days ago we had a visit from a mother and her two sons who were selling koumiss. They weren't the same people who came last year – they were quiet and looked very poor. Lyovochka keeps insisting he doesn't want koumiss and refuses to drink it, but he has had a bad stomach upset these past few days.

3rd June. A German from Berlin came and spent the whole of yesterday with us.* He had come to "take a look at Tolstoy", and ask Lev Nikolaevich for an article that he could take back and translate for his German Jews – Loewenfeld and the others. He himself is a merchant and travels around Russia buying wool. He was a most unpleasant, ingratiating fellow, and ruined the whole day. That evening Lyovochka, my sister Tanya and I had a discussion about abstract matters. Lyovochka maintained that there were certain actions which were simply *impossible*, and this was why some Christians were martyred; they were *unable* to worship sacrificial idols, the peasant was *unable* to spit out the communion wafer, and so on. I said that of course one couldn't do such things, but for some cause, or to help or save a person close to one, anything was possible. "Like killing a child, you mean?" he said. "No, not that," I said, "because *that* is the worst crime one could imagine, and there couldn't be any possible justification for it." He didn't like this at all, and contradicted me in a terrible angry voice. Then he began shouting, and I grew so exasperated I said a lot of unpleasant things to him. I told him one could never hold a conversation with him – his friends had realized this long ago – for he always *preached* at people. I couldn't talk to him when he shouted and made those horrible noises, I said, any more than I could talk to a barking dog... I was far too hard on him, but I was feeling very angry.

Lyovochka has only two "extreme" topics of conversation now: against heredity and in favour of vegetarianism. There is a third subject which he never mentions, but which I think he is writing about, and that is his ever more bitter denunciation of the Church.

5th June. A warm fine day. My soul is uneasy. Lyovochka and I went to the village to look in at the boot-maker's and visit poor sick Timofei Fokanov.* I sometimes long to be close to Lyovochka and talk to him, but he makes this impossible at the moment. He has always been severe, but now one is always touching on old wounds – as happened last night. We started talking about the children and he said that twelve years ago he had undergone a great change, and that I too should have changed with him and brought up the children in accordance with his new beliefs. I replied that I could never have done so on my own – I simply wouldn't have *known how* – and that he had always *talked* a lot, and over the years he had *written* a lot, but in fact he had not only not brought up the children himself, he had actually quite often forgotten about them altogether.

It ended quite amicably however, and we parted as friends. I have just finished yet another page of proofs for *The Kreutzer Sonata*. It is now 2 in the morning.

7th June. Lyovochka went to Tula at the request of one of his "dark ones", some follower of his I don't know by the name of Dudchenko, to visit this gentleman's mistress who is being transported from Tula, where she has been in exile. They told her she could make the journey on her own if she wanted to, at her own expense, but she refused, so now she will travel with the other prisoners. Why is he going? So he can brag and boast about his "principles", or from a sense of conviction? I won't decide before seeing for myself. It turned out the girl wasn't in Tula anyway, and Lyovochka was evidently pleased to have done his *duty* without actually having to see her. He went to the slaughterhouse again, and told us in great distress what a frightful spectacle it was, how terrified the bulls were when they were led out, and how the skin was ripped off their heads while their legs were still twitching and they were still alive. It is indeed terrible – but then all deaths are terrible! I've had a visit from Lyovochka's sister Maria Nikolaevna, the nun. She talks only of monasteries, Father Ambrosius, priests and nuns, John of Kronstadt and the holy powers of this or that icon, but she herself likes to eat well and frequently loses her temper, and seems to have no love for anyone. We went swimming this evening. It was terribly hot all day. I was cutting Vanechka's hair and accidentally nicked his head with the scissors. The blood spurted out and he cried and cried. "Forgive Maman, careless Maman," I said, but he went on crying. Then I stretched out my hand to him and said: "There, hit it!" But he seized it and kissed it fervently, still sobbing. What a dear little boy he is. I fear he will not live long.

9th June. Whit Sunday. A heavenly summer day, bright, hot and beautiful, and a lovely, warm, moonlit evening. To think of all the Whitsuns I have lived through! The children went off to church this morning in the carriage, looking very solemn in their best clothes and carrying flowers. After I had had a rest and read, I took Vanechka and Mitechka into my room and told them fairy stories in bed. One must develop their minds. Then suddenly we heard the strains of peasant women singing as they approached the house, and we went out and followed the smartly dressed crowd to Chepyzh, where they wove crowns. There is something very moving about this endlessly repeated spectacle. Every summer, for almost thirty years, ever since

I have been at Yasnaya, they have woven crowns and thrown them in the water. Almost three generations have grown up here before my eyes, and this is the one time in the year I see them all together. Today I felt such tenderness for these people with whom I have lived for so long, and for whom I have done so little.

Ilya came yesterday, and in the evening we had yet another discussion about the division of the property. Lyovochka is eating very badly and won't touch eggs, milk or koumiss, just stuffs his stomach with bread, mushroom soup and chicory or rye coffee. He has made himself a spade and says he is going to dig the wheat field instead of ploughing it. Yet another mad scheme of his – wearing himself to death digging the dry earth, which is hard as stone. I should be happy to see him healthy again, instead of ruining his stomach (in the doctor's words) with all this harmful food. I should be happy to see him an artist again, instead of writing sermons which masquerade as articles. I should be happy to see him affectionate, attentive and kind again, instead of this crude sensuality followed by indifference. And now this new fantasy of digging the earth – it will be the death of him! And in this heat! He is a continual torment to me with his perpetual dreams and his restless heart.

12th June. Yesterday we had a visit from two "dark ones", called Khokhlov and Alekhin. Alekhin used to be a learned chemist and university teacher, but now wears a peasant shirt and wanders the country with his comrades in the faith. The same old Russian pilgrims served with another sauce – this wandering life is in the Russian blood. But it seems sad that he spent ten years working at the university and is now going to waste. Khokhlov is a technician, young and somewhat unformed. They are a silent, gloomy pair, like all the disciples; they won't eat meat and wear rough peasant clothes. I cannot understand that scientist. He must realize this is no way to live, wandering about and living off others. Lyovochka keeps telling me that they *do* work, but I have yet to see any evidence of this: as far as I can see they do nothing but sit around in silence with downcast heads.

13th June. I got up at four this morning to see the children off to Ilya's. It was a bright cold day. Then Lyovochka announced that he and his "dark ones" were setting off on foot to see young Butkevich, some 20 miles away. I am afraid it will exhaust him and I'm unhappy about the friendship, but I realize he's in a restless mood and if it's not this it will be something else – some wild venture he'll think up just for a change I suppose. So they slung their rucksacks over their shoulders and all three set off in the blazing heat. The nights are very cold, but the days are hot and dry. It is dreadful to hear people complaining on all sides about the probability of famine. I can't imagine how most Russians are going to get through this year. In places there has been an almost complete crop failure, and they've had to plough the land all over again. The situation at Yasnaya Polyana is still tolerable, but there are parts of the country where people have no crops for themselves or their cattle.

We all gathered on the veranda this evening to drink tea, shivering in the cold, while Masha told us in horrified tones about the debauchery that goes on among the servants. I was appalled that she and the little girls should know such things, but it could hardly be avoided I suppose, considering the sort of life she has led. She spends all her time with the common people, and they talk of little else.

14th June. I had a pleasant busy day, although I didn't sleep at all last night. This morning I read some Russian stories in a journal, then tidied the house until it was all neat and clean. I don't know why, but whenever Lyovochka is away I am always filled with energy. Then we all went for a swim. Before dinner I read the German proofs of a biography of Lyovochka that Loewenfeld had sent us. After dinner I gathered up the children and we all walked across the rye field, picking cornflowers as we went, to the Cherta forest. There we gathered bunches of night violets, then sat down to marvel at the evening. How extraordinarily lovely, peaceful and fresh it was! Then I took another turn around the park and examined the oaks and firs I had planted. I went into the house, read through the Russian proofs of the *Second Reader*, wrote some letters and drank tea with Tanya.

15th June. I went to Tula with my daughter Masha, to attend to the division of the property and apprentice the boy Filka to a boot-maker – which she did. The reason for our visit was her refusal to accept her share of the property. I realize that the poor girl doesn't know what she is doing, and can't imagine what it will be like to be left without a kopeck after the life she is used to, but she is acting under hypnosis, not conviction. She is waiting for her father to return so she can ask his advice, since she must at least sign some papers and accept my guardianship.

This evening we discussed death, premonitions, dreams, and all the things that affect our imagination. We were interrupted by a visit from a lady from the Caucasus, the wife of Doctor Kudryavtsov. She had come to see Lyovochka, and she missed him. Then my sister Tanya's son Misha arrived, and told us some fascinating stories about a madwoman here. What had happened was that various things of Tanya's had disappeared from the pavilion,* and there was clear evidence that it was the mad sister of Mitya's wet nurse who had made off with them. So Misha went off with the wet nurse to see the woman, and tactfully asked what she had done with the things. It was a highly peculiar business. Gradually she showed him where everything was: she had buried the little work box with its keys in the cemetery near the church and covered it with stones; she hid two towels and a shirt under the bridge; she trampled her own peasant dress and a pair of her husband's trousers into a muddy ditch; and she hung the antique silver ink pot on its chain from a tree in the orchard at Telyatinki. She remembered exactly where everything was, and slowly went round collecting it all except for the ink pot, which they couldn't find in the dark. It rained this evening, and got a bit warmer. But it didn't rain enough. God grant us more.

16th June. It rained all day and there was a thunderstorm; the countryside and people are looking more cheerful. Lyovochka has returned from the Butkeviches in a sombre, silent mood. My daughter Masha is learning the most frightful things from the workers and peasant girls in the village. All this moral corruption grieves and shocks her dreadfully, and she insists on bringing this filth home with her and telling us about it. It's quite horrifying! When I told Lyovochka, he said we mustn't turn away from such things, we must help them forsake their vile ignorance. Help them – yes indeed, he and I might possibly try to help them, but she is an innocent girl of 20!

18th June. Sasha's seventh birthday. I gave her some presents this morning, and started on the translation of the preface to an English book on vegetarianism.*

This evening we packed some plates and crockery, the samovar, some berries and various other nice things to eat, and all went off to Chepyzh, where we made a bonfire and had a "picnic", as the children say. The little girls played rather half-heartedly, but we had great fun. Then just as it was growing dark two women came rushing out of the Kuzminskys' house and told us the bull had escaped and was charging towards Chepyzh. We gathered up our things in a flash and raced home. It turned out that the bull had gone for the cowherd, and very nearly gored him to death. I was worried about Lyovochka, who was out swimming. But he soon came back, put on his dressing gown and announced he had a stomach ache and a chill and wasn't feeling well. It's hardly surprising, considering his abominable diet recently – almost nothing but bread, stuffing his stomach with it despite the doctor's warning that it won't do him any good. He's completely given up eggs, drinks enormous amounts of rye coffee – and on top of that he insists on walking to Butkevich's, carrying a heavy rucksack that strains his stomach. I've never met anyone so stubborn once he gets some outrageous idea into his head.

16th July. I went to Moscow and ordered 20,000 copies of Volume 13; they had printed only 3,000, and had sold out almost immediately. I exhausted myself getting the paper and finding a printer prepared to do it in 2 weeks. I also ordered some silver for my niece Masha Kuzminskaya's dowry. Her sister Vera and I went to the French exhibition.* I wanted to see the paintings, but it was closing for the evening when we got there so we hardly saw anything. I was terribly tired, and decided not to go up in a balloon as I didn't want to waste 5 rubles.

Lyovochka wrote to me in Moscow saying he wanted to make Volumes 12 and 13 public property* so that anyone could print them. On the one hand I don't see why my family should lose the money, and on the other, since the censored articles in these volumes have been allowed to appear only in the *Complete Collected Works*, I think it would be wicked to release these to the public, and would involve them in all sorts of expense and confusion. But it grieves me more than anything to annoy Lyovochka, so yesterday I told him he could do what he liked, print what he wanted, I wouldn't stop him. He hasn't mentioned it again and hasn't yet done anything about it.

We have crowds of visitors. Repin left today. He has finished a small head-and-shoulders painting of Lyovochka writing in his study, and has started a larger full-length painting of him standing barefoot in the forest with his hands in his belt.* He is going to finish this one at home.

The sculptor Ginzburg is sculpting a large bust of him, which is most unsuccessful, but he has also done a smaller figure, writing at his desk, which isn't so bad.*

It's hot and terribly dry, the nights are cool, and people talk of nothing but this dreadful, terrible famine. It preys on my mind every moment of the day. The situation seems utterly *hopeless*.

Lyovochka is in poor health. He ate such quantities of peas and watermelon yesterday that I was quite alarmed. He paid for it in the night with an upset stomach. He still refuses to drink koumiss.

I took Vanya and Sasha for a walk yesterday evening and today; we went to the ravine at Zakaz, and today I walked to the well by the felled plantation. Vanya loves to exercise his imagination – he was pretending to be terrified that there were wolves in the forest, and that the water in the well was "special".

21st July. I must write down the whole foolish, sad story of what happened today. I don't know whether it is I who am foolish, or the life I am forced to live, but I now feel crushed, exhausted in body and soul.

Just before dinner today Lyovochka told me he was sending his letter to various newspapers renouncing the copyright on his latest works.* The last time he mentioned doing this I decided to endure it meekly, and that is what I would have done this time too. But when he mentioned it again I simply wasn't prepared, and my immediate feeling was of outrage. I felt how terribly unfair he was being to his family, and I realized for the first time that this protest of his was merely another way of publicizing his dissatisfaction with his wife and family. It was this more than anything else that upset me. We said a great many unpleasant things to each other. I accused him of being vain and greedy for fame. He shouted at me, saying I only wanted the money, and that he had never met such a stupid, greedy woman. I told him he had humiliated me all my life, and he had never learnt how to behave towards a decent woman. He told me I would only spoil the children with the money. It ended with him shouting "Get out! Get out!" So I went out and wandered about the garden not knowing what to do. The nightwatchman saw me crying and I was so ashamed. I went to the apple orchard, sat down in the ditch and signed his statements with a pencil I had in my pocket. Then I wrote in my notebook that I was going to Kozlovka to kill myself. I was exhausted by these endless quarrels with Lev Nikolaevich and no longer had the strength to settle all our family business on my own, so I was going to put an end to my life.

When I was younger, I remember I always felt like killing myself after an argument, but I never thought I could. Today though I would have done it – if circumstances hadn't saved me. I ran to Kozlovka completely deranged. When I had almost reached the footbridge across the great ravine, I lay down to get my breath back. It was growing dark but I wasn't at all afraid. It was strange, but my main feeling was that I would be *ashamed* to go home without carrying out my plan. So I got up and walked on, in a calm, dispirited way and with the most frightful headache, as if my head were in a vice. Then suddenly I caught sight of a figure in a peasant shirt, walking towards me from Kozlovka. I was overjoyed, thinking it was Lyovochka and we would be reconciled. But it turned out to be my brother-in-law Alexander Kuzminsky. I was furious that my plan had been thwarted, and felt sure he wouldn't let me go on alone. He was greatly surprised to meet me, and saw from my face that I was upset. I certainly hadn't expected to see him, and tried to persuade him to go home and leave me, assuring him I would soon be back myself. But he wouldn't go, and urged me to walk with him, pointing to a crowd of people in the distance and saying they might frighten me. God knows who was wandering in these parts.

Then he told me he had intended to take the roundabout route back, through Voronka and Gorelaya Polyana, but he was attacked by a swarm of flying ants, and had to run for cover into a thicket and take off his clothes. After waiting there for a while he decided to set back along the same road. Realizing that God didn't want me to commit this sin, I had no choice but meekly to follow him. But I didn't want to go home and decided to walk alone through Zaseka and go for a swim. There is another way out, I thought, I can drown myself; for I was still pursued by the dull despairing desire to leave this life with all its impossible problems. By then it was quite dark in the forest. Then all of a sudden, just as I was approaching the ravine, a wild beast leapt at me across the path. I couldn't see what it was, a fox or a wolf – I'm so short-sighted I can see nothing from a distance – but I screamed at the top of my voice. The animal jumped away and darted off with a great rustling of leaves, and at that point all my courage deserted me and I set off home. I got back and went straight in to Vanechka, who was already in bed. He kissed me and said, "My Maman! My Maman!" over and over again. In the past, when I used to go to my children after these episodes, they seemed to give meaning to my life. Today I realized to my horror that on the contrary, my despair merely grew deeper, and the children made me even more sad and hopeless.

I lay down in my bed, then was seized with anxiety about Lyovochka, who had gone out, and went into the garden to lie in the hammock and listen for his returning footsteps. One by one all the others came out to the veranda, and eventually Lyovochka returned. Everyone was chattering, shouting and laughing, and he was as merry as if nothing had happened; for him these are *rational* issues, in the name of some idea, which have no effect whatsoever on his heart. As for the pain he caused me – he has already hurt me so often in the past. As for the fact that I was close to killing myself – he will never know about that, and if he did he wouldn't believe it.

Exhausted by the emotional and physical torment I had endured, I dozed off in the hammock. Masha then came looking for something with a candle and woke me up, so I went in for tea. We all gathered together and read Lermontov's play *A Strange Man*. Later on, Lyovochka came up to me, kissed me and tried to make peace. I begged him to print his statement and say no more about it. He said he would print it only when I *understood* why it had to be. I said I had never lied and never would, and I would never "understand". Days like these are hastening my death. Something inside me has broken, and left me feeling sad, hard and old. "Let them strike but let them finish me off quickly!" I thought.

I am haunted again and again by thoughts of *The Kreutzer Sonata*. Today I again told him I could no longer live with him as his wife. He assured me this was exactly what he wanted too, but I didn't believe him.

He is asleep now and I cannot go in to him. Tomorrow is my niece Masha Kuzminskaya's name day, and I have got the children to rehearse a game of charades. I hope to God nothing goes wrong and no one quarrels.

23rd July. This latest quarrel has broken something in me that will never mend. I went in twice to ask him publicly to renounce the copyright on his recent works. Let him tell the world about our family arguments! I am not afraid of anyone, my conscience is clear. I spend all the money from his books on *his* children; I merely regulate the amount *I* give them, since if they had it all at once they might spend it unwisely. Now I have but one desire: to clear myself of this charge, this crime I am accused of. I have too much on my shoulders already: the division of the property, foisted on me against my will, the education of the boys, for whose sake I should go to Moscow, all the business with the publishers and the estate, and the entire emotional responsibility of my whole family. These past two days I have felt crushed by the weight of my life; were it not for the flying ants that attacked Kuzminsky and forced him to return, I might not be alive on this earth today. I was never so calmly determined about it as I was then.

Yet despite this stone on my heart, I organized the children's charades yesterday. We did "horse-pond". Masha, Sanya, Vasya Kuzminsky, Boris Nagornov, Andryusha and Misha all joined in. Sasha appeared briefly as an angel, and also made a *tableau vivant*. They all played nicely together; these games are essential for the boys I think, for they develop their imaginations and occupy their minds.

26th July. A young peasant woman died in the village – the wife of Pyotr, Fillip the coachman's son. Masha, who was looking after her, had mentioned she had a bad sore throat, and eventually told us she thought it was diphtheria. I told her she wasn't to go there again. But if she has been infected it will be too late anyway. I was so sorry for that dear little peasant woman, but also very angry with Masha for exposing two families and several small children to the risk of infection. Judging from her reports it certainly seems like diphtheria, but she was keeping it to herself in her usual sly way. Now she is distraught, complains of a sore throat and is obviously terrified. This daughter of mine brings nothing but grief, anxiety, irritation and pity; she was sent to me as the cross I must bear.

I spent all day working on the proofs for *ABC*. The Academic Committee has not approved it in view of various words, such as "lice", "fleas", "bedbugs" and "devil".

27th July. Horribly dissatisfied with myself. Lyovochka woke me this morning with passionate kisses... Afterwards I picked up a French novel, Bourget's *Un cœur de femme*, and read in bed till 11.30, something I normally never do. I have succumbed to the most unforgivable debauchery – and at my age too! I am so sad and ashamed of myself! I feel sinful and wretched and can do nothing about it, although I do try. Because of all this, I didn't get up early, see off the Bashkirs and make sure they didn't miss their train, write to the notary and send for the papers, or visit the children to see what they were doing. Sasha and Vanya romped with me for a long time on the bed, laughing and playing. Then I told Vanya the story about Lipunyushka,* which he loved.

What a strange man my husband is! The morning after we had that terrible *scene*, he told me he loved me passionately. He was completely in my power, he said; he had never imagined such feelings were possible. But it is all *physical* – that was the secret cause of our quarrel. His passion dominates me too but I don't *want* it, my whole moral being cries out against it, I never wished for *that*. All my life I have dreamt sentimental dreams, aspired to a perfect union, a *spiritual* communion, not *that*. And now my life is over and most of the good in me is dead, at any rate my ideals are dead.

Bourget's novel fascinated me because I read in it my thoughts and feelings. A woman of the world loves two men at the same time: her former lover (virtually her husband, though not officially), noble, affectionate and handsome; and her new lover, who is also handsome and also loves her. I know how possible it is to love two men, and it is described here very truthfully. Why must one love always exclude another? And why can one not love and remain honest at the same time?

29th July. Nikolai Strakhov is here, wonderfully pleasant and clever as always, as well as some woman student from Kazan, who asked Lyovochka all sorts of questions about life and morality.*

15th August. Marvellous weather. The children lured me outside to pick mushrooms and I was out for 4 hours. How beautiful it was! The earth smelt heavenly and the mushrooms were so lovely: shaggy caps, sturdy brown caps and wet milk caps glistening in the moss. The soothing forest silence, the fresh dewy grass, the bright clear sky, the children running about with happy faces and baskets full of mushrooms – this is true happiness!

20th August. Two Frenchmen have arrived,* Richet, a learned psychologist, and a relative of his.

19th September. It always happens that when life is most eventful I have no time to write my diary, yet this is just when it would be most interesting.

Before 25th August, we were all cheerfully preparing for my niece Masha Kuzminskaya's wedding. We went shopping and made lanterns, decorations for the horses, flags, and so on. On the morning of the 25th, my brother Sasha and I blessed Vanechka Erdeli, and I then drove with him in the carriage to the church. We were both very moved. I felt so sorry for this gentle boy, so pure, so young to be taking on all these responsibilities and so alone in the world. I wasn't there to see Masha being blessed, but they told me she cried a lot, and so did her father. Then there was the ceremony. I kept swallowing the tears.

We had dinner on the croquet lawn. It was a heavenly day, fine and warm, and everyone – family, neighbours and relatives – was in high spirits. We spent the evening playing games, dancing and singing. The party went on very late, and I sat up until dawn with the guests.

It wasn't until the 29th that I again raised the question of the move to Moscow, and whether we should send the boys to the gymnasium. I told Lyovochka I realized how hard it was for him and that I just wanted to know how much of his life he was prepared to sacrifice for me by living in Moscow with me. "I am definitely not going to Moscow," he said.

"Splendid," I said. "The question is decided. I won't go either in that case and won't take the boys, but I'll look for tutors instead."

"But I don't want that!" he said. "You *must* go to Moscow and send the boys to school, for that's what you think is right."

"Yes but that means a separation – you wouldn't see me or your five children all winter."

"I see little enough of the children as it is, and you can always come and visit me here."

"Me? Not for anything!"

At that moment I felt overwhelmed with regrets: all my life I had loved nobody but him, belonged to him alone, and even now, when I was being thrown out like a threadbare garment, I was still in love with him and couldn't leave him.

My tears embarrassed him. If he had one iota of the psychological understanding which fills his books, he would have understood the pain and despair I was going through.

"I feel sorry for you," he said. "I see you suffering but I don't know how to help you."

"Well I know!" I said. "I consider it immoral to tear your family in two, there's no reason for it. I shall sacrifice Lyova's and Andryusha's education and stay with you and our daughters here in the country."

"You keep talking of *sacrificing* the children – then blame me for it."

"Well what should I do then? Tell me what I should do!"

He was silent for a moment, then said: "I cannot tell you now. Let me think it over until tomorrow."

We parted on the Grumond field, and he went off to visit a sick man in Grumond while I walked home. The heartless, cynical way he had thrown me out of his life hurt me deeply. Yet another funeral of my happiness. I walked home sobbing. It was growing dark. Some peasant men and women drove past, looking at me in amazement. I walked through the forest terrified, and eventually reached the house. There the lights were on and everyone was drinking tea. The children ran up to meet me.

The following day Lyovochka calmly said: "You go to Moscow and take the children. I shall naturally do whatever you want." Whatever I *want*? Why, the word was ridiculous. When did I last *want* something for myself, rather than thinking only of *their* health and happiness?

That evening I packed my things and the children's and collected my papers, and on the evening of Sunday 1st September the boys and I travelled to Moscow. I am still beset with doubts and fears as to whether I have done the right thing, but I really had no choice. Just before we set off, Lyova told me the most terrible story about my nephew Misha Kuzminsky, who has sinned with Mitechka's wet nurse – and my boys apparently know all the details. One blow after another. My heart was filled with disgust, grief for my sister and anxiety for my innocent boys. The pain went with me when I left, and was with me throughout my stay in Moscow. But material worries and the need to help the boys in their new life had a somewhat soothing effect on me. Lyova told me my sister had taken the news very hard and was in despair, and Tanya was hurt because she felt my response was cool and insufficiently sympathetic. But this was unfair. Calm compassion can be just as genuine as passionate sympathy, which is all very well at the time, but may last no longer than a couple of days.

I stayed with them in Moscow for two weeks, had the house papered and painted, the furniture reupholstered and the rooms rearranged, made sure the children had settled in, and then left. My three sons are still there, with their tutors M. Borel and Alexei Mitrofanovich.

I arrived home on the morning of the 15th, and that same morning Lyovochka accused me of leaving the children "in a cesspit". Another argument flared up, but it soon calmed down for this was no time for quarrels. I told Tanya how disgusted I was with Misha, and mentioned the possibility of us living apart until the following summer – Lyova had assured me that this would be best for the children's sake, but I found the idea terribly painful, and I knew Tanya would too. She flushed and said: "Don't, Sonya! You've made me suffer quite enough as it is." So we have decided to leave it until next spring, and see how Misha behaves in the meantime. Then Lyovochka and I discussed the letter he had written to the newspaper on the 16th, renouncing the copyright on the articles published in Volumes 12 and 13. The source of all he does is vanity, the greed for fame and the desire for people to talk about him all the time. Nobody will persuade me otherwise.

Then that evening a letter arrived from Leskov with a cutting from *New Times*, headed 'L.N. Tolstoy and the Famine'. Leskov had taken extracts referring to the famine from a letter Lyovochka had written to him, and had allowed them to be published. Lyovochka's letter was extremely clumsy in parts, and quite unsuitable for publication.* He was terribly upset that they had printed it, and didn't sleep that night. Next morning he said he was tormented by thoughts of the famine; we should organize canteens where the hungry could be fed, he said, but above all people should take some personal initiatives. He hoped I would donate money (after his letter renouncing the copyright, which meant there wouldn't be any! What one is to make of him!) and said he was going immediately to Pirogovo to organize and publicize the campaign. Since he couldn't write about something of which he had no first-hand experience, he would start by setting up two or three canteens, with the help of his brother and some local landlords, and then publicize them.

Before going off he said to me: "Please don't imagine I'm only doing this to be talked about. It's just that one cannot stand aside and do nothing."

Yes indeed, if he were doing it because his heart bled for the suffering of the starving, I would throw myself on my knees before him and give him everything I had. But I don't feel, and never have, that he was speaking from the heart. Well at least he can move people's hearts with his pen and his brain!

Yesterday my husband again aroused violent passions in me; today everything is bright, holy, quiet and good. Purity and clarity – these are my ideals.

8th October. I couldn't wait, and went to Moscow to collect the boys. It happened like this: my sister Tanya and I had a falling out over the Misha business. She thought I didn't show her enough sympathy or concern, and I was very hard on Misha, for I was furious with him for corrupting my boys. Tanya left for Moscow and I decided to accompany her. Everyone was well at home, and Liza Obolenskaya and her daughter Masha were staying. On 26th September we set off. Our own separate carriage was attached to the train at Tula, the Tsar's suite was made available to us at the station, and Zinoviev saw us off. In Moscow my three boys soon returned from an exhibition in a lively, cheerful mood, and on Saturday the 28th I took them back to Yasnaya with me.

Now the nerves of my heart are so exhausted that I had an asthma attack and neuralgia in my temple. I cannot sleep, speak, enjoy myself, do my work – nothing. I go off and weep for hours on end, weeping for everything that has happened to me, weeping for this period of my life that is over. And if I was asked what was at the heart of my grief, I would say it was Lyovochka's lack of affection. We were talking about the various letters we had written and he started by reading his – to some dark ones. I asked him where Popov was, and Zolotaryov, and Khokhlov. The former is a retired officer of Oriental appearance, and the other two are young men from the merchant class. All of them call themselves disciples of Lev Nikolaevich. "Well, Popov is with his mother," he replied, "because that was what she wanted. Khokhlov is at the technological institute, because that was what his father wanted. And Zolotaryov is stuck in some small town in the south with his father, who is an Old Believer, and is having a very hard time of it!"

So they are all having a "hard time", living with their parents because that is what their parents want. Now I know that this Popov, whose mother is an extremely coarse woman, found it hard to live with his good and beautiful wife, so he left her. He then went to live with Chertkov for a while, but Chertkov couldn't abide him and he found it hard there too. I know for a fact that Lyovochka has a "hard time" living with me – his peculiar principles make it hard for him wherever he is and whoever he's with. There have been a number of Tolstoyan communities, but they all collapsed because people had such a "hard time" living together. It was on this unpleasant note that our discussion ended.

I was looking at an earlier passage in my diary, where I wrote about Lyovochka and Tanya's visit to the famine-stricken areas around Pirogovo.* Lyovochka's brother Seryozha greeted them very coldly and said they had come to lecture him: you're much richer than I am, you can afford to help, he said, I am a pauper, and so on and so on. Lyovochka and Tanya travelled on to the Bibikovs', where they wrote down the names of all the starving people. Tanya stayed with the Bibikovs while Lyovochka went on to visit Svechin and a certain woman landowner.* This woman and Bibikov both responded very coolly to the idea of canteens for the starving. They are preoccupied with their own affairs and say they have no money to spare, although the Svechins were more sympathetic.

When they came back and announced that they wouldn't be going to Moscow but would be spending the winter on the steppes, I was appalled. This means us being separated all winter, them living 15 miles from the nearest station – with his indigestion and bad intestines – the little girls alone in the middle of nowhere, and me endlessly worrying about them. I felt particularly crushed by the news since, with a great deal of pain and effort, we had just settled one question, and I had agreed, so as to make it easier for Lyovochka to live in Moscow, that he should print his announcement about Volumes 12 and 13. It made me quite ill. And on top of this, Lyova wrote urging us all to remain in Yasnaya, saying my presence in Moscow would disturb the three boys in their studies and that I wasn't needed there. This was yet another grief. For 29 years I have lived *only* for my family, denying myself all the joys and pleasures of youth, and now *nobody* needs me. I have cried so much recently! I suppose I must be very bad, yet I have loved so much, and love is said to be a noble feeling...

I have no idea what Lyovochka and the girls intend to do. Personally I have doubts about these canteens. It's the free, strong, healthy people who will go there for food, while the children and old people, the pregnant women and those with babies won't go, and it's they who need it most.

Before Lyovochka published his statement about the copyright, I had intended to give 2,000 rubles to the starving; I wanted to choose one district and give every starving family there so many pounds of flour, bread or potatoes per month. Now I simply don't know what to do. If I do donate money it will be for Seryozha to dispose of, for he is the secretary of our local Red Cross. He has a clear duty to do famine-relief work; he is free, young and honest, and is here on the spot.

16th October. It was snowing all day. I drove to Tula in the large sledge, harnessed to a pair of horses, and when I came back it was 8° below freezing. Some gypsies had put up their tents and were camping just outside our estate, with children, hens, pigs, about 40 horses and a large crowd of people. The girls went to see them and brought them back to the side kitchen. Last night Lyovochka sent off his article 'On the Famine' to Grot's journal *Questions of Philosophy and Psychology.** Sasha and Vanya have just drawn lots for the property: Sasha drew her own, and got the left half of Bistrom. Vanechka drew for Misha and Andryusha; Misha has got the land at Tuchkov and Andryusha the right half of Bistrom and...

The directors of the St Petersburg theatres have refused to hand over the royalties for *The Fruits of Enlightenment*, and I was furious with them and with Lev Nikolaevich for depriving me of the pleasure of giving this money to the starving. Yesterday I wrote to the Minister of the Court, Vorontsov, requesting that this money be paid to me, but I don't know what will come of it.* We are packing our things and preparing for the journey to Moscow. Wherever I look – in our family, all over the place – I see nothing but arguments and strife. Everything and everyone is oppressed by this famine.

19th October. Petya Raevsky is here, as well as Popov (a dark one) and some other itinerant intellectual, sent here by Syutaev. A glum, dissatisfied, disillusioned, sickly fellow.* Lyovochka is strangely, selfishly cheerful – physically cheerful, but not emotionally.

12th November. I have been in Moscow since 22nd October, with Andryusha, Misha, Sasha and Vanya. On the 26th my husband Lyovochka left with his daughters for the Dankovsky district to visit I.I. Raevsky at his estate in Begichevka, and on the 25th my son Lyova left for the village of Patrovka, in the province of Samara. We all had one thing on our mind: to help the starving people. For a long time I didn't want them to go, and hated the idea of parting with them, but I knew in my heart that this had to be and at last agreed. I even sent them 500 rubles when they had gone, on top of the 250 I had already given then; Lyova took just 300 and I sent another 100 to the Red Cross.* But how little this is compared to what is needed! I felt terribly homesick when I arrived in Moscow, and was in the most frightful emotional state. Words cannot describe how I felt. My health was shattered and I was close to suicide.

One night I was lying in bed unable to sleep, and I suddenly decided to issue a public appeal for charity. The next morning I jumped out of bed, wrote a letter to the editors of the *Russian Gazette* and set off at once to deliver it. On the following day, Sunday, it was published. Suddenly I began to feel well and cheerful again. Donations poured in from all sides. I was so moved by people's compassion; some were crying when they brought the money in. Between the 3rd and the 12th I received no less than 9,000 rubles, of which I sent 1,273 to Lyovochka, and 3,000 yesterday to Pisaryov to buy rye and maize. I am now waiting to hear from Seryozha and Lyova, who will tell me what to do with the rest of the money. All morning I receive donations, record it in the books and talk to people, and it is all very absorbing. But there are times when I suddenly lose heart and long to see Lyovochka and Tanya, even Masha, although I know she is always much happier when she is away from me.

Andryusha and Misha are studying at the Polivanov gymnasium; Misha is doing poorly, Andryusha is average. I always feel sorry for them; I want to cheer them up and entertain them, and in general am prone to spoil them, which is no good. I was sitting down to dinner with the children today when I thought how selfish, fat and sleepy our bourgeois city existence was, without contact with the people, never doing anything for others! I couldn't eat. I felt so wretched thinking of all those at that moment dying of hunger, while the children and I were mentally dying in this atmosphere, without any useful work to do. But what can we do?

I received a reply from the Minister of the Court. In view of the fact that I want the money for charity, he has promised to give me the royalties on *The Fruits of Enlightenment*, and I have written to the director about this.

1892

Famine encourages formation of populist groups, who join liberals in calling for some form of representative government.

December to January – Sofia Tolstoy again joins Tolstoy in setting up canteens in famine-stricken areas. Government campaign against Tolstoy intensifies, with local priests exhorting peasants to refuse his bread.

16th February. I decided to visit Begichevka myself with Lyovochka and Masha, leaving Tanya in Moscow to look after the boys. The day we left, someone brought us an article in issue 22 of the *Moscow Gazette.* They had paraphrased Lyovochka's article 'On the Famine' (written for *Questions of Philosophy and Psychology*), treated it as a proclamation and declared him to be a revolutionary.* Lyovochka and I sat down and wrote a denial, which he made me sign, then we set off.

On 24th January we caught the train from Tula to Kletkotka, travelling on the desolate Syzran–Vyazma line. On the train I had asthma and a nervous attack. Lyovochka was restless and taciturn, and kept going to the corridor. The weather was ghastly; it was raining and thawing, a heavy grey sky bore down on us and a fierce wind howled. We finished the journey in two sledges: Masha, Maria Kirillovna and Fedot, the Raevskys' cook, in one, and Lyovochka and I in the other, which was smaller. It was dark and eerie and very cramped. Masha was sick the entire journey and I was worried Lyovochka would catch cold in the wind.

It was night when we got there. We were met at the Begichevka house by Ilya, Gastev, Persidskaya, Ilya's sister-in-law Natasha and Velichkina.* Ilya was in a strange, jumpy mood, terrified of seeing the ghost of Raevsky. He left the following morning, and we stayed on with our two women volunteers.

Lyovochka and I lived in one room. I took on all the bookkeeping and tried to put it in some order, then went to inspect the canteens. I went into one hut; there were about ten people there, but there were soon about 48. They were all in rags, wretched and thin-faced. They came in, crossed themselves and sat down quietly. Two tables had been moved together, with long benches to sit on. There was a basket filled with slices of rye bread. This was taken round by the serving woman, and everyone took one slice. Then she put a big dish of cabbage broth on the table. There was no meat in it, just a bit of hemp oil. The young boys all sat together on one side of the table, laughing and enjoying their meal. Afterwards they get potato stew or peas, wheat gruel, oat porridge or beetroot. They generally have two dishes for lunch and two for supper. We drove out to inspect various canteens. At first I wasn't sure what people really thought of them. In the second canteen I visited I met a pale peasant girl who looked at me with such sadness that I almost burst into tears. It cannot be easy for her, or the old man with her, or any of them, to accept this charity. "Lord, let us give and not take" – how true the old saying is. Then I began to feel easier in my mind about the canteens, without which things would have been so much worse.

The hardest thing for us is having to decide which people are the neediest, who should go to the canteens, who should get the firewood and clothes that have been donated, and so on. When I made my list a few days ago there were 86 canteens. Now as many as a *hundred* have been opened. The other day Lyovochka and I drove out to the neighbouring hamlets; it was perfect weather, bright and clear. First we visited the mill and enquired about the grinding; then we called in on another food store where we told them to release the millet (from Orlovka) and made general enquiries about distribution; and finally we opened a canteen in Kulikovka, where there had been a fire. We visited the village elder, asked him which families were the poorest, and told him to call the other elders and peasants to a council meeting. They came in and sat down on benches, and we began by asking them which families were worst off, then decided how many people per family were to be fed. While I was taking down their names, Lyovochka told them to come on Tuesday to fetch their provisions, and suggested to the elder's wife that she set up a canteen in her own house for the victims of the fire.

We got back at dusk. On one side the red sun was setting, and on the other the moon was rising. We drove along the steppes, following the course of the Don. It is a flat, bleak place, but there are several old and new estates picturesquely scattered along the banks of the river.

In the mornings I helped the tailor make coats for the men from material people had donated. I managed to do 23. The boys were delighted with their new coats and fur jackets. They were *warm and new* – some of them have never in their life had such a thing.

I stayed in Begichevka for 10 days.

When I got back to Moscow I heard more and more reports about Lyovochka's letters to England about the famine, and had letters from St Petersburg saying they had threatened to send us into exile, urging me to go there immediately and do something about it. I delayed doing anything for a long time as I had to visit the dentist almost the whole of that week. But eventually I wrote to Durnovo, Minister of Internal Affairs, and Plehve, his deputy, explaining the true facts, refuting the lie put about by the *Moscow Gazette*. They refused to publish my denials in the newspapers, even though I had written to the *Government Herald*.* So I made an appointment to see Grand Duke Sergei Alexandrovich, and asked him to order them to publish my denials. He said that it wasn't in his power, and that Lev Nikolaevich should himself write to the *Government Herald*, to "soothe excited minds and satisfy the Emperor". So I wrote to Lyovochka begging him to do so. I have just received his letter today,* and have sent it off to the *Government Herald*. I am now waiting to hear whether or not it will be published.

Lyovochka, Tanya, Masha and my niece Vera Kuzminskaya have all gone back to Begichevka.

Tomorrow is the first day of Lent. I shall fast.

1893

The Kingdom of God Is within You *is finished in April; banned by the censors, it circulates unofficially nonetheless.*

2nd August. I have just learnt from Chertkov that most of Lev Nikolaevich's manuscripts are either with him or in St Petersburg – with his friend *Trepov* of all people.* Our children must be told of this at once.

Chertkov subsequently removed all of Lev Nikolaevich's manuscripts and took them with him to Christchurch in England. [This last paragraph was added later.]

5th November (Moscow). I believe in good and evil spirits. The man I love has been taken over by evil spirits, but he doesn't know it. His influence is pernicious: his son is being destroyed, his daughters are being destroyed, and so is everyone he comes into contact with. I pray day and night for my children and it is a hard spiritual struggle, and I am thin and physically exhausted, but my spirit will be saved, because my communion with God can never be destroyed so long as I don't fall under the evil influence of people who are blind and cold, too proud and presumptuous to acknowledge their God-given responsibilities.*

1894

Vigorous government action against members of such increasingly popular religious sects as the Stundists, much like the Baptists, and the Dukhobors "spirit-wrestlers", whose primitive communal brand of Christianity, denouncing hierarchies, sacraments and violence, is considered especially subversive. Hundreds of them are harassed and imprisoned, yet this does little to check the huge growing population of religious dissidents. November – Tsar Alexander III dies. His twenty-six-year-old son Nicholas becomes Tsar.

Sofia Tolstoy brings out ninth edition of Tolstoy's Complete Works.

2nd March. Tanya has left for Paris to stay with Lyova. His health is worse. I am haunted by the thought that he isn't long for this world. He is too exceptional, too good and too unbalanced. I live from day to day – but it is no life. My health is shattered. Today I coughed up blood – a lot too. Feverish nights, painful chest, sweat. Lev Nikolaevich is depressed too. But his life goes on as usual: he gets up early, cleans his rooms, eats a bowl of oatmeal cooked in water, then goes off to work. Today I found him playing patience. He ate a hearty lunch, then went off and had a sleep. He woke up in an extraordinarily cheerful mood. Looking out at the bright sun and picking a handful of dates from the window sill, he set off for the mushroom market to take a *"coup d'œil"* at the people selling honey, mushrooms and cranberries.*

4th August. Doctor Zakharin has told us Lyova is very ill. I always knew it in my heart. How am I to survive the loss of my son, so young, so good and so dearly loved? My heart is breaking with the strain. I must live – for little Vanechka, for Misha, for Sasha, even for Andryusha, who still has a glimmering love and tenderness for me even though so much in him has been destroyed. But it is all so hard. My husband has worn me down over the years with his coldness, and has loaded absolutely everything onto my shoulders: the children, the estate, the house, his books, his business affairs, and then, with selfish, critical indifference, he despises me. And what about *his* life? He walks and rides, writes a little, does whatever he pleases, never lifts a finger for his family and exploits everything to his own advantage: the services of his daughters, the comforts of life, the flattery of others, my submissiveness, my labours. And fame, his insatiable greed for fame, continually drives him on. You have to be heartless to live such a life. My poor Lyova, how deeply he has suffered for his father's unkindness. The sight of his sick son spoils his easy sybaritic life – and that annoys him. It's painful for me to recall Lyova's dark suffering eyes, the sad reproachful look he gave his father when he blamed him for being ill and wouldn't believe he was suffering. He has never experienced such pain himself, and when he is ill he is always impatient and demanding.

23rd November. The whole family is staying in Moscow. Poor sick Lyova is the centre of my life and concerns. I shall never get used to this grief. I think constantly of his sad sick stare and I suffer painfully for him. I see almost nobody and almost never leave the house. We have a new English girl, a Miss Spiers. Lyovochka, Tanya and Misha have gone over to the Pasternaks to hear some music.

I am preparing Volume 13 for publication* and reading *Marcella* by Mrs Humphry Ward.* Lyovochka and I have been on friendly terms, although I was angry he was so indifferent to Andryusha's activities and never gave me any help with him. But it's my own fault if after 32 years I still hope he will do something for me and the family. I should be grateful for all the good qualities he *does* have.

1895

Revolutionaries form clandestine Marxist discussion groups and take their propaganda into the factories. Autumn – Marxists in the capital unite in the Union of Struggle for the Emancipation of the Working Class, led by Lenin. November – Lenin and other revolutionaries arrested, imprisoned and exiled. The Dukhobors in the Caucasus refuse to bear arms and continue to be arrested and persecuted.

January – Tolstoy attends a meeting organized by landowners. February – Lyova Tolstoy has electrical treatment for his nervous illness. 23rd February – Vanechka dies. March – Tolstoy makes his first will, leaving his unpublished papers to his wife and Chertkov. He resumes work on Resurrection. *Summer – Anton Chekhov visits Yasnaya Polyana; the composer Sergei Taneev spends the summer there; Chertkov moves to a nearby estate. July – Sergei Tolstoy marries Maria Rachinskaya. September – Nicholas II authorizes production of* The Power of Darkness, *at St Petersburg's Alexandra Theatre (opening shortly afterwards in Moscow's Skomorokh People's Theatre).*

1st and 2nd of January (Moscow). I was woken at 4 this morning by a ring at the door. I waited, terrified, and then there was another ring. The servant went to open the door, and who should it be but Khokhlov, one of Lyovochka's followers, who has gone mad and keeps pursuing Tanya and proposing marriage to her! Poor Tanya can't go out into the street now, for this *dark one*, dressed in rags and covered in lice, follows her everywhere. These are the people Lev Nikolaevich has brought into our family circle – and it's I who have to send them packing.

How strange that it should be these weak foolish people, who for whatever morbid reason have strayed from the path of normal life and thrown themselves into Lev Nikolaevich's teachings, then follow the road to certain ruin.

I am afraid I cannot resist complaining about Lev Nikolaevich whenever I write my diary. But I must complain, for all the things he preaches for the happiness of humanity only complicate life to the point where it becomes harder and harder for me to live.

His vegetarian diet means preparing two dinners, which means twice the expense and twice the work. His sermons on love and goodness have made him indifferent to his family, and mean the intrusion of all kinds of riff-raff into our family life. And his (purely verbal) renunciation of worldly goods has made him endlessly critical and disapproving of others.

When it all gets too difficult I fly into a rage and say harsh things which I then regret; but by then it is too late, and that makes me even more miserable.

I have very tender feelings for my daughter Masha. She is a sweet, gentle good creature and I should so love to help her! I don't love Tanya quite so much as I used to, as I feel she has been contaminated by the love of the "dark ones", Popov and Khokhlov. I pity her, she has grown old and withered. I am sorry that her youth is behind her – so full of beauty, happiness and promise. I am sorry she never married. How little my lovely big family has given me. I mean, how little happiness they have had. That is the most painful thing for a mother.

This morning I read Jules Verne's *20,000 Leagues Under the Sea* to Sasha and Vanya. "It's difficult, you won't understand it," I said to them. But Vanya said, "It doesn't matter, Maman. Read it, and you'll see how clever we get after that and *In Search of the Castaways*."*

3rd January. I got up late. I went to see Masha and Lyova, and scolded Misha for not practising his violin and not getting up until midday. Then Lyova went off to the clinic for his electrical treatment. The streets, the courtyards, the garden and the balcony are all covered in snow. 4° below freezing.

5th January. I didn't write yesterday as I was reading Fonvizin's story to Lyova. We found it interesting but rather coarse.

Then I did the accounts till 3 in the morning and got in a great muddle. I can't get it right. I spent a lot of the day sitting with Vanya and reading to him. He has been ill all day. Everything terrifies me nowadays, but especially Vanechka's fragile health. My life is inextricably bound up with his – there is almost something wrong and dangerous about it. He is such a weak, delicate little boy – and so good!

8th January. Vanechka has been ill for three days with a fever and a bad stomach. It breaks my heart to see him grown so thin and pale. Andryusha, Misha and Sasha went to a children's party at the

Glebovs' yesterday, while Vanechka sat on my knee all evening, weak and feverish. I hated to make him miss the party. Before this he was ill in bed with influenza, and it's three weeks since he had any fresh air. I have given up trying to teach the older boys a sense of their responsibilities; the struggle to do so has quite set my heart against them. Oh how painful it is, how painful to see Ilya ruining himself in this stupid vulgar way, and Seryozha with his immoral life, and Lyova ill, and my daughters unmarried, and poor darling Vanechka with hardly a flicker of life in him.

Busy all day. I paid the laundresses and the others and gave the labourers in the workshop their orders. The servants asked for leave to attend a wedding; some documents arrived from the police station about the theft at Yasnaya Polyana;* then wages, overdue passports, and so on and so on. Then Lyova, Vanechka and I sat together and looked at the pictures in the history books; I told him everything I could remember about the Egyptians, then read him some of Grimms' fairy stories.

The episode with the photograph still hasn't died down.* Posha came and blamed me, and I blamed all the others. They had persuaded Lev Nikolaevich on the sly, without telling us, to have his photograph taken with a group of "dark ones". The girls were highly indignant, all his friends were horrified, Lyova was grieved and I was furious. Group photographs are taken of schools, picnics, institutions, etc., so I suppose that means that the Tolstoyans are an "institution"! The public would seize on it, and all want to buy pictures of "Tolstoy with his pupils" – that would make them laugh! But I wasn't going to let them drag Lev Nikolaevich from his pedestal into the mud. So the following morning I went to the photographer and got all the negatives from him before a single print had been made. The photographer, an intelligent, sensitive German called Mey, was very sympathetic and gladly handed over the negatives.

I have no idea what Lev Nikolaevich thought of this. He has been very affectionate to me, but he'll blame me "on principle" in his diary, where he never has a sincere or kind word to say nowadays.

The English governess Miss Spiers is not nice. She is dry and unfriendly and keeps her distance from the children, and is concerned only with learning Russian and having a good time.

10th January. This evening I went to the bathhouse and took a bath. Then Masha and I drank tea together and talked about the Olsufievs and Tanya. It is pouring with rain, 3° above freezing, and very muddy.

This evening I smashed the negatives of the photographs of the dark ones. I tried to scratch Lev Nikolaevich's face out of it with my diamond earring but couldn't. I went to bed at 3 a.m.

11th January. Vanya has a rasping cough. I have been sitting with him and reading him Grimms' fairy stories. I then tried to draw our garden, but was out of practice. I went out and swept the snow from the skating rink, for the exercise. Through the window I could see that Vanya had jumped out of bed and was running about without any clothes on. I went in and shouted at the nurse, and she screamed back at me and Vanya started crying. We all dined at home. It is Misha's name day; I gave him 10 rubles. This evening they took Ilya's peasant coachman Abramka to the circus, and were enchanted by his naive enjoyment of it.

12th January. I got up early and gave Vanya some apomorphine for his cough, which is worse. I opened the ventilation pane in the window – it was 10° below freezing – and had a wash in cold water, but didn't feel any livelier. I was in very low spirits. I sat with Vanya and read to him, then received guests. Chicherin came, and Lopatin, with whom I had an interesting talk about death. He said among other things that life wouldn't be so interesting if we were not faced with the eternal mystery of death at the end. Then Petrovskaya and Tsurikova came. Tsurikova dined and spent the night here. She is one of those aristocratic old-fashioned unmarried ladies who tells fortunes with cards, has a huge circle of acquaintances and falls in love at the age of 40.

This evening Vanechka again had a temperature of 38.3, and I was dreadfully worried. Something has broken in me – I ache inside and cannot control myself. Chicherin was talking about Lyovochka today; there are two men in him, he said, a writer of genius and a mediocre philosopher who impresses people by talking in paradoxes and contradictions. He cited several instances of this. Chicherin loves Lev Nikolaevich, but that is because he has known him for so long. He sees in him the Lev Nikolaevich he knew as a young man, who wrote him a vast number of letters which he treasures.*

15th January. I spent the whole day frantically trying to entertain Vanechka. Doctor Filatov came this afternoon and didn't find any complications in his lungs or his throat, and said his spleen wasn't enlarged. It's influenza, nothing more. I drove to the Glebovs' to collect Sasha, who had just had her first dancing lesson there. My brother came this evening with his sad, thin wife. Afterwards I told Masha's fortune with cards. I told Misha Olsufiev's too, and it showed death. I was very upset, and afraid for Tanya and Lev Nikolaevich.

16th and 17th of January. Vanya is just the same. He becomes feverish at noon and this lasts until night. His cough is better, but his cold is the same. I sewed, and spent the whole day sitting with him. My life is empty and cheerless.

18th January. Today is the anniversary of my little Alyosha's death. He died nine years ago.

I got up at 6 a.m., gave Vanya 4 g of quinine, then went back to bed. I got up again at 8.30 and took his temperature – which was 36.7. Then I lay down again and dozed off. I got up late, and my temple was aching. I went out shopping and bought cloth, stockings, bobbins and various other essentials. I also bought the children more pieces for the ariston.* After dinner I accompanied Misha, who played first a Mozart violin sonata then one by Schubert. It's a pity I sight-read so badly. He was enjoying it enormously and I was sorry to have to tear him away and make him revise his lessons with his tutor. Andryusha has a stomach ache, and his illness makes him lazy and disagreeable.

Lev Nikolaevich and Tanya have returned from the Olsufievs'. It wasn't a very joyful reunion after 18 days apart – not as it was in the old days. Tanya had a sharp, censorious manner, and Lyovochka is indifferent to everything. I had a talk with Miss Spiers this morning about her general inadequacy. She is very disagreeable and doesn't like children. I shall have to get rid of her. There are no good governesses to be had these days. It's all very depressing.

19th January. I got up early and sat with Vanya. He did a still-life drawing of some baskets, without any help, and I tried my hand at a watercolour sketch of our garden – with disastrous results.

Goltsev is with Lyovochka, reading him the Tver address and the petition presented to the new Tsar.* Dunaev is also here. Vanya is still ill. His temperature shoots up at 3.30 every afternoon. It's fine, 6° below freezing, a moonlit night. So beautiful! But I am depressed and my soul is asleep.

20th January. Vanya is very ill, with a high temperature. I went to see Doctor Filatov this evening, and he prescribed large doses of quinine. Lyovochka is annoyed that I consulted him, although he evidently has no idea either what to do. He is healthy, draws his own water from the well and writes. This afternoon he read, and has just gone off to see Sergei Nikolaevich. 17° below freezing, with a mist and hoar frost; a fine day and a bright night. My heart is heavy, it's unbearable!

26th January. Vanechka has had a high temperature for the past week. It tortures me body and soul to look at him. He is a little better today, and we have been giving him 4 g of quinine twice a day. I left the house for the first time in many days and bought some sheet music, toys, cheese, fresh eggs and so on. I sat with Vanya for a little while, played duets with Lev Nikolaevich after dinner, and chose a piece for Sasha and Nadya Martynova to play at the forthcoming children's musical evening. Then everyone left but Lyova, who told me about the house he wants to build in the courtyard, and curtly asked me for the money to do so. When I refused, he soon changed his tune and became more friendly. Then Masha and I corrected and transcribed the proofs for Lyovochka's story 'Master and Man'. I am angry that he gave it to the *Northern Herald* to publish. What is one to make of him? If he had published it for *nothing* in the *Intermediary*, I would have understood, for then anyone could have bought it and read a story by Tolstoy for just 20 kopecks. But now the public will have to pay 13 rubles to read it. This is why I cannot share my husband's "ideas" – because they are dishonest and insincere. His whole philosophy is so strained, artificial and unnatural, based as it is on vanity, the insatiable thirst for fame, and the compulsive desire for popularity. No one ever believes me when I say this, and it's painful for me to recognize it – especially when others don't see it. But then what does it matter to them!

It's now 2 in the morning. Lyovochka has gone off to some meeting, I don't know what about, called by Prince Dmitry Shakhovskoi.* The lamps are still burning, the servant is waiting up. I have boiled his porridge and pasted up the proofs. Meanwhile they just sit there *talking*. Tomorrow I shall get up at 8, take Vanechka's temperature and give him his quinine, while he sleeps on. Then he'll go and draw his water from the well, without even asking whether his child is better or his wife is exhausted. How little kindness he shows his family! With us he is never anything but severe and indifferent. His biographers will tell how he helped the porter by drawing his own water, but no one will know that he never once thought to give his wife a moment's rest, or his sick child a drink of water. How in 32 years he never once sat for five minutes by his sick child's bedside to let me have a rest, or a good night's sleep, or go for a walk, or simply sit down for a while and recover from my labours.

11° below freezing. Hoar frost, silence, moonlight.

1st February. Vanya hasn't had a temperature for 3 days, and for 4 days I have been giving him 5 or 6 drops of arsenic twice a day after dinner. I feel much happier about him now. I am still concerned about Lyova. Relations with Lyovochka are good.

I measured him the other day, by the way. He is 6 foot 3 inches.

5th February. Either I have a bad character or I am being perfectly reasonable. Lev Nikolaevich wrote a marvellous story called 'Master and Man'. Now that scheming half-Jewish Gurevich woman is always buttering him up, trying to inveigle him into sending her things for her magazine, and it makes me furious.

Once on my name day Lev Nikolaevich brought me a file containing 'The Death of Ivan Ilich', for the new edition. Then he took it away again and published an announcement saying he was making it public property. That made me angry and I wept bitterly. Why does he give so little thought to *my* feelings? How sad it all is!

Yesterday Masha visited Professor Kozhevnikov, who was not at all reassuring about Lyova's health. This morning I told Andryusha off for deceiving his father and me the other day and going off with Kleinmikhel and Severtsev to see the gypsies, rather than coming straight home as he had promised. Andryusha flared up and said the reason he deceived his father was that for the past year the only two words he had heard from him were "Come home!" His father never took any interest in them, he said, and never had anything to do with them or gave them any help. It made me sad to hear this – but there's much truth in it.

I started thinking about Turgenev, and that spring when he stayed with us in Yasnaya Polyana and we went out shooting snipe. Lyovochka was standing behind one tree and he and I were behind another, and I asked him why he didn't write any more. And he stooped down, looked around in a rather comical way and said, "Nobody can hear us but the trees I think, my dear." (He called everyone "my dear" as he got older.) "So I shall tell you. You see, before I write something new I need to be inflamed by love – and that's all over now!"

"What a shame!" I said, adding as a joke: "You can fall in love with me if you like, then you could write something!"

"No, it's too late!" he said.

He was such good company. That evening he danced a Paris cancan with my daughters and the Kuzminsky girls, and argued good-naturedly with Lev Nikolaevich and the late Prince Urusov. I remember he asked me if we could have chicken soup with semolina, and beef and onion pie, saying that was something only Russian chefs knew how to make. He was gentle and affectionate with everyone and to Lev Nikolaevich he said: "What a good thing you did when you married your wife." He was always urging him to write more fiction, and spoke passionately about his supreme talent as a writer. It's painful to recall all this now.

21st February. I am passing through yet another painful period, and another dreadful *episode* between us. It's all my fault of course, yet how did I get dragged into it in the first place?

As I said earlier, I was upset about his story 'Master and Man'. But I tried to keep this to myself, and worked hard on the proofs with him. Then just as they were about to be sent off I asked him if I could take a copy for myself, so I could publish them in Volume 13 of the *Complete Collected Works*.

I couldn't bear the idea of the *Northern Herald* having the sole rights; I recalled the words of Storozhenko, who said that Gurevich (the editor) must have bewitched the Count, since she had got two articles out of him in one year, and I was quite determined that, come what may, I would see that my own edition was published simultaneously. We were both furious and upset. Lyovochka got so angry that he rushed upstairs, put his clothes on and said he was leaving home for ever and wouldn't be returning.

Since I felt my only crime was wanting to take a copy, it suddenly flashed across my mind that there must be some more serious reason why he should want to leave me, and I immediately thought of the Gurevich woman. I ran out of the house and tore off down the road in my dressing gown. He came chasing after me in his long underpants and waistcoat, without a shirt. He pleaded with me to go back, but at that point my only wish was to die, never mind how. I was sobbing and shouting: "I don't care, let them take me away and put me in prison or the mental hospital!" Lyovochka dragged me back to the house, I kept falling in the snow and got soaked to the skin. I had only a nightdress on under my dressing gown, and nothing on my feet but a pair of slippers, and I am now ill, demented and choked, and cannot think clearly.

Somehow we smoothed things over. Next morning I again helped him to correct the proofs for the *Northern Herald*. He finished them after lunch and was about to take a nap. "Well, I'll take a copy now if I may," I said. He was lying on the sofa, but when I said that, he leapt up, glared at me and again refused to let me do it, without giving any reason. (I still don't know what it might be.) But I didn't lose my temper, and merely begged him to let me copy it; I had tears in my eyes and could hardly speak. I promised I wouldn't release the story without his permission; I was only asking him to let me copy it. He didn't refuse in so many words, but his anger stunned me. I couldn't understand anything. Why were Gurevich and her journal so precious to him that he wouldn't let his story be published simultaneously in Volume 13?

Feelings of jealousy and rage, the mortifying thought that he *never did anything for me*, the old grief of having loved him so much when he had never loved me – all this reduced me to a state of despair. I flung the proofs on the table, threw on a light overcoat, put on my galoshes and hat and slipped out of the house. Unfortunately – or perhaps fortunately – Masha had noticed my distraught face and followed me, although I didn't realize this at the time. I stumbled towards the Convent of the Virgin, intending to freeze to death in the woods on Sparrow Hills. I remember I liked the idea that Vasily Andreich froze to death in the story, and that I too would meet the same end. I didn't regret what I was doing. I had staked my whole life on one card – my love for my husband – and now the game was lost and I had nothing to live for. I wasn't sorry about the children either. I always feel that however much *we* may love them, *they* never love *us*, and I was sure they would survive quite well without me. Masha, as it turned out, hadn't let me out of her sight and eventually managed to take me home. But my despair didn't subside, and for two days I kept trying to leave. The following day I hailed a cab in the street and set off for the Kursk station. How my children guessed I had gone there I shall never know. But Seryozha and Masha caught up with me and once again took me home. Each time I get back I feel so foolish and ashamed of myself.

After I had been sobbing for a long time he came in, kneeled before me on the floor and begged me to forgive him. If he could keep just a fragment of that compassion for me alive, I might still be happy with him.

Having tortured my soul, he then called in the doctors to examine me. It was comical the way each prescribed medicine according to his own speciality. So the neurologist prescribed bromide, and the specialist in internal diseases prescribed Vichy water and drops. Then the gynaecologist Snegiryov was called in, referred cynically to my "critical time of life" and prescribed *his* particular medicine. I haven't taken any of it. I don't feel any better either. I've been running around the streets for three days and nights with barely a stitch on, in 16° of frost, frozen to the marrow and at my wits' end – naturally I'm ill. The girls were timid with me, Misha sobbed and Andryusha went off to share his grief with Ilya. Sasha and Vanya were childishly puzzled, Lyovochka was alarmed. The nicest of all was Seryozha – gentle, affectionate and completely uncensorious. Lyovochka, Christian that you are, I saw in you more judgement than love or compassion. This whole *episode* was due only to my limitless love for him. He is always seeking *evil* in me; if only he would realize this isn't one of my vices, although there are plenty of others to be sure. Is it my fault that God has given me such a restless, passionate temperament?

His sister Maria Nikolaevna was also very sweet and kind and told me what I said in my frenzy was quite true, but that I'd gone too far. Yes, this frenzy is an unforgivable, incorrigible vice!*

We have made peace again. Lyova has left for Ogranovich's sanatorium.* He is morbidly resentful of his family and wants nothing to do with us, which may be for the best while he is in this nervous condition. A doctor arrived from there yesterday and spoke reassuringly about him. God grant that I don't live to see any of my children die, and that I may be the first to join Him in the place where all is love and an end to suffering.

The story has been given to both me and the Intermediary. But at what a price.

22nd February, morning. Vanya has been ill ever since yesterday evening. He has now developed scarlet fever, a sore throat and diarrhoea.

23rd February. My darling little Vanechka died this evening at 11 o'clock. My God and I am still alive!

1896

18th May – Tsar Nicholas II marks his coronation with the distribution of presents to his subjects on the Khodynka Field near Moscow. 1,300 people crushed to death in what becomes known as the "Khodynka catastrophe". The 1890s see an unprecedented rapid growth (supported by foreign capital) of mining, metallurgical and manufacturing industries, railways and oilfields, with a corresponding growth in the working class. May to June – a huge wave of textile workers' strikes in St Petersburg (spreading to other places in Russia) against the fifteen-hour working day. Some 260 factories hit; hundreds of strikes and revolutionaries arrested. November – large demonstration to mourn the Khodynka victims, in which over 700 people are arrested. Pobedonostsev, the Tsar's chief adviser, exhorts him to imprison Tolstoy.

Tolstoy working on Hadji Murat. 15th May – Lyova Tolstoy marries Dora Westerlund in Sweden. The composer Sergei Taneev spends the summer at Yasnaya; his friendship with Sofia provokes Tolstoy's jealous rage.

1897

First comprehensive census in Russia. Another disastrous harvest, followed by famine.

January – Tolstoy starts work on What Is Art? *(also referred to in the text as* On Art*). February – Tolstoy's disciples Biryukov and Chertkov arrested and sent into exile. Summer – Tolstoy proposed for Nobel Peace Prize. 2nd June – Masha Tolstaya marries Nikolai Obolensky (Kolya). Tolstoy refuses to allow Taneev to spend the summer at Yasnaya and threatens to leave. Sofia working on fourteenth edition of Tolstoy's* Complete Works. *November – first part of* What Is Art? *published to storms of protest.*

1st June. It was two years ago, on 23rd February, that my little Vanechka died. Since that time I closed the last page of my diary as I closed my life, my heart, my feelings, my joy. But this utter spiritual solitude has made me want to write my diary again. Let my words give a picture of this last period of my life – particularly my *married* life. I shall keep strictly to the facts, and later on when I am able to I shall describe those two years of my life, so rich in emotion and significance.

Today is Whit Sunday, bright and lovely. This morning I saw Tanya and Seryozha off to Moscow for Masha's wedding, which is tomorrow.* Then I read the proofs for Volume 12 of the new edition I am bringing out. Lev Nikolaevich is writing his article about art,* and I see nothing of him from breakfast to dinner time. We ate at 2. At 3 he asked me to go for a ride with him. I said no, then became terribly keen to go, mainly because I hate being left alone. So the three of us set off (the third being Dunaev),* and rode through some lovely parts of Zaseka. We visited the mines, where a Belgian company is digging for ore, and the abandoned "Kingdom of the Dead", then rode down the ravine and up again. Lev Nikolaevich was extraordinarily kind and attentive to me, and I was so grateful to him. In the past his kindness would have filled me with joy, but now that I've learnt from his diaries what his true attitude to me is I am merely touched by this kindness in his old age – I'll never again abandon myself to those paroxysms of love, happiness and despair as I did before reading his diaries.

3rd June. Masha and Kolya arrived, as husband and wife. Taneev came, and Turkin, Misha's new tutor. All other feelings are overshadowed by the dread of scenes over Taneev's visit. I feel sorry for Masha, and this makes me terribly fond of her, and of course I shall love her and do everything I possibly can for her. Kolya makes the same impression as before – a nice young man, but the thought of him as my daughter's husband excludes any good feelings I might have for him. He can't possibly be the mainstay of her life. My heart is happy and at peace at present. But it was deeply painful to see the horror on Lev Nikolaevich's face when he heard of Taneev's arrival. He is morbidly jealous, and his suffering is unbearable to me.

4th June. A distressing conversation this morning with Lyovochka about Taneev. The same unbearable jealousy. I choked back the tears, bitterly reproached my suffering husband and ached with regret for the rest of the day. I read the proofs for *The Power of Darkness*. What a pure, whole, truthful work of art. Then I went for a swim and met Taneev, which sadly reminded me of our daily meetings last year. After dinner he played Tanya some of his songs. I love his music and I love his character, calm, noble and good.

He played two of Mendelssohn's 'Songs Without Words', which transported my soul. I copied out more of Lev Nikolaevich's article before bedtime.

5th June. Sergei Ivanovich left today and Lev Nikolaevich immediately became calm and cheerful again, and I am calm too. It is only because he is suffering that he makes these jealous demands that I have nothing more to do with Sergei Ivanovich. But to break off relations with him would make me suffer too. I feel so little guilt and so much calm joy in my pure, peaceful friendship with this man, that I could no more tear him from my heart than I could stop seeing, breathing or thinking. I read proofs this morning, then waited on the balcony for Sergei Ivanovich to have coffee with me. He came just when I had gone out to the garden to talk to Vanechka in the watchtower. I asked him whether there was anything wicked in my feelings for Sergei Ivanovich, and today I sensed he wanted to draw me away from him, probably out of compassion for his father; but I know he doesn't judge me and wouldn't want to take Sergei Ivanovich from me, for it was he who sent him to me in the first place.

Later on Maria Vasilevna and I went for a swim. I am horrified by my strength and capacity for exercise! After dinner Lev Nikolaevich,

Sergei Ivanovich, Turkin and I all went for a walk. I picked a wonderful bunch of flowers, and was amazed to hear Lev Nikolaevich
expound his views on art to Sergei Ivanovich with lively enthusiasm
after all his jealous scenes.

There is very little life in the house at present; there are not many
of us here, and I miss Sergei Ivanovich more than anything.*

6th June. I couldn't sleep last night; my head and back ached, and I
felt unbearably depressed. I suppose this painful physical condition
is due to my critical female time of life. I went swimming with
Tanya, Vera and my sister-in-law Masha. There are no proofs to
correct at present, so I spent the whole day busily copying for Lev
Nikolaevich. It's a fascinating article and has given me all sorts of
new ideas.

The others drove out to Ovsyannikovo, while Lev Nikolaevich
and I stayed at home. I was just going upstairs to write and he was
going to his study, when we stopped to have a talk about Masha,
who has apparently given up her religious views, which once had
such an influence on her life. Lev Nikolaevich commented that *his*
life had been utterly transformed by religion. I said, his *inner* life
maybe; externally it hadn't changed a bit. That made him furious,
and he shouted that in the past he used to hunt, farm, teach and
make money, whereas now he didn't do any of those things. And a
great pity too, I said. It had been much better for his family in the
past; it had been a great deal better for the district when he farmed
the estate, for he had planted trees and improved the land; and it
had been a great help to me when he made money and taught the
children; now he bowls about on his bicycle, goes out on whichever
of his horses he feels like riding, eats the large meals cooked for
him, and not only refuses to bother with his children, but frequently
forgets about their existence altogether. At this he exploded with
rage, saying I had ruined his life.

I haven't experienced such spiritual anguish for a long time. I ran
out of the house intending to kill myself, go away, die, anything
not to have to suffer like that again. What joy it would be to live
out the rest of one's days amicably with a good quiet man and
not to be tormented by more insane jealous scenes. Yet the sky
is so clear, the weather is radiantly beautiful and peaceful, and
nature is so rich, bright and abundant, as though to show man
how insubstantial are his endless passions and griefs beside her
splendour.

Towards dusk I went for a swim in the Voronka. Lev Nikolaevich collected me in the trap and spoke to me kindly, and said it was time for us to stop loving and quarrelling so passionately. I had never expected such an offer of tender spiritual friendship from him. Later that evening I walked alone through the forest, weeping and praying for Vanechka, for the love we had had for each other, the one truly great and sacred love of my life. I shall never again know such love – now it's merely this insane jealous physical passion which drives all other attachments out of my heart.

7th June. My feelings for the beauty of nature today reawoke for the first time. These feelings of mine are utterly *chaste* – without memories, without regrets for people with whom I have loved this beautiful Yasnaya countryside in the past. Recently I devised a complete theory for myself concerning this *chaste* attitude to *religion*, *art* and *nature*.

Religion is chaste and pure when it isn't linked with all those Father Johns, Father Ambrosiuses and a lot of Catholic priests and confessors, but is focused within one's own soul, alone before God. Only then does religion help us.

Art is chaste and pure when one loves it for its own sake, regardless of the personality of the artist (like Hoffmann, Taneev and Gué, for whom Lev Nikolaevich has such a high regard, or my own feelings for L.N., for that matter). Only then can art be a truly pure and lofty joy.

The same with *nature*. If all the oak trees, flowers and beautiful places are linked with memories of people one has loved and lived with and are no more, then we cannot see nature as she truly is, but will merely identify her with whatever mood we happen to be in at the time. We should love nature as God's supreme gift – the gift of beauty. Only then will she give us that pure joy.

I worked hard copying for Lev Nikolaevich all morning. Then I gave Sasha her lesson. I enjoyed working with her – but, oh, what an insufferable temper she has.

I long desperately for music; I would like to play myself, but I never have the time. I did play two of Mendelssohn's 'Songs Without Words' today, however. Oh, those songs! One of them in particular moves me to my soul.

8th June. I must make a great effort to regain my energy, not for the sake of being happy but because of all the work I have to do. Proofs all morning, then a walk to the Voronka for a swim. I put on a white dress for dinner. (Why? For whose benefit? Well one mustn't let oneself go!) After dinner I walked to the tennis court to watch Tanya, Masha, Misha, Kolya, Sasha and Lev Nikolaevich playing. The place is so empty without Taneev! I went to the rose beds, tied back the bushes and cut off the dead heads, did some pruning and picked a great bunch for Lev Nikolaevich. Then more proofs. Later on we drove to the river in the trap, and had a swim. Then I sorted out the accounts, checked the table of contents for the new edition and did more proofs. It is now 2 in the morning. The weather is splendid: warm, bright, hot and beautiful. Tanya is also trying to keep her spirits up. Poor thing, she is *entitled* to want love, the love of a husband and friend, the love of children. The latter are certainly a great and pure joy; the former, however, is nothing but impure pleasures, deceptions and...

I was going to bed last night feeling calm and happy, and began talking to Lev Nikolaevich in a low, gentle voice. He responded affectionately: "How sweet and feminine your voice is tonight," he said. "How I hate it when you shout."

I was proofreading *The Kreutzer Sonata* today, and it again made me so sad. How cynical it is, how blatantly it exposes the evil side of human nature.

10th June. Maria Schmidt was here yesterday. She simply lives for L., whom she worships fanatically. She used to be an extreme adherent of the Orthodox faith, then she read Lev Nikolaevich's articles, took down her lamps and icons and hung up portraits of him instead. Now she possesses a complete collection of his banned works, and earns her living by copying and selling them. She is incredibly thin, works herself practically to death, does everything for herself and delights in her kitchen garden, her cow Manechka, her calf, and all of God's creatures. We women cannot live without our idols, and hers is Lev Nikolaevich. Mine used to be Vanechka, but now... my life is empty.

12th June. I visited Tula with Seryozha and Nurse. I went with Nurse to the savings bank to collect her interest, settled Masha's financial affairs* with Seryozha, and got the application forms for Misha to appoint me as his guardian.

13th June. I slept badly, got up late and ran straight out for a swim. On the way to the river I came across some peasant children taking lunch to the haymakers. They were such adorable little creatures, with their gentle, serious, inquisitive eyes, and they reminded me of Vanechka. I walked on with my heart full of tears, and met my daughter Tanya at the bathing hut.

"Fancy that, I was just thinking of you," she said.

"Yes? What were you thinking?" I said.

"Oh, about Vanechka," she said. "I was remembering the way he puckered his lips when he cried – the way he never cried from anger or naughtiness, but only when he was unhappy – and I was thinking, if *I* have painful memories of him, how much more painful it must be for *you*."

And I said: "Was it those peasant children who put you in mind of him?"

"Yes," she said. And at that we both burst into tears. It often happens that I hear echoes of my own soul in Tanya's words. We hadn't spoken to each other, yet we both experienced the same feeling at the same moment, prompted by the same thing.

This afternoon we all went for another swim, and after dinner we piled into the trap and drove over to the Belgian iron foundry near Sudakovo. We watched the machines and saw the molten cast iron being poured out, and it was all highly interesting – although depressing too, to see people being roasted day and night in this inferno. The heat was intense, and the ground beneath our feet was littered with iron and rocks. Some horses broke away but were caught. Lev Nikolaevich is tender and attentive to me, and that is my greatest joy. How long will it last? It's a fresh, peaceful night, the glow of evening will soon be followed by the glow of dawn, and my head is filled with memories of the drives we took last year.

15th June. I didn't sleep a wink all night. Towards morning I dozed off, but was shaken awake by sobs. I was dreaming of Vanechka; Nurse and I were going through all his toys, and I was weeping. Intense grief, like intense love, is something you can never suppress, however hard you try. There are days when I feel as though I cannot make my life stretch far enough. Life is like a piece of cloth which has to be stretched over something. Sometimes it's too big, and there's a surplus; sometimes, there's exactly the right amount you need to be happy, and sometimes there just isn't enough, and when you stretch it, it tears.

17th June. I dreamt last night that I was lying in a strange bed in a strange room. Sergei Ivanovich comes in and goes straight to the table without seeing me; on the table is a bundle of torn-up scraps of paper – notes or bills – and he puts on his glasses and hurriedly starts writing on them. I lie there quite still, terrified that he will see me. Then, having covered all the bits of paper with his writing, he bundles them up again, takes off his glasses and leaves the room. I jump out of bed, run to the table, pick up the bits of paper and read. On them is a detailed description of the state of his soul, his struggles and his desires. I am hurriedly reading them when there is a loud knock at the door and I wake up. I hadn't managed to read to the end and was annoyed at being woken up, for I had wanted to sleep on and continue reading – but of course I couldn't.

More proofs, then a swim in the cold river and a solitary walk home in the cold. I thought of our walks to Kozlovka last year. How happy and energetic I was then!

The other difference is that at this very moment, instead of the sweet elegant music Sergei Ivanovich played for us last year, Lev Nikolaevich is banging away on the piano, trying to pick out some chords to accompany Misha on the balalaika – which he plays quite nicely, although I am not particularly fond of these Russian folk songs. I couldn't help making the comparison – and it could hardly be to the advantage of the latter!

Relations with Sasha are no better. She is rude and wilful, and has worn me down by mocking me and insulting my feelings. Lev Nikolaevich went to visit a dying peasant called Konstantin twice today. When we went out for a walk he kept scribbling notes, then he went for a bicycle ride. He is cheerful and well.

18th June. Today is Sasha's 13th birthday. What dreadful memories I have of her birth! I remember we were sitting that evening having our tea – the Kuzminskys were still staying with us, and Mme Seuron the governess was there with her son Alcide (the poor boy later died of cholera) – and we were talking about horses. I said to Lev Nikolaevich that he was always losing money: he bought the most marvellous stud horses from Samara then bred them to death – no pedigree, no money, nothing – and it cost him thousands. It was true of course, but that wasn't the point. He was always finding fault with me when I was pregnant. Because he didn't like the look of me I suppose, and he had been especially irritable with me in the last months. This time however he completely lost his temper with me and said a number of truly terrible things, and putting some things in a linen bag, he said he was leaving for good, possibly for America – and despite my pleading he left.

At that point my labour pains started. I was in agony – and he wasn't there. I went into the garden and sat alone on a bench. The contractions came stronger and stronger – and still he didn't come. My son Lyova came to me, and Alcide, and they both pleaded with me to go in and lie down. But I felt paralysed by grief. Then the midwife came out with my sister and the little girls, who were in tears, and they took my arm, led me upstairs and put me to bed. By that time the contractions were more frequent. At last, at 5 in the morning, he returned.

I went downstairs to him and he glared sullenly at me. "Lyovochka," I said, "the contractions are very strong – I'm about to give birth. Why are you so angry? If I'm to blame forgive me, for I may not survive this labour…" Still he didn't speak. Suddenly it flashed across my mind that he might be jealous again, or suspicious of something I had done. So I said to him: "It doesn't matter if I live or die, but if I do, I shall die pure in body and spirit. I have never betrayed you, never loved anyone but you…"

He jerked his head and stared at me, but not one kind word did he say to me. I went out of the room, and an hour later Sasha was born.

I gave her straight to the wet nurse. How could I breastfeed my baby when Lev Nikolaevich had handed all the work over to me and I was having to labour both as a woman and as a man?

What an agonizing time that was! It was then that he was undergoing his conversion – to *Christianity*! For this Christianity the *martyrdom* was mine of course, not his.

19th June. I dealt today with the unpleasant business of the felled trees. The poor Grumond peasant came in dressed in rags, throwing himself to the ground and begging my forgiveness. I could have wept, but I felt furious too to have been forced into this position of having to run the estate, which means I have to guard the woods – and now I am responsible for punishing these wretched peasants. I never liked running the estate, I never wanted to, I never knew how to. All I know is that estate management means defending private property against the people, and that is something I am not capable of.

It was decided the matter wouldn't be reported to the village policeman, and that they would keep the trees they had already used for building and would repay us with labour.

Another unpleasantness was a letter from Kholevinskaya, the woman who was exiled to Astrakhan for giving some banned books to a clerk in Tula, after Tanya had sent her a note asking her to do so. Kholevinskaya is worn out and very bitter, and has begged me to help her.* I cannot think what more I can do, but I should dearly like to get her released.

20th June. Proofs all morning. I worked hard on them all day, and now, joy of joys, I have finished! I have been working on them for six months and today they're done. I just hope they're all right. I went for a swim with Tanya and Maria Vasilevna – the water is 12° and the nights are cold. Lev Nikolaevich went to Tula this evening to send a telegram to Chertkov in England.* Apparently Chertkov has been worrying about Lev Nikolaevich's *feelings* for him. But Lev Nikolaevich simply *loves* him! This evening I played some of Mendelssohn's 'Songs Without Words', and as I listened to them I remembered how Sergei Ivanovich played them.

Tanya did some copying and played the guitar then the mandolin. Sasha tidied up her room, made jam and arranged flowers. Misha has taken 22 rubles and gone off somewhere. He has been singing at the top of his voice, banging out chords on the piano, walking around in Sasha's dress and doing almost no work.

21st June. I didn't sleep, got up late and sat down at once to work with Sasha. But I saw she was looking very pale and she said she felt sick and had a headache. So that was unfortunately the end of the lesson. Then she vomited and had to lie down. She often gets migraines, like her father. I called Tanya and Maria Vasilevna, and the three of us went for a swim in the Voronka. I cut out a dress, then we had dinner. The Obolenskys came and they all played lawn tennis, while I wandered off on my own to sit in the watchtower talking to Vanechka, then picked a bunch of flowers for his portrait. I started back and saw them all coming in my direction, but I went home alone, sat down at the piano, stretched my fingers and was just about to start playing when Ilyusha arrived. I feel very sorry for him. I know his affairs are going badly, but I really cannot blindly hand money over to the children without having any control over their affairs. I never know what they want it for or where I should draw the line. I have tried not to refuse – but then I realize there is no limit to their demands. I need what money I have now to live on and pay for the new edition – and I don't have enough even for that. Financial matters are the bane of one's life.

Later we took a walk to Grumond; it was a lovely evening and my soul was at peace.

And now I have to write out the menu for dinner: *soupe printanière* – oh, how I've grown to loathe *soupe printanière*! For 35 years, day in day out, it's been *soupe printanière*... I don't want to have to write *soupe printanière* ever again, I want to listen to the most difficult fugue or symphony, to the most complicated musical harmonies, to strive with all my soul to understand the composer's private complicated musical language, and what he experienced in the depths of his being when he was composing them...

Misha and Ilya have been banging out chords on the guitar and the piano, bawling Russian folk songs at the top of their voices. I would dearly love not to have to listen to this ugly banging and to hear once again those elegant sounds that brought me back to life last summer. Yes, that was a true joy. I thank my good fortune for the memories.

22nd June. A lovely bright summer day. This morning I played scales, studies and exercises on the piano. Then we went swimming. Ilya and Kolya Lopukhin stayed for dinner, and afterwards I played the piano again for an hour. After tea all of us women went for a walk. Sasha grumbled at me for calling her away from the tennis court, even though she was only watching.

Tanya ran to catch us up and I was so pleased to see her. "You know mother," she said, "I'm growing closer and closer to you all the time – I shall soon become a baby again and start sucking at your breast!" Yes, I am growing more and more attached to her too. I didn't give Ilya the money. He said a great many cruel things to me: it made no difference that Lev Nikolaevich had made over the property to me by deed of purchase rather than for life, he said, I would start hoarding money in my old age... and much more besides. My God! Is there nothing more to my relations with my elder sons than money, money, money? And Andryusha is the same – it's nothing but give me money, give me money! It's frightful!

23rd June. The beauty of nature has stirred my soul, driven out the pain that was lodged there and filled it with light.

24th June. A letter from Mikhail Sukhotin – his wife has died. Both Lev Nikolaevich and I are extremely distressed by Tanya's relations with him and their correspondence.

25th June. I didn't sleep last night; I was so feverish I felt I was in a steam bath. It's a very difficult time for me physically. I am reading a disgusting French book that I found lying around. I picked it up and was horrified by its lewd contents. The title was bad enough – *Aphrodite.** What debauched people the French are! And yet reading it does give one a true assessment of a woman's physical beauty – and of my own too.

The greatest happiness a beautiful woman can hope for, however, is to live her whole life until she is old in complete ignorance of her beauty and her body, for then she will remain morally pure and fresh. Books like this would be her ruin.

26th June. Heat, haymaking, I have a bad headache.

After dinner I played the piano with our English music teacher Miss Welsh; I'm going to learn Beethoven's E-flat Major Sonata. It's a pleasure to work with her. Tanya and Sasha have gone to Tula. Seryozha has arrived, and tomorrow Sasha and I will visit him and Ilya. I spent the evening copying for Lev Nikolaevich. I've seen almost nothing of him, as usual. He rode his bicycle to Tula to be mended, walked back part of the way and was taken the rest of the way in some carts that were going in his direction.

30th June. Sasha and I returned yesterday evening from visiting Seryozha and Ilya. It was Seryozha's birthday on the 28th, and I wanted to spend it with him and make at least that day a little less lonely for him. His confused runaway wife, who is now expecting his child, hasn't an ounce of pity in her icy heart for her poor husband who never did her any harm. Ilya and his way of life I found utterly depressing: four lovely children (Misha especially), and what ideas does he put into their heads apart from horses, dogs, whether or not the hounds were in good voice, and whether or not they hunted down old Velvet? Then he goes off drinking at every opportunity with the most unspeakable characters – and that's all he ever does! If he doesn't change, his children will turn out very badly indeed. Sonya, his wife, vaguely senses this, and I feel very sorry for her. She does all she can to make things better and works hard at it too – but he is no help to her, and she simply isn't up to managing the house and the children's education all on her own.

At Nikolskoe with Seryozha we went for a lovely walk through some picturesque places. Guests came. Seryozha and I had a discussion about musical theory. On the train back I read a frightful book by Prévost, called *Les Demi-vierges;** I felt ashamed and physically disgusted, as I always do when I read a dirty book. Love without purity is a terrible thing, yet even the noblest love is inevitably reduced to the same desire for possession and intimacy. What is so disgusting in this French book isn't the woman's fall, it's her life of semi-debauchery: she doesn't actually take the final step, but she does everything but, and that's even worse.

At home I found that Misha had a bad attack of dysentery and there was no one to look after him, since Masha was busy with her young husband and Tanya had gone off. As for his father, well my children haven't had a father for a long time.

Lev Nikolaevich himself was rude and unwelcoming when I got back, and I was mortified to realize yet again how uninterested he is in me and my life when I am sitting at home with the family and seeing no one.

2nd July. I was sitting in my room copying his article when Misha rushed in terrified and said: "Papa is screaming and groaning with pain!" I ran downstairs. He was sitting in his chair, bent double and groaning, with the sweat pouring off him. I at once got him into a clean shirt, then Masha, Misha and I got busy with linseed poultices, soda water and rhubarb. But it didn't do him any good; the medicines made him vomit, and the vomiting induced excruciating pains. He didn't sleep all night, the pain got no better, and that night I feared for his life. And I thought how dreadfully lonely I would be without him. For although I suffer because his love for me is purely physical, not emotional, he is a part of my life and I couldn't live without him. He stroked my hair when I was changing his poultice today, and when I finished he kissed my hands, then followed me round the room with his eyes while I tidied up for him.

Doctor Rudnyov came today and said he had an excellent constitution. He had a severe catarrh of the stomach and liver, he said, but was in no danger. It will be hard to keep him on a sensible diet. It was eating all those radishes and cucumbers that made him ill in the first place, although I had begged him not to while there was an epidemic going around and he had a stomach ache. Misha is ill too – his dysentery still hasn't cleared up; his illness makes him so sweet and childish. I went swimming. It's warm and damp and there's a wonderful moon – but fate has ordained that instead of walks, the wonders of nature, music and everything that makes life beautiful, I must fuss around with compresses, go without sleep, and try to conquer my longing for happiness and beauty. I finished *Les Demi-vierges* on my own.

3rd July. Lev Nikolaevich is better today; he has moved his bowels and is no longer in pain, and my soul is relieved of a terrible anxiety. But he stayed in bed all day. A young man came to visit him, a sectarian, and stayed talking to him for a long time.* He was extremely dogmatic and narrow-minded, like all sectarians, but has read a lot and is fascinated by abstract questions and the wisdom of the ages. He has read Epictetus, Plato, Marcus Aurelius and others, all in the Intermediary edition.

Today I left the room in which I have slept for almost 35 years and moved into Masha's old room. I have started to want more privacy, besides it was stiflingly hot in the bedroom, and I am drenched in sweat all day as it is. This evening I walked to the Voronka on my own for a swim.

I coached Sasha for a while this morning; she has worked much better ever since I threatened to send her to the Institute. Misha is studying hard, although I am sometimes alarmed by his wild behaviour – putting out candles with his gun, making liqueurs, thumping out chords on the piano and yelling folk songs in a stupid, ugly voice. But he is only eighteen, and may become more sensitive as his soul matures. I had a cool note from Sergei Taneev to say he would be coming this Sunday. I haven't yet told Lev Nikolaevich, and fear the news will distress him. I hope he won't be jealous again – what a dreadful thought!

4th July. Everyone has been a lot better, but there have been more unpleasant scenes. At dinner today Misha mentioned Sergei Ivanovich's visit, and Lev Nikolaevich flushed crimson and said: "Well that's the first I've heard of it!" After dinner there were yet more painful discussions, accusations of lying and demands that I either extinguish my special feelings for Sergei Ivanovich or break off all relations with him. Both suggestions are preposterous. One cannot simply *extinguish* the feelings one has for a person.

5th July. Neither my tender caresses, nor my loving care, nor my patience in the face of Lev Nikolaevich's rude and unjustified accusations can soften his rage over Sergei Ivanovich's visit. So now I have decided to keep quiet. It is my own business after all, and concerns no one but God and my conscience.

10th July. My worst fears about Tanya have come true: she is in love with Sukhotin and they have discussed marriage. She and I came to the subject in the most natural fashion, quite by chance. She evidently felt a great need to talk about it, for she is on the road to ruin and is desperately seeking salvation. She has also spoken to Lev Nikolaevich. When I first told him he was stunned and suddenly looked wizened with grief – only it wasn't grief, it was despair. Tanya has been weeping a lot, she seems to realize now that this marriage would bring her nothing but grief, and has written to refuse him.

My relations with Lev Nikolaevich have improved again.

13th July. Sergei Ivanovich left today. The past few days have been peaceful and happy. He played several times. The first time, on the evening of the 10th, Lev Nikolaevich had gone in to Tanya to talk about Sukhotin, and I begged him to play a Mozart sonata for me. We were alone in the drawing room, and it was wonderfully peaceful. He played two sonatas – what joy! Then he played the lovely andante from his own symphony, which I heard in Moscow and love so much.

Later that evening, when everyone had gathered for tea, he played again, a Chopin sonata. Nobody in the world plays like he does. What nobility, what integrity, what a sense of timing. Sometimes it's as though he forgets himself, abandons himself, reaches out for something beyond himself, and then he captivates his audience. The next morning, the 11th, he played again – a Beethoven rondo, Mozart's variations on a theme of '*Ah! Vous dirai-je maman*', some Schubert, Marguerite's song from *Faust* and a Polonaise and Ballade by Chopin.

He was obviously trying to choose pieces that would appeal to Lev Nikolaevich. His playing tore me apart; when he had finished the Polonaise I could no longer hold back the tears, and was shaken by sobs. Yesterday, at midday, he again played the Chopin sonata.

Today the weather broke. I have spent such a happy week with Sergei Ivanovich. We took two walks to the Belgian foundry, and one to Gorelaya Polyana by the roundabout route, and went swimming under the bridge by the main road. We strolled over to the mines, and through the lovely Zaseka woods, and yesterday we walked through Lemon Groves to Kochak and back again. Every day we made up a party to go swimming. Turkin and I took photographs of everyone, and most of mine came out very well indeed. I took a lot of Sergei Ivanovich, and Lev Nikolaevich didn't mind so much this time. In fact he has suddenly grown calm and kind. Yesterday he went for a spin on his bicycle and rode his horse, and he didn't once lose his temper with me. But why should he? What possible harm can there be in my friendship with this pure, kind, talented man? How sad it is that our relations have been spoilt ruined by Lev Nikolaevich's jealousy!

Tanya has had a reply from Sukhotin – he has doubtless written her all those sentimental banalities with which he has already seduced many another woman! Masha and I wept today for this mad, blind love of hers.

Andryusha visited us on his way from Moscow. He stayed only an hour, but it's always the same thing with him – give me money, give me money!

14th July. I have been developing photographs all day, making prints of the ones people have asked for. Misha started talking to me today with unwonted frankness and passion about his tormenting sexual urges, which are making him feel ill; he longed to remain pure, he said, but feared he would succumb. My poor boys! They have no father, and what advice can I give them in these matters? I know nothing of this side of a man's life. Lev Nikolaevich is in high spirits; he was telling me about his cycle ride to Tula to attend a meeting of the cycle club, where they discussed races and various bicycle matters. Yet another interest of his!

15th July. I got up late, developed prints, then went swimming with Sasha and her governess. Afterwards I did more developing and gave Sasha her lesson, which went very well.

I thought a lot about Sergei Ivanovich. I long passionately for music, and to play myself. But there's never any time, and Lev Nikolaevich is always working or sleeping, and every sound disturbs him. I try to convince myself that true happiness comes from fulfilling one's *duty*, and I force myself to copy out his writings and do all my other duties, but sometimes I weaken, and yearn for some *personal* happiness, a private life and work of my own, rather than constantly toiling for others as I have done all my life…

16th July. I got up late today, as I had stayed up copying until 3 a.m. I went on with it all morning until dinner time, then went out to the apple orchard to watch the gardener grafting trees, and walked through the plantation with him, giving him various essential instructions. I picked some russula mushrooms on my way back, and came across the man who has rented the orchard from us. I shouted at him disgracefully for failing to prop up the trees, which means many of them have collapsed.

17th July. I did more copying and developed more photographs. I gave them all away today, and shall soon abandon this hobby. We went for a swim. Later we had a visit from the Shenshins, our neighbours from Sudakovo, and went for a walk with them around the plantation and to the bathing hut. It was a marvellous evening, the deep-pink sun setting against the pure bright sky. Tanya was sad, Lyovochka somewhat distant – and I was sad at heart. Misha went off to bless Ivan the servant's baby daughter. Sasha is making jam for Masha and has written her composition. She giggles all day, and is fat, red and rude to everyone. Masha and Kolya were here and played tennis.

My granddaughter Annochka arrived with her Russian governess. My daughter-in-law Sonya is arriving tomorrow with the 3 boys, and Ilya will be here on Saturday. They all leave Ilya's estate now whenever the neighbours come round for a drinking bout. I love and admire Sonya for trying to remove Ilya and her family from this hideous immorality.

18th July. Tanya was sitting in the drawing room today weeping bitterly. Maria Schmidt and I came in and started crying too. Poor thing! She doesn't love Sukhotin boldly, joyfully, as young people love when they have faith in the future and the feeling that everything is possible, everything is happy and the world is theirs. She is almost 33 and is morbidly in love with an old, weak-willed man of 48! I know those *morbid* feelings, when love doesn't light up God's world but darkens it – when it is *wrong* and even *evil*, but one hasn't the strength to change things. God help us!

Sonya is here with my grandchildren. I am delighted to see them, but alas they cannot fill my life. All my love for my own children has run dry, and I can no longer live only for them. The three little boys went to bed and the others drove off to Ovsyannikovo, and I went to practise the piano. But then Obolensky arrived with young Count Sheremetev and interrupted me. I am always being disturbed, and it is very painful and annoying.

Both Lev Nikolaevich and I have stomach aches today and feel under the weather. I attended to a lot of business – wrote to the Samara steward and the newspaper announcing the appearance of the new edition, drafted a petition to the president of the local *zemstvo* about the neglected state of the apple trees, sent some books off to Lyova, sorted out various business papers and passports and sent them to Moscow, wrote back to Loewenfeld in Berlin, made a list of the things I had to do in Tula tomorrow, and so on and so on. All these things have to be done, but oh, how tedious, how tedious they are!

20th July. I did no writing yesterday. First I played with my grand-children, then I stayed up late working on some photographs that had come out unsuccessfully. Today was a day of disasters. Sasha pinched Annochka and Tanya lost her temper with her. Sasha then burst into tears and wouldn't come down for dinner. I was angry with her for spoiling Ilyusha's name-day dinner and shouted at her to come down, threatening to punish her if she didn't. She came eventually, but cried all through dinner and wouldn't eat a thing. I remembered how darling little Vanechka used to suffer when Sasha was unhappy – he couldn't bear to see another person suffer – and I felt so sad, so sad. I wasn't particularly sorry for Sasha though, for I had heard her tormenting Nurse from three rooms away while she was dressing for dinner.

I played the piano for an hour yesterday and today, and it's not enough! I get no better at it, but it's good for my nerves and as a pastime.

21st July. I dreamt of Vanechka yesterday, lying in bed looking so thin, stretching out his pale little hand to me. Today I dreamt of Sergei Ivanovich. He was lying in bed too, smiling and stretching out his arms to me.

Masha told me Ilya was mortified to discover that my intimacy with S.I. was the talk of Kiev – he said they were all discussing it at my sister Tanya's and the Filosofovs'. Public opinion is so odd! Why should it be wrong to *love* someone? I'm not at all troubled by this gossip. I am happy and proud to have my name associated with such a fine, moral, kind, gifted man. My conscience is clear before God, my husband and my children; I am as pure in soul, body and thought as a newborn child. I know that I have never loved anyone as deeply and intensely as I love Lev Nikolaevich, and never shall. Whenever I see him somewhere unexpectedly I always feel so happy – I love his personality, his eyes, his smile, the way he talks, which is never the slightest bit vulgar (except when he is angry, of course, but I won't mention that), and his perpetual desire for perfection.

22nd July. Lev Nikolaevich was ill again last night. He had a violent gastric upset in the middle of the night and was vomiting continuously for four hours. He wasn't in great pain however, and towards morning it stopped. He ate an unbelievable quantity of baked potatoes yesterday and drank *kvas** even though he had a stomach ache, and the day before yesterday he had had nothing but Ems water and a peach. His lack of self-control and ignorance of hygienic matters is remarkable in one so clever.

Seryozha came and played the piano charmingly.

Today he said: "Maman is in her second childhood. I shall give her a doll and maybe a china tea set too." That may sound very funny, but in fact it's anything but funny, it's tragic. I never had time to do anything for *myself*, I've always had to subordinate my energy and time to the demands of my husband and children at any given moment. And now old age has crept up on me and I have used up all my mental and physical strength on my family, and have remained a child, as Seryozha says.

23rd July. Ilya and Andryusha arrived this morning with Misha's new tutor, Sobolev, who has come to replace Turkin. How I miss Turkin! This man is an enthusiastic chemist, a lively free-and-easy man, who had a long discussion with Seryozha about chemistry and the university. Andryusha has squandered all his money on the gypsies again and has borrowed 300 rubles. I am depressed and disgusted at his appalling life. What will become of him? He has already gone to the bad, and worst of all he has taken to drink, and he's a complete daredevil when he is drunk. Ilyusha came into my room today and accused me of having changed, of no longer loving the children and shutting myself off from them. I denied this and reminded them (Tanya, Sonya and Andryusha were there too) that I had spent my entire life labouring for the children, copying for their father and being constantly at his beck and call. I reminded them of that dreadful time just after Vanechka was born. Lyova was taking his final examinations, the boys had no governess, and I was having to feed my poor sick baby with aching breasts, see to the spring cleaning, look for tutors, do the packing – when I was still weak from the birth – and Lev Nikolaevich had set off on foot for Yasnaya and abandoned me, ignoring my tears and pleas for help. I reminded them of all the difficulties, sleepless nights, tears and doubts I had endured, all the years I had moved to the city in the spring so as not to abandon my boys while they were taking their examinations – and now all I got was reproaches and criticisms. I had listened long enough, I wasn't going to justify myself any longer, I couldn't endure any more – and I burst into tears.

They were attacking me about Sergei Ivanovich too. Well, let them! This man has brought such richness and joy into my life; he has opened the door to the world of music, and it was through hearing him play that I found happiness and consolation. His music brought me back to life after Vanechka's death, when life had deserted me. His gentle happy presence has soothed my soul, and even now I feel so peaceful, so comfortable, after I have seen him. And they all think I am in love with him! How quick they are to cheapen one's feelings. Why, I'm far too old – it would be quite inappropriate.

24th July. This evening Ilya, Andryusha, Lev Nikolaevich and Vaka Filosofov played tennis, my grandsons ran around brandishing whips, and Tanya, Sonya and I kept an eye on them and followed the game. But I don't like sitting still for long, so I got a saw and some secateurs and cut off the dry and dead branches on the avenue. When I got back I had a serious talk with Ilya, Andryusha and Vaka, warning them all of the evils of alcohol and strongly urging them not to touch it. All my sons' failings and mistakes have been due to the excesses of wine. Tanya went to Tula to see Sukhotin and came back in lively spirits; but I find this forced cheerfulness very sad. Our darling is walking towards her ruin. Will she turn back in time? Oh how sad it is, how sad!

I am now going to read A. Rubinstein's *Letters on Music*. Lev Nikolaevich has a dark one with him called Yartsev. He seems to find him insufferably tedious.

25th July. Tanya and I bought some Russian lace from an old woman in the village. After supper Lev Nikolaevich read us a foolish play from *La Revue blanche*. Sonya and the children are leaving tomorrow morning and I am very sorry. They didn't disturb me a bit, they brought me great joy.

I was sitting alone on the balcony today, thinking how fortunate I was: Yasnaya Polyana is so beautiful, my life is so peaceful, my husband is devoted to me, I am financially independent – why am I not happy? Is it my fault? I know all the reasons for my spiritual suffering: firstly it grieves me that my children are not as happy as I would wish. And then I am actually very lonely. My husband is not my friend; he has been my passionate lover at times, especially as he grows older, but all my life I have felt lonely with him. He doesn't go for walks with me, he prefers to ponder in solitude over his writing. He has never taken any interest in my children, for he finds this difficult and dull. To each his fate. Mine was to be the auxiliary to my husband. And that is good; at least I have served a great writer who is worthy of the sacrifice.

I went to visit a sick boy in the village. I put a compress on his stomach and gave him medicine, and he was so grateful to me for everything.

26th July. I copied out music all morning, then went for a swim. Very cold and windy. Boulanger, Zinoviev, Nadya Feret and the Englishman Maude* came, a dull, pompous man.

Sonya and the children left early this morning, and Andryusha drove over to see Bibikov. He keeps promising not to drink, but cannot go two days without seeking out the company of drunken dissolutes like the Bibikovs. Tanya seems a bit calmer, but how thin she is! Sasha went to pick nuts with her governesses. It is colder. There are a huge number of apples and they look lovely; they're being picked today.

28th July. I got a letter from Sergei Ivanovich. I had been expecting to hear from him; I had sent him some photographs and knew he would write to thank me, for he is such a courteous man.

An affectionate letter from Lyova in Sweden; he misses Russia, and worries that his wife may miss her parents. You never get everything you want in life!

29th July. Maude the Englishman was here all day.

Fine days again, terribly dry, wonderful moonlit nights. If only all this natural beauty could be put to some *use*! As it is the days pass in such a mundane fashion…

30th July. The moon is so lovely, shining through my window! I used to love looking at the moon when I was young, speaking in my heart to the man I loved who was far away, and knowing he was gazing at the same moon and that his eyes too were bewitched by its beauty, so that through it we seemed to be secretly speaking to each other.

I played the piano for four hours today; music lifts me off the ground and makes all my worries and difficulties easier to bear. Today a telegram came from Danilevskaya in Poltava saying Misha was well and happy and wouldn't be back before Saturday. This tactless, dishonest self-indulgence of Misha's drove me to despair. I managed to persuade the director of the Lycée to let him take his exams in the autumn, so while he enjoys himself strolling around Poltava, it's I who have to endure his disgrace, first with his teacher, then with the director. No, I can no longer bear the burden of bringing up my weak, wretched sons! They torment me! I wept when I received that telegram. Even Lev Nikolaevich, generally so indifferent to everything concerning the children, was indignant. I sent a third telegram to Misha, but almost two weeks have been wasted already!

The other worry is Sasha. Her work with me has been going very badly and I made her repeat her lesson, and again she failed to learn it, so I didn't let her go riding with Tanya. I don't like punishing the children, but all the governesses have given up with Sasha.

A terribly dry day, African heat. An owl is hooting – an evil, piercing sound. But what a marvellous night, how still it is!

1st August. Today I was copying Lev Nikolaevich's *On Art*, in which he refers to the exaggerated importance of love (the erotic mania) in all works of art. Yet only this morning Sasha said to me, "How cheerful Papa is today – when he's happy everyone else is too!" If only she knew that her "papa" was always cheerful after enjoying the love he denies!

The days are still fine and very dry. Dust and poverty everywhere. We went swimming. I posed standing up for Ginzburg. We went for a walk in the moonlight. Goldenweiser played the Chopin 'Sonata and Funeral March' beautifully. What a marvellous heartfelt musical epic! It tells the whole story of death – the monotonous funeral knell, the wild notes of agony, the tender poetic memories of the dead one, the wild cries of despair – you follow the whole story. I should hope even Lev Nikolaevich would recognize *this* as a true work of art. Goldenweiser went on to play some Chopin Preludes, Beethoven's Sonata Opus 90 and some Tchaikovsky variations. What a delight!

The Obolenskys came. Tanya has already started making up to the new tutor, so powerfully accustomed is she to flirting. Lev Nikolaevich played lawn tennis energetically for about three hours, then rode to Kozlovka; he had wanted to ride his bicycle, but it's broken. He also did a lot of writing today, and is youthful and active. What vitality he has! Yesterday he told me sadly that I had aged recently. I don't expect I shall outlive him, despite our sixteen-year age difference and my healthy, youthful appearance (as everyone keeps telling me).

2nd August. Misha returned from the Danilevskys' this morning. I had meant to scold him for delaying, but I didn't have the heart: he came back so cheerful, so full of his experiences of the journey. How lovely it is to be young; one's impressions of nature and people – especially nature – are such a *novelty*. And he needed a break in his life, for he has been painfully worried by sexual temptations.

I went swimming with Nadya Ivanova today and swam a long way. Then I came back and copied for several hours, and managed to get a lot done. "How well you copy for me and tidy my papers," Lev Nikolaevich said to me today. Thank you for those few words; one never expects gratitude from him, however hard one works.

Lev Nikolaevich has some factory worker* visiting him; he keeps saying what an intelligent man he is, but seems to find him very dull and evidently has no idea what to do with him or how to get rid of him. I finished A. Rubinstein's book on music and told Sasha about it on our walk.

This evening Misha's tutor, Sobolev, told us some fascinating things about the gold and platinum mines in the Urals. It is warm and still and there is a moon, although the sky is overcast. Lev Nikolaevich was annoyed today because his bicycle is broken, so he couldn't ride it to the bathing hut and had to go on horseback instead. There's still so much of the young man in him!

3rd August. This morning I sorted out my letters to Lev Nikolaevich and his to me. I must now copy them and hand them over to the Rumyantsev Museum in Moscow. I am completely at his service at present, and he is calm and happy. Once again he consumes my life. Does this make me happy? Alas, no. I do my duty towards him, and there's some happiness in that, but at times I yearn for something different and have other desires.

4th August. Crowds of people all day. The moment I got up Lev Nikolaevich had a visit from a Frenchman who had been travelling around Europe doing geological research. He is a cultured but uneducated man, a landowner who lives on his estate in the Pyrenees. Then Kasatkin the artist arrived and showed us his huge collection of photographs, paintings and drawings he has brought back from abroad. This was a great pleasure for me. I swam on my own again, and again posed for Ginzburg. Lev Nikolaevich also posed standing up for his statuette. This evening we went for a walk; it was dry and quiet, the sun was setting in a rosy sky, and now the moon is up. Two

more guests came for half an hour, doctors from Odessa on their
way to a medical conference in Moscow. One was called Schmidt,
the other was an army doctor called Lyubomudrov. They were both
very unpleasant. Goldenweiser played us a Beethoven sonata and
Schumann's 'Carnaval' before retiring. Lev Nikolaevich complains of
feeling weak and chilled. He went swimming and·drank a lot of tea;
he really shouldn't swim.

6th August. I am exhausted, having just copied out a long chapter of
On Art for Lev Nikolaevich. Goldenweiser played us the Grieg Piano
Concerto beautifully; it is a powerful, original work, and I enjoyed
it immensely. Then he played two Chopin Nocturnes, something of
Schubert's and a waltz by Rubenstein.

My daughter Masha and her husband Kolya are here. Masha is
wretched, pale and thin; I would love to be able to help her, poor
thing. About Tanya I prefer to say nothing. I am still terrified for
her. Misha is very upset by all the gossip at Yasnaya, with everyone
hounding everyone to death and out for what they can get. It
distresses him terribly – but it's always like this! It's better not to
think about it.

8th August. Masha has fallen ill and Doctor Rudnyov has diagnosed
typhus. The news fills my heart with grief; I am choking back the
tears, terrible familiar tears of fear and alarm, constantly ready to
flow. She had been dreaming of Vanechka – maybe he will call her
to him and release her from her wretched difficult life, married to
that lump of a husband. She lived a good, useful, self-sacrificing life
before she married Kolya. God knows what lies in store for her. But I
feel so sorry for her, she has been so pitiful ever since she left home.
I couldn't help recalling Sasha Filosofova's death, also from typhus,
and it terrifies me.

The house is seething with guests. There were 20 people at the table
today. Individually they're all very nice, it's just a pity there are so
many all at once. No walks, no time to oneself, no work, no copying
– just this crush of people. I am not doing any real *work*; something
has disappeared irrevocably, something has taken the wrong turning,
something has gone wrong.

Yesterday I accidentally left my diary on the table. Lev Nikolaevich
had another read of it and was annoyed by something. Why should
he be annoyed? I never loved anybody in the whole world as I love him
– and for such a long time too!

There was a telegram from Lombroso, the learned anthropologist, who has arrived in Moscow for a medical conference and wants to pay Lev Nikolaevich a visit.

Ginzburg is sculpting Lev Nikolaevich and they read *On Art* together during sittings. It's a good thing Lev Nikolaevich attacks the modern decadent movement in his article. This vile, senseless tendency must be put a stop to, and who better to do it than he.

11th August. I haven't written anything for three days. They brought poor Masha here from Ovsyannikovo the day before yesterday. She has typhus, and for several days now she has had a fever of 40°. At first we were all very frightened, but we have now become used to the idea of her being ill. Doctor Rudnyov visited and said it was a mild case, but I feel so sorry for her, tossing and turning and unable to sleep at night. Yesterday I sat with her till 3 in the morning, copying out Lev Nikolaevich's article. I had already done a lot when she suddenly had violent stomach pains. Lev Nikolaevich got up and said he would put on the samovar to make poultices, but he found the oven hot enough to warm up some napkins instead. It always makes me laugh when he embarks on some practical task, he is always so clumsy. He got soot all over the napkins, singed his beard with a candle and was furious with me for trying to put it out with my hands.

At 3 in the morning Tanya took my place by Masha's bed. Lombroso arrived this morning, a little old man with weak legs, who looks very decrepit for someone of 62. He speaks bad French, with a lot of mistakes and an appalling accent, and even worse German. He is Italian and very learned; as an anthropologist he has done a lot of work on human criminality. I tried to draw him into a discussion, but he had little of interest to say. He said crime was on the increase everywhere except in England, and that he didn't trust statistical information about Russia as we don't have a free press. He also said he had studied women all his life and still couldn't understand them. French and Italian women – "*la femme latine*" – are incapable of working, their sole interests in life are clothes and the desire to please. "*La femme slave*", however, which includes Russian women, is capable of any kind of work and is far more moral. He then spoke about education; he feels it has almost no influence on innate qualities, and I quite agree.

Ginzburg left today. He has finished his statuettes of me and Lev Nikolaevich. He was working on the one of Lev Nikolaevich yesterday when three young ladies arrived and begged to have a look at Tolstoy.

They were taken into his study and he enquired whether they had any questions to ask him and they said no, they just wanted to see him. So they looked at him and left. A little later some young man arrived with the same thing in mind, but was told Lev Nikolaevich was out. Then just as we were having our tea a man wheeling a bicycle and covered in blood arrived asking for him. He turned out to be a teacher from the Tula gymnasium who had fallen off his bicycle and hurt himself. He was taken into the pavilion, where his wounds were washed and bandaged, and he then stayed for supper.

13th August. Masha still has a high fever – over 40° all day. Poor girl, I feel so sorry for her and powerless against the implacable course of this terrible illness. I have never before seen such a bad case of typhus. The doctor called again – Lev Nikolaevich rode over to fetch him; he said she was in no danger, but I have a great weight on my heart.

I have copied out a great deal of Lev Nikolaevich's manuscript *On Art.* I spoke to him about it yesterday, and asked him how he expected art to exist without all the specialist "schools" he attacks. But one can never have a *discussion* with him; he always gets irritable and shouts, and it becomes so unpleasant one loses sight of the subject under discussion, and merely wants him to stop talking as soon as possible.

14th August. Lyova and Dora have arrived from Sweden, looking cheerful and well. Thank God – they'll cheer us up too. The doctor came and said Masha was in no danger, which reassured us. I also consulted him about my own health; he said my nervous system was in a bad state but there was nothing organically wrong with me, and prescribed bromide.

Lev Nikolaevich rode to Baburino at the invitation of some schoolmistress from St Petersburg. I spent a lazy day, for I had an exhausting night sitting up until 4.30 a.m. with Masha, who was very restless and had a fever of 40.7. I went for a swim, pasted up some photographs, read a little of Taine's *Philosophie de l'art* and sat with her. Still this terrible drought continues!

16th August. Life is hard. Masha is still very ill. I felt dazed when I got up today. I had watched over her all night in a state of terror until 5 a.m. She was terribly delirious, and has been so all this morning. At 5 I went to my room but couldn't sleep. Nothing but trouble on all sides. Tanya had another meeting with Sukhotin in Tula and sat

with him in his hotel, then travelled back with him on the train.
As far as I can see, she has never for one moment given up the idea
of marrying him. Misha didn't go to Moscow, where his tutor is
waiting for him – he's doing no work and is bound to fail his exams.
He just loafs around the village playing his harmonium until 2 in the
morning with the peasant lads and that silent, stupid Mitya Dyakov.
Andryusha arrived this morning, and will stay for a month and a half.
He said he wanted to go to Samara and visit Ilya, which is good. But
the hardest thing is my relationship with Lev Nikolaevich. There's
no pleasing him, one can say nothing to him. Boulanger was here
yesterday; we talked to him and agreed it would be a good idea to
go through *On Art* with the censors in mind, discard a few passages
to which they might object, then publish it simultaneously in the
Intermediary and in Volume 15 of the *Complete Collected Works*.
I didn't want to be the first to suggest this, as I am terrified of the
angry way he almost always speaks to me – and to almost everyone
else who dares contradict him.

Boulanger* talked it over with him and told me he had agreed.
But he was furious when I mentioned it to him, and said Chertkov
had expressly asked that none of his works should be published
here before they had appeared in English.* That Chertkov has Lev
Nikolaevich completely in his power again, even in England!

Today we had a talk about Tanya. He said we should keep our
thoughts to ourselves – we might want the wrong thing for her or
give her the wrong advice. But I said we shouldn't lie, and should
tell her what we thought, even if we were wrong, and shouldn't be
dishonest merely for fear of being mistaken. I don't know which of
us is right – maybe he is, but it's not a question of being right, it's a
question of being able to say what one thinks without losing one's
temper.

Just today, as he was coming out of his study, he went for Misha
and said some terribly – though deservedly – harsh words to him and
Mitya Dyakov. But what did he achieve by it? How much better if he
had had a quiet talk with Misha this morning and firmly told him
to go to Moscow, stop shirking and work for his exams. As it was,
this rebuke only made his sons angry; they were saying their father
never gave them any sympathy or advice and did nothing but scold
and shout at them. Only their mother had the right to scold them,
they said, for she was the only one who cared for them. I have indeed
cared for them – but what good has it done, what have I achieved?
Absolutely nothing! Andryusha has failed to do anything so far, and

I cannot think what will become of Misha – he has absolutely no strength of character... Oh, how sad it all is, how terribly sad...

17th August. A nurse has arrived to look after Masha; she is a little better today, and her temperature is down to 38.6°. Lyova and Dora are both lethargic and under the weather. Poor Dora, I feel sorry for her, it's hard for her in Russia, so far from her family. Another dry, windy day, but much cooler since morning. I walked back from the bathing hut with Tanya and we had a talk about Sukhotin. She says she hasn't come to any definite decision. Misha left for Moscow yesterday evening, and Andryusha has gone off to some mysterious destination. I have been copying again for Lev Nikolaevich and sitting with Masha, but there's no satisfaction in merely fulfilling my duties, and I feel melancholy. Then there was distressing news of another fire on Ilya's estate; the whole of this year's harvest was burnt, as well as the barn, the farm implements and various other things. Oh, how cruel life is!

I remember how I used to wait for my pages of *War and Peace* to copy after Lev Nikolaevich had finished his day's work. I used to write on and on in a state of feverish excitement, discovering new beauty as I went along. But now I am bored. I must work on something of my own, or my soul will wither.

18th August. Masha is much better. Maria Schmidt visited. There was a shower. We went swimming. The nurse arrived in the evening yesterday to take Masha's pulse and keep an eye on her, and Doctor Rudnyov came. I saw to various tedious domestic matters – mattresses, lamps, jam-making – and put the house in order. I then did some copying for Lev Nikolaevich and managed to do a great deal. My lower tooth is loose, which has put me in a bad mood. Oh, how I dread growing old. I must get used to the idea.

21st August. I have been terrified for Masha these past three days. First she had a temperature of over 40°, then this morning it suddenly dropped to 35.6°. We made her take some wine and champagne, but today she couldn't drink a thing, and everything made her vomit. She started shivering and we sent for the doctor, then her temperature shot up to 40° again. It's frightful! Poor thing, I feel so sorry for her, she's worn out.

Sasha is embroidering a table napkin, which she is giving me for my birthday tomorrow. 22nd August. I shall be 53.

23rd August. Masha is better and everyone is more cheerful. But I have another weight on my heart: Sukhotin is coming tomorrow and Tanya is very excited. Tomorrow I am going to Moscow, where I have a mass of things to attend to and must stay with Misha for his exams. I have no desire to go, it's a great nuisance, but I feel I must.

26th August. This is my second day in Moscow. I went to the banks yesterday, withdrew the interest and paid in 1,300 rubles for the mortgage on Ilya's property. I shall soon have to pay the same again, and then he had the fire and lost a further 2 thousand rubles on the deposit on an estate he and Seryozha rashly decided to buy in the province of Volhynia. How depressing and annoying it all is. Ilya is incapable of doing *anything* – studying, managing his affairs or conducting any sort of *business*.

Seryozha's wife Manya gave birth to a son on the 23rd. Poor Seryozha and that poor little boy with a mother like her!

Moscow is quiet and dull with everyone away. Sergei Ivanovich isn't in Moscow yet, and I am very sad that I won't be seeing him.

It rained, and now it's cold and overcast. Tomorrow Misha will sit his exams; I have an appointment with the board of censors, then with the accountant at home.

28th August. Today is Lev Nikolaevich's 69th birthday. It must be the first time in the whole of my marriage that I haven't spent it with him. How sad. I wonder what sort of state he is in today?

Misha took his last exam today, and I am anxiously waiting for him to return. Will he go up to the 7th form?

For the whole of the past two days I have been busy with the accounts, adding up endless rows of figures with the accountant.

I am living a calm, healthy life on my own, and shall return here on 10th September. It has become cold – or rather cool – and cloudy. I went to the bathhouse today.

31st August (Yasnaya Polyana). It's all so sad, everything has gone wrong. Misha failed, and will now have to stay down in the 6th form. Andryusha made another painful scene in Moscow, and the poor boy went off in tears with Misha to visit the Gruzinskys. I thought he might have been slightly drunk, for he was veering most oddly between extremes of violence and tenderness. Misha's attitude to his failure also saddened me: he was completely unperturbed, and went straight out to the garden with Andryusha, Mitya Dyakov and Boris

Nagornov, where they started yelling folk songs in coarse, tuneless voices. My children haven't turned out at all as we would have liked: I hoped that they would be cultured with refined aesthetic tastes and a sense of duty. Lev Nikolaevich wanted them to lead simple lives of hard work. And we both wanted them to have high moral standards. But alas this hasn't happened! I set off for Yasnaya Polyana the day before yesterday feeling worn out and depressed. Lev Nikolaevich met me not far from the house, got into the carriage beside me and didn't ask once about the children. How painful that always is! The house was packed with guests: Dunaev, Dubensky and his wife, Rostovtsov and the writer Sergeenko. The rooms were full of bustle and chatter, and it was all extremely tiresome. These gentlemen come here expecting to get something out of Lev Nikolaevich, and now he has decided to write an open letter to be published abroad.* It seems a Swedish kerosene merchant named Nobel has left a will bequeathing all his millions to the person who made the greatest contribution to peace (*la paix*), and against war. They held a meeting in Sweden to discuss it, and said the prize should go to Lev Nikolaevich. He would never accept the money of course, but he did write them a letter, saying it was the Dukhobors who had done most for the cause of peace by refusing military service and suffering cruelly for it.

Now I would have had nothing against that, but in this letter Lev Nikolaevich went on to abuse the Russian government in the most crude and provocative terms – quite inappropriately too, merely for the love of being outrageous. I was terribly distressed by the letter, my nerves were overwrought, and I became quite desperate, sobbing and blaming him for risking his life by needlessly provoking the government. I actually wanted to leave; I cannot live this nerve-racking life any longer, under the constant threat that he will write something truly desperate and evil against the government and get us all deported.

He was touched by my despair and promised not to send the letter. Today, however, he decided he would, although a modified version of it. But all of a sudden I no longer cared – simply from a sense of self-preservation. One cannot endure endless sleepless nights such as I endured yesterday, one cannot endlessly weep and torture oneself.

1st September. All our guests have left and we are on our own again, I'm glad to say. I had a short but unpleasant conversation with Lev Nikolaevich yesterday evening. I had been feeling unwell, he kept finding fault with me, and we brought up the subject of our diaries.

But we are friends again today. I copied out two chapters for him, tidied his room and put a lovely bunch of flowers there, and went swimming with Sasha. The water is 11°, the nights are cold and bright, with little clouds passing across the moon. The days are beautiful, dry and sunny. Tanya went to Tula to visit an exhibition. Masha is better. Sasha is upset about the disappearance of her pet hare from the barn. Lev Nikolaevich went for a ride and received a visit from a Catholic canon who has come here to make a study of Russian monasteries.

I have been yearning for music all day – I *dream* of it. I shall soon be going to Moscow, where I shall hire a piano and play, and I hope Sergei Ivanovich will come and play to me. How good that will be, the very thought of it revives my spirits.

2nd September. I sorted and arranged the books in the library, had a swim – the water was 11° – went for a walk, took a photograph of the apple trees covered in apples, and copied out a rewritten and modified version of Lev Nikolaevich's letter in which he says the Nobel Prize should go to the Dukhobors. I haven't finished it yet, but the first part is quite moderate.

There was a shower but it's not cold yet.

4th September. I try and try, but I cannot stretch life far enough. Every member of our family feels isolated, however friendly we may appear to be. Even Lev Nikolaevich complains of loneliness and of feeling "abandoned". Tanya is in love with Sukhotin, Masha has got married, and I haven't felt close to any of them for a long time. And we're all tired of devoting our whole lives to the service of Lev Nikolaevich. He considered himself fortunate to have enslaved the lives of three women, his two daughters and me. We wrote for him, looked after him, diligently supervised his elaborate vegetarian diet (which can be extremely inconvenient when he is ill), and never left his side. And now we have all suddenly announced that we have a right to some life of our own, his friends have been deported* and there are no new followers – and he is wretched.

I strain every last drop of my energy to help him and I copy out his article; yesterday I copied his 15-page letter calling for the Nobel Prize to be awarded to the Dukhobors. But at times I find it intolerable to have no work, no friends or interests of my own, no free time, no music, and I lose hope and lapse into depression.

Lev Nikolaevich is forever writing and preaching about universal love and serving God and the people, but it puzzles me to hear him say these things. He lives his entire life, from morning to night, without any sort of contact with others. He gets up in the morning, drinks coffee, goes for a walk or a swim without seeing anyone, then sits down to write; later he goes for a bicycle ride or another swim, eats dinner, plays a game of lawn tennis, goes downstairs to read, and spends the whole of the afternoon sitting in his study. It's only after supper that he comes and sits with us for a while, reading newspapers or looking through the illustrated magazines. And so this ordered selfish life goes on, day after day, without love, without any interest in his family or the joys and griefs of those closest to him. His coldness is a torture to me, and I have started to seek other things to fill my inner life, and have learnt to love music, to read into it and discern the complicated human emotions contained in it. But not only is music disapproved of in this house, I am bitterly criticized for it, so once again I feel that my life has no purpose, and bowing my back I copy out his dull essay on art for the tenth time, trying to find some consolation in doing my *duty*. But my lively nature resents it and I long for a life of my own, and when there's an icy wind blowing I rush out of the house, run through the forest to the Voronka and throw myself into the freezing water, and there's some pleasure in the physical sensation.

And the sweetest dream of all is of the heavenly kingdom awaiting us after we die, the dream of being united with God and reunited with our loved ones.

Ah, Vanechka! Today I came across a scrap of cloth from his blue sailor jacket, and I wept bitterly. Why did he leave me alone on earth without love? I cannot live without him – I often feel as though he took my soul with him, and my sinful body is merely dragging out its life here on earth.

8th September. A lot of commotion and a new crowd of guests: Dunaev, Boulanger and an Englishman named St John, evidently sent here by Chertkov.* Boulanger is being deported, charged with dangerous activities – propagating Lev Nikolaevich's ideas and writing and publishing a letter in the *Stock Exchange Gazette* about the wretched condition of the Dukhobors.* He was summoned to St Petersburg to the 3rd Department (in other words the police), which is responsible for administrative order (in other words administrative tyranny), and they reprimanded him.

Now Boulanger is a very clever man, lively and full of energy, and they were quite daunted by him. But Heavens, what a despotic government we have! It's as though we had no Tsar at all, just a lot of ignorant blackguards like Pobedonostsev and Goremykin (Minister of Home Affairs), who behave in such a way as to bring down people's wrath on the head of the young Tsar, which is a great pity. Lev Nikolaevich is plagued by a pimple on his cheek and keeps talking about death. I feel quite alarmed, he has a terror of dying. He is coming to the end of his essay *On Art*, and we have a young lady staying here who is copying it out on the Remington; they want to send an English translation to Chertkov in England so he can publish it there.

12th September. I've been in Moscow for 2 days, alone with Nurse, and am thoroughly enjoying myself. Misha goes to the Lycée and comes home only for dinner, Tanya is staying with the Wulfs and I see hardly anything of her. I spend the mornings at the dentist, who measures my mouth and tortures me with hot red mastic and various other nasty things. The painful moment has come when I need false teeth – another one in the front has fallen out now and the ugliness and inconvenience are unbearable. I am going to find my false teeth a real trial, I can see that. The main reason I like it here is that there are none of those tiresome guests and strangers who are constantly coming to visit Lev Nikolaevich in Yasnaya, none of those complicated family and conjugal relations, no conversations about the Dukhobors and the government, about sending articles and letters abroad to expose the activities of the government, no reproaches and criticism... How tired I am of it all and how badly I need a rest! I played the piano this afternoon, and scribbled down some notes for a story I want to write. I've had no news from home yet. I still haven't seen anyone here, but I very much want to see Sergei Ivanovich and hear him play. I hope he'll come on my name day and play for me.

14th September. I went to the dentist again yesterday, and spent the rest of the day reading and sewing at home. I played the piano this afternoon; I am learning two pieces, a Bach two-part invention and a Beethoven sonata. I play badly and must practise a lot. We spent the evening talking and dancing with the children and young folk. I danced a waltz with my brother Sasha, and was foolishly delighted when they told me how gracefully I moved.

Today was a very busy day. I hurried out first thing with my basket and took a tram to the Smolensk market to buy mushrooms. There was an enormous quantity of them. I bought some to give Tanya to take back to Yasnaya Polyana, where these white mushrooms are not to be found. I also bought some grapes. I took everything round to the Wulfs', where Tanya has been staying, then summoned a cab and went with Nurse to visit the graves of Vanechka and Alyosha. Their little graves always fill me with sweet, tormenting memories and a grief that will never heal.

I longed to die, to be borne off into the unknown where my little boys had gone. Nurse sobbed while I recited the Lord's Prayer, striving to unite my soul with my infants and asking them to pray for us wretched sinners, then I fled from my grief.

Wanting to please Nurse, I took her and the village girls to look for mushrooms in the woods, but we didn't find any. I arrived home for dinner to find a crowd of boys who had come to see Misha: Mitya Dyakov and the Danilevskys. After dinner Nurse and I made jam and pickled mushrooms. We finished late, and I spent the rest of the evening playing the piano; I sight-read some songs by Taneev, Pomerantsev and Goldenweiser. Taneev called here today, but I was out. I was so excited when I heard he had called; I long to see him, but I don't see how it's to be done. God will help me; maybe I won't see him – whatever is best.

I have heard nothing from home. Lev Nikolaevich hasn't written and Lyova doesn't mention him in his letter, just asks me to do some errands for him.

15th September. I got up late and scurried round the house all day. The double windows had to be put in, the floors and doors washed, the mattresses and upholstery beaten, the mushrooms and grapes pickled, etc., etc. At about 8 in the evening Sergei Ivanovich arrived, and the two of us spent the evening alone together. It is very sad that Lev Nikolaevich should persecute me for knowing him, for we have such a good, calm, profound friendship. We talked all evening about art, music, Lev Nikolaevich's writing – Taneev is so fond of him – of how we would spend the summer, and the boundless hopes of youth. He played me his beautiful symphony, which affected me deeply. It's a marvellous work, lofty, noble music.

17th September. My name day, I've been foolishly busy all day. I rearranged the furniture, bought some inexpensive flowers, and tidied and decorated the house like a child getting ready for a holiday. I remember how my darling Vanechka loved to "celebrate", as he used to say. I received a letter from Sasha, which delighted me. Lyovochka still hasn't written, as if he was deliberately ignoring me, and it hurts me. Today the house is in a real "name-day mood"; I cooked a meal for the servants too, which they appreciated, with pie, goose, tea and biscuits. Uncle Kostya, Alexei Maklakov, S.I. Taneev, Pomerantsev and Kursinsky came this evening, followed by various friends of Misha's – Golitsyn, Butyonev, Dyakov, the Danilevskys, Lopukhin – who all sang, jumped around, fought, ate and drank. Uncle Kostya begged Sergei Ivanovich to play, and he played his symphony again. Sergei Ivanovich's music has a quality one finds in certain people: the better you know it the more you love it. I have listened to this work three times now, and discover new beauty in it every time.

18th September. I got up late, sat down to play the piano and diligently practised the Bach two-part invention. When the rain stopped I left the house to visit the dentist and the Gubner factory for some fustian. And totally unexpectedly I met Sergei Ivanovich in the street! I didn't recognize him at first, and was amazed. Fate is always playing these tricks on me! He was on his way to the Monastery of the Virgin. We got into conversation and I accompanied him to the tram stop. I didn't get to the factory, but arrived in good time at the dentist's, who seems to have done a splendid job on my teeth. I shouldn't have told Sergei Ivanovich about the time I tried to kill myself by freezing to death on the Sparrow Hills. (I spared him the causes and details of course.) It's just that these agonizing memories make me need to talk about them.

I got home, had dinner with Misha, then practised the piano for four hours, by which time I was exhausted.

19th September. A talented man puts all his understanding, all the sensitivity of his soul, into his work, while his attitude to real life is obtuse and indifferent. I immersed myself yesterday in Sergei Ivanovich's songs, trying to understand them more deeply. (I now have so many of them.) The music corresponds not only to the mood of the poem but to almost every word too (so powerful in places), yet in real life he is so calm and reserved, never expressing his feelings, seldom speaking his thoughts, appearing indifferent to everyone and everything. And as for my incomparably more gifted husband! What extraordinary understanding of people's psychology in his writings, and what incomprehension and indifference to the lives of those closest to him! Me, the children, the servants, his friends – he doesn't know or understand them.

22nd September. I am back at Yasnaya Polyana, and have left Misha in Moscow with Nurse and Ivan the drunkard. I am sorry to have ended my solitary life where I could play the piano, and to have returned to the hectic existence Lev Nikolaevich has organized for me here. We had a visit from some Molokans* whose children were taken away from them because of their sectarian beliefs. Lev Nikolaevich wrote to the young Tsar about it, but has had no response. He has written again, but fortunately the Tsar is abroad and the letter will probably not reach him. I would do anything in the world to console the mothers and their children, but what is the point of risking one's life when it's *impossible* to do *anything*. He is always seeking noise, publicity, risk. I simply don't believe in his goodness and love of humanity, for I know what is at the bottom of it all – fame, the insatiable, frantic desire for yet more fame. How can one believe in his love, when he doesn't love his own children, his grandchildren, his *family*, but has suddenly developed this great love for the Molokans' children? He has a boil on his cheek and his face is tied up in a handkerchief. He looks wretched, and is terribly worried about it.

He paid two visits to the doctor while I was away, and the third time he asked him to call. He kept insisting he had cancer and would soon die, and was very depressed and couldn't sleep. He is better now. Poor man, how he hates suffering, and how hard it will be for him to leave this life. God help him!

26th September. The days rush past. The 23rd was our wedding anniversary, and we spent it very pleasantly, although we didn't arrange any special celebration. We have been married 35 years, and however hard my life has been at times, I thank God that we have remained faithful to each other and now live peacefully, even affectionately, together. My two eldest sons came, and all the family were together except Misha, who has now arrived, I am pleased to say. Our guests included Sergeenko and Boulanger with his 9-year-old son. Boulanger is leaving for England on the 28th; he is being deported for spreading the ideas of Tolstoy.

Lev Nikolaevich has already written the conclusion to his essay on art and has made yet more changes to it, so I shall copy it again, and I have just finished copying his letter to the *Russian Gazette*. Various papers have published articles saying it is unthinkable that the Molokans' children should be taken from them. But since this has in fact happened, and the parents have been visiting Lev Nikolaevich to ask him to take up their cause, he has decided to publicize the whole story in the *Russian Gazette*. Whether they publish it or not is another matter.

My niece Liza Obolenskaya arrived last night and today we went for a walk with her. How beautiful it was! We walked through the fir plantation to the river, came out at the bathing hut, and walked through the great fir trees, returning home along the forest path. The bright-yellow tints, shading into green, red, dark brown and all the colours of the autumn foliage, were extraordinarily lovely. A few young birch trees have grown up here and there among the tall firs, and their brilliant leaves are etched against the black background like lace.

On the way home I told Liza about my friendship with Sergei Ivanovich and Lev Nikolaevich's jealousy of my feelings for him. It upset me to talk about it, and there were yet more trying discussions at home with Masha about her future, and the fact that they are planning to live with Kolya's mother in Pokrovskoe. I told her I didn't approve, and said he should go out and earn his own living or enter government service, rather than living first off her mother, then his.

29th September. Masha and Kolya left for the Crimea yesterday. I wasn't sorry to see them go, although I am fonder of them now than when they were first married. My fears for Masha's life when she was so ill have brought me closer to her. And Kolya is a good kind boy, just terribly lazy and phlegmatic. He cannot and will not work, and that isn't a pleasant sight.

More Molokans came. They have been in St Petersburg, where they took Lev Nikolaevich's letters to Koni, the Public Procurator, as well as to various other people who were out of town.* The case of the children is to be taken up in the Senate, and Koni is hopeful that it will be decided to return them to their parents. But their case may be passed on to the State Council, which means it might drag on for years. The Molokans were telling us that one little girl of two was being cared for by a nun who loved her very much and was incensed she had been taken away, and was looking after her very well. The boys have been sent to a monastery but are being badly cared for; their clothes are filthy and they're covered in lice. They asked the monks to let them go outside the gates to watch for their parents' horses, but the monks told the Molokans they would only be allowed to see their children in church. But when they got to the church their children weren't there, just some more Molokans who were being converted to Orthodoxy as an example to them. The Father Superior embraced and kissed them when they came in, and said: "Just as you grieve for your children, so Mother Church grieves for you who have left her." But the Molokans stood their ground.

My sister Tanya, Liza Obolenskaya, Vera and I sat up late sewing, telling each other's fortunes with cards and chatting about intimate matters. Women can be open with one another about *everything* – one can only be relaxed and unguarded with people one has loved since childhood, when one knows every detail of their character, every event of their life. I am closer to Tanya than to anyone else.

30th September. My daughter Tanya has left for the Crimea, and has taken Ilya's son Andryusha with her. The house feels empty with only Sasha here, and Lyova and Dora in their wing. I feel sorry for poor Lev Nikolaevich. For years he spent the quiet months of autumn with his daughters: they served him, wrote for him, became vegetarians for him and sat through the long, dull autumn evenings with him. I always used to spend the autumn in Moscow to be with my sons while they were at school, and I missed my husband and daughters terribly and was with them in spirit, since Lyovochka and my daughter Tanya were always my favourites. But now all that has changed: Masha has married and poor Tanya has fallen in love, and this disastrous love for a man who is unworthy of her has exhausted both her and us. She is going to the Crimea to think things over. God help her! And in 6 days I am leaving for Moscow with Sasha. I have put it off as long as possible, but it's high time she went to school; she is 14 now, and is doing next to no work. I am concerned about Misha too; I fear he is being morally corrupted, and feel that family life is the best thing for the boy. Lev Nikolaevich will be staying here with Lyova, but it is plain that neither of them is overjoyed at the prospect. I shall take Sasha to Moscow, settle her in there, then come straight back to be with Lev Nikolaevich. Oh how trying and complicated it all is!

2nd October. The peace of autumn, with the yellow leaves turning to gold in the sunlight. I had a good day today. This morning I read Seneca's *Consolation à Marcia* and *Consolation à Helvini*, then I tidied the books in the library. After dinner we walked to Kozlovka and back; the road looked so sad and deserted – what memories that road evokes! Oh, I don't need memories, or regrets!... Why does every experience leave such a deep impression on my heart? When I got home I heard that Lyova had gone off to Krapivna leaving Dora on her own, so I ran in to keep her company. Then Lyovochka gave me Chapter 10 of his essay on art, and using that as a model I was able to revise the other chapters. It's hard work, laborious, exacting and mechanical, and I was at it for three hours. I am glad he has attacked the decadents and exposed their tricks. He cites some utterly meaningless poems by Mallarmé, Griffin, Verhaeren and Moréas among others by way of example. Lyovochka invited me out for a game of shuttlecock this evening for some exercise, but I asked him to play a duet with me instead. We played a Beethoven septet quite nicely, and I was in such high spirits afterwards! We went to bed late and I read Menshikov's article 'On Sexual Love' in the *Week*. This matter will never be settled, however much people talk about it.

The best, the most painful and the most powerful thing in the world is love, and love alone; it guides and determines everything. Love gives life to the artist, the scientist, the philosopher, the woman, the child; love lifts up the soul, gives us strength and the energy for work, inspiration and joy. And I don't mean just *sexual* love, but any kind of love. In my case the best, most powerful, most unselfish love of my whole life was for my little Vanechka. With my husband, however much he repelled me with his slovenly habits and his immoderate physical inclinations, it was his rich inner existence that made me love him all my life. My attachment to Sergei Ivanovich too was based not on his physical appearance but on his extraordinary musical talent; the nobility, purity and seriousness of his music flows from his soul.

It was for this reason that of all of my children I loved Vanechka the best: he was all soul, such a tiny, disembodied child, so sensitive, tender and loving – he was made of the very finest spiritual material, and wasn't made for this world.

May God help me to leave behind this physical life and to cleanse my soul, and with a purified heart to pass over into that world where my Vanechka is now.

6th October (Moscow). I have come to Moscow with Sasha and Mlle Aubert. I left Lyovochka yesterday with a heavy heart; I have rarely felt so sorry for him as I did then. He is so old, lonely and bent. (He stoops more and more these days, probably because of the sedentary life he leads, writing hunched over his desk sometimes for days on end.)

I tidied his study, sorted his things and his linen and made sure he had all his small household needs: porridge oats, coffee, saucepans and dishes, honey, apples, grapes, Albert rusks, all the things he likes. He said goodbye to me affectionately, almost shyly, and didn't want me to go; so I shall be back in 6 days, and we shall both go over to Pirogovo to visit his brother Sergei Nikolaevich. I am relying on young Lyova and Dora to look after him. His boil is better, but now his nose is hurting and he is terribly anxious. I hope it's nothing serious.

10th October. I haven't written for four days, days filled with hectic activity and a mass of things to attend to. No music, no reading, no happiness, nothing. I started looking for suitable Russian governesses for Sasha; today I decided to hire Sofia Kashkina, the daughter of Seryozha's former music teacher, Nikolai Kashkin. Misha has fallen and hurt his leg; he has been off school for three days and is lying in bed doing nothing. The drunken footmen are insufferable. First one drinks himself into a stupor and has to leave, then another is blind drunk for three days on end. I've never known anything like it, it's infuriating and tedious.

Sergei Ivanovich spent this evening with me, and there was something unsatisfactory about our relations, even a certain coldness. I didn't feel happy with him, in fact I felt awkward and even uncomfortable at times. Perhaps it's because of the kind letter I received from Lev Nikolaevich today, which transported my soul back to him in Yasnaya, or perhaps it torments me that Sergei Ivanovich's intrusion into my life has brought Lev Nikolaevich so much grief – and may be distressing him even now. Whatever the reason, something has changed in my feelings for him, even though I always defied Lev Nikolaevich's displeasure and refused to give up my freedom to feel and behave as I liked, seeing there was never anything wrong in it.

Tomorrow is the Czech concert. They're playing quartets by Beethoven, Haydn and Taneev. That will be nice!

11th October. I received letters from Lev Nikolaevich, Lyova and Dora, all saying that Lev Nikolaevich wasn't well, so I made up my mind to leave for Yasnaya Polyana this evening. The concert was marvellous, and Taneev's quartet was a musical triumph. What a delightful piece! It's absolutely the last word in modern music, but so profound and so intricate too, with such unexpected harmonic shifts and such a wealth of ideas and skill. A truly sublime musical experience.

20th October. I stayed with Lev Nikolaevich at Yasnaya from the 12th to the 18th, during which time his health improved greatly. By the 17th he was riding over to Yasenki and had stopped drinking Ems water. I copied *On Art* all day without drawing breath, and there were moments when I felt like laughing, screaming or crying from exhaustion. First I transferred the corrections from the ten revised chapters to the fair copy. Then I did an unbelievable amount of fresh copying. Then Lev Nikolaevich scribbled yet more corrections on my copy, so I had to make all these changes in the fair copy. He has such tiny, untidy, illegible handwriting, he never completes his sentences or puts in any punctuation... What a strain it is trying to decipher this muddle and make sense of all his footnotes, signs and numbers!

My husband was so kind to me; he sweetly put compresses on my aching arm and shoulder, thanked me for copying his article, and when I was leaving he kissed my hand, something he hasn't done for a long time.

I returned to Moscow on the 18th and rushed around all morning attending to my affairs, and was fitted for my new dress. That evening I went to a symphony concert. It was an all-Mendelssohn programme: his 4th Symphony, *A Midsummer Night's Dream* with a choir, and his Violin Concerto. I thought Safonov conducted very poorly.

Sergei Ivanovich has fallen and hurt his leg, and will be in bed for several days. I couldn't resist paying him a visit, as I felt concerned about him. I don't know if he was pleased to see me, it may have been the reverse. Professor Maklakov was there and they were playing chess together. Sergei Ivanovich was looking pale and wretched, like a punished child, complaining that lack of exercise and fresh air made it impossible for him to work.

I had letters from Tanya and Masha. Still the same sorry news from my daughters, Masha with that lazy foolish boy-husband of hers, Tanya with her morbid infatuation for Sukhotin. I feel I have lost both daughters at once.

Sasha is working hard and doing very well with her new teacher.

21st October. I called on Sergei Ivanovich. He has to stay in bed and I couldn't but go and see him. We talked together in our usual serious, simple, quiet fashion. He told me about a sect called the

Self-Burners, and I told him about the decadent poems from which I was copying out quotations for Lev Nikolaevich. Then we talked about music and Beethoven, and he told me various things about his life and gave me a two-volume biography to read. As always I left him with a feeling of peace and contentment. He begged me to call again, but I don't know whether I can bring myself to. I went on to visit Natasha Dehn but didn't find her in, although I did see the wretched hole she lives in. These daughters of ours go off and lead impoverished lives with the men they love, yet they are used to grand houses, servants and good food... Well, there's obviously nothing more precious than love.

I received a cold and haughty letter from Lev Nikolaevich. I expect he is angry with me for living here in Moscow rather than with him in Yasnaya, where I would be copying for him from morning to night. But I cannot do it any more, I simply cannot! I am tired and old, my spirit is crushed, and maybe I'm spoilt. I remember that week I spent there: the filthy yard, the two filthy rooms where I lived with Lev Nikolaevich, the four mousetraps that never stopped snapping, and mice, mice, endless mice... The cold bleak house, the grey sky, the drizzle, the darkness; traipsing through the mud with a lantern, writing, writing, morning, noon and night; smoking samovars, no servants, deathly silence... What a depressing, difficult week it was. I prefer it here; I must live a fuller, more *useful* life.

25th October. I long to see Lev Nikolaevich, I missed him all day and played the piano for four hours to distract myself. I spent a long time being tortured by the dentist, but my false teeth still hurt. So here I am, reduced to the misery of false teeth – I have always dreaded this...

Pomerantsev and Igumnov came this evening, and Igumnov played for us – his own overture, some Scriabin pieces, a Bach fugue (for the organ) and something by Pabst. He also played us some songs by Sergei Ivanovich and his pupil Yusha Pomerantsev. But I am deaf to music today and half asleep. On Monday I want to go back to Lev Nikolaevich and visit Pirogovo with him.

26th October. I took Sasha and her friend Sonya Kolokoltseva to a public concert held in memory of Tchaikovsky, and from there to an exhibition of Russian paintings at the Historical Museum. There was nothing outstanding. I was struck by the enormous number of autumn landscapes. Autumn was indeed very lovely this year; the leaves were on the trees for a long time, the days were long and sunny – a truly golden autumn. Seryozha came to visit. My love and tenderness for him is always checked by a certain embarrassment. I long to kiss him, tell him how much I love him and how I suffer for him. This evening Goldenweiser came, with Natasha Dehn and her husband. Goldenweiser played marvellously – a Chopin Nocturne and several other things. He has such taste, such a lovely delicate touch. It was a truly great pleasure – I have had a lot of *art* today, and am happy.

27th October. It has snowed and the garden is dazzling white in the sunshine. But I no longer feel that leap of energy, that simple uncomplicated joy I used to experience at the sight of the "first snow".

Went to town on business; played the piano a little. Leaving now for Yasnaya Polyana.

2nd November. I was in Yasnaya Polyana with Lev Nikolaevich for five days. As I rode there from Kozlovka by sleigh on the morning of the 28th, I was so full of energy and love, so looking forward to working and helping him. It was a bright sunny day, the snow was dazzling, a huge moon was setting and a brilliant sun was rising – a beautiful, magical morning!

But the moment I arrived at Yasnaya everything went wrong. Lev Nikolaevich was surly and hostile to me. Then while I was cleaning out my room I reset one of the innumerable mousetraps, which snapped shut and struck me in the eye, and I fell to the ground and thought I had been blinded.

So instead of copying for him I had to lie down with a compress on my eye for a day and a half. Next day he rode over to Tula; it was 15 degrees below freezing, and I felt very anxious, but I had to lie there on my own in the great stone house with my eyes closed, pursued by gloomy thoughts about my children and my relationship with them and with Lev Nikolaevich.

I got up several times to write, using only one eye, and managed despite this slowly to copy out the whole of Chapter 12 of *On Art*. I had dinner and supper with Dora and Lyova in their wing, which made me feel more cheerful.

The next day Lev Nikolaevich and I went to Pirogovo to visit his brother, Sergei Nikolaevich. But the evening before our departure we had a dreadful row that made one of those *cuts* which always leave a deep scar and drive two people who love each other still further apart. What was it about? Impossible to say. Nothing at all really, yet the result was that I shuddered, as so often before, to realize what an icy heart he has, and how indifferent he is to me, the children and our life. When I asked him whether he would be coming to Moscow or not, he replied vaguely and evasively; when I said I wanted to be closer to him, to help him with his work, copy for him, cook him healthy vegetarian food and generally look after him, he peevishly told me he needed nothing and asked for nothing, that he enjoyed being alone and didn't need any copying done – he wanted, in other words, to deprive me in every possible way of the pleasure of thinking I could be of any use, let alone pleasure, to him.

I cried, then became hysterical, overwhelmed with a despair so extreme that I wanted only to die.

And the worst thing is that his iciness makes me yearn to attach myself to someone else, someone to fill the void in my heart left by this man, my lawful husband, who has spurned and rejected my love. This is a great tragedy that men will neither acknowledge nor understand.

After I had almost gone mad with tears and grief, we managed somehow to patch it up, and by the time we got to Pirogovo the next day I was already copying for him again. Then he needed his warm cap which I had thought to bring for him, as well as fruit, dates, my body, my labours and all the copying he wanted me to do for him. It was all suddenly indispensable to him! Help me, Lord, to do my *duty* to my husband to the end of his life, in other words to serve him patiently and humbly. But I cannot stifle my need for the sort of quiet, friendly, considerate relations that should exist between two people who are close to each other.

And despite the pain he caused me, I still went through agony when he rode the 20 miles to Pirogovo on horseback, and worried he would get tired and cold! He stayed on in Pirogovo with his brother, while I left for Moscow yesterday and went to a delightful symphony concert: Tchaikovsky's C Major String Serenade and the Schumann Piano Concerto. I met a number of people, but not Sergei Ivanovich, who still has a bad leg.

Sasha is doing well, although she doesn't get on with Mlle Aubert. Misha told me he got nothing but twos for his unseen translations, and I lost my temper with him.

Tanya has a cough and is leaving for Cannes.

7th November. I returned to Pirogovo on Monday morning to stay
with Lev Nikolaevich's brother, and we didn't leave until yesterday,
Thursday. Staying with Sergei Nikolaevich was a great strain. He
is 71 years old, mentally alert, but the most dreadful despot with
his family and a terrible misanthropist; he is well read and takes an
interest in everything, but he curses the whole world – apart from
the gentry. He never stops railing against professors ("sons of b—s",
"scoundrels") and merchants ("thieves and swindlers") – and as
for the common people, they come in for every foul word he can
think of. The musical world too is nothing but fools and villains...
It was dreadfully difficult with him. They live like paupers and the
food is terrible; his poor daughters never say a word in front of
their despotic father, but they long in that backwood of theirs for
some human contact with living souls. So Vera organizes magic-
lantern shows for the village children and gives a peasant boy
English lessons, and they talk about philosophy and religion with
the peasants, the saddlers and the carpenters. This enrages their
father, and Masha their mother (the gypsy) gets very upset about
it. Besides this the three girls have a horse and two cows that they
feed and milk themselves, and they drink the milk too, since they
are vegetarians.

Lev Nikolaevich continued with his writing there, and I copied
for him all day. One evening I played their out-of-tune piano and
everyone was in ecstasies; it's so long since they've heard any
music.

We intended to leave on Tuesday, but it rained and the roads
were icy, so we stayed. Next day there was a frightful wind and I
was afraid Lev Nikolaevich would catch cold, so we again decided
to stay. By yesterday, however, my depression was so extreme that
we decided to leave for Yasnaya. There was still a strong wind, but
Lev Nikolaevich cheerfully rode home on horseback while I sat in
the sleigh and worried about him – more than I have worried for
a long time. How insignificant all my other interests, fantasies and
friendships seem beside the fear that my husband might catch a cold
and fall ill or die!

The journey took three hours and we didn't catch colds, thank
God. Lyova and Dora were waiting for us and warmly welcomed
us, and Yasnaya seemed heaven after Pirogovo! We had dinner with
them, and that evening we lit the stove in our part of the house.
Lyovochka made more corrections to Chapters 12 and 13 and told
me to enter these into the other copy.

We sat cheerfully together and drank tea. This morning soft feathery flakes of snow were falling; there was no wind, just a light frost in the clear air. We drank coffee together, tidied our rooms, received letters from almost all the children, which delighted us, and looked through the newspapers. Then I was driven in the sleigh to Yasenki station and left for Moscow. Lyovochka and I parted on friendly terms, and he even thanked me for my help.

A lot to do in Moscow with publishers and banks – all very tedious. Sasha and Misha were delighted to see me, but they're not doing very well; they do no work and Sasha is persistently rude to her governesses.

This evening I managed again to play a little...

10th November. I returned today from Tver, where Andryusha is stationed with his regiment. He met me at the gates of the barracks and said he had been waiting for me all morning, and fondly told me over and over again how pleased he was to see me. He had burnt himself with carbolic acid and was in bed for three weeks, but the burns are all healed now. We spent a very pleasant day together; he sat with me while I worked, then we had a talk about intimate matters and his personal life. He has matured a lot – life seems to be having a sobering effect on him. He is alert, doesn't drink or lead a disorderly life, and is very good company and full of energy. I am going to apply, at his insistence, for him to be transferred to Moscow to the Sumsky regiment.

11th November. I visited the Lycée to discuss Misha, and was distressed by their complaints of his laziness and bad behaviour. What a misfortune it is that all my life I have had to listen, blushing with shame, to all these directors and schoolteachers criticizing and belittling my boys.

Yet there are some fortunate mothers who hear very different things about their sons! At home I had yet another painful discussion with Misha and decided to do all I could to get him taken in as a boarder. He doesn't like the idea, but I shall stand my ground.

I went out to do some errands; it was sleeting and windy. This evening I sight-read some Beethoven sonatas – without much success but with great interest.

12th November. I went to a musical evening at the Conservatoire with Sasha. It was delightful. There are some excellent women pianists studying there.

13th November. Went shopping for Dora and wrote her a letter, then had a music lesson with Miss Welsh. I feel depressed today, and long for the friendly company of someone I love.

Misha has gone to the theatre and Sasha is doing her lessons. I am going upstairs to play the piano; maybe that will lift my dismal spirits.

I played the piano all evening, without much success. What endless pleasure there is in the music of Beethoven.

14th November. Spent the whole day from morning to night doing dull accounts with the accountant. Maklakov came this evening and we did some duets, but he's quite hopeless. We attempted a Mendelssohn symphony, some Schubert (his lovely *Tragic Symphony*) and some Mendelssohn overtures, but we made a terrible job of it. I could have wept – I'm incapable of playing anything properly.

Andryusha has come for a couple of days. He was so bored and lonely in Tver after I left that he applied to his squadron commander for leave. An affectionate letter from Lev Nikolaevich.

16th November. Music again all day. I was busy all morning with accounts, then played the piano for about two and a half hours, and still didn't master that 8th Invention by Bach. After dinner I sight-read a Schubert symphony and played a Beethoven sonata. Then Goldenweiser, Dunaev and Varya Nagornova came. Goldenweiser played a Beethoven sonata (the '*Appassionata*') and some Chopin Preludes and Nocturnes, and played beautifully; although when I remember Taneev's interpretation of that sonata, the difference between them is as between earth and heaven. I have a desperate, helpless desire to hear that man play again – will it *never* again be granted me?

19th November. I had another music lesson with Miss Welsh, and afterwards I couldn't tear myself from the piano and played for another 4 hours. I had a great urge to play Schubert's last unfinished symphony as a duet, but there was no one to play with. I had a letter from Lev Nikolaevich; he says that although he is missing me he needs to be alone to write now that he is getting old and hasn't much longer to work. These arguments may ring true for humanity at large, but it would take a lot to persuade me personally that writing articles is more important than my life, my love and my desire to live with my husband and find happiness with him, rather than seek it *elsewhere*.

I was telling my fortune with the cards, and twice I drew "death", and suddenly I felt terrified of dying. Yet only recently I was longing for it! It is all in God's hands! It hardly matters whether it comes sooner or later.

23rd November (Moscow, Khamovniki Street). I am starting a new notebook on a terrible day. It is certainly true that there is a great deal more grief than joy in this world. Yesterday evening Andryusha and Misha invited a large crowd of boys here, and they all set off together to Khilkova's house on the Arbat to lie in wait for a ghost. That, at any rate, was the reason they gave for disappearing all night and not returning until 9 in the morning. I waited up for them until 8 a.m., choking with exasperation. I wept, raged and prayed... When they finally woke up (at one o'clock), I went in and gave them a severe talking-to, then burst into tears, which brought on an asthma attack and palpitations in my heart and throat, which meant I had to take to my bed all day, and I now feel destroyed.

The boys were very subdued, especially Misha, whose conscience is younger and purer.

Frost and snow. I am reading part 3 of the Beethoven biography and am delighted by it. I had another music lesson, then practised from 11 to 1.

24th November. This morning I went to the Lycée to talk to the director about Misha. He again urged that he attend as a boarder; more attempts to persuade Misha, his objections – I feel defeated.

I posted off his application to the Duma to volunteer in the army.* Then I took Lyova's article – a translation from the Swedish – to the *Russian Gazette.*

I got home and changed, then went off to a name-day party for Dunaev, Davydov and Ermolov. I love worldly brilliance, lovely clothes, masses of flowers, refined company, cultured conversation and good manners. As always, as at every age in my life, there was general astonishment at my unusually youthful appearance. Istomin was particularly agreeable.

Sergei Ivanovich hasn't once come to see me. He must have heard reports of L.N.'s jealousy, and his cordiality towards me has changed to coldness. How sad, and how sorry I am! There is no other possible explanation for his aloofness – why else would he not come to visit? Could L.N. have written to him?

25th November. Tanya has returned from Yalta in a much better state, emotionally and physically. Ilyusha came – wanting money as usual.

Tanya tells me L.N. has described life in Moscow as "suicide". So if he comes to Moscow for my sake, *I* shall be killing him. But that's frightful! I wrote to tell him so and begged him not to come.*
I want to live with him because I love him, but according to him I am "killing" him. I *have* to live here, for the children's education, yet he reproaches me for it! I am so tired of life!

26th November. I spent all day in theatres. This morning I took Sasha, Vera Kuzminskaya and my niece Zhenya to the Korsh Theatre to see Griboedov's *Woe from Wit*. It was a poor production and I was terribly bored. Then this evening Tanya persuaded me to accompany her to see the Italian actress Tina di Lorenzo. She is a beautiful woman, with an Italian temperament, but since I didn't know the language or the play (*Adrienne Lecouvreur*), I didn't find it very interesting. I was exhausted today and hardly played at all; all I want now is to sit at home.

29th November. I received a long, kind, reasonable letter from my husband yesterday. I tried very hard to absorb what he was saying, but there was such an old man's coldness about it that it made me wretched. I often forget he will soon be 70 – I forget this discrepancy in our ages and the degree of tranquillity we have attained; and this fault of mine isn't mitigated by my youthful appearance and emotions. *Tranquillity* is more important than anything to L.N. now; but I still want him to long impetuously to see me, and to live with me again. I have been pining for him these past two days – but I have got over it: something in my heart has snapped shut...

I am rereading Seneca, and continuing with the Beethoven biography. It's so long, and there's so little time.

30th November. S.I. came for lunch and was his usual delightful self, calm, gay and kind. I was observing him with Tanya, but detected nothing.

Safonova* also came with her two little girls to visit Sasha, and Sonya Kolokoltseva came too, and all the girls cheerfully went skating in the garden. Then Makovitsky* arrived from Yasnaya and told me in his broken Russian that L.N. was well and working hard.

10th December. I haven't written my diary for ten days. What has happened? It is hard to assemble all the events on paper, especially since it has all been so painful – and now yet more painful facts have come to light. But I shall try to recall everything.

On 2nd December, I went to a Beethoven evening. Auer and d'Albert played four of his violin sonatas. It was an utter joy, and balm to my soul. But the following day I saw in the papers an advertisement for L.N.'s essay in the *Northern Herald*. Then on top of this Tanya picked an argument with me, reproaching me for my supposed relations with S.I. – when I haven't seen him for a whole month. I feel dreadfully hurt; my family is always so quick to accuse me of crimes I haven't committed the moment I stop serving them like a slave and submitting to their demands.

I was waiting eagerly for L.N. to come. I longed to write to him, to help him in every way, to love him, not to cause him any more unhappiness and to see no more of S.I. if it was really so painful for him, and the news that he wasn't coming to see me after our month's separation – and that he was publishing his article in the *N.H.* – reduced me to the depths of despair. I packed my things and decided to go off somewhere. I got into a cab, with no idea where I was going. First of all I went to the Petersburg station, intending to go to St Petersburg and take the essay from Gurevich, then I thought better of it and set off for the Troitsa monastery. That evening, alone in a dirty hotel room lit by one candle, I sat alone as if turned to stone, overwhelmed by feelings of grief for and resentment of my husband, and his utter indifference to me and my love for him. I tried to console myself with the thought that one's feelings are less passionate when one is almost 70 – but why the deception, why all these secret negotiations behind my back with the *N.H.* over his essay? I thought I would go mad.

I went to bed and had just fallen asleep when I was woken by Nurse and Tanya knocking on the door. Somehow Tanya had guessed that I had gone to Troitsa, and had grown worried and decided to come and fetch me. I was very touched, but it did nothing to dispel my despair. Tanya told me that L.N. was coming the next day. But the news left me completely unmoved. I had waited for him too eagerly and for too long, and now something inside me had snapped, and I felt morbidly indifferent to everything.

Tanya left and I went to church. I spent the whole day there – nine hours – and I prayed fervently to be delivered from the sin of killing myself or avenging myself for the pain my husband had caused me; I prayed for a reconciliation, for a miracle to unite us in love, trust and friendship; I prayed for my sick soul to be healed.

My confession was before God, since Father Fyodor, the Church elder, was so decrepit he couldn't hear a word I was saying, and just let out a short sob of nervous exhaustion. There was something mysterious and poetic about this monastic existence: the stone corridors and cells, the monks wandering about, the simple folk – prayers, long services and complete solitude amidst a crowd of supplicants who didn't know me. I went back and spent the evening poring over the precepts and prayers in a book I found at the hotel. The next morning I received the Eucharist at the Trapeznaya Church. It was a royal day (6th December), and a magnificent dinner was being prepared for the monastery – four fish dishes, honey and beer. The tables were covered in tablecloths, the plates, dishes and mugs were all of pewter, and the meal was served by novices dressed in white aprons.

Having stood through the service, I went off to wander around the monastery buildings. A gypsy woman pursued me as I was walking across the square: "A fair-haired man is in love with you, but dares not tell you. You are a noble, distinguished lady, refined and educated, and he is not of your class... Give me 1 ruble and 6 10-kopeck pieces and I'll give you a charm! Come to my house and I'll give you a charm to make him fall in love with you like your husband..."

I was quite unnerved and wanted to take her charm. But when I got back to my room I crossed myself and realized this would be foolish and wicked of me.

I felt very depressed – there was still no telegram from Tanya to inform me of L.N.'s arrival. After I had something to eat I drove to the telegraph office and there were two undelivered telegrams waiting for me: one from Tanya, and the other a long, touching one from L.N. asking me to return to Moscow.

I went straight to the station.

At home Lev Nikolaevich was waiting for me in the hall with tears in his eyes, and we fell into each other's arms. He agreed not to publish his essay in the *Northern Herald* (he had already said this in the telegram to me that Tanya had sent); I promised faithfully not to see S.I. again, and to serve and care for him and do all I possibly could to make him happy.

We had such a pleasant talk, it was a joy for me to promise this, I loved him very deeply and was eager to love him...

Yet today in his diary he writes that I had "acknowledged my crime"* for the first time, which had brought him much joy! God help me endure this! Once more he has to present himself to future generations as a *martyr*, and me as a *criminal*. But what is my *crime*? L.N. was angry with me for visiting S.I. with Uncle Kostya a month ago when he was in bed with a bad leg. It was because he was so furious about this apparently that he didn't come to Moscow; this, according to him, was my "crime".

Yet when I told him that considering my pure and blameless life with him, he could surely forgive me paying a visit to a sick friend – and with my old uncle too – the tears came to his eyes and he said: "Of course that is true, your life has indeed been a pure and blameless one." No one saw his tears of contrition, no one knows about our life together, and in his diaries he writes only of my "crimes"! God forgive him for his cruelty and injustice to me.

11th December. Gurevich visited Tanya, weeping and telling her how wretched she was not to have L.N.'s essay. He didn't go out to see her. He has now asked her for the article back. What will happen now! I no longer trust him after he deceitfully sent it to the *Northern Herald*.

If I wasn't living under this domestic despotism I would go to St Petersburg for the Nikish concert. As it is, I've had to abandon my music again. Dora and Lyova left for Yasnaya today. He was very irritable in Moscow.

14th December. Today I took Vera Kuzminskaya and my Sasha to Gluck's *Orpheus*. It is a marvellous opera, graceful and melodious, and the choruses, the dances and sets were airy and elegant. Yesterday I went to a symphony concert – Beethoven's lovely 'Pastoral', Tchaikovsky's 1st Symphony, and some other works of no interest.

The fact is that although I put a brave face on it I feel a deep grief in my heart that L.N. and I are not on better terms, and a lot of anxiety about his health. I have done my best – I truly want us to be friends. But oh how difficult it is! As I was leaving for the theatre today I was waylaid by some woman – the wife of a chemist – sobbing and imploring me to give her 600 rubles, then 400 rubles, to settle her debts. It's even harder for her. But we are all tempting the Lord...

16th December. Yesterday I paid social calls. Everywhere I go it's the same question: "What is the Count writing at present?", "*Qu'est-ce que vous faites pour rester toujours jeune?*"* and so on. My youthful appearance has become an invariable topic of conversation in society. But what is it to me when my soul is sad? And Lev Nikolaevich is so unfriendly. There is definitely something he is concealing from me. I see nothing of S.I. and try not to think about him.

17th December. This morning I had a piano lesson with Miss Welsh. Then a call from Annenkova and a visit to the bathhouse.

An astonishing incident there. There has been a lot of talk in Moscow recently of the Solovyov family, whose three children all died of scarlet fever in one week. Well, I just happened to be sitting next to the mother of these children. We got into conversation, and I shared with her my painful memories of Vanechka's death; I told her of my grief, and of the (religious) solution I had sought and partly found, and this consoled her a little. Then she asked me who I was, and when I told her she burst into tears and threw her arms around me, kissing me and begging me to stay with her a little longer. What a dear, lovely, pitiful woman.

This evening there were guests: Chicherin, Masha Zubova, Annenkova, Rusanova and Taneev. His appearance alarmed me for Lev Nikolaevich's sake, and at first I felt awkward and anxious. Then I had to preside at the tea table. I was happy to see him of course, and would have been even happier to hear him play, but he didn't.

I had a dream last night; there was a long narrow hall and at the end of it was a piano, on which S.I. was playing one of his own compositions. I observed him more closely, and saw Vanechka was sitting on his knee. I could only see him from the back, his golden curly hair and his white shirt. He was leaning his head against S.I.'s right shoulder, and I felt so peaceful and happy listening to the music and seeing Vanechka and S.I. together. Then someone banged the shutters and I woke up. The tune he was playing stayed clearly in my mind even after I had woken up, but I didn't manage to retain it for long. And I was overwhelmed with sadness.

Lev Nikolaevich was telling us today about a woman who was giving birth in the Kremlin. It was a difficult birth and she was thought to be dying, so they sent to the monastery for a priest. A monk came with the sacraments, and it turned out that this monk had once been a doctor, and saw that he could save the mother and baby with the standard forceps procedure. It was the middle of the night; he went back to his cell, fetched his surgical instruments and performed the operation, and both mother and baby were saved. It is said when this news reached the ears of the Metropolitan he was going to defrock the monk, but in the end he was merely transferred to another monastery in another town.

21st December. Where is it, human happiness?

Today was yet another painful, dreadful day. Tanya had a letter from Gurevich, insisting that L.N. give her his essay. Both Tanya and Seryozha, who came today, berated me for my unwillingness to do so (I find these dealings with the *Northern Herald* so disagreeable), and they sent me to L.N. to beg him to let her have his 'Preface' to the translated Carpenter article. So I went in to him and asked him to give it to her, since he and his family wanted it so much.

But when I foolishly said something to the effect that I found his relations with Gurevich as unpleasant as he found mine with Taneev, I looked at him and was terrified. His face has changed so much recently: his thick bushy eyebrows beetle over his angry eyes, and his expression is wild, ugly and full of suffering; his face is pleasant only when it has an expression of kindly sympathy or passionate affection. I often wonder what he would do to himself if I really did something sinful! I thank God for sparing me from sin and temptation.

This morning L.N. swept the skating rink in the garden and went skating, then rode to Sparrow Hills. He is doing no work at present.

25th December. The day before yesterday Lev Nikolaevich went off to Nikolaev station as he wanted to catch Sulerzhitsky and the Englishman St John to give them some money for the Dukhobors, whom they were going to visit. But he didn't find them in. He walked home, chilled and exhausted, and went straight to bed, and when I got back he was already quite ill, with a temperature of 38.5. The doctor prescribed Ems water as usual, and said he should have a warm massage and keep his stomach warm. I did all I could, and yesterday he was a little better and his temperature was down to 38.6. Today it is 37.5. He is still very weak but no longer ill, and today he had something to eat. At 3.30 I brought him some puréed oatmeal soup. "How clever of you to think of bringing me soup," he said. "I was beginning to feel a little weak." Then he ate dinner with the rest of us.

We received an anonymous letter:

Dear Count Lev Nikolaevich,

There can be no doubt that your sect is growing and putting down deep roots. However misbegotten it may be, you have nevertheless succeeded, with the aid of the Devil and the stupidity of the people, in insulting our Lord Jesus Christ, whom we must now avenge. In order to do underground battle with your underground sect, therefore, we have formed a secret society, the Second Crusaders, whose aim is to kill you and all your disciples, the leaders of your sect. We fully recognize that this is not a Christian act – may the Lord forgive us and pass judgement on us in the next world! But once a hand is infected with gangrene it must be sacrificed, however much it grieves us. I grieve for you too, as a brother in Christ, but you must be annihilated if we are to weaken the forces of evil! It has fallen to me, unworthy as I am, to kill you! The day I have appointed for your death is 3rd April of the coming year, 1898. In doing this I am fulfilling my great and sacred mission, and enabling you to prepare for your journey to the other world.

You may well ask me, quite logically, why we attack your sect alone. It is true that all sects are an "abomination before God"! But their instigators are numbskulls, and are no match, Count, for you. And secondly, you are the enemy of our Tsar and country!

The Second Crusader Who Drew the First Lot, December 1897

It was sealed in wax with the initials E.S., and a royal crown. The postmark was Pavlograd, 20th December.

I am so worried about this letter I can think of nothing else. I thought of informing the governor of Ekaterinoslav province and the local police chief, so they could take appropriate measures against these dangerous people and order a police search if they wanted to. But Lev Nikolaevich is totally unperturbed, and says we mustn't notify anyone and it is in God's hands.*

26th December. I saw Tanya and Sasha off to Grinevka and Nikolskoe this morning, and Seryozha left yesterday evening. We rushed about packing boxes: I filled one with Christmas presents for my grandchildren, one with gifts and fruit for Dora, and one with some silver and a fur coat for Masha. All these will travel with Tanya; I also packed a basket with food and fruit for them to eat on their journey. Lev Nikolaevich and I are all on our own now; there's nothing to do, and it's nice and quiet. He is much better; he had a temperature of 36.9 this morning, and this afternoon it went up to 37.5. This evening he asked for some soup and a baked apple, and was in much better spirits. I am haunted by the letter.

I spent the whole day playing the piano. This wordless musical conversation with Beethoven, Mendelssohn, Rubinstein and so on gives me enormous pleasure, even though I play so poorly.

1898

1st–3rd March – founding of Marxist Social Democratic Labour Party.
Tolstoy finishes What Is Art? *The complete work appears, mutilated by the censor, in the fourteenth edition of his works and also in an Intermediary edition. Sofia writes a romantic short story, 'Song Without Words'. Tolstoy works in the villages to alleviate the famine and appeals for funds. He helps the Dukhobors raise money to emigrate and supports the Molokans. December – Sergei Tolstoy accompanies a shipload of two thousand Dukhobors to Canada.*

1st January (Moscow). Lev Nikolaevich, Andryusha, Misha, Mitya Dyakov, the Danilevsky boys and I all saw in the New Year together. We drank Don champagne, and Lev Nikolaevich drank tea with almond milk.

This morning I played the piano and kept an eye on Misha to make sure he studied. Then I went to visit my old aunt Vera Shidlovskaya and chatted with her and my cousins. Lev Nikolaevich and I had dinner on our own. He is not yet fully recovered, and ate just a bowl of mushroom soup with rice, some semolina with almond milk and coffee. He is lethargic and bored, for he is not used to being ill and debilitated. How hard it will be for him when he finally loses his strength and grows even weaker! He has such an appetite for life! Yet he'll soon be 70 – in August this year, i.e. in 6 months. He has been reading alone in his study upstairs and writing a few letters; today he walked over to visit Rusanov, who is ill – and simply worships him. Lying on the sofa in his study is Tanya's black poodle, a gift from Countess Zubova. He took it out for a walk today.

Our Masha is arriving tomorrow for a consultation with the doctor. Tanya and Sasha are still in the country; they'll probably go to Yasnaya Polyana tomorrow to visit Lyova and Dora. I should like to go to Yasnaya too. How I love it, and what a lot of good experiences I have had there!

3rd January. Stasov,* Ginzburg the sculptor, a young painter and Vereshchagin (a bad writer) were here yesterday morning. Stasov took advantage of his 74 years to fling his arms round me and kiss me, repeating "Oh, how pink and slender you are!" I was so embarrassed – I couldn't get away from him. We then went upstairs to the drawing room and discussed Lev Nikolaevich's article *On Art*. Stasov said he thought L.N. had got it all back to front. He didn't have to tell me that – he certainly hit the nail on the head!

L.N. and I had a nasty argument because I was complaining that the public should have to take out a two-year subscription to the *Journal of Philosophy and Psychology* to read his essay, which is in the November–December and February–March issues, when if I had brought it out in the *Complete Collected Works*, I would have sold it for 50 kopecks and everyone could have read it. L.N. then shouted in front of everyone: "I shan't give it to you! I'm giving it to everyone! Everyone has criticized me ever since I started giving things away for nothing!"

But he never gives me anything. He sent 'Master and Man' to the *Northern Herald* behind my back. He also returned the Preface on the sly, and has been at pains not to let me have his essay either. God be with him! He's quite right, they're *his* works, *his* inalienable property – but he oughtn't to shout at me like that.

Masha arrived yesterday with Kolya. She is completely taken up with her husband, we hardly exist as far as she's concerned – and she means very little to us too. I was pleased to see her; I am sorry she is so thin, but I'm happy she is living for love, for that is a great joy! For a long time I too lived for this simple love, without judging or criticizing. I regret that I am now more experienced and have lost so many illusions. I would have preferred to remain blind and besotted to the end of my days. What I tried to accept as love from my husband was nothing but sensuality, now degenerating into sullen severity, now flaring up into jealousy, demands – and occasionally tenderness.

6th January. I drove to Patriarch Ponds today and went skating for a long time with the Maklakovs and Natasha Kolokoltseva. Then it started to rain and thaw. Skating is such a bracing, healthy activity. This evening I did some reading, sat with Sasha, then listened to an unknown young man named Pol from Kiev, playing us some of his works on the piano – very well too. L.N. is gloomy because he is still unable to work. He went skating too – at some institution for young waifs and strays.

He is reading all he can find about the Caucasus at present – Caucasian life, Caucasian scenery, everything.*

8th January. The artist Repin dined with us yesterday and kept asking Lev Nikolaevich to suggest a theme for his next painting. He said he wanted to devote his last efforts in life to a good work of art, something really worth working on. Lev Nikolaevich hasn't suggested anything to him yet but is thinking about it. He himself can do no work. The weather is frightful: there's a terrible wind, and floods everywhere – even more than during a Moscow spring. It's 3° and dark.

13th January. Yesterday was Tanya's name day, and we bustled around all morning organizing a *party*. First Tanya invited some guests, then I invited some. One has a *duty* to one's society friends. I was sorting through some cardboard this morning, with my hair awry and my morning cap on, when Sergei Ivanovich and his pupil Yusha Pomerantsev suddenly came into the room. I hadn't heard a thing, and was so agitated I blushed crimson and couldn't say a word. I had given express orders that no one should be admitted, but for some reason they had been let in. They sat there for almost an hour, talking about *Sadko* and Rimsky-Korsakov among other things. When Sergei Ivanovich left I felt deeply depressed – to pacify L.N. I should hate this man, or at least treat him as a stranger. But that is impossible.

16th January. Tanya is leaving for St Petersburg. I mentioned that I should like to attend some of Wagner's operas there, but this provoked Lev Nikolaevich into such an angry flood of criticisms and biting references to my insane love of music, my stupidity, my ineptitude, etc., etc., that he has completely killed my desire to go.

I spent the day checking the accounts with the accountant, and diligently set all my publishing, family and household affairs in order, and I am now exhausted and my head is aching. Late this evening Lev Nikolaevich and I walked Marusya Maklakova home, and Dunaev and my brother Styopa came.

Seryozha and Ilyusha arrived. A painful discussion with Lev Nikolaevich this evening. He is becoming more and more suspicious, jealous and despotic. He resents every independent move I make, every innocent pleasure, every hour I spend at the piano.

Marusya Maklakova and our Tanya were looking through photographs of various men today, discussing which of them they would marry. When they came to Lev Nikolaevich's portrait they both cried, "No, no! Not for anything!" Yes, it is difficult to live under any sort of despotism, but jealous despotism is frightful!

17th January. L.N. has been nagging me all day, begging to be "released" to go back to the country; he wasn't necessary to me here, he said, life in Moscow was murder for him – on and on in the same vein. The word "released" is absolutely meaningless – as though I could "hold" him here! I wanted him to come to Moscow because it is quite natural for me to want to live with my husband, and it's a pleasure too, for I am used to loving and caring for him. I have done all I could to spare him from his tormenting jealousy, but I still haven't earned his trust. If he went to the country he would torment himself even more; if we all went, what would happen to Misha and Sasha? What about their studies? I have been racking my brains... Lev Nikolaevich's apathy and indifference to his children's education is always painful to me, and I blame him bitterly for it. How many fathers not only educate their own children, but also support them with their own labour, as my father did? But L.N. considers that even to *live* with his family would be murder.

20th January. Yesterday morning Sasha was collecting money for the young son of our footman Ivan, who has just left. This little boy, Lyonya, was badly burnt by some scalding water from the samovar, and is now in hospital.

An extraordinary thing happened the day before yesterday. My sons had gone to the theatre – Seryozha to see *Sadko* at the Solodovnikov – and I had a sudden overwhelming fear that the theatre would burn down. I told Lev Nikolaevich of my premonition, and sure enough, that night after the audience had left, it burnt down and the roof collapsed.

Today I took Sasha to buy her some shoes and a corset. Then I swept the snow off the skating rink in the garden; Lev Nikolaevich joined me and we both swept together, then he took a turn on his skates while I went indoors and practised the piano for an hour and a half.

22nd January. I played the piano all morning. I feel intensely anxious. Biryukov is leaving Bauska for England.* Wiener, Prince Khilkov's former mistress, also left for England yesterday and he too has been deported.

26th January. I have been ill these past few days. It started as neuralgia on the right side of my head, and was followed by a high fever and a sore throat. Young Doctor Usov came; he feared at first that it might be diphtheria, but when he examined me it proved not to be. These young doctors are quite extraordinary. Malyutin refused to take any money for treating Sasha, and now Usov too refuses to be paid. I have sent him a signed copy of L.N.'s works instead. As Tanya is still in St Petersburg, L.N. sweetly offered to paint my throat, which he did very cautiously and clumsily. My illness has frightened him, and he has suddenly started to look older and sadder. How strangely we love each other! He is happy when I sit quietly at home, bored and inert, copying or reading. The moment I become more lively, tackle something new or make new friends, he becomes anxious, then angry, and starts treating me harshly. Yet it is sometimes very hard for me to stifle my natural spontaneity!

I was lying in bed yesterday when three more Molokans from Samara came to see L.N. again, begging for letters of introduction to take to St Petersburg.* They are going there to plead once more for their children who were taken away from them by the government and sent to monasteries. Those poor children, and their poor mothers! What a barbaric way to convert people to Orthodoxy! It won't convert them at all, quite the opposite.

Yesterday and today I was lying in bed reading the proofs of *Childhood*, which always touches me deeply. My back aches, I feel weak and am afflicted by a constant gnawing depression.

L.N. just came in and said: "I've come to keep you company for a bit." Then he showed me the two seven-pound weights he bought today for his gymnastics exercises. He is very lethargic at present and keeps saying: "I feel as though I were 70." But in 6 months, that is in August, he *will* be 70. He went skating today and swept the snow. But he cannot do any mental work, and that mortifies him beyond words.

28th January. I got up with great difficulty, still feeling very unwell. My body aches, I feel sick and have a headache. But I managed to do a lot of work on the proofs and on the children's affairs; yesterday and today I have been copying accounts from the general housekeeping book into three separate ledgers – for Andryusha, Misha and Lyova. Dear M.E. Leontyeva came to see me and we had a frank and intimate discussion about the serious matters of life.

Sergei Ivanovich sent his dear old nurse, Pelageya Vasilevna, to ask after my health.

Lev Nikolaevich had a visit from a lady named Kogan, and they discussed lofty matters concerning human purpose and happiness and the paths to its attainment.

29th January. Tanya has returned from St Petersburg. She went to get her paintings published and had a very pleasant time there. She visited Pobedonostsev, Chief Procurator of the Synod, to discuss the case of the Samara Molokans who were robbed of their children. He told her the local bishop had exceeded his authority, adding that he would write to the governor of Samara about it and "hoped the matter would soon be settled". What cunning! He pretended not to know that Tanya was Lev Nikolaevich's daughter, and when she was on her way downstairs he asked her, "Are you the daughter of Lev Nikolaevich?" When she said "Yes", he said: "Ah, so you are the renowned Tatyana Lvovna!" To which Tanya replied: "Well, I certainly didn't know I was renowned!"

My brother Styopa has come again with his sick, deaf, sad wife. He and Seryozha have concluded their negotiations over the property they are buying in the Minsk province. The question is, is it worth it? Our friend Misha Stakhovich had dinner with us. Lev Nikolaevich corrected the proofs of *What Is Art?* all day. It is now evening; he has taken the poodle for a walk and is eating porridge and drinking tea.

A blizzard all day. Between three and five degrees of frost.

30th January. Today Sergei Ivanovich came to see me – he has an undoubted power and influence over me, I must confess. We were alone together for only a short while as my brother Styopa and my son Seryozha came in, but when he left my nerves felt soothed, and I felt a calm joy I haven't experienced for a long time. Was this wrong of me? We talked only of music, of his compositions and of the musical range of the alto, soprano and tenor voices. Then we spoke of the way one assuages one's conscience by dealing severely with one's own actions; and how hard it is when someone close to us dies to accept the wrongs we did them. He enquired with such sympathy and affection about my recent illness, my children, and what I had been doing recently – and there was so much simple, calm kindness in it that it made me extraordinarily happy. What a pity it is that Lev Nikolaevich is too jealous to tolerate our friendship, or allow himself and our family to be friends with this marvellous, idealistic man.

31st January. I have been out for the first time since my illness. I paid 1,000 rubles into Ilyusha's account at the Bank of the Nobility, withdrew the interest and made various other payments. *Business –* all very dull but necessary. Andryusha came, more discussions about money and why he perpetually needs so much of it. Will the happy moment ever come when I am free of these financial ordeals with my children? I thought I would be spared all this when the property was divided up, but in fact this division has been the ruin of my children.

2nd February. We went to bed late yesterday, and I hardly slept at all. It's a long time since I've been in such an exalted, religious mood. All those feelings I experienced after Vanechka's death reawakened in me and swept through my soul. It was as though I had raised a curtain and looked at the light – at that pure, disembodied, spiritual state besides which all earthly concerns are as nothing. And this mood inspired me to pray, and prayer brought consolation.

3rd February. Today is Nurse's name day. She and I have been avoiding each other all day for fear of both bursting into tears, as we did last year and the year before, remembering Vanechka, who was always so eager to "celebrate" her name day. He would always ask me to buy a cup, some handkerchiefs or some sweets for her. All day I restrained my grief and spoke to no one of it, although it was choking me, and it was only in the evening that I sat down to pour out my feelings into those pieces of music which soothed my grief before, when that man made himself so dear to me by playing them for me.

5th February. I went to a concert given by the Conservatoire students. I arrived late unfortunately, as I hadn't realized it was meant to start at 8. I sat beside Sergei Ivanovich throughout – I love his explanations and interpretations of the music. I gave him a lift, and he was naively delighted by the horse's brisk trotting.

When I got home I suddenly felt afraid, as though I were concealing some shameful secret. But I felt so sorry for Sergei Ivanovich wearing his thin coat in the wind and cold, and it seemed only natural to give him a lift. Besides, he still has a bad leg and is hobbling with a stick.

Tomorrow he and Goldenweiser are coming to play us his symphony and the *Oresteia* overture, arranged for four hands.

6th February. A tense, difficult evening. Sergei Ivanovich and Goldenweiser played Taneev's symphonic overture as a duet, and the whole family listened with patronizing indifference and no one praised it. It was terribly awkward. Thankfully Lev Nikolaevich, with his customary good breeding, went up to them afterwards to tell them how much he had liked the *theme*. The only ones who liked it and were excited by it were Taneev's friend Anna Ivanovna Maslova and myself. We had heard the *Oresteia* before and heard the overture performed by an orchestra, so for us the piano version was only an echo of the original.

8th February. L.N. again complains of feeling ill. His back aches from the neck down and he felt sick all day. It must be his diet. Today he ate pickled mushrooms, marinated mushrooms and stewed dried fruit – all of which produces fermentation in the stomach, and there's no nourishment in it so he loses weight. This evening he asked for a mint infusion and drank a little. He is in low spirits. Today he was saying his life was coming to an end, the machine had broken down, it was all over. But I can also see he has a very hostile attitude to death. Today he reminded me a little of his aunt Pelageya, who died in our house. She also dreaded death, and was violently angry when she realized it had come. L.N. hasn't actually said as much, but surely his depression and indifference to everything and everyone mean the thought of death is terrible to him.

When I looked in on him this evening there were some strangers sitting there – a factory worker, some peasants and another "dark one". This is the wall that has stood between me and my husband over recent years. I overheard their conversation: the factory worker was naively asking, "And what are your views, L.N., on the second coming of our Lord Jesus Christ?"

My Misha has vanished for the whole day. I am very displeased about these disappearances from the house, but an eighteen-year-old boy finds it dull to be with factory workers and old men, and misses the company of young people. Fat, sulky Sasha is too young for him and doesn't interest him as a companion. What a difference between her and our sensitive, clever little Tanya at her age!

12th February. I walked to Kuznetsky Most yesterday, and returned to find L.N. skating in the garden. I quickly put my skates on and joined him. But after Patriarch Ponds I found our garden cramped and dreary. L.N. skates confidently and well; he has been much healthier and happier these past three days.

I was on my way to a concert yesterday when I suddenly had a vivid picture of the peasant poverty which will follow the bad harvest that is on everyone's lips at present. I saw it as clearly as if it were before my eyes – children begging for food when there is no food, mothers suffering as their children starve, when they themselves are starving – and I was consumed with horror and the most helpless despair...

Nothing grieves me more than the thought of starving children. When I was breastfeeding my own children my heart would bleed for any child who was hungry, and ever since then I have felt sorry not only for my own children but for all children on earth.

This morning there was an unpleasant scene with Misha. He had stayed out all night, I scolded him, he answered back, and I lost my temper and he went off whistling. I then burst into tears, completely beside myself, and said: "Your mother cries and you whistle, have you no heart?" He was ashamed then and apologized. To soothe my nerves and my heart I went to the piano and played Beethoven's 'Pathétique' Sonata. I played for an hour and a half and practised another sonata. Then L.N. came in and I started telling him about Misha, but he wasn't interested as he had come to give me some work – copying more corrections from one copy of *What Is Art?* to another.

I felt outraged when I read his condemnation of Beethoven. Not long ago I read Beethoven's biography and learnt to love and appreciate this genius more than ever. But my love is always quick to arouse his loathing, even for the dead. I remember when I read Seneca and was so enchanted by him, and he told me Seneca was a pompous Roman fool with a fondness for fine phrases. One must conceal one's feelings.

I had an affectionate letter from Andryusha. I wrote to Masha yesterday. It's her 27th birthday today. And to think she's my *fifth*! I never feel old – I am still young in every respect: my eagerness for work, my impressionability, my capacity for love and grief, my passion for music, my delight in skating and parties. My step is light, my body is fit – only my face has aged…

13th February. I worked on proofs all evening, transferring corrections and translations from one copy of *What Is Art?* to another. Yesterday I agreed that L.N. should let Gurevich publish his preface to Seryozha's translation of Carpenter's article on the meaning of science. I have done so because I want to publish his views on science after *What Is Art?* in Volume 15, as this will continue the sense of the article perfectly.* L.N. was delighted with my suggestion.

He wrote a great many letters this evening. Today and yesterday he had nothing but dry blinis and soda water for dinner. Poor man! His principles won't allow him to eat butter or caviar. This restraint of his is very fine, but it's much worse if the temptation is there.

14th February. Hectic preparations for Shrovetide. I went to buy
some things for this evening, then went skating with Tanya, Sasha,
Lyova and Dora, who stood and watched as she is pregnant. We had a
family dinner and everyone was in a good mood, which was pleasant.
L.N. is still working on the proofs of *What Is Art?* This evening he
visited an old merchant of seventy-two, a follower of his, who has
cancer of the liver. He complained to L.N. how bored he was living
with his family, and told him his wife and son both prayed to the
"boards" (i.e. the icons).

A large crowd of boys and children came round this evening. At
first they were rather listless, then they played games and charades,
sang together and did gymnastic tricks, while some of the boys sat
down to a hand of vint.

The evening ended with Goldenweiser playing a Nocturne and a
Scherzo by Chopin, followed by a Liszt Étude.

15th February. Heavy snow all day, overcast; the house is silent.
Andryusha was telling me the most frightful tales of debauchery and
fallen women; how sad that such things should interest him. L.N.
again sat at his proofs. Tanya is sad, Sasha is unwell. I sat here all
day immersed in household business and ordered seeds, which always
demands a lot of thought. I didn't go out. I wanted to play the piano
but kept being interrupted.

16th February. It is Monday in the first week of Lent. I love this time;
I love the quiet orderly atmosphere and the religious calm. I used to
love it because spring was near – but I have lost that feeling now. What
is spring to me! It doesn't add anything to my happiness, it lessens it
with its compelling pressure to search for a happiness that doesn't
exist and never will.

I spent the morning altering Sasha's dress, then played the piano
for two and a half hours. I called on Sofia Filosofova before dinner,
and we chatted about our children and grandchildren, our trials and
tribulations, and various family matters. When I left her I longed for
some fresh air, exercise, solitude and freedom, so I set off for a walk.
I was late for dinner. When I got back the others were all sitting round
the table and scolded me good-naturedly while I ate my Lenten soup.
I shall fast all through Lent, God willing.

17th February. This morning I again managed to play the piano for
over two hours. Afterwards I bought a saddle to give Lyova tomorrow

for his name day, and for Lev Nikolaevich I shall buy some honey, dates, special prunes, pears and pickled mushrooms. He loves to keep a supply of these things on his window sill so he can eat fruit or dates with bread when he is hungry. He wrote a lot today. I don't know what, he won't say. Then he went skating with Lyova. We had a cheerful dinner together. Dunaev sat here this evening while I did my embroidery – I can't bear to do nothing, no matter who our guests are. And I have certainly had a lot of them foisted on me today. There was a certain Aristov who arrived to see L.N. But Lev Nikolaevich had disappeared off to the bathhouse with Sergeenko and didn't return for two hours, so I had to listen to this Mr Aristov's endless tales about irrigation, fish-breeding and his family affairs, and advise him as to whether or not he should let his twenty-two-year-old daughter marry a rich old man of fifty. What a strange question to ask a woman he has never met before!

18th February. It is Lyova's and Lev Nikolaevich's name day, although L.N. never recognizes special days, especially name days. I gave Lyova a very fine English saddle from Zimmerman's, and spent the day working; I altered and mended Lev Nikolaevich's grey flannel shirt, then sewed a band of embroidery on some white linen – my old, beautiful, stupid work. It's best to have some sewing to do when all these guests are here, otherwise it can be very dreary.

We had a family dinner, with Uncle Kostya Islavin and Lev Nikolaevich's nieces Liza Obolenskaya and Varya Nagornova. A lot of the children were here too – Seryozha, Tanya, Lyova, Dora, Misha and Sasha. I love celebrating these family occasions.

We drank their health in Don champagne. But there was a certain emptiness about the day.

I was astonished by what L.N. said yesterday evening about the woman question. He announced, as usual, that he was against women's emancipation and so-called "equal rights", and went on to say that no matter what work a woman did – teaching, medicine, art – she had only one real purpose in life, and that was sexual love. So that whatever she might strive to achieve, all her strivings would merely crumble to ashes.

This made me terribly indignant, and I admonished him for his perpetually cynical attitude to women, which has made me suffer so much. I told him the reason he regarded women like this was that he hadn't known a single decent woman before he was 34. It's precisely this lack of friendship and spiritual affinity (rather than physical intimacy), this indifference to my spiritual and emotional life, which torments me to this day. All this has become blatantly obvious to me over the years – it has spoilt my life and disillusioned me and has made me love my husband less.

19th February. L.N. is hiding his diary somewhere. I always used to be able to guess where it was and search it out, but now I am at a loss to know where he has put it.

22nd February. I visited L.N.'s friend Rusanov, who is sick, and we talked about L.N., vegetarianism and Chertkov, whom the Rusanovs strongly disapprove of; they said that he was an abnormal person, prone to attacks of insanity, manifested by his extreme suspiciousness, garrulousness, fussiness and despotism. There's really very little good in him. We had a lot of people to dinner and there were blinis; I arrived home half an hour before dinner and was told that Count Olsufiev and Sergei Ivanovich Taneev were there. I was delighted, ran straight upstairs and found them sitting with Tanya, who was lying on the couch. Sergei Ivanovich has brought me *The Sunrise*, his work for four voices set to words by the poet Tyutchev, and he played it to me. It is beautifully written and is divided into two moods: waiting for the sun, and its final triumphant appearance.

Tanya said a great many spiteful things to me yesterday about his visit. That's the way to stop a good sympathetic friendship between two people!

23rd February. The anniversary of Vanechka's death – three years have passed since he died. The moment I got up I went to church and prayed and thought about my dead infants, parents and friends. I had a requiem service performed for me. Then we went to the maternity home to visit the cook's wife Masha, who earlier today had given birth to a baby boy. From there I called on Zhilyaeva, the wife of a poor landowner from Kursk, to find out how she was getting on, but she wasn't in. She has an extraordinarily musical son, a pupil of Sergei Ivanovich's. I bought some flowers to put round Vanechka's portrait, and some rolls and honey for Nurse.

4th March. Bad news about *What Is Art?* The secular censors passed it, but there was a telegram from St Petersburg saying it must now be presented to the church censors. Which means that this essay, the second part of it anyway, is sunk for good. It's exasperating! So now

I've printed and corrected it all for nothing. It will just have to be published abroad.

7th March. L.N. is listless and fractious. He cannot work and he is exhausted by all his visitors, who are often most unwelcome, and despite my pleading with him to send them away and enjoy his leisure, he stubbornly refuses to do so. He has a boundless *curiosity*, which makes him receive absolutely everyone who comes to see him, as well as that eternal stubbornness, and the desire to contradict and defy me all the time.

I had a very unpleasant conversation with him this morning. He wants to make a lot of additions to *On Art*, but I am afraid the censors will seize on these additions and stop the book again, and I want to print 30,000 copies. One word led to another, and soon we were shouting at each other. I blamed him for depriving me of my freedom and not letting me go to St Petersburg; he blamed me for selling his books; I replied that it wasn't me who took that money, most of it went to his children whom he had abandoned, and had neither educated nor trained to work. I also said that it was with this money that I paid for his saddle horse, his asparagus, his fruit, his charity work, his bicycles and so forth, and that I spent less on myself than on anyone else... But I wouldn't have said all this if he hadn't shouted at me that I had forgotten myself, that he could *forbid* me to sell his books. Very well, I said, forbid me, I shall be delighted to support myself by going out to work as a schoolteacher or a proofreader or some such thing. I love work, and I do *not* love this life, which doesn't suit me at all, and has been organized, through sheer inertia, to suit my family – my husband and children.

What Is Art? has apparently returned from the church censors, who have underlined one or two things, but passed it. L.N. and I didn't argue after that – in fact we were both thoroughly ashamed and made up.

8th March. I am battling with myself. My soul is torn between my passionate desire to go to St Petersburg for the Wagner and various other concerts, and the fear of distressing Lev Nikolaevich and having this on my conscience. I cried last night for this painful *lack of freedom*, which is becoming more and more oppressive. Materially of course I am free: I have money, horses, dresses – everything. I go to bed, sit down, drive around. I am free to read proofs, buy apples for L.N., make Sasha's dresses and my husband's shirts, take his photograph from every conceivable angle, order dinner, manage our family affairs – I am free to eat, sleep, be quiet and submit. But I am not free to *think* as I please, to *love* whom I choose, to come and go according to my own interests and intellectual pleasures; I am not free to pursue my music, I am not free to drive away all these innumerable, unwanted, dull and often extremely evil people, and instead receive people who are good, clever, gifted and interesting. We have no need of such people in our house – for one would have to take them seriously and treat them as equals, whereas he likes to enslave people and preach at them...

And I'm not happy, my life is hard... No, that wasn't the right word: I don't need *happiness*, what I need is a life that is *full* and *peaceful*, not this difficult, anxious, pointless existence.

9th March. The Day of the Forty Martyrs. On the morning of this day when I was a child and when my children were young, Trifonovna, our old cook in my father's house, and Nikolai, the cook at Yasnaya Polyana, would bake delicious rich lark cakes, with blackcurrants for eyes and crisp beaks. There was something so poetic about them. And then the live larks would fly up and settle on the thawed patches of brown earth poking through the snow, before soaring into the sky with their sweet silvery song. I used to love springtime in the country. In those days spring brought all those happy, impractical hopes for the future... Now it brings nothing but sad memories and helpless, impossible longings... Ah, old age is no joy!

This evening, to my great delight, L.N. gave me *Hadji Murat*, his story about the Caucasus, to copy. I copied with great enthusiasm, despite the pain in my arm, until Sergeenko came in and interrupted me. Then Dunaev and Uncle Kostya came, and my brother Sasha, and Seryozha. We had a long talk about government affairs, and this new fleet of ships it has bought for 90 million rubles. Sergeenko told us the Japanese had ordered these ships from Britain for 130 million, but the Japanese couldn't pay on time as the money was held by the Chinese-Russian Bank, which delayed in releasing it. So the contract lapsed, and the Russian government then offered 90 million, and with that they bought an entire fleet from the British.

14th March. I can't remember a thing, just more long sleepless nights. One night I sat up happily copying *Hadji Murat* for L.N. until 4.30 in the morning. The past few days I have either stayed at home working and proofreading, or gone out shopping for summer clothes. L.N. writes endless letters, which he finds a great strain, and reads a lot. He hadn't been so gentle and affectionate with me for a long time, then the other day his voice suddenly changed. I was terribly busy with the proofs for Volume 15. I had been working all day, and hadn't been attentive to his mood. I went on working that evening, with short rests (I had 12 printed pages to read), and as I knew my insomnia wouldn't let me sleep anyway, I asked my husband to go to bed without me, then got undressed, put on my dressing gown and slippers and promised to come in quietly as soon as I had finished. L.N. threw a tantrum: go to bed, he said, and let that be the end of it. Well, my work had to be done urgently – it had to be sent to the printers that morning – so I didn't pay him any attention and went on working. An hour and a half later he came in and started shouting at me: I was torturing him, he said, he had a headache and he wanted to sleep and I wasn't letting him. I sat there and patiently heard him out, then went into the bedroom (I had been sitting in the dining room, which is next to it), and went to bed without finishing the last page. But there my nerves snapped. All that hard work, that unpleasant scene, and most of all my husband's unfairness to me, produced such feelings of despair in my suffering soul that I felt a terrible spasm in my heart and chest, and barely managed to say "I am dying" into the darkness, before I started to choke. My heart was pounding. I had spasms in my chest and a feeling of utter horror, as though my life had stopped. I have never before had such an attack. I splashed cold water on my heart and made enormous efforts to control myself, which helped me eventually to stop the attack. Lev Nikolaevich was beside himself and began to shudder and sob... We slept badly, for we were both exhausted... But why, oh why should these things happen! Lord help me care for my husband and be patient to the end... The following morning I went to him and said I was sorry about what had happened. He seemed to apologize, and the peace was restored. But will it last?

Yesterday S.I. Taneev came, and his presence had an immediately soothing effect on me. He is such a calm, kind, even-tempered, gifted man. He played us his lovely symphony and asked Lev Nikolaevich for his opinion of it. L.N. considered the question with great seriousness and respect, then expounded his views: namely, that his symphony, as all modern music, was completely lacking in consistency, in either the melody, rhythm or harmony. The moment you began to follow the melody it stopped short, the moment you mastered one rhythm it jumped into another, so you felt constantly dissatisfied. Whereas in a genuine work of art you feel it could not be otherwise; one thing flows from another, and you think to yourself: "Why, I would have done it just like that." Sergei Ivanovich listened attentively and respectfully to what he had to say, but was obviously mortified that L.N. hadn't liked it. Today he is going to St Petersburg, where his symphony will be performed by an orchestra.

Yesterday morning I got up feeling exhausted after our argument the night before. Then L.N. brought my grandson Misha in to me, and I was so pleased to see this pure, sweet, clever child. I spent the whole day with him; I took him to the Zoological Gardens, the toy shops, the cake shop and the Kremlin, and he was delighted by everything but surprised by nothing. So yesterday was God's reward for last night's unpleasant scene with my husband.

17th March. Yesterday I copied Lev Nikolaevich's letter 'Aid to the Dukhobors'. (They are now hoping to emigrate.) L.N. thinks the *St Petersburg Gazette* will publish it, but I'm sure they won't. He appeals for two kinds of aid: finding them a place to emigrate, and collecting money for this.* There are 10,000 of them – how much money will they need?

Still the same harsh winter weather. It was 10 degrees below freezing today, and very windy and cold, despite the sun.

18th March. Things were going well and we were on good terms. Then today I was reading the proofs of Lev Nikolaevich's 'Preface' to Carpenter's article 'Contemporary Science', when I suddenly realized it was all different, everything had been changed. I was astonished and hurt. When the *Northern Herald* took this article I begged L.N. to give me the *final* proofs, so I could send the *final* version off to be printed in Volume 15. I went to him and reproached him, quite mildly, for deceiving me, and he grew terribly angry. These arguments opened up old wounds and it was utterly unbearable. He had concealed these final proofs from me merely out of consideration for the *Northern Herald*'s profits, because he didn't want to delay its publication. It would have taken him just one day to make these corrections in my edition.

Many, many guests this evening – Belskaya and her daughter, Toliverova and her daughter, Maklakov and his sister, Varya Nagornova and Gorbunov. Toliverova, editor of the magazine *The Toy*, wants to publish a journal called the *Woman's Cause*, and the woman question was discussed. L.N. said that instead of speaking of women's inequality and oppression one should talk of *people's* inequality in general. And he said that if a woman raises this question herself there is something immodest, unwomanly and impertinent about it. I think he is right. It's not freedom we women want, but *help*. Help mainly in educating our sons, setting them on the right road to life, influencing them to be brave, independent, hard-working and honest. A mother cannot educate her sons all on her own, and the reason the younger generation is no good is because their fathers are no good. They are too lazy to educate their own sons, and would gladly throw themselves into anything that lets them avoid their most important duty – educating the future generation, which must go forward and continue humanity's work.

2nd April. Two weeks have passed since I last wrote my diary!

Tomorrow is the day appointed by the anonymous letter for Lev Nikolaevich's murder. I am worried of course, but I don't really believe it. Two Dukhobors came to see L.N., strapping peasants, strong in body and soul. We told them to go and see Suvorin and Prince Ukhtomsky in St Petersburg, so that these two influential newspaper editors can give them advice and help. They have promised to do so, but it's unlikely they will. These two Dukhobors are now sitting with L.N., along with a young factory worker called Bulakhov who is being sent with the petition and 300 rubles to Verigin, their exiled leader.

I spent four days in St Petersburg. Ever since autumn I had the fixed idea of going there to hear Taneev's symphony – which he played several times for me on the piano – performed by an orchestra. I thought it would be magnificent. I had also dreamt of hearing some Wagner, as there was a visiting German opera company performing him in St Petersburg at the time. At first L.N. refused to let me go, which resulted in depression, sleepless nights and apathy. Then he agreed to release me, but the trip was no pleasure. It rained incessantly; Taneev's symphony was atrociously performed and conducted by Glazunov, I didn't hear any Wagner, and life with my sister Elizaveta, who is on bad terms with her husband and servants, and is interested only in the management of Russia's financial affairs (a strange interest indeed for a woman), was so depressing, and the whole trip was so unsuccessful that I was delighted to get back to L.N. and my life in this house, which is at least free in spirit, and I shan't be in a hurry to leave again.

The floor-polishers were here all day and the locks were cleaned. Noise, visitors, Dukhobors. Sulerzhitsky is here; the children are outside in the sunny garden playing muskets; Sasha is singing with the Friedman children and thumping out dance tunes on the piano; L.N. is chatting with the Dukhobors, and composing a long petition to the Tsar which I have been copying. These past few days I have been making clothes for L.N. I embroidered his handkerchiefs in satin stitch, made him a new shirt and am about to make him some trousers. When my friends asked me why I have "collapsed" and become so silent and sad, I reply: "Look at my husband, that is the reason he is so cheerful and energetic."

3rd April. Well, the day is almost over, it's gone ten and there have been no attempts on L.N.'s life. This morning I cut out some trousers for him and stitched them on the machine. He then decided to go out for a walk, and I went with him so as not to stay at home worrying.

My whole life passes in a way that's not to my liking. L.N.'s life and interests are so particular, so personal, they just don't concern his children. They can't interest themselves in sectarians and Dukhobors, or the renunciation of art or ideas about non-resistance. They need their own personal life. And since they have no leader in their father, no ideals within their grasp, they create this undisciplined life, with card games, idleness and entertainments, rather than serious work or art. I have neither the strength nor the skill to make a better life for them – and I doubt it would be possible anyway, with a father who renounces *everything*!

6th April, Easter Monday. I spent the whole day with the children. I went to the fair with Sasha, Verochka the maid and the Litvinov and Kolokoltsev children, and we watched the marionettes and the theatre, and went on the toboggans and merry-go-rounds. After dinner we rolled eggs. The children had a lovely day. Tanya is ill, with a fever and a swollen cheek. We had a letter from Masha. The boys paid some calls. After dinner Varya Nagornova and I played Taneev's quartet as a duet; the more one studies his music the more one loves it – and him, for his profound and noble soul.

10th April. I should go mad if I had to live like Lev Nikolaevich. He writes all morning and wears himself out mentally, and all evening he talks non-stop, or rather preaches, as his listeners generally come to him for advice or instruction.

There were thirteen people here after dinner today – two factory workers, three young schoolteachers, a lady studying the market for Russian handicrafts in England, a doctor, a correspondent for the *Messenger*, Sergeenko, Dunaev and various others.

Seryozha came today and sat down at the piano to compose a piece of music. Tanya is not well: her cheek is swollen and she has a stomach ache. Andryusha left yesterday. It rained all day. I visited the sales again and bought some furnishing material. At home I attended to *business* – accounts, banking matters, all the bookkeeping for my trusteeship of the children, letter-writing, etc. I didn't touch music or my story* all day.

There were moments today when the familiar grief welled up in my soul – it is still with me, after all these years I have still not really recovered from it.

15th April. I did various jobs in town – took things to be mended and altered, left books to be bound, etc. This evening we had a visit from young Prince Trubetskoy, a sculptor born and educated in Italy. An extraordinary young man, exceptionally talented, but utterly primitive. He hasn't read a thing, doesn't even know *War and Peace*, hasn't studied anywhere – he is naive, rough and totally engrossed in his art. He is coming here tomorrow to start on a sculpture of Lev Nikolaevich and will dine with us.

Sergei Ivanovich came, and it was all wonderfully straightforward and natural. He talked in my room with Seryozha about some musical translation, and Seryozha was asking him various questions.*

L.N. announced today that he was leaving for the country to see Ilyusha the day after tomorrow, that it was a great strain for him to live in town and that he had 1,400 rubles he wanted to give to the needy. It was all perfectly reasonable of him, but I felt so wretched at the thought of living here on my own with horrid Sasha, and Misha, who is never here, that I burst into tears and pleaded with him not to leave yet and to stay just one more week. If only he knew how fragile my soul is, how terrified I am of myself; I am terrified of suicide, despair, my desire to be entertained... Everything *terrifies* me, and mainly I terrify myself... I don't know whether he'll listen to my entreaties. He is always insisting that he only lives in Moscow *for my sake*, and that it's torture for him! Which is to say I torture him. Yet he is far gloomier in Yasnaya Polyana, and I know that despite what he says he actually finds city life very interesting and entertaining and it only occasionally tires him.

16th April. Lev Nikolaevich was sculpted today by Prince Trubetskoy, who has come from Italy and is in fact an Italian citizen. He is apparently considered a very good sculptor. Nothing visible so far. He has made a start on a huge bust. L.N. is being kind to me again and we are on good terms. Yesterday evening my nerves were in a terrible state – almost abnormal.

18th April. Lyova has come. He has decided to sell the house* through some broker, without consulting me in advance. Any sort of trouble or change terrifies me at present. And I am very sorry about this house, as I had reserved it for myself, and shall now be left almost penniless, with money owing on the new edition. It would cost me a great deal to buy this house too – almost 58,000 rubles. Trubetskoy has done more work on his sculpture of Lev Nikolaevich, and I can now see how exceptionally talented he is.

19th April. Tanya had an extremely painful operation on her nose. They pulled out a tooth and got through the opening to her nose to let out the pus. She is now very ill, weak and pale. I feel so sorry for her and long to stroke her, comfort her and kiss her, but one never does, and just feels wretched instead. I dismissed Mlle Aubert today and hired a new governess for Sasha, who is much quieter already. Trubetskoy is still working on his bust of Lev Nikolaevich, and it's extremely good – majestic, distinctive and lifelike.

We had a visit from S.T. Morozov, an ailing merchant who has just finished a course at the university and wants to lead a better life. He gave Lev Nikolaevich 1,000 rubles for the starving peasants. On Wednesday I am going with L.N. to visit Ilya at Grinevka, where L.N. will stay and help the poverty-stricken peasants in the surrounding countryside.

21st April. L.N. and I were going to leave for Nikolskoe and Grinevka yesterday to see our sons, and I was so excited by it all – the trip, the spring and our grandchildren. But we decided to postpone it again until tomorrow evening, as Trubetskoy hadn't finished his bust and it was so good it seemed a pity not to let him do so. He has caught perfectly the tilt of the head, the expression of the eyes and body – it is beautifully and expressively conceived, although I am disturbed by that unfinished quality the sculptor is so pleased about. Lev Nikolaevich is in a great hurry to leave, as he has 2,000 rubles in charitable donations, which he wants to give to the peasants in the most poverty-stricken areas.

I visited the notary and the bank this morning, and when I got back I packed my things and my husband's. (I had laid in a good stock of vegetarian supplies, bread and so on.) Sergei Ivanovich called this evening, and L.N. and he had a fascinating and very lively conversation in which Trubetskoy also took part. They talked about art and the Conservatoire, about how short life is and how best to make use of one's time so as to spend each moment profitably – for work, service, people (I put that in myself) and happiness. I was delighted to see that L.N. no longer treated this marvellous man as an enemy.

29th April. Trubetskoy finished his bust of Lev Nikolaevich on the 23rd, and it is excellent. That evening L.N. and I left for Grinevka. We travelled first class; it was very crowded. That evening on the train I heated up some porridge for L.N. that I had brought ready-cooked. First he said he would do it himself and grabbed the hot saucepan lid, burning his fingers. I offered to get him some water to ease the pain and he stubbornly refused. But without saying anything I bought him a mug of water anyway, and the moment he dipped in his fingers he felt better. But it meant he slept badly that night.

In Grinevka we were met by our sons Ilya and Andryusha on horseback, and by our grandchildren Annochka and Misha, who were on foot. It was delightful to see them again and arrive in their village. L.N. set to work at once. He travelled round the villages making enquiries about the famine. It is worst of all in Nikolskoe and the Mtsensk district. They eat bread there once a day and that's not enough, and the cattle have either been sold or eaten or are frightfully thin. There is no disease. L.N. is organizing canteens.* We sent Andryusha off to Oryol to discover the price of bread. We walked around Grinevka a lot. I read some French with Annochka, sewed for the boys, looked after all four children and did some painting and drawing with them. I also had to keep an eye on their atrocious cook to make sure he didn't prepare anything too horrible for Lev Nikolaevich. But Ilya and Sonya's housekeeping is so wretchedly meagre and inadequate. *I* don't mind, but I am afraid Lev Nikolaevich's stomach won't tolerate the bad food and he'll fall ill.

I didn't at all like Ilya's behaviour at home. He takes no interest in the children, he is rude to the peasants, he has no serious interests and cares for nothing but horses. Sonya on the other hand is kind to the peasants, gives them medical treatment and takes the trouble to see they are properly fed, and distributes flour and buckwheat to the women and children.

We also visited our son Seryozha in Nikolskoe. He is still wretchedly miserable. He keeps busy with his music and has written a lovely song, which Sonya sang very sweetly for us with her attractive young voice.

L.N. wasn't in a happy state. There was something dispirited and despondent about our relations, which saddened me very much. And I couldn't have been gentler or more attentive to him.

I was sorry to have to leave him in Grinevka. But then perhaps it's better for us to part for a while!

On my way back to Moscow I stopped briefly at Yasnaya Polyana, and after Grinevka I was in ecstasies over the beauty of the Yasnaya countryside. I dashed about the garden and woods, picking lungwort and planting saplings in the park, then I tidied the house and prepared a room for Lev Nikolaevich.

On the 28th, yesterday, there was the first thunderstorm and the first cuckoo. The trees are turning green, and there is cheerful hard work on all sides, planting the kitchen garden, digging round the apple trees and clearing the orchards. Dora and Lyova were friendly and cheerful. She is a lovely woman, cultured and even-tempered. They too are digging their newly laid-out little garden and decorating the house, in readiness for her confinement and the arrival of her parents.

I returned to Moscow this morning... and am wretched here. Sergei Nikolaevich came with his daughter Masha. Lyovochka will be sorry to have missed his brother.

1st May. I didn't write yesterday, my life is empty. This morning a pupil from the 1st Gymnasium called Veselkin brought round 18 rubles and 50 kopecks, which his comrades had collected to give to the starving. These contributions from young souls and poor people move one to tears. Then Brashnin's widow brought 203 rubles, and a woman called Kopteva from Zurich sent me another 200. I am sending it all on to Lev Nikolaevich.

I had a letter today from Sonya saying that L.N. was fit and well and was continuing to travel around visiting the needy, but I still haven't had a word from him. My warm feelings for him are again beginning to cool. I have written him two letters, filled with sincere love and expressing my desire for spiritual closeness, and he hasn't written me so much as a word!

5th May. I had two letters from L.N. today. He is cheerful and well, thank God. He says he has opened eight canteens and has no more money. It always seemed to me that it was enough to feed one or two people – not several hundred. But today nine canteens suddenly seemed so paltry when one thinks of all the millions of poor people. We haven't appealed for money, as L.N. isn't strong enough to do all the work, but if we did, people would certainly send us a lot.

10th May. This morning I read proofs, then went to collect theatre tickets, then on to the Dunaevs' to try to find an assistant for Lev Nikolaevich in his famine work. They suggested Strakhov, who would be excellent. Today I read Chertkov's letter to L.N. The whole letter is unnatural – all the same old arguments about the struggle with the flesh, money and the sin of possessing it, but the fact is he is in debt all over the place, and is asking Tanya for a loan of 10,000 rubles.*

It's such *hypocrisy, that's* what I can't endure. Which of us does *not* struggle with our passions? And what a struggle it is too! Sometimes you feel it is draining you of all your strength, and you have none left. What sort of passions do they have anyway? They're all so dull and austere... Besides, if you have passions you should keep quiet about them, not perpetually shout about them.

This evening I went to the theatre with Seryozha, Andryusha and Sasha to see a benefit performance of *Der Freischütz*, which the Conservatoire students had put on to raise money for the starving. I was sitting in the second row of the stalls, the same row as Sergei Ivanovich.

19th May (Yasnaya Polyana). A lot of coming and going these last few days. I packed up and moved the whole house, Sasha, and her new Swiss governess, Mlle Kothing, to Yasnaya. The servants all left Moscow on 15th May, and Sasha and I arrived at the empty Yasnaya house on the morning of the 16th. This is the second year I have come here like this! The horses, the cow, the grand piano and the boxes arrived later the same day, and we all threw ourselves into unpacking and tidying up; we had dinner and supper with Lyova and Dora, who made us very welcome. I was off again to Grinevka to see Lev Nikolaevich on the morning of the 17th, and was delighted to see him and my children and grandchildren. But my warm feelings are always drowned in cold water. When I arrived, Lev Nikolaevich had some sectarian sitting with him to whom he was reading his article.

My arrival interrupted him, and he was slightly cross about this, although he tried hard not to show it. I went out for a long walk in the garden with my darling little grandsons Misha and Andryusha, and we wandered all over the place while I told them nature stories about the flowers, the apple trees and the insects. I enjoyed myself with them for about three hours, and after dinner I again went in to see Lev Nikolaevich. The sectarian was with him again, this time reciting some long verses of a spiritual nature which had been composed for sectarians to sing, and once again L.N. irritably sent me packing. I left the room and burst into tears. We hadn't seen each other for nearly three weeks; our life in Moscow, our children, Misha's exams, Tanya – none of it means a thing to him. When he realized I was upset he came looking for me and excused himself with some embarrassment.

We all had tea on the terrace together this evening, then set off to the station to meet Dora's parents, who didn't arrive till late at night.

L.N. wasn't very well at Grinevka, and had a high backache and heartburn. He was better today though. He is working hard to develop his muscles, doing gymnastics with his dumb-bells, swimming in the pond and washing on the bank. He eats so poorly and so little – then grumbles and panics and groans, wraps himself in his quilted dressing gown and talks about death, which terrifies him.

It's fine and cool, especially at night. A bright moon in a clear sky, dry and dusty again – we'll have another bad harvest!

A telegram from Tanya to say she is arriving tomorrow. Misha continues to pass his exams, thank God! I shall go and see him the day after tomorrow.

20th May. What a dazzling, beautiful spring! Fine sunny days, bright moonlit nights, the lilacs, extraordinarily thick and white this year, drifting apple blossom, nightingales... It enchants and intoxicates us, we try to grasp these fleeting impressions of the beauty of spring, and regret them eternally.

Dora's dear kind parents, the Westerlunds, arrived yesterday. How pleased she was to see them, the dear little girl with her big stomach, her domestic worries and her concern for their comfort.

My Tanya came this morning looking pale and listless, talking of nothing but love, her desire to have children and the difficulties of being unmarried.

I feel comfortable and happy with her. We know each other through and through, and love and understand each other.

A still moonlit night. The days are hot again, and the nights warm. I reread the life and teachings of Socrates with new understanding. All great people are alike: their genius is a deformity, an infirmity, because it is exceptional. There is no harmony in people of genius, and their unbalanced characters are a torment to others.

22nd May. I arrived in Moscow this morning.

25th May. Whit Sunday. Misha has gone to the Martynovs. He has passed his exams – just. I went with Nurse to Nikolskoe to visit the graves of Alyosha and Vanechka. We planted flowers and edged them with turf. I then said the Lord's Prayer, and silently begged my infants to pray to God to forgive my sick and sinful soul.

It was a bright cheerful day, and the peasants were in a festive mood. A little girl took me to a nearby convent, where I chatted with the nuns. One of them said she had been "in love with Christ" from an early age, and was possessed by the notion that she should remain in every way the "bride of Christ" and of no one else.

There was absolutely no "atmosphere" about this place, with its neatly laid-out little garden, the peasants, and the countryside and dachas near by. We returned to Moscow late that evening.

26th, 27th, 28th, 29th May. Proofs, solitude, sadness. I was playing the piano in the corner room one evening, longing to see Sergei Ivanovich again and hear him play, when through the window I saw three figures approaching. I didn't recognize them at first, then saw to my amazement that it was Maslov, Taneev's pupil Yusha Pomerantsev and Taneev himself. Maslov left first, and Yusha played to me. Then Sergei Ivanovich played his songs, and he and Yusha played his quartet as a piano duet.

30th May. Speech day at the Conservatoire. A hot, sunny day. A Schumann sonata, the Saint-Saëns piano concerto and various minor pieces were beautifully performed by the women students Friedman, Bessy and young Gediker, and gave me enormous pleasure. There wasn't a single person who didn't come up to me afterwards and say: "How young you look today!" or "Oh, you look so fresh!" or "It makes one cheerful just to look at you…" This was largely thanks to my new pale-lilac muslin dress. But I always find it very pleasant, I am ashamed to say, when the public comment on my youthful appearance and say friendly things to me.

I arrived home and went out on to the balcony, and who should I see but Sergei Ivanovich, sitting on a bench in the garden reading the newspaper. I was terribly pleased. Dinner had been laid in the garden for Misha and me, and they laid a third place for him. And what a nice cheerful dinner we had. We were all hungry, and it was delightfully cosy and fresh outside! After dinner the three of us strolled around the garden together. Sergei Ivanovich told us stories about the Caucasus, and Misha, who was leaving the next day, was fascinated. Misha went off and left the two of us together, and we drank tea and Sergei Ivanovich played me some variations composed by Kolya Zhilyaev, a pupil of his. Then we sat and talked, as people talk when they trust each other completely – frankly, seriously, without shyness or stupid jokes. We talked only of things that genuinely interested us, and there wasn't a dull or awkward moment.

What an evening it was! It was my last in Moscow – and perhaps the last such evening in my life.

At nine o' clock he stood up to go and I didn't hold him back. He took his leave, merely saying wistfully: "One has to go some time." I didn't reply – I wanted to cry. I saw him to the door, then went out to the garden. Then I packed, tidied and locked up, and at midnight we set off for Yasnaya.

31st May. A dismal reception at Yasnaya this morning. No Tanya, no Lev Nikolaevich, just three telegrams announcing that he was ill and was staying with the Levitskys!

1st June. Lev Nikolaevich didn't return. I wept all day, then feeling quite ill I set off with Maria Schmidt first for Tula, via Kozlovka, then took the Syzran-Vyazma line train to Karasei, where I arrived early this morning, hired a coach and went straight to the Levitskys. Lev Nikolaevich was very ill and weak, and it was unthinkable that he should go home.

2nd, 3rd, 4th, 5th June (at the Levitskys). A wonderful family, busy, liberal in a good sense, him especially – a clever, strong-minded man.

It's hard nursing and caring for L.N. and cooking his complicated vegetarian diet in a strange house. I sent for the doctor, and we gave him bismuth with opium and applied compresses. It was dreary, cold and exasperating. Lev Nikolaevich was already ill when he left. What sort of folly is this? He should be ashamed of making a nuisance of himself in another person's house, making a lot of complicated and outlandish demands for things like almond milk, rusks, porridge oats, special bread and so on.

6th June. When we returned to Yasnaya I had a bad cough and felt weak and exhausted from looking after him.

We spent the night at the house of the Ershovs, who weren't at home. A dreadful thing has happened! A young woman called Tulubyova (born Ershova) threw herself into the river there in a fit of depression and drowned herself. I envied her courage. Life is very hard.

8th June. At 12.45 today Dora gave birth to a son. How she suffered, poor girl, how she pleaded with her father in her guttural young voice to give her something. Lyova was very gentle with her and reassured her, and she was so sweet and loving with him, pressing herself close to him as if begging him to share her suffering. And he did, and so little Lev was born, a normal, healthy birth.

11th June. I had the grand piano moved into Tanya's studio and played for three hours today and wept bitterly, overcome with a helpless desire to hear Sergei Ivanovich's music once more. How happy those two summers* were after the death of Vanechka! To think that after such a frightful tragedy I should have been sent such a consolation! I thank the Lord for that joy.

12th June. I was wondering today why there were no women writers, artists or composers of genius. It's because all the passion and abilities of an energetic woman are consumed by her family, love, her husband – and especially her children. Her other abilities are not developed, they remain embryonic and atrophy. When she has finished bearing and educating her children her artistic needs awaken, but by then it's too late, and it's impossible to develop anything.

Young girls often develop spiritual and artistic powers, but these powers remain isolated and cannot be carried on by subsequent generations, since girls do not create posterity. Geniuses often have older mothers, who developed their talents early in life, and Lev Nikolaevich is one of these; his mother was no longer young when she married and had him.

14th June. I spent the day with my children. My grandson Lev was christened at 1 o' clock. Dora was very agitated, and the Swedish grandparents were horrified by our primitive Russian christening ceremony.

We dined very grandly in the garden, with fruit, bunches of flowers and champagne on the table, and the weather was lovely and sunny. Then everyone played tennis, including L.N. He is not flagging, and his health is completely restored, thank God. Masha and Kolya left this evening, and Ilya left with Misha, whom I was terribly sorry to part with. Yet the feeling that *he isn't mine*, that loving him will bring nothing but sorrow, makes me afraid to love him, and I deliberately withdraw from him.

18th June. Sasha's 14th birthday. An unbearably hot day – 40 degrees in the sun at 2 this afternoon. L.N. is still ill, with bad heartburn and a temperature of 38.3. This evening he improved a little and his temperature dropped to 37.5; he ate two plates of porridge and drank some coffee.

I raced down to the Voronka with Sasha for a swim. It was a wonderful evening, and I couldn't stop gazing at the glorious countryside, the sky and the moon.

When I got home I found L.N. dictating a newspaper article to Tanya, which they subsequently decided not to send. Then 6 girls and boys, gymnasium pupils from Kharkov, arrived at Yasnaya with 100 rubles which they wanted to give to the needy peasants. L.N. sent them to the priest, who is the guardian of this area, and the man told them which peasants were the poorest. The girls and boys then went to Yasenki to buy flour to give to the poor peasants. But the sergeant and the district police officer appeared and strictly forbade the Yasenki merchant to supply flour to the peasants in exchange for the credit notes we had given them. It's outrageous! Let no one in Russia give alms to the poor – the police won't allow it! Tanya and I were deeply distressed, and would willingly have gone straight to the Tsar or his mother and warned them against the anger that may arise in the people.

20th June. Lev Nikolaevich is still ill. He has only a slight fever, 37.8, but is burning hot and still very thin and weak. His stomach aches only when he moves or puts pressure on it. Last night I massaged it for a long time with camphor oil, then we applied spirit of camphor compresses and I gave him some bismuth with soda and morphine. He ate a plate of porridge today, some rice gruel made with half almond milk and half ordinary milk (without telling him), and

Doctor Westerlund finally, after three days, managed to persuade him to eat an egg.

The district police officer was here enquiring about the Kharkov schoolgirls and boys who came here wanting to help the peasants and work with them. They have all disappeared without trace, but two more little girls, one of whom was only 13 years old, arrived here today with the same purpose. They have all been banished from the district, and I gave the officer a piece of my mind for forbidding the merchant at to sell them flour. The priest had ordered that it should be given to the poorest inhabitants of our area, and it is already paid for.

I read four pages of proofs. My eyes are growing weaker.

21st June. What with all these illnesses and anxieties I have made a terrible mess of Volume 15 of the 9th expensive edition; I am very worried about it and cannot think how to extricate myself. I forgot that what stands as the appendix to Volume 13 wasn't included in the expensive edition, and I went straight into Volume 14 without including it. Now I shall have to add it at the end, regardless of chronological sequence. I have too much to hold in my head. It's all right so long as everything else is going well. But "even the old woman has a blunder up her sleeve", as the saying goes, and I really have blundered this time. And it's all because of Lev Nikolaevich being ill, and having to travel all over the place to nurse him.

There's an eclipse of the moon, which I can see through the window... It's already moving away...

22nd June. Peasant women have been at the porch all day begging for flour, money, a bit of bread to eat, a little tea, medicine, and so on. I try patiently to give them what they want, but I'm exhausted. It's impossible to help them. I spent the whole day running up and down the stairs, looking after Lev Nikolaevich and attending to business, and by this evening I was half dead. As I massaged L.N.'s stomach I was dreaming of the sea and rocks and mountains of Norway, where we have been invited to stay with the Westerlunds, who are leaving tomorrow.

26th June. I spent an extremely difficult afternoon yesterday. Our young neighbour Bibikov has appropriated the land we bought from his father, and we now have to defend ourselves, and the court case has started. Yesterday they had to collect all the local witnesses, but the only witnesses called were from the village of Telyatinki, which belongs to Bibikov. It was quite obvious that the witnesses, the judge and the land-surveyor had all been bribed and feasted by Bibikov yesterday, and the whole case was conducted in the most corrupt fashion. At first I was distressed, then utterly bewildered: the judge, the questioning, the oath – it was all chicanery, from beginning to end.

I stayed out of curiosity though, sitting until late that night in the village elder's cottage. Everyone, judge and peasants, seemed to grow rather confused and subdued towards the end of the twelve peasants' interrogation: we were obviously in the right.*

Afterwards I wrote a petition to the Tula court asking them to set boundaries to the estate, otherwise the peasants will simply appropriate more and more of our land each year.

The night is still, and the moon is shining through the open window. I love being alone at night with my thoughts, in spiritual communication with my loved ones who are absent or dead.

27th June. This thundery atmosphere is insufferable; we are quite debilitated by the heat and electricity in the air. L.N. has a stomach ache again. My God! Help me not to grumble, and to bear my responsibilities to the end with patience and dignity.

I gave him a bath today, ran it myself and tested the water with the thermometer. I then laid tea in the drawing room and he brightened up. I very much wanted to visit Seryozha tomorrow for his birthday, but couldn't bring myself to leave my husband. I tried to take my grandson's photograph, but he fell asleep, and then the thunderstorm made it impossible. I practised my Bach Inventions, but only managed to play for an hour. Sick peasant women, work, business. I wrote a letter to some peasant at L.N.'s request.

Westerlund said I spoilt my husband terribly. I was astounded today by something L.N. wrote in his notebook concerning women: "If a woman is not a Christian she is an animal."* That means that throughout my life I have sacrificed all my personal life to him and suppressed my own desires – even a visit to my son, today – and all my husband can see is animal behaviour.

The real animals are those men who through their own egotism consume the lives of their wives, children, friends – everyone who crosses their path.

28th June. Misha has returned from the Caucasus in ecstasy over his trip, the magnificent scenery, the friendliness of the people and all the parties they organized for him and Andryusha. He arrived with my brother Sasha, looking manlier and uglier than ever.

L.N. is looking very pinched, thin and subdued.

He regarded Doctor Westerlund as a bourgeois, dull-witted German peasant, whose medical thinking was 30 years behind the times. He didn't see the doctor's goodness, his self-sacrificing life in the service of humanity, his eagerness to help every peasant woman and anyone he met, his concern for his wife and daughter, his unselfishness...

1st July. Annenkova came today and we went to Ovsyannikovo. We called first on Maria Schmidt. She has a large portrait of Lev Nikolaevich over her bed. She has a fanatical faith in his ideas and is in love with him as only a woman can be, and this gives her the strength to endure her austere, hard-working life. Without that she would have died long ago, so weak is her organism. I love her ardent nature.

6th July. Rain, cold; Tanya is in bed with a stomach ache. I strolled round the garden and picked a lovely bunch of flowers for her. I played the piano for about two and a half hours, but badly. I corrected proofs all day. I have a lot of running about to do and a mass of petty, boring matters: sending documents to the council, paying the servants' wages, buying mushrooms and raspberries, tending the sick, giving food to the beggars, ordering dinner and supper, keeping Dora and my grandson company, giving the servant girls their work for the day. I should do some copying for Lev Nikolaevich, but there's a pile of proofs to do first. And I have to look after Tanya, who stubbornly refuses to take any medicine.

12th July. I left the house to make some visits, and called first on my daughter Masha. It pierced my heart to see her, so bent, weak and nervous, tearful and thin as a skeleton. It is such an impoverished life, and the food there is disgusting.

16th July, Kiev. A warm welcome from my sister Tanya and her family, the Kuzminskys. They have a pretty, well-appointed little dacha, her sweet boys were there, and Sasha the cordial host, and my beloved, my dear, sweet beloved sister. The sight of little Mitechka tore at my heart: he was the same age as Vanechka, his first friend, his first childhood comrade. And Mitya is already a big boy of ten – and Vanechka is gone!

I went for a walk in the Kitaev forest, through ancient pines and old oaks, past hills and monasteries... Sasha, Vera, Mitya and little Volodka came too. We went swimming in the pool of a monastery, drank tea and rambled in the hills. It's so pleasant being a guest, everything is new, there's nothing to worry about.

17th, 18th, 19th, 20th July. I have spent the past four days with the Kuzminskys. We had a picnic with some other dacha folk on an island in the river Dnieper, went to the peasant theatre in Kitaev and swam in the Dnieper. On the 20th I went to Kiev with Tanya and we visited the cathedral. The best painting there was *The Raising of Lazarus*, by Svedomsky. Vasnetsov's paintings – especially the *Baptism of Vladimir and the People* – were beneath criticism: one was amazed by the complete lack of formal elegance. Eve's legs, for instance, when she is being tempted by the serpent in Paradise, are frightful.

The monument to Vladimir stands in a charming place, with a lovely view over the Dnieper below. Ancient monuments are generally so much better than the modern ones, like that hideous statue of Pirogov in Deviche Pole in Moscow.

We also visited the caves in Kiev. I forced myself to go this time, but felt nervous as soon as we had walked a little way down that airless underground passage, illuminated only by the candles we held in our hands. It was impossible to turn back, and it suddenly came into my mind that the devil was obstructing my path. And just then the monk who was leading us said to me: "No need to be afraid, Mother! Why, people used to live here, and you're afraid to walk through. This is a church, so pray!" I mechanically crossed myself and repeated the words of a prayer, and my fear vanished and I walked on fascinated. It was extraordinary to see those little round windows in the walled-up cave rooms where the holy men used to immure themselves. People would hand them food through the windows once a day, and there they would die, in these cells, these living coffins.

My sister's family made a good impression on me; I envied the fact that Sasha was so concerned about his sons and was on such good terms with them. Tanya's and her husband's concern for each other was also very touching.

I persuaded her to accompany me back to Yasnaya, to my great joy.

22nd, 23rd, 24th, 25th July. Early in the morning of the 22nd my sister Tanya and I arrived in Tula. It was cold and wet and they hadn't sent horses for us, so we hired a cab and drove back. Then the trouble started – a whole series of unpleasant remarks from L.N. about my meeting with Sergei Ivanovich in Moscow on the way to Kiev. Yet I had asked him before I left whether he would mind, and said I wouldn't go if he did. I had leant over him to say goodbye, kissed him while he was still half-asleep, and put it to him quite candidly. And he snapped back ironically: "Why should I mind? By all means go," adding: "It's your business anyway."

There is a huge wall painting at the threshold to the cave in Kiev, depicting the ordeals to which St Theodora is subjected. The pictures alternate: two angels, with the soul of Theodora as a young girl dressed in a white robe, followed by a group of devils in inconceivably hideous poses. And these devils, forty groups of them, portray the forty sins, which are inscribed in Old Church Slavonic beneath. I suppose L.N. is cursing me for committing all the forty sins in those three or four days.

28th July. I took Tanya to Yasenki and she left for Kiev, apparently happy with her stay in Yasnaya. We have grown even closer, if that's possible. I feel bereft – I have no one to cling to now.

I walked through the forest alone, swam and wept. Late that night we resumed our discussion about jealousy, with yet more shouting, cursing and recriminations. Suddenly my nerves snapped. Some valve maintaining the equilibrium in my brain flew open. I lost all self-control and had the most terrible nervous attack. I was terrified, shaking, sobbing and raving. I don't remember what happened to me, only that I ended up stiff with cold.

29th, 30th July. I have been lying in bed in a darkened room for the past day and a half, without food or light, without love, hate or emotions, just the deathly gloom of the grave. They all came in to see me but I didn't care about any of them. I just wanted to die.

I pushed the table a moment ago and Lev Nikolaevich's portrait fell on the floor, just as this diary of mine has pushed him off the pedestal he has spent his entire life erecting for himself.

3rd August. I spent yesterday and the day before industriously copying L.N.'s story *Father Sergei*, an artistic work written in a lofty style, excellently conceived although still unfinished.* It takes from the

Lives of the Saints the story of the saint who sought God and found Him in the most ordinary, lowly woman, who had sacrificed herself entirely to work and toil. In this story Father Sergei, a proud monk who has experienced all life's vicissitudes, finds God in Pashenka, a woman no longer young, whom he has known since childhood, who leads an industrious life in her old age and lives for her family.

There is some hypocrisy in the story though – the ending in Siberia. I hope it won't be left like that, for it really is very well devised and constructed.

I copied it from 1.30 to 5 a.m., by which time it was growing light and my head was spinning. But I finished the whole thing, so L.N. can start working on it the moment he gets up.

He wants to finish *Hadji Murat*, *Resurrection* and *Father Sergei* together, publish the 3 stories simultaneously and sell them for as much as possible in Russia and abroad, so he can use the profits to finance the Dukhobors' emigration scheme.*

This is an insult to us, his family: he would do better to help Ilyusha and Masha, who are both extremely poor. And two Dukhobors came here whom I had to hide in the pavilion, which was most unpleasant.*

Windy, dry, fine and beautiful.

I have been keeping Dora company and getting to know my little grandson Lev. I have lost that direct, almost animal passion for small children, and in my grandchildren I love only my *dreams* for the future and for the continuation of our life.

5th August. I copied L.N.'s essay on art yesterday: the same rejection of absolutely everything, all under the pretext of Christianity – it's pure socialism.

This morning I went to Tula, where I had a lot of business to attend to at the bank and the council, visiting the notary, looking for a teacher for Misha and going to the shops. I was so exhausted my legs were shaking. I was longing for a rest when I got home, but a huge crowd of guests unexpectedly arrived – Sergeenko, the two Dieterichs girls, my sister Liza with her daughter and governess, Zvegintseva with her daughter, Volkhonsky, Prince Cherkassky and his boys – and they all stayed to supper. My heart sank. Goldenweiser came for the evening too and played some Chopin. The music awakened that wonderful mood of elation which I have lived for these past two years.

A lot of noise and shouting and mindless youthful merriment. I am very tired. L.N. on the other hand is cheerful and excited; he enjoys guests and Misha Kuzminsky's balalaika and Princess Volkhonsky's chatter, and any sort of entertainment and diversion.

11th August. Bad news from the censors, who have seized the last volume of the expensive edition I have just had printed. It won't be passed unless I make a fuss. I have written to Solovyov, the chief censor, in St Petersburg.

19th August. I have been ill with a high fever and stomach pains. I stayed in bed until yesterday, and barely managed to get up even then. The time flashed past so quickly – I have only a dim memory of it. Everyone was very kind to me, looked after me, stayed with me constantly, anticipated all my needs and comforted me. There was one day when I thought I was dying but was quite happy about it. Now I am up again, back in life's whirlpool, with all its demands, griefs, worries and irresolvable questions that have to be resolved.

I am reading an interesting book called *Le Réveil de l'âme*. I also read Anatole France's *La Bûche* and *La Fille de Clémentine*. Being ill didn't bore me at all; I enjoyed the solitude, being able to concentrate on my thoughts, and the absence of material anxieties.

22nd August. My 54th birthday. Tanya, Masha and Sasha all gave me presents; Tanya and Sasha gave things they had made themselves, which was nice, but Masha bought me a little table, which I didn't like, for I know she has no money and it's a pity to waste it on things I don't need. But I suppose it was a kind thought. She is always ill, first her headaches, then her stomach, then something else... She thinks too much about her health – it's simply *neurasthenia*.

24th August. Windy, raining and cold. We all stayed indoors talking. Everyone is interested in this latest statement from the Tsar in favour of universal peace and disarmament. L.N. actually had a letter from the *World* in America, asking his opinion of it. So far it was only *words*, he said, first of all one had to abolish taxes, military service, and much more besides. I think many generations will need to be educated to hate war if it is to be eradicated.

Some Munich professor came to visit, a stocky red-faced German. Sulerzhitsky came here after seeing the Dukhobors, and is going on to England for more information. Meanwhile the Dukhobors, 7,000 of them, are living on the coast in Batumi in Georgia, waiting for a decision as to where they should go. And from whom? Why, from Chertkov* of course. It's an appalling, disgraceful situation.

26th, 27th August. I spent the whole day shopping in Tula with my sister-in-law Maria Nikolaevna, buying provisions, straw mattresses, crockery and so on for our guests.

More Dukhobors came; they are still waiting for something to happen, and hope for a favourable response to their petition from the Tsar, *and* help from Lev Nikolaevich. This is quite ridiculous, since help from one necessarily excludes help and sympathy from the other.

How the day of 28th August 1898 was spent. Today Lev Niko-laevich is 70 years old. I went in to greet him this morning while he was still in bed, and he looked so pleased, as though this was his own special day. All the family were here, with their wives and children. Altogether we had about forty people for dinner. P.V. Preobrazhensky started to drink Lev Nikolaevich's health in white wine, and made a clumsy toast which everyone deliberately ignored. One can hardly *drink* L.N.'s health, since he preaches total abstinence. Then someone proposed a toast to me, and in a unanimous, noisy show of affection they all raised their glasses to me, which agitated me so much that my heart started to pound. It was a very cheerful dinner, and was a completely *family* affair, which was just what we had wanted. L.N. was writing *Resurrection* all morning, and was very pleased with his day's work. "You know," he said when I went in to see him, "he doesn't marry her after all. I finished it today, or rather I decided that, and I know it's right!" And I said: "But of course he doesn't marry her! I always told you if he did it would just be *hypocrisy*."*

We received about a hundred telegrams from an enormous variety of people. This afternoon the sun came out and we took all the children, grandchildren and guests for a walk. Muromtseva sang at length, and was unpleasantly over-excited. Then Goldenweiser played the piano, very badly. More guests arrived for supper, but it remained just a simple, good-natured family party.

The day finished with singing – choruses and solo songs. We were all very tired, and the food and sleeping arrangements required a great deal of work...

29th August. The servants have been drinking and quarrelling. It is raining. Misha left for Moscow to resit an exam.

30th August. I received a clever, charming letter from Sergei Ivanovich this morning and showed it to Lev Nikolaevich, who thought the same. He writes that one doesn't have to be a follower of L.N. to be stirred by his works, for his ideas imperceptibly enter one's mind and remain there. Then, just an hour after I got his letter, Sergei Ivanovich himself arrived. This evening after a short nap, he played a game of chess with Lev Nikolaevich, then sat down at the piano. And how marvellously he played! Such depth, such intelligence, such seriousness and experience – it would be impossible to play better. Both L.N. and Mashenka were in ecstasies – and so of course was I. He played Schumann's *Davidsbündlertänze*, Beethoven's Sonata Op. 30, a Chopin Mazurka and Barcarolle, Rubinstein's '*Près d'un ruisseau*' and an aria by Arensky. Lev Nikolaevich said his performance was superb, no one could match Sergei Ivanovich's playing, he said. The following morning, the 31st, I fell ill with a fever. I looked at the thermometer and saw I had a temperature of 38.4. Sergei Ivanovich left that morning and I took to my bed. Lev Nikolaevich was touchingly anxious about me. My dear, sweet old man! Who else could ever love me or need me as much as he does? I was moved to tears as I thought of him, and lay in bed praying that God would prolong his precious life.

I was ill all day, so couldn't go to Moscow as I had intended, to visit Misha and do business.

1st September. I am better. It's a lovely warm day and there are masses of bright fragrant flowers in the garden… I am full of the joys of life again, and I love people and nature and the sun. I was deeply touched by the love everyone lavished on me, and rejoice in my recovery.

I went out with my camera and dashed about taking photographs of the park, my grandchildren, L.N. and his sister, the forest, the path to the swimming pool and the charming Yasnaya countryside…

This evening I quickly packed my things, made a note of all the errands I had to do and left for Moscow, carrying the bunches of flowers Sasha had given me. L.N. and Sasha took me to Kozlovka in the carriage. I was tired, tearful and overwrought; I bade Lyovochka a tender farewell, then Nurse and I got into the train. That night who should come into our compartment but Seryozha; he had gone back to Yasnaya to talk to his father, and is now leaving for England to discuss the Dukhobors' emigration. It seems from our correspondence that their plans are no further advanced, and we don't know how seriously Chertkov is dealing with it; there's so little money besides.

2nd September (Moscow). I arrived in Moscow this morning with Nurse. It was raining, the house was dark and gloomy and my soul was oppressed... I unpacked, hired a cab and went out shopping, and oh dear, I was so jolted and shaken! But by this afternoon the lights were on, the house was filled with flowers, I had cleaned and tidied everything and hired a piano. Misha came; he has passed the exam he was resitting, and is now going up to the 7th form, but I am sure he is keeping something from me. Things became more lively later on. My brother Sasha, Uncle Kostya, young Yusha Pomerantsev and Sergei Ivanovich came and we had a merry evening.

Sergei Ivanovich astonished me by something he said. He told me when I was at the Maslovs' this summer I had deeply offended him by laughing at his ugly white cycling socks, saying they made him look like a clown.

3rd September. More shopping and business... Seryozha was here and has now left for England... It keeps raining. No guests. Misha and I both went to the bathhouse.

4th September. I spent the day in my dressing gown going over the bills with the accountant, checking the sales of books and entering figures into ledgers; I didn't even take a walk. But Uncle Kostya came to dinner and prevented me from finishing, which was a nuisance, as it means I probably won't be able to leave for Yasnaya tomorrow and shall have to pay more calls instead.

I read my future in the cards today, and drew death on the king of clubs. I was terrified, and longed suddenly to be with Lyovochka, to make him happy, not to waste one moment of my life away from him. Yet when Sergei Ivanovich left, the thought that I wouldn't be seeing him again for some time made me wretched. And torn between these two conflicting emotions, I longed to run off somewhere and take my life. I stood alone in my room in a state of torment... Oh, if only one could see into a person's soul at such moments and *understand* what takes place there... But gradually suffering passed into prayer. I prayed long and earnestly, summoning up all my best thoughts, and began to feel better.

6th September. This morning I corrected one or two mistakes made yesterday in my calculations with the accountant, and left by the fast train. Home was friendly, peaceful and familiar, and I was glad to be back. I force myself to pray constantly, and rely on God to help me in my weakness.

A lot of Obolenskys are here – Liza and her three children.

12th September. Chaos at home. The footman has fallen in love with Sasha the dressmaker and is going to marry her. My maid Verochka, a mere baby of eighteen, is going to marry the bailiff on the 18th, and the cook has been taken to hospital. Ilya and Nurse are in Moscow. There has never been anything like it. Meanwhile a never-ending stream of guests keep arriving and staying. Today Maslov and Dunaev came.

This morning L.N. read us *Resurrection*, the novel he is currently working on. I had heard it before – he said he had reworked it, but it's still exactly the same. He read it to us three years ago, the summer after Vanechka's death. And then as now I was struck by the beauty of the incidental details and episodes, and the hypocrisy of the plot – Nekhlyudov's relationship with the prostitute in jail and the author's own attitude to her. It's just sentimentality, toying with strained, unnatural feelings that don't exist.

13th September. Rain all day and guests – an Englishman, a Mr Wright, I believe, and a stupid old maid called Ivanova who believes in spiritualism. These guests are a terrible burden imposed on our family, and especially on me. Only one thing interests me about them, the fact that they have been staying in England with Chertkov and the rest of the exiled Russian community. They found them in a bad way, and told us they couldn't stay there any longer, because of the emotional tensions between them and the general hardships of their life. L.N. has been at pains to keep this from me, but I always sensed it...

We went for a walk in the rain, which pours dismally without ceasing. I was about to play the piano, when I was startled by a frightful noise at the window; it was Lev Nikolaevich, summoning me to come and hear him read the end of his story. I was sorry to have to abandon the piano and the beautiful Bach aria I have been studying and learning to appreciate, but went all the same.

Music has a strange effect on me; even when I play myself it suddenly makes everything clear, fills me with peaceful joy and enables me to see all life's worries in a new light, calmly and lucidly.

Not at all the effect *Resurrection* has on me. Everything in it is disturbing and worrying, everything induces discord... It torments me that an old man of seventy should describe with such extraordinary gusto, like a gourmet relishing a delicious piece of food, the scenes of adultery between the chambermaid and the officer. I know he is describing here his own liaison with his sister's chambermaid in Pirogovo, he told me about it himself in great detail. I have since seen that Gasha, now an old woman of about seventy, for he has pointed her out to me, to my deep despair and disgust. It torments me too that Nekhlyudov the hero should be described in terms of his transformation from a state of degradation to a state of grace, and I see Lev Nikolaevich himself in this, and it's the way he sees himself too. He describes all these moral transformations very well in his books, but never actually achieves them in his life. While he is telling everyone about these beautiful feelings of his, he is moved to tears by his own words, yet he goes on as he always has, with his fondness for sweet foods, his bicycle, horse-riding and physical love...

All in all, as I thought the first time, this novel contains some brilliant descriptions and details, and a deeply, bitterly hypocritical state of affairs between hero and heroine.

It put me in such a distressed frame of mind that I suddenly decided I would leave for Moscow, that I couldn't possible *love* this work of my husband's, that we had less and less in common... He noticed my mood, and accused me of never liking the things he liked and was working on. I replied that I loved his artistic work, that I had been in ecstasies over *Father Sergei*, was fascinated by *Hadji Murat*, highly valued 'Master and Man' and cried every time I read *Childhood* – but was repelled by *Resurrection*.

"Yes but you don't like me working with the Dukhobors either," he said reproachfully.

"I simply can find no pity in my heart for people who refuse military service, force the poorest peasants to enter the army in their place, and then demand millions of rubles to allow them to leave Russia," I replied.

I helped the *starving* in 1891, 1892 and this year too – I felt for them, worked for them and gave them money. No, if one is going to give money to anyone it should be to our own peasants who are dying of hunger, not to those arrogant revolutionary Dukhobors.

Meanwhile his children and grandchildren have to eat black bread!

15th September. Yesterday I felt so sad that L.N. and I had been on bad terms the day before, and he had listened so meekly to my criticisms of his story and the way it was being sold, that a sudden compassionate impulse made me go down to him in his study and tell him how sorry I was for the sharp things I said, and how much I longed for us to be reunited as *friends.* We both wept, and felt that despite all the things that separated us *externally,* we had nonetheless been bound together these past thirty-six years by *love,* and that was more precious than anything.

17th September (Moscow). I arrived in Moscow yesterday evening.

I went out first thing to buy provisions, then paid some calls, and this evening some young lads came round to see Misha, while I entertained Natasha Dehn, Miss Welsh, Goldenweiser, Dunaev and his wife, the Maklakovs, Uncle Kostya and Sergei Ivanovich. According to Yusha Pomerantsev, he had practised for three hours today to play for me this evening. He played Schumann's *Davidsbündlertänze,* but the boys were sitting beside him playing cards and their shouting irritated him.

19th September. I went to three banks today, paid in Ilya's money and closed the account I had opened three years ago in Vanechka's name. The little darling won't need money now! Oh, when shall I pass into that blessed state!

A letter from Mashenka, who says Lyovochka was sad on my name day. This was because he knew Sergei Ivanovich would be playing for me and was jealous again. But what could be more pure and innocent than the aesthetic pleasure of listening to marvellous music?

22nd September. Ilya and Andryusha arrived to prepare me to receive Chertkov's sister-in-law Olga Dieterichs, to whom Andryusha has just proposed.

I hired a new governess for Sasha today, an elderly lady, the mother of three daughters. I have been busy with practical matters, and played the piano for three hours.

I made a great mistake and personally delivered some books to Sergei Ivanovich. I very much regret this now, but I have been quite beside myself recently, lying awake until four in the morning, haunted by the stench of corpses, the misery of loneliness and the vanity of life, and desperately searching for something to grasp hold of, something to save me from this depression.

23rd September. My wedding anniversary. Today I have been married to Lev Nikolaevich for thirty-six years – and we are apart.

28th September (Yasnaya Polyana). I have come home. I turned off the highway at Yasenki in the dark and drove towards the church. It was a dismal journey in the dark through melting snow along the bad road, and I was weighed down with worries about Misha, whom I had left in a despondent state. But then what a treat to get back to the bright house at Yasnaya, filled with my dear ones who love me. I went straight to Lyovochka's study, and we fell into each other's arms as we used to when we were young, and kissed over and over again. His eyes shone with joy and love – it's a long time since I have seen him so happy.

3rd October. L.N. is buried in his work; he keeps putting more finishing touches to *Resurrection*, and has sent several chapters abroad to be translated. Today he was talking to a wandering man who was thrown into jail for four months after a strike, and was deported. L.N. was mesmerized by his stories.

5th October. We have had news of Tanya. She has apparently refused Sukhotin, and they were both crying; Nurse writes that Misha told her she was pining and weeping.

Misha has arrived very depressed; he has been carousing in Moscow, and has returned to his family in the country to come to his senses. We had an interesting French couple here called M. and Mme de Gercy. They are extreme socialists and atheists, and have instigated several strikes in Paris. They are both passionate people, very fond of each other and very French, with their lively, temperamental natures and their capacity to live entirely for some cause, something beyond themselves.

6th October. This morning I had a talk with Misha about his recent disorderly life and he said how remorseful he felt and how much he longed to do better and be more disciplined. What I found so touching was that he had come to be with his family and seek salvation in nature – and he seems to have found it too.

Pasternak the artist came; L.N. invited him here as he wants him to do some illustrations for *Resurrection* for a French journal – called *Illustration*, I believe. What a lively, clever, educated man this Pasternak* is.

17th October (Moscow). Sasha and I have been in Moscow since Sunday evening, the 11th. She is studying hard and behaving well at present. Long may this continue. It's very hard having to keep an eye on Misha all the time, it's a constant strain and worry that he'll do something wrong, yet I feel he relies on me to worry about him. My life is constantly busy, selling the oats according to the plan, tidying the house, then publishing business and work. I am also copying Lev Nikolaevich's diaries, which is one more torment for my soul.

22nd October. Something ripens then falls. My depression came to a head – and yesterday it fell away. I wrote Lev Nikolaevich a bad letter, and today I had one from Lyova, who writes that his papa has a headache and is exhausted by this business with the Dukhobors and his work on *Resurrection*. Oh, why did he involve himself with these Dukhobors! It's so unnatural. We have quite enough to worry about in our own family; our children need a father who takes an interest in them, instead of searching the world for sectarians.

Today I was examining a photograph of him, looking at his thin old arms which I have kissed so often and which have caressed me so many times, and I felt so sad – it's an *old man*'s caresses I long for now, not a lover's.

Uncle Kostya, Marusya and Sergei Ivanovich visited yesterday evening. We read some poems of Tyutchev's, and Sergei Ivanovich was in ecstasies over them. He was in a tender mood – he seemed quite inspired, and had the idea of setting the words of one of these poems to music. Marusya opened the book at random at the verse "Do not trouble me with your just reproaches", and Sergei Ivanovich immediately began composing and wrote a song to the words and played it to us. Such a clever man.

Pomerantsev was telling us about a soldier on the Arbat square who didn't salute his drunken officer and the officer slashed him to death with his sabre. What hideous brutality!

26th October. I travelled to Yasnaya this morning via Kozlovka. Rain and slush, everything grey. I was chilled and soaked. At home everyone was asleep. I went straight in to see L.N. The room was dark and he jumped out of bed and kissed me.

In the mornings he works hard on his *Resurrection*. He says for the past few days he couldn't work for thinking of me, and that on the morning of my arrival he dreamt about me. Every so often he comes in to see me, smiles and kisses me. Tanya and Vera are both very sweet and cheerful. Tanya is her old, lively, playful laughing self, lovable and cheerful. To tease Dunechka they took everything out of the larder and hid it in the cupboard, so when she got back from Tula she was convinced everything had been stolen and was about to go to the fortune-teller. Having made her thoroughly worried, they then opened the cupboard, roaring with laughter, and showed her all the bread and jam and other things inside. Then they brought a herring from Lyova's wing, and ate it, still roaring with laughter. The atmosphere is happy, and I feel healthy and carefree.

27th October. We slept badly last night as it was so cold. L.N. has a chill. I have asked him a lot of questions about *Resurrection* and have approved of the new ending and a number of other things. It's much less *hypocritical* now.

28th October. I bade a tender farewell this morning to L.N., Tanya, Vera and Lyova. It was frosty and windy, and Adrian the coachman regaled me all the way to Yasenki with a hideous story about the murder of four people near Rudakova at Kosaya Hill. Our neighbourhood has been ruined by that Belgian factory. It was a tedious journey; I read Maximov's book on hard-labour convicts, about their lives, the convict trains and so on. A depressing picture!

6th November (Moscow). I have only two interests now: my morbid anxieties about Misha, and making the arrangements for an evening in honour of *Tolstoy*. L.N. has sent me an extract from a beautifully conceived short story he is writing, called 'History of a Mother'. It tells of a mother of eight children, a beautiful, tender, considerate woman, who at the end of her life is all on her own and goes to live near a convent, with the bitter unacknowledged awareness that her entire life has been wasted upon her children, and that not only do they give her no happiness, but they too are unhappy.

The evening is being organized by the Society for Popular Entertainment. Tomorrow I am taking this extract to the censors; Sergei Ivanovich has been asked to play, but refused. He said to me: "I would gladly spend the time and effort if it would give Lev Nikolaevich pleasure. But *who* will I be playing for, and what can one play apart from the *Kreutzer Sonata*?" He and the singer Lavrovskaya are coming on Sunday evening to console me with music, and I am terribly happy.

8th November. I am starting on another book of diaries, the fifth. I wonder if I'll live to finish the whole of this thick book? Is it possible under these circumstances that I will? I did no writing yesterday. I went to rather a dull symphony concert, and Marusya, Sergei Ivanovich and I walked home together under the starry sky. Marusya and I both wanted to look at it through binoculars, then Sergei Ivanovich happened to join us. But the stars were glimmering motionlessly, and only the firmament seemed to be swaying. When I got home I stood in the garden and gazed at the sky through binoculars for the first time in my life, amazed by the extraordinary spectacle of the innumerable stars.

11th November. Misha came home late today. I was sitting up sewing, waiting for him. He seemed genuinely contrite, kissing me and begging me not to cry (for I couldn't restrain my pent-up tears by then), that for the time being I felt consoled.

But I myself am bad too. I fear my mania for spending money, I fear my foolish love of dressing up – those are *my* sins, which I cannot control.

13th November. Marusya, Sasha, Misha and I left on the 13th for Yasnaya Polyana. We enjoyed the journey and laughed all the way. We arrived on the mail train at 11 at night, and drove in the moonlight to Yasnaya through drizzle, white fog and frightful slush. But it was nice in the country and even nicer to be at Yasnaya. We found them all well and friendly. Masha appears to be well. The doctors say the baby couldn't have moved yet, but that it will soon; so either she *imagined* the movement or simply lied to herself and us. She is very cheerful and full of energy, and so pale, delicate and pretty.

L.N. was tender and passionate with me but I couldn't respond.

14th November. I had a long talk with him about Misha, about me and about his work. He says he hasn't been in such a creative mood since writing *War and Peace*, and is very pleased with *Resurrection*. He rode over to Yasenki and is full of energy; his body is fit and he is in high spirits, because he is doing the sort of *artistic* work to which he is temperamentally suited.

16th November. I woke this morning in tears. I dreaded returning to Moscow and having to leave L.N. We were deeply, genuinely touched to see each other this time, and these past few days we were good friends and in harmony with each other – even loving.

I was sorry too to leave Tanya, whom I love so much, and peaceful, beautiful Yasnaya Polyana. L.N. was astonished to see me crying, caressed me and shed some tears too, promising to join me in Moscow on 1st December. I would dearly love this, but it would be wicked to make him come here and tear him from his work.

Misha was there to meet us in Moscow, but he immediately got ready to go out. I was very distressed. And I was even more distressed when he came home at three in the morning and I was again obliged to give him a scolding. So the moment I arrived I was waiting up for him, darning linen and worrying.

18th November. Misha didn't return until three a.m. again. I waited up listening for him, then couldn't sleep all night for worrying. This morning I went to see the director of the Lycée and asked him to take him on as a full boarder. "*Nous jouons gros jeu,*"* he replied, meaning that Misha might well go off for good. He looked very crestfallen when he eventually returned and said I was right about everything, but that he simply forgets about my anxiety when he is sitting up all night with his comrades. This evening he suddenly presented me with three pears.

22nd November. If my diary could express the groans in my soul, I would groan and groan. Misha is ruined. His moments of remorse are short-lived. The day before yesterday he again disappeared all night with the gypsies, and didn't return until seven in the morning. Yesterday he stayed at home, and today he went off again, and where he is or who he is with I have no way of knowing. He has a new set of friends every day, wild, rough strangers.

25th November. I dragged myself around Moscow all day in the rain, wandering senselessly, aimlessly through the mud – the depression is insufferable! This afternoon I lay down for a sleep. I got up and Sasha came in. "Are you ill, Maman?" I said no. She threw herself into my arms and kissed me. "Oh, if only you know how pink and pretty you are when you've been asleep." Am I really *pretty*? Or is it her love that sees beauty in her darling Maman? This evening we went to the theatre to see *Mozart and Salieri*, and *Orpheus*.* Sergei Ivanovich was with us, as well as Marusya, Sasha, Goldenweiser, and Butyonev. Various other acquaintances were in the boxes. It started off cheerfully and interestingly enough, but I was annoyed by the atrocious singing in *Orpheus* and barely managed to sit through it.

27th November. Letters from home, from Lev Nikolaevich (who still plans to come to Moscow on 1st December), and from Tanya. Mine to her was lost – what a nuisance! I had written to urge L.N. not to come to Moscow. I can't bear to think of him suffering in the city. He cannot endure the visitors, the noise, the crowded streets, the lack of leisure, being away from the country and his daughters, who have been such a help to him. Besides, it would be hard for me to curtail *my* interests – the children's education, my music, my friends, my visits, rare as they are, to concerts and theatres – and that will annoy him. And then my failing eyesight and frequent blood rushes now make it impossible for me to go on copying his endlessly revised writings as I used to, and he will be angry about this too.

S.I. Taneev arrived this afternoon while Masha, Misha and I were having tea together. How pleased I was to see him! I love him best when he comes like this, just to see me. He had just finished composing the most beautiful work for two choirs, set to words by Tyutchev, and had come to play and sing it through for me. We sat chatting quietly and read an article of music criticism. One always has such sincere, interesting talks with him. We get on so well – it is a great shame that L.N.'s jealousy weighs so heavily on this pure, simple friendship.

30th November (Yasnaya Polyana). Tanya has lost her voice and has a slight fever. Still nothing definite about Masha, but she seems calm and well. L.N. rode to Pirogovo the day before yesterday and rode back the following day, which is why he's worn out and lethargic now. Having promised to come to Moscow on 1st December, he now seems to be trying to wriggle out of it. And I was counting on the pleasure of taking him back to Moscow and living with him there. I had brought some dates, spirits and bran bread with me for the journey, I had told them to prepare a room for him in Moscow and had ordered the dinner and fruit, and I was going to pack his things myself and organize his departure as inconspicuously as possible. But by evening it was decided he wasn't going. I cried, my heart was aching and I took to my bed.

1st December. I am in Moscow again. I didn't sleep all night because of the uncertainty. "I'm coming to Moscow on the first," L.N. had written to me. Today is the 1st and I prepared to catch the fast train to Moscow, thinking: he couldn't not be packing and coming with me. My heart was pounding and I was in a fever, and this morning he got up and went downstairs without saying a word. I got up at about 10 to discover he wasn't packing and wasn't leaving. Choking back the tears, I dressed and ordered the carriage to be harnessed – he didn't say a word. Then Maria Schmidt, Tanya and L.N. all start clamouring – why am I leaving? What do they mean – why? I had already arranged to go, the horses have been sent, my children and grandchildren are expecting me in Moscow. I am suffocated by uncontrollable sobs. I pick up my bags, order the carriage to catch up with me and start walking, for I don't want to upset them by letting them see me in this state, or give Lev Nikolaevich the pleasure of achieving his goal year after year and of seeing me so unhappy when he refuses to live with me in Moscow. But it's impossible, his cruelty is driving me to despair. Then I see him in his sheepskin coat driving towards me in the carriage: "Wait! Don't go!" he shouts. We return home. He reads me a lecture in a hateful tone of voice. I am choking back the sobs. We sit together for half an hour, while I suffer the most unspeakable pain and struggle with my despair. Tanya comes in and says: "I understand how difficult it is for you." Eventually I say goodbye to them all, ask them to forgive me and leave. I shall never forget that journey to Yasenki as long as I live. What a terrible wind there was! I was doubled up all the way, sobbing so hard I thought my head would split open. How could they let me go like this! Only one thing prevented me from lying down under the train, the thought that then I wouldn't be buried next to Vanechka, and that is my *idée fixe*. In the train the other passengers all stared at me weeping – then I dozed off. Not a bite of food had passed my lips all day. I arrived home to a cheerless welcome from my children and grandchildren and wept again. I had a telegram from L.N.: "I'll come the day after Sonya arrives."

2nd December. I had a letter from Lev Nikolaevich this afternoon. He asks me to forgive his apparently unintentional cruelty to me, the misunderstandings, his tiredness and the various other reasons why he couldn't come and why he tormented me. Then he arrived... I have neuralgia in my right temple, my insides are aching, I didn't sleep all night, and I am completely cold and numb. I don't feel a thing, no joy, no anger, no love, no energy for life, nothing. I just want to cry and cry – for my lost health and freedom, for my friends, since if I do manage to see them now it's simply not the same as if I were alone and they belonged entirely to me. One day of suffering has destroyed me!

I shall try to do *my duty*. I shall look after L.N., copy for him, satisfy his physical love – for I don't believe in any other sort now – and there's an end to it! And what then?!!! Patience, faith and kind friends.

5th December. Still the same depression, which even my grandchildren are unable to lift.

There was a most unpleasant discussion. My daughter-in-law Sonya wanted to hear some good music, so I suggested inviting Lavrovskaya, Goldenweiser and Taneev to play for us and organizing a musical evening at home. Sonya and I then shyly told L.N. that we wanted some music. He looked furious. "Well, in that case I'm going out," he says. "God forbid you should be driven out of the house," I say. "We'd better not have any music in that case." "No, that's even worse – it would be as though I was stopping you." Well, it soon led to an argument, and a very nasty one, after which of course there was no point in thinking about music.

10th December. Relations with L.N. have improved, but I don't believe they are pure or lasting. I am copying the latest chapters of *Resurrection*. My eyes ache, I have no free time, yet I still copy.

I went to the bank with Andryusha and handed him all his money and documents. I also gave him a fur coat and 2,000 rubles, and ordered a dozen pieces of silver for his bride. And after everything I'd done for him and all my presents, he not only didn't say thank you, he actually looked disgruntled.

13th December. I invited Lavrovskaya to sing, Taneev to play and some close friends to listen. Raevskaya, the Kolokoltsevs, Uncle Kostya, my brother and his wife, the Maslovs and various others came. Sergei Ivanovich played delightfully, and also accompanied. Lavrovskaya sang a lot, and beautifully too. It would have all been so pleasant and cheerful if one didn't feel Lev Nikolaevich was angrily condemning every entertainment I organized.

14th December. I copied for Lev Nikolaevich for 7 hours without stirring from my chair, then answered his letters. My head was spinning. He is gloomy and sullen. Misha is a trial: he disappears every evening to parties, stays out all night, sleeps to three in the afternoon and hasn't been to school.

15th December. This evening L.N. read us a translation of Jerome K. Jerome – no good. It's thawing heavily.

16th December. Spent the day going over the bills with the accountant again. L.N. read us more of the Jerome K. Jerome – I haven't seen him laugh like that for a long time.

19th December. We have just returned from an evening at the Korsh Theatre in honour of seventy-year-old Tolstoy. And what a wretchedly unsuccessful evening it was! Bad singing, bad reading, bad music and some appalling *tableaux vivants* utterly lacking in truth, beauty, artistry or anything else. Mikhailovsky received shattering ovations for some reason, then began shouting for Tolstoy and sent him a telegram… It was all so trite, so vulgar – one had no sense of it as a genuine cry from the people's heart. L.N. himself had earlier today set off alone for Yasnaya Polyana on the mail train. He worked all morning, ate some porridge and drank coffee at one, then left.

Ilyusha and Andryusha have arrived. Andryusha is terribly anxious: this summer in the Caucasus he frivolously proposed to a certain Princess Gureli, then wrote her a letter of rejection. The princess shot herself, the parents sprang to her defence, and Andryusha now lives in terror of being murdered or having to fight a duel. It's nothing but sorrow! Misha left for Oryol, and from there will visit Ilyusha, then Yasnaya.

The princess has since died.

20th December. I discovered that those taking part in yesterday's so-called Tolstoy evening, Ilya included, all went off to the Hermitage to dine, i.e. get drunk – and this *in honour of Tolstoy!* It's disgraceful!

Numerous distressing discussions at home about this Princess Gureli who has killed herself; Andryusha is terrified of the Caucasian parents' revenge.

24th December (Yasnaya Polyana). I got up early, massaged L.N.'s back and stomach again and gave him his Ems water, and again my closeness disturbed him. Terrible weather – damp and windy, 3 degrees of frost. L.N. is more cheerful and was able to work again today, but he hasn't written anything recently and has grown terribly weak and lethargic. Whenever I am away he is unable to write, is prone to illnesses and sleeps badly.

Today he is like another person, and when I said this to him he smiled and agreed. I am happy to be here, but not all my family are in good spirits, and I fear that *my* energy alone isn't enough to compensate for the generally sour mood. I went to "the other house" to see Lyova and Dora and my adorable six-month-old grandson Levushka. I took a walk round the garden in a prayerful mood, filled with all my old sentimental feelings about Yasnaya and memories of my youth and recent past.

25th December, Christmas (Yasnaya Polyana). Everyone has been in a holiday mood: we made presents and unpacked all the good things we had brought from Moscow. The moment I enjoyed best was my walk through the woods. It was especially lovely in the young fir plantation – three degrees of frost, silence and brief moments when the sun peered out after disappearing all autumn. Everything was covered with fresh pure snow that had fallen during the night. The young green fir saplings were lightly covered in snow, and across the horizon stretched the broad black band of the old Zaseka forest, frozen for the winter, and everything was quiet, still and severe. Nature and art are the best things in life. How well Sergei Ivanovich understands this. With one's family and in the company of others there is so much unnecessary aggravation, so much pain and spite...

We had a nice cheerful family dinner. M.A. Schmidt came. At five o' clock Dora and Lyova entertained us around the Christmas tree with tea and refreshments. Poor Dora was so tired, but she loved the whole thing – she is only nineteen, virtually a little girl still, and she *needs* this holiday. My grandson Levushka was startled and amazed. A splendid, adorable baby.

By eight o'clock everyone was in low spirits again, for L.N. had a temperature of 38°.

26th December. L.N. was feverish all night. He was shrieking, groaning and tossing, and I didn't get a wink of sleep. It would be hard to find a more impatient, selfish invalid, he is so stubborn. He wouldn't take his rhubarb yesterday, but took it at 11 today. This means he cannot take his quinine for the fever now on a full stomach, but must wait another twenty-four hours – all because of his stubbornness and his unwillingness to listen to me and take his laxative at the proper time. Oh, how bored and weary I am of putting all my energy into *persuading*, *convincing* and getting angry with him, with the sole purpose of saving and helping a cross, grumbling, stubborn man for whom I have sacrificed my entire life and killed every personal desire, even the simple need for peace, leisure, reading and music – not to mention that I have never travelled anywhere, neither abroad nor within Russia.

Some Tula working man came here with an extraordinary picture by a peasant icon-painter. It is a pencil drawing, an *arshin* and a half* wide. Lev Nikolaevich is sitting in the middle, to his left is a school and some children, beyond them is an angel, above them is Christ in the clouds with the angels, then further off are various wise men – Socrates, Confucius, Buddha and so on. On the right is a church with a gallows and some hanged men in front of it. In the foreground are bishops, priests and gentlemen-in-waiting, and beyond them in the background are soldiers on foot and horseback. Then there are various national types reading books, and in the foreground for some reason a Turk in a turban reading a huge book. L.N. is not strictly true to life but his general appearance is. He is sitting cross-legged.

Appalling stories about the Yasnaya peasants. One brother has stolen from another, a widow has killed her illegitimate child, a father pushed his little son through a narrow crack into a storeroom and told him to steal things and hand them out to him, the windows of the library have been smashed and some children have made off with our books. It is sad and infuriating. Oh, the power of darkness!

I am reading a wonderful book about Buddhism entitled *The Soul of a People*.* What beautiful truths there are in Buddhism. It is as though one knew them already, but to see them written down and the laconic way they are expressed is a delight to the soul.

27th December. Tanya, Sasha, Sonya Kolokoltseva and I left at five for Grinevka to visit Ilya. Misha was there looking thin, restless and confused. It's nice and friendly with Sonya and Ilya. The children were all asleep apart from Annochka.

28th December. This morning we all decorated the Christmas tree and gave one another presents. My three grandchildren are such healthy, fair-haired youngsters, they're a joy.

We went for a long walk. The fresh snow that had fallen in the night on the boundless fields gleamed in the bright sun, and it was silent, pure and beautiful. I walked a long way on my own, thinking of the people I love. My soul too is pure, peaceful and happy.

This evening there were guests, a magnificent Christmas tree (I had brought everything from Moscow), neighbours, servants and peasants, singing, dancing and mummers, with a rough-and-ready performance of *Tsar Maximilian and his Unruly Son Adolf*. Sasha and Annochka dressed up and danced round in masks. Sasha is so fat and clumsy, she's a sorry sight. I like the way at Ilya's they keep open house for *everyone* to come and enjoy themselves. They had laid in quantities of food so the guests could eat and drink all day long, and had covered the floor of the office with straw and fur jackets so they could lie down and sleep. It was all very hospitable, friendly and chaotic, and they live in grand style, but I couldn't live like that.

29th December. A heavenly day; the trees and fields were all covered in thick hoar frost, everything was white, and sky and earth were fused into one vast kingdom of whiteness. I took a long walk on my own, and the children went tobogganing on the hill. The only genuine, serious interest in Ilya's life is horses and dogs, and that is very sad. We left at six o'clock, taking my granddaughter Annochka with us. It was a fearsome journey from Yasenki to Yasnaya. I wasn't used to this country road in winter; we got lost on the way from Grinevka to the station, and ended up at the house again. All is well at Yasnaya. L.N. is healthy and passionate.

31st December. The last day of the year. What will the New Year bring! Masha collapsed this morning. We are waiting in anguish for her either to miscarry or deliver a dead baby. It is now gone nine p.m.; the midwife is here and we are waiting for Doctor Rudnyov. The house is silent, and everyone is in a state of agonizing suspense.

At five minutes to midnight Masha was delivered of a stillborn four-month son.

The whole family calmly gathered to welcome in the new year. Goodbye old year, which brought me so much grief – although a few joys too. And thanks to those that caused them.

1899

February – University of St Petersburg convulsed by student riots and demonstrations, which spread to Latvia and Poland. All universities in Russia closed. Students expelled and drafted into army.

8th January – Andrei Tolstoy marries Olga Dieterichs (the sister of Chertkov's wife). 13th March – first part of Resurrection *published in the journal* The Cornfield, *and the money sent to the Dukhobors. 14th November – Tanya Tolstaya marries Mikhail Sukhotin. End of the year – Tolstoy finishes* Resurrection.

1st January. A disappointing start to the new year. We got up late, and I drove Sasha, Sonya Kolokoltseva and my grandchildren Misha and Annochka to the woods in the big sledge, with my camera. It was lovely in the woods, and the children were such fun. We laughed and took photographs; the shaft of the sledge broke, but strong Sasha repaired it. We got back for dinner. This afternoon I had tea with Dora and Lyova and lit the candles on the Christmas tree again. Back in our house the children and both sets of servants dressed up and danced, first to dance tunes on the piano, then to two concertinas. I went to sit with Masha, developed photographs and made a peasant shirt for Lev Nikolaevich.

Masha is recovering, thank God. Lev Nikolaevich's work is going badly. He always ascribes every emotional state – his own, mine and everyone else's – to physical causes.

4th January. More guests this evening – the three Cherkasskys, the two Volkhonskys and the Boldyryovs. Mary is utterly delightful. Accordions, dancing, some unsuccessful choral singing… Dreadful! The appalling Princess Cherkasskaya is an ageing sinner who doesn't want to grow old. She and I woke Masha, who then had a hysterical attack. It was extremely regrettable, and it was partly my fault for making so much noise with that old harridan.

Lev Nikolaevich has again been in a good mood for work.

8th January. I spent the morning in Tula alone in my room in the Petersburg Hotel. It was so cheerless, and I felt depressed and upset about Andryusha's wedding.* I read a French pamphlet about Auguste Comte, which was sent to Lev Nikolaevich and written as a letter to Émile Zola. It preached peace, brotherhood and sociology.

Then my sons arrived – poor thin Lyova, plump jolly Ilya, anxious Andryusha and wild Misha, incoherent, noisy and selfish, who hadn't received his uniform and was searching for a tailcoat to wear.

Ilya and I blessed Andryusha there in the hotel room. He seemed to be in a dream, deeply affected, yet bewildered as to why he was getting married or what would happen. I still can't make Olga out. A wedding is always a frightening, mysterious occasion. I kept wanting to cry.

We dined at the Kuhns', got a little drunk, then took them to the station. Lev Nikolaevich rode there wearing his fur jacket. The public surrounded us: Tolstoy and a wedding; they were all fascinated. He has grown to love his fame. He loved the sight of those people at the station, I could see he did.

12th January (Moscow). Tanya's name day. A lot of tedious guests arrived at midday with a great deal of chocolate and chatter and an endless number of boys – schoolfriends of Misha's, etc. I feel even worse. I was expecting Sergei Ivanovich all day, but he didn't come. I am told he is at Tchaikovsky's estate in Klin, working on a production of his ballet *The Sleeping Beauty* with the composer's brother. This afternoon Masha Kolokoltseva, Liza Obolenskaya and the pianist Igumnov came, just back from Tiflis. He played us the Chopin Tarantella and Nocturne, Rubinstein's 'Ballade', the andante from a Schubert sonata and something by Mendelssohn – but I wouldn't have recognized his playing, it was so lifeless. Either that or I was ill and I couldn't listen properly.

I have seen almost nothing of Lev Nikolaevich all day. He wrote a lot of letters and was busy with his own writing. He still complains of a stomach ache and I gave him another massage.

13th January. Misha arrived; he was telling me that a crowd of drunken students, magistrates, old men and all sorts of other people had gathered yesterday at the Hermitage and Yar's nightclub to celebrate St Tatyana's Day (the university holiday), and 200 people had danced the *trepak* together. They ought to be ashamed of themselves! I spent half the day in bed.

14th January. We had a splendid evening: Lev Nikolaevich read us two Chekhov stories, 'Darling' and one whose name I have forgotten, about a suicide, more of a sketch really.

16th January. A telegram from Sulerzhitsky saying he has arrived safely in Canada with the Dukhobors, and they like the country and have been well received there. Our Seryozha ought to be there in six days' time. I am waiting impatiently for his telegram, I think constantly about him and tell his fortune.

I went with Modest Tchaikovsky to a rehearsal of Tchaikovsky's ballet *The Sleeping Beauty*. Lovely music, but I am too old for ballet now, and I soon grew bored and left.

17th January. Lev Nikolaevich had a visit from Myasoedov and the inspector of the Butyrki prison fortress, who gave him a lot of technical information about prison affairs, the prisoners' lives and so on for *Resurrection.**

20th January. I didn't sleep all night. We had some good news this morning – a telegram from Seryozha in Canada saying he has arrived safely with the Dukhobors. Three died on board, a baby was born and there was an outbreak of smallpox, which means they are all in quarantine.

Lev Nikolaevich has been entertaining some dark ones – Nikiforov, Kuteleva, a midwife who did famine relief work, a certain Zonov, Ushakov...

22nd January. I paid seven calls today, and this evening endless guests arrived. I am exhausted. I called on Sergei Ivanovich to thank him for giving us such pleasure yesterday and to enquire about his fingers, which he hurt when he was playing for us yesterday.

The Annenkovs, taciturn Rostovtsov, dear Davydov, pathetic Boratynskaya, Sukhotin the student and Butyonev *père*. My temple aches insufferably, which makes me depressed and listless, and my soul is melancholy.

A friendly letter from Andryusha, to which Olga added a few lines. At the moment they are quite happy. Who knows what the future holds!

I have no contact with Lev Nikolaevich all day. He writes all morning, then takes a walk. This afternoon he went off to see Misha at the Lycée, then this great wall of guests separates us, which is very depressing. Misha is bored, he cannot sleep at the Lycée and I fear he won't last long there.

23rd January. I spent a quiet day on my own, and found time for everything – I read a little of *The Greek Conception of Death and*

Immortality, did some work, played the piano for about four hours, sat with Lev Nikolaevich, did a little copying from the revised proofs for him. Not a soul here all evening – heavenly! Tanya took Sasha to a dance and Misha went too – Misha Mamonov that is, such a nice intelligent boy. I love children, I never really grew up myself and joined the adults, and children are so grateful, so forgiving, they observe God's world with such eager, inquisitive eyes.

24th January. 10 degrees of frost, fine. This morning I paid some unsuccessful calls, and this evening a crowd of guests came – the Naryshkins, Princess Golitsyna, Count Sollogub, Stakhovich, Olsufiev, Ermolova, the boys and so on – 30 people in all. I was in bed with neuralgia when Tanya got me up and called me to them. Lev Nikolaevich was there throughout, reading Chekhov's 'Darling' to the ladies and chatting animatedly to everyone. Then Goldenweiser played a Mozart sonata and some things by Chopin. We went to bed late, then Misha called me out to tell me he didn't know how much longer he could go on living at school. I'm sure he'll leave.

25th January. I stayed in all day, but couldn't do a thing because of all the visitors. The Olsufiev brothers came, read *Resurrection* and drank tea. Then Stakhovich came to dinner. He seems rather gloomy. Tanya went to see Chekhov's *The Seagull* with Trepova.

Wind, frost, fires on the street. Sitting at the dinner table today I scolded myself for being unable to be happy. There was a heated discussion. Lev Nikolaevich said it was important to have principles and to strive for spiritual perfection, but that one's actions might nevertheless be inadequate, the result of human passions. I said if despite all these principles it was still possible to sin and succumb morally, then what could I stake my faith on in future? It was better to have no principles at all, I said, just an inner sense that would lead one to the right path. Lev Nikolaevich said the desire for spiritual perfection automatically led one to the right path. And I said that while a man was perfecting himself he could sin twenty times or more. No, I said, better to *know* what is right and what is wrong and not sin, rather than expect some sort of perfection.

It is almost two a.m. Lev Nikolaevich has just sent for Maklakov for some reason, and has ordered some food to be heated up for him. What a lot of trouble he makes for others without realizing it.

26th January. I was copying the revised proofs of *Resurrection* and was repelled by the desire to shock when he describes the Orthodox service. For instance: "The priest extended to the people the gilt image of the cross on which Jesus Christ was executed – *instead of the gallows.*" The sacrament he calls "*kvas* soup in a cup". It's scurrilous and cynical, a crude insult to those who believe in it, and I hate it. I read a little today, and copied out a little of his diaries. There were no guests – what a blessing!

29th January. I don't remember the past two days: I paid visits with Tanya, played a little, pined and fretted for my absent children. I cut out and sewed today and am very tired. I thought about my son Seryozha and remembered him composing and playing for me his song that begins: "We met once again after a long parting…" and ends: "…we pressed each other's cold hands and wept…"* I know he was expressing his own fears, his emotional state at the time. He is *awkward* but so profound in his feelings, and in all his other faculties too. He just hasn't been able to *make the best* of his good qualities. We women – and especially his wife – love to act like characters out of a *novel*, even at times with our husbands; we love sentimental strolls, we love to be emotionally cherished. But one doesn't expect this from the Tolstoys. So often one feels an outburst of tenderness for one's husband – but if, God forbid, it is expressed, he recoils with such disgust one feels mortified and ashamed of one's feelings. He only cherishes me when his passions are aroused – which alas is not the same!

30th January. I sewed all morning, first a sash for the coachman, then a silk skirt for myself on the machine. Lev Nikolaevich had a visit from old Soldatenkov, the publisher, who brought him 5,000 silver rubles for the Dukhobors. I greatly dislike this business of asking rich people for money – considering that L.N. wrote an article denouncing the *evils* of *money* and refusing to have anything to do with it. It doesn't bother him that while he now curses music, just to be contrary, Modest Tchaikovsky told me that he once wrote a letter to Pyotr Ilich Tchaikovsky saying he considered music the supreme art, and gave it *first* place in the world of art.

I often think: Lev Nikolaevich should be *ashamed* of living a life of such contradictions. Everything with him is *ideological*, everything is for a purpose – the main purpose being to *describe* everything, as he did in that wonderful article of his about the famine last summer. Maybe he's right: to each his own path and his own cause.

I visited the Lycée the other day and talked with the director. This splendid man, Georgievsky, treats Misha better than his own father does. Misha is in good spirits; he has left the boarding house again to be a day boy, but has started to work.

31st January. Lev Nikolaevich, much to my disapproval, continues to ask rich merchants for money for the Dukhobors.

1st February. Dunaev, Almazov and the student Strumensky came this evening and there were discussions again: about disarmament and whether the Tsar was sincere in his talk of peace, about Marxism, about music. I wasn't bored, for they talked very interestingly and without acrimony.

3rd February. I was pacing about aimlessly, with an anxious heart, then at dinner, what joy, a letter from Seryozha in Canada. There was an outbreak of smallpox on the boat, and Seryozha and the Dukhobors were put down on a small island and quarantined for nineteen days. About himself he writes almost nothing, but is evidently exhausted by his role as interpreter, and worn out by seasickness, anxiety and so on.

There was a special symphony concert this evening in honour of Paderewski, the famous and utterly loathsome pianist. Sergei Ivanovich was there.

4th February. A hectic day. I went this evening to a concert. I met Sergei Ivanovich as we were taking off our coats, and we had a most unpleasant exchange: he said he had walked there yesterday and had driven back with M.N. Muromtseva, telling me all this with a foolish laugh. I was seething with rage – what business was it of mine?

When I got home I found Lev Nikolaevich standing at the long table in the drawing room which had been laid for tea, and around it was a group of Molokans who had arrived from Samara. Dunaev, Annenkova, Gorbunov, Nakashidze and some peasant or other were all there drinking tea, Lev Nikolaevich was explaining something about St John's Gospel to them, and I overheard a discussion about religion going on.

I don't understand religious discussions: they destroy my own lofty relations with God, which cannot be put into words. There is no precise definition of eternity, infinity and the afterlife – there are no words for these things, just as there are no words to express my attitude and feelings about the abstract, indefinable, infinite deity and my eternal life in God. But I have no objection to the Church, with its ceremonies and icons; I have lived among these things since I was a child, when my soul was first drawn to God. I love attending mass and fasting, and I love the little icon of the Iversk Mother of God hanging over my bed, with which Aunt Tatyana blessed Lev Nikolaevich when he went to war.

The Molokans are staying the night here, unfortunately.

5th February. Paid calls this morning. An interesting conversation with Maslov and Scriabin about music. Terrible depression all day: I can't bear to think I have brought about a break with Sergei Ivanovich. I didn't sleep all night.

7th–27th February. I haven't written my diary for twenty days. On the morning of Sunday 7th I received a telegram from my niece Vera Kuzminskaya in Kiev: "Pneumonia. Maman very ill." I left for Kiev on Monday morning* and found my sister Tanya with pneumonia of both lungs; she was very weak, her face was inflamed and she was in great pain, but she was delighted to see me. I shall not describe her illness here, or the effect my presence had on her, the terror I felt at the prospect of losing my best friend and the sudden *insight* I had into the question "*what is death?*" One's feelings can only be truly described directly, and this I have done in my letters.

I returned to Moscow on the 19th, visiting Yasnaya Polyana on the way to see Lyova's little nest which I love so much, with Dora and Levushka. In Moscow I found everyone well. But no sooner had I arrived than Lev Nikolaevich reduced me to tears by saying: "Well, I'm glad you're back, now I can go off to the Olsufievs'." I was worn out by the journey from Kiev, and it was more than I could endure. "But I was looking forward to living quietly with you again!" I sobbed. He was alarmed by my tears, and said of course he was pleased to see me too and wouldn't leave for a while. I am painfully sorry for my daughter Tanya. She has to syringe out her nose through the hole left by the teeth she had taken out, and it has broken her spirits. She still pines terribly for Sukhotin, and cannot forget him. Her life is poisoned by misfortunes. An interesting letter from Seryozha about his life in quarantine with the Dukhobors. They haven't been cleared yet to enter Canada.

10th March. Lev Nikolaevich goes to the Myasnitskaya art school every day to visit Trubetskoy in his studio, who is doing two sculptures of him simultaneously, one a small statuette and the other of him sitting astride an unfamiliar horse.* It is very tiring for him and I am amazed he agreed to pose. He works away every morning on *Resurrection*, and is well and cheerful. He still stubbornly and silently eats his breakfast on his own, at two in the afternoon, and dines, also on his own, at about 6.30, sometimes as late as 7. We never see him; the cook just has to seize the opportunity to give "the Count" his food, and the servants never get any peace or free time.

Today three young ladies came wanting to help the starving peasants in the Samara region. My sympathies are with the starving Russians and the wretched Kazan Tartars, who are dying of scurvy and swollen with hunger; they need help far more urgently than the Dukhobors, whose hard lives have been of their *own* making.

11th March – 21st June. I fainted at a symphony concert on 11th March and was confined to my bed until 8th April. I was very weak for a long time afterwards. I haven't really been well since my return from Kiev. On 27th February I collapsed with influenza, forced myself to get up, then took to my bed again.

21st June. I haven't written my diary for almost three months, and have been more dead than alive, sick in mind and body. The doctors talked about a "weakening of the heart", and at times my pulse rate was just 48; I was fading away, and was filled with a quiet joy at this gradual departure from life. I had a lot of love and sympathy from my family, friends and acquaintances during my illness. But I didn't die; God ordained that I should live. For what?... We shall see.

Can I remember anything of significance in these three months? Not really. Seryozha has returned safely from Canada, which is a relief. Then there were three magnificent concerts by the Berlin Philharmonic, conducted by Nikish, which were a great pleasure.

On 14th May Lev Nikolaevich went off to the country, travelling with Tanya first to Pirogovo, then on the 19th to Yasnaya. Sasha and I left for Yasnaya on the 18th. On 20th May poor Tanya left with Marusya for Vienna. Hajek operated on her; she suffered greatly, and I suffered doubly for her.

On 30th May Lyova, Dora and Levushka left for Sweden. We are in Yasnaya with Andryusha, and his wife Olga, Sasha, Miss Welsh, Nikolai Gué (who copies *Resurrection* for Lev Nikolaevich), Misha and his teacher, and a young student called Arkhangelsky.

Sergei Ivanovich and Lavrovskaya visited us on the way from Moscow. He played my favourite Beethoven sonata in D Major, the Chopin Nocturne with six sharps – he picked out all my favourite pieces – and something else; next day he played his new quartet and interpreted it so interestingly for my son Seryozha. It was an absolute joy.

Then on 14th June Lev Nikolaevich fell ill with a stomach ache and was in great pain, and he still hasn't recovered.

A cold, rainy summer.

Lev Nikolaevich leads a monotonous life at present, working every morning on *Resurrection*, correcting now the proofs, now his manuscript. He is drinking Ems and is thin and quiet and has aged much this year.

Relations between us are good – peaceful and considerate, without reproaches or fault-finding. If only it could always be like this! Although I am occasionally saddened by a certain coldness and indifference on his part.

I had a depressing experience yesterday: he gave some self-educated peasant a number of books to bind, and in one of these he had accidentally left a letter, which I saw. Something was written in L.N.'s hand on a blue envelope, which was sealed. I was horrified when I saw what it said: he wrote on the envelope that he had decided to take his life as he could see I didn't love him and loved another, and he couldn't endure it… I wanted to open the letter and read it, but he snatched it out of my hands and tore it into pieces.

It transpired he had been so jealous of my relationship with T— that he wanted to kill himself. Poor darling! As if I could ever love anyone as I love him! But how I have suffered from this mad jealousy of his throughout my life! And how much I have had to give up because of it – friendships with good people, travelling, improving myself and generally everything interesting, valuable and important.

I fainted again the day before yesterday. I welcome death and am ready for it – I don't feel this to be the end. For me it's the replacement of one moment of eternity (our earthly life) by another; and this other is *interesting*, as my friend said to me.

My soul is torn and tormented. I have accumulated so much depression and remorse, such powerful longings for love and a different life, that I don't think I can bear the strain much longer.

"Grant me the spirit of wisdom, humility, patience and love."

Very hot. I swam today for the first time.

26th June. Yet another warning. Yesterday I choked several times, and that evening I had such a bad asthma attack it almost killed me. I had a terrifying, uncontrollably violent burst of hiccups and yawning – I was suffocating, gasping for air, couldn't breathe. Then it passed. There were plenty of reasons for it: Lev Nikolaevich's suicide letter, and Misha's flood of reproaches two evenings ago that no one *understood* or *sympathized* with him.

I have exercised all my maternal devotion, all my energy and skill, and I have achieved nothing. It wasn't that I didn't *want* to – I have evidently been *unable* to do so.

I haven't been able to educate my children (having married as a young girl and spent 18 years shut up in the country), and this torments me.

While I was playing the Beethoven Variations yesterday, I remembered Andryusha saying half-jokingly the other day: "Do give me a music lesson, Maman, then you can slap me again..." It made me unbearably sad to remember this. If I had children now I would be far too tender-hearted to lift a finger to them, but when I was young I had *goals* to achieve, the children were stubborn and lazy, it was hard to teach them, I wanted them to know everything and more, I had such a lot to do, such a lot of time was wasted and I would get upset and lose my temper and slap them – lightly of course, for a mother would never hurt her children badly. Yet they still remember it, and I longed to say: "Forgive me, children, I'm so sorry I hit your soft little heads. I wouldn't do it now – but it's too late!"

Lev Nikolaevich is stuck at the Senate trial in his *Resurrection*. He badly needs to ask someone about sessions of the Senate, and jokingly says to us: "Quick, find me a senator!" He might as well not exist: he lives completely alone, immersed in his work. He walks alone, sits alone, emerges halfway through dinner or supper merely to eat, then disappears again. His mind is obviously working all the time and it exhausts him – he is working too hard and I have advised him to take a break. He swam yesterday for the first time.

4th October. Tanya's birthday. She went yesterday to Moscow where Sukhotin is staying, and now feels she must decide once and for all whether to marry him or not. My poor Tanya! 35 years old, brilliant, clever, talented, happy and loved by all – and she hasn't found happiness. She is miserable – thin, pale, nervous. Her treatment in Vienna did no good at all in my view. She still has to keep rinsing out her nose through the cavity in her mouth and forehead, and her general health is wretched.

11th October. Yet more busy monotonous days have passed at Yasnaya. We had a letter from Tanya, saying she is calm and happy in the knowledge that she is in good hands. That means she has decided to marry Sukhotin.

Two days ago Lev Nikolaevich went for a walk in the afternoon without telling me where he was going. I thought he had gone for a ride – when he had just had such a bad cough and cold. Then a storm blew up. It rained and snowed, roofs and trees were smashed, the window frames rattled, it grew dark – there was no moon – and still he didn't appear. I went out to the porch and stood on the terrace, waiting for him with a spasm in my throat and a sinking heart, as I used to when I was young and he went out hunting and I would wait hour after hour in an agony of suspense. Eventually he returned, tired and sweating after his long walk. It had been hard going through the mud, and he was worn out but in good spirits. I burst into tears, reproaching him for not looking after himself and not telling me he was going out and where he was going. And to all my passionate and loving words his ironic reply was: "So what if I went out? I'm not a little boy, I don't have to tell you."

31st December. The last day of a sad year! What will the new one bring?

On 14th November our Tanya married to Mikhail Sukhotin. We should have expected this. One had the feeling she had simply come to the *end* of her unmarried life.

For her parents this marriage was a tragic blow, such as we hadn't experienced since Vanechka's death. Lev Nikolaevich lost all his outward calm. When Tanya, tormented and grieving, went upstairs in her simple little grey dress and hat to say goodbye to him before leaving for the church, he sobbed as though he was losing the most precious thing in his life.

Neither of us went to the church, but we couldn't be together either. After seeing Tanya off I went into her empty room and sobbed.

There were almost no guests, just our children, minus Lyova and Misha, and his children, and one or two others.

As they were unable to get a sleeping compartment on the train, Tanya and Sukhotin couldn't leave for the continent that day and she spent another night in her parents' house, while Sukhotin went off to stay with his sister.

The following day we saw them off for Vienna, which they have now left for Rome. Is she happy, I wonder? I cannot tell from her letters, which are very long, but more descriptive than personal.

Lev Nikolaevich grieved and wept terribly for Tanya, and on 21st November he fell ill with bad stomach and liver pains; his pulse was very weak for two days, and his temperature was 35.5. We gave him stimulants: wine, Hoffman drops, caffeine – which we sprinkled into his coffee without telling him. He was treated by dear kind Doctor Usov, who had treated me last spring. I won't describe how we looked after him, and the emotional and physical effort it cost me. Spoilt by the flattery and admiration of the whole world, he accepts my back-breaking labours for him as his due... But it's not *fame* we women want in our husbands, it's love and affection.

Almost six weeks have passed now, and he is better, but not fully recovered yet. He still has weak intestines, a sick liver and bad catarrh of the stomach.

We gave him Ems water, Ceria powder, sparkling Botkin powder, caffeine and wine. Then some Kissingen Rakóczí. Oh, yes, and I forgot – for the first three days he drank Karlsbad water, and once, with great difficulty (after I had wept and pleaded with him), we got him to drink some bitter Franz-Josef water.

Throughout his illness I found distraction in painting. I had never painted in watercolours before or had any lessons, but at my son Ilya's request I copied Sverchkov's two paintings of horses – young Kholstomer, and Kholstomer as an old horse. They came out so well that everyone praised them excessively and I was delighted.

I suffered a great deal emotionally. For the first time in my life I realized I might lose my husband and be left alone in the world, and that was an agonizing realization. If I thought about it too much I might fall ill myself.

Masha and Kolya are staying, as well as Andryusha and Olga, who is five months pregnant and has just lost her father.

And here too there is nothing but suffering. Andryusha is so rough, despotic and critical with dear, clever, compliant Olga. I can't bear to see her suffer; I am forever scolding and shouting at him, but he is more like a madman than a normal person at present, for he has a bad liver. The poor girl will have to suffer a lot more from that wretched inherited complaint. Lev Nikolaevich also suffered a lot from his liver, and I suffered too because of it.

I live from day to day, without any goal or serious purpose in life, and I find this exhausting. I am writing a novel,* which interests me. If I cannot please those around me I try not to poison their lives, and to bring peace and love to my family and friends.

My eyes ache, I am losing my sight. But in this, as in everything else: "*Thy* Will Be Done!" The end of 1899.

1900

Discussions within the government about Tolstoy's excommunication. Sofia becomes trustee at a Moscow orphanage.

5th November (Moscow). I haven't written my diary for almost a year. The hardest thing has been my failing sight. There is a broken vein in my left eye and, according to the eye specialist, an almost microscopic internal haemorrhage. I now have a permanent black circle in front of my left eye, a rheumatic pain and blurred sight. This happened on 27th May, so all reading, writing, working and any sort of strain was forbidden. A difficult six months of inactivity and ineffective treatment, with no swimming, no light and no intellectual life at all.

I have hardly played the piano, but have done a lot of exhausting work on the estate. I planted a number of trees, including some apple trees, and painfully observed our endless struggle with the peasants: their thieving and debauchery and the injustice of our rich lives, making them work for us in the rain, cold and mud, and not only adults but children too, for 15, sometimes 10 kopecks a day.

On 20th October I left with Sasha for Moscow in high spirits, looking forward to enjoying myself, meeting people, and the pleasure of seeing my beloved friends. But now I have lost heart again.

Lev Nikolaevich left Yasnaya Polyana to see his daughter Tanya in Kochety on 18th October, and returned to Moscow on 3rd November – ill, of course. The roads were icy after a month of rain and mud, and it would have been an impossibly bumpy journey. So he set out for the station on foot, but didn't know the way, and for four hours he wandered along, lost and covered in sweat, eventually getting a ride in a jolting cart which took him to the station. Now there are yet more stomach aches, massages and the rest of it.

It was pure joy when he arrived. He had been gloomy, anxious and unable to work ever since we parted. Yet before this he had been cheerful and full of energy, happily writing his play *The Corpse** and working hard.

When I met him at the station he gazed at me and said, "How lovely you are! I'd forgotten you were so pretty!"

All yesterday and today he was putting his books and papers in order. Then *his* friends came – Gorbunov, Nakashidze, Boulanger, Dunaev and the rest of them. They are thinking of starting a journal with contributions from talentless scribblers like Chertkov and Biryukov, and they want Lev Nikolaevich to give his spiritual support to the scheme.*

I went to see Misha at his new property, and felt very sorry for him – he is so childish and shy, and has made such a clumsy start in life. I spent the summer with Tanya and the autumn with Andryusha. They're all *starting* new lives. Today I took Sasha and Misha Sukhotin to a rehearsal of Koreshchenko's *The Ice House*.* V.I. Maslova was there, as well as the Maklakovs, Sergei Ivanovich and various other friends. Things have changed somewhat with Sergei Ivanovich. We seldom meet, but when we do it's as if we never parted.

My heart has been heavy all autumn – no snow, no sun, no joy, as though I was asleep. Shall I wake up to new joys, or to death, or will some great grief arouse my joyless soul? We shall see...

This evening I prepared an enema for Lev Nikolaevich with castor oil and egg yolk, while he lectured the obsequiously attentive Goldenweiser about the European governments, which he said were becoming increasingly shameless and provocative.

6th November. I got up early and visited the Krutitsky barracks on behalf of a woman who had begged me with tears in her eyes to intercede for her son, a soldier named Kamolov, who wanted to stay in Moscow. I arrived at the courtyard of a huge building, milling with young recruits, their wives and mothers, a huge crowd of people. I asked a soldier where the military commander was. "There he is!" the soldier said and pointed. And sure enough, two men were approaching. If I'd come two minutes later I couldn't have done anything, but now I was able to plead my case, which was heard very courteously, then I went on to demand the royalties due to the author of *The Fruits of Enlightenment*. This money has always gone either to the starving or to peasant victims of fires. It is now going to the latter. I received 1,040 rubles, covering several years.

I arrived home exhausted and sat down to check the accounts on the book sales. When I went out into the dining room I found Lev Nikolaevich's copier Alexander Petrovich standing by the door drunk and cursing. I quietly urged him to go to bed, but he cursed even louder, so I had to restrain him even more energetically. What an emotional ordeal this is for me! Ever since I was a child I have had a horror of drunk people, and to this day the sight of them makes me want to cry. Lev Nikolaevich tolerates them quite easily, and when he was young I remember him laughing at old Voeikov the landlord monk when he had too much to drink, making him jump around, talk nonsense and do all sorts of tricks to amuse him.

12th November. This morning I visited the orphanage where I am a patron, and took a good look at these children picked off the streets and from the drinking houses, children carelessly born to fallen girls or drunken women, children who are congenital idiots, born with fits and defects, hysterical children, abnormal children... And it occurred to me that this work I'm doing isn't really such a splendid thing after all. Is it necessary to save lives that offer no hope for the future? And according to the rules of the home, we only have to keep them till they are twelve.

Seryozha has come, and sits absorbed in chess problems for days on end. Most odd! This evening I went to the Maly Theatre with Sasha to see *The Fruits of Enlightenment*. I don't like comedies, I can never laugh – it's my great failing. We returned to find guests there.

The day before yesterday, Sergei Ivanovich came and played his symphony, arranged as a duet, with Goldenweiser.

Lev Nikolaevich told me today that when he left Tanya's house in Kochety the roads were so bad he had decided to walk to the station, but he didn't know the way and got lost. He saw some peasants and asked them to walk with him, but they were afraid of wolves and didn't want to, although one finally agreed to walk him to the main road, where Sukhotin and the Sverbeevs overtook him on their way to the station. By then he had been wandering around for four hours, and by the time he got back to Moscow he was ill and exhausted.

Then on the way he pinched his finger in the train, and the nail came off, so he has been going to the clinic ever since he got back to have it dressed, and has been unable to write for three weeks.

13th November. Tanya came with her husband and visited Doctor Snegiryov, who diagnosed a completely normal pregnancy. Lev Nikolaevich was so overjoyed to see her he could hardly believe his eyes, and kept repeating: "She's back, she's back!"

Lev Nikolaevich, Misha and Seryozha went to the bathhouse this afternoon and later we all sat with Tanya; she has become a stranger to us now and is totally absorbed in material worries about the

Sukhotin family. As she herself was saying only today, "I've become a perfect Martha."

My soul is weary and my body aches with neuralgia. It's a hard life; the inner fire that should warm my life devours it instead, for one has to smother it as soon as it bursts through.

15th November. I am ill, with a cold, nausea and headache, and have stayed at home for three days. Today I played the piano for about three hours – Mendelssohn's studies, *Auf Flügeln des Gesanges* and a Beethoven sonata. We had guests all day. Much too much commotion for my poor head; worries about food, a lot of talk.

I see almost nothing of Tanya, who is completely absorbed in her husband. Lev Nikolaevich feels slightly unwell; he has a bad stomach and has had no dinner. Both he and I are in low spirits. It makes him angry and anxious whenever I see Sergei Ivanovich, but I miss him and his music – I don't want to hurt Lev Nikolaevich, but I can't help missing him dreadfully. It's all very sad.

20th November. Our guests yesterday were a man from the island of Java who spoke French, and another from the Cape of Good Hope who spoke English. The first talked interestingly about Java, and told us that in the capital there were electric trams, an opera house and higher educational institutions, while in the provinces there were cannibals and heathens. This Malayan had read all of Lev Nikolaevich's philosophical works and had come here *especially* to talk to him.*

The house is full: my daughter-in-law Sonya has come with her sons Andryusha and Misha, Tanya is here with her husband and stepson, and Tanya's artist friend, Yulia Igumnova. Seryozha and Misha are here too. Yesterday there were two romances: Misha and Lina Glebova, who spent the day in our house for the first time yesterday, such a sweet, serious girl; and Sasha, who has fallen in love with Yusha Naryshkin. Who knows what *that* will lead to?

I love it when there is a lot of passion and excitement around me, but I can no longer join in as I used to. My own intense, impetuous life and my relations with my family and with outsiders have burnt out my heart and it is exhausted.

22nd November. I printed photographs, tried on dresses and called on Sergei Ivanovich to examine his gymnastic equipment, and he played me two choral works he has just completed. As usual I didn't understand them straight away; one was set to words by Tyutchev, the other to the words of Khomyakov's 'The Stars'.*

As usual, his "*intérieure*" made a very good impression. His student Zhilyaev was sitting there busily immersed in some musical proofs, his old Nurse was asleep in her semi-darkened room, and Sergei Ivanovich came out to greet me, calm, serious and affectionate. We had a quiet talk together, and he took an affectionate, unaffected interest in everything.

Sonya came back late and I stayed up chatting with her, Tanya and Yulia Igumnova, and we all went to bed at around two in the morning.

23rd November. Tanya and her husband returned to their house in the country today, intending to return to Moscow for the birth. We won't be seeing her again until the end of January. Seryozha and Misha are leaving too, and Sonya will leave tomorrow with the grandchildren. But I don't care about any of them, I'm not particularly keen to see anyone – there's just a nagging sense of something irretrievably lost, a helpless sense of the emptiness and pointlessness of existence, the absence of a close friend, the absence of love and concern.

I struggle to elicit from my husband *what* he lives for. He never tells me what he is writing or thinking, and takes less and less interest in my life.

24th November. Visits to various Ekaterinas on their name day. Ekat. Davydova is ill, Ekat. Yunge is in tears because her son has been taken into the army for three years, Ekat. Dunaeva is in deep mourning for her beloved brother-in-law. More cheerful at Ekat. Ermolova's, with a lot of flowers, fine gowns and social brilliance. The dear Sverbeevs and their friends were good-natured but dull.

This evening I visited sick Marusya, and Lev Nikolaevich went to a musical evening at the lunatic asylum.* I often feel sorry for him: he seems to want music and entertainment, but his principles and his peasant shirt prevent him from going to concerts, or the theatre or anywhere else.

27th November. Ill again. Stayed in bed all of the 25th and yesterday until three in the afternoon, and could barely get up. No thoughts, no desires, depression... This evening Prince Shirinsky-Shikhmatov, Dunaev, Sneserev, secretary of the *New Times*, and someone else. We talked about Eskimo dogs, and the fire at Muir and Merrilees – so dull!

Today I am a little better. I spent the day going over bills with the accountant, checked the book sales, got receipts for everything. He tried to cheat me out of 1,000 rubles, but I spotted it in time.

I was lying in bed this morning listening to the wind howling, and all at once a cock crowed, and I had a sudden vivid memory of Easter Sunday at Yasnaya Polyana; I looked out of the window and saw a red cockerel on a heap of straw crowing. I opened the ventilation window and heard the distant church bells ringing and remembered how in the old days no one in our home cursed the Church, no one condemned the Orthodox faith as Lev Nikolaevich did yesterday with Shirinsky-Shikhmatov. The Church is the idea that preserves the Deity and unites all who believe in God. The Church has created its fathers and its worshippers, those who fast and appeal to God with purified souls and prayers such as: "Our Father, Lord of Life, grant me not the spirit of idleness, sorrow, self-love and empty talk. Grant me instead the spirit of wisdom, humility, patience and love..."

30th November. This morning I went to buy shoes and jerseys for my grandchildren, wool for blankets, dresses for Dora and Varenka, and plates and dishes in the sale. For two days I have been cutting out underwear and making a layette for Tanya's baby. But I don't enjoy it, I hate it, I'm tired of working.

The secretary of the orphanage visited: things aren't going well there. Some little boys were brought in yesterday and turned away because they were too young.

3rd December. I have been busy with the orphanage, without success. I went there today, and for the first time since I was made a patron I felt sorry for these children. I want to organize a concert to raise money for them, but it will be hard, I'm too late, and it's such an unusual scheme.

Misha was here, and has gone elk-hunting with Ilya.

4th December. Lev Nikolaevich said today he was much better and felt motivated to work again. He joked that he had been drained of all his talent by *Puzin*, and that Puzin would now be the wiser for it. This Puzin, a nobleman and horse-dealer, is a young ignoramus who lives with the Sukhotins. Lev Nikolaevich stayed in his room and slept in his bed when he visited them, and afterwards said he must have been invaded by Puzin's soul, for he couldn't work and had grown as stupid as Puzin. But today this has passed. Lev Nikolaevich has resumed his old life now that I am looking after him, and is physically and mentally fit again.

I went to greet the Varvaras on their name day. I spent a long time at the Maslovs; all very good-natured, friendly, simple and interesting, with refreshments, chocolate and a lot of guests. Sergei Ivanovich came and livened things up.

I am preoccupied with the concert for the orphans' home.

5th and 6th December. Lev Nikolaevich is writing a letter to the Tsar appealing to him to allow the Dukhobors' wives, who emigrated to Canada with the others, to be reunited in Yakutsk with their husbands.

I returned some essential calls, then sent invitations to a meeting at my orphanage and asked members to pay their dues.

7th December. Lev Nikolaevich and I were invited to the Glebovs' for a concert of 23 balalaikas conducted by Andreev. The orchestra also includes *zhaleiki,** psalteries and bagpipes.

It was splendid, especially the Russian folk songs; then a waltz, and Schumann's '*Warum?*' This was played for Lev Nikolaevich's benefit, as he had expressed a desire to hear it. The dear Trubetskoy children were there. V.I. Maslova, Dunaev and Usov came this evening.

There was a slight unpleasantness with Lev Nikolaevich. We had planned to spend the holidays with Ilyusha near Moscow, but Lev Nikolaevich now says he wants to go to Pirogovo to see his brother. Ilya's estate is so close to Moscow, I could have looked after him there. But Pirogovo is such a godforsaken hole and Sergei Nikolaevich, that proud and despotic man, is very ill. Lev Nikolaevich is sorry for him and will suffer to see him; then there's the exhausting journey and the bad food, and he'll be living away from me so I won't be able to look after him. I felt very hurt and told him: he would ruin the holiday for me if he went. I couldn't and wouldn't go to Pirogovo, which I hate, I wanted to visit Ilya, Andryusha and Lyova and see my grandchildren.

He kept a cold and stubborn silence throughout – a murderous new habit of his. I was sobbing all night until 4 in the morning, trying not to wake him.

8th December. I went to town to do some errands for my children, and to the bathhouse. The driver turned the horse too abruptly on the Kuznetsky Most and tipped over the sledge, tumbling off the coach box and throwing me onto the ground. It was a very busy street, with trams jingling and carriages dashing past, and a large crowd gathered around me. I hurt my elbow, leg and back, but it doesn't seem too serious. Lev Nikolaevich was very upset though, which pleased me. I sewed a kidskin finger-guard for his sore finger and carried it upstairs to give him; he took it and drew me towards him, kissing me and smiling. How seldom he shows me affection these days! But thanks for this kindness, anyway.

This evening's guests were Gagarina, Gayarinova, Martynov, Gorbunov and a peasant writer called Semyonov. Lev Nikolaevich started a discussion about children. He says women and children are egotists, and it is only men who are capable of self-sacrifice. We said only women were capable of self-sacrifice, and there was a nasty argument.

10th December. A meeting at the orphanage. Very flattering for me, because the other members told me I was the life and soul of their society, it was a joy to work with me, and I inspired them with my passionate devotion to our cause.

But what made me happiest was that when they showed the children to Tsvetkova, the wife of our *benefactor*, the little ones all jumped into my arms and hugged me and kissed me. That means the children *like* me, and that's the most precious thing for me.

This evening I went to a concert to hear the interlude to Taneev's *Oresteia*, a marvellous work, but badly performed by Litvinov's orchestra. Then Sobinov sang a song which his pupil Yusha Pomerantsev had dedicated to me.

Throughout the concert I was making enquiries about the meeting hall, finding out when it was free, how much it cost and so on. I was in a businesslike frame of mind. I went home with Sergei Ivanovich, again quite by chance – we happened to meet on the stairs. I begged him to play at my concert, but he refused, logical, self-centred and perfectly correct, as usual. "I am composing at present and cannot play," he said. "In order to play for just a quarter of an hour I would have to waste two months practising." He is quite right of course, but I am sorry no one will agree to play or sing.

Good-natured Ilya arrived today with his endless jokes, and Misha has brought his gramophone, which amused everyone with its horribly tinny sounds. Seryozha has come too; he played a piece by Grieg beautifully.

17th December. I returned yesterday evening from Yasnaya, worn out mentally and physically. When I got there I found my little grandson Levushka in a fever, and Dora anxious and also ill. Lyova left for St Petersburg to buy a house while I was there, and it was pitiful to see the worried mother with her baby, crying and groaning day and night.

I spent two days paying out money for some casual labour we had had done, entering it all in the book and checking the accounts. Then I walked around the estate. It's a never-ending struggle with the peasants; all this thieving is justified from the poor peasants' point of view, but so unpleasant. It's particularly painful that the Grumond peasants have chopped down the birch trees on the bank of the pond where we used to have picnics, drink tea and fish. I wanted to pardon the peasant who pulled up some apple trees at the threshing barn, as he had asked permission to do so, but the case had already been referred to the village policeman while I was away.

I spent four days with Dora and helped her with the children, and drove to Ovsyannikovo to see Maria Schmidt. It was a frosty evening, with a beautiful sunset, hoar frost, the sharp outline of the half-moon, boundless expanses of snow, and everything silent, stern and cold. She seemed weighed down by her earthly life after her illness. Tolstoy's follower, young Abrikosov, is also there, living an ascetic life. I cannot think what reason he had to settle there in an alien village, with no purpose in life and no work, simply making some sort of chest for a local peasant for money, when his father owns a sweet factory and a wealthy estate in the Crimea and lives in luxury.

I found Olga alone in Taptykovo, as Andryusha was out on a wolf-hunt. She sits there alone with her little daughter all day, like a bird in a cage. I feel so sorry for her. I spent the night there and left for Moscow the following day. Still 24 degrees of frost.

23rd December. More terrible days. It turns out Lyova's son Levushka has tuberculosis of the brain and is dying. One more sweet creature to whom my soul has grown attached is leaving this life. *This* child, with his delicate moral constitution, wasn't made for this world, just like my Vanechka.

Lev Nikolaevich is constantly besieged by people. Yesterday seventeen Americans, fifteen women and two men, came to look at the famous Tolstoy. I didn't see them, I had no wish to.

1901

A socialist Revolutionary terrorist shoots dead Minister of Education. Students demonstrate to applaud the deed. More students drafted into the army. Tolstoy writes open protest letter to the Tsar.

22nd February – Tolstoy excommunicated, excommunication order appearing on all church doors in Russia. Sofia Tolstoy writes to the Synod and the Metropolitans to protest. Tolstoy is revered and reviled. He works on his pacifist 'Notes for Soldiers' (published the following year in England). Sofia starts work on her autobiography, My Life. *June – Tolstoy seriously ill with malaria. September – Tolstoy family goes to Crimea for him to convalesce. He is mobbed along the way.*

6th January. The old year ended and the new year started with a great tragedy. On 25th December, Christmas Day, I heard of Levushka's death. He passed away the previous day, at nine in the evening. Despite being ill I packed immediately and set off for Yasnaya, accompanied by Ilya. I arrived that evening and Dora threw herself into my arms, sobbing hysterically, while Lyova stood there looking thin and distraught, blaming himself, his wife and everyone else for his son's death. He blamed them for letting him catch cold, for letting him go out in a thin coat, for neglecting his poor health and delicate constitution; and these accusations were harder to bear than anything else. But their grief was unspeakable! All the emotional agony I had endured with Vanechka's death surfaced from the depths of my soul, and I was suffering both for myself and for my children, the young parents. I was unable to help them; Westerlund, Dora's father, arrived and managed to relieve Lyova's conscience a little. Dear Maria Schmidt was there with them all the time, and Andryusha arrived for the funeral. And then once again it was the open pit, the little waxen face surrounded by hyacinths and lilies, the harshness of death and the frantic grief of the mourners.

Then news came that Tanya had given birth to a dead baby girl. I was stunned. No sooner had I attended Levushka's funeral than I had to set off again that evening to see Tanya; Andryusha came with me. It tore my heart to see her so ill and grief-stricken, her husband away and her hopes of being a mother cruelly dashed. She bore it so bravely, playing with her stepchildren, reading, knitting and chatting as if nothing had happened. But I could see the grief and despair in her eyes. Her stepchildren, especially Natasha, are very sweet to her, but she said to me: "Looking at my dead baby gave me a hint of the maternal instinct, and I was horrified by its power."

I returned to Moscow on 3rd January. Sasha, L.N. and the servants gave me a very warm welcome. We have announced Misha's wedding to Lina Glebova. She is madly in love with him. I went to the Glebovs' today for the blessing, which moved me to tears. Lina is radiantly happy.

8th January. I spent the day doing essential tasks. I went to the bank, ordered an enlarged portrait of Levushka, went to the bathhouse and did some shopping, and took my dress to the cleaners for Misha's wedding. L.N. is ill – first it was a chill, now it's a bad stomach. He is feeling wretched. He doesn't want to die – the idea clearly terrifies and depresses him.

10th January. I went to the Rumyantsev Museum, and took out his unpublished comedy *The Nihilist, or The Infected Family*, which I think I shall read at my charity concert. I looked through a few things with An. Al. Goryainova this evening, but there doesn't seem to be anything interesting to read all the way through. We decided on Friday that we would all read something aloud.

19th January. Very worried about Lev Nikolaevich's health. He has been taking quinine for three days and seems to be feeling better, but his legs ache in the evening. His mind has simply dried up, and this depresses him. These family griefs have taken their toll. Then all the arrangements for Misha's wedding. He and Lina spend the whole time swooning over each other unpleasantly.

28th January. We spent the week preparing for Misha's wedding, paying visits, going shopping, making clothes, sewing little bags of sweets and so on.

Today we heard from poor Masha; her baby has just died inside her, and she is in bed in a state of collapse, grieving inconsolably, like Tanya, for her lost hopes. I want to cry all the time. I feel terribly, terribly sad for my two little girls, starved by their father's vegetarian principles. He couldn't have known, of course, that they would be too undernourished to feed the children in their wombs. But he has always gone against *my* wishes and my maternal instinct, which is never mistaken if a mother loves her children.

31st January. Misha and Lina Glebova were married today. It was a splendid society wedding. The Grand Duke Sergei came from St Petersburg for the day, the Chudovsky choristers sang, there were a mass of flowers and fine clothes, some beautiful prayers for the newly-weds and a lot of vanity and glitter. What an unemotional way to introduce these two young creatures, so in love with each other, to their new life together.

Nothing *amuses* me any more. I feel sorry for my darling young Misha embarking so *irrevocably* on this new life. Still, he has a wife who is worthy of him, thank God, and who loves him.

We left the church for the Glebovs', where the Grand Duke was very affable to me, and – I am ashamed to admit this – flattered my vanity, as did people's comments as we were leaving the church: "That's the mother of the bridegroom, she's still a very beautiful woman, isn't she", and so on.

L.N. stayed at home for the wedding, but came out at four to say goodbye to Misha and Lina. This evening he entertained some sectarians from Dubovka and various "dark ones", and they read aloud that article by Novikov the peasant about the suffering people.

12th February. Bad news today from my daughter Masha, who has given birth to her dead baby boy. Poor, suffering creature!

Tanya and I visited Yasnaya together. My darling, kind Tanya was determined to visit Lyova and Dora after their grief. They are a little more cheerful now, and they love and care for each other. Maria Schmidt was also in Yasnaya, and Olga, who is feeling very lonely at present. Aren't we all!

I have been feeling acutely so today. The children are always so eager to judge me – Tanya was criticizing me for the untidiness at home, Misha berated me when he and Lina were leaving for foreign parts for worrying about them on their travels. And they simply don't see anything! How can one keep things tidy when there are people constantly coming to stay, dragging yet more guests after them – crowds of people milling around from morning to night? And I do all the work for everyone on my own. I take care of business on my own, without any help from my husband or sons. I do a man's work: I run the estate, supervise the children's education and deal with them and the servants – all on my own. My eyesight is failing, my soul is weary, yet there are these endless demands on me...

We had a musical evening here on the 9th. Sergei Ivanovich played his *Oresteia*, Muromtseva sang Clytemnestra's aria with a choir of her pupils, and Melgunova and Khrennikova sang too. Everyone enjoyed the evening immensely, but L.N. tried to cast it in a negative and ridiculous light, and as usual my children were infected by his hostility to me and my guests.

Long after all the respectable people had left and he had put on his dressing gown and gone to bed, some students, one or two young ladies and Muromtseva stayed on in the drawing room. They had all had a great deal to drink at supper, and broke into rowdy Russian folk songs, gypsy songs and factory ballads, whooping, dancing and going wild... I went downstairs and who should I see there but L.N., sitting in the corner and urging them on. He sat up with them for a long time.

15th February. I have just seen Tanya off to Rome with her family. It's a long time since I've cried when parting with my children, for I seem to be forever meeting them or seeing them off somewhere. But today with the bright sunset lighting up our garden and Lev Nikolaevich's sad, grey, balding head as he sat by the window seeing her off with such mournful eyes that she came back twice to kiss him and say goodbye – it broke my heart, and I am weeping now as I write. We evidently need suffering to make us better people. Even the small grief of today's parting had the effect of ridding my heart of spite and anger, especially with my family, and I wished them all well and wanted them all to be good and happy. I feel terribly sorry for L.N. at present. Something is tormenting him, I don't know if it's the fear of death, or that he's unwell, or some secret worry. But I don't remember ever seeing him like this, constantly dissatisfied and depressed by something.

16th February. Sasha has a sore throat. Doctor Ilin called and said she had a fever and swollen tonsils, but nothing serious. I went with Sem. Nik. the cook to the mushroom market and bought mushrooms for myself, Tanya and the Stakhoviches, then bought some Russian furniture. Crowds of people, folk handicrafts and a lot of peasant atmosphere. They were ringing the bell for vespers when I drove home. Then I changed my dress and went out again on foot with L.N.; he went to buy 500 grams of quinine for the Dukhobors, and I went to church. I listened to the prayers and prayed fervently to myself; I love being alone in a crowd of strangers and leaving behind all cares and earthly concerns. From the church I went on to the orphanage, where the children all surrounded me, welcoming and kissing me. I stayed there a long time finding out how they were doing and what they needed.

It was almost 2 a.m. and we had just gone to bed, when there was a sudden desperate ringing at the doorbell. Some woman, a widow called Berg, who had been in a lunatic asylum for 13 years, wanted to see Lev Nikolaevich. I didn't let her in, but she talked to me at the door for a whole hour, in a terribly agitated state, recalling, among other things, how my Vanechka had picked some little blue flowers in the garden of the lunatic asylum seven years ago and asked if he could keep them. A pathetic, neurotic Polish woman. We got to bed very late, but on calm, friendly terms. At 6 in the morning I painted Sasha's throat.

18th February. I went to bed late yesterday, burdened by oppressive memories of a discussion between Lev Nikolaevich and Bulygin about religion. They were saying that a priest in a brocade cassock gives you bad red wine to drink and people call this "religion". Lev Nikolaevich was jeering and raging against the Church in the coarsest possible tones, and Bulygin said he thought the Church was the Devil's work on a massive scale.

These remarks made me angry and sad, and I loudly protested that *true* religion saw neither the priest's brocade cassock, nor Lev Nikolaevich's flannel shirt, nor the monk's habit. Such things simply do not matter.

6th March. On 24th February it was announced in all the newspapers that Lev Nikolaevich has been excommunicated.* This incensed public opinion and bewildered and dismayed the common people. For three days Lev Nikolaevich was given ovations, brought baskets of fresh flowers and sent telegrams, letters and salutations, and expressions of sympathy and indignation with the Synod and the Metropolitans are still pouring in. That same day I myself wrote and circulated a letter to Procurator Pobedonostsev and the Metropolitans. I am attaching it here.*

This stupid excommunication coincided with the upheavals in the university. For the past three days the students and the population of Moscow were in turmoil. The students had risen up because students in Kiev had been drafted into the army for rioting. But what was unprecedented about these disorders was that whereas people had previously been against the students, now everyone's sympathies are with them, and the cab-drivers, shopkeepers and workers are saying the students are on the side of truth and the poor.*

That same Sunday, 24th February, L.N. was walking to Lubyanka Square with Dunaev, and met a crowd of several thousand people. One of them saw L.N. and said: "Look, there he is, the Devil incarnate!" At this a lot of people turned round, recognized him and began shouting, "Hurrah L.N.! Greetings L.N.! Hail to the great man! Hurrah!"

The crowd grew bigger, the shouts grew louder, the cab-drivers fled...

At last some technical students managed to find a cab and put Dunaev and Lev Nikolaevich inside, and a mounted gendarme, seeing people grab the horse's reins and hold its bridle, stepped in and dispersed the crowd.

For several days now there has been a festive spirit in our house, with an endless stream of visitors from morning to night...

26th March. It's a great pity I haven't kept an accurate account of the various events and conversations that have taken place. What interested me most were all the letters, especially those from abroad, sympathizing with my letter to Pobedonostsev and the Metropolitans. None of Lev Nikolaevich's manuscripts have reached such wide or speedy distribution as this letter of mine, and it has been translated into all the foreign languages.* I was delighted, but it did *not* make me conceited, thank God! I dashed it off spontaneously, passionately. It was God's will, not mine, that I should do it.

Lev Nikolaevich has written a letter 'To the Tsar and His Assistants'.* What will come of it! I wouldn't want us to be exiled from Russia in our old age.

Another event was my concert in aid of the orphanage. Some very pleasant people took part, and this lent it an exceptionally elegant, respectable tone. The young ladies selling programmes all wore white dresses, and there were baskets of fresh flowers on the tables. Mikhail Stakhovich did a fine rendering of an excerpt from L.N.'s 'Who is Right?', and I wasn't disgraced before all these people whose opinion I esteem. We didn't make much for the orphanage, only 1,307 rubles.*

An unpleasant scene with Sasha on Palm Sunday. I called her to go to vespers with me and she refused, saying she had lost her faith. I told her if she wanted to follow her father's path she must go the whole way like him: he was extremely Orthodox for many years – long after he got married too – then he renounced the Church in the name of pure Christianity, and also renounced all earthly blessings. Sasha, like so many of my children, was of course simply jumping at the easy way out – in this case not going to church. I burst into tears and she went to ask her father for advice, and he told her: "Of course you must go – you mustn't distress your mother."

So she came to the orphanage church with me and attended vespers, and now she will fast with me.

27th March. The other day I received Metropolitan Antony's reply to my letter, perfectly correct but completely soulless.* I wrote mine in the heat of the moment, it has gone round the entire world and has *infected* people with its sincerity.

These public events have exhausted me and I have turned to introspection; but my inner life is tense and joyless too.

30th March. Things have gone from bad to worse with Sasha. She wouldn't fast with me: first she pleaded a sore leg, then she refused outright. Yet another worsening in our relations.

I received the Eucharist today. I have found it very difficult to fast; there are such vast contradictions between what is genuine – the Church's *true* foundations – and all these rituals, the wild shrieks of the deacon and so on, that it is hard to persevere and one sometimes feels like giving up altogether. This is what disgusts young people so much.

I was standing in the church today and the invisible choir was singing so beautifully, and I thought: the simple people go to church as we go to a good symphony concert. At home there is poverty, darkness and endless, backbreaking toil. They come to church and there is light, singing, beauty... There is art and music here, and a spiritual justification for all this entertainment too, since religion is approved of, and considered good and necessary. How could one live without it?

I fasted without much conviction, but went about it in a serious, sensible way, and was glad to exert myself physically and spiritually – getting up early and standing for a long time in church, praying and reflecting on my spiritual life.

18th May. We have been in Yasnaya Polyana for ten days. We travelled with Pavel Boulanger in a well-appointed private carriage, and L.N.

had a very comfortable journey. I warmed him up some pre-cooked porridge, boiled him an egg and made coffee, then he ate some asparagus and went to sleep. We were seen off in Moscow by Uncle Kostya, Dunaev, Fyodor Maslov and his sister Varvara, as well as some young people we had never met before – technical students I think – who shouted "Hurrah!" and took pictures of Lev Nikolaevich. It was very moving.

6th June. I went to Moscow and did my business there, and lived alone with the maid in my big empty house. I visited Vanechka's and Alyosha's graves and went to see my living grandson, Seryozha's little boy. He's a splendid child, serene and straightforward. I saw Misha and Lina, who always make an excellent impression, and I also saw Sergei Ivanovich. There has been a cooling in our relations recently, and I have neither the energy nor the inclination to maintain our former friendship. Besides, he really isn't the sort of person one can be friends with. Like all gifted people he is always seeking new experiences and he looks for other people to provide them, while giving almost nothing of himself.

I returned to Yasnaya Polyana, and it was hot, stuffy, lazy weather. L.N. is taking salt baths and drinking Kronenquelle. He is fairly cheerful after a winter of illnesses.

14th June. What a lovely summer! Through my window I can see the moon in the clear sky. It is still and silent, and the air is caressing and delightfully warm. I have been spending almost all my time outside with nature; I go swimming and in the evenings I water the flowers and go for walks. My beloved Tanya is staying with her husband, with whom I am becoming reconciled since she loves him. He has a sweet nature but is terribly selfish, which makes me fear for her.

Pasternak the artist has been here and has drawn me, Lev Nikolaevich and Tanya in a variety of poses and angles. He is planning to do a genre painting of our family for the Luxembourg.

Lyova, Dora and little Pavlik have left for Sweden. It was terribly painful to part with them. They lead such irreproachable Christian lives, with the finest ideals and intentions. They have nothing to hide, one could look into the depths of their souls and find nothing but purity and goodness. At 5 in the morning poor little Dora ran to Levushka's grave to say goodbye to her darling baby; I suffered so much for her and wanted to sob.

20th June. I went to Moscow to negotiate the sale of Sasha's land; another frightful waste of time and energy. It was hot, I spent two nights on the train, talked to the barrister, did some shopping and so on.

When I returned exhausted next morning, they hadn't sent any horses, so I had to walk back from Kozlovka. I was in a thoroughly bad temper, the heat was insufferable and the house was crowded with good-for-nothings – Alyosha Dyakov, Goldenweiser, some sculptor, the Sukhotins. Tanya is the only one I care about.

3rd July. Something frightful is drawing near, and it is death.

Lev Nikolaevich fell ill on the night of 27th–28th June. He felt wretched, couldn't sleep and had difficulty breathing. Sasha and I planned to visit my son Seryozha on the 28th, but I wasn't sure I could leave him. In the end we did go, at 8 that morning. He slept well that night, but the following day he set off for a walk and could hardly manage to get home. The pain in his chest grew worse, but they put a hot blanket on it and that eased it. He again had a fever on the evening of the 29th when I returned. No one had looked after him properly while I was away! It broke my heart to see him. It must be his heart, I told him. The following morning Doctor Dreyer from Tula discovered he had a high fever and a dangerously high pulse of 150 per minute. He prescribed 10 grains of quinine a day, and caffeine and strophanthus for the heart. But when his temperature fell to 35.9° his pulse was still 150.

We wired Doctor Dubensky in Kaluga (chief doctor at the local hospital and a good friend of ours) who said it was the pulse of the death agony. After several doses of quinine the fever passed, and for two days running his temperature has been normal, 36.2°. But he has just had another two sleepless nights, with a slight chill, a fever and profuse sweating, and he is now feeling exhausted, and what is more serious, his heart has been weakened.

The children have all arrived – apart from Lyova, who is in Sweden, and Tanya. Ilya's children are here too. Yesterday he invited his three grandsons and Annochka his granddaughter into his room, gave them all chocolates out of a box, made four-year-old Ilyusha tell him about the time he almost drowned in a rainwater tub, and asked Annochka about her hoarseness. Then he said: "Off you go now, I'll call you again when I'm next feeling bored." And when they had gone out he kept saying: "What marvellous children."

Yesterday morning I was putting a hot compress on his stomach and he gazed at me intently and began to weep, saying: "Thank you

Sonya. You mustn't imagine I'm not grateful or don't love you…" His voice broke with emotion and I kissed his dear familiar hands, telling him what pleasure it gave me to look after him, and how guilty I felt when I couldn't make him happy. Then we both wept and embraced. For such a long time my soul has yearned for this – a deep and serious recognition of our closeness over the thirty-nine years we have lived together…

Today he said to me: "I am now at a crossroads. I would just as soon go forwards (to death) as backwards (to life). If this passes now, it will just be a respite." Then he reflected a little and added: "But there's still so much I want to tell people!"

Yesterday he was anxiously enquiring about some peasant victims of a recent fire in a faraway village, to whom he had asked me to give 35 rubles. He wanted to know if any of them had come to the house, and asked us to tell him if they came asking him for anything.

He had a terrible night last night, 2nd–3rd July; I was with him from two to seven in the morning. He didn't sleep a wink, and his stomach was aching. Later his chest started hurting, so I massaged it with spirit of camphor and made a cotton-wool compress, which eased the pain. Then he started having pains in his legs and they grew cold, so I massaged them with spirit of camphor and wrapped them in a warm blanket. He began to feel a little better, and I was happy to relieve his suffering. But then he began to feel very low and miserable, so I took his temperature. It was up again – from 36.2° to 37.3° – and he remained feverish for about three hours. Then he went to sleep, and I went off to bed as I was dropping with exhaustion.

I was sitting in his room today reading the Gospels, in which he has marked the passages he considers especially important, and he said to me: "Look how the words accumulate. In the first Gospel it says Christ was simply christened. In the second it has been expanded to: 'And he saw the skies open,' and the third makes the further addition: 'He heard the words, "Sit down and eat, my son,"' and so on."

Now my Lyovochka is sleeping. He is still alive, I can see him, hear him, look after him… What will happen next? My God, what unendurable grief, what horror to live without him, without his love, his encouragement, his intelligence, his enthusiasm for the finest things in life.

14th July. Tanya came with her husband, Doctor Shchurovsky arrived from Moscow, and a lot of our friends visited. Telegrams, letters, a great crush of children, grandchildren and acquaintances, one anxiety after another... Eventually I fell ill too. I had a high fever all night, my heartbeat was weak, my pulse was 52, and I had to stay in bed for two days, unable to move.

He is now very thin and weak, but has a good appetite, is sleeping well and is out of pain; he works every morning on his article about the labour question.

Thank God, thank God, for yet another reprieve! I wonder how much longer we will live together! His sunken face, his white hair and beard and his emaciated body and the persistent ache in my heart become unbearable, and I feel as though my life were at an end and I had lost all my interests and energy.

Yes, a phase of my life has just come to an end. A line has been drawn between that period when life *went on*, and now, when life has simply *stopped*.

I kept thinking: "Salt baths will help, he'll get better, he'll live another ten years; Ems water will repair his digestion, and the warmth of summer and lots of rest will restore his strength..."

But now suddenly it is the *end*. No health, no strength, nothing to restore, nothing to repair – there's so little left of Lyovochka now, too little to repair. And what a giant he used to be!

22nd July. Lev Nikolaevich is on the mend. He is taking long walks through the forest, and eating and sleeping well. Thank God!

We received letters from well-wishers in Tula yesterday evening. He burst out laughing and said: "Well, next time I start dying I shall have to do so in earnest, I mustn't joke about it any more. I'd be ashamed to make people go through all that again, with everyone gathering round, the journalists arriving, the letters and telegrams – and all for nothing!"

We had a delightful letter from Queen Elizabeth of Romania today. She has sent L.N. a brochure she has written, and writes how happy she will be if "*la main du maître*" lies for a moment on her little book.*

A hot, dry, dusty day. The oats are being harvested. Bright, sunny days, moonlit nights; it's so beautiful, one longs to make better use of this lovely summer.

30th July. It's hot again today and there's a smell of burning, as if there was smoke in the air. It's impossible to see anything, and the sun has turned into a tiny red ball.

I lead a dreary life, sitting all day by my sick husband's door and knitting caps for the orphanage. All the life and energy in me has died.

I received a letter from Countess Panina offering us her dacha in Gaspra, in the Crimea, and we are planning to go, although I don't want to leave before September.

3rd August. Lev Nikolaevich's latest illness has robbed him of even more of his strength, although he is a little better today. Terrible heat, very dry again, I swim every day. We were visited this morning by the Myasoedovo villagers who were burnt out in the fire, and we gave them all 7 rubles in the courtyard. There have been so many fires this summer, and there are so many people to be helped!

Then another visitor we didn't know, called Falz-Fein, who has just lost his young wife and has been left with three young children, desperate and ill with grief. L.N. took him out for a walk and talked to him.

26th August. We're leaving for the Crimea on 5th September. I went to Moscow on business and shall go again before we leave, probably on the 1st. Cold, windy, damp and vile.

Housekeeping, bills, taxes, packing, endless practical tasks... No walks, no music, nothing but boredom and low spirits. It seems we will be staying in the Crimea for the winter, and this makes me terribly sad! Well, whatever God ordains. A line has been drawn and a new phase in our life is starting. Just as long as Lev Nikolaevich is alive and well.

2nd December (Gaspra, the Crimea). We have been living here since 9th September for the sake of Lev Nikolaevich's health, and he is making a slow recovery. He was 73 in August, and has aged and grown very much weaker this year.

I haven't been writing my diary; it has taken me such a long time to get used to the new living conditions and emotional deprivations I have to endure here. But I am now used to it, helped by the knowledge that I am fulfilling my stern duty and my wifely obligations.

Last night I wrote letters to our four absent sons (Andryusha has just arrived), and was then kept awake all night by tormenting memories of my children's early years, my passionate, anxious relationship with them, the unwitting mistakes I made in their education and my relationship with them now they are *grown-up*.

Then my thoughts turned to my dead children. I saw with agonizing clarity first Alyosha, then Vanechka, at various moments of their lives. I had a vivid vision of Vanechka, thin and ill in bed, when after his prayers, which he invariably said in my presence, he would curl up into a cosy little ball and go off to sleep. I remember how it broke my heart to see his little back and feel his tiny bones under my hand.

And as for the spiritual and physical solitude I endured last night! Things have happened exactly as I imagined. Now that physical infirmity has forced Lev Nikolaevich to abandon amorous relations with his wife (this wasn't so long ago), instead of that peaceful, affectionate friendship I have longed for in vain all my life, there remains nothing but emptiness.

Morning and evening he greets me and leaves me with a cold and formal kiss. He loses his temper and tends to regard the world about him with utter indifference.

I think more and more of death, imagining with a calm joy the place where my infants have gone.

3rd December. A hot day. I went to Yalta and sent a letter to Seryozha authorizing him to buy 150 acres of land in Telyatinki to add to the Yasnaya property. Oh, this endless unbearable business, which is all so unnecessary to me! I wandered round the town on my own and went to Chukurlar, where I met a consumptive young man begging for a living. Everything here is dreary and chaotic. And there's more to come. Ilya and Andryusha have just arrived and, to my great displeasure, were playing cards with Sasha, Natasha Obolenskaya, Klassen the German bailiff and my daughter-in-law Olga. I sat sewing silently on my own, then studied some Italian.

4th December. Another hot day, brighter and lovelier than yesterday. The sun is as hot as summer. What a strange changeable climate here, and one's moods are equally changeable. Lev Nikolaevich, Sukhotin and his son and tutor, Natasha Obolenskaya and I walked to Orianda. The walk tired us a little but the "Horizontal path" was very lovely. We drove home with Sonyusha and Olga, and the sea and sunset were magical.

7th December. I have just said goodbye to Andryusha and my good-natured, childish Ilya. Lev Nikolaevich will accompany them to Yalta and spend the night there with Masha, which he has wanted to do for a long time. Either the arsenic or simply the good weather has had an excellent effect on him, and he is feeling much more fit and energetic. And this bustling activity shows how glad he is to be better. Yesterday he was on his feet from morning to night, and that evening he walked to the hospital, marvelling at the view in the moonlight. Today he got ready to leave for Yalta.

I wanted to help him pack so he wouldn't exert himself, but he snapped at me so peevishly I almost burst into tears, and went off without saying a word.

I incline more and more to the view that every kind of sectarianism, including my husband's teachings, tends to dry people's hearts and make them proud. Two women I know well, his sister, Mashenka the nun, and his cousin Alexandra, have both become better, nobler people without leaving the Church.

My poor Tanya gave birth to another dead baby, a boy, on 12th November. She is even more devoted to her frivolous selfish husband. There is nothing left of her now, she has been completely absorbed by him; he *allows* himself to be loved, and loves her very little himself. Well, thank God if that is to her liking! We women are able to live for love alone, even when it's not reciprocated. And even then one can live a full and active life!

Various pieces of news from Moscow and Yasnaya. Our affairs are being neglected, our friends are forgetting us; I am tantalized by all the wonderful recitals and symphony concerts, but it's no use, I just have to sit here and mope.

8th December. Lev Nikolaevich didn't return from Yalta today.

9th December. It's just as I thought – Lev Nikolaevich has been taken ill in Yalta and his heart is irregular. I have just spoken to him on the telephone; he sounded quite cheerful, and said it was his stomach again; the long ride to Simeiz and back irritated his intestines. It must be the hundredth time he has done this. Just before he left he wolfed down some treats we had got for little Andryusha's sixth birthday – some dumplings and grapes, a pear and some chocolate. And now look what happens. The moment he gets better he undoes everything with his immoderate appetite and activity. He takes fright, is treated, gets better, then ruins everything again... And so it goes on, in a vicious circle.

I went to church. The girls sang beautifully and I am in a happy, calm state of mind. Unlike other people I'm not bothered by foolishness like "with ranks of angels bearing spears" and "at the right hand of the Father" and so on. Above and beyond all this is the Church – the place that reminds us of God, where millions of people have brought their noble religious sentiments and their faith, the place where we bring all our griefs and joys, at every moment in our fickle lives.

13th December. Lyovochka's niece Liza Obolenskaya and I took him back to Gaspra with us today.

At first, after drinking some coffee with milk, he was very lively, and this evening he played two games of chess with Sukhotin; then he felt weak and took to his bed. We had been urging him to go to bed all along as the doctor had ordered, but he wouldn't listen.

The Sukhotins have had some bad news. Their Seryozha has fallen ill with typhus at Naval School, and they have been informed by telegram that his condition is serious. Tanya is wretched and has been weeping. She takes such a childish view of her fate; she thinks someone is forever out to hurt her.

We heard to our great joy today that a son, Ivan, had been born to Misha and Lina on the 10th. May my Vanechka inhabit this little boy's soul and pray for him to grow up to be a happy, healthy child.

14th December. Lev Nikolaevich moved downstairs yesterday so as not to have to climb the stairs. His room next to mine is empty, and there is something ominous and poignant about the silence upstairs. I no longer have to put the washbasin down quietly on the marble table and tiptoe around and refrain from moving chairs.

Liza Obolenskaya is sleeping downstairs next to his room at present, and he gratefully accepts her help and is glad not to have to bother me.

15th December. Lyovochka has recovered now and we have all cheered up. He had dinner with us and walked as far as the gates of the estate.

He had a call from Doctor Altschuler, who is treating him here, a pleasant, clever Jew, not at all like most Jews, whom Lev Nikolaevich trusts and likes. He was given his thirtieth arsenic injection today, and took five grains of quinine.

We have a Slovak Doctor Makovitsky* here, whom we have already met, accompanied by some Georgian called Popov, who is apparently a Tolstoyan.

23rd December. Lev Nikolaevich is fully recovered. He went for a long walk today, and looked in on Maxim Gorky* – or rather Alexei Peshkov; I dislike it when people write under assumed names. Lev Nikolaevich, Olga, Boulanger and I all came home in the carriage. It is fine, windy and warm – 6°. He brought a large mauve-pink wild flower into the house and it has blossomed again. The almond tree is also trying to come into blossom, and the snowdrops are in flower. So beautiful! I am beginning to love the Crimea. My depression has lifted, thank God, mainly because he is better now.

24th December. This evening he played vint with his children and Klassen (the bailiff). They all shouted and got very worked up over a grand slam no trumps – I find this excitement over card games incomprehensible, shouting a lot of nonsense as if they've all lost their reason.

25th December. We had a festive Christmas. Lev Nikolaevich is better – his fever has passed and his arms aren't hurting him.

26th December. We spent the evening at Klassen's – German conversation, strange people and sweet food – not at all to my liking.

29th December. The Tartars had a festival today. They were seeing a Mullah off to Mecca for three months and had prepared a dinner for him, and the streets of Koreiz and Gaspra were crowded with cheerful people of all nationalities in their best clothes. The Turks danced in a circle, looking very picturesque. I tried to take a photograph of them, but they were moving too fast and it came out badly. Lev Nikolaevich walked off on his own to Ai-Todor. He was gentle and kind today, and we are getting on well together – what a joy!

30th December. A very mixed lot of people came to see Lev Nikola-evich – three revolutionary workers filled with hatred for the rich and dissatisfaction with the present social arrangements, then six sectarians who have lapsed from the Church, three of whom are true Christians, in that they lead a moral life and love their neighbour. The other three were originally Molokans and are still sympathetic to their beliefs.

There was also an old man, better off and more intelligent than the rest, who apparently wants to go to the Caucasus and found a monastery by the sea based on new principles. He wants all the brothers to be highly educated, so that this monastery could be a sort of centre of learning and civilization. The monks would work the land and support themselves through their own labour. A difficult venture, but a worthy one.

This evening we went to the public library, where a dance had been organized. The music was provided by three travelling Czech musicians and a young man with a big harmonium, and chambermaids, and craftsmen's wives and daughters all danced waltzes, polkas and *pas de quatre* with men from various social classes. Two Tartars did some Tartar dances, two Georgians did a *lezginka* with a dagger, and a lot of people – including Volkov the *zemstvo* doctor, a highly capable and energetic man – danced the *trepak*, squatting and leaping Russian-style. We all went to watch, even Lev Nikolaevich.

31st December. The last day of a difficult year! Will the new one be better?

Lev Nikolaevich walked over to see M. Gorky and returned with Goldenweiser, who is staying with us.

I have copied out the first chapter of 'On Religion', and so far I don't like it. I don't at all like the way he compares people's faith in religion to an outworn appendix.

I went with Sasha to Koreiz to buy wine, oranges and refreshments for the servants' New Year party. We are having a party too, although I don't much like these *semi*-celebrations. People just sit around and eat, then at midnight something is suddenly supposed to *happen*.

1902

April – a young student shoots dead Minister of Interior. July – a worker shoots governor of Kharkov. Waves of peasant riots in the countryside; some ninety estates plundered, with the help of Socialist Revolutionary "expropriators".

June – Tolstoys leave the Crimea. Tolstoy works on two plays, The Light Shines Even in Darkness *and* The Living Corpse, *a few short stories, an essay on Shakespeare and a popular anthology,* Thoughts of the Wise Men for Every Day. *Sofia works on the eleventh edition of his* Complete Works.

1st January. We had a quiet family New Year party yesterday. (Lev Nikolaevich had to go to bed early, as he felt ill after his bath.) Klassen came this morning with some lovely violets.

I am copying Lev Nikolaevich's article 'On Religion' a little at a time, but it lacks something – it needs more passion, more conviction.

I took a walk to the Yusupovs' Park and the coast, with Olga and Tanya. It was a warm, summery day, and by the sea we met Gorky and his wife. Then Altschuler called. Our servants all came in dressed as mummers and stamped and danced about; it was terribly tedious – I am much too old for that sort of thing.

I wrote five letters, finished knitting a scarf and gave presents to Ilya Vasilevich and the cook. I received charming letters from my daughters-in-law Sonya and Lina, and felt so pleased that at least two of my children, Ilya and Misha, are happily married. What will this new infant Vanechka Tolstoy be like?

4th January. For the past three nights I have been sleeping on the leather sofa in the drawing room, or rather not sleeping but listening out all night for Lev Nikolaevich next door. His heart has been very irregular. Yesterday and today he came down to dinner, but grew dreadfully weak afterwards, and today we summoned Tikhonov, the Grand Duke's doctor, from Dülber. He warned of dire consequences if Lev Nikolaevich continued to lead this reckless life, overtiring himself and overeating.

Seven inches of snow fell in the night, and it is still on the ground. Yesterday there was a north wind and 3 degrees of frost; today it is half a degree above freezing, with no wind. I knew this weather would have a bad effect on him. It always does.

I am looking after him on my own, but his obstinacy, his tyrannical behaviour and his complete ignorance of hygiene and medical matters makes it terribly hard, even unbearable at times. For instance, the doctors order him to eat caviar, fish and bouillon, but he refuses because he is a vegetarian – it will be the ruin of him.

I have been reading an extraordinary little book, a translation of Giuseppe Mazzini's *On Human Duty*.*

5th January. Palpitations, difficulty in breathing, insomnia, general misery. Several times during the night I got up and went to him. He drank some milk with a spoonful of cognac, took some strophanthus, which he asked for himself, and managed towards morning to get a little sleep. Doctor Tikhonov called yesterday evening, and again today, and said there was an infiltration of the liver, a weakness of the heart and a disorder of the intestines. These complaints appeared long ago, but are now following their course in a more pronounced and malignant fashion, and manifest their ominous symptoms yet more frequently and painfully.

L.N. is very dejected, and keeps us all at a distance, calling us only if he needs something. He sits in a chair, reads or goes to bed. He slept very little again today.

There is snow on the ground and the temperature is at freezing point. A terrible wind has been howling all day. The whole place is cheerless and desolate. I have put all thoughts of Moscow out of my mind for now – although it's essential that I go!

I sit at home all day sewing and ruining my eyes; I am sunk in torpor, as I used to be in my youth at Yasnaya Polyana. But then I had children!...

8th January. Doctor Altschuler and Doctor Tikhonov came yesterday and prescribed a twice-weekly dose of extract of buckthorn, in tablet form, and five drops of strophanthus three times a day for six days. But he refuses to take anything. I am tired of this forty-year struggle, I am tired of having to employ tricks and stratagems to make him take this or that medicine and help him get better. I no longer have the strength to struggle. There are times when I long to get away from everyone and withdraw into myself, if only briefly.

All this morning I was copying out his 'On Religion'. This is more of a socialist work than a religious one.

I told him this yesterday. A religious work should be poetic and exalted, I said; his 'On Religion' was very logical but didn't capture the imagination or elevate the soul. He replied that it needed only to be logical, a lot of poetry and lofty obscurity would only confuse the issue.

I was thinking about my trip to Moscow again.

10th January. The atmosphere here is so gloomy at times. I am sitting alone after dinner sewing in the dark drawing room. Lev Nikolaevich is next door in his room. Tanya is tapping away on the Remington on the other side, Seryozha is silently reading the newspapers in the dining room, and Olga is upstairs with Sonyusha. There is silence in the house, broken at times by terrible gusts of wind, which howls and groans and stalks the rooms, filling them with cold.

He is so weak at present, he often calls me simply to cover him with a rug or adjust his blanket. I have to make sure he doesn't overeat, that people don't make a noise when he is trying to sleep and that there are no draughts. I have just put a compress on his stomach. He drinks Ems water twice a day.

11th January. I went to Yalta with Tanya to do some business and shopping, and brought her a hat for her name day. Masha was looking very thin and wretched.

Poor Olga's baby has stopped moving inside her in her sixth month. I feel so sorry for her. I brought Sasha home. Yesterday she rode her horse over to Gurzuf, and today she attended a rehearsal of *It's Not All Cream for the Cat*, in which she plays Fiona. I have now finished copying 'On Religion', which I began to like better towards the end. I like what he writes about the freedom of a man's soul illuminated by religious feeling.

12th January. The whole day was absorbed by worries. First I played with my granddaughter, then comforted poor Olga who was weeping for her baby; then I washed and mended Seryozha's cap; then I gave Sasha some advice about her theatrical costume; then the doctor came to see Olga; then this evening I prepared an enema for Lev Nikolaevich; then I put a compress on his stomach and brought him some wine, and he drank some coffee that had been heated up for him.

Tanya's name day. She has arrived from Yalta and is in a melancholy mood. Andryusha too is sad and quiet: his marriage is in difficulties and I feel very sorry for him. Seryozha has just left for Yalta, intending to celebrate the first day of the Moscow University year. He has spent the last few days playing the piano on his own in the side wing. I have been deprived of even that pleasure now! I cannot leave the house, I cannot leave Lev Nikolaevich or Olga with anyone. My old age is turning into a sad time. Yet that storm of desires and aspirations for a more spiritual, more significant life has not been extinguished in my soul.

14th January. How time flies... There is no winter here and no certainty. There is nothing to rejoice about either. Lev Nikolaevich's health isn't improving. This great man has a dreadfully obstinate nature. He refuses the diet of fish and chicken that has been recommended, and insists on eating carrots and red cabbage as he did today, then suffering for it.

I sat by his room until half-past three in the morning yesterday, waiting for Andryusha and Seryozha to return from an evening of cards. He slept well. At the moment I am copying out his letter to the Tsar.

16th January. A terrible night. L.N.'s temperature went up to 38. I spent the night in the drawing room next to his bedroom and had no sleep at all. Yesterday and today we rubbed him with iodine and applied a compress. He had five grains of quinine at 2 in the afternoon, and has been taking 5 drops of strophanthus twice a day. Despite all this he got up, did some writing and played vint with Klassen, Kolya Obolensky and his sons.

17th January. The same medicine, the same pain in his side, although he is a little more cheerful. Chekhov called,* and Altschuler. The weather is warm and fine. Tanya has left to see her husband in the country. I have just copied out L.N.'s letter to the Tsar – an angry insulting letter, abusing everything on earth and giving him the most absurd advice on how to run the country. I do hope Grand Duke Mikhailovich understands it is the product of a sick liver and stomach and doesn't give it to the Tsar; if he does, it will infuriate him and he may take action against us.

18th January. I put my husband to bed every evening like a child. I bind his stomach with a compress of spirit and camphor mixed with water, I put out a glass of milk, a clock and a little bell, I undress him and tuck him up; then I sit next door in the drawing room reading the newspapers until he goes to sleep. I have summoned up all my patience and am doing my utmost to help him endure his illness.

20th January. I went to see Sasha in the role of Fiona the old house-keeper in *It's Not All Cream for the Cat*, which is being performed in the local library. It was Sasha's first acting attempt, and she wasn't at all bad. The cast was a strange mixture of people – a doctor's wife, a blacksmith, a nurse, a stonemason and a countess. This is all good.

Lev Nikolaevich is better, his stomach isn't hurting and his temperature was 36.9 this evening, as it was yesterday. He took some strophanthus, but refused to take quinine. We didn't apply a compress today.

There has been a thick fall of wet snow.

23rd January. Doctor Bertenson (a distinguished physician-in-ordi-nary) arrived from St Petersburg yesterday evening. Today clever Doctor Shchurovsky came from Moscow, and the two of them had a serious consultation with Altschuler. I shall note down their recommendations for Lev Nikolaevich:

Regime:
1. Avoid all exertion, physical and emotional.
2. Not to go for long walks. Horse-riding and climbing strictly forbidden.
3. To rest for 1 to 1½ hours every day, taking his clothes off and going to bed.
4. To have three meals a day and eat no peas, lentils or *red cabbage*. To drink no less than four glasses of coffee with milk every day (¼ coffee to ¾ milk). If milk is drunk on its own, it must be taken with salt (¼ teaspoonful per glass).
    Wine may sometimes be replaced by porter (no more than two Madeira glassfuls per day).
5. To take a bath every two weeks. The water to be 28 degrees and the soap (half a pound) to be dissolved into it. To sit in the bath for five minutes and sponge himself with clean water of the same temperature.
    In the interval between baths to rub the body with a solution of soap spirit and eau de Cologne.

Treatment:
1. A twice-weekly enema made from 1 pound of oil slightly warmed, to be administered at night.

For the other days, 1–5 pills to be taken at night. If the pills prove ineffective, to administer a water enema in the morning.

2. Glass of Karlsbad Mühlbrun, slightly warmed, to be drunk three times a day for one month.

3. Three camomile capsules a day for three days; repeat after two days, and so on.

4. Should heart medication (strophanthus) be required, this must be administered by a doctor.

5. In the eventuality of a bad nervous illness, capsules (+ Coff) should be taken for the pain.

If the doctor considers it necessary to give quinine under the prescribed regime, this must not be obstructed.

Lev Nikolaevich's diet must consist of: four glasses of milk and coffee a day.

Gruels: buckwheat porridge, rice, oats, semolina with milk.

Eggs: fried, whisked raw, in aspic, scrambled with asparagus.

Vegetables: carrots, turnips, celery, Brussels sprouts, baked potatoes, potato purée, pickled cabbage chopped fine (?), lettuce scalded in hot water.

Fruits: sieved baked apples, stewed fruit, raw apples chopped small; all oranges to be sucked.

All sorts of jellies and creams are good; meringues.

Written later, on the evening of the 23rd. Lev Nikolaevich had a terrifying attack of angina and his temperature went up to 39°.

24th January. The doctor listened to his heart this evening and diagnosed pleurisy in the left lung. Shchurovsky has returned and is treating him.

25th January. They have decided it is pneumonia of the left lung, which subsequently spread to the right one too. His heart has been bad all this time.

26th January. I don't know why I am writing – this is a conversation with my soul. My Lyovochka is dying... And I know now that my life cannot go on without him. I have lived with him for forty years. For others he is a celebrity, for me he is my whole existence. We have become part of each other's lives, and my God what a lot of guilt and remorse has accumulated over the years... But it is all over now, we won't get it back. Help me, Lord. I have given him so much love and tenderness, yet my many weaknesses have grieved him! Forgive me Lord! I ask for neither strength from God nor consolation, I ask for faith and religion, God's spiritual support, which has recently helped my precious husband to live.

27th January. I would like to record everything concerning my dear Lyovochka, but I cannot; I am suffocated by tears and crushed by the weight of my grief... Yesterday Shchurovsky suggested Lyovochka inhale some oxygen, and he said: "Wait a bit, first it's camphor, then it's oxygen, next it'll be the coffin and the grave."

Today I went up to him, kissed his forehead and asked him: "Is it hard for you?" And he said: "No, I feel calm." Masha asked him: "Is it horrible, Papa?" And he replied: "Physically, yes, but emotionally I feel happy, so very happy." This morning I was sitting beside him and he was groaning in his sleep, when he called out suddenly in a loud voice: "Sonya!" I jumped up and bent over him and he looked at me and said: "I dreamt you were in bed somewhere..." Then the dear man asked me whether I had slept and eaten... This is the first time *anyone* has asked about me! Oh Lord, help me not to expect anything from people, and to be grateful for everything that I may receive from them.

His pleurisy is pursuing its terrifying course, his heart is growing weaker, his pulse is quick, his breathing is short... He groans day and night. These groans carve deep scars into my heart – I shall hear them for the rest of my life. He often talks at length about what has been preoccupying him lately: his letter to the Tsar and other letters he has written.

I once heard him say: "I was wrong," then "I didn't understand."

He is generous and affectionate with everyone around him, and is evidently well pleased with the treatment he is receiving. "That's wonderful," he keeps saying.

No, I cannot write, he is groaning downstairs. He has had several injections of camphor and morphine.

He once said in his delirium: "Sevastopol is burning." And then he called out to me again: "Sonya what are you doing? Are you writing?"

Several times he asked: "When is Tanya coming?" and "What time is it?" He asked what the date was, and whether it was the 27th.

28th January. Tanya, the Sukhotins and Ilya have come, bringing a lot of noise and worries about food and accommodation. How frightful it all is: the painful struggle of a great soul in its passage to eternity and oneness with God, whom he has served – and all these earthly cares in the house.

It is so hard for him, the dear, wise man... Yesterday he said to Seryozha: "I thought it was easy to die, but it isn't, it's terribly hard."

He has just called Tanya in to see him. He was so happy when she arrived. He was also pleased to get a telegram from Grand Duke Nikolai, saying he had personally handed his letter to the Tsar.

Doctor Volkov is on duty one night, Altschuler the next, and Elpatevsky the third; Shchurovsky is here all day.

29th January. 9 o'clock in the morning. They insisted I go up-stairs and get some sleep, but having spent the past hour sobbing I now feel like writing again. My Lyovochka (although he isn't mine now but God's) had a terrible night. The moment he dropped off he started choking and shrieking and couldn't sleep. First he asked Seryozha and me to sit him up in bed, then he drank some milk, followed by half a glass of champagne and some water. He never complained but he was tossing about and suffering terribly.

I have a spasm in my chest every time he groans. How can I not suffer too, when my other half is suffering?

Every loved person's passage to eternity enlightens the soul of those who tenderly bid him farewell. Oh Lord, help my soul remain to the end of my life in this lofty enlightened state that I experience increasingly these days! He has just gone to sleep and Liza Obolenskaya and Masha have taken my place. I sat with him until 4 in the morning.

30th January. Yesterday morning he was feeling so well that shortly before 1 he sent for his daughter Masha and dictated into his notebook roughly the following words: "The wisdom of old age is like carat diamonds: the older it is the more valuable it is, and must be given away to others." Then he asked for his article on freedom of conscience, and began to dictate various corrections to it.*

His temperature was normal all day and he was in good spirits, and we all cheered up. This evening I took up my nightly vigil by his bed; I sat with him until four in the morning, listening to his breathing, and all was well.

Lyova arrived yesterday evening. I always love to see him.

Misha too came this evening, bubbling with life as usual.

At about three he began choking and tossing, then he went to sleep.

It is now eight in the evening and he is sleeping peacefully.

He generally calls for Andryusha when it is time for him to change position, and he eats most happily from Masha's hand. My suffering for him is involuntarily communicated to him, he often strokes my hand and tries to spare my strength, and will accept only the lightest personal attentions from me now.

31st January. He had a bad night. He tossed and gasped until 4 a.m., called twice for Seryozha and asked him to sit him up in bed.

Yesterday he said to Tanya: "What was it they said about Count Olsufiev? That he had an easy death?* Well it's not at all easy, it's hard, very hard, to cast off this familiar skin," he said, pointing to his emaciated body.

He was better today and called for Dunaev and Misha; every new arrival delights him. Ilya's wife Sonya also arrived today. It's noisy and crowded here, but the death of my beloved husband pursues its natural course.

He has been dictating notes for his notebook again, as well as for some articles he has already started. He looks so peaceful and serious in bed. He dictated a long telegram to his brother Sergei.

1st February. He has had a terrible night. He was awake until seven in the morning, he had a stomach ache and was gasping for breath. I massaged his stomach several times, but it didn't help. Once he fell asleep for ten minutes while I was massaging, and I stopped rubbing and froze, kneeling on the floor, with my hand on his left side. I thought he would take a nap, but he soon woke up and started groaning again. At five in the morning I went out and Liza and Seryozha took my place. At seven o'clock we woke Doctor Shchurovsky, who gave him a morphine injection. Doctor Elpatevsky also kept watch over him, but by then he was so exhausted he went to sleep. He had a fairly peaceful day, and Shchurovsky put another plaster on his left side.

He dictated some notes to Masha for his notebook.

2nd February. Ilya's wife Sonya came yesterday evening, as well as old Uncle Kostya and Varya Nagornova. Lev Nikolaevich is delighted to have visitors.

At three in the morning he had a small morphine injection (a sixth of a grain), and ten minutes later fell asleep and slept till morning. Today for the first time his temperature was 35.9 instead of 36.9. He tucked into an egg and some tapioca with milk, and is looking forward to a meringue for dinner – the doctor has allowed this.

He dictated to Masha some corrections to his article 'On Freedom of Conscience'.

Yesterday all the children and I had our photograph taken – in memory of a sad but important time.

3rd February. The *Russian Gazette* has at last published news today of Lev Nikolaevich's illness.

Yesterday morning Lyova left for St Petersburg.

He has taken a little soup, an egg and a meringue. He asked Sonya, "Where did you bury your mother last year?" "We took her body to Paniki, at my brother's request." "How senseless," he said. "What's the point of moving a dead body?"

5th February. The situation is unchanged. A night under morphine – they gave him an injection of ⅛ of a grain. He drinks champagne and milk with Ems water, and eats puréed oat soup, eggs and gruel. We applied a compress today. I am sitting here exhausted and numb; it has all been too much for my heart, and now I have slumped, waiting.

6th February. A sleepless night, two injections of morphine, nothing helped. At 5 a.m. I went to bed exhausted. A morning of anxieties.

Elpatevsky and Altschuler came. They say this is the crisis. The pneumonia has suddenly started to clear from both lungs. But what will happen when his temperature falls? We are living in terror. "Everything is in the balance," he said today to his niece Varenka. He is taking his own pulse and temperature, and is very frightened; we are forced to deceive him and reduce the degrees.

The cold and wind make things worse.

7th February. The situation is almost hopeless. Until 5 o'clock I was doing all I could to relieve his suffering. The only time my darling Lyovochka dropped off was when I lightly massaged his stomach and liver. He thanked me and said: "Darling, you must be exhausted."

Olga's pains began this morning, and at seven she gave birth to a dead baby boy.

Today Lev Nikolaevich said: "There, you've arranged everything perfectly, give me a camphor injection and I'll die."

He also said: "Don't try to predict what will happen. I can't foresee anything."

He asked for the medical notes on the progression of his illness – his temperature chart, medicines, diet and so on – and read it closely. Then he asked Masha what she had felt during the crisis in her typhus attack. Poor, poor man, he so wants to go on living, yet his life is slipping away…

There is thick snow on the ground and a strong wind. Oh this hateful Crimea!

Tonight there were eight degrees of frost.

8th February. He spent a slightly more comfortable night.

He called Masha today and dictated a page of ideas to her – against war – "fratricide", as he calls it.*

I sat with him until five in the morning; I turned him over with the help of Boulanger, changed his soaking underwear and gave him his medicine (digitalis), and some champagne and milk.

When I examine my soul I realize that my entire being aspires only to nurse this beloved man back to life. But when I'm sitting with my eyes closed, all sorts of dreams suddenly creep up on me, and plans for the most diverse, varied and improbable life… Then I come back to reality and my heart aches again for the death of this man who has become so much part of me I couldn't imagine myself without him.

A strange double life. The cause, I tell myself, is my own indestructible health, my enormous energy, that demands an outlet and finds nourishment only in those difficult moments when it is really necessary to *do* something.

9th February. The other day he said: "It keeps hurting. The machine has broken down. Pull the nose and the tail gets stuck, pull the tail and the nose gets stuck."

Yesterday was a fine day, and he was better. It is snowing again today, and it's dark, overcast and freezing.

10th February. Another fine day – it was 3 degrees. Our dear invalid had a good night and was in less pain during the day, although he is still dreadfully weak and had a temperature of 36.3. He hasn't said a word all day, nothing interests him, he just lies there quietly. He had three small glasses of coffee, asked for some champagne and was given two camphor injections. He is peaceful and I feel fairly calm.

12th February. He has been very weak and drowsy, and hardly speaks at all. Yesterday he asked Doctor Volkov how the common people cured old men like him – did they give them camphor injections? Who lifted them up in bed? What did they give them to eat? Volkov answered all his questions, saying they treated them just the same, and it was generally the family or the neighbours who attended to them, lifted them up and helped them.

14th February. An anxious night. It's a long time since I felt so weak and exhausted.

I read my unfinished children's story 'Skeletons'* to the children, Varya Nagornova and some young ladies, and they seemed to like it.

As for Lyovochka, I simply don't know what to think: I don't know whether this weakness is temporary or terminal. I keep hoping, but today matters have again taken a gloomy turn.

How I should love to look after him patiently and gently to the end, and forget all the old heartaches he has caused me. But instead I cried bitterly today at the way he persistently scorns my love and concern for him. He asked for some sieved porridge, so I ran off to the kitchen and ordered it, then came back and sat beside him. He dozed off, the porridge came and when he woke I quietly put it on a plate and offered it to him. He then grew furious and said he would ask for it himself, and that throughout his illness he had always taken his food, medicines and drinks from other people, not me. (Although when someone has to lift him up, go without sleep, attend to him in the most intimate ways and apply his compresses, it is of course me whom he forces mercilessly to help him.) With the porridge, however, I decided to employ a little cunning, so I called Liza and sat down in the next room, and the moment I left he asked for the porridge, and I began weeping.

This little episode summarizes my whole difficult life with him. This difficulty consists of one long struggle with his *contrary spirit*. My most reasonable and gentle advice to him has always met with protest.

15th February. I received a letter from the St Petersburg Metropolitan Antony exhorting me to persuade him to return to the faith and make his peace with the Church, and help him die like a Christian. I told Lyovochka about this letter, and he told me I should write to Antony that his business was now with God, and to tell him his last prayer had been: "I left Thee. Now I am coming to Thee. Thy will be done." And when I said if God sent death, then one should reconcile oneself in death to everything on earth, including the Church, he said: "There can be no question of reconciliation. I am dying without anger or enmity in my heart. What is the Church?"

The pains in his side are worse, his lungs are still inflamed, and tomorrow they will apply a plaster.

It's foggy and cool. There is a steamer in the sea beyond Gaspra, and its sirens are hooting mournfully. The ships are all at anchor at the moment; I suppose they are afraid to move in the fog.

16th February. Lev Nikolaevich is a little better today: he is not in pain and is lying quietly; he slept much better too.

It's extraordinary how selfless these doctors are: neither Shchurovsky nor Altschuler nor the *zemstvo* doctor Volkov, the poorest but kindest of them all, will accept any money; they are so generous with their time, and never begrudge the labour, the financial loss or the sleepless nights. They put a plaster on his right side today.

My head was aching this evening and it felt as if it would burst, so I lay down on the divan in Lev Nikolaevich's room. He called out to me. I got up and went to him. "Why are you lying down?" he said. "I can't call you if you do that."

"My head is aching," I said. "What do you mean, you can't call me? You call me at night." And I sat down on a chair. He then called to me again: "Go into the other room and lie down. Why are you sitting up?" "But I can't leave – there's no one here," I said. I was terribly agitated and almost hysterical with tiredness. Masha came and I left, but then urgent tasks awaited me on all sides – business documents from the accountant in Moscow, summonses and translations, and everything had to be entered in the book, signed and sent off. Then the washerwoman and the cook had to be paid, the notes had to be sent to Yalta...

19th February. I haven't written my diary for several days: the nursing is very hard work and leaves me little time – barely enough for housework and essential letters and business.

My poor Lyovochka is still very weak. He has been thirsty, and today drank four half-bottles of *kefir*. The doctors say the pneumonia is making slow progress in clearing from the right lung.

20th February. He was better yesterday; his temperature was only 37.1 and he was much more cheerful. "I see I shall now have to live again," he said to Doctor Volkov.

"Are you bored then?" I asked him, and he said with sudden animation: "Bored? How could I be? On the contrary, everything is splendid." This evening, concerned that I might be tired, he squeezed my hand, looked at me tenderly and said: "Thank you, darling, that's wonderful."

22nd February. He is much better; his temperature was 36.1 this morning and 36.6 this evening. They are still giving him camphor injections, and arsenic every other morning.

I received a letter from the orphanage suggesting I resign as patron, as I am away and cannot be useful to them. We shall see who they choose in my place and how they run their affairs.

23rd February. Another bad night. Towards evening his temperature rose to 37.4 and his pulse was 107, although it soon dropped to 88, then 89.

At night he called out to me: "Sonya?" I went in to him. "I was just dreaming that you and I were driving to Nikolskoe in a sledge together."

This morning he told me how well I had looked after him in the night.

25th February. The first day of Lent. I yearn for the mood of peace, prayer and self-denial, the anticipation of spring and all the childhood memories that assail me in Moscow and Yasnaya with the approach of Lent.

But everything is so alien here.

Lev Nikolaevich is more cheerful, and for the first time last night he slept from 12 to 3 without waking. At 5 a.m. I went off to take a nap and he stayed awake. This morning he read the papers and took an interest in his letters. Two exhort him to return to the Church and receive the Eucharist, two beg him to send some of his works as a gift, and two foreigners express feelings of rapture and reverence.

I too received a letter, from Princess Maria Dondukova-Korsakova, saying I should draw him back to the Church and give him the Eucharist.

These spiritual sovereigns expel L.N. from the Church – then call on me to draw him back to it! How absurd!

27th February. Seryozha looked after his father all night with extraordinary gentleness. "How astonishing," Lev Nikolaevich said to me. "I never expected Seryozha to be so sensitive," and his voice was trembling with tears.

Today he said: "I have now decided to expect nothing more; I kept expecting to recover, but now what will be will be, it's no use trying to anticipate the future." He himself reminds me to give him his digitalis, or asks for the thermometer to take his temperature. He is drinking champagne again and lets them give him his camphor injections.

28th February. Today he said to Tanya: "A long illness is a good thing, it gives one time to prepare for death."

And he also said to her today: "I am ready for anything; I am ready to live and ready to die."

This evening he stroked my hands and thanked me. But when I changed his bedclothes he suddenly lost his temper because he felt cold. Then of course he felt sorry for me.

A terrible blizzard, with one degree of frost. The wind is howling and rattling the window frames.

I spilt some ink and got it all over everything.

5th March. He is better; his temperature was 35.7 this morning and 36.7 this evening. The doctors say there is still some wheezing, but apart from that everything is normal. He has such a huge appetite he cannot wait for his dinner and lunch, and has drunk three bottles of *kefir* in the past twenty-four hours. Today he asked for his bed to be moved to the window so he can look out at the sea. He is still very weak and thin, he sleeps badly at night and is very demanding. He once called out five times in one hour – first he wanted his pillow adjusted, then he needed his leg covered up, then the clock was in the wrong place, then he wanted some *kefir*, then he wanted his back sponged, then I had to sit with him and hold his hands... And the moment one lies down he calls again.

We have had a fine day and the nights are moonlit, but I feel dead, dead as the rocky landscape and the dull sea. The birds sing outside, and for some reason neither the moon nor the birds, nor the fly buzzing at the window seem to belong to the Crimea, but keep reminding me of springtime in Yasnaya Polyana or Moscow. So the fly takes me back to a hot summer at harvest time, and the moon evokes memories of our garden in Khamovniki Street, and returning home from concerts…

6th March. Last night was frightful. Agony in his body, his legs, his soul – it was too much for him. "I can't imagine why I recovered, I wish I had died," he said.

8th March. I had a nasty scene with Seryozha. He shouted at a servant about Lev Nikolaevich's new armchair: he said we should wire Odessa about it, but had absolutely no idea where or whom. I said we should first decide what kind of chair was needed. This made him lose his temper and he began shouting.

10th March. I went out for my first walk today and was astonished to see spring was here. The grass is like the grass at home in Russia in May. Various coloured primulas are in flower, and there are dandelions and dead-nettles all over the place. The sun is bright, the sea and sky are blue and the birds, sweet creatures, are singing.

Lev Nikolaevich has made a marked improvement in this fine weather – his temperature was 35.9 today and his pulse was 88. He has a huge appetite, drinks *kefir* day and night with great relish and reads the papers and letters. But he doesn't seem very cheerful.

11th March. He is getting better. I went to Yalta. It was a lovely day, the sea and sky were blue, the birds were singing, the grass was springing up everywhere.

We rubbed him all over with spirit and warm water, and at ten we put him to bed.

12th March. He is slowly but surely improving. Today he read the *Herald of Europe* and the newspapers, and took an interest in the latest Moscow news.

13th March. It is warmer, 13 degrees in the shade, and there was a warm rain. He continues to recover. I am still sitting with him until

5 in the morning. Sasha took my place yesterday, and Tanya will do so today.

Late yesterday evening I read a translation of an essay by Emerson. It was all said long ago and much better by the ancient philosophers – that every *genius* is more closely connected to the dead philosophers than to the living members of his family circle. It is rather a naive conclusion.

For a *genius* one has to create a peaceful, cheerful, comfortable home. A *genius* must be fed, washed and dressed, must have his works copied out innumerable times, must be loved and spared all cause for jealousy, so he can be calm. Then one must feed and educate the innumerable children fathered by this genius, whom he cannot be bothered to care for himself, as he has to commune with all the Epictetuses, Socrateses and Buddhas, and aspire to be like them himself.

I have served a *genius* for almost forty years. Hundreds of times I have felt my intellectual energy stir within me, and all sorts of desires – a longing for education, a love of music and the arts… And time and again I have crushed and smothered these longings, and now and to the end of my life I shall somehow continue to serve my *genius*.

Everyone asks: "But why should a worthless woman like you need an intellectual, artistic life?" To this I can only reply: "I don't know, but eternally suppressing it to serve a genius is a great misfortune." However much one loves this man who people regard as a *genius*, to do nothing but bear and feed his children, sew, order dinner, apply compresses and enemas and silently sit there dully awaiting his demands for one's services, is torture. And there is never anything in *return* for it either, not even simple gratitude, and there's always such a lot to grumble about instead. I have borne this burden for too long, and I am worn out.

This tirade about the way geniuses are misunderstood by their families was provoked by my anger at Emerson and all those who have written and spoken about this question since the days of Socrates and Xantippe.

15th March. He was awake all last night with terrible pains in his legs and stomach. It's a little warmer, the parks are slightly green, but it's just the same old rocks, the same crooked trees, lifeless earth and tossing sea.

I did a lot of sewing today.

19th March. Life here is so monotonous, there's nothing to write about. His illness has almost run its course.

Whenever I come into his room he is intently counting his pulse. Today he was looking through the window at the sun, poor man, and begged me to open the door of the terrace for a moment.

5th April. A lot of time has passed and little has happened. Tanya left on 30th March with her family and Andryusha arrived on the 24th. L.N.'s various treatments continue – he has been having arsenic injections since 2nd April, and today they gave him electrical treatment for his stomach. He was taking nux vomica but is now taking magnesium, and at night he has bismuth with codeine and ether-valerian drops. His nights are very disturbed, and his legs and stomach ache, so his legs have to be massaged, which I find very tiring: my back aches, the blood rushes to my head and I feel quite hysterical. He rejected all such things, of course, when his health was good, but with the onset of his first serious illness every conceivable treatment is set in motion. Three doctors visit practically every day; nursing him is extremely hard work, there are a lot of us here, we are all tired and overworked, and our personal lives have been completely eaten up by his illness. Lev Nikolaevich is first and foremost a writer and expounder of ideas: in reality and in his life he is a weak man, much weaker than us simple mortals. I couldn't endure the thought of writing and saying one thing and living and acting another, but it doesn't seem to bother him, just so long as he doesn't suffer, so long as he lives and gets better... What a lot of attention he devotes to himself these days, taking his medicines and having his compresses changed, and what a lot of effort he takes to feed himself, sleep and lessen the pain.

13th April. Saturday, the evening before Easter Sunday, and my God, the depression is unbearable! I am sitting on my own upstairs in the bedroom, with my granddaughter Sonyushka sleeping beside me, while downstairs in the dining room there is the most vile heathen commotion going on. They are all playing vint, they have wheeled Lev Nikolaevich's armchair in, and he is enthusiastically following Sasha's game.

I am feeling very lonely. My children are even more despotic, rude and demanding than their father. Day and night, hour after hour, he attends to and cares for his body, and I can detect no spiritual feelings in him whatsoever. With me he is rude and demanding, and

if I do something careless out of sheer exhaustion he shouts at me
peevishly.

11th May. I am ashamed of the unkind things I wrote in my diary
last time about Lyovochka and my family. I was angry about their
attitude to Holy Week, and instead of being mindful of my own
sinfulness I transferred my anger to my nearest and dearest. "Grant
me to see my own sins and not judge my brother..."

What a long time has passed since then, and what a ghastly time
we are going through once again!

He was at last beginning to recover from the pneumonia; he was
walking about the house with a stick, eating well and digesting his
food. Masha then suggested that I attend to my urgent business
in Yasnaya and Moscow, and on the morning of 22nd April I set
off.

My trip was very pleasant and successful. I spent a day at Yasnaya
Polyana, where Andryusha joined me. The weather was delightful;
I adore the early spring, with its soft green hues and fresh hopes
for a new and better life... I busied myself with the accounts and
bills, toured the apple orchards, inspected the cattle and walked over
to Chepyzh as the sun was setting. The lungwort and violets were
blooming, the birds were singing, the sun was setting over the felled
forest, and this pure natural beauty, free of all human cares, filled
me with joy.

In Moscow I was delighted by the way people treated me. Everyone
was so friendly and cheerful, as though they were all my friends.
Even people in the shops and banks welcomed me back warmly
after my long absence.

I dealt successfully with my business, visited the Wanderers'
Exhibition* and the exhibition of St Petersburg artists, went to
an examination performance of Mozart's cheerful opera *Così Fan
Tutte* and saw a lot of friends, and on Sunday invited a group of
my closest friends to the house – Marusya, the Maklakovs, Uncle
Kostya, Misha Sukhotin and Sergei Ivanovich, who played me
some of Arensky's lesser-known pieces, a Schumann sonata and
his own charming symphony, which gave me more pleasure than
anything.

Soothed and satisfied, I set off for Gaspra, assuming from the
daily telegrams that everything there was in order. But on my return
I discovered that L.N. had had a fever for the past two or three
evenings, and eventually typhoid fever was diagnosed. These past

days and nights have been agony and terror for all of us. At two in the morning I called on Doctor Nikitin, who is staying here with us, and he administered some strophanthus, stayed a while, then went off to bed.

Lev Nikolaevich is now lying quietly in the large gloomy Gaspra drawing room and I am writing at the table. The house is silent and ominous.

13th May. He is better, thank God. His temperature is falling steadily and his pulse has improved. Seryozha is being insufferable and keeps finding new reasons for being angry with me.

I live only for *today*, it's enough for me if everything is all right. I played the piano alone for two hours in the wing while L.N. slept.

15th May. This unpleasantness with Seryozha has taken its toll. Yesterday I had such terrible pains all over my body that I thought I was dying. I am better today. L.N.'s typhus is passing; his temperature was 36.5 after his bed-bath this evening, and his pulse was 80; his maximum temperature today was 37.3. But he is weak and terribly wretched. I was told not to go downstairs but couldn't resist visiting him. It is cold, 11 degrees.

16th May. He is much better and his temperature is down to 37, not even that. He is very bored, poor man. I should think so too! He has been ill for almost 5 months now.

He is dictating ideas about the unequal distribution of the land and the injustice of land ownership; this is his major preoccupation at the moment.* I feel I am about to break. If only I could leave!

22nd May. Lev Nikolaevich is gradually recovering: his temperature is back to normal, no higher than 36.5, and his pulse is 80. He is upstairs at present, as the downstairs rooms are being cleaned and aired. The weather is cool and rainy. Everyone in the house has become terribly homesick all of a sudden, and even L.N. is in low spirits, despite his recovery. We are all longing to be back in Yasnaya. Tanya is missing her husband, and Ilyusha his family. To be perfectly frank, all of us are feeling the need for some sort of personal life again, now that the danger is past. Poor Sasha, it's quite reasonable for her to want this at her age.

Yesterday and today I played the piano on my own in the wing. I am practising the very difficult Chopin Scherzo (the second, in five flats).

What a lovely piece it is, and how it harmonizes with my present mood! Then I sight-read the Mozart rondo (the second, the minor), such an elegant, graceful work.

I was lying in bed today wondering why a husband and wife so often find estrangement creeping into their relations, and I realized it was because married couples know *every aspect of each other*, and as they grow older they become wiser, and see everything more clearly. We don't like people to see our *bad* side, we carefully conceal our flaws from others and show ourselves off to our best advantage, and the cleverer a person is the more able he is to present his best qualities. With a husband or wife though, this isn't possible. One can see all the lies and the masks – and it's not at all pleasant.

I am reading Fielding's *The Soul of a People*, translated from the English. It is quite delightful. How much better Buddhism is than our Orthodoxy, and what marvellous people these Burmese are.

29th May. I haven't written for a whole week. On Saturday the 25th Tanya went home to Kochety. On the 26th Lev Nikolaevich was carried downstairs and taken outside to the terrace, where he sat in his armchair. Yesterday he even took a spin in the carriage with Ilyusha. Professor Lamansky was here yesterday, and some peculiar fellow who talked about the low cultural level of the peasants and the necessity to do something about it. He kept saying "*pardon*" in French, and deliberately didn't pronounce his "r"s. Lev Nikolaevich got very angry with him, but when I sent him away to take his pulse – which was 94 per minute – he angrily shouted at me in the presence of Lamansky: "Oh, I'm so tired of you!" which hurt me deeply.

The lovely white magnolias and lilies have come into flower.

5th June. Still in the Crimea. It is very pleasant here at the moment; the days are hot and fine and the moonlit nights are beautiful; I am sitting upstairs, admiring the reflection of the moon in the sea. Lev Nikolaevich is walking about with a stick now and seems well, although he is very thin and weak. He only lost his temper once with me yesterday, when I cut and washed his hair. He writes every morning – a proclamation to the working people, I think, and also something about the ownership of the land.

11th June. Today he went for a drive with Doctor Volkov to the Yusupovs' Park in Ai-Todor, which he enjoyed very much.

Sofia Tolstoy in 1863

Sofia Behrs and her younger sister Tatyana,
photographed some time in the early 1860s

Yasnaya Polyana, the general view
of the Tolstoys' estate, 1897

Sofia Tolstoy, Lev Tolstoy, Sofia's younger brother Stepan Behrs,
Sofia's daughter Maria and Maria Petrovna Behrs, Stepan's wife, 1887

Peasant women gathering apples in the
Tolstoys' orchard at Yasnaya Polyana, 1888

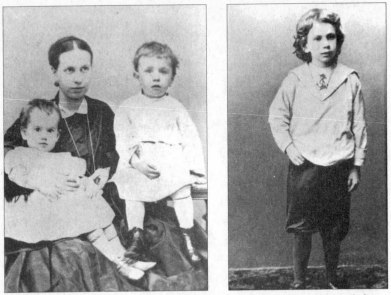

Sofia Tolstoy with her children Tatyana and Sergei, 1866 (above left),
Ivan Tolstoy (Vanechka), the Tolstoys' youngest child, photographed
in 1893 in Moscow by the firm of Scherer and Nabholz (above right)

Sofia Tolstoy with her younger children: left to right, Mikhail (Misha),
Andrei (Andryusha), Alexandra (Sasha) and Ivan (Vanechka)

Lev and Sofia Tolstoy at Yasnaya Polyana, with
eight of their children, 1887 (Sofia's photograph)

Lev Tolstoy and Sofia in his study

Sofia Tolstoy copying a portrait by Repin, 1904

Maria Tolstaya (Masha) haymaking at Yasnaya Polyana, 1895
(photograph by P.I. Biryukov)

Yasnaya Polyana, 1896 (Sofia Tolstoy's photograph)

The house in Dolgokhamovnichesky Lane, Moscow

Moscow, 1896: at the back, Sofia Tolstoy and Sergei Taneev; at the front, from left to right, Maria Tolstaya, Tatiana Tolstaya, Konstantin Nikolaevich Igumnov

Vladimir Chertkov with colleagues at the Free Word publishing
house in Christchurch, England, *c.*1901

Gaspra, Crimea, 1901: left to right, Anton Chekhov,
Sofia Tolstoy, Lev Tolstoy and their daughter Maria

Tula schoolchildren visiting Lev Tolstoy at Yasnaya Polyana, 1907

Sofia and Lev Tolstoy during his illness at Gaspra, 1901

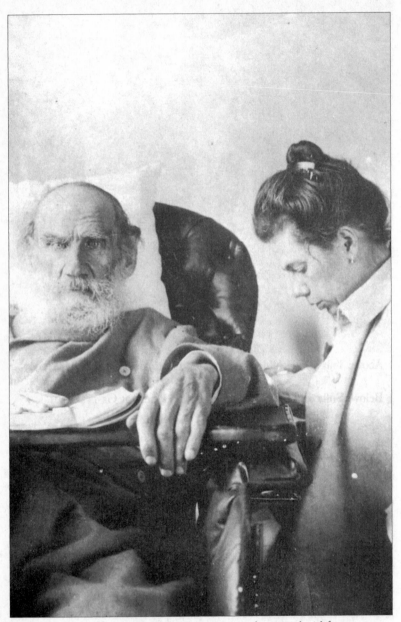

Gaspra, May 1902: Tolstoy recovering from typhoid fever,
with his daughter Tatyana (Sofia's photograph)

Sofia Tolstoy in the park at Yasnaya Polyana, 1903 (Sofia's photograph)

Yasnaya Polyana, 1904: the Tolstoys' eldest sons: left to right,
Lev, Ilya, Sergei, Andrei and Mikhail (Sofia's photograph)

Sofia Tolstoy at the window of the stationmaster's house at Astapovo
station, where Tolstoy was dying, November 1910

Tolstoy's sons carrying his coffin, 8th November 1910,
at Astapovo station

Sofia Tolstoy by Tolstoy's grave at Yasnaya Polyana, 1912

Sofia Tolstoy and her granddaughter Tanya, 1917

Altschuler's wife visited, as well as Sonya Tatarinova, the Volkov family and Elpatevsky with his son. A large crowd of strangers came and peered through the window at Lev Nikolaevich.

We have been enjoying life here, the weather is fine and L.N.'s convalescence is progressing well. I went riding twice, once to Orianda with Klassen and once to Alupka with him and Sasha. It was most enjoyable. I play the piano, sew and take photographs. Lev Nikolaevich is writing an appeal to the working people, 'On the Ownership of the Land', in which he says much the same thing as he wrote to the Tsar. We are planning to leave on the 13th.

13th June. Yet again it looks as though we won't be leaving Gaspra for a while. In Russia it's damp, raining and very cold – only 12 degrees – and Lev Nikolaevich has an upset stomach.

He is still writing his proclamation to the workers. I copied the whole thing for him today. Much of it is illogical, impractical and unclear. The fact that the land is owned by the rich, and the great suffering this imposes on the peasants, is indeed a crying injustice. But this matter will not be resolved in a hurry.

17th June. Arguments about the Bashkirs.* Numerous visitors milling around all day.

26th June. Yesterday we finally left Gaspra. I thank God He has granted us to take Lev Nikolaevich home once more! I pray he never has to leave again!

27th June (Yasnaya Polyana). Today we returned home from the Crimea. We rode to Yalta on horseback, with Lev Nikolaevich and Sasha, travelling in the Yusupovs' rubber-tyred carriage. There were Lev Nikolaevich, Sasha and I, my son Seryozha, Boulanger, Yulia Igumnova and Doctor Nikitin in our party. In Yalta we boarded the steamer *Alexei*. Ladies, bouquets, crowds of people waving farewell… On the steamer L.N. sat on deck, ate in the public dining room and felt extremely well… In Sevastopol we disembarked onto a skiff and sailed round the harbour to the station; the sun was bright and it was very beautiful. A specially large, comfortable carriage with a saloon had been set aside for L.N. Sasha was ill and miserable and had an upset stomach. At Kharkov station, people – mostly women – welcomed him with ovations. At Kursk there were crowds of people who had just been to an exhibition on popular education. The police pushed them back, and deputations of men and women teachers and students boarded the train – Misha Stakhovich, Dolgorukov, Gorbunov and Lodyzhensky, among others.

It was a joy to get back to Yasnaya, but our joy was short-lived. That evening Masha began to have pains, and soon afterwards she gave birth to a dead baby boy. ·

30th June. Lev Nikolaevich had a temperature of 37.8 this evening and we were very anxious about him. I sat with Masha all morning. It is cold and raining. The saffron milk caps* are out.

3rd July. Lev Nikolaevich walked to the side wing to see Masha, and this afternoon he played Haydn's second symphony as a duet with Vasya Maklakov. Sasha brought in some saffron milk caps.

4th July. Lev Nikolaevich is well; he went to the side wing and back. This afternoon he had a long talk with Doctor Nikitin about psychiatrists, whom he was criticizing.

23rd July. The time is passing terribly fast. On 5th July I went to see Ilyusha at Mansurovo, his estate in the province of Kaluga, and spent a delightful two days with him, Sonya and my grandchildren. We went for walks and drives through the lovely woods and countryside, and had long heart-to-heart talks.

On 7th July, I went to Begichevka to see Misha and my lovable little grandson Vanechka. Lina is a sensitive, serious, loving woman. Misha is young and arrogant, but this will pass. On the night of the 8th I returned to Yasnaya with Misha. Lev Nikolaevich is well but weak. Sasha had a nervous attack on the 10th.

On 11th July, Sasha and I went to Taptykovo to visit Olga on her name day. We had a pleasant day, and returned home late that night after a heavy downpour of rain.

My son-in-law Mikhail Sukhotin is gravely ill with suppurative inflammation of the lung. I felt so anxious and so sad for poor Tanya, and on the evening of 16th July I set off for Kochety. The atmosphere there was cold and depressing. Mikhail Sergeevich looked thin and wretched, and Tanya, who had been sitting up with him every night, was tense and exhausted. I spent four days there and returned on the morning of the 21st.

It is still cool, and yesterday it poured with rain. The rye still hasn't been sheaved and the oats aren't cut. It is afternoon now, and only

10 degrees. Before it rained yesterday I took a drive round Yasnaya Polyana and the plantations. How wonderfully beautiful it all is!

26th July. A full and happy day. Ilya's family came with Annochka and the grandsons, and we took a walk with Zosya Stakhovich and Sasha. This evening Goldenweiser played beautifully, a Schumann sonata and a Chopin Ballade. Then we talked about poets and Lev Nikolaevich recalled Baratynsky's poem 'On Death'. We straight away got out the book and Zosya read us this lovely poem.

On the 22nd another son was born to Lyova and Dora; we had a telegram from them today.

Lev Nikolaevich is well. He played vint all evening and enjoyed the music. In the mornings he writes his novel *Hadji Murat*,* to my great delight.

27th July. Music continues to have its usual healing effect on me. This evening Goldenweiser played, excellently, the Chopin sonata with the funeral march. L.N. was sitting near me and the room was filled with my nearest and dearest – Ilyusha, Andryusha, Sonya, Olga, Annochka, Zosya Stakhovich and Maria Schmidt. And moved by the music, I felt a quiet joy creep into my heart and fill it with gratitude to God for bringing us all together once more, happy and loving, and for allowing Lev Nikolaevich to be with us still, alive and comparatively well... And I felt ashamed of my weaknesses and resentments and all the evil that spoils this good life of mine...

9th August. What a long time it is since I wrote my diary! The past month has been filled with anxieties about Sukhotin's health; he is now worse again. My poor darling Tanya. She loves him too much, and is finding it very hard; nursing him is difficult enough as it is. I went to Moscow on the 2nd and was busy checking accounts, attending to business and ordering the new edition. Sergei Ivanovich is immersed in work on a musical textbook* that he wants to finish before leaving for Moscow. I asked him to play something, but he refused, and was stern, unapproachable and even rather unpleasant. There is something sad and serious about him nowadays; he has aged and changed, and this makes me unhappy. I was glad to get home. Lina came yesterday with little Vanechka, and this morning Misha arrived. His whole family is utterly charming in every respect. Lina's mother came yesterday with her sister Lyuba. My nephew Sasha is here, and Annochka and Maude, and Liza Obolenskaya arrived. A lot of commotion, but most enjoyable.

Lev Nikolaevich played a game of vint and asked for something to eat. He is still writing his story *Hadji Murat*, and today his work evidently went badly, as he played patience for a long time – a sure sign he can't work something out. The priests keep sending me religious books which curse him.* Neither he nor they are right; all extremes lack the *wisdom* and *goodness* of inner tranquillity.

A grey day, but no wind. A bright sunset and a moonlit night.

11th August. Misha's family left yesterday, and Olga arrived with Sonyushka. What a sweet, affectionate, clever little girl she is! I love her so much. Liza Obolenskaya left, and Stasov arrived, and also Ginzburg, who has sculpted a bas-relief of Sasha which is very bad and not at all like her. I have now learnt how to do this myself, and would very much like to attempt a medallion of L.N. and me.

We all went to pick saffron milk caps yesterday; I left the others and had a lovely time wandering through the forest on my own. The old fire in my heart is extinguished, and I am obviously growing old.

Lev Nikolaevich has been very lively and talkative. He told us when he was in Sevastopol he had asked to be assigned a *post*, and they sent him and the artillery to the fourth bastion. But he was removed from there on the Tsar's orders, after Nicholas I sent Gorchakov a message saying: "Remove Tolstoy from the fourth bastion and spare his life, for he is worth something."

Rain all day. The oats are still in the field. 13 degrees.

28th August. Lev Nikolaevich's 74th birthday. We went out to meet him on his way back from his walk. Four of our sons have come; Lyova is in Sweden, and my poor darling Tanya couldn't be here as her husband is still ill. We celebrated my great husband's birthday in the most banal fashion: dinner for twenty-four ill-assorted people, with champagne and fruit, and a game of vint afterwards, just like any other day. Lev Nikolaevich simply cannot wait for evening, when he can sit down to a hand of vint. And they have now dragged Sasha into their games, which greatly distresses me.

He is working hard on *Hadji Murat*.

2nd September. On 31st August two doctors arrived from Moscow for a consultation – capable, lively Shchurovksy and P. Usov, a dear cautious man who has treated L.N. before. They both decided it would be best to spend the winter here in Yasnaya, which is far more to my liking than having to travel here, there and everywhere. I personally find it much easier in Moscow; there are people I love there, and a lot of music and serious innocent entertainments – exhibitions, concerts, lectures, interesting friends, social life and so on. But I realize Lev Nikolaevich finds Moscow *insufferable*, with all the visitors and noise, so I shall gladly live in my dear Yasnaya and visit Moscow only when I am exhausted here.

Meanwhile life is very eventful, time speeds past, I am kept busy all day long, and there isn't any music or a chance to rest. All these guests can be very tiresome at times. I have started to sculpt a medallion of L.N.'s and my profiles. I'm in despair that I won't be able to finish, but I do so want to; I occasionally sit up all night, as late as 5 a.m., straining my eyes.

10th October. I haven't written for so long – time has flown. On 18th September I saw my Tanya and her family off to Montreux in Switzerland. My heart ached to see her, wretched, pale and thin, bustling about on the Smolensk station with all the luggage and her sick husband. But we have just had good news from her, thank God.

I spent my name day in Moscow. I invited a lot of guests, who came to say goodbye to the Sukhotins, and Sergei Ivanovich, whom I had run into on the street. He was solemn and austere; something in him has changed, he has become even more impenetrable than before.

At 11 o'clock on 11th September we had a fire in the attic and four beams were burnt. By a sheer stroke of luck I had gone up to inspect the attic and noticed the fire. If I hadn't, the whole house would have burnt down and the ceiling might have collapsed on top of Lev Nikolaevich, who was asleep in the room directly below. I was led there by the hand of God, and I thank Him for it.

Lev Nikolaevich's health is good; he went horse-riding, worked on *Hadji Murat* and has started on a proclamation to the clergy.* Yesterday he said: "How hard it is. One must expose evil, yet I don't want to write unkind things as I don't want to arouse bad feelings."

But our peaceful life here and our good relations with our daughter Masha and her shadow – her husband Kolya – have now been disrupted. It is a long story.

When the family divided up the property, at Lev Nikolaevich's insistence, our daughter Masha, who had already reached the age of consent, refused to partake of her parents' inheritance. As I didn't believe her at the time, I took her share in my name and wrote my will, leaving this capital to her. But I didn't die, and then Masha married Obolensky and took her share, as she had to support both herself and him.

But as she had no rights in the future, she decided without telling me to copy out of her father's diary for 1895 a whole series of his wishes after his death. Among other things, he had written that it made him unhappy that his works should be sold, and that he would prefer his family not to sell them after his death. When L.N. was dangerously ill last July, Masha asked her father, without telling anyone, to sign this passage she had copied from his diary, and the poor man did so.

It was exceedingly unpleasant for me when quite by chance I found out about it. To make L.N.'s works *common* property would be senseless and wicked, in my opinion. By making his works public property we only line the pockets of rich publishing companies like Marx, Zetlin and so on. I told L.N. that if he died before me I would *not* carry out his wishes and would *not* renounce the copyright on his works; if I thought that was the right and proper thing to do, I would give him the pleasure of renouncing it *during his lifetime*, but there was no point in doing so after his death.

As I didn't know the exact contents of this document, I asked Lev Nikolaevich to give it to me, after he had taken it from Masha.

He readily agreed, and handed it over to me. Then Masha flew into a rage. Yesterday her husband was shouting God knows what nonsense, saying they had planned to make the document "public property" after Lev Nikolaevich's death, so as many people as possible would know that he hadn't wanted to sell his works, but his wife had made him do so.

So the upshot of this whole episode is that Masha and Kolya Obolensky will now be leaving Yasnaya.

23rd October. Masha and I have made peace; she has stayed on in the side wing at Yasnaya, and I am very glad.

An unbearably muddy, cold, damp autumn. It snowed today.

Lev Nikolaevich has finished *Hadji Murat* and we read it today; the strictly epic character of the story has been very well sustained and there is much artistic merit in it, but it doesn't move me. We have only read half of it though, and will finish it tomorrow.

4th November. It is very frosty; the little girls are skating. The sun is bright, the sky is blue, and as I came up the avenue to the house I had a sudden vivid memory of the distant past, walking up this same avenue from the skating rink carrying a baby on one arm, shielding him from the wind and closing his little mouth, while the other dragged a child in a sledge, and behind us and before us were happy, laughing red-cheeked children, and life was so full and I loved them so passionately... And Lev Nikolaevich came out to meet us, looking healthy and cheerful, having spent such a long time writing that it was too late for him to go skating...

Where are they now, those little children whom we reared with such love? And where is that giant – my strong, cheerful Lyovochka? And where am I, as I was in those days? If only I could live a little better and not store up so much *guilt* towards people, especially my family.

8th November. Yesterday the sun shone, we were all in high spirits and I went skating with the little girls – Sasha, Natasha Obolenskaya and their young pupils. We all had a fine time on the ice. Today we had a discussion about divorce. I said divorce was sometimes necessary, and cited the case of L.A. Golitsyna, whose husband abandoned her three weeks after the wedding for a dancing girl, and whom he told quite cynically he had only *married* in order to have her as his mistress, otherwise he would never have managed to get her.

Lev Nikolaevich replied that marriage was merely the Church's seal of approval on adultery. I retorted that this was only the case with bad people. He then snapped back in the most unpleasant way that it was so for *everyone*. "What about in reality?" I said. To which he replied, "The moment I took a woman for the first time and went with her, that was marriage."

And I had a sudden painful insight into our marriage as Lev Nikolaevich saw it. This naked, unadorned, uncommitted sexual coupling of a man and a woman – that is what he calls marriage, and after that coupling it doesn't matter to him who he has gone with. And when he started saying one should only get married once, to the first woman one fell with, I grew extremely angry.

It is snowing, and there seems to be a path in the snow. I looked through the proofs of *The Cossacks*. What a well-written story, what brilliance, what talent. A man of genius is always so much better in his works than in his life!

25th November. I feel more and more lonely here in the company of those members of my family I still have with me. Today I returned from Moscow to find that Dr Elpatevsky had just arrived from the Crimea, and this evening L.N. read him a legend he has just written, about devils.*

This work is imbued with the most truly negative, malicious, diabolical spirit, and sets out to mock everything on earth, starting with the Church. The supposedly Christian feelings that L.N. puts into these discussions among the devils are presented with such coarse cynicism it made me sick with rage to hear him read it: I became feverish, and felt like weeping and shouting and stretching out my hands to ward off the devils.

I told him in no uncertain terms how angry it made me. Would it not be more fitting for an old man of seventy-five, whom the whole world respects, to do like the Apostle John, who when he was too weak and debilitated to speak simply said, "Children, love each other!" Neither Socrates, Marcus Aurelius, Plato nor Epicurus had any need to attach ears and devils' tails to the truths they wanted to proclaim. But then maybe contemporary man, whom L.N. is so clever at pleasing, needs this sort of thing.

And my children too – Sasha, who is too young to know better, and Masha, who is a complete stranger to me – both imitated their father's laugh with their own hellish laughter after he had finished reading his devilish legend, and I felt like sobbing. Did he have to survive death to do work like this!

7th December. My soul is again filled with despair and the terror of losing my beloved husband! Help me, Lord… Lev Nikolaevich has a fever – 39 this morning – his pulse is weak, his strength is failing… The only doctor who has seen him cannot understand what is wrong.

We have summoned Dreyer from Tula and Shchurovsky from Moscow, and are expecting them today. We have wired our sons too, but none of them has arrived yet.

While there is still hope and I still have the strength, I shall write down everything that has happened.

When Lev Nikolaevich was having lunch I came in and sat with him. He ate porridge and semolina with milk, and asked for some curd pancakes from our lunch, which he ate with the semolina. I remarked that these pancakes were a little heavy for him while he was drinking Karlsbad – which he has been taking for four weeks now – but he wouldn't listen.

After lunch he set off for a walk on his own, and asked to be driven to the highway. I assumed he would take his usual walk along the main road, but without saying a word he set out for Kozlovka, turned off into Zaseka – 3 miles in all – then put on a frozen fur coat over his sheepskin jacket and drove home, flushed and exhausted, in a cold north wind and 15 degrees of frost.

The following morning, 5th December, about midday, he felt chilled and wrapped himself in his dressing gown, but remained at his desk with his papers all morning and ate nothing. He went to bed in the afternoon and his temperature went up to 38.8. That night he started having bad stomach pains; I stayed with him all night and kept his stomach warm. That evening he had a temperature of 39.4, but then Masha suddenly ran in, beside herself, and said, "His temperature is 40.9!" We all looked at the thermometer, and sure enough it was – although I am still not sure there wasn't something wrong with the mercury. We were all distraught; we sponged him down with alcohol and water, and when we took his temperature it was 39.3 again.

I am going in to Lyovochka again – oh, these groans, how I suffer for him... Forgive me, my darling, God bless you!

8th December. His temperature has gone down now and the fever has passed in a profuse sweat. But his heart is still weak. The doctors have diagnosed influenza and now fear these bacteria may lead to pneumonia.

We had a visit this morning from those two dear selfless doctors, always so bright and kind – warm-hearted Usov and cheerful Shchurovsky. Doctor Chekan from Tula stayed the night here and our own Doctor Nikitin has been kind, sensible and diligent.

Seryozha, Andryusha and his wife and Liza Obolenskaya arrived yesterday, and Ilya arrived today.

I looked after Lev Nikolaevich until five this morning, when Seryozha took my place. The doctors also took turns – first Nikitin, then Chekan.

12th December. It is now six in the morning of 12th December. I have spent another night sitting beside Lyovochka's bed and can see him slipping away.

A cheerless life looms ahead.

Long sleepless nights, with a heart full of anguish, a terror of life and a dread of living without Lyovochka.

As I was leaving the room just now he said, "Goodbye, Sonya!" in a distinct and significant tone of voice. And I kissed his hand and said "Goodbye" to him too. He thinks I might be asleep when he dies... No, he doesn't think anything of the sort, he understands *everything*, and it's so hard for him...

13th December, evening. Lyovochka has come back to life again and is much better – his pulse, temperature and appetite have improved. Boulanger was reading Kropotkin's *Notes** to him.

Today the following announcement from Lev Nikolaevich appeared in the *Russian Gazette*:

We have received this letter from Count Lev Nikolaevich Tolstoy:

Dear Sir, Most Honoured Editor,
Due to my extreme age and the various illnesses which have taken their toll, I am obviously not in particularly good health, and this deterioration in my condition will naturally continue. Detailed information about this deterioration may be of interest to some people – and in completely opposite senses too – but I find the publication of this information most unpleasant. I would therefore ask all newspaper editors not to print information about my illness.
                                              Lev Tolstoy, 9th December, 1902

18th December. Lev Nikolaevich is still in bed. He sits up, reads and takes notes, but is very weak...

I have been reading Hauptmann's *The Weavers*: all we rich people, landowners and manufacturers live such extraordinarily luxurious lives, I thought; I often don't go to the village simply to avoid the awkwardness and shame I feel for my wealthy, privileged life and their poverty. Yet I am constantly astonished at how meek and gentle they are with us.

Then I read some of A. Khomyakov's poems. There is so much genuine poetry and feeling in them. 'To Children' simply pours from his heart, honest and passionate. If one has never had children, one couldn't possibly understand the feelings of a parent, especially a mother.

You go into the nursery at night and look at the three or four little cots with such a feeling of fullness, richness and pride... You bend over each one of them, look into those lovely innocent little faces which breathe such purity, holiness and hope. And you make the sign of the cross over them or bless them in your heart, then pray for them and leave the room, your soul filled with love and tenderness, and you ask nothing of God, for life is full.

And now they have all grown up and gone away... And it's not the empty cots that fill one with sadness, it's the disappointment in those beloved children's characters and fates.

27th December. It's again a long time since I have written. I spent three days in Moscow – the 19th, 20th and 21st. I got the accounts for the book sales from the accountant, did some shopping and got presents for the children, servants and so on, which they loved.

Lev Nikolaevich improved greatly while I was away, and got up, went into the next room and worked. Then on Christmas Day he suddenly grew worse. He ate nothing, was given strophanthus and caffeine, and the doctor was evidently nonplussed. Yesterday he was much better again.

When Lev Nikolaevich was so ill, he said half-joking to Masha, "The Angel of Death came for me, but God called him away to other work. Now he has finished he has come for me again."

Every deterioration in Lev Nikolaevich's condition causes me greater and greater suffering, and I am terrified of losing him. In Gaspra I didn't feel nearly so much pain and tenderness for him as I feel now. What agony it is to see him suffering and sinking, weak and stricken in mind and body!

I take his head in my hands and kiss him with tender love and solicitude, and he looks at me blankly.

What is happening to him? What is he thinking?

29th December. First Lev Nikolaevich gets better, then worse. Today he said to me: "I am afraid I shall be exhausting you for a long time."

We talked about the English. Two Englishmen from some spiritual society had walked to London dressed only in jackets and open shirts, and from there they travelled to Russia without so much as a kopeck, with the sole purpose of seeing Tolstoy and asking him to clear up their religious doubts. They stayed with Dunaev, and we sent a couple of L.N.'s fur coats and caps over to them so they wouldn't freeze.

1903

Riots in the countryside continue. 6th April, Easter Day – massacre of Jews in Kishinev, Bessarabia. (Tolstoy writes to governor of Kishinev to protest.) May – a railway worker blows up governor of Ufa with high explosives. August – another great pogrom in Gomel.

Tolstoy visited by increasing numbers of radical students and revolutionaries. Eleventh edition of his Complete Works *published.*

1st January. A sad start to the new year. We had a letter from Tanya yesterday saying her baby has stopped moving again and she is in despair... L.N. read her letter first and when I went in to see him this morning he said to me, "It's all over for Tanya now, you know." His mouth trembled, he burst into sobs and his thin sick face was filled with grief.

I feel desperately sorry for Tanya, and it's torture to see Lyovochka slipping away from life. These are the two people I love best in my family.

Then today a poor peasant woman called Domna came from the village to beg a bottle of milk to feed her twin baby daughters.

We saw in the New Year yesterday. My daughters-in-law Olga and Sonya are here with the children. Ilyusha and Andryusha arrived last night. There are a lot of people – nineteen in all, including the servants. Two more Englishmen have come, some sort of crazy spiritualists from the partly educated working class. They took L.N. by the arm and suggested praying for his recovery; they are quite convinced this will save him.*

His pulse was weak this morning and very irregular; he had a morphine injection and has been asleep all day.

At five this morning I went into my bedroom, raised the blind and opened the ventilation window. The white moonlight streamed over the countryside and poured over the linden avenues and into my room. Then the cocks started crowing in the village – such an eerie sound! Today I went for a long walk through the woods, along the path to the swimming pool and back. Silence, solitude, nature – wonderful! Goldenweiser played beautifully for us this evening.

2nd January. News from Tanya: she gave birth to dead twin boys yesterday! We are all feeling crushed, but at least the birth wasn't too difficult, thank God. Heaven knows what will happen now.

19th January. I returned today from Moscow, where I placed a new order with another printer. There is not a single copy of the *Complete Works* for sale at the moment, and not one copy of *War and Peace*.

I heard a lot of music in Moscow. Arensky played his study with Ziloti, and conducted his musical poem to the words of 'The Goblet' – it was delightful.

I had a most disturbing conversation yesterday with Sergei Ivanovich, which made me realize just why I had always loved and appreciated him so much. He is an extraordinarily good and noble man.

The weather is still and warm, 1 degree below freezing. The silence of nature is so good, for God is there. How I long to merge with nature and join Him. Instead of reading proofs I sit here and cry all day. Help me, Lord!

21st January. Seryozha was rude to me the other day because I spoke to Sasha while they were playing vint and interrupted their game. I burst into tears, went to my room and lay down on the bed. After a little while L.N. came in leaning on his stick, looking very weak and thin, and was so kind and understanding and told me he had reprimanded Seryozha.

I was very touched by this, and felt such tenderness and reverence for him that I started sobbing again, kissing his hands with that involuntary sense of guilt which has lately been leading me down some fateful path I know not where.

28th January. My inner torment reached a pitch of suffering and guilt and I longed to see and talk to the man I love. I was taken ill, and felt very bad; then I collapsed and couldn't stand up all evening. They put ice on my head and I lay there all night, tense and overwrought; my body simply stopped living. But today, three days later, I am feeling much better, for the illness put a stop to all my anguish and emotional torment.

9th February. I went to Moscow again. There was a chamber music recital at which they played Taneev's quartet (I saw him briefly), the Mozart clarinet quintet (delightful, it gave me enormous pleasure) and Tchaikovsky's sextet *Memories of Florence*. I felt calm and happy afterwards. The old ladies, Uncle Kostya and Sergei Ivanovich all came to see me the following day and we read Lev Nikolaevich's 'Destruction and Reconstruction of Hell', about the devils. This again had the most unpleasant effect on me, and the other listeners too. Sergei Ivanovich was in a lively mood and I found him quite charming. I went to the Hoffmann concert, at which he played the wonderful Chopin piano concerto. I also had a lot of work to do – finding a proofreader, publishing, binding and so on – and I left much of it unfinished. I also attended to Sasha's financial affairs... It is emotionally exhausting, and such a waste!

20th February. Lev Nikolaevich has an old man sitting with him, a soldier from the days of Nicholas I, who fought in the Caucasus and is relating his memories. He went for a drive through the woods yesterday, and this morning he sat outside on the upper balcony. He is healthy and calm. I did a little work on his correspondence – mostly begging letters and notes asking for his autograph.

What has happened recently? 1) A son, Ilya, was born to Andryusha on the night of 3rd–4th February. I went to see him and congratulate Olga. 2) Masha and Kolya have gone abroad. The house seems empty without them, but I feel relieved – they were almost daily guests here.

We lead a secluded existence. Our landowning life is so unnatural – just a few individuals living here among the rural population, with absolutely no contact with the people. It would be quite unnatural anyway to make contact with a class that hasn't been educated to our level.

I receive many letters concerning mine to the *New Times*. Many condemn Lev Nikolaevich as the creator of sordid literature, with his *Resurrection, The Power of Darkness* and *The Kreutzer Sonata*.

But this is a misunderstanding, mere foolishness. Many people are overjoyed, and thank me for my letter – mainly because I wrote it as a mother. The government has its defenders though, and all this makes me feel as if I had scattered Persian powder on bedbugs. I write one letter to the newspaper, and it provokes countless letters, articles, notices and caricatures.

Music is one consolation, and the other is knowing I am doing my duty looking after Lev Nikolaevich and easing his suffering.

22nd February. A daughter, Tanya, has been born to Misha and Lina.

6th March. I went to Moscow to see Andryusha, who is ill, check the book sales, have my teeth filled, go shopping, place orders and go to concerts: Taneev's cantata and various other pieces, performed by the philharmonic orchestra, a symphony concert, the *Manfred* overture, *Der Freischütz* and so on, some Beethoven and Mozart quartets, and the pianist Buyukli played Chopin's 'A Major Polonaise'.

I then went to St Petersburg. Lyova and Dora were very sweet, and so were their dear little boys; my sister Tanya was wretchedly short of money; my brother Vyacheslav was there with his ugly wife and was so kind and sensitive. I spent one day there and two nights on the train, then it was Moscow again and a lot of dashing around, entertaining guests, visiting sick Andryusha – and all this anxious, senseless waste of physical and emotional energy gave me such a sense of powerlessness, dissatisfaction and depression.

It is better in Yasnaya. The beauty of the bright days, the sun shining on the smooth glassy expanse of frozen water, the blue sky, the stillness of nature and the twittering birds are all a premonition of spring.

I have finished the proofs of *Anna Karenina*. By following the state of Anna's soul, step by step, I grew to understand myself and was terrified... But people don't take their lives to *avenge themselves* on someone, they take their lives because they *no longer have the strength to live*... At first struggle, then prayer, then reconciliation, then despair – and finally powerlessness and death.

And I had a sudden clear vision of Lev Nikolaevich weeping his old man's tears and saying no one had ever seen what was taking place in my soul, no one had ever helped me...

How could they have helped me? To allow Sergei Ivanovich to be invited here again and help restore our old peaceful, friendly relations. And to forgive me for my feelings, so I needn't feel guilty about them.

10th March. Lev Nikolaevich is well. We went for a lovely drive today along the forest paths through Zaseka, although the thaw has already started. Yet when I go into my room I am overwhelmed by the evil mystery of my emotional state, and I long to see the man who is now at the centre of my disgraceful, untimely madness. I must *live*, I must think of my husband and children, I mustn't betray my madness, I mustn't see the person I love to distraction...

All I can do is pray to be cured of this sickness...

1st July. I have written nothing all spring and summer, and have spent the whole time outside with nature, taking advantage of the delightful weather. I can't remember such a beautiful summer or such a dazzling spring. I didn't want to think or write or examine my soul. What would be the point?

There was a hateful conversation at dinner today. L.N., in front of large numbers of people and with a naive grin on his face, began cursing doctors and medicine in his usual way. I found this insufferable now that he is well, after those nine doctors in the Crimea worked so selflessly and intelligently to restore his health. I felt no honourable man should regard those who saved his life in this way. I would have kept quiet, if he hadn't then added that according to Rousseau all doctors were in league with women. At that I couldn't contain my rage. I am sick and tired of eternally acting as a screen for my husband to hide behind. If he didn't trust the way these doctors treated him, why did he summon them in the first place and submit to their diagnoses?

Our painful conversation of 1st July 1903 is no mere chance event, it is a result of the solitude and the dishonesty of my life.

My husband blames me for everything: his works are sold against his will, Yasnaya Polyana is kept and managed against his will, the servants serve against his will, the doctors are summoned against his will... There's no end to it... And meanwhile I work like a slave for everyone and my life is not my own.

9th July. The children have returned from abroad – Masha and Kolya Obolensky on the 6th, Andryusha on the 7th, and Lyova on the 8th. Andryusha looks weak and wretched, but he is being very agreeable. Poor Lyova is in a state of emotional turmoil; he is so pathetic, and so dear to me. Masha has recovered and is as much a stranger as ever.

10th July. L.N. was better yesterday evening. A young officer of the household cavalry called Adlerberg came with his immensely fat wife, and L.N. invited him into his room and questioned him closely about his military activities: "What do you do when you troop the colour? When does the Tsar get on his horse to review the troops? Who leads the horse?" and so on and so on. He is studying the history of Nicholas I's reign at present, and is collecting and reading a lot of material for *Hadji Murat*.

12th July. I wanted to write something good today, but instead I became engrossed in reading, and now I am too tired. Yesterday I went to Taptykovo to see Olga on her name day. Andryusha is sick and exceedingly thin. I find Olga incomprehensible. What exactly does she live for? I went there with Lyova, and this son brings me no joy either. His wife is ill with nephritis in Sweden, and he is making plans, says he wants to enrol in the medical faculty and live in Moscow; there is a terrible restlessness about him. Lev Nikolaevich is not well: he still has difficulty breathing and an irregular pulse. The weather has turned – it's terribly windy and only 11 degrees. This evening he played a lively game of vint with Masha, Kolya, Sasha and Nikitin.

13th July. We had a visit from an old man and his wife who had been arrested for blaspheming against Athanasius;* they were very pathetic, but it seems impossible to do anything for them. L.N. sent a letter to the Tsar via Count Olsufiev, making enquiries about this Athanasius.

10th August. It's said no one but God can judge a husband's treatment of his wife. So let this letter which I am copying here not provide grounds for judging anyone.

It was in the year of my beloved little son Vanechka's death. He died on 23rd February, 1895, at just seven years of age, and his death was the greatest tragedy of my life. At that time I clung with all my soul to Lev Nikolaevich, in whom I sought comfort and some purpose in life, and I worked for him and wrote for him. Once, when he went to Tula, I found his room hadn't been properly cleaned, so I went in to tidy it up... How many tears I shed later as I wrote this letter.

Here it is; I found it today, 10th August, amongst my papers. It is a rough draft, dated 12th October, 1895, and ends:

Forgive me if I have been so base as to read your diaries; I was tidying your room and dusting a cobweb off your writing desk, and the temptation to look into your soul was too great...

And then I came across the words:

"S. came back from Moscow. Butted into my conversation with Bool. Pushed herself forward. She has become even more frivolous since Vanechka's death. One must bear one's cross to the end. Help me Lord..."

And so on.

I try to rise above the suffering that torments me now.

But if it is not very hard for you to do so, please delete those angry words about me from your diaries – for this is the Christian thing to do. I cannot beg you to love me, but please spare my name.

Forgive me if you can.

S. *Tolstoy*

At the time we did manage to reach some sort of agreement, and L.N. crossed out one or two things in his diary. But I wasn't seeking love and comfort from him then, and my heart never again turned to my husband with that spontaneous love and trust that had once been there. It closed for ever then, irrevocably.

17th November. I went into Lev Nikolaevich's room this evening as he was getting ready for bed, and realized I *never* hear a single word of comfort or kindness from him nowadays.

What I predicted has indeed come true: my *passionate* husband has died, and since he was never a friend to me, how could he be one to me now?

This life is not for me. There is nowhere for me to put my energy and passion for life; no contact with people, no art, no work – nothing but total loneliness all day while L.N. writes, with games of vint all evening for his recreation. Oh, those hateful shrieks of "Little slam in spades! No threes!" It's like the raving of lunatics, and I can't get used to it. I have tried joining in this madness myself so as not to have to sit on my own, but whenever I play I always feel ashamed of myself and more depressed than ever.

1904

January – Russia declares war on Japan. Disastrous defeats for Russia unleash more demonstrations, riots and strikes. June – Russian governor of Poland assassinated. July – Minister of the Interior, V.K. Plehve, blown up. Summer – south and west Russia see a wave of pogroms. October – Union of Liberation formed by liberal landowners. December – Port Arthur, Russia's stronghold in the far east, surrenders to Japan.

January – Tolstoy starts on the Circle of Reading. *August – Andrei Tolstoy joins the army. Pavel Biryukov, released from exile, settles at Yasnaya Polyana where he writes biography of Tolstoy. 23rd August – Tolstoy's brother Sergei dies. Sofia writes a short story, 'Groans', under the pseudonym "A Tired Woman" and works on* My Life. *She becomes increasingly distant from Taneev.*

18th January. Life flies past so quickly. From the 6th to the 27th December my daughter Tanya stayed with her family. The elections, the Christmas party and the holidays were so exhausting that there was no time to rejoice. An attack of influenza has left me feeling very weak. L.N. fell ill just before the New Year, and we had a sad party with Seryozha, Andryusha, Annochka, Sasha and the Sukhotin boys. Then my sister Tanya came to stay, happy and irresponsible as ever; but she has been broken by life, hence that peculiar *manner* of hers. There was an unpleasant scene at the card table, and I felt ill with chagrin. On 8th January three students from the St Petersburg Mining Institute arrived with a letter. I had a long talk with them; they were very intelligent, but like all young people nowadays they don't know where to put their energy.* That evening we all left for Moscow, where I stayed until the evening of the 15th.

I took Sasha everywhere with me. We went to a symphony concert at which Chaliapin performed. He is the most intelligent, talented singer I have ever heard in my life. We went to a Goldenweiser concert too – he played with more spirit than usual – then a rehearsal of Chekhov's *The Cherry Orchard*,* which gave me immense pleasure. Sensitive and intelligent, humour alternating with a genuine sense of the tragedy of the situation – just right.

But my main business in Moscow was to transport nine boxes containing Lev Nikolaevich's manuscripts from the Rumyantsev to the Historical Museum. They had asked me to remove these boxes from the Rumyantsev Museum because they were repairing the building. It seemed strange to me that there should be nowhere in the building to store nine boxes, 28 inches long, so I asked to speak to the director, a former professor called Tsvetaev. He made me wait for half an hour, then didn't even apologize and addressed me rudely:

"You see, we're putting up new shelves in the room where the boxes were kept, and we now need the space for *more valuable manuscripts*," he said, among other things.

That made me very angry. "What sort of rubbish could be more important than Tolstoy's manuscripts and the diaries for his whole life?" I said. "I suppose you support the views of the *Moscow Gazette*?"

After this I left for the Historical Museum to see its director, eighty-year-old Zabelin. A white-haired old man with kind eyes and a ruddy face came out to see me, barely able to move his legs. When I asked if he could store Lev Nikolaevich's manuscripts, he took my hands and kissed them, saying in a sweet voice: "Can we take them? But of course we can, bring them immediately! Oh, what a joy! My dear lady, this is history, you know!"

The next day I went to visit Prince Shcherbatov, who said how pleased he was that I had decided to store Tolstoy's manuscripts at the Historical Museum. I also met his dear wife Princess Sofia Alexandrovna (née Princess Apraxina) and his lovely little girl, Marusya. The following day we went to inspect the place where the manuscripts would be stored – they are giving me two rooms directly opposite Dostoevsky's rooms.

The staff of the Historical Museum – Stankevich the librarian, his assistant Kuzminsky, Prince Shcherbatov and his wife – all treated me with the respect and esteem due to me as Lev Nikolaevich's representative.

In Moscow I discovered that the March issue of the *Journal for All* is to print my prose poem 'Groans', which will appear under the pseudonym "A Tired Woman".

3rd February. L.N. is well. Three days ago he was out for a very long time. He appeared at almost six and we discovered he had ridden to Tula and back to buy the last telegraph for the latest news about the war with the Japanese.* This war has stirred us all up, even here in the peaceful countryside. The mood of elation here and the general sympathy with the Tsar are astounding. This is because the Japanese attack was so utterly brazen and unexpected. As far as Russia is concerned, neither the Tsar nor anyone else had the slightest desire for this war. It was simply *forced* on us.

26th May. Lev Nikolaevich told us the story of how he entered military service. Once, after he had lost badly at cards in Moscow and squandered a lot of money, he decided to go to the Caucasus to see his brother Nikolai Nikolaevich, who was serving there. At the time he had no intention of serving in the army; he went to the Caucasus in his civilian coat, and when he went on a raid for the first time he wore the same coat and a service cap. He stayed with Nikolai Nikolaevich in Stary Yurt (known as Hot Springs, as there were sulphur springs there), and from there they went on a raid on Grozny. (Lev Nikolaevich has described this raid elsewhere.)

Once L.N. rode over to Khasav Yurt with an old Cossack to visit some acquaintances. The old Cossack had a falcon on his arm. On the road, which was thought to be very dangerous, they met his cousin Count Ilya Tolstoy driving along in his carriage, surrounded by Cossacks. Count Ilya invited L.N. to go with him to see Baryatinsky, and Baryatinsky praised Lev Nikolaevich for the calm and courage he had displayed during the raid, and urged him to join the army, so that was what he did: he applied to the brigade commander and entered the artillery as a cadet. He remained a cadet for two years without being promoted, although he took part in several dangerous operations.

It was only after two years that he was transferred to the ensigns. When war with Turkey broke out, he applied to enter the Danubian army under Gorchakov, then applied to go to Sevastopol, when the military operations there commenced.*

8th August. On 5th August, just three days ago, I saw off to war my sweet, devoted, loving son Andryusha (even though he has lived badly). I want now to describe his departure with the staff of the 6 Kromsk Infantry Regiment from Tambov. He enlisted in this regiment as a non-commissioned officer, a senior cavalry orderly. He went to war voluntarily. He had just left his wife and children, having fallen in love with Anna Tolmacheva, daughter of General

Sobolev, a weak, empty-headed woman who nonetheless knew how to be tender and loving to him. I shall not judge either my son or my pretty, virtuous, intelligent daughter-in-law Olga. Only God can judge a husband and wife. But I struggled with myself for a long time before I finally decided to petition for Andryusha to be taken into the army. He convinced me by saying it was all the same to him whether they took him or he went without my help – only that way would be much harder for him. And indeed if anywhere is the right place for him at present, it is certainly the regiment. His warm, open charm makes him universally liked, and the regimental commander told me, "Andrei Lvovich had so far given full satisfaction."

Having made all the necessary purchases for him in Moscow and completed my own financial transactions, I went with Lyova to Tambov, where Misha, Ilya and his wife Sonya had all gathered. We stayed in the Evropeisky Hotel, which by Tambov standards was quite magnificent. I was feeling very ill, and couldn't sleep all night, and got up early. That morning I set off for the camp with Andryusha, and he took me to the stables, where we met his fellow orderlies. Like all my children Andryusha loves horses, and he showed me his mare, the best horse in the regiment, which he had bought from Mary Boldyreva (née Cherkasskaya). Twelve men, Andryusha's comrades, were running about the stables, their red shirts flashing; I had bought these shirts for them and they put them on with great excitement. Andryusha introduced me to an adjutant of their regiment, a very decent man called Nikolai Ruzhentsov, and we walked round the square, chatting and waiting for the horses to be harnessed to the military carts. We were also approached by Ruzhentsov's elderly mother, who looked like a merchant's wife. She was bitterly lamenting her fate, sobbing that her youngest and only remaining son was going to war, leaving her alone in the world. She wept uncontrollably, and I tried to comfort her, inviting her to join me in my cab and follow the officers and soldiers as they left the camp. She was delighted to accept, and said God had sent me to help her endure the parting in better spirits. Yet despite all this, that unhappy mother is now completely alone!

When she and I got into the cab, we saw a crowd of people approaching in the distance. These were the soldiers, accompanied by their relatives and loved ones. There was something melancholy about the distant music and drumbeats. The orderlies were riding along with them, and my Andryusha, in his sand-coloured shirt and cap, led them all on his lovely mare. It is all etched vividly in my memory: the mare's legs bound with white bandages, Andryusha looking so handsome in the saddle, and the old woman's words: "Oh, how your son rides that horse – what a picture he makes, just like the one in the study at home."

The crowds of friends and relatives kept growing larger and accompanied the soldiers to the waiting train, not far from the station.

The wives, mothers, fathers and little children were all carrying things – parcels and bundles of ring-shaped rolls. Not far from me stood a young soldier boy with his wife and mother. The old woman stopped and said in a heart-broken voice: "I can't go any further!" The soldier embraced her, kissed her and ran off to catch up with his regiment. His wife followed him, but his mother stood there as if turned to stone.

When they reached the train they were given the order "Stand at ease!" The soldiers loosened their uniforms and began to load the horses. Andryusha helped and gave orders. The crowd milled around the carriages. Some started eating, some soothed their children, some cried. Almost no one was drunk. The task of loading the horses and vehicles on the train was completed quickly and efficiently. They had a long struggle with one bay horse, however, that had to be dragged on by force.

By now the crowd around the train was even denser. The soldiers were getting into their compartments, and the wives and relatives were handing them their things and food for the journey. One soldier leant out and shouted to his four-year-old son: "Don't cry, Lyonka, I'll bring you some chocolate back!" Another soldier, whose hair was already grey, lay down, tipped back his head so his cap fell off, raised his legs in the air, and sobbed with such despair that it broke my heart. A pale young ensign stood on the platform, his eyes dull and his white face tinged with yellow, like a wax doll. He didn't say a word. A few soldiers were weeping. I went to the regimental commander and thanked him for being so good to Andryusha, and he said it was a "great pleasure to have him in the regiment". I was then introduced to the head of the division – Lieutenant-General Klaver, I think it was. He kissed my hands and said: "We are certainly living through extraordinary times."

Andryusha took us to his first-class compartment. He had a folding seat by the door. It will be hard for him, spoilt and ill as he is, to endure the discomforts of the journey and army life.

Eventually the third and final whistle went, there was a flourish of music and everyone wept. I kissed Andryusha, made the sign of the cross over him and could look at no one else. His flushed, distraught face, wet with tears, nodded to us out of the window. Further and further away, then he disappeared completely, and for a moment I lost consciousness of life and its meaning. I felt something similar to this, only much more intensely, when I left Vanechka's funeral. Only mothers will know what I mean.

Everyone was suffering, everyone was leaving against his will, bewildered and unhappy. General Klaver shouted to the soldiers, as they said goodbye to him from the train: "Give them hell!" But his words sounded vile and absurd. It was as if he had suddenly realized he was supposed to encourage them as they left, but knew how pointless it was.

Yet again something has broken in my heart. Seeing my son and the other soldiers off to war marks the end of one phase in my life. What is war? Is one foolish man, Nicholas II, really capable of creating so much evil?

17th August. When I saw Andryusha off to war I suddenly felt connected with everyone grieving over the fate of their children, husbands, brothers and loved ones. I lost all pleasure in life, and was terrified for my son, and the horror of war, which had lain buried for so long in the depths of my soul, suddenly surfaced with terrible power and clarity and wouldn't let go of me.

Andryusha sent a cheerful letter from Ufa, where the train had stopped. But he says nothing of the future... His poor wife Olga and the children are staying here with me, and it breaks my heart to see them. His daughter Sonyusha is such a sad and touching sight, with her sensitive little soul.

But Misha's family is a joy. What charming children – what cheerful, lovable, warm-hearted little mites; it's a pleasure to be with them. And Misha's wife, what a lovely, warm, intelligent woman she is. I sometimes long to hug her and tell her how much I love her and how sorry I would be if she were ever unhappy.

L.N. has been staying in Pirogovo with Masha for the past week. He went there to see his brother Sergei Nikolaevich, who is dying of cancer of the face, eyes and jaw. The poor man is suffering very much, but his emotional state is far worse; no patience, no faith, no love of people... Save us from such an end.

1905

Sunday, 9th January – thousands of workers assemble outside the Tsar's palace to present their petition for a constitution. Cossacks fire on the peaceful crowd and many hundreds killed. Bloody Sunday is the start of Russia's first revolution. Waves of strikes follow, the countryside is ablaze with riots, and hundreds of estates are looted and burnt. February – Russian army defeated at Mukden. The Tsar announces the formation of a new consultative assembly, or Duma. May – Russian fleet annihilated in the Tsushima Straits. As riots continue, extreme right-wing organizations unleash a wave of pogroms. Summer – general strike in Odessa, supported by the battleship Potemkin. *August – Treaty of Portsmouth ends war. Universities become forums for great protest meetings. September to October – general strike in Moscow. 17th October – Tsar issues manifesto promising more freedom and the formation of a Council of Ministers. Workers' councils (soviets) formed in St Petersburg and elsewhere. November – St Petersburg soviet delegates arrested. Moscow soviet organizes armed uprising in protest. Troops sent into Moscow; hundreds killed.*

January – Andrei Tolstoy discharged from army with nervous disorder. Tolstoy writes 'On the Social Movement in Russia' and letters and articles condemning violence. His influence on the revolution is in decline. November – Tanya Sukhotina gives birth to a daughter, Tanya (Tanechka, Tanyushka).

14th January. I went in to see Lev Nikolaevich on the morning of 1st January, kissed him and wished him a happy new year. He was writing his diary, but stopped when I came in and stared at me. "I feel so sorry for you, Sonya," he said. "You are always so unhappy." And at that he burst into tears, caressed me and started telling me how much he loved me and how happy he had been with me all his life. Then I began to cry too; I told him if I wasn't very happy sometimes it was my own fault, and I asked him to forgive me for my unstable state of mind.

L.N. always weighs up his life at the beginning of every year. And just before this new year Pavel Biryukov, who was recently released from exile in Switzerland,* was reading his diaries and his letters to me. L.N. glanced at these from time to time and read through one or two passages, and his whole life seemed to flash before him, and he told Biryukov he couldn't dream of any greater family happiness, that I had given him everything, that he could never love anyone so much... It made me so happy when Biryukov told me this.

On the night of 10th–11th January, our son Andryusha returned from war, thank God. He has been given a year's leave. His head is sick and his nerves are shattered. He is as childish as ever, but the war has left its mark and he seems changed for the better. The cruelty of war is atrocious. Shooting aside, people are punished like martyrs; they are beaten with sabres and bayonets, then cast aside, before receiving the final blow, to die in frightful agony; they are tied up and burnt alive on fires; they are thrown into wolf-holes with stakes at the bottom... And so on. To think human beings could do such things!... It's beyond my understanding. It makes me suffer terribly to hear of people's brutalization and this endless war.

Lev Nikolaevich is writing an article saying the government must act, voicing the demand for a constitution and an assembly of the zemstvo.*

Dreadful news from St Petersburg. 160 thousand workers came out on strike, the troops were called in, and it is said 3,000 were killed.*

1906

Events prove the freedoms promised in the Tsar's October manifesto to be a fraud, and his Duma a fiction. January – first congress of the new Constitutional Democrat (Cadet) Party, which supports a constitutional monarchy. 27th April – opening of the First State Duma. All its demands for reforms rejected by the Tsar. 9th July – Duma dissolved. Strikes and riots continue, but with less intensity than the previous year.

Sofia's son-in-law Mikhail Sukhotin elected to the Duma. She prepares twelfth edition of Tolstoy's Complete Works. *Tolstoy writes 'On the Meaning of the Russian Revolution', and starts on 'The Children's Law of God'. June – peasants steal wood from the Yasnaya estate and Sofia calls police, which provokes bitter arguments with Tolstoy. August – Sofia critically ill with peritonitis, and has operation to remove fibroma of the womb. 26th November – Masha Tolstaya dies of pneumonia.*

1907

Some 2,500 terrorist murders in this year. Terrorist campaign reaches its climax, then collapses, with hundreds of terrorists in prison, Siberia and exile. 3rd June – second Duma dissolved as too radical, and Social Democrat deputies arrested and imprisoned. July – announcement of Russo-Japanese reconciliation. August – Anglo-Russian entente. November – third Duma, dominated by conservatives, completes its full term (until June 1912).

19th May – Sofia's brother Vyacheslav murdered by terrorists. Marauders break into Yasnaya Polyana and Sofia applies to police for guards to protect the property. (The occasion for more bitter arguments with Tolstoy.) September – Tolstoy receives a telegram from an extreme right-wing organization threatening his life. October – his secretary, Nikolai Gusev, arrested for "revolutionary propaganda" and exiled to the Urals. November – Andrei Tolstoy marries his second wife, Ekaterina Artsimovich. Tolstoy starts evening class for peasant children and writes Children's Circle of Reading *and 'Thou Shalt Not Kill'. Winter – he has several strokes and memory losses. Chertkov returns to Russia from exile in England, and takes control of his diaries. Sofia continues work on* My Life *(referred to in this period as her* Autobiography*).*

1908

Spring – revolution defeated, reaction once more triumphant, most revolutionaries in exile or prison. Under the patronage of Nicholas II, ultra-conservative organizations multiply. Large numbers of people move to Siberia to colonize its barren places.

Tolstoy writes 'I Cannot Be Silent', a manifesto to the Tsar begging for an end to the carnage. It is banned, but circulates nonetheless (those found reading it are punished heavily). Sofia working on My Life *and a series of short stories for her grandchildren. Summer – Chertkov buys estate near Yasnaya Polyana and is a constant visitor. Sofia's battles with him begin in earnest. September – Tolstoy's eightieth birthday celebrated in grand style. He suffers more strokes and phlebitis. Violent quarrels with Sofia over the copyright to his post-1881 works.*

7th September. It is a long time since I have written my diary.

Living here in Yasnaya at present are Lev Nikolaevich and I, our daughter Sasha, Doctor Makovitsky, Sasha's companion and assistant Varvara Mikhailovna Feokritova and Lev Nikolaevich's secretary, Gusev, to whom he dictates corrections and new ideas every morning for the new edition of his *Circle of Reading*.

We have recently celebrated Lev Nikolaevich's eightieth jubilee. What an enormous amount of love and respect people have for him. This was evident from all the articles, letters and telegrams – some 2,000 in all. I am saving everything and shall send it to the Historical Museum in Moscow, which is going to open a "Jubilee Archive".

There were some very touching presents too: the first was from waiters at St Petersburg's Bouffe Theatre, and was accompanied by a charming letter. The present was a nickel-plated samovar with engraved inscriptions which read: "Not in God our Strength but in Truth", "The Kingdom of God Is within You", and 72 signatures.* Some artists sent a lovely album of watercolours,* and there were numerous portraits of Lev Nikolaevich, one embroidered on silk, and another done from tiny words taken from a short story of his.* There was a beautiful embroidered red cushion from some craftsmen; the Borman bakery sent chocolate, of which 100 boxes were given to the Yasnaya village children. Someone else sent 100 scythes for our peasants; there were 20 bottles of St Raphael wine for Lev Nikolaevich's stomach, and from the Ottoman factory a box of cigars, which he returned with a letter of thanks, saying he was against tobacco and smoking.

There were also a number of malicious presents, letters and telegrams. For instance, there was a box containing some rope and a letter, signed "A Mother", saying: "Since Tolstoy has no reason to think the government will hang him, he had better do it himself."*

This mother probably had a child who died in the revolution, and she blames its propaganda on Tolstoy.

24 people gathered at the table for his birthday party, including Seryozha, Ilya, Andryusha and Misha and the Chertkovs (father and son). Then Chertkov's wife Galya arrived, and the Nikolaevs. Everyone was calm, quiet and very moved, not least Lev Nikolaevich himself.

He felt fairly well today, although he was again confined to his wheelchair with his slightly swollen leg stretched out in front of him. He ate a hearty lunch with us, and told us he had received a letter from some colonel he had never met, who asked him the name of the horse on which he had galloped away from the Chechens when he was in the Caucasus.*

The story went like this:

An "exploration party" had been organized, and they all set off in carriages and on horseback, accompanied by soldiers. Three of them, wanting to prance about and show off their horses, detached themselves from the main party and galloped on ahead – these three being Lev Nikolaevich, Sado his "*kunak*" (or friend) and Major Poltoratsky. Lev Nikolaevich was on a large, very beautiful grey horse, which had cost a great deal of money and had a lovely gait, but was very heavy, in other words a dawdler. His dear Sado suggested they change horses, so he could experience the speed of his own Nogai horse. They had just done so when some armed Chechens suddenly appeared from under the brow of the hill, advancing towards them. Neither Lev Nikolaevich nor Poltoratsky had a gun. Poltoratsky was on a slow artillery pony and fell behind; they shot at him, attacked his horse and slashed him with their sabres on the spot, but didn't kill him. While Sado was brandishing his rifle and shouting something in Chechen to his fellow tribesmen, Lev Nikolaevich managed to gallop away on his "*kunak*'s" fleet-footed little Nogai horse. So yet again Tolstoy's life was saved by a sheer lucky chance.

The contractor came and drew up estimates for rebuilding the floor in Sasha's room, repairing the bathhouse and the coach house, building a poultry yard and so on. I don't even have the chance to take a walk: first I sit with Lev Nikolaevich, then there are things to be done in the house. I listen to Goldenweiser play the piano and long with my whole being to study music...

8th September. Today L.N. and his secretary Gusev were composing a letter of thanks to everyone who had honoured him on his eightieth birthday. Gusev read it out to me this evening and I made one or two corrections and suggestions, with which both he and Lev Nikolaevich agreed.

Sasha has gone to a concert in Tula with Varvara Mikhailovna. Davydov came and we spent a very pleasant day with him. We had a long talk about literature and everyone deplored the pornography, lack of talent and crude audacity of our modern writers. We discussed the death sentence, and Davydov said how utterly senseless and ineffective it was. The days fly past – and so fruitlessly it makes me wretched.

10th September. I am completely taken up by the estate. I give orders for the potatoes to be dug up, and go to the field, and find they have all gone to dinner, and there is no one there but a puny lad of fourteen, "guarding" the potatoes from thieves. "What are you sitting there for?" I say to him. "Why don't you dig some potatoes?" So he and I pick up sacks and we set to work digging potatoes and putting them in the sacks until the rest of the labourers return. It is so much more enjoyable to work than to be a housewife and make others work. My taking part seemed to infuse the others with energy, and on that day they dug a great many potatoes. We then sorted them out and carried them to the cellar, with me supervising and helping. The guards looked on in amazement.

Lev Nikolaevich is much better and played vint all evening with Sasha, Varvara Mikhailovna and his niece Liza Obolenskaya, who arrived today. It is 10 degrees outside and very peaceful; everything is still green, and there are some lovely phlox outside my window.

13th September. Reading the newspapers in search of any mention of Lev Nikolaevich's name takes a great deal of my time and has a very depressing effect on me. People have so little real understanding of him.

A red-haired, barefoot peasant came to see him and they had a long talk together about religion. Chertkov brought him, saying what a good influence he had on all those around him, despite his poverty. I wanted to listen to their conversation, but whenever I stay in the room when Lev Nikolaevich has guests he gives me a questioning glance, that tells me he doesn't want to be disturbed.

Seryozha's crops have burnt down and he has lost 1,000 rubles' worth of wheat. L.N. sat out on the balcony for breakfast, and this evening he played chess with Chertkov.

14th September. This morning I paid off the Yasnaya day-labourers. The girls and young men all gathered at the office, Varvara Mikhailovna came to give me a hand, and later on Sasha came too. We worked away, checking their tickets, noting them down and paying them. The girls broke into song and cracked jokes, and the children ran about gleefully. I paid out 400 rubles in all. I went on working in the house, and stamped "paid" in their books. It has been a still grey day – 8 degrees towards evening. Sasha has picked a few large honey agarics and saffron milk caps.

L.N. was inundated by guests all day. Eight young revolutionaries came who recently published a proclamation urging people to rise up and kill the landowners. L.N. had sent for these young men himself after learning about them from others in their group, and tried to make them see reason and inspire them with good Christian feelings.* God knows what all this will lead to.

Then I found a young man sitting with L.N. and weeping piteously. It transpired he had been ordered to do his military service and this was abhorrent to him; first he wanted to refuse, then he weakened, now he weeps incessantly and still cannot decide what to do. Then a simple old fellow came for a chat. Two soldiers who came with a civilian weren't allowed in, but were given books.

16th September. After two months sitting at home, L.N. went out for the first time with Gusev in the carriage. He himself drove, and they went to see Chertkov in Telyatinki. His appetite is good and he seems to be making an excellent recovery.

17th September. My name day. I went for a walk with Varya Nagornova, and was enchanted by the youthful beauty of the autumn countryside.

I also took a walk with Andryusha and his new wife Katya. Maria Schmidt came too, to celebrate my name day. I don't usually like "celebrations", but today was most enjoyable. L.N. went for a drive with Sasha in the rubber-tyred carriage, with Chertkov riding on the box. Late this evening he began talking about his *Circle of Reading*, and read us some of his own sayings and those of other writers. He is very absorbed in this work at present, and obviously loves it. He said human happiness consists of universal love, constant communion with God and the aspiration to experience and fulfil God's will throughout one's life. He has never clearly defined exactly *what* he means by God's will, however, or how to apply this to one's life. "Through love," he replies when one asks him.

He has aged greatly over the past year; he has now passed over to the last stage. But he has aged well. His spiritual life evidently predominates now. He likes to go for drives, he likes good food and a glass of the wine the St Raphael wine company sent him for his jubilee, but his body seems to live a separate life, and his spirit exists on an altogether higher plane, independent of his body and indifferent to this earthly life.

30th September. I am consumed by estate matters.

I walked to see how they were progressing with the dam and the slope on the lower pond. Then I picked a bunch of flowers in the garden for Lev Nikolaevich, but he didn't want it. I don't know whether it's this illness that has kept him at home and had a depressing effect on him, or whether it's old age, or this wall of Tolstoyans – mainly Chertkov, who has practically moved in with us and almost never leaves him alone – but he has become not merely distant but even bad-tempered with me and with everyone else. Yesterday we had a letter from his sister Maria, a delightful letter full of warmth – and he didn't even bother to read it.

Heavenly weather. A bright sun, 11 degrees in the shade, the leaves haven't fallen yet and the birches in front of our windows, bright yellow against the blue sky, are astonishing.

The day before yesterday we had a visit from a former revolutionary called N.A. Morozov, who was in prison for twenty-eight years, first in Schlüsselburg, then in the Peter and Paul Fortress. I longed to hear him talk about his psychological state during his imprisonment, but he talked more about the way they had starved them with bad food that gave them scurvy. They would cure the scurvy then starve them again, so that of eleven prisoners in the fortress at the time only three lived out their term, and eight died.

Morozov still looks very fit though, and got married last year. He is full of life and absorbed in his passion for astronomy. He has written and published a book about the Apocalypse,* and his work now consists in discovering references to astronomy in old sacred texts.

8th December. I want to write down something I overheard yesterday evening. Chertkov, who visits us every day, was in Lev Nikolaevich's room and was talking to him about the sign of the cross. L.N. said he made the sign of the cross sometimes from habit, as though even if his soul wasn't praying at that moment, his body was making the sign of prayer. Chertkov replied that it was possible he might make the sign of the cross when he was dying or in pain, and that those with him might think he had returned to Orthodoxy; so in order that people should think no such thing, Chertkov would make a note in his notebook of exactly what he had said.

What a narrow-minded individual this Chertkov is, what an unimaginative view he takes of everything! He isn't interested in the psychology of Lev Nikolaevich's soul at that moment when, alone before God, he blesses himself with the sign of the cross, as he himself was blessed by his mother, his grandmother, his father, his aunts and his little daughter Tanya, who used to bless her father every evening when she said goodnight to him, moving her little hand over him and saying, "Bless Papa!" All Chertkov ever does is to *collect information*, *make notes* and *take photographs*.

Chertkov told us an interesting story of two peasants who came and asked him to make them members of any "party" he wanted, saying they would sign anything he wanted, with whatever he wanted – ink, blood, they didn't mind, just so long as they were paid for it.

This happened because of all the appalling characters who have gathered in Chertkov's house. There are thirty-two people living and eating there at present; the house is a large one and it is completely full. Among them are four young Yasenki peasants, comrades of his son Dima, who do absolutely nothing, eat with their masters, collect 15 rubles a month each and are the envy of all the others. Also living there with their mother, his cousin, are my poor little grandchildren Sonyushka and Ilyushok. It grieves me to see them there.

1909

March – Tolstoy ill again. Chertkov expelled from his estate for "subversive activities" and moves to Kryokshino, near Moscow. October – Chertkov and Sasha Tolstaya prevail upon Tolstoy secretly to draw up a new will bequeathing all his post-1881 works to Tanya, Sasha and Sergei Tolstoy, making Chertkov sole heir to his literary estate. Sofia driven nearly mad by suspicion.

14th January. Today I resumed my old work – copying out a new fictional work Lev Nikolaevich has just completed.*

The subject is revolutionaries, punishments and where all this springs from. It may be interesting. But it's still the same old themes, and the same old descriptions of peasant life. He relishes that peasant girl with her strong female body and her sunburnt legs, she allures him just as powerfully now as she did all those years ago: the same Axinya with the flashing eyes, almost unrecognizable at the age of eighty, has risen from the depths of his past. Axinya was a Yasnaya peasant girl, Lev Nikolaevich's last mistress before his marriage, and she still lives in the village. He didn't want to give it to me to copy at first, and if he had slightly more sensitivity he wouldn't have called his peasant heroine Axinya. Then there is his peasant hero, who is meant to be sympathetic, with his smile and his accordion, who becomes a revolutionary. Maybe I shall change my mind, but so far I don't like it at all.

Wanda Landowska came today and performed for us.* She played a Chopin Mazurka and a Mozart sonata to perfection, bending low over the keys as if forcing them to reveal the meaning of the music to her. The refinement and expressiveness of her playing were taken to the very extremes of beauty. Apart from our family, the Chertkovs, father and son, were here, and my daughter-in-law Olga.

1910

Furious arguments between the Tolstoys over possession of his diaries and the copyright to his works. January – Tolstoy writes 'On Suicide' (later titled 'On Madness'). Summer – Tolstoy rewrites his will, leaving everything to his daughter Tanya, should Sasha die before him, and giving Chertkov sole power to change or publish anything after his death. His sons Andrei and Sergei contemplate certifying him as insane to invalidate his will. July – Tolstoy calls in a psychiatrist to examine Sofia. Diagnosis: paranoia and hysteria. A mounting crescendo of reproaches and recriminations. 28th October – Tolstoy leaves home with his daughter Sasha and his doctor. 7th November – Tolstoy dies at Astapovo station. His death triggers student riots across Russia.

26th June. Lev Nikolaevich, my husband, has given all his diaries since the year 1900 to Chertkov, and has started writing a new diary at Chertkov's house, where he has been staying since 12th June. In this diary, which he started at Chertkov's and gave me to read, he says amongst other things: "I must try to *fight* Sonya with love and kindness." Fight?! What is there to fight, when I love him so passionately, when my one concern is that he should be happy? But to Chertkov, and to future generations who will read his diaries, he must present himself as unhappy and magnanimous, "fighting" some imaginary evil.

My life with Lev Nik. becomes more intolerable each day because of his heartlessness and cruelty to me. And it is Chertkov who has brought all this about, gradually and consistently. He has done everything in his power to take control of this unfortunate old man, he has separated us, he has killed the creative spark in L.N. and has kindled all the protest, castigation and hatred that one sees in these recent articles, which his stupid evil genius has reduced him to writing.

Yes, if one believes in the Devil, he has been embodied in Chertkov, and he has destroyed our life.

I have been ill these past few days. I am tired and depressed by life, and exhausted by my endless tasks; I live alone, without help, without

love, and I pray for death – it is probably not too far off now. Lev
Nikol. is an intelligent man, he knows the best way to get rid of me,
and with the help of Chertkov he has been killing me gradually; soon
it will be all over for me.

I fell ill all of a sudden. I was lying here on my own, as Lev Nikol.,
Sasha and the whole retinue – his doctor, secretary and servant – had
left for Meshcherskoe to see the Chertkovs. For the sake of Sasha's
health (she has been ill), I was obliged to paint the house and repair
the floors. I hired some workmen, and with the help of good Varvara
Mikhailovna I moved out all the furniture, pictures and so on. There
were also a lot of proofs to read, and things to attend to on the estate.
All this exhausted me, and by that evening I was feeling very bad
indeed. The spasms in my heart, my aching head and unbearable
feelings of despair were making me shudder all over; my teeth were
chattering, I was choking and sobbing, I thought I was dying. I was
terrified, and in a desperate attempt to save myself I naturally threw
myself on the mercy of the man I love, and sent him a telegram:
"Implore you to come tomorrow, 23rd." But on the morning of the
23rd, instead of taking the 11 a.m. train and coming to my help, he
sent a telegram saying: "More *convenient* return morning 24th. If
necessary will take night train."

I detected the cold style of the hard-hearted despot Chertkov in
that "more convenient". My despair, my nervous anguish and the
pains in my head and heart reached the limits of endurance.

The violinist Erdenko and his wife had come to visit the Chertkovs
that day, and Chertkov had urged Lev Nikol. that it would be tactless
to leave. And L.N. was only too happy to spend one more day with
his beloved idol.

On the evening of the 23rd he returned, with his hangers-on, in a
disgruntled, unfriendly mood. For while I regard *Chertkov* as having
come between *us*, both Lev Nik. and Chertkov regard *me* as having
come between *them*.

We had a painful talk, and I said everything on my mind. Lev
Nik. sat on a stool looking hunched and wretched, and said almost
nothing. Then a wild beast suddenly leapt out of him, his eyes blazed
with rage, and he said something so cutting that at that moment I
hated him and said: "Ah, so that is what you are really like!" He grew
quiet immediately.

The next morning my undying love for him got the better of me,
and when he came into the room I threw myself into his arms asking
him to forgive me and take pity on me; he embraced me and wept,

and we both decided that henceforth everything would be different, and we would love and cherish each other. I wonder how long this will last.

Today I read Lev Nik.'s diary that he gave me, and was again chilled and shocked to learn that he had given Chertkov *all* his diaries since 1900 so that he could copy out extracts from them for his future advantage. Lev Nik. has always deliberately represented me in his diaries – as he does now – as his tormentor, someone he has to fight and not succumb to, while himself he presents as a great and magnanimous man, religious and loving...

I must try to reach a higher spiritual plane, and see how petty are Chertkov's intrigues and L.N.'s attempts to destroy me, in the face of death and eternity...

Evening. Yet another conversation, yet more anguish and heartache. No, it's impossible, I must kill myself. When I asked Lev Nik. why he wanted to fight me, he replied: "Because you and I are in constant disagreement, about the land question, the religious questions, everything." "But the land isn't mine," I say. "I consider it belongs to all of us, to the family." "Well, you could give away *your* land," he says. "But why aren't you bothered by Chertkov's million rubles and all his land?" I ask. "Oh, I'm not going to talk to you any more, leave me alone!..." First he shouted, then he withdrew into angry silence.

At first, when I asked him where his diaries since 1900 were, he mumbled something and admitted Chertkov had them. Then I asked him again: "So where are your diaries? Are they with Chertkov? What if his house is searched and they're taken?" "He has taken all the necessary measures. They are in the bank," he replied. "Which bank? Where?" "Why do you want to know?" "Because I am your wife, the person closest to you." "Chertkov is the person closest to me, and I don't know where my diaries are. Anyway, what does it matter?"

Everything is a plot against me, and it will end only with the death of this poor old man, who has been lead astray by the devil Chertkov.

Just before he left to visit Chertkov the other day, he was angrily criticizing the life we led, and when I asked: "But what is to be done?" he cried out indignantly: "Leave here, abandon everything, not live in Yasnaya Polyana, not see the beggars, the Circassian guard, the servants waiting at table, the petitioners, the visitors – it's all loathsome to me!"

"Where can we old people go then?" I asked. "I'll go with you wherever you want – Paris, Yalta, Odoev."

I listened to his angry words, then took 30 rubles and went out, intending to go to Odoev and settle there.

It was terribly hot. I ran to the highway, gasping with agitation and exhaustion, and lay down in a ditch by the side of the road, beside a field of rye. Then I heard the coachman approach in the cabriolet, and I climbed in, defeated, and returned home. Lev Nikolaevich had been having palpitations while I was away. What was to be done? Where could we go? What should we decide?

So now I have returned home, back to the old life and its burdens. My husband keeps a sullen silence, and there are the proofs, the painters, the bailiff, the guests and the housekeeping... I am answerable to everyone, I have to satisfy everyone...

This evening, pacing the avenue in the park for the tenth time, I made up my mind: without any arguments or discussions I would abandon all my old responsibilities, my old life, and rent a small corner in someone's hut and settle there, a poor old woman living in a hut with some children whom I would love. That is what I must try to do.

But when I told Lev Nikolaevich that not only was I ready to adopt a more simple life with him, I regarded this as a happy idyll, and asked him to tell me exactly *where* he wanted to go, he initially replied: "To the south, to the Crimea or the Caucasus," then said: "All right, let's go, but first..." And then he started telling me that the main thing was human *goodness*. Of course he won't go anywhere as long as Chertkov is here.

Lev Nik. accused me today of disagreeing with him about *everything*. About what? I asked. The land question, the religious question, everything... But that is not true. It's simply that I don't understand Henry George's ideas on the land question, and I consider it utterly unjust to give it away and deprive my children. It's the same with the religious question. We both believe in God, in goodness, and in submitting to God's will. We both hate war and capital punishment. We both love and live in the country. We both dislike luxury. The only thing I don't like is Chertkov, and I love Lev Nik. And he doesn't love me, he loves his idol.

30th June. I was watching Lev Nik. play chess with Goldenweiser, when Bulgakov came in and said Chertkov's exile was over and he was going to stay with his mother in Telyatinki.* I jumped up as if bitten, the blood rushed to my head and heart and I couldn't sleep all night.

He spent almost the whole day in bed, where he received Sutkovoy, Goldenweiser and Chertkov. I overheard his conversation with Sutkovoy, to whom he said, among other things, "I made a great mistake in getting married..." A mistake?

He considers it a "mistake" because his married life interferes with his spiritual life.

Later that evening he got up, played chess with Goldenweiser and corrected proofs of *The Power of Darkness*. We had a peaceful evening – without Chertkov.

1st July, evening. I spent the day correcting proofs for the new edition of *The Fruits of Enlightenment*, and felt wretched. Lev Nikolaevich didn't like my letter to Chertkov,* but what could I do? One should always write the truth, and never mind the consequences, and I sent the letter all the same. Then this evening Lev Nik., Sasha and Chertkov all retired behind closed doors for some secret conversation, of which I overheard very little, apart from frequent mention of my name. Sasha came outside to check whether I was listening, and when she saw me she ran back to tell the others that I had probably heard their conversation – or confabulation – from the balcony. And again my heart froze and I felt unbearably hurt and sad. I then went into the room where they were all sitting, faced Chertkov and said to him: "What, another plot against me?" At which they all looked embarrassed, and L.N. and Chertkov both started talking at once about the diaries, but in such an incoherent and unclear fashion I never found out what they had been discussing, and Sasha went straight out of the room.

I then had a painful conversation with Chertkov. (Lev Nikol. went out to greet Misha, who had just arrived.) I repeated what I had written in my letter and asked him to tell me *how many* of the diaries he had, *where* they were and *when* he had taken them. At this Chertkov flew into a rage and said that since Lev Nikol. had trusted him he didn't have to answer to me or anyone else, and that Lev Nik. had given him the diaries so he could cross out any unpleasant intimate details.

He soon calmed down and suggested we should work together to love and care for Lev Nikolaevich, and that we should both devote ourselves to his life and work. As if this wasn't what I had done for almost my entire life – for the past 48 years! But no one came between us then, we lived one life. Chertkov then announced that he was Lev Nikol.'s "spiritual confessor" (?), and that I should eventually have to reconcile myself to this.

During our conversation, the crudest words and thoughts kept breaking into Chertkov's speech. For instance, at one point he shouted: "You're afraid I'll use the diaries to unmask you! If I wanted to I could *drag you and your family through the mud!*" (a fine expression for a supposedly decent man!) "I have enough connections, the only thing that has stopped me is my love for Lev Nikolaevich." And to show just what was possible, he cited the example of Carlyle, who had a friend who "unmasked" his wife and showed her in the worst possible light.

What a vile way Chertkov's mind works! What do I care if some stupid retired officer "unmasks" me after my death to various ill-intentioned gentlemen? My business in life and the state of my soul concern me and God alone. I have devoted my entire life on this earth to my passionate, self-sacrificing love for Lev Nikolaevich, and no mere Chertkov could possibly wipe out the past, the half-century of my life I have given to my husband.

Chertkov also shouted that if he had such a wife as me he would have shot himself or run off to America long ago. Then as he was coming down the stairs with my son Lyova, I heard him say angrily: "I can't understand a woman who spends her *entire life* murdering her husband."

Well, this murder is certainly a slow business, considering that my husband has already lived to be 82. But he has now put this idea into Lev Nik.'s head, which is why we are so unhappy in our old age...

What is to be done now? Alas, I shall have to dissimulate if Lev Nikolaevich is not to be taken away from me entirely. I must be sweet and kind to Chertkov and his family; knowing what he thinks of me and me of him, I shall find this intolerably difficult. I must visit him and do my utmost not to upset Lev Nikolaevich, seeing that he has been coerced, controlled and enslaved by Chertkov. I have lost his love for ever if the Lord doesn't see my plight. And I feel so sorry for him! He is so unhappy under the tyrannical Chertkov's yoke – and he was happy when he was with me.

After the business with the stolen diaries, I managed to get Chertkov to write a note undertaking to finish his work on them as soon as possible and to give them straight back to L.N.*

I find Sasha's behaviour very painful.* My daughter has betrayed me. If someone urged her to draw her father away from me, telling her this was for the sake of his peace of mind, she would do so at once. Today she shocked me by holding a secret whispered conversation with her father and Chertkov, constantly looking over her shoulder and running out of the room to see whether I had heard what they were saying about me. They have surrounded me with an impenetrable wall. I sit and pine in my solitary confinement and take this as a punishment "for my sins", the cross I must bear.

2nd July. I am incapable of doing anything, I have been too upset by my recent discussions with Sasha. What spite, what coldness, what injustice! We are growing ever more estranged. How sad it is! Wise, impartial old Maria Schmidt talked to me, which I found a great help. She urged me to rise above Chertkov's criticisms and curses; she said when my daughters pestered me to go and live "elsewhere" with Lev Nikolaevich, since he finds it intolerable now in Yasnaya, they were talking rubbish, as his visitors and petitioners would find him wherever he went, and it would make matters no easier, and it would be folly to disrupt our life in our old age.

Lev Nikolaevich rode over to visit the Chertkovs, and was evidently exhausted by the heat.

A crowd of people arrived after dinner, and my son Lyova got home in time for dinner in a lively, happy mood. He is delighted to be back in Russia and to see Yasnaya Polyana and his family again.

Chertkov's mother came. She is a good-looking woman, extremely aged, very agitated and not quite normal. She is a "Radstockist",* a kind of sectarian, and believes in redemption; she believes that Christ dwells within her and that religion is a kind of inspiration.

Lev Nik. had a bath today; his stomach has been upset, but in general his health is not too bad, thank God!

3rd July. Before I was even dressed this morning I learnt that there had been a fire on Tanya's estate at Ovsyannikovo.* The house where the Gorbunovs are living was burnt down, as was Maria Schmidt's cottage. She had spent the night with us, and they had set fire to it while she was away. Everything was burnt, and what distressed her most was that her trunkful of manuscripts was destroyed. She had copied out everything Lev Nik. had ever written and stored it in a trunk, along with 30 letters to her from him.*

It breaks my heart when I remember her rushing up to me, throwing her arms round my neck and sobbing in despair. How could I comfort her? I could only sympathize with all my heart. All day I have been sadly recalling her last words to me: "Darling, we have such a heavenly life in Ovsyannikovo." She called her cottage her "palace", and she grieved too for her old three-legged mongrel dog who was burnt to death under the stove.

Tomorrow Sasha is going to Tula to buy things for her immediate needs. We shall replace her clothes and furniture as best we can, but as to *where* she will live I have no idea. She doesn't want to live with us, for she is used to her independence, her cows and her dogs, her own kitchen garden and strawberry bed.

Goldenweiser and Chertkov came this evening, and Lev Nik. played chess with Goldenweiser, while Chertkov sat there looking haughty and unpleasant. Lyova is being sweet and sympathetic and gives me a lot of encouragement, yet I still feel so sad!

I have corrected proofs and am now going to send them off.

5th July. This is no life. Lev Nikolaevich's heart is as cold as ice, Chertkov has taken complete control of him. This morning he went over to see him, and this evening Chertkov came to see us. Lev Nik. was sitting on a low sofa and Chertkov was sitting very close to him, and I was beside myself with rage and jealousy.

They then embarked on a conversation about madness and suicide. I left the room three times, but wanted to stay and drink tea with the others. And as soon as I came back Lev Nikol., turning his back on me and facing his idol, again started talking about suicide and madness, cold-bloodedly discussing it from every angle,* accurately and calculatedly analysing the condition in terms of my present suffering. This evening he cynically told me he had forgotten everything, everything he had ever written. "And what about your old life?" I asked. "And your old relations with those close to you? I suppose now you live only for the present?" "Well yes, I do live only for the present now," replied Lev Nik. This had a terrible effect on me! I truly believe that a heartbreaking physical death, with our former love intact to the end of our days, would be preferable to this misery.

Something is hanging over me in this house, some great weight is crushing and destroying me.

I was determined to be calm and to be on good terms with Chertkov, but it was no good; still the same icy relations with Lev Nikol., still the same adoration of that idiot.

I called on his mother today, to return her visit and see my grand-children.* She is a harmless old woman; I was particularly struck by her large ears, and the quantities of food she ate in my presence – sour milk, berries, bread: she simply never stopped.

I sewed some shirts for Maria Schmidt, made her a skirt on the machine and cut out some handkerchiefs. I had a headache.

6th July. I didn't sleep all night. I kept seeing the hateful Chertkov before my eyes, sitting very close to Lev Nik.

I went for a swim on my own this morning, praying as I went. I prayed for this delusion to go away. If it doesn't, I nurture the idea of drowning myself in my beloved Voronka. Today I was remembering that time long ago when Lev Nik. came to the river where I was swimming alone... All that is forgotten now; what we need is quiet, affectionate friendship, sympathy and closeness...

7th July, morning. Rain, wind and damp. I have proofread *The Fruits of Enlightenment* and finished sewing Maria Schmidt's skirt. I took the proofs of *Resurrection* from Lev Nik.'s divan, before Chertkov could sniff them out and take them away. Lev Nik. went to see his idol today, despite the weather, and I realized that although his last diaries are very interesting, they have all been *composed* for Chertkov and those to whom it pleases Mr Chertkov to show them! And now Lev Nikol. never *dares* to write a word of love for me in them, for they all go straight to Chertkov and he wouldn't like this. What made them valuable in my hands was their sincerity, their power of thought and feeling.

I have guarded Lev Nik.'s manuscripts very badly. But he never gave them to me – before he used to keep them with him, in the drawers of his divan, and never allowed anyone to touch them. When I decided to move them to the museum we weren't living in Moscow, so I could only move them and couldn't sort them out. And when we were living in Moscow I was preoccupied with my large family and business that couldn't be ignored, which was our daily bread.

Lyova also quarrelled with that rude, uncouth idiot yesterday.

It's pouring with rain, but despite this Lev Nikol. rode over to Chertkov's, and I waited for him in despair on the porch, worrying and cursing that he lives so close to us.

Evening. No, Lev Nik. has not been taken from me yet, thank God! I went into his room as he was going to bed and said: "Promise me you won't ever leave me without telling me." And he replied: "I wouldn't ever do such a thing – I promise I shall never leave you. I love you," and his voice trembled. I burst into tears and embraced him, saying how afraid I was of losing him, and that despite some innocent, foolish passions in the past I had never stopped loving him for a moment, and still in my old age loved him more than anyone else in the world. Lev Nik. said he felt exactly the same, that I had nothing to fear, that the bond between us was too strong for anyone to destroy, and I realized this was true, and I felt happy. I went into my room, and returned a moment later and thanked him for taking this weight off my heart.

I said goodnight to him then, and went off to my room, and after a little while the door opened and he came in.

"Don't say anything," he said. "I just want to tell you our conversation made me happy too, so very happy..." He burst into tears again, embraced me and kissed me... "Mine! Mine!" I said in my heart. I shall be much calmer now, I shall come to my senses, I shall be kinder to everyone, and try to get on better with Chertkov.

The cocks are crowing, dawn is breaking. Night. The trains rumble, the wind rustles the leaves on the trees...

9th July. Lord, when will these vile episodes and intrigues end! My daughter-in-law Olga arrived, and there was yet another discussion about my relations with Chertkov. He was rude to me again, and I didn't say one impolite word to him – and they all go into corners and pick over my bones, gossip about me and accuse me of I know not what. I cannot get used to the fact that some people simply *lie* – I find it quite astonishing. Sometimes one is horrified and tries naively to establish the truth, to remind them or explain... But all such attempts are useless; people often *simply don't want the truth*, it is neither necessary nor to their advantage. But I shall say no more about it, I have enough worries as it is. Today Lev Nikol. and Lyova went for a ride through the woods. There was a large black rain cloud ahead, but they rode straight into it, and Lev Nikol. was wearing just a thin white shirt, and Lyova a jacket.

They arrived home soaked to the skin. I wanted to rub Lev Nikolaevich's back, chest and legs with spirit of camphor, but he angrily rejected my help and only grudgingly agreed to let his valet Ilya Vasilevich give him a massage.

Olga got angry for some reason and took her children away without staying for dinner. I was feeling quite debilitated this afternoon and went to my room, where I fell asleep and unfortunately slept on and off all evening.

Chertkov and Goldenweiser came, and Lev Nik.'s follower, the economist Nikolaev, who evidently annoys him with his talk. L.N. played chess with Goldenweiser, who then played the piano for a while. That heavenly Chopin Mazurka transported my soul! My son Lyova is very anxious about his foreign passport; they wouldn't give him one in Tula, demanding evidence from the police that he was free to leave Russia, and he is under arrest for publishing two pamphlets in 1905 called 'What Is the Solution?' and 'The Construction of Hell'. It's a very worrying business.

10th July. Lev Nikolaevich naturally didn't *dare* write in his diary how he came into my room late at night, wept, embraced me and said how happy he was that we had reached some understanding and closeness. Instead he writes: "I must restrain myself." What does this mean? No one could possibly love or care for him as I do, no one could desire his happiness as I do. Yet he gives his diaries to Chertkov, who will publish them and repeat to the whole world what he said to me – that a wife like me would make one want to shoot oneself or run off to America.

L.N. rode with Chertkov into the forest today, where they had some sort of discussion. They gave Bulgakov a horse too, but made sure he kept his distance as they didn't want him to disturb their privacy. It is *I* who have to "restrain myself" every day at the sight of that odious figure.

In the forest they dismounted twice for some reason, and in the gulley Chertkov pointed his camera at Lev Nik. and took his photograph. As they were riding back, Chertkov noticed he had lost his watch, and got as far as the balcony before telling Lev Nik. where he thought he had lost it. And L.N., looking so pathetic and submissive, promised to go to the gulley after dinner *to look for Mr Chertkov's watch.*

We had some very pleasant guests to dinner – Davydov, Salomon and the artist Gué. Davydov brought me *Resurrection*, which he had read for the new edition, but I still have a great deal of work to do on it. My son Seryozha is also working on it.

I thought Lev Nik. would be embarrassed to drag these respectable people off to the gulley in search of Mr Chertkov's watch. But he lives in such fear of him that even the thought of being made to look *ridiculous* didn't deter him from taking a crowd of 8 out to the forest. We all stamped around in the wet hay, but couldn't find the watch – heaven knows where that absent-minded idiot lost it! Why did he have to take a photograph in the soft wet hay anyway? Then for the first time this summer Lev Nik. asked me out for a walk with him. I was overjoyed, and waited anxiously to get away from the gulley and the watch. But I was wrong, of course. The following morning Lev Nik. got up early, went to the village, summoned some peasant lads, went off to the gulley again and found the watch.

This evening I felt quite ill and was thrown into another fit of despair. I lay down on the bare boards of the balcony and remembered how it was on that same balcony 48 years ago, when I was still a girl, that I first became aware of my love for Lev Nikolaevich. It was a cold night, and I liked the idea that I should find my death where I had found his love. But I had evidently not earned this yet.

Lev Nikolaevich heard a rustle, came out to the balcony and shouted at me to go away, as I was preventing him from sleeping. I then went to the garden, and lay on the damp ground for two hours in my thin dress. I was chilled through, and longed to die – and I still do.

They raised the alarm, and Dushan Makovitsky, Gué and Lyova came out and shouted at me and helped me up off the ground. I was shaking all over from cold and nerves.

Well, what now! What is to be done! I cannot live without his love and tenderness, and he cannot give it to me. 4 in the morning...

I had already told Davydov and Salomon about Chertkov's malicious intrigues against me, and they were sincerely horrified. They were astonished that my husband could tolerate these insults to his wife, and unanimously spoke of their dislike for this proud, spiteful fool. Davydov was particularly incensed that Chertkov had stolen all Lev Nik.'s diaries since the year 1900.

"But these should belong to you and your family," raged dear Davydov. "And that letter Chertkov wrote to the newspapers when Lev Nik. was staying with him was the height of stupidity and insensitivity."*

All this seems quite clear to everyone else – but what about my poor husband?...

11th July. I slept only from 4 to 7.30 a.m. Lev Nik. also slept very little. I am ill and exhausted, but my soul is happy. Relations with Lev Nik. are friendly and straightforward again. I love him so intensely and foolishly! He needs me to make concessions and heroic sacrifices, but I am incapable of doing this, especially at my age.

Seryozha came this morning. Sasha and her shadow, Varvara Mikhailovna, are cross with me – as if I *cared*! Lyova is being very sweet to me, and the clever fellow has started working on a sculpture of me.

We all went to bed early. L.N. himself asked Chertkov not to come this evening. Thank God! Just to breathe freely for one day is a rest for one's soul.

12th July. I posed for Lyova; his bust of me is beginning to look quite lifelike. What a talented, good person he is. Alas, what a contrast with Sasha!

Lev Nik. waited in for Goldenweiser, as he wanted to go for a ride with him, but he didn't appear. So he sent Filka the stable boy to Telyatinki, and Filka invited Chertkov by mistake instead of Goldenweiser. I didn't know about this, but L.N. eventually decided not to wait any longer for Goldenweiser and went to the stable to saddle his horse and ride out to meet him. I thought he would be all on his own in this fierce heat and might get sunstroke again, so I ran to the stable and asked where he was going and if he was meeting anyone. Lev Nik. was trying to hurry up the coachman, and Doctor Makovitsky was there too, and as soon as he left the stable I saw the odious figure of Chertkov, approaching from under the hill on his white horse. I shrieked that I had been deceived again, that they were trying to hoodwink me, that they had lied about Goldenweiser and invited Chertkov instead, and I had a hysterical attack right there, in front of all the servants, and ran off to the house. Lev Nik. told Chertkov he wouldn't ride with him, Chertkov went home and L.N. rode on with the doctor.

Fortunately it turned out there had been no plot, merely that Filka had been half-asleep and forgotten where he had been told to go, and had accidentally invited Chertkov instead of Goldenweiser. But I am in such a state of torment that the merest mention of Chertkov, and especially the sight of him, drives me into a state of frenzied agitation. When he arrived this evening I left the room and shook like a leaf for a whole hour. Goldenweiser and his wife were here, and were both very kind.

Chertkov's mother, Elizaveta Ivanovna, wrote inviting me to call on her today. Two preachers have come to visit her; one is called Fetler, and the other was some Irish professor whom I could barely understand, but who ate very heartily and occasionally made religious pronouncements in a mechanical sort of way. But Fetler was a man of principle and spoke beautifully and tried to convert me to his faith in Redemption. He got down on his knees and started praying for me, for Lev Nikolaevich, for the peace and happiness of our souls and so on. It was a beautiful prayer, but it was so strange! Elizaveta Ivanovna was there all the time, and at one point she called me over to ask me why I hated her son. I told her about the diaries, and explained that her son had taken my beloved husband from me. To which she replied: "And I have been unhappy because your husband has taken my son from me!" And she is quite right.

13th July. After sending Chertkov away yesterday for my sake while he was out riding, Lev Nik. spent the whole evening waiting for him to come so he could explain the reason. Chertkov didn't come for a long time. Sensitive to my husband's moods, I saw him anxiously looking for him, waiting like a lover, and becoming more and more agitated, sitting out on the balcony downstairs staring at the road. Eventually he wrote a letter, which I begged him to show me. Sasha brought it, and soon I had it in my hands. It was "dear friend", of course, and endless endearments... and I was again in a frenzy of despair. Nevertheless he gave this letter to Chertkov when he arrived. I took it under the pretext of reading it, then burnt it. He never writes me tender letters, I am becoming even more wicked and unhappy and close to my end. But I am a *coward*. I didn't want to go swimming yesterday, because I was afraid of *drowning*. I need only *one moment* of determination, and am incapable of even that.

Lev Nik. went for a ride with Goldenweiser and the Sukhotins, and I looked for his last diary but couldn't find it. We are like two silent enemies, constantly suspecting, spying and sneaking up on each other! Lev Nik. hides everything he can from me by giving it to that "spiteful pharisee", as Gué called him. Maybe he gave his last diary to Chertkov yesterday.

Lord take pity on me and save me from sin!...

Night of 13th–14th July. Let us assume I have gone mad, and my "fixation" is that Lev Nik. should get his diaries back and not allow

Chertkov to keep them. Two families have been thrown into confusion, there have been painful arguments – I have been driven to the
very limits of my endurance. (I haven't eaten a thing all day.) Everyone
is depressed, and my tormented appearance annoys everyone like a
bothersome fly.

What can be done to make everyone happy again and put an end
to my sufferings?

*Get the diaries back from Chertkov, all those little black oilcloth
notebooks, and put them back on the desk, letting him have them,
one at a time, to make excerpts. That's all!*

If I do eventually summon up the courage to kill myself, everyone
will look back and realize how easy it would have been to grant my
wish.

When they explain my death to the world they won't give the real
reason. They'll say it was hysteria, nerves and my wicked nature –
and when they look at my dead body, killed by my husband, no one
will *dare* say that the *only* thing that could have *saved* me was the
simple expedient of returning those four or five oilcloth notebooks to
my husband's desk.

Where is their Christianity? Where is their love? Where is their
"non-resistance"? Nothing but lies, deception and cruelty.

Those two stubborn men, Chertkov and my husband, have joined
forces and are crushing me, destroying me. And I am so afraid of
them; their iron hands crush my heart, and I long to tear myself from
their grip and escape. But I am still so afraid...

Thoughts of suicide are growing stronger all the time. Thank God
my sufferings will soon be over!

What a terrible wind! It would be good to go now... I must try once
more to save myself... for the last time. If they *refuse*, it will be even
more painful, and even easier to deliver myself from my suffering; I
should hate to keep making threats, then pester with my presence all
the people whose lives I have made a misery... But I should love to
come back to life so I could see my husband carrying out my wishes,
and see that gleam of love that has warmed and saved me so many
times in my life, but which Chertkov now seems to have stifled for
ever. Without that love my life is over.

14th July. I haven't slept all night. These expressions of my suffering,
however extreme, can't possibly do them justice. Lev Nikol. came in,
and I told him in terrible agitation that everything lay in the balance: it
was either the diaries or my life, he could choose. And he did choose,

I'm thankful to say, and got the diaries back from Chertkov. In my nervousness I have made a bad job of pasting into this diary the letter he gave me this morning;* I am very sorry about this, but there are several copies, including the one I made for the collection of Lev Nikolaevich's letters to me, and the one our daughter Tanya has.

Sasha drove over to Chertkov's to fetch the diaries and give him a letter from Lev Nikolaevich. But the thought of suicide, clear and firm, will always be with me the moment they open the wounds in my heart again.

So this is the end of my long and once happy marriage!... But it is not quite the end yet; Lev Nik.'s letter to me today is a scrap of the old happiness, although such a small, shabby scrap!

My daughter Tanya has sealed up the diaries, and tomorrow she and her husband will take them to the bank in Tula. They will fill out a receipt for them in the name of Lev Nik. and his heirs, and will give this receipt to L.N. I hope to God they do not deceive me, and that Jesuit Chertkov doesn't wheedle the diaries out of Lev Nik. on the sly.

Not a thing has passed my lips for three days now, and this has worried everyone terribly for some reason. But this is the least of it... It's all a matter of passion and the force of grief.

I bitterly regret that I have made my children Lyova and Tanya suffer, especially Tanya; she is being so sweet and kind and compassionate to me again! I love her very much. Chertkov must be allowed to come here, although this is very, very difficult and unpleasant for me. If I don't let them meet, there will be page upon page of secret, tender letters, and that would be much worse.

15th July. Another sleepless night. I kept thinking if it was so easy for Lev Nik. to break his promise in his letter not to leave me, then it would be equally easy for him to break all his promises, and where would all his "true and honest" words be then? I have good reason to worry! First he promised me in front of Chertkov that he would give *me* his diaries, then he deceived me by putting them in the bank. How can one keep calm and well when one lives under the constant threat of "I'll leave, I'll leave!"

I had another frightful nervous attack and longed to drink opium, but again lacked the courage, and instead told Lev Nik. a wicked lie and said I had taken it. I confessed immediately, and wept and sobbed, and made a great effort to regain my self-control. How ashamed and wretched I felt. But... no, I shall say no more: I am sick and exhausted.

My son Lyova and I went out in the cabriolet to look at a house in Rudakovo to replace Tanya's house in Ovsyannikovo.* Lev Nik. went for a ride with Doctor Makovitsky. I thought we were going together, but L.N. deliberately went in the opposite direction. I shall go along the highway, he said, and home via Ovsyannikovo. He then went a completely different way, turning off just before Ovsyannikovo, as though quite by chance. But I notice everything, remember everything and suffer deeply.

I forced myself to let Chertkov visit us, and behaved *correctly* with him, but I suffered terribly as I watched their every movement and glance. How I loathe that man!

Chertkov's son Dima was here too, a sweet, straightforward boy accompanied by his English friend who drives motorcars. The papers have published a short article by L.N. called 'From My Diary', about his conversation with a peasant.

A mass of dull people here: the Englishman, Dima and his comrade (they aren't so bad), the tedious Nikolaev, Goldenweiser and Chertkov. And since none of these gentlemen had anything to talk about, they played the gramophone. I tried to read some proofs – but couldn't. Lyova is sculpting me: I feel calmer with him. He understands everything and loves and pities me.

Taking these diaries from Chertkov has cost me dear, but I would do it again if I had to; I would gladly give the rest of my life to ensure they never went back to Chertkov, and I don't regret the health and strength I have lost in rescuing them. This must now lie on the conscience of Chertkov and my husband, who clung to them so stubbornly.

They will be deposited in the bank in Lev Nik.'s name, and he will have the sole right to take them out. What an insensitive, distrustful attitude – and how unkind to his wife!

16th July. Now they have discovered I am keeping a diary every day, they have all started scribbling *their* diaries. They are out to attack me, condemn me and bring all sorts of malicious evidence against me for daring to defend my conjugal rights, asking for a little more love and trust from my husband, and for the diaries to be taken away from Chertkov.

God be with them all: I need my husband, while I am still not completely frozen by his coldness; I need justice and a clear conscience, not the judgements of others.

I went to Tula with Tanya and we deposited Lev Nikolaevich's seven notebooks in the State Bank. This is a half-measure, i.e. a partial concession to me. They have been removed from Chertkov, thank God, but now I shall never be able to see or read them in Lev Nik.'s lifetime. This is my husband's revenge on me. When they were brought back from Chertkov's I took them frantically and leafed through them to see what he had written (even though I had already read most of them before), and I felt as though my beloved lost child had just been returned to me and was about to be taken away again. I can imagine how furious Chertkov must be with me! This evening he visited us again. I am still tormented by hatred and jealousy of him. A mother whose child is lured away by the gypsies must feel what I felt today.

I know hardly anything about his work; at night I go into the so-called "office", where Sasha and her companion Varvara Mikhailovna are copying for him, and look through his papers.

There are various letters there, an introduction to the kopeck booklets, the article about suicide, several beginnings, but nothing important.*

There was the most terrible thunderstorm all evening. Lord, what rain! The noise of the storm and wind and the leaves on the trees makes it impossible to sleep...

17th July. My daughter Tanya left this morning. The storm has passed. I went to bed late and slept till 12; I got up feeling exhausted, and my first thought was of Lev Nikolaevich's diaries. Last night I read Tanya my letter to Chertkov, which is affixed to this diary, and I thought if Chertkov really loved Lev Nik. he would have given me the diaries when I asked him to, seeing what a desperate state I was in, instead of making us all so unhappy.

So are things better now? This business has brought grief to our entire family for the past two weeks; the diaries are completely inaccessible now, and Lev Nik. has offered *never* to see Chertkov again if I wish. Chertkov is now openly at war with me. I am winning so far, but I confess honestly that I have paid for those diaries with my life, and I know there is more to come. When Lev N. told me he was coming this evening too, I protested with all my strength, then eventually had to accept the idea. But then Lev Nik. himself asked Varvara Mikhailovna to drive over to Chertkov's and tell him not to come.*

Lev Nikolaevich told me today that his diaries had first been hidden with our daughter Sasha, and that, at Chertkov's insistence, she had given them to young Sergeenko, who had taken them to Chertkov behind my back on 26th November.

What vile, secretive behaviour! What a web of plots and intrigues against me! Lies! Isn't my daughter Sasha a traitor? What a sham that was, when I asked Lev Nikol., "Where are the diaries?" and he took my arm and led me to Sasha, as though he didn't know, but she might know where they were. And Sasha too said she didn't know, and she too was lying. Though Lev Nikol. had probably forgotten that he had given them to Chertkov.

All these people surrounding Lev Nik. have grown so skilled in lying, cheating, justifying themselves and planning endless conspiracies! I hate lies; it's not for nothing they say the Devil is the father of lies. It was never like this before in our bright, honest family atmosphere; it has only started since Chertkov's devilish influence appeared in this house. For good reason his name derives from the word "devil".*

It is he who has filled our house with this stench that is choking us all, and this gentleman accuses me of "murdering" him. He wants his revenge, but this doesn't frighten me.

19th July. They break my heart and torture me, and now they call for the doctors – Nikitin and Rossolimo. Poor men! They have no idea how to cure someone who has had wounds inflicted on her from all sides! The chance reading of a page from his old diary has disturbed my soul and opened my eyes to his present infatuation with Chertkov, and irrevocably poisoned my heart. First they suggest the following remedy: that Lev N. should live in one place, and I in another; he would go to Tanya's and I would go who knows where. When I realized everyone around me was intent on separating me from Lev Nikolaevich, I burst into tears and refused. Then seeing how weak I was the doctors began prescribing baths, walks, no excitement… It was absurd! Nikitin was amazed to see how thin I had become. It's all because of my grief and my wounded loving heart – and all they can say is leave him! Which would be more painful than anything else.

I drove to the river for a swim, and felt even worse. The water is very low in the Voronka, like my life, and it would be hard to drown in it at present; I went there mainly to estimate how much deeper it might get.

I washed Lev Nik.'s cap. He went over to Ovsyannikovo in the heat and ate no dinner. He now looks very tired. No wonder! 14 miles on horseback in 36 degrees, in the glare of the sun! This evening he played chess with Goldenweiser. I didn't say a word to him all day as

I am afraid to upset him, and myself too. I posed for Lyova; I always enjoy being with him. I then corrected proofs, but still haven't sent them off – I cannot work… It is late now and I must go to bed, although I am not sleepy.

20th July. We have had two peaceful days without Chertkov. The doctors left earlier on. I suppose they were asked here to testify that I am mad, just in case. Their visit was completely pointless. I would be quite well if every day was like the past few days.

Lev Nik. went for a ride with Filka, our stupid, good-natured stable boy, then sat on the balcony outside his room all evening, quietly writing, reading and resting. Goldenweiser came and they played a quiet game of chess, then we all drank tea on the balcony together. I feel so sorry for Lyova. He has been sad and preoccupied all day. Has he suddenly recalled some painful experience in Paris, or is he worried they won't give him his documents for a foreign passport, or are all the painful problems of our life here too much for his nerves?…

I went swimming with Liza Obolenskaya, Sasha and Varvara Mik-hailovna, and we drove home together. Insufferable heat, a lot of white mushrooms, the rye is being harvested.

I read some proofs – the new edition of the *Collected Works* in Russian, and Maude's biography of Lev Nik. in English – and posed for Lyova.

21st July. Lev Nik. has a bad pain in his liver, his stomach is upset and the bile isn't flowing. But the main reason I feel so tormented is that it is my fault he is not getting better.

This evening he played chess with Goldenweiser on the balcony upstairs. Then Chertkov came. The moment I heard his cabriolet approaching I began to tremble all over. Earlier I had walked round the garden for an hour and a half trying to regain my self-control.
. But then they all sat out on the terrace together with Maria Schmidt, and I felt wretched that everyone but me was enjoying Lev Nik.'s company, and here we were, coming to the end of our life together on earth, and I couldn't be with him. Three times I tried to go out on the terrace to drink tea with the others, and when I eventually summoned up the courage to go, what happened? I was so agitated that the blood rushed to my head, my pulse was barely perceptible, I could hardly stand and couldn't see Chertkov. I tried to say something, and it was as though my voice wasn't mine

but that of some wild creature. Everyone stared at me. I struggled desperately to be calm, to avoid creating a scandal and distressing Lev Nikolaevich, but with little success. Lord help me! How sad and painful it is!

22nd July.* Early this morning the doctor applied leeches to the small of my back to stop the blood rushes to my head. I got up, reeling after a night without sleep.

Lev Nik. again lost his temper with me at dinner today, after I had voiced my chagrin at never being shown any copies of his latest works to read, since Chertkov immediately takes away all his manuscripts. I again burst into tears, left the table and went upstairs to my room. He thought better of it and came after me, but our conversation soon turned acrimonious again. Eventually though he invited me to take a stroll around the garden with him, which I always appreciate, and all our resentment seemed to pass.

Chertkov came after receiving a note from me to say he could visit Lev Nikolaevich if he wished; I want to be magnanimous to him, despite his rude and unpleasant behaviour. I managed to conquer my feelings and sat down to a game of draughts with my granddaughter Sonya, which distracted me from thinking about him.

Lev Nik. is listless, his liver is aching, he has no appetite and his pulse is quick. I implored him to take some rhubarb and apply a compress, but he became irritable and stubbornly refused.

23rd July. Lev Nik. was much worse this morning. But I did have one great joy – my darling grandchildren visited: first Sonyushka and Ilyushok with their mother, then Lyova, Lina and Misha came from Chifirovka with Vanechka and Tanechka. They are all such sweet, loveable children. But I couldn't spend much time with them, as I was looking after Lev Nik., watching over him and listening for his call, which made me sad.

When I learnt Chertkov was coming again, I burst into tears and started trembling all over, and Sasha virtually spat in my face as she went past, shouting, "Oh, what the devil is it now! I'm so sick of these scenes!"

What a horribly rude creature. And what a terrible, wicked expression she had on her face when she said it. Oh, how one longs for death in the midst of all this evil, deception and hatred.

I read the little two-act play Lev Nik. wrote in Kochety after his peasant pals had put on his play *The First Distiller*, and asked him to write something else for them. It's just raw material so far, but he has thought it all out and parts of it are very good. I kept being reminded of *The Power of Darkness*.

In the past, when I used to copy everything for Lev Nikol., I used to point out the mistakes and clumsy bits, and we would correct them together. Nowadays the others do all his copying for him, very accurately, but like machines.

24th July. Chertkov came again this evening, and I overheard Lev Nik. whispering to him: "Do you agree with what I wrote?" And he replied: "Of course I agree!" Yet another plot! Lord have mercy!

When I asked Lev Nik. with tears in my eyes to tell me what "agreement" they were talking about, he made a spiteful face and stubbornly refused to tell me anything. He is unrecognizable! And once more I am in the throes of despair. There is a phial of opium on my table, and the only reason I haven't drunk it is because I don't want to give them all, including Sasha, the satisfaction of seeing me dead. But how they persecute me! Lev Nik.'s health is much better now and he will certainly do everything he can to survive me so as to continue his life with Chertkov. I long to drink that phial and leave a note for Lev Nik. saying, "Now you are free."

This evening he said to me spitefully: "I have decided today that I want to be free, so I am not going to pay attention to anything any more." We shall see who will be the winner if he does declare open war on me. My weapon and my revenge is death, and it will be his and Chertkov's disgrace if they kill me. "She is mad!" they will say. Yet who is it who drove me mad?

25th July. He has been *writing* something with Chertkov. Today he gave him some large documents, probably a new will depriving his family of his works after his death. He has renounced money, yet he always has several hundred rubles on his desk to give away. He has renounced *travelling*, yet he has already made three journeys this summer, he visited his daughter Tanya in Kochety twice this year, he has been to see Chertkov in Kryokshino and Meshcherskoe, and his son Seryozha with me – and now he wants to go to Kochety again.

On the evening of the 24th I sat down at my desk in a state of great agitation, and stayed there *all night* in just a light summer dress, without once closing my eyes. At five in the morning I decided to go outside for some fresh air, even though it was pouring with rain. But then my daughter-in-law Olga ran out of the room next door, grabbed me with a strong arm and said: "Now where are you going? I know you're about to do something silly and I'm going to stay with you!" And that dear, sweet, kind woman sat up with me all night, without sleeping a wink, poor thing, and tried to comfort me... Stiff with cold, I moved to a stool and dozed off. (Olga told me I moaned pitifully in my sleep.) The next morning I decided to leave so as not to see Chertkov and simply to get some rest and give Lev Nikolaevich a rest from my presence and my suffering soul. I packed my case, took some money, and writing work and my permit, and decided either to move into a hotel in Tula or to my house in Moscow.

I drove to Tula in the trap which was being sent to collect Andryusha and his family. I met him at the station and decided that after seeing them off to Yasnaya I would go on to Moscow that evening. But Andryusha immediately sensed my state of mind and firmly announced he wouldn't leave me on my own for a moment. There was nothing to be done, and I agreed to return to Yasnaya with him, although all the way back I was shuddering at the memory of my recent experiences.

I straight away lay down in bed, for fear of meeting my husband and being the butt of his jibes. But in fact, to my great joy, he entered my room with tears in his eyes and thanked me tenderly for returning: "I realized I couldn't live without you," he said weeping. "I felt shattered, I went to pieces... We are so close, we have grown so used to each other... I am so grateful to you for coming back darling, thank you..."

26th July. Sad news this morning from Tanya, who is ill in bed. She begs Lev Nikolaevich (but not me) to go to Kochety.

My sons have been splendid, and have united to defend me. Sasha looks maliciously at me, like all guilty people. Having insulted me and spat in my face, she is now sulking and unconsciously wants to take her father away from me; but of course for his sake I would abandon everything and leave here.

It is a warm damp day, with a lot of little clouds but no rain. They are cutting the oats now, although the rye has still not been harvested and some of it has been stolen.

27th July, morning. Another sleepless night. Anxiety is gnawing at my heart. I cannot bear not knowing about the conspiracy with the document Lev Nik. has just signed (evidently a supplement to his will, drafted by Chertkov and signed by Lev Nik.). That document is his revenge on me for the diaries and for Chertkov. Poor old man! What sort of memories will he leave behind after his death?!

The moment I got up this morning I took Vanechka's basket and wandered off to the woods, and who should I see there but L.N., sitting on his shooting stick and scribbling something. He seemed taken aback to see me, and hurriedly covered up his piece of paper. I suspect he was writing to Chertkov.

I was out for two and a half hours, and it was good to be with nature, far away from cunning, spiteful people. Silly little Parasha who watches our calves is such a happy, kind-hearted creature; she had picked some inedible mushrooms which she gave me, but with such good nature! Two shepherds greeted me amiably as they drove our cattle past. I gazed into the cows' eyes and realized they were just *nature*, and had no soul.

The boys were out picking mushrooms, such cheerful, artless fellows... In the barn the men who guard our orchards and the girl labourers (who have come from far away) were all sitting down on the threshing floor for their dinner. They looked so bright and cheerful; not one of them had ulterior motives, or was drawing up plots and documents with sly fools like Chertkov. Everything is simple and honest with them! We should learn to merge with nature and the common people; our lives would be much simpler without the stench of false non-resistance.

29th July. We have regained our old calm existence again, and life has returned to normal. Thank God! Chertkov hasn't visited us for five days now, nor Lev Nik. him. But at the mere memory of him, and the possibility of their renewed intimacy, something rises from the depths of my soul and torments me. Well at least it's a rest!

Zosya Stakhovich has cheered us all up and is very pleasant company. Lev Nik. went out for a ride, even though it is still pouring with rain. I have been working on the proofs and was delighted by *The Cossacks*. How weak his later stories are by comparison!

I wrote to my daughter Tanya and my nieces Liza Obolenskaya, Varya Nagornova and Marusya Maklakova. Nikolaev came after dinner and Lev Nik. talked to him about Henry George and "justice". I heard snatches of their conversation, which evidently exhausted him. Zosya Stakhovich talked animatedly about Pushkin, whom she has just been reading, and recited some of his poems. Then they played a game of vint; Sasha wanted to exclude me, and when I firmly took a card she pulled a face and left the room, whereupon Lev Nik. and I cheerfully took a grand slam no trumps. I don't really like cards, but it's so depressing sitting on my own when my family are enjoying themselves at the card table. The day passed quietly, without Chertkov. Lev Nik. was in better spirits today.

30th July. I have been unable to do a thing all day: nothing but humdrum tasks, tedious worries about food, making guests comfortable, supervising the rye harvest and the repairs to the storeroom and so on and so on, and nothing in return but endless criticisms and homilies about my "materialism".

31st July. How hard it is to move from reading proofs to ordering dinner, to buying rye, to reading Lev Nik.'s letters – and finally to writing my diary. How fortunate are those people who have leisure, and can spend their entire lives concentrating on one abstract topic.

While I was reading through L.N.'s letters to various people I was struck by his insincerity. For instance he writes frequently and with apparent affection to a Jew named Molochnikov* – a carpenter from Nizhny Novgorod. Yet my daughter-in-law Katya and I were remembering just today that Lev Nik. once said: "I am always careful to be friendly to Molochnikov, which is hard for me as I dislike him and have to make great efforts to behave well with him." L.N. also writes to his wife, who he has never met. And all this because Molochnikov was sent to prison, apparently for distributing Tolstoy's books – although I am told he is simply an embittered revolutionary.

I was also struck by his frequent laments in these letters that "it is hard to live in luxury as I do, against my will…" Yet who but he needs this luxury? There are doctors for his health, two typewriters and two copiers for his writings, Bulgakov for his correspondence, Ilya Vasilevich, his valet, to look after a weak old man, and a good cook for his weak stomach.

And the entire burden of finding the money for this, supervising the estate and getting his books published rests on my shoulders, in order that he can have the comfort and leisure he needs for his work. If anyone took the trouble to examine *my* life, any honest person would realize that I personally need nothing. I eat once a day, I go nowhere. I have just one maid, a girl of eighteen, and I dress quite shabbily. Where is all this luxury I am supposed to have forced on him? How cruelly unjust people can be! May the sacred truth contained in this diary survive to cast light on all these matters that have been obscured.

The Lodyzhenskys came, bringing with them the Russian Consul to India.* He had little of interest to say, but the Lodyzhenskys have travelled widely, have been to India and Egypt and studied religion, and are interesting, lively people.

1st August. I have felt very ill all day; again everything torments and worries me. Lev Nik. is being cold and withdrawn and is evidently pining for his idol. I am trying to work out whether I can bear the sight of Chertkov – and I realize I cannot, I cannot…

Three villagers came to visit Lev Nik.; we had asked them for the names of our poorest peasants so we could buy rye seeds for them with the money the Englishman Maude sent us in aid of the starving. The peasants had a talk with Lev Nik. and promised to make a list of the poorest peasants. He told me the names of two of them, but not the third – it must be Timofei, his son by that peasant woman. (In fact it was Alexei Zhidkov.)

I told fortunes with the cards tonight. For Lev Nikolaev., I drew that he would live with a young woman (Sasha) and the King of Diamonds (Chertkov), and that he would have love, marriage and happiness (all hearts). I drew death (the Ace of Spades and the Nine). For the heart I drew an old man (the King of Spades) or a villain. Then I drew all four tens, which means that my wish will be granted, and my wish is to die, although I should hate to yield Lev Nikolaevich to Chertkov when I do. And how they would gloat and rejoice after my death! The first blow against me was well aimed and has done its work. *It is these sufferings that will bring about my death.*

2nd August. Writing his diaries has lost all meaning for Lev Nikola-evich now. His life and his diaries – with their revelations of both the good and bad impulses of his soul – have become two completely separate things. His diaries are now composed for Mr Chertkov, whom he doesn't see, although from the evidence I assume they are corresponding, and their letters are passed on by Bulgakov and Goldenweiser, who come here every day.

Last time Chertkov was here, Lev Nikol. asked him if he *"received his letter, and whether he agreed with it"*. To what new abomination has Mr Chertkov given his approval now? If his visits put a stop to this clandestine correspondence, then let him visit here by all means; but they continue to write even when they are meeting, so it's better they don't see each other – they just have their letters now, and no meetings. L.N.'s love for Chertkov intensified after he stayed with him this summer without me, and it weakens with distance and time.

Lev Nik. rode *alone* to Kolpna today to inspect the rye that we are buying for the peasants. I couldn't do a thing; my heart was pounding wildly, my head was aching, and I was terrified he had arranged to meet Chertkov and they would go there together. Eventually I ordered the cabriolet to be harnessed and drove out to meet him. He was alone, thank God, followed, it so happened, by a peasant of ours called Danila Kozlov.

I have such a lot of work to do and proofs to read, but can do nothing while Chertkov is in the neighbourhood, and I am afraid of getting things in a muddle. I forced myself to go to dinner, but immediately afterwards felt so ill I had to go to my room and lie down. Lotions and mustard plasters on my head eased the pain, and I eventually dropped off to sleep.

Lev Nik. was kind and solicitous. But later on, when I heard Bulgakov had come with some mail, and I asked if there was a letter from Chertkov, he grew furious, and said: "I think I have the right to correspond with whomever I please... He and I have a vast amount of business connected with the printing of my works and various writings..."

Ah yes, but if it was only *that* sort of business, then there wouldn't be any of this *secret* correspondence. When things are secret there is bound to be something bad hidden away. Christ, Socrates – none of the ancient philosophers did things in secret; they preached openly on the squares before the people, fearing nothing and no one. And they were killed for it too – but then they joined the gods. Criminals – conspirators, libertines, thieves – always do things in secret. And Chertkov has inveigled poor saintly Tolstoy into this situation which is alien to his nature.

3rd August. When Lev Nikol. learnt that Mr Maude had revealed in his biography of him various loathsome things about Chertkov (even though he didn't name him and merely referred to him as "X"), he stooped so low as to write to Maude begging him to delete these vile truths and remove an excerpt from a letter written by our late daughter Masha, which refers contemptuously to him. I received two letters from Maude today, one to me, the other to Lev Nikolaevich. What a terrible thing it is that L.N. should love

Chertkov so much that to protect him he is prepared to humiliate himself to the point of lying.

I wanted to explain to Lev Nik. the source of my jealousy of Chertkov, so I showed him the page of his old diary, for 1851, in which he writes that he has never fallen in love with a woman but has frequently fallen in love with men. I thought he would understand my jealousy and reassure me, but instead he turned white and flew into a terrible rage such as I haven't seen for a long, long time. "Get out! Get out!" he shouted. "I said I'd leave you and I will!" He rushed from room to room and I followed him horrified. Then he went to his room, slammed the door and locked me out. I stood there stunned. Where was his love? His non-resistance? His Christianity?

When the others had gone to bed, Lev Nik. came to my room and said he had come to apologize. I trembled for joy. But when I followed him out and suggested we should try to live out the end of our lives in a more friendly fashion, he refused to listen and said if I didn't go away he would regret coming in to see me. What is one to make of him!

4th August. Today passed without any mention of Chertkov, thank God! Things have become slightly easier and the air has cleared somewhat. I am grateful to my dear Lyovochka for taking pity on me. If everything started all over again I don't think I would have the strength to endure it. I hope everyone will leave Telyatinki soon, so I can stop living in terror of their secret meetings, trembling with anxiety every time Lev Nikol. goes out for a ride.

There is an evil spirit in Chertkov, and he frightens and disturbs me.

5th August. I heard today that there are 30 people at Telyatinki furiously copying something. What can it be? Didn't Lev Nikol. take his diaries back yesterday? It's impossible to discover what is happening! With sly, malicious obstinacy Lev Nikolaevich hides *everything* from me, and we are strangers.

I am to blame for a great deal, of course. But I have suffered such remorse that a *kind* husband would forgive me the wrongs I have done him. How happy I should be if he would only draw me closer and say nice things to me. But this will never happen – even if Chertkov is kept away from him!

6th August. Yet another sleepless night. Each morning I wake in terror at what the day will bring. And this is what happened today.

I looked into Lev Nikolaevich's room at 10 o'clock and he wasn't there, and had gone out for his walk. I dressed hurriedly and ran to the fir plantation, where he usually takes his morning walk. I met some village children and asked them: "Have you seen the old Count, my little ones?" "Yes, we saw him sitting on the bench." "Alone?" "Yes, alone." I took myself in hand and calmed down a little. The children were so sweet, and seeing that I couldn't find any mushrooms they gave me five brown caps, saying pityingly: "You can't see a thing, can you! You're completely blind!" Lyova came into the plantation – I don't know if he was looking for me or it was by chance; and a little later he met me again on horseback by the swimming pool.

I stayed out for four hours and grew a little calmer. The house has been invaded by the apple merchant, the guards, bearing apples and bowing – and later on the baker. Lev Nik. is being cold and severe; when I see him so cold I keep hearing that cruel cry: "Chertkov is the *person closest to me*!" Well, at least Chertkov isn't closer to him *physically*.

7th August. Still the same weight hanging over us, the same gloomy atmosphere in the house. The rain pours incessantly and has beaten down the oats in the field, which have sprouted. Our peasants came and we distributed Maude's money amongst them.

I have no idea if the Chertkovs will go soon, or if L.N. wants to see him again. He says nothing and does nothing. Anger and grief are written all over his face. Oh, to melt the ice in his heart!

We lived quite happily without Chertkov for several decades, and what now? We are the same people, but now sisters quarrel with their brothers, the father is ill-disposed towards his sons, the daughters towards their mother, the husband hates his wife, his wife hates Chertkov, and all because of that gross, stupid, corpulent figure who has insinuated himself into our family and ensnared the old man, and is now destroying my life and happiness...

8th August. I lay awake all night thinking I should suggest to Lev Nikol. that he sees Chertkov again. When he got up this morning I said this to him, and he waved his arm, and said he would discuss it later, then went out for his walk. At 9 o'clock I went out too, wandered all over the woods and parks of Yasnaya and tripped and fell on my face, scattering all my mushrooms; I then gathered a big bundle of oak branches and grass, laid them on a bench and lay down, weeping and exhausted, until I eventually dozed off into fantastic dreams. The oak branches were wet from the rain, and I was soaked, but I lay there in the silence, gazing at the pine trees, for more than an hour. I was out for more than 4 hours altogether – without eating anything, of course.

When I got back, Lev Nik. called me into his room and said (and by then I was so happy to hear his voice): "You suggest I see Chertkov again, but I don't want to. What I want more than anything is to live out the end of my life as calmly and peacefully as possible. I cannot be calm if you are agitated. So I think it would be best if I were to visit Tanya for a week and for us to part for a little while, to give us both the chance to calm down."

At first the idea of another parting was unbearable to me. But after a while I realized Lev N.'s separation from Chertkov was the best possible alternative and what a good idea it was, for it would give both of us a rest from this emotional aggravation.

Today he wrote an appeal to young people wanting to refuse military service.* It was very good, and Sasha has already copied it out, but where has the original gone? Can they have given this too to Chertkov?

I did some work on the new edition, wrote to Maude about the peasants' money, and to the accountant. This afternoon I slept. Goldenweiser played a Beethoven sonata, which I didn't hear unfortunately; but I did hear him play a Chopin waltz and a Mazurka beautifully.

9th August. I have been sewing for Lyovochka all day; first I altered his shirt, then his white cap, and it soothed me. I deliberately did no other work today, to give my nerves a rest. It would all be perfect if it weren't for these extraordinary outbursts of vile rudeness from Sasha. She keeps going to see the Chertkovs, and they do all in their power to turn her against me for making my husband sever connections with the Telyatinki clique. I could never have imagined it possible that my daughter would dare to treat her mother like this. When I told her father about her intolerable rudeness, he said sadly: "Yes, it's a great shame, but this rudeness is in her nature. I shall speak to her about it."

10th August. Tanya arrived at four a.m. today. I was listening out for her all night but didn't hear her arrive. This morning I had another long talk with her about the same thing, and I became so upset that we eventually agreed not to talk any more about this subject that so torments us all.

Some soldiers came today to Yasnaya to see us for some reason. Four of them managed to slip into the house to see Lev Nik., although I never did discover what he discussed with them. He has such a strange attitude to my presence on such occasions. If I am interested in what he is talking about and go into his room, he looks at me angrily, as if I was in the way. And if I don't go in and seem uninterested, he takes this as a sign of indifference, and even outright disagreement. So I often don't know what to do.

I read *Christianity and Patriotism* for the new edition, and regretfully deleted some passages that hadn't yet been censored.* I find all this so hard to understand!

12th August. I was out picking mushrooms for 3½ hours today with Ekaterina Vasilevna, Andryusha's new wife. It was delightful in the fir plantation, with the red saffron milk caps nestling amongst the green moss, and everything so fresh, peaceful and secluded. Then I worked on the new edition. What hard work it is!

This evening Tanya made a number of painful accusations against me, almost all of which were unfounded, and I detected Sasha's suspicions and lies there, for she is trying to slander me in every way she can, turn everyone against me and separate me from her father. She is the greatest cross I have to bear. Such a daughter is worse than all the Chertkovs in the world; she can't be sent away, and no one will marry her with her frightful character. I often come in through the courtyard merely to avoid having to see her, for I never know if she is going to spit in my face again, or viciously attack me with a choice selection of oaths and lies. What a grief in one's old age! How has it happened?

I have just read through my diary and was horrified – alas! – by both myself and my husband. No, it's impossible to go on living like this.

14th August. Agitation much worse, blood rushes, pounding heart all day. The thought of parting from Lev Nik. is unbearable. I hesitated between staying in Yasnaya and going with him to see Tanya in Kochety, and eventually decided on the latter and hastily packed. I am very sorry to be leaving Lyova, who is awaiting trial in St Petersburg for his pamphlet, 'The Construction of Hell',* which means they won't give him a foreign passport. But I simply won't be parted from my husband again, I can't bear it.

I went to the woods with Katya, but the saffron milk caps had all been picked. Lev Nik. wrapped up warmly and went for a two-hour ride through Zaseka with Dushan Makovitsky. He is much better.

This evening Goldenweiser played Beethoven's sonata 'Quasi una Fantasia', but his playing was cold and lifeless. He also played two Chopin pieces excellently, and Schumann's 'Carnaval', which wasn't bad technically, although he failed to convey the different character of each separate piece.

I felt so ill all day that I went without dinner. A lot of people came – Dima Chertkov, a simple, good-natured lad, quite unlike his father; Goldenweiser and his wife, Maria Schmidt, and a stranger called Yazykova. I finished packing and went to bed late.

15th August (Kochety). We got up early and drove to Zaseka, seen off by a great many people including Lyova; then we set off for Kochety with Tanya, Sasha and Doctor Makovitsky. It was a long and difficult journey, and we had to change trains at Oryol for the Blagodatnaya line. Lev Nik. slept most of the way, hardly ate a thing and seemed very weak. But this evening in Kochety he played vint with great enthusiasm until midnight – then complained of feeling weak.

Our little granddaughter Tanechka met us touchingly at Kochety. What a sweet, adorable, loving child! How affectionately she kissed and caressed me – at least someone was pleased to see me! That sacred innocence is always so moving in a child. So unlike us adults! When I went to say goodnight to my husband this evening, he was asking Sasha (in my presence) for his notebook. She mumbled something, and I realized there was yet another plot afoot. "What are you asking for?" I said. Lev Nik. realized I had guessed something and told me the truth, thank God, otherwise I would have been terribly upset. "I am asking Sasha for my diary," he said. "I give it to her to hide, and she copies my thoughts out of it."*

They are *hiding it from me*, of course, *copying out his thoughts for Chertkov.*

Dear Tanya unselfishly gave me her room, which makes me feel *guilty*; I shall worry all night.

16th August. How can there be any joy or happiness in life when Lev Nik. and Sasha, at his wishes, are taking enormous pains to hide his diaries from me. I didn't sleep all night, my heart was pounding, and I kept devising new ways of reading what L.N. is so frantic to hide from me. If there is nothing there, wouldn't it be simpler to say: "There, take them, read them and calm down." But he would die rather than do that, because that is his nature.

He complained of feeling drowsy and weak today, lay in his room, then went for a walk. I saw him for a moment though, and handed him a scrap of paper on which I had written that I considered it quite fair and reasonable to hide the diaries from *everyone*, and not let *anyone* read them. But to give them to Sasha to read and copy for Chertkov, and then furtively hide them in cupboards and desks from *me*, his *wife*, was hurtful and insulting. "Let God be your judge," I ended my note, and I shall say no more about it.*

There are crowds of people here; it is all rather tiring, but a relief not to have any responsibilities for the housework. It is hard work for poor Tanya though, and I feel badly that the four of us have come when she already has her own large family to look after. This evening we all played vint, and I was grateful to spend an evening with my husband. He is a keen player and is always scolding me for playing so badly and tries to exclude me from the game. But yesterday I beat them all.

17th August. I spent the day hard at work correcting the proofs of *Childhood*. It's astonishing to see exactly the same traits of character in his youth as in his old age – his worship of beauty (Seryozha Ivin), the way he suffers such agony from his ugliness and longs to be beautiful in exchange for being a *good*, *clever* boy. The chapter 'Grisha' has an extraordinary passage in the manuscript version, omitted from the book: that sensual scene in the storeroom with Katenka directly after they witness Grisha the holy fool alone in his room in a state of tender, exalted religious ecstasy.

Beauty, sensuality, sudden changes of emotion, the eternal search for religion and truth – that is my husband through and through. He tells me his growing indifference to me is due to my "lack of understanding". But I know that what he actually dislikes is that I understand him all too well, and see all too clearly things I hadn't seen before.

He took a walk round the park, and was visited by a *skopets*,* with whom he talked for more than two hours. I don't generally like sectarians, especially the *skoptsy*, but this one seemed intelligent enough, even though he boasted disagreeably of his time in exile.

Lev Nikolaevich seemed sad and distant again today. I expect he is pining for his idol. I should remind him of the wise words: "Thou shalt not make graven images." But there's nothing you can do with a person's heart if they love someone intensely.

18th August. I read some terrible news in the papers today: the government has given Chertkov permission to stay in Telyatinki!* Lev Nikolaevich instantly cheered up; he looks years younger and his gait is brisk and sprightly. But I am aching with unbearable anguish, my heartbeat is 140 a minute, and my head and chest are aching.

This cross I have to bear is God's will; it was sent to me by His hand, and he has chosen Chertkov and Lev Nikolaevich to be the instruments of my death. Maybe the sight of me lying dead will open L.N.'s eyes to my enemy and murderer, and he will grow to hate him and repent of his sinful infatuation with the man.

Tanechka's nurse has been a marvellous comfort to me. "Pray to your guardian angel to soothe and calm your heart," she said firmly, "and everything will turn out for the best. You must take care of yourself," she added.

We went to the village school, where the peasant children were performing *The Screw* by Chekhov, adapted from a short story of his. It was stuffy and tedious.

19th August. I awoke early, and at the thought of Chertkov living so close to Yasnaya all the old suffering started up again. But then my husband managed to console me. He came into my room before I got up and asked how I had slept and how my health was, and he didn't ask in his usual cold manner, but with genuine concern. Then he repeated his promise:

1) *Never to see Chertkov again,*

2) *To give his diaries to no one,*

3) *To let neither Chertkov nor Tapsel take his photograph.* This was at my request. I found it most distasteful that his idol should photograph him in forests and gulleys like some old coquette, despotically dragging the old man here, there and everywhere so he could build up a collection of photographs to add to his archive.

"But I shall remain in correspondence with Chertkov," he added, "it's essential for my work."

I went with Tanya to pick mushrooms, of which there were masses, then played with the children and cut out paper dolls for them. I cannot work, my heart is *physically* aching, and the blood keeps rushing to my head. L.N. and Chertkov between them have half-killed me already – another two or three heart spasms like the one yesterday will finish me off. Or I shall have a nervous attack. That would be good! They will *certainly* torment me to death at this rate – I don't want to kill myself and yield Lev Nik. to Chertkov.

20th August. Two bulky parcels were posted this afternoon addressed to Bulgakov – i.e. for Mr Chertkov.* Having given up all meetings with him for my sake, Lev Nikol. is now consoling his idol with all sorts of papers for his collection, and sending these to him via Bulgakov. Lev Nik. took a long ride through the forest to Lomtsy today; this evening he played vint but was very sleepy.

21st August. Childhood is now ready for the printers. I reread the chapter 'The Ivins' and was struck by the words: "Seryozha made a great impression on me the moment I saw him. His unusual beauty astonished and captivated me. I felt irresistibly attracted to him..." And further on: "Just the sight of him was enough to make me happy, and at one time the whole strength of my soul was focused on that desire. If by chance I didn't see that lovely little face for three or four days I would fret and become sad and cry. All my dreams were of him..." And so on.

Night... I cannot sleep. I prayed and wept for a long time, and realized that what I am going through must be the means by which I appeal to God and repent of my sins – maybe too it spells the return of *happiness* and inner peace...

22nd August. My 66th birthday. I still have all my old energy and passion, the same acute sensitivity and, I am told, the same youthful appearance. But these past two months have aged me considerably and, God willing, have brought me closer to my end. I got up exhausted after a sleepless night and went for a walk round the park. It was delightful: the old avenues of various trees, the wild flowers, the saffron milk caps and the silence, the solitude. Alone with God, I walked and prayed. I prayed for reconciliation, prayed that I might with God's help stop suffering, and that He might return my husband's love to me before we died.

Lev Nik. rode a long way off to see the eunuch who was here previously and had earlier visited Chertkov while Lev Nikolaevich was there. He played vint again this evening. I played at the other table with Tanya's stepdaughter Lyolya, who had asked me to teach her the game.

25th August. This morning I had the unexpected joy of seeing Lev Nikolaevich at my door. I couldn't go to him at once, as I was washing, but I hastily flung a dressing gown over my wet shoulders and ran up to him. "What is it, Lyovochka dear?" I asked. "Nothing, I just came to ask how you slept and how you were feeling," he said. A few moments later he was back again. "I wanted to tell you that at midnight last night I kept thinking about you and wanted to come in and see you," he said. "I thought you might be lonely on your own, and wondered what you were doing – I felt so sorry for you..." At this the tears came into his eyes and he began to weep. I was overcome with joy, and this sustained me through the day, even though my imminent departure for Yasnaya and Moscow fills me with alarm.

I spent the day working on *Resurrection* for the new edition. Some uncensored passages have to be deleted, some omitted passages have to be inserted – all important and responsible work.

I enjoy myself with Tanyushka, take walks and grieve for my daughters' unjust attitude to me and the way they favour Chertkov.

26th August. I haven't read any of L.N.'s letters to Chertkov, or from Chertkov to him, but can deduce everything in them from the way he refers to me: "S.A. (Sofia Andreevna) is very pathetic, I try to stand my ground and remember the role I have been called on to fulfil... More than ever I realize how spiritually close to you I am... I think of you constantly, I should like to see you... but this is not necessary if we know that our souls are in communion and we both serve the Father... I pray to God for patience, I kiss you..." and other tender words of this pharisaical nature, in which, with the genius of a writer, he laments the suffering he has to endure from his wicked wife. And this correspondence between him and Chertkov, based entirely on that theme, will be preserved for future generations to read...

They all treat me as though I were *ab*normal, hysterical, even mad, and everything I do is attributed to my morbid condition. But other people, and the Lord above, will judge for themselves.

27th August, morning. My jealousy for Chertkov is a living wound! Why did it please God to open my eyes to these things?

I woke sobbing this morning from an agonizing dream. I dreamt Lev Nik. was sitting there wearing a new fur jacket with a hood at the back, and a tall sheepskin hat, and an unpleasant, hostile look on his face. "Where are you going?" I asked him. "To see Chertkov and Goldenweiser," he said in an offhand manner. "I have to look through an article with them and clear up a few things."

I was in despair that he had broken his promise, and I burst into agonizing sobs that woke me up. And now my heart and hands are trembling and I can hardly write.

Evening. I took a walk on my own in a state of great agitation, praying and weeping. I am terrified of the future. Lev Nik. has promised never to see Chertkov, to have his photograph taken at his bidding or give him his diaries. But he now has a new excuse that he uses whenever it suits him. He just says "I forgot", or "I never said that", or "I take back my promise". So that one is afraid to believe a word he says.

I have done a lot of work on the proofs, correcting *On Art*, 'On the Census' and *Resurrection*. Mine is a hard task! I have a terrible headache – and oh, the depression, the depression!

When I said goodnight to Lev Nik. I told him everything on my mind: I told him I knew he was writing letters to Chertkov addressed to Bulgakov, Goldenweiser and the other spies, and said I hoped he wouldn't go back on his promises behind my back, and asked him whether he wrote to Chertkov every day. He told me he had written to him twice, once in a note he had added to a letter of Sasha's, and once on his own. That is still two letters since 14th August.

28th August. Lev Nikolaevich's 82nd birthday. A marvellous, bright summer day. I got up feeling very anxious after another sleepless night, and felt even more so after going in to greet him. I wished him a long life, without secrets, tricks or plots – and said I hoped he would soon be completely *at peace with himself*, now that he is reaching the end of his life.

At this he pulled an angry face. The poor man is possessed – he considers that he and Chertkov have already reached the pinnacle of spiritual perfection. Poor, blind, proud man! How much more spiritually exalted he was a few years ago! How sincerely he aspired to live simply, to sacrifice all luxuries and to be good, honest, open and spiritually pure! Now he enjoys himself quite openly, loves good food, a good horse, cards, music, chess, cheerful company and having hundreds of photographs taken of himself.

He is kind to people only if they flatter him, look after him and indulge his weaknesses. All his old responsiveness is gone. Is it merely his age?

Evening. When he was out walking today, L.N. gave apples to all the village children, and this evening he spent two hours playing chess, and another two hours playing vint. He soon grows bored without these entertainments, and all this talk of living in a hut is merely an excuse to rage at me, so that with his writer's skill he can describe his disagreements with his wife in such a way as to present himself in the role of a martyr and saint.

29th August. Lev N.'s anger yesterday affected me so badly I didn't sleep a wink; I prayed and cried all night, and first thing this morning I went out to wander about the park and the wood. Then I called on a dear young nurse called Anna Ivanovna, and she and her sweet, sympathetic mother comforted me.

I received a telegram from Lyova saying his trial had been fixed for September the 3rd, and that he was leaving on 31st August. I was glad of the excuse to leave, and I badly wanted to see my son, say goodbye to him and give him some encouragement. So Sasha and I travelled to Oryol on the Blagodatnaya line, and from there we went on to Yasnaya. L.N. and I bade each other a tender, loving farewell, and we both cried and asked each other's forgiveness.

I was sleepy and exhausted on the train – I felt shattered. It was terribly cold, only 2 degrees, and Sasha and I were shivering and yawning all the way. We arrived home at five in the morning.

1st September. Bulgakov and Maria Schmidt were here for lunch, as well as Liza Rizkina (née Zinger) with her two boys. She is well educated and no fool, but I find her erudition and materialism rather alien. I didn't take a walk today; I didn't want to wash my favourite haunts at Yasnaya with my tears. For most of my life I have darted about with a light step and a light heart, conscious of nothing but the beauties of nature and my own joy! And now too it's all extraordinarily beautiful, and the days are clear and brilliant, but my soul is sad, so sad!

I did a lot of work on the proofs and various other things connected with the new edition, and gave orders around the estate. But nothing is going well. I was intending to go to Moscow, but I have no energy and haven't prepared anything, and it all seems futile and unimportant.

2nd September. Today I sent for the priest, who performed a service with holy water.* The prayers were lovely, apart from the last one: "Victory to the Lord our emperor", and so on. After all those prayers about the softening of hearts and the deliverance from griefs and troubles, it seemed utterly inappropriate to pray for victory, i.e. the murder of people.

In Lev Nik.'s room I found Chertkov's letter to the Tsar begging to be allowed to return to Telyatinki. It's a truly pharasaical letter, but what struck me most was his desire to be close to Lev Nikolaevich. What has happened though is that the Tsar allowed him to return, and now Tolstoy's *wife* has driven him away. He must be furious with me! And I am delighted!

Still the same enchanting weather – bright days, cool nights and a dazzling variety of greens on the bushes and trees. The potatoes are being dug now, the painters are finishing work on the roofs and outhouses, the earth is being removed from the hothouses, and here and there in the woods there are still a few mushrooms.

4th September. I am becoming increasingly impatient to see my husband, and shall go to Kochety tomorrow without fail. Today I went for a walk on my own, feeling sad at heart; I received a sweet letter from Lyova saying his trial would now be on the 13th. I worked on *Resurrection* with Sasha's companion Varvara Mikhailovna, and took a stroll round the estate. It's warm, with a light breeze and little clouds in the sky, with wild flowers everywhere and the most marvellous garden flowers and bright coloured leaves – how good it is! But how sad to be alone! I like people and movement and life... That is why it's better at the Sukhotins', where there are a lot of people and life is simpler. Lev Nik. is more cheerful there too; he plays chess for a couple of hours after dinner with Sukhotin or the local doctor, then takes a walk, reads letters, goes into the dining room, asks where everyone is and for the table to be laid as soon as possible. Then he plays a game of vint, and that goes on in the most lively fashion for about three hours, until 11.30 p.m. He doesn't have to strike attitudes, since none are expected of him; there are no petitioners, no beggars, no responsibilities – he just lives, writes, plays, talks, sleeps, eats and drinks...

I am very afraid he will miss all this in Yasnaya Polyana. I shall try to make sure there are more people here. But we have managed to drive everyone away from our house, and now I have driven away Chertkov and co.

5th September (Kochety). I left for Kochety early on the morning of the 5th, travelling via Mtsensk. Deep in my heart I hoped Lev Nik. would return to Yasnaya with me, as I am tied to this essential work on the new edition and must stay close to Moscow, where I have all the books and materials to hand.

I travelled the 20 miles from Mtsensk in a strong wind and driving rain, and the muddy road and the ferry crossing and the agitation left me exhausted.

I had a cold reception in Kochety from my husband and my daughter. Lev Nik. had just ridden over to visit the eunuch, 16 miles there and back, and in this appalling weather!

But how warmly I was met by the two little five-year-olds, my granddaughter Tanechka and her little cousin Mikushka Sukhotin!

6th September. Lev Nik.'s big toe is red and swollen after yesterday's ride, and he keeps saying: "It's senile gangrene and I shall surely die."

8th September. I felt much calmer when I arrived in Kochety, but now it has all started again. I didn't sleep all night and got up early. Drankov filmed us all again for the cinematograph, then filmed a village wedding they had put on especially for his benefit.

When I eventually plucked up the courage to ask Lev Nik. when he was returning home, he grew furious, shouting angrily about his "freedom", waving his hands and making the most unattractive gestures. Then to cap it all he said he regretted his promise to me never to see Chertkov.

I received a letter from Chertkov – a lying pharisaical letter in which he asked for a reconciliation with the evident desire that I should let him into the house again.

9th September. I wept and sobbed all day; I ache all over, my head, my heart and my stomach hurt, and my soul is torn apart by suffering!* Lev Nik. tried to be a little kinder to me, but his egotism and malevolence won't let him concede to me in anything – *not for anything* will he tell me if he is planning to return to Yasnaya, and if so, when.*

I wrote a letter to Chertkov, but haven't posted it yet. This man is the cause of all my suffering and I cannot reconcile myself to him.

10th September. I stayed in bed all morning, then took a long walk round the garden. Lev Nik. flew into a rage with me again today and said: "I shall never give in to you on anything ever again! I bitterly regret my promise never to see Chertkov, it was a terrible mistake!"

Then he got up, and taking both my hands in his, he stared at me, smiled so sweetly, then burst into tears. "Thank God!" I said to myself. "He still has a glimmer of love for me in his soul!"

12th September. I avoided meeting Lev Nik. all day. His stubborn refusal to tell me *approximately* when he might be leaving has made me feel desperate. His heart has turned to stone! By the time I left I had suffered so deeply from his coldness and was sobbing so wildly that the servant who was seeing me off started crying too. I didn't even look at my husband, my daughter and the others. But then Lev Nik. suddenly came round to the other side of the trap and said to me with tears in his eyes: "Well, give me another kiss then, I'll be back very, very soon..."

13th September. I have been working hard on the proofs, and try to be calm and remind myself of Lev Nik.'s words: "I'll be back very, very soon." Annenkova and Klechkovsky came to visit me.

It's hard to talk to anyone, for they all consider me abnormal and think I am being unjust to my husband. But I only write true facts in my diary. People can draw their own conclusions from them. I am tormented by life and material concerns.

17th September. My dream that my husband would return for my name day has been dashed; he hasn't even written, nor have any of the rest of them from Kochety – apart from my dear granddaughter Tanechka, who sent me a greetings card. The others just sent an impersonal collective telegram!

My name day was the day when Lev Nik. proposed to me. What did he do to that eighteen-year-old Sonechka Behrs, who gave him her whole life, her love and her trust? He has tortured me with his coldness, his cruelty and his extreme egotism.

I went to Taptykovo with Varvara Mikhailovna. Olga and her children, Ilyushok and my granddaughter and namesake Sofia Andreevna, were very sweet to me.

19th September (Moscow). I corrected proofs, packed my suitcase and left this afternoon for Moscow on business. In Tula I met my son Seryozha, to my great joy, and he said his wife and sons were travelling to Moscow in the same carriage.

21st September. I was preoccupied with business in Moscow on the 20th and 21st. I also paid a visit to Taneev's old nurse to find out how he was. He was still in the country. I should love to see him and hear him play. But this is not possible now; I no longer love him as I did, we don't see each other any more for some reason, and I have done nothing for a very long time to bring this about.

22nd September. I arrived back in Yasnaya this morning. It is a bright frosty day, and my soul is a hell of grief and despair. I went round the garden and wept myself senseless, yet I am still alive, walking, breathing and eating – although I cannot sleep. The frost has withered the flowers, like my life. It looks so desolate, and my soul is desolate too. Will the spark of joy and happiness be rekindled in our lives?

Not a word from Lev Nik. He couldn't give me one day of his epicurean life at the Sukhotins', with his daily games of chess and vint. So when he, Sasha and Nakovitsky returned tonight I met him with reproaches instead of joy, burst into tears, then went off to my room to let him rest after the journey.

23rd September. Our wedding anniversary. I stayed in my room for a long time this morning, weeping on my own. I wanted to go in to my husband, but opening the door to his room I heard him dictating something to Bulgakov, and went off to wander about Yasnaya Polyana recalling the happy times – what few of them there were – in my 48-year marriage.

I then asked Lev Nik. if we could have our photograph taken to-gether. He agreed, but the photograph didn't come out, as Bulgakov is inexperienced and didn't know how to do it.

L.N. was a little nicer to me this evening, and I felt easier in my mind. It was a comfort to feel I had found my "other half" again.

24th September. Lev Nikol.'s kindness to me didn't last long, and he shouted at me again today. Olga's former French governess told me in Taptykovo that they had read a tale by L.N. called 'Childhood Wisdom' at the Chertkovs', so I asked him to let me read it. When it transpired that there wasn't a copy of it in the house, even in Lev Nik.'s personal possession, I said of course Chertkov was in a hurry to take the manuscript, as he is nothing but a *collector*. This made Lev Nikol. frightfully angry and he shouted at me. I started crying inconsolably and went off to the fir plantation, where I sawed some branches, then developed photographs and read proofs, and saw almost nothing of my husband for the rest of the day.

25th September. I am happy he is actually *here* with me, and am beginning to feel calmer. But his soul is so distant!

He is reading Malinovsky's *Blood Revenge** with great interest at the moment, and went for a ride today.

26th September. As I was passing Lev N.'s study today I saw that Chertkov's portrait, which I had removed to the far wall while he was away and replaced with a portrait of his father, was again hanging in its former place above the armchair where he always sits.

The fact that he had put it back drove me to despair – he can't bear to part with it now he isn't seeing Chertkov every day – so I took it down, tore it into pieces and threw it down the lavatory. Lev Nik. was furious of course, and quite rightly accused me of denying him his freedom. He is possessed by the idea at present, although never in his life has he bothered about it before – he never gave it a thought. What did he need his "freedom" for when we always loved each other and wanted to make each other happy?

I went to my room, found a toy pistol and tried to fire it, thinking I would buy myself a real one. I fired it a second time when Lev Nik. returned from his ride, but he didn't hear.

Maria Schmidt, thinking I was planning to kill myself, without finding out what was really happening, wrote to Sasha in Taptykovo begging her to come home as her mother had shot herself – or some such story.

I knew nothing about this until that night, when I heard a carriage approaching the house and someone knocking at the door. It was very dark and I couldn't imagine who it might be. I went downstairs and to my amazement saw Sasha and Varvara Mikhailovna standing there. "What has happened?" I asked. And all of a sudden two voices were showering me with such angry words and foul names that I was stunned. I went upstairs, followed by Sasha and Varvara Mikhailovna, still shouting at me. Eventually

I lost my temper with them. What have I ever done to those two? Why was I to blame?

Unfortunately I started shouting too – I said I would throw them both out of the house tomorrow, and dismiss Varvara Mikhailovna, who merely lives off us and licks Sasha's boots. Maria Schmidt, realizing her mistake, began to cry and begged the two loud-mouths to leave the room.

But these shrews were in no hurry to calm down, and next morning they packed their things, took a couple of horses, the dogs and the parrot, and set off for Sasha's house at Telyatinki. It is they who are in the wrong; they lost their tempers and acted disgracefully.

29th September. Relations with Lev Nik. are calmer and I am happy! I sat with him after he had had his lunch today, and I ate something too – pancakes with curd cheese. It was wonderful to see the joy on his face when after asking who the pancakes were for, I said, "For myself." "Ah, how glad I am that you're eating again!" he said. Then he brought me a pear and tenderly begged me to eat it. When other people aren't here he is generally kind and affectionate to me, just as he used to be, and I feel he is *mine* again. But he hasn't been cheerful lately, and this worries me. I was very active all day: I sawed some dry branches off the young fir trees, then drove to Kolpna to buy rye and flour. A lovely bright frosty autumn day.

1st October. Goldenweiser came this morning, and played chess with Lev N. this afternoon. Sasha arrived too, and took Goldenweiser back to the Chertkovs. I was going to suggest that L.N. went there too, but the moment I mentioned the idea to my husband, I started choking back the tears and shaking with agitation; the blood rushed to my head and I felt I was being flayed alive. When I saw the joy on Lev N.'s face at the prospect of seeing Chertkov again, I felt desperate, and went off to my room to cry. But my dear husband didn't visit Chertkov, bless him, and instead took another ride through the woods and gulleys, and exhausted himself. I finished work on *Childhood* and read the proofs of 'On Money'.* It is windy and pouring with rain.

2nd October. This morning dear Pavel Biryukov arrived; he is always so kind, gentle, intelligent and understanding, and I wept as I told him of my grief. He dislikes Chertkov too, and understood me completely. Lev Nik. had a stomach upset, ate nothing, didn't leave the house and slept all day. After dinner we had a good talk, my son Seryozha arrived and everyone played chess.

3rd October. Lev Nik. took a walk this morning, then went for a short ride and returned stiff with cold; his legs were numb and he felt so weak he collapsed on the bed and fell asleep without taking off his cold boots. He was so late for dinner I grew worried and went to see him. He looked vacant, kept picking up the clock and checking the time, talking about dinner, then falling into a doze. Then to my horror he started to rave and things went from bad to worse! Convulsions in his face, terrible shuddering in his legs, unconscious, delirious raving. Three men couldn't hold down his legs, they were thrashing so violently. But I didn't lose my composure, thank God. I filled hot-water bottles at desperate speed, put mustard plasters on his calves and wiped his face with eau de Cologne. Tanya gave him smelling salts to sniff, we wrapped his cold legs in a warm blanket and brought him rum and coffee to drink. But the paroxysms continued, and he had five more convulsions. As I was clasping my husband's feet I felt acute despair at the thought of losing him.

I brought the little icon with which his Aunt Tatyana blessed her Lyovochka when he went off to war, and attached it to his bed. He regained consciousness during the night, but could remember nothing of what had happened to him. His head and limbs ached, and his temperature was 37.7 at first, then 36.7.

All night I sat beside my patient on a chair and prayed for him. He slept quite well, groaning occasionally, and the shuddering stopped. My daughter Tanya arrived in the night.

4th October. Tanya's birthday; we all celebrated. The others went off to visit the Chertkovs. Lev Nik. has regained consciousness and has his memory back now, although he keeps asking what happened and what he said. His tongue is coated, his liver hurts slightly and he has eaten nothing. We summoned Doctor Shcheglov from Tula, who gave him Vichy water and rhubarb with soda. I made him a vodka compress for the night.

Sasha and I had a moving and heartfelt reconciliation, and decided to forget our quarrel and both work to make Lev Nik.'s life as peaceful and happy as possible. But my God! How hard this will be if it means resuming relations with Chertkov. It is impossible, I am afraid this sacrifice will be beyond me. Well, everything is in

God's hands! Meanwhile the joy of Lev Nik.'s recovery has made us all calmer and kinder to one another.

5th October. Lev N. has been better today. He ate some rusks and a whole gingerbread, and drank so much coffee and milk I grew quite alarmed. He took some Vichy water, then had dinner with the rest of us. Seryozha left this morning, and Tanya spent the day at Ovsyannikovo. Sasha and Varvara Mikhailovna have returned, and life is now more cheerful. Tanya is being very harsh; she keeps scolding and threatening us, then assuring us she wants to help make the peace. I feel shattered; the left side of my stomach is hurting and I have a headache.

6th October. Lev Nik. is better, but still very weak, and says he has heartburn and an aching liver. He got out of bed this morning and was going out for a walk later, but he hankered after his daily ride, and rode off to Bulgakov without telling me, which upset me terribly.

We had visitors. It's better when there are guests, it isn't so depressing. I asked them for some advice on the new edition, and we spent the evening chatting quietly. Sasha went to see Chertkov during the day, and with my consent she invited him to come and visit Lev Nikol. Chertkov wrote a mean and characteristically unclear letter* – and didn't come. Thank God for at least one day without that loathsome man!

7th October. There was yet another discussion about Chertkov, then Tanya and Sasha went to see him and he promised to come at 8 this evening. But I arranged with the doctor that he would order Lev Nik. to take a bath this evening – for this would be good for his liver and would shorten his visit.

So that is what happened. I spent the day preparing myself for this dreaded visit, worrying and unable to concentrate on anything, and when I heard the sound of his sprung carriage through the ventilation window I had such palpitations I thought I would die. I rushed to the French window and took out the binoculars, straining to catch any special expressions of joy. But L.N., realizing that I was watching, merely shook Chertkov's hand with a blank expression. Then they had a long talk about something and Chertkov leant closer to L.N. and showed him something. Meanwhile I started his bath, and sent Ilya Vasilevich to tell him the water was ready and would get cold if he didn't hurry. Chertkov then said goodbye and left.

I felt terribly shaken all evening. What an effort it cost me to let that idiot come, and how I struggled to control my feelings!

8th October. I got up early to see my daughter Tanya off, then went back to bed feeling ill and exhausted. When I had got up, Lev Nikolaevich came in to see me, and as I was already dressed I followed him out. He was flustered and evidently displeased about something. He asked me to listen to him in silence, but I couldn't help interrupting him several times. What he had to say, of course, concerned my jealous, hostile behaviour to Chertkov. He put it to me, in an extremely agitated and angry manner, that I had made a fool of myself and must now stop, that he didn't love Chertkov *exclusively*, and there were many other people who were much closer to him in every way, such as Leonid Semyonov, for instance, and some complete stranger called Nikolaev, who has just sent him a book and lives in Nice.* This of course is simply not true. I have now released him from his promise not to see Chertkov again, but he saw what his meeting with that repulsive idiot cost me yesterday, and he reproached me for never giving him any peace of mind, as he has my disapproving attitude to Chertkov constantly hanging over his head like the sword of Damocles. But why do they have to meet at all?

9th October. I tidied the books – a dull chore! – and was so tired I spent the whole afternoon asleep, or rather in bed. I read a small part of the book by this unknown Nikolaev from Nice, and liked it very much. It is logical and well thought-out – what a pity L.N. doesn't have people like that around him.

Lev N. and I have lived lives of such moral and physical purity! And now he has revealed the most intimate details of our life to Chertkov and co., and this repulsive man draws his own conclusions and observations from his letters and diaries, which are often written merely to please him – often in his tone of voice too – and then he writes to Lev N. about it, for instance:

1st October 1909
I am particularly anxious to collect all such letters relevant to your life, so that I may in due course provide an explanation of your position for the benefit of those who have been seduced by hearsay and rumour...

I can well imagine the sort of "explanation" he will provide, and what sort of "selection" he will make when he launches his attack on L.N.'s family – concentrating especially on the moments of struggle...

11th October. I went out to the fir plantation and sawed some branches, then sat down exhausted on the bench and listened to the silence. How I love my plantation! I used to come and sit here with Vanechka. I have done very little work. I am in too much pain.

My daughter-in-law Sonya has left. She too has suffered with her husband, poor woman, for Ilya has fallen in love with someone else and ruined himself – and he has 7 children! We had a good talk to each other as wives and mothers, and we understood each other perfectly. The writer I. Nazhivin has left too. I told him everything I had endured with Chertkov, my husband and my daughters.

12th October. Chertkov has now persuaded Lev N. to give instructions that the copyright shouldn't go to his children after his death, but should be public property,* as are his last works. And when L.N. said he would talk to his family about it, Chertkov was *hurt* and wouldn't let him! Scoundrel and despot! He has taken this poor old man in his dirty hands and forced him into these despicable deeds. But if I live, I shall have my revenge, and he won't be able to do any such thing. He has stolen my husband's heart from me and the bread from my children's and grandchildren's mouths,* while his son has millions of stray rubles in an English bank, quite apart from the fact that those rubles were partly earned by me, because of all the help I gave L.N. Today I told Lev Nikol. I knew about these instructions of his, and he looked sad and guilty but said nothing. Yes, an evil spirit has guided Chertkov's hand; it is no coincidence that Lev Nik. wrote in his diary: "Chertkov has drawn me into a struggle. And this struggle is painful and hateful to me."* I am in a hurry to publish the new edition before Lev Nik. does something desperate; he is capable of anything in his present mood.

13th October. Thoughts of suicide are growing again, but I nurture them in silence. Today I read in the newspapers about a little girl of fifteen who took an overdose of opium and died quite easily – she just fell asleep. I looked at my big phial – but lacked the courage.

Life is unbearable. It has been like living under bombardment from Mr Chertkov ever since Lev Nik. visited him in June and succumbed to his influence.

Monster! What business has he to interfere in our family affairs?

Lev N. has been infected by Chertkov's vile suggestion that my main motive was *self-interest*. What "self-interest" could there possibly be in a sick old woman of 66, who has a house and land, and forests and capital – not to mention my 'Notes', my diaries and my letters, all of which I can publish?!

I went for a long walk – 4 degs. below freezing – then drove to Yasenki to the post.

14th October. I woke early and straight away sat down and wrote my husband a letter.

When I timidly opened the door to his study, he said, "Can't you leave me in peace?" I said nothing, closed the door and didn't go in again. He came to see me later, but there were yet more reproaches, a blank refusal to answer my questions, and such hatred!*

He is reading Dostoevsky's *Karamazovs* at present and says it is no good; the descriptions are excellent, he says, but the dialogue is very bad – it's always Dostoevsky speaking, rather than the individual characters, and their words are simply not characteristic of them.

I have done a lot of work on the new edition, and am feeling weak, my head is aching, and I keep falling asleep over my books and papers. Yesterday evening I wrote to Andryusha. Magnificent weather, clear, starry, frosty and bright, but I didn't go out.

16th October. I woke early and couldn't get back to sleep for worrying about how to retrieve Lev Nik.'s diaries from the Tula State Bank. I went down to breakfast, and he announced he was off to see Chertkov.

I cannot express what I felt! I ran out to the woods and clambered down some gulleys where it would have been hard to find me had I been taken ill. Then I came out into the field and raced to Telyatinki (carrying the binoculars, so as to be able to see everything from a long way off). When I got to Telyatinki I lay in the ditch near the gates leading to Chertkov's house and waited for Lev Nik. to arrive. I don't know what I would have done if he had – I kept imagining I would lie down on the bridge across the ditch and let his horse trample over my body.

Fortunately though he didn't come. I saw young Sergeenko and Pyotr, who had gone to fetch water. (Chertkov, in the name of some sort of Christian charity, has recruited various young men to work for him, as our servants work for us.)

At 5 o'clock I wandered off again. I entered our grounds as it was growing dark, went to the lower pond and lay down for a long time on the bench under the large fir tree. I was in agony at the thought of Lev Nikolaevich's exclusive love for Chertkov, and a resumption of their relations. I could just imagine them locked away together in some room with their endless *secrets*, and these frightful imaginings turned my thoughts to the pond, in whose icy water I could that very moment have found eternal deliverance from my tormenting jealousy! Then I lay on the ground and dozed off.

When it was completely dark and I could see Lev N.'s light through the windows, they came out to search for me with lanterns. Alexei the yard-keeper found me. I got up, beside myself with cold and exhaustion, and sat down on my bed without undressing and stayed there like a mummy, without eating dinner or taking off my hat, jacket or galoshes. This is how you kill people – without weapons but with perfect aim!

When I asked L.N. why he made me so unhappy, and whether he would be going to see Chertkov later, he started shouting in a rage: "I want my freedom, I won't submit to your whims and fancies, I'm 82 years old, not a little boy, I won't be tied to my wife's apron strings!..." and many more harsh and hurtful things besides.

He cannot live without Chertkov, of course, and this is why he gets so angry with me: because I simply *cannot* force myself to endure a resumption of relations with that scoundrel.

I went in to see Lev Nik. twice during the night, in a desperate state, and tried somehow to repair our relations. I managed with great difficulty to do so, and we forgave each other, kissed and said good-night. He said, among other things, that he would do all he could not to grieve me and to make me happy. I wonder what tomorrow will bring?

17th October. A quiet day. I managed to do a lot of work on the proofs and the new edition. Lev Nikolaevich, in his Gospel for children, writes among other things about anger (quoting from the Gospel): "If you think your brother has done you a wrong, choose a time and a place to talk to him eye to eye, and tell him *briefly* about your grievance. If he listens to you, then instead of being your enemy he will be your friend for life. If he doesn't listen, take pity on him and *have nothing more to do with him*."

This is exactly what I want from Chertkov – I want nothing more to do with him and an end to our relations.

I have decided not to go anywhere, neither to Moscow nor to concerts. I now treasure every moment of my life with Lev Nik. I love him intensely, like the last flicker of a dying fire, and I couldn't possibly leave him. Maybe if I am gentle with him he will grow more fond of me too, and won't want to leave me. God knows!

18th October. I got up late feeling shattered, haunted by new fears of some quarrel or unpleasantness. When I look back on the past four months of my ordeal, I am reminded of a cat-and-mouse game. It tortured me that his seven diaries were with Chertkov, and I begged him to get them back. But he kept refusing to do so. He went on torturing me for three weeks, by which time he had driven me to despair, then he took them back, only to deposit them in the bank. I had fallen ill with a nervous disorder long before this episode with the diaries.

Then he deliberately stayed on in Kochety because he *knew* I had to be near Moscow for the new edition. The separation and worry were agony for me, yet he stubbornly stayed on and wouldn't return to Yasnaya. And when, at the end of my stay there, I begged him with tears in my eyes to tell me *roughly* when he might return, even if only for my name day, he grew furious and stubbornly refused.

Terrible weather – a driving blizzard and thick snow. By this evening it was completely white and 6 degs. of frost.

19th October. E.V. Molostvova came to visit. She has made a study of various religious sects and is writing a book about them. She is a sensitive intelligent woman, and understands a great deal. I told her about my woes, and she dismissed much of what I said, insisting that beside me, Lev Nik.'s wife, Chertkov represented such an insignificant figure that I demeaned myself by imagining he could ever occupy *my* place in his relations with him. But I wasn't convinced; I am still terrified they will resume their friendship.

Last night I grew very anxious when I saw his diary had disappeared from the table where it invariably lies in a locked attaché case. And when he woke in the night, I went into his room to ask him if he had given it to Chertkov. "The diary is with Sasha," he said, and I grew a little calmer.

Clear, frosty weather. It is now 8 degs. below freezing, and starry and silent. Everyone is asleep.

20th October. Sasha was busy looking after her sick horses and writing for her father; she also went to a meeting in our village to talk to the local peasants about the consumers' store in Yasnaya Polyana.

Lev Nikol. worked on his writing and played patience, rode over to Zaseka, came into my room several times and spoke kindly to me. Some peasants came to see him – Novikov,* a clever peasant from Tula who writes articles, and some of our villagers, one of whom went to prison for two years for being a revolutionary.*

How avidly he reads everything about himself in the newspapers! He obviously couldn't do without this now!

21st October. Today I saw in the newspaper *Spark* the photograph taken of Lev N. and me on our last wedding anniversary. Thousands of people can see us there together, hand in hand, as we have lived all our lives. I had a long talk with Sasha today. She knows nothing of life and people, and there is an enormous amount she doesn't understand. Telyatinki is her entire world; she has her beloved little home there, and nearby live the dull-witted Chertkovs.

I am continuing to read Lev Nik.'s pamphlets for the new edition, and find them terribly monotonous. I warmly sympathize with his denunciation of war, violence, punishments and murders, but I don't understand his denunciation of governments. People *need* leaders, masters and rulers; any sort of human organization is unthinkable without them. It is essential however, that the ruler is wise, just and self-sacrificing in the interest of his subjects.

23rd October. Now that he lacks Chertkov's *closeness*, Lev Nikol. seems to have grown closer to me. He occasionally talks to me, and today I had two joys – my dear husband, the *old* Lyovochka, noticed my existence *twice*. Early this morning when guests were leaving and there was a great deal of bustle and commotion, he thought it was me walking about and came and told me how worried he had been. Later on he ate a delicious pear and brought one for me to share with him.

Recently he has started writing articles about socialism, suicide and something about madness. What he was working on this morning I don't know. This evening he was frantically sorting out his kopeck booklets for distribution, dividing them into good, middling and bad, as well as deciding which ones were for the most intelligent and which were for the less educated.

I took the dogs Belka and Marquise for a walk to Zakaz, following the horses' hoofprints in the direction where Lev Nik. and Doctor Makovitsky had ridden.

Thawing, no roads, grey and windy.

I have done a lot of reading for the new edition. My eyes are bad, I soon grow tired and am worried about the uncensored state of Lev Nikolaevich's later works.

24th October. We had a visit from a young lady called Natalya Almedingen, who edits children's magazines. Also Gastev, a long-standing Tolstoyan who lives in the Caucasus, and Bulgakov.

I went for a walk with the young lady, and suddenly on the hillock in front of the swimming pool we saw two riders, Lev Nikol. and Bulgakov. I was delighted to see L.N. as I had been thinking about him, wondering if he would go home without me and worrying he might have an accident on the slippery road.

Towards evening it poured with rain and grew warmer. There was no mention of Chertkov today, but every day when L.N. sets off for his walk I wait in terror for him to return, in case he has gone to see him. I fret and cannot work, and calm down only when I see him approaching from the other direction, and am then happy for the rest of the day.

25th October. I got up early, spent the morning with Almedingen and read six pages of proofs. Then I went to our village school, where one young, inexperienced teacher is in charge of 84 girls and boys. This evening our son Seryozha came; he played chess with his father, then played the piano. I read Almedingen the 'Notes' I wrote about my girlhood and marriage, and she seemed to like them.

Lev Nik. exchanged letters with Chertkov's wife Galya today. I asked what they were about, and he made another excuse and pretended to have forgotten. I asked to see Galya's letter, and he said he didn't know where it was, which wasn't true. Why not just say, "I don't want to show it to you"? But recently it's nothing but endless lies, excuses and evasions... How morally weak he has become! Where is his kindness, his clarity, his honesty?

An evil spirit rules our house and my husband's heart.

I am coming to the end of this terrible diary, the history of my sad sufferings, and shall seal it up for a long, long time!

Curses on Chertkov, curses on the person who was the cause of it all!

Forgive me, Lord.

7th November. On 7th November, at 6 o'clock in the morning, Lev Nikol. died.

9th November. I have not recorded the events of October the 26th and 27th, but on the 28th, at 5 in the morning, he slipped out of the house with Doctor Makovitsky. His excuse for leaving was that I had been rummaging through his papers the previous night. I had gone into his study for a moment, but I didn't touch one paper – there *weren't* any papers on his desk. In his letter to me (written for the entire world) the pretext he gave for leaving was our luxurious life and his desire to be alone and live in a hut, like the peasants.* But then why did he have to write telling Sasha to come with her hanger-on, Varvara Mikhailovna?

When I learnt from Sasha and the letter about his flight, I jumped into the pond in despair. Sasha and Bulgakov pulled me out, alas!* Then nothing passed my lips for the next five days, and on 31st October at 7.30 a.m. I received a telegram from the editors of *Russian Word*: "Lev Nikolaevich in Astapovo. Temperature 40°." Andrei, Tanya and I travelled by special train from Tula to Astapovo. They didn't let me in to see Lev Nik.* They held me by force, they locked the door, they tormented my heart. On 7th November, at 6 in the morning, Lev Nik. died. On 9th November he was buried at Yasnaya Polyana.

II

Daily Diary

1906–7 and 1909–19

1906

20th November. Masha is very poorly; her temperature was 40.8 this evening. My heart is like lead; I feel so sorry and afraid for her. The house is sad and silent.

21st. Masha is very ill. Day and night her temperature is 41.3. Doctor Afanasyev came.

23rd. Masha has a fever of 40.7, and has difficulty speaking. I am terrified. I don't sleep at night, my soul is oppressed.

Lina and Misha came for dinner, and it became a little more cheerful; there are still plenty of people to love, so long as I have my grandchildren.

24th. Masha is still very ill. Doctor Shchurovsky and Doctor Afanasyev came. There is inflammation of the left lung and pleurisy.

Lina and Misha have left. Ilya came – wanting money as usual. 1° of frost, snowing. We can think of nothing but Masha's illness.

25th. Masha is in a terrible state – groaning, tossing and delirious. I was sitting with her and it was unbearable to see her. I walked along the avenue and thought: *why* do people so value their own lives and those of their loved ones? We are all tense with anticipation.

27th. Masha died quietly at twenty to one this morning. Lev Nikolaevich was sitting beside her, holding her hand. She sat propped up on the pillows, and we were all with her in the room under the arches. I kissed her forehead and stood beside L.N. Kolya kept weeping and kissing her hands even after she had fallen quiet. A terrible wind was howling and tearing at the house. I cannot believe Masha has gone; it is very painful.

28th. Masha has been laid in her coffin, and Marfa Kub[asova], Olga Ershova, Matryosha and her mother are all sitting with her. Lev Nikolaevich, Kolya and Tanya went in to see her and a funeral service will be held. I have been with Kolya and Andryusha, who are making all the arrangements.

29th. We buried Masha.

30th. I do nothing all day, life has stopped. I went to the side wing to see my granddaughter Tanyushka, who is adorable.

1907

8th August. Alexei the yard-keeper told us a strange tale of how some hooligans had questioned him about our house and offered him a hundred rubles if he turned informer. We are all terribly frightened and can't sleep. I wrote to the governor, and sent someone to buy a gun. Tanya's husband Mikhail Sukhotin came. We read her splendid article about the fire, and were very moved.*

9th. Four policemen were sent over here with an officer. Nothing has happened, but yesterday some tramps told Alexei to bring them some bread.

A Czech journalist was here.

19th. A tragic accident. A 7-year-old boy has drowned in the middle pond; his 16-year-old sister waded in to save him and was also drowned. The poor mother! She is the sister of Varya, our washerwoman. Lev Nikolaevich and I went to the Chertkovs. Endless talk and crowds of young people, mainly peasants. He preached – utter hypocrisy. His follower Abrikosov came, and two schoolmistresses from Kazan.

22nd. My 63rd birthday, I cannot believe I'm so old. The Chertkov family was here, the Goldenweisers, Maria Schmidt, Rostovtsova and Abrikosov. I thought of my children and longed to see them. I played the piano for a long time during the day, and this evening read Zosya Stakhovich my memoirs. Lev Nikolaevich visits the Chertkovs almost every day.

23rd October (Moscow). L.N.'s secretary Gusev has been arrested for inserting the words "the brainless Tsar" into L.N.'s article 'What Is the Solution?' and for not having a passport.

26th October. L.N. visited Gusev in jail.

27th November. The anniversary of our daughter Masha's death. Exactly one year. How sad and strange it is that she is gone. Our life is so quiet and lonely now. I have developed a passion for painting portraits, which is a great waste of concentration and energy. Lev Nikolaevich goes riding and muddles up his *Circle of Reading*: it's like Penelope's labours – one day he works, the next day he does it all over again.

1909

31st August. This morning we had a visit from a 30-year-old Romanian who had castrated himself at the age of 18 after reading *The Kreutzer Sonata.** He then took to working on his land – just 19 acres – and was terribly disillusioned today to see that Tolstoy writes one thing but lives in luxury. He questioned everyone, seeking an explanation of this contradiction. He was obviously very hurt, and said he wanted to cry, and kept repeating, "My God, my God! How can this be? What shall I tell them at home?" Then a rich deaf mute arrived from Kiev with his friend, a barber, especially to make Tolstoy's acquaintance. Goldenweiser came and played chess with L.N.

2nd September. Lev Nikolaevich's preparations to visit Chertkov are very painful for me. I corrected the proofs of Maude's English biography of him, and drew some illustrations. Our visitors today were the Nikolaevs, Goldenweiser, Kalachyov, the deaf mute and some cinematographers from Paris.*

1910

18th April (Yasnaya Polyana). Easter Sunday. A decorated officer visited, who had written some scurrilous verses about Lev Nikola-evich.* Very remorseful. We rolled eggs on the balcony with the children. A warm summery day, 18° in the shade. The birches are delightful with their soft green leaves. The cheerful sounds of humming bees and singing birds. Clear, bright days, intermittent rumbling of thunder, peasants singing in the village. Seryozha has left. He played the piano a little, his own works too, which were lovely. This evening Nikolaeva came to visit. Endless talk, they all prevented me from doing any work.

19th. There are some lovely bulbs out in the meadow, and marguerites and violets. Still the same heavenly fine weather – it could be June. We had dinner on the veranda and rolled eggs. Two real Japanese men* visited; one runs a lot of schools in Japan, the other is a student in Moscow. Maria Schmidt came, and Gorbunov. Then Mezhekova the typist arrived with her little girl. After church they played the gramophone at the village library, and a lot of people came to listen. Lev Nikolaevich talked to the peasants, who asked him about the horn, and about the construction of the gramophone. Tanya is packing – unfortunately: I shall miss my granddaughter Tanechka. I played "opinions" with the children. Tanechka thought and thought, then said, "Granny is an angel."

20th. My two darling Tanechkas, mother and daughter, left this morning. I worked hard on the proofs of *Childhood*. I miss my daughters and worry about Sasha. This evening I sat down to play the piano – the whole of Beethoven's '*Pathétique*', and another sonata of his. Lev Nikolaevich listened happily.*

29th May (Yasnaya Polyana). Painful discussion with Lev Nikolaevich. Reproaches flung at me for our privileged life, after I complained about the difficulties of running the estate. He wants to drive me out of Yasnaya to live in Odoev or Paris or some other place. I went out of the house. Terrible heat, aching leg, wild pulse. I lay down in a ditch and stayed there, and they sent a horse for me.* Stayed in bed all day, wept, didn't eat. The sculptor Paolo Trubetskoy came with his wife.

4th June. Too many visitors. Lev Nikolaevich is distraught because the Circassian guard has brought Prokofy in for stealing a beam, and he is an old man who once worked with him.* Oh, I've had enough of the estate!

28th October. Lev Nik. has left! My God! He left a letter telling me not to look for him as he had gone for good, to live out his old age in peace. The moment I read those words I rushed outside in a frenzy of despair and jumped into the pond, where I swallowed a lot of water. Sasha and Bulgakov dragged me out with the help of Vanya Shuraev. Utter despair. Why did they save me?

29th. All the children have come, apart from Lyova, who is abroad. They are so kind and attentive, but they can't help or comfort me. Mitasha Obolensky has come. Seryozha, Ilya and Misha have left. Vanya discovered that L. Nik. had gone to Belev – maybe to see his sister Maria Nikolaevna?*

30th. I cry day and night and suffer dreadfully. It's more painful and terrible than anything I could have imagined. Lev Nik. did visit his sister in Shamordino, then travelled on beyond Gorbachevo – who knows where.* What unspeakable cruelty!

31st. I haven't eaten or drunk anything for four days, I ache all over, my heart is bad. Why? What is happening? Nothing to write about – nothing but groans and tears. Berkenheim came with some stupid doctor called Rastorguev, and a young lady fresh from medical school.* These outsiders make it much more difficult, but the children don't want to take *responsibility*. What for? My life? I want to leave the dreadful agony of this life... I can see no hope, even if L.N. does at some point return. Things will never be as they were, after all he has made me suffer. We can never be straightforward with each other again, we can never love each other, we shall always *fear* each other. And I fear for his health and strength too.

1st November. I am growing weak; I have eaten nothing for five days, and have just drunk a little water. Today I feel slightly better, and am not such a prey to my passionate love for L.N. that has tormented my heart and is now poisoned. I received the Eucharist, talked with the priest and decided to take a little food, for fear of not being strong enough to go to Lev Nik. should he fall ill. My son Misha has arrived. I did a little work.

2nd. I received a telegram from *Russian Word* at 7.30 this morning: "Lev Nik. ill in Astapovo. Temperature 40°." Tanya, Andryusha, the nurse and I all left Tula for Astapovo by special train.

3rd (Astapovo). Doctor Nikitin arrived, then Berkenheim. Lev Nikolaevich has pneumonia in the left lung. They won't let me see him. Seryozha is here, and Tanya. Lev Nik. wired for Chertkov in person.*

4th. Lev Nik. is worse. I wait in agony outside the little house where he is lying. We are sleeping in the train.

5th. Shchurovsky and Usov have come. There is evidently little hope. I am tormented by remorse, the painful anticipation of his end, and the impossibility of seeing my beloved husband.

6th. Dreadful atmosphere of anticipation. I can't remember anything clearly.

7th. At 6 o'clock in the morning Lev Nikol. died. I was allowed in only as he drew his last breath. They wouldn't let me take leave of my husband. Cruel people.*

8th. We are leaving with the body. They have lent us the train carriage in which we were staying.

9th. Back in Yasnaya. Crowds of people at Zaseka. We lowered the coffin onto the station and they came to pay their last respects. Masses of young people and delegations. They all followed the coffin from Zaseka to Yasnaya Polyana. We buried Lev Nikolaevich.

10th. I am ill with a cough and a fever of 40.4 – I cannot remember anything. Varya Nagornova and my sister Tanya are here with me. It's good to be with them. Sasha left this morning for Telyatinki.

11th. I am ill. They have hired a nurse, Ekaterina Terskaya.

13th–15th. Ill. My sons were here.

16th–18th. Ill in bed. Many letters and telegrams.

25th. Better, but still in bed. Sleepless nights.

27th. Got up. Bulygin, Biryukov, my sister Tanya, the Sukhotins and others came. They brought my granddaughter Sonechka.

28th. Health better. Anna Maslova came, Drankov the cinematographer and Spiro the journalist. All very painful, but it's a little easier with other people. What will happen when I'm alone? Terrible! No future.

29th. Unbearable depression, remorse, painful feelings of pity for my late husband's sufferings – what he must have endured at the end!... I cannot go on living. My sister Tanya has a sore throat.

30th. Sasha arrived with Maria Schmidt and Vaka Filosofov. Tanya is better. Zero degrees. A damp, overcast November, with almost no snow. A dismal, frightening life ahead – in a few days I shall be alone.

2nd December. Everyone is still here, thank God. What will happen afterwards? Sasha arrived with Varvara Mikhailovna.

4th. A journalist from the *New Times* has arrived – a certain Ksyunin. Windy and overcast. No snow. I haven't done a thing. A lot of chatter on all sides.

5th. Seryozha and others came. We show Lev Nik.'s room to visitors.

6th. More people came to visit the grave with the physicist Alexander Zinger. A dear man. I showed them the rooms. Bulgakov was here. I read him my memoirs. My two darling Tanechkas have left. It's even more sad and difficult.

7th. Deep despair all day. I didn't sleep all night and wept all morning. My daughter-in-law Sonya came, Ilya arrived for dinner, and things became more cheerful. Bulgakov and Belinky came. Zero degrees.

8th. My sister Tanya left this morning, and I wept. The loneliness is unbearable. No one to care for, no one to talk to. I don't remember what I did. I wrote something and went to L.N.'s grave with Sonya.

9th. I translated some letters from French and copied them for the new edition. Proofs. The artist Rossinsky came. My daughter-in-law Sonya left this evening.

10th. Read proofs all day. Rossinsky is still here. My son Misha arrived for dinner and left at eight to see Sasha, from where he will return to his estate in Chifirovka. I took a bath. A wind has blown up. I wrote to Maslova, Taneev,* Lyova and Andryusha.

11th. I tidied Lev Nikolaevich's things to protect them from moths. It was terribly painful – life is torture. I wrote to Tanya and fell asleep this afternoon to the sounds of a terrible gale. Loneliness, remorse, despair!

12th. Read proofs, walked to the village with the nurse. Everyone weeps when they see me. I sorted through the newspapers. Dushan Makovitsky has left to see Misha, whose son Petya has pneumonia. A publisher called Lenkovsky was here. This evening there was a telegram announcing Seryozha's arrival.

13th. I didn't sleep last night. Oh, these ghastly sleepless nights, alone with my thoughts, my agonizing conscience, the darkness of the winter night and the darkness in my soul! Two ladies from St Petersburg came with a letter from Misha Stakhovich – one was called Elena Timrot. Gué, Nikitin and my son Seryozha came too. Life is easier with them here. But soon there'll be loneliness again!

14th. My guests haven't left yet, and I am glad! I wept all day and visited the grave. There I found an artist and the village policeman – most unpleasant. I catalogued the library books, most of them Lev Nikolaevich's. What a warm winter! It's 2° today. I wrote to Lyova.

15th. Seryozha, Maria Schmidt, Bulygin and Gué spent the day with me. Sasha came – we are friends. I weep incessantly, tormented by my separation from Lev Nik. My one consolation is that I too haven't long to live. I have done a little work on the proofs and feel unwell.

16th. All the villagers from Yasnaya Polyana – peasants, women and children – gathered today, 40 days after his death, at Lev Nikolaevich's grave, which they tidied and laid with branches and fir wreaths. They knelt on the ground three times, took off their caps and sang 'Eternal Memory!' I cried and suffered deeply, but felt moved by the peasants' love for him. At that moment we were all experiencing the same thing together, and they were so sweet to me. I wrote to my sister and to my daughter Tanya, and to Ilya and Andryusha. So sad and lonely!

17th. I took a sleeping powder and slept, but waking was frightful! Yet more visitors from far-off places to see the grave and the house. Proofs, newspapers – such a lot to be done. I live here with the nurse, Ekaterina Terskaya. Proofs, copying and depression day and night. It sometimes seems all this is temporary and things will soon return to normal.

18th. I walked around the garden in the heavy snow, then visited Lyovochka's grave. I feel so puzzled whenever I go there – can it really be my beloved Lyovochka lying under the ground? And every time I cry until my chest aches. I copied his articles and read proofs. Oh, the loneliness! 52 girl students from St Petersburg came to visit the grave and look around the house.

19th. I copied out a play by L.N., then walked to the village to find out about the taxes and ask who was selling what to pay them. Biryukov visited briefly, with a journalist from *Russian Word*, and yet more visitors. They come from all corners of the world. There were four Slavs from Austria, a man from the Caucasus and a Mohammedan who brought a wreath. A lot of snow. It is white, quiet and beautiful. 5° below freezing. But where is *He*? Where?

23rd. Ilya has left. He visited Sasha and Chertkov, about whom we are discovering more and more bad things. A sly, malicious man. I went to photograph the grave, and wept. A delightful, fine, bright day, with the white hoar frost and the blue sky. But the beauty made me even sadder. 13–17° below freezing. This afternoon I developed my photographs of Lev Nik.'s grave.

24th. Another sleepless night – torture! I was woken by a mouse. This morning I printed the photographs of L.N.'s grave. Then I wrote letters to my sister Tanya, Chefranov the accountant, the editors of *Herald of Europe* and *Russian Wealth*, the stationmaster and Sergeenko. This evening I copied L.N.'s manuscript of *The Light Shines Even in Darkness*. A rough draft, not very good. Andryusha is a little calmer but still irritable.

25th. A painfully sad Christmas! I was pleased to have Andryusha here, but he left at three. I visited L.N.'s grave with the nurse, and decorated it with white and pink hyacinths, leaves and primulas. I wept bitterly. The beauty of nature and the light of the sun were astonishing. Dushan Makovitsky, the nurse and I wrote quietly for a long time in the drawing room together. 15° below freezing.

26th. Slept badly, as depressed as ever. Wrote all day. Another beautiful day, hoar frost, sun and ice. Didn't leave the house. Wrote letters, two business replies.

27th. Took some veronal for my insomnia and slept till 12. Felt dazed, but it's better like this – the suffering is less acute, the body loses the capacity to respond to spiritual pain. But where is the soul? I did a lot of copying and wrote to Lina, Vanya and Tanya, Sonya and Ilyushok, plus two business letters. 15° below freezing as before, and windy.

28th. It is two months today since Lev Nik. left. I went to the grave. Life is just as unbearably painful. I wrote to my daughter Tanya in Rome and sent her a photograph of the grave. 10° below freezing, windy and not quite so beautiful outside. I am copying manuscripts. My daughter Sasha came, and Andryusha with his wife and daughter. There have been a lot of visitors to Lev Nik.'s grave and his rooms.

29th. I wrote all day and corrected proofs – there were a lot to do. Andryusha is a sorry sight with his unstable nerves. We're all like that now! And so depressed. The weather is warmer; I didn't go out. I copied a very good excerpt from a work of Lev Nikolaevich's about God. He *wrote* well, but what did he *do*?

30th. My son Ilya arrived with his wife and three eldest boys. Andryusha is a little better today, but still very tense. Windy. 6° below freezing. A sleepless night, slightly feverish all day, didn't leave the house. I'm glad my sons are here, I don't feel so lonely. Read a lot of proofs, and copied a lot of Lev Nik.'s story 'What I Dreamt About'.

31st. I read proofs, copied *Father Sergei* and played for a while with my granddaughter Mashenka. My son Seryozha arrived before dinner. When the clock struck 12 we all gathered in the drawing room and talked about Lev N.'s last days. Then we went into the dining room and drank tea. There was a cake, fruit and fruit juice for the children. The atmosphere was sad but very touching. Ilya told me something interesting old Professor Snegiryov had told him about Lev Nikol.'s death. Apparently there's a certain kind of pneumonia that starts as an unnatural excitement of the brain, and the patient, infected by the poison, rushes out of the house, goes off he knows not where and roams around. Just like Lev Nik. leaving the house and visiting Shamordino, then rushing off. He bought tickets that were valid for three months. Snegiryov assumes Lev Nik. was already ill when he left Yasnaya Polyana.

1911

January–February – student riots, followed by arrests and depor-
tations; 125 professors resign. Universities come under police control.
Jews further disenfranchised. September – Stolypin, President of
the Council of Ministers, assassinated by agent of security police.
Ascendancy at court of the monk Rasputin and his increasing influence
on government decisions. The start of a series of wars in the Balkans
for control of the Ottoman Empire.

Battle over Tolstoy's manuscripts begins, with Sofia and her sons
against Chertkov and Sasha (who obtains injunction forbidding her
mother access to her room at the Historical Museum and halting
publication of her editions). Government declines to buy Yasnaya
Polyana so as not to honour Tolstoy's memory, but the Tsar provides
his widow with a generous pension. Sofia's brother-in-law Mikhail
Kuzminsky and her sons Lev, Mikhail, Andrei and Ilya negotiate with
American businessmen against her will over the possible purchase
of Yasnaya (it comes to nothing). March – official opening of the
Moscow Society of the Tolstoy Museum. Sofia starts work on an
edition of Tolstoy's letters to her.

1st January. Made a copy of Lev Nikol.'s diary for July and August
to give to Lyova. Lovely weather, 5°, moonlit nights and such sadness!
My children, grandchildren, guests and people in general are no real
consolation, only a diversion. I even love my sadness, as my final
contact with my Lyovochka. The tears are there, every moment of the
day, but I try to restrain myself and fear them. Seryozha is closest to
me, we grieve more than the others.

2nd. Proofs all morning. Took fresh flowers to the grave and scattered
seeds to the birds. Wept bitterly; inconsolable, irreparable grief. Prayer is
no comfort. My three grandsons have left. Andryusha returned and told
me of L.N.'s fears that I might chase after him, and his tears and sobs
when they told him I had tried to drown myself. It was very painful.

4th. A snowstorm this morning. The artist Orlov has arrived. Seryozha
has left. I tidied the books again – so tedious! This evening my sons

Ilya, Andrei and Misha rushed over and demanded 1,500 rubles to send Ilya to America to sell Yasnaya Polyana.* I find this most distasteful and distressing. I should like to see Yasnaya Polyana in Russian hands, as public property.

5th. A lot of proofs, all to no purpose, it seems. There's no spiritual centre to the world now, no lofty, abstract life in this house – and it's very sad! There's no love either – although I was robbed of that long ago, the expression of it anyway, and my place in Lev Nik.'s heart.

6th. Makovitsky left here for good today. I wept; one more link with Lev Nik. is now broken. I corrected some page proofs of Volume 20 and wrote Tanya a postcard. Then I tidied some books, although there are still a lot of new ones from Makovitsky to be sorted. This evening I pasted cuttings into the album and wrote to Lev Nik.'s French translator Halpérine-Kaminsky in Paris.

8th. I am tormented by discussions with my sons about the sale of Yasnaya Polyana and Andryusha's attempts to contest the will. I can sympathize with one aspect of this, however: his desire to disinherit the hateful Chertkov.

11th–15th (Moscow). Sasha has again fallen under the same influence that destroyed both Lev Nik. and me – Chertkov. He has set her against me, and through Muravyov, her attorney, she has issued a legal injunction barring me from my room at the Historical Museum, halting publication of my edition at the press and other similarly despicable acts. And she has found yet another ally in her persecution of me – Goldenweiser. I visited the Historical Museum, talked to the administrators and gave them a document in response to Sasha's, also forbidding anyone to enter my room or have access to his manuscripts. Sasha has threatened to damage my edition in every way possible – let her! I left this evening for Yasnaya Polyana without coming to any agreement with her. How her late father would have grieved at her behaviour.

19th. Spent the morning reading proofs, and was about to go to the grave when my son Misha arrived from Moscow. Long discussions about how to defend ourselves against Chertkov's and Sasha's malevolence. Terribly painful and nerve-racking! If it wasn't for my impoverished sons I would have given up.

20th. Painful discussions with Andryusha: "If there's no money I'll shoot myself!" How terrible to think like that! The newspapers and lawyers have stood up for my rights.* But how much better it would be to have peace and friendly agreement.

21st. Very depressed, the tears keep coming to my eyes. The same as usual – reading proofs and pasting in newspaper cuttings. Hypocritical feuilleton by Mr Chertkov in all the papers. The more I think about it, the more clearly I realize Lev Nik. preferred Chertkov at the end of his life, and the more sad and painful it is. Very frosty, minus 20°. Everything is bright and beautiful. How white and pure it all is…

22nd. Read 3 pages of proofs and marvelled at the artistry of Lev Nik.'s writing.

23rd. Read probably the *last* proofs of *Youth* I shall ever read. A telegram from Spiro telling me to prepare a reply to a letter from Chertkov in today's papers, which I haven't yet read.

24th. Wrote to Ksyunin and the State Bank. Most unpleasant to read Sasha's letter next to Chertkov's in all the newspapers. The persecution continues. How will it all end! At times like these one longs for death. The articles in the papers are so unpleasant; they have cheapened my beloved Lyovochka's name, and this is unbearably painful. S.P. Spiro, a journalist for *Russian Word*, came to visit. I begged him not to publish anything on my behalf. Cold, minus 16°, wind. I didn't leave the house all day. Such depression!

4th February. Oh, what sadness! The wind howled all day. I copied out some interesting pages from Lev Nik.'s notebooks – material for an unwritten work about the Peter the Great period.* Fascinating.

9th. Copied my letter to Koni.* Initialled handkerchiefs. Went to Lev Nik.'s grave and wept and prayed, begging him to forgive me for being unable to make him happier at the end of his life. I should have accepted that he preferred Chertkov, but I couldn't. I pasted newspaper cuttings and grieved.

10th. Terrible snowstorm this morning. Copied the diary L.N. kept when he wooed and married me. Did a little sewing. I'm depressed and afraid of going to Moscow – although I must; I have to clear up things for future generations.

13th (Moscow). Sasha came, fat, red-cheeked and stubborn, secretive and spiteful as ever. Painful discussion. What a cross this daughter of mine is. A lot of tedious business and bustle. The new edition has appeared in 20 volumes.

16th. We are hurrying to sell and distribute the new edition.

17th. Went to the warehouse this morning to give various instructions, then to the bank and to Howard's to ask about the account and the cheques. Learnt that Volumes 16, 19 and 20 of the *Complete Collected Works* have been seized.* This complicates everything. Home this evening.

20th. The lawyer Maklakov recommends that Sasha and I go to a court of arbitration. All courts are so painful. Ilya and Andryusha came, and briefly Misha. I went to see him and his family off from Paveletsky station. Endless partings – life is so lonely! Endless problems.

21st. Worked frantically on the sale of the new edition all morning. Paid Howard 20,000 rubles for paper and the Kushneryov printers over 15,300. Went to the bank to see Dunaev, who is a director. Did some shopping. Thawing snow and terrible mud in Moscow. Spent the evening quietly at home. Depression.

22nd. Went to the bank. Visited the museum and talked to Prince Shcherbatov about the manuscripts. The police sealed up Vols. 16, 19 and 20 in the warehouse today.

23rd. I went to the warehouse early this morning to ask the police officer not to spoil the books when they're sealing them up, then walked to the mushroom market with my maid Verochka. Thawing. Went home, copied my summer diary and painfully relived it. Went to church. Today is the day of my Vanechka's death. May the Lord reunite me soon with my Lyovochka and Vanechka.

2nd March. Spent the day copying out the sad story of my life during the summer of 1910. I weep for things that can never be put right, yet it was all foreordained. Stakhovich was here. Negotiations are starting today between him, Belgard and Stepanov (procurator of the Palace of Justice). Tomorrow they will be summoning me too.

3rd. Misha Stakhovich came this morning and Alexei Belgard, chief press censor, a most sympathetic man. They are defending my interests over the seizure of the 3 volumes of the *Complete Collected Works*, and I am grateful to them. But then one *has* to take L.N. Tolstoy's widow's wishes into account; one could hardly put her in prison or lock her in a fortress. I stayed indoors all day.

4th. My negotiations over the seizure of the 3 volumes are going badly. I shall have to reprint two volumes at least – that's the best that can happen. At worst they can throw me in the fortress and put me on trial. I spent the day copying and weeping.

7th. Visited the editorial boards with an announcement of the sale of Lev Nik.'s works. Sat up late copying and did 4 pages – 90 more to go.

9th. Prince Shcherbatov, president of the Historical Museum, called on me and stayed a long time, telling me how I could get the manuscripts back, although he said they hadn't come to any agreement and everything was exactly as it was before. He advised me to write to Kasso, Minister of Education, and to take up the matter in St Petersburg, and if I didn't achieve any results with the ministers to go and see the Tsar himself. I stayed at home all day and copied.

10th. I wrote two letters to Kasso, one asking them to return everything of mine to me (diaries, letters and so on), the other asking to be allowed to use various documents for my memoirs. I also prepared to leave for St Petersburg. Sonya Mamonova, Misha Olsufiev and Count Geiden dined with us, which was very pleasant. I visited the Rumyantsev Museum and the Historical Museum, asked for copies of the paintings of Lev Nik. and visited the exhibition.

12th. I worked all morning and late into the night, and finished copying my diary from June to October, when Lev Nik. left. This evening I went to vespers at the Palace Church in the Kremlin, where L.N. and I were married. The service was very crude, the deacon and the singers had the most disagreeable bass voices, the church was empty and dark, and the whole thing had a dismal effect on me. Maslova and Prince and Princess Odoevsky came to pay their respects and compliments.

14th. Took my last diary to the Historical Museum, as well as three notebooks containing Lev Nik.'s first and last diaries, and copies of various letters of his; I shall receive a receipt for these tomorrow. Then I rushed around the town – I am planning to leave for Yasnaya tomorrow. A wonderful spring day, the sun is shining, the streams are thawing – and everything is so melancholy! I long for home and the grave.

15th. Took back a book to Taneev. He is *weeping* for his nurse, I am weeping for my husband, and we had a good heart-to-heart talk. This evening I left for Yasnaya.

16th. I cried as I approached the house, cried when I went to the grave and cried when I went into Lev Nikol.'s room. It was as if he was still here and was about to come in and I would tell him something. Tanya's friend Yulia Igumnova is staying, who has become very stout, and the artist Orlov. Old Dunyasha and Nurse are quietly living out their last days here. All so empty and sad! Nothing but bills, housekeeping and business.

21st. Copied out the diaries. What a lot of careful, conscientious background work on his books he put into these diaries!

23rd. I have finished copying Lev Nik.'s diaries – to my great sorrow! Now I have nothing of his to work on! Endless sadness, I sit here at home on my own all day! I have hung the large portraits of Lev Nik. on the walls. But they don't speak to me. There are so many of them – they're everywhere!

24th. Today I have been vividly recalling the events surrounding Lev Nik.'s last days, and despite all the anguish I feel it *could not* have been otherwise, it was foreordained.

27th. Went to Lev Nik.'s grave and wept inconsolably. I thought about my daughter Sasha. She must be so lonely among all those strangers, poor thing. She has left her mother, her brothers don't love her – even her dogs come to see me, especially Belka, but she never pays her grieving mother a visit.

4th April. We read aloud my son Lyova's letters from America.* I went to bed, then got up and talked to Lev Nik.'s translator Halpérine, and read some of his article about his departure.

10th. A warm, windy day; I went out for the first time – to Lev Nikola-evich's grave of course. In the distance they were ringing the church bells, and 'Christ is Risen!' rang out over Russia. But in the forest and beside the grave there was silence, and the wind shook the withered wreaths as I prayed and wept. Then I sat in silence for a long time on a board that had been laid on a tree stump. Did Christ rise in my beloved husband's heart when he cruelly left me and his home, and disinherited his poor sons and their families? May the Lord forgive him!

14th. My daughter Tanya arrived at 5 this morning, full of energy, common sense and sympathy as always. She has gone off to see Sasha in Telyatinki.

16th. My son Seryozha arrived. I had a good day resting my soul with people I love; my health seems better too. We had a cosy evening together – Seryozha, Tanya, Maria Schmidt, Yulia Igumnova, Andryusha, his Katya and I.

20th. How uninteresting my life is! I went out twice to visit the grave and couldn't find the fence – they've broken the lock again. I read some Chekhov – very clever, but he sneers a lot and I don't like that.

A fine morning, then a thunderstorm and a short, fierce shower. I haven't been crying recently – I've grown cold, my life is a matter of *endurance*. "To *live* is to *submit*!" according to Fet.

21st. I read some unpleasant news in the papers today: the Palace of Justice has decided to destroy Volumes 16, 19 and 20 of my edition.* This is extremely annoying and means huge financial losses.

25th (Moscow). I went to the Palace of Justice and asked Stepanov the procurator to speed up the decision of my case concerning the seizure of the 3 volumes of the new edition.* He promised to send the decision to Sidorov, the chief censor. I then went to the Censorship Committee, where Sidorov promised to remove the ban the moment he received the court's decision.

27th. Visited the censorship inspector at Chernyshevsky Street, then on to the Censorship Committee. They are doing all they can, and the ban on the books will be lifted tomorrow; Chefranov was here and I have assigned him to reprint the three volumes.* I worked on Volume 20 until 2 in the morning.

29th (St Petersburg). I was met by Andryusha and my sister Tanya. Everything's so friendly and informal at the Kuzminskys'. I wrote to Countess Geiden, a maid-of-honour, about gaining an audience with the Empress, Maria Fyodorovna.

30th. Countess Geiden visited. The Empress has refused me an audience.*

1st May. Crowds of visitors. This evening was the first meeting of the Society of the Tolstoy Museum. My son Seryozha came too; he is president, I am an honorary member. A lot of dull speeches.

2nd. I visited the Winter Palace to see Naryshkina, a lady-in-waiting, and asked her to arrange an audience with the Tsar. She promised rather feebly.

3rd. Spent the morning at home, then visited Minister P.A. Stolypin; my sister Tanya came too. He understands the necessity of buying Yasnaya Polyana and giving me the manuscripts, but is afraid to announce this to the Tsar, especially now, with this new "religious" spirit at court.

5th. A lot of guests. At 8.30 this evening I visited Minister Kokovtsov about the purchase of Yasnaya Polyana.

6th. Visited my lawyer Shubinsky this morning, who promised to defend me if Sasha takes the matter to court. I am writing to Naryshkina about an audience with the Tsar in Tsarskoe Selo, and to Stolypin and the Tsar explaining the main points of my case. I cannot bear the thought of losing Yasnaya Polyana.

7th. Stayed at home and wrote to the Tsar and Minister Stolypin. Drove around town with Tanya. I'm being pestered by journalists; I miss home and long to get back and see the grave again. The sale of Yasnaya Polyana is tormenting me.

8th. My trip to Tsarskoe Selo didn't take place; Naryshkina wrote to say it had to be cancelled because of the arrival of Grand Duchess Elizaveta Fyodorovna, but she will see me on Tuesday in the Winter Palace. So annoying! I want to go home as soon as possible. Mitya Olsufiev was here, and S.P. Auerbach. I mended sheets for Tanya and am staying at home.

10th. Went to the Winter Palace to see Naryshkina. She was most affable and gave me a copy of her memoirs, and undertook to give the Tsar my letter.* I left for Moscow this evening.

12th (Moscow). I gave the printers all the material for the reprinting of the 3 previously banned volumes.

13th. Visited the Duma and talked to Guchkov about the sale of the Moscow house.* It breaks my heart to destroy all my nests, which contain so many memories of a full and happy life.

15th. Didn't go to the grave – there were too many visitors, and Lyovochka and I need to be alone together.

16th. Went to the grave, laid a bunch of wild flowers there and sat for a long time weeping and praying. My life is over, I am numb and indifferent to everything, my soul is heavy with suffering.

17th. I read about my Lyovochka in the books by Bulgakov, Lazursky, Rolland, Maude and the others. It's all wrong, all wrong!

24th. Worked on my photographs. Very tired. Visited the grave. Every time I go I weep, as if I were responsible for my husband's death. But how passionately I loved my Lyovochka – to the very last moment of his life! What happened is a complete mystery, we will never understand it.

28th. Photography all morning. This afternoon my son Seryozha arrived with Bogdanov, secretary of the Tolstoy Society in Moscow, and played some Chopin and Schumann beautifully.

30th. A lot of visitors to the grave and the estate. Spent the evening knitting, and listening with an aching heart to the gramophone.

6th June. Read an old French book called *De l'Amour** – naive and insubstantial, but the language is beautiful. Copied my daily diaries.

9th (Moscow). Dined at the Praga restaurant. A pleasant conversation with the artist Nesterov and a friendly meeting with Alexei Maklakov. This evening Biryukov visited.

10th. Went shopping, finished my business in Moscow, looked at a little house I might buy after selling this one. A hot, bright day. Left this evening for Yasnaya. I gave photographs to Mey for his album.

11th. Painfully sad homecoming to a deserted Yasnaya Polyana. A nasty scene with the Circassian guard, who had robbed a woman in the village of her grass; I ordered him to give it back.

15th. Some valuers from Tula and St Petersburg came to look over the estate. Endless bustle all day. The plan is for me to move to the Kuzminskys' wing.* Everything is different, life is in decline, and it's all very hard.

16th. Seryozha, Misha and Ilya left, and Lyova unexpectedly arrived. I did nothing all day. Endless discussions about this nightmarish sale of Yasnaya Polyana, inventories and all the other matters concerning that dear, beloved man. I put a brave face on it, but it is hard! There was a distant thunderstorm and a brief shower, and people have picked the first berries, white mushrooms and milk caps. Later this evening there was a heavy thunderstorm and it poured with rain.

17th. I have made a list of the things in the bedroom, and am giving almost all of them to the government, care of the Museum. All very sad, but I know it must be done.

18th. Today is Sasha's 27th birthday. I thought about her all day. Poor girl! It must be sad for her to be alienated from her beloved father's family. It has been raining and thundering on and off all day.

20th. I took a walk with my Lyova and we had a long talk. There are no happy people in this world! It was very hot today; they've been gathering the hay and picking berries and white mushrooms.

21st. The same – it rained, I read Naryshkina's fascinating memoirs of her life at the palace. A brilliant life and an intelligent one – unlike my own naive memoirs about my life as a mother.

23rd. I have started painting a copy of Pokhitonov's view of Chepyzh. Andryusha is back. It rained all day. Lyova is tense and nervous and his plans are erratic. I live only for today, with the happy certainty that every day brings me closer to death.

24th. No rain today. Very warm, the hay is still lying on the ground. I did a painting in oils and am very dissatisfied with the results. One cannot get far if one has no training and is almost blind.

25th. A wonderful evening – the light, the sunset, the fresh green, the flowers... and the more beautiful it is, the sadder I feel. At the grave I met some young people who had come to pay their respects; I asked them not to touch my flowers and roses.

28th. My son Seryozha's birthday today. I was going to visit him but who needs me there? I sobbed as I remembered his birth 48 years ago. I was just 18.

29th. Today is fine and cool. I tried hard to stifle my grief – mowed hay, pumped water and took a long walk with Yulia Igumnova to the plot of land I have bought in Telyatinki and the birch grove. I spent the evening with my sons. None of them is happy – how sad!

4th July. Worked hard photographing Lev Nik.'s private diary "for himself alone". It makes painful reading! My poor Lyovochka, we were so estranged at the end! I feel it was my fault, yet I was so unhappy myself! I took a long walk after dinner with Andryusha, Katya and Yulia. Mown hay lying everywhere. We walked across the meadow and along the Voronka, returning by the swimming-pool path, to the grave. I knitted all evening. Painful discussions about the will.

6th. Today Biryukov brought two hundred peasant teachers, men and women, to look round the house, the estate and Lev Nikolaevich's grave. I helped and talked to them, and met with a great deal of sympathy. This evening I pasted newspaper cuttings. Another

insufferable polemic inspired by an article of Chertkov's! The rain
has ruined the hay.

10th. There were about 140 visitors to the house today, and even more
at the grave. I took some of them round the house myself and read
the second notebook of Lev Nik.'s letters to me. It's sad to recall the
past, but sometimes it's good too.

16th. Couldn't sleep last night, took some veronal and got up late.
Went to Sasha's house in Telyatinki to see my sister-in-law Maria
Nikolaevna. Discussions and tears. I learnt nothing new, apart from
the fact that a chapter in *Resurrection* called 'The Liturgy' has been
published abroad.* Lev Nik. had promised his sister not to publish
this chapter, but Chertkov has already done so.

17th. A very busy day. Crowds of visitors to the grave and house.
Artists taking photographs for Merkurov the sculptor, who has
been commissioned to produce a relief map of Yasnaya Polyana.

19th. Our dear nun, L.N.'s sister Maria Nikolaevna, came for the day.
Discussions, memories... I have seen my daughter Sasha twice now,
and we are getting on better.

21st. Endless bustle all day, but I feel free of it all. My grief at losing
Lev Nikolaevich is so solemn and profound, nothing else seems
important.

24th. What turmoil. My son Ilya, his wife Sonya and my nephew
Sanya Kuzminsky paid a brief visit. Maria Nikolaevna came, and
some Serbian doctor, an acquaintance of Makovitsky. Then Gusev,
who has just returned from exile. There were 15 for dinner.

26th. Maria Nikolaevna said Chertkov had taken six photographs of
her, and in all of them he had been in the picture, and Sasha too. How
unpleasant! More gales, thunderstorms and rain. A dead branch has
come down over the grave.

31st. More guests. All these visits are completely lacking in soul, love
or joy. It makes me sad. I have given so much love to other people, and
have met so much injustice, coldness and censure.

6th August. Went to Telyatinki to see Sasha, and had a talk with my sister-in-law Maria Nikolaevna the nun. I was touched by something she said about Lyovochka, who shortly before he died kept repeating: "What is to be done? What should I do now?" She said he spoke with such anguish and despair. I feel so sorry for him! His soul was not at peace before his death. In Telyatinki Olga made a spiteful remark and Sasha ostentatiously left the room.

12th (Moscow). Went to the Duma this morning and delivered an application for the sale of our house in Khamovniki Street.* Everything there is just as it was in the old days, it's like a grave! Where is Vanechka? Where is Masha? Where is Lyovochka? They all lived there once…

13th. Did some shopping, and this afternoon went to the cinematograph to please my maid Verochka. Most depressing! Stupid subjects for an uncultured audience.

14th. We left Moscow and returned to Yasnaya this afternoon. Sadness everywhere! On the train I read 'Does Woman Represent God'.*

16th. I printed some photographs and sent them to Mey, then made jam – apple and peach – and marinated some red plums. A lot of bustle, and all for what? Eating is the only sweet and purposeless activity. A widow visited today with her 2 little mites, and how they grabbed at the white bread I gave them! I also gave her 4 rubles. Gusev came. Is he sincere, I wonder? I wrote to Mashenka about the portable chairs.

22nd. My 67th birthday. Why was I born? Who needed me? Surely my wretched life must soon end.

28th. Lev Nikolaevich's birthday. About 300 visitors came to the house, and many more to the grave. I didn't go: I can't bear to see so many policemen, and there's so little real feeling for Lev Nik.*
    My son Seryozha came, and my grandson Seryozha with his teacher M. Kuez. A crowd of guests. My soul is sombre and my head is a fog.

30th. I went to the grave and got soaked in the rain. Chatted to the peasant Taras Fokanov. Worked hard taking notes for *My Life*, and suddenly rediscovered my interest in my old work. My eyes were better today. This evening Prince Dolgorukov came to discuss the peasants' library.*

3rd September. Worked hard on my memoirs and read some sad family letters written in 1894, when Lyova was so ill, then wandered sadly about the garden. What a hard life! Rain all day, a blazing red sunset and starry night.

7th. A delightful warm, bright day, but the leaves already have their autumn colouring. I couldn't stay indoors – too sad! – and went out to saw dead branches off the apple trees. Then I had to tidy up the cellar and boil jam. I sat in the barn and thought intensely about eternal life. *Where* do we all go? Where has my Lyovochka gone? This evening I copied out my Daily Diary for 1910.

11th. I walked to the fir plantation, and my Sasha was here, with the peasant Frolov boy. She and I are friends, thank God.

12th. I didn't sleep last night and felt wretched this morning, and got up early and went to Lev Nik.'s grave. On the way I found some mushrooms – honey agarics and milk caps – and picked a whole basketful. At the grave I wept and prayed as usual, and spoke to L.N. No one was there for a change. I spent the day painting the autumn leaves in watercolours and wandering around Yasnaya Polyana.

19th. I wrote to Minister Kokovtsov about the sale of Yasnaya Polyana, painted and sat with the writer Almedingen. Life is dull and tedious these days, my soul is unbearably sad.

22nd. I painted, copied, knitted and didn't leave the house. News of Liza Obolenskaya's arrival. I am so pleased. How good Socrates's last discussion with his pupils* was. One *must* believe in *eternal* life, otherwise it would be impossible to go on.

23rd. Our wedding anniversary! When I got up I picked some white flowers and roses – emblems of my vanished youth – and took them to the grave. I stood alone there and wept. Where are you, my bridegroom, my beloved husband? Liza Obolenskaya came, and my son Ilya paid a brief visit. Then dear Maria Schmidt arrived. This evening we read *The Living Corpse*.* Not very good.

1st October. Dmitry Obolensky came with two engineers from St Petersburg who have come to inspect the Belgian factories at Sudakovo. Andryusha has returned from Krapivna. He was unanimously voted a town councillor of the Krapivna district.

2nd. I played the piano for a long time – sonatas by Beethoven and Weber. I wanted to forget myself but couldn't. Then I copied out my Daily Diary, painted an autumn leaf and read various articles about *The Living Corpse*. Frightful weather, 2° below freezing, dark sky. It distresses me that I haven't visited the grave for so long.

4th. Tanya's 47th birthday. Already! How vividly I remember her birth. Lev Nik. had a broken arm, and sobbed with emotion when his first daughter was born. How he loved me!

8th. Lovely weather. Clear, still, 7°. I went to the grave and talked to the peasant Taras Fokanov, who loved Lev Nikol. and now guards his grave. This evening I finished reading aloud 'Tolstoy and Turgenev'. I have tried to work on my memoirs but still haven't written anything. My spiritual life is severe and contemplative. I must be brave!

9th. Not many visitors today – eight in all. Andryusha, Yulia Igumnova and I visited the grave. Taras, Ivan Drozd and I measured the space for the new wrought-iron fence. I don't like their plans. I worked hard on my memoirs for 1894. Life was hard then, but it got worse.

16th. Andryusha returned from Moscow, and told us about *The Living Corpse* and the Tolstoy exhibition.* He understands a lot. I spent the day drawing autumn leaves; I didn't feel disposed to write. A warm wind. The workmen have arrived to mend the path by the grave and dig ditches.

18th. At 7.20 this morning Maria Alexandrovna Schmidt died in Ovsyannikovo. Yet another dear, close friend is no more – yet again my heart is like lead! She died suddenly, as she lived, without bothering anyone, all alone with her maid. I went to Ovsyannikovo to look at her stern, yellow face and say goodbye to my dear friend. A fine sunny day, with a freezing north wind. Before going to Ovsyannikovo I visited the grave. The workmen are there mending the ditches and the road, and it's seething with activity.

19th. I went to the grave; everyone was hard at work there, as they were yesterday. Then I went to the barn and the threshing machine. There they all were, peasants and young folk, laughing and joking and threshing – life goes on around me, but my heart is sad and silent. As silent as the small, thin, dead figure of Maria Alexandrovna in her coffin. The artist Baturin has arrived. A warm, windy day, with fleecy clouds in the sky. I drew and wrote.

20th. We buried Maria Schmidt today. Andryusha and Katya are packing up and preparing for a new life in Taptykovo. A still day. 5°, and a starry, moonlit night. It's good to be with nature, even though it's autumn.

21st. This morning I went to the grave. Yesterday and today they've been putting up another sort of fence. There are a lot of workmen there.

23rd. I wept bitter, painful tears as I walked back from the grave and recalled Lyovochka's tortured mental state at the end, and I am still weeping now. Visitors arrived from Moscow and I showed them everything. I attended to the day-labourers' records and accounts, and packed my bag for Moscow.

25th (Moscow). Visited the banks and delivered the album and *Skeleton Dolls*.* Everyone was very pleasant. Had dinner and spent a pleasant evening with Seryozha and Masha, and my grandson Seryozha.

27th. Shopping and business all morning. Dined with Seryozha again. Saw my grandchildren, Misha's children, and was very, very happy.

28th. It was on this day that Lev Nikol. left Yasnaya Polyana. Spent the morning at the Tolstoy Exhibition. Various gentlemen kept following me around so I had to force myself not to cry. It was very distressing, but interesting!*

29th. Back at Yasnaya. The moon was still shining at 7 this morning. The house is silent, sad and empty.

31st. I have started copying Repin's portrait of Lev Nik. – very hard. This evening I read Arabazhin's book about Lev Nikolaevich;* very well written. A grey, windy day. I took a bath. Lev Nik. lives in me, like a pregnant woman with her baby. I'm forever thinking: "Oh, I'll tell Lyovochka that, I must show him that…" But he was so indifferent last year to everything that concerned me, he lived only for Chertkov. It was on this day that he stopped at Astapovo. But I survived, and, alas, I am still alive!

1st November. I wrote letters to my sister Tanya, Marusya Maklakova, Lyova and my daughter-in-law Katya. Also letters about the waltz and the poems.* I worked on my copy of Lev Nik.'s portrait and went to the grave; they're finishing the work on the fence and the paths.

7th. A sad day. A year ago today Lev Nikolaevich died. All my sons came, apart from Lyova, and a crowd of journalists and members of the Tolstoy Society – about 500 visitors in all. Our peasants followed me to the grave and sang 'Eternal Memory'. My granddaughter Tanyushka Sukhotina was with me. Endless bustle, long discussions about the sale of Yasnaya Polyana and sadness in my heart.

11th (Moscow). The Sukhotins, Yulia, my maid Verochka and I are all staying for the last time in my house in Khamovniki Street, and are happy to be here. Sukhotin and Makovitsky stayed with my son Seryozha in Staro-Konyushenny Street.

12th. I visited the Duma to discuss selling my house to the city of Moscow.

17th. Ilya complains about his affairs, and says: "I'll shoot myself." I have been visiting Speshnev the notary about the sale of the house. Dzhunkovsky the governor came to give me some advice about my letter to the Tsar. I wrote him a letter about the sale of Yasnaya Polyana,* and Ilya and I decided to send it straight to his palace in Livadia with my son Misha. I still don't know whether it has been sent.

20th. The Moscow Arts Theatre gave me a ticket for a box to see *The Living Corpse.*

22nd. This evening we went to the Arts Theatre and sat in the director's box with Zosya and old Alexander Stakhovich. *The Living Corpse* is remarkable more for the performance of the actors (often in a bad sense, as in the part of Fedya) than for its literary merits. It's better to read it.

23rd. Spent the morning at the Merchant Bank and the Duma. I received 125,000 rubles for the house and sent 60,000 rubles of this to my 6 children. Sasha is very rich now, but she is all alone.

26th. I tidied the old house in Khamovniki Street and choked back the tears as I said farewell to the past. Yet one more thing has been torn from my heart. I dined with Seryozha. He then left for the English Club, and this evening I set off home for Yasnaya.

27th. I am back again; the house is cold and empty. The artist Orlov is here. I went to bed and slept till one, then drank some coffee and went to the grave. The grey sky looming overhead, the forest silence, our peasants chopping brushwood in the gulley – everything is sombre and severe here in the country. Letters from Lyova, tender but sad.

28th. I got up late feeling rested but lonely. I had letters from the children, which was a consolation. I learnt that Sasha had walked over to the house and hadn't come in! What a strange creature!

30th. I went to the village and took over the peasants' library from Maria Valentinovna, who is leaving. The villagers take out books and don't return them, which is most annoying. The library will have to be closed, and that will be the end of it. Our peasants are still so uncultured. I worked on newspaper cuttings until late tonight and pasted them in.

5th December. I went to Taptykovo with Verochka to visit Andryusha. The road was terrible! Not much snow, frozen mud, potholes and unbearably bumpy. They were all touchingly pleased to see me, and I was glad I went; Katya, Andryusha and little Mashenka warmed me with their love, and I looked round their comfortable house.

6th. Andryusha's 34th birthday. We all spent the day together.

7th. We spent the morning together again, and Katya and Andryusha thanked me touchingly for coming. A strong wind, the road was terrible, 2½° below freezing. I was exhausted and fell asleep on the sofa in the drawing room. This evening I read Alexandrine's 'Reminiscences', which I found fascinating, and her correspondence with Lev Nik., published in a splendid Tolstoy Museum edition.

12th. I collected the library books from the peasant children – some were lost, some were torn and filthy. Then I drew up a contents table for my memoirs. I didn't go out all day. There was a heavy fall of snow. I relive my whole life when I read my memoirs.

15th. Wanda Landowska and her husband arrived here from Sasha's. Their talk upset me. Before they came I went to the grave and fed the birds. The silent forest, hoar frost, 5° below freezing.

22nd. The house was cleaned and I tidied my Lyovochka's rooms myself. He is always in my thoughts, and I am glad to be able to live on in this house as if he was still here. Nyuta and I played Haydn's 20th Symphony, which I used to play with Lyovochka. I painted wooden dolls for my grandchildren, who will soon be here.

24th. 27–30° of frost. 18° this evening, but windy. I did some copying on the Remington for my daughter Tanya. I also wrote her a letter. Then I read 'The Forged Coupon'.* What a lot of murders! It is painful to read.

25th. Christmas. Alone with Yulia. I walked on my own to the grave, weeping and praying. I entered the library books into the catalogue (the returned ones), gave the peasants presents and worked hard on my memoirs for 1895, the year of Vanechka's death. It's strange, when I go back to the past, even the painful times, I stop living in the present and live entirely in my memories – they're so vivid, they're almost real.

26th. Dushan Makovitsky was here. I worked all day on my memoirs, preparing material for each month. 13° of frost, slight snow. They're doing a performance in Telyatinki of *Poverty's No Sin*, and everyone is hurrying over to see it.

29th. We are decorating the Christmas tree and listening to the gramophone, which I dislike very much.

31st. I was busy with the children and the Christmas tree, and talked to Ilya. Such a depressing year – yet I'm still alive! Cold wind and a blizzard, so Sonyushka and Ilyushok couldn't come. Ilya's elder sons didn't come either, and the Christmas tree and New Year's party were dreadfully unexciting. So much sadness – not to speak of Sasha's estrangement; she must be lonely surrounded by strangers. Sonya went to visit her in Telyatinki.

1912

An increasing number of strikes, including a large one at the Lena goldfields, in which workers are shot.

Sasha Tolstaya receives 120,000 rubles for the copyright on Tolstoy's posthumous works, and 28,000 rubles for the exclusive licence to publish a complete edition of his works. More conflicts with Sofia (who has already produced eight editions of Tolstoy's works). Excerpts from Sofia's My Life *(covering the years 1862 to 1901) published.*

2nd January. The two Ilyas, my son and grandson, have left, and 33 women students arrived from St Petersburg; I myself showed them around the house, 11 young ladies at a time. Then I worked on my 'Memoirs' (*My Life*). For the time being I am still collecting material. This evening I pasted newspaper cuttings and read.

4th. I worked hard on my Memoirs and finished the material for 1895. This evening I made notes of all the books that had been returned to the peasant library. The whole business has become disastrously muddled. Silence, nobody here.

7th. I wrote my 'Life' for 1895. I kept having to stop and weep as I described Vanechka's illness and death, and all the terrible things I experienced at that time.

19th (Moscow). Visited the Tolstoy Museum, where there were some *English guests.* Prince Dolgorukov gave a speech, and an Englishman replied beautifully in French. The young lady typist came and I dictated my memoirs to her.

24th. Ilya came, I gave him 1,000 rubles. He is pathetically poor, and blames everyone else for his poverty. I wrote to V.N. Kokovtsov thanking the Tsar for my pension.*

29th. More negotiations about the sale of the editions. We hope to win Sasha and Chertkov over, but I don't think we will, for they are devising all sorts of traps to make me recognize Sasha as the heir to all her father's writings – even those in the Historical Museum. I dictated to the typist again.

7th–13th February. We are exhausted by all these promises to buy my edition and bring Sasha to some agreement with the publishers. And of course Chertkov spitefully interferes with everything. I read three books, two French and one Russian – Fonvizin's *Two Lives*, which wasn't bad. I went to three art shows and three concerts: two were recitals by the Czechs, who played magnificently, especially the Beethoven quartets. Taneev's quintet was also very good, but hard to understand at once. He played himself. I also went to Wanda Landowska's concert. She played marvellously, both the harpsichord and the piano. I am indifferent to everything, I died with my Lyovochka! But it seems I shall have to bear my healthy body for a long time yet!

15th. I did a lot of work on the village library. It's hard to put it all in order, and I got Vasily Orekhov from the village to help me. What an extraordinarily backward lad! Dushan Makovitsky came and checked his memoirs from my notes.

23rd. I copied Lev Nik.'s notebook for 1908. I endlessly relive the past. There is no present, nothing excites me, nothing consoles me. It's a most unpleasant spring. Fog all morning, then it cleared, but the wind was terrible, a real tempest. The barometer is at zero. I read nothing but the Gospels these days.

27th. A large crowd of strangers unexpectedly arrived to see the grave and take a look at the house and Lev Nikol.'s rooms. I showed them round myself and talked to them.* Some had come from the Chertkovs, and heard some bitter truths from me. I went to the grave and decorated it with roses, primulas, stocks and hyacinths – it looked beautiful. I read a lot about Herzen today. Yulia has left for Moscow and I am alone here at Yasnaya. I worked again on my memoirs for 1896, but there is very little material and I remember almost nothing.

28th. I read letters from my children for 1896 as material for my memoirs. Andryusha unexpectedly arrived; I was delighted to see him and spent the rest of the day with him. It's sad to realize that *not one* of my children is happy, and they are all short of money.

29th. There were some workers from the Brashnin factory here, some women teachers and various other visitors. Their attitude to L.N.'s memory and to me was very touching. I stayed up late writing *My Life*. I am sitting on my own, with a frightful wind howling outside.

4th April. Went with some workmen to the forest to visit the grave, and had a very pleasant talk with them. This evening I played the piano and wrote a little.

6th. News of the death of Lev Nik.'s sister Maria Nikolaevna. How sad! I wrote to her daughters Varya and Liza, and to Tanya and Lyova. I have finished working on 1896. It was very painful to write about it. Last night I dreamt of Lev Nikol.; he was walking along the street straight towards me, gazing seriously into the distance, and as he got closer he melted away.

9th. I gave 77 Yasnaya Polyana schoolchildren 3 yards of calico, which I received from Burylin in Ivanovo-Voznesensk. It was a joy to see so many children and I wanted to give them a treat.

10th. I took fresh flowers to the grave, then read an article about my sister-in-law Maria Nikolaevna.* It was well written and affectionate. She had prayed away all her sins, lucky woman!

11th. I went to Tula, and met my sons Ilya, Misha and Seryozha at the Chernyshevsky Hotel; they are all wretchedly poor. They told me about Maria Nikolaevna's touching death and funeral.*

21st (Moscow). My daughter Tanya and her family left early this morning, I received 100,000 rubles for the books, sent my sons some money and gave Tanya a bank draft for 20,000. I stayed with my brother Sasha and my sister Liza, and left for St Petersburg this evening.

22nd (St Petersburg). I was met in St Petersburg by my son Lyova, who took me to his house on Tavricheskaya. The darling children were there, and I had a delightful time with them all. I was glad to see my sister and her husband too.

26th. Wrote to Kasso, Minister of Education, about the manuscripts.*

28th. Half the day in the train, the other half at home in Yasnaya, where I arrived at 8 this evening. Three artists are here, Orlov, Saltanov and Yulia Igumnova.

5th [May]. Spent the whole day copying my 50th-wedding-anniversary article on the Remington. A worrying letter from my sister, who wants to spend the summer with me in Yasnaya.

15th (Moscow). Andryusha and I tidied the Khamovniki house, deciding what was to go to the Stupin warehouse, what was to be sold and what would go to Yasnaya. How sad that everything is coming to an end – the beautiful old life has died, and it won't be continued by the children.

21st (Yasnaya Polyana). 80 women students came with Professor Valentin Bochkaryov. They took an interest in everything and walked to the grave, then went off to Telyatinki. I too went to the grave this afternoon and planted it with forget-me-nots and other flowers. This evening I copied some documents to send to the Senate.

27th. A mass of visitors all day. Unpleasantness with the gardener, the assistants and the visitors.

2nd June. I am rereading Pascal's *Pensées*.* Books and ideas like these are good, and help to explain our inner spiritual life.

16th. Sasha arrived with her companion Varvara Mikhailovna. We are friends again, thank God!

22nd. The surveyor Korotnyov brought an estimate for the forest and the parts of Yasnaya Polyana that will be left after the sale.*

28th. In Nikolskoe for Seryozha's name day and 49th birthday. My sister Tanya came too, and my daughter-in-law Sonya, and Varya Nagornova with her son, daughter and grandson. Sonya and Tanya sang and everyone sang together, then Tanya danced with Orlov the artist. His whole family was here, and we had a good-natured, cheerful time. We all went for a walk. The day was marred by a distressing discussion with Sonya about money.

5th [July]. More distressing discussions this afternoon about Lev Nik.'s flight and his relations with Chertkov. My sister Tanya's husband is very wise and sympathetic in his judgements. I wish I could say the same for Tanya; she is much changed.

6th. The peasants from the new settlements came here: 23 households were burnt to the ground. I gave 10 rubles to each family and waived their rent for the rest of the year.

8th. This morning I received various visitors who had come to see Lev Nikol.'s rooms, and wasted time chatting to them. This evening the Kuzminskys and I read aloud Snegiryov's letter to me.*

13th. Stayed in bed all day reading and got up this afternoon. Sasha came and we spent a very pleasant evening together.

16th. Went to the grave. A lot of young people on bicycles.

19th. I am copying Pascal's *Pensées*; there's a strange essay called 'Passion et l'amour'.* I took a great bunch of flowers to the grave this evening. There were some white lilies there that someone had brought, and there are always visitors.

29th. Biryukov and Bulgakov were here. The same conversations for two years now about Lev Nik., his flight, the will and so on. And the same thing again this evening with Kuzminsky. Kuzminsky is an extraordinarily good and logical person. Tanya is quite the opposite. She shouts, loses her temper, puts wholly unjustified nuances into everything. How she has changed! What a shame!

6th August. I copied out Lyovochka's last diary "for himself alone" on the typewriter. What happened? It's incomprehensible! A lot of it is very unjust. My soul is in mourning.

9th. My granddaughter Annochka came with my darling little great-grandson Seryozha. Annochka and my sister sang some duets very prettily and my son Seryozha played the piano. Dushan Makovitsky visited and I spent the day with guests; a lot of commotion, but it's good that Yasnaya Polyana is again becoming a place where people gather. Tears in my throat all day.

14th. I went to the grave as soon as I got up, and decorated it with flowers. Then I went to the village library. About 175 books have been stolen or torn by the peasants, and I find this so depressing I no longer feel like working on it. I am reading a series of articles 'On Tolstoy's Religion', and for a rest I read Potapenko's 'The Janitors of Fame'. This evening I read biographies of various people from portraits published by Grand Duke Nikolai.

19th. This morning I sat with my sister while she read me her notes about our genealogy;* it's not badly written. Biryukov came, visitors came to see the study, and L.N.'s old secretary Gusev arrived asking for money for the consumers' shop.

22nd. My 68th birthday. A very pleasant day. Andryusha's family came and my sons Ilya and Seryozha. We went to the grave, then my sister and her family arrived. There were 19 people to dinner. Yasnaya Polyana came to life again! This evening we sang and danced. It was so cheerful I wanted to weep with emotion and a bitter sense of loss. I am even closer to the children now, thank God!

27th. Sasha asked if she could spend the winter in the Kuzminskys' wing; she wants to extricate herself from the hateful Chertkov.

9th September. I packed for Moscow and went to the grave to say goodbye to Lyovochka. It's all very sad! Bulgakov came, then Martynov the artist, who asked in a very familiar manner where he and his wife could stay.

12th (Moscow). To the editorial offices of the *Russian Word* about my article and my grandchildren's portraits, then to the banks.

13th. More business. Went to the Historical Museum and corrected some mistakes in an earlier copy of Lev Nik.'s diary.

28th (Yasnaya Polyana). It poured with rain all day. I did a little work and felt very melancholy. Lev Nik.'s old black cap fell to pieces in my hand, and suddenly I saw before me his old head that I had loved so much.

1st October. The artist Martynov is here again. Linev came too (a member of the Tolstoy Museum), and took away all the photographs of the estate. I do almost no work, merely squander my energy on trifles and feel constantly ill. My daughter Sasha visited.

12th. Andryusha came to visit and took 2,000 rubles from me; we talked about the sale of Yasnaya Polyana and how they had chosen him as an elector. I wrote to Kuzminsky, who wants me to visit St Petersburg to petition for a cinematographic lampoon about me* to be banned.

13th. My health is much worse, I feel as though I were half asleep, and have no energy, particularly after this distressing news about the cinematograph.

15th. Sasha sent Popov the valuer and his assistant to see me, and we looked at the plans. Sasha has bought a house in Moscow across the Moscow river.

19th (Moscow). I visited the Governor to discuss the cinematograph, which has now been banned.

20th (St Petersburg). I have arrived in St Petersburg and asked the ministers for a meeting.

22nd. I was received by the Minister of Justice, and gave him my complaint about Lev Nik.'s manuscripts, which I had sent to the Senate.* Shcheglovitov seems well disposed towards me and my campaign.

23rd. Today I visited the Minister of Internal Affairs, Makarov, about the cinematographic lampoon against me, and he promised to ban it throughout Russia. We still have to write to Poland, Finland and the Caucasus.*

24th. I wrote registered letters to Zein, Skalon and Count Vorontsov-Dashkov about the cinematograph, and dined at home with the Kuzminskys, saw Lyova, then left for Yasnaya Polyana. My sister Tanya saw me off.
25th (Yasnaya Polyana). I was happy to get home. Makovitsky was here.

28th. Painful memories of Lev Nikolaevich's flight two years ago today; I got up with an aching heart. After dinner I read Chirikov's

'Banishment', then sewed under the lamp – the first lamp in our house, which my Lyovochka lovingly bought for me.

1st November. A photographer arrived this morning from Pathé. I didn't leave the house.

7th. The anniversary of Lev Nikolaevich's death. All sorts of visitors to the house and grave all morning – police, cinematographers, journalists, the general public. Andryusha came, and Seryozha arrived shortly afterwards. This afternoon when the visitors had all left, I went to the grave with Andryusha. Seryozha went on his own. Dushan Makovitsky came for the evening.

9th. I read a great many articles about Lev Nikol. in the newspapers, and a spiteful note by Chertkov in *Speech.**

10th. I went to the grave as soon as I got up. Whenever I am there on my own I weep and talk to Lyovochka and pray. I scattered crumbs to the birds, and a flock of them flew up and chirped cheerfully at me. I went back and wrote a lot of *My Life*, and this evening I played both pianos and read a French article about Rod.* We read many articles about Lev Nik., and Yulia cut them out and pasted them in the book.

19th. I rose early and went to the grave, where I chatted there to some peasants I had never met before, who were carrying logs. Then I wrote all day. An unpleasant article about the manuscripts in the *Russian Gazette*.

12th December. Today a young priest I didn't know held a funeral service – at his own request – over Lev Nikolaevich's grave, then performed a requiem mass in his bedroom. He left this evening. An energetic, intelligent man, just 27. Bulgakov, Yulia, Verochka and I attended the service, and Nurse and Semyon the cook came for the requiem.*

13th. I started on some difficult work today, copying and editing all Lyovochka's letters to me. That's a job I won't finish in a hurry. I shall relive the whole of my married life as I read them. It will be very hard at times.

22nd. I wrote an article for *Russian Word* in reply to Pankratov's lying article about the priest's visit.* I also wrote to my sister Tanya, and to the editors of the Clan publishing house about the *Illustrated Anthology on War and Peace*, which has been banned by the censors.*

24th. I stood for a long time at the grave in spiritual communion with my husband. This evening I copied and read aloud to Yulia and Bulgakov the letters he wrote from the Samara steppes in 1871.

25th. Went to L.N.'s grave as soon as I got up, taking fresh flowers and seeds for the birds. Taras was there. On the way back I met the village policeman and the guard – not a pleasant experience. I spent the day with outsiders – Yulia, Bulgakov, Saltanov. This evening an Englishwoman travelling around Russia on foot arrived with some Jew. I copied some of L.N.'s letters and one from N.N. Strakhov, which I sent to *Contemporary World*.

31st. I worked on the letters a little this morning, and Andryusha and Katya came for dinner. We spent a pleasant day together, and saw in the New Year in a nice friendly fashion. Makovitsky also paid a brief visit.

1913

8th March – huge Women's Day demonstrations under the auspices of the Bolsheviks and Mensheviks, in Moscow, St Petersburg and other cities. May – armistice signed with Turkey. Divisions emerge within anti-Turkish coalition over spoils, and Tsar Nicholas urged by many in his government to take Straits of Constantinople.

 26th February – Sasha Tolstaya buys Yasnaya Polyana from her mother and brothers for 40,000 rubles, which Sofia divides between her thirty-eight dependants. 26th March – over two-thirds of Yasnaya Polyana's land, including forests, is transferred to the peasants (according to the conditions of Tolstoy's will), while Sofia retains the rest of the estate, including the house and orchard. She starts work on an edition of Tolstoy's diaries. More excerpts from My Life *published.*

7th January. Sasha and Varvara Mikhailovna came; we drank tea, talked and parted on friendly terms. I collected some books to be bound, wrote to *Russian Word* and the *Sun of Russia*, and spent the rest of the day copying my late husband's letters.

20th. I had a visit from my son Andryusha, still unwell, and Ilya; I lent him 6,000 rubles and he cheered up immediately. But will it last? The visitors arrived and looked around the house. I did more copying.

31st. I am reading nothing but French books. I have never read Zola's *Fécondité* and am curious to do so. More unpleasantness with Sasha; she wants to gain possession of the property and the Yasnaya Polyana library. What will this strange – to say the least – girl think up next? More threats and blackmail!

8th February. Dreadfully upset by news in the papers about the Senate's decision on the manuscripts; it seems they'll refuse again, the cowards!*

13th. I copy Lev Nik.'s letters, and my heart suffers at our gradually dwindling happiness. My daughter Sasha visited briefly – a stranger, alas! This evening I played a Mozart quintet and symphony as a duet with Varya.

24th. Various people arrived early this morning to look at the study – Academician Sreznevsky, a dentist, and a member of the Tolstoy Museum. We visited the grave with Biryukov, and took flowers, and were surrounded by a flock of hungry birds. I spent the rest of the day embroidering underwear, and gave Biryukov a lot of material for his biography of Lev Nik.

25th. Biryukov has left. I did some embroidery and numbered L.N.'s letters.*

26th. Went to Tula this morning to discuss the buying and selling of Yasnaya Polyana.* I was joined by Ilya and Sonya, Andryusha, Misha, Sasha (in another hotel), Vaka Filosofov and many friends. Painful business discussion, visit to the notary, exhaustion. The streets are rivers and the sun is shining, but the countryside is still plunged in grim winter.

3rd [March]. Printed photographs all day. Ilya visited. He keeps coming up with plans to make enough to live on, and has none of his Yasnaya Polyana money left. He took my memoirs to use them to write his reminiscences of his father.

10th. Yulia and I left by express train for the Crimea, via Tula, to stay with my daughter Tanya. We were given a lovely large compartment just for the two of us.

11th (Yalta). We arrived in Yalta by automobile at 5.30 in the evening, after various adventures with a burst tyre and so on. The Sukhotins welcomed us warmly, especially little Tanechka. It's a pity my room is downstairs and theirs is on the 4th floor.

14th. Tanya, Tanechka and I visited my mother's grave, high on a hill with a view of the sea and mountains. Painful memories of Mother's suffering and death, followed by the murder of her son Vyacheslav, still in deep mourning at the time.

22nd. I went to Gaspra with Yulia. Everything was so lovely, even memories of Lev Nikol.'s illness, because we, his *family*, looked after him with love, and he was *mine*, not Chertkov's!

28th. We sailed to Sevastopol, where we went for a walk to the Malakhov burial mound, and this evening we returned home by train. I had a pleasant journey with the Sukhotins in a spacious international carriage. The weather was fine, and we were very comfortable.

30th (Yasnaya Polyana). This morning we said goodbye to the Sukhotins, who are staying in Oryol. My heart ached at the parting, but it was good to get home. Dear Bulgakov was happy to see us, and the servants seemed so too. I went to L.N.'s grave and decorated it with Crimean flowers.

3rd April. Endless bustle all day. The surveyor Korotnyov came to discuss the boundaries of my property at Yasnaya Polyana. Ganeev called about the workmen who are digging the ditch and the dam. Some people arrived from Belobrodov regarding my sons' payment for the trees.* I printed photographs of Lev Nik. and visited the grave, and this evening I read Andreev's 'He'. Rubbish.

4th. Most upset this morning by Sasha's article in the newspapers about her right to the manuscripts.* Yet more vileness. She says *I* refused to go to a court of arbitration, when it was *she* who refused to go.

20th. I wandered about Yasnaya Polyana for a long time, then sat down on the bench in the fir plantation where Lev Nik. used to sit, and where I once lay down and sobbed for hours, without noticing the rain or damp. I cried today too and prayed. Then I went back and worked on L.N.'s letters to me.

1st May (Moscow). I dined with Seryozha and spent the evening with him. On the train I read Pascal.

3rd. I went to the warehouses, paid Stupin for storing our furniture, and collected the books from the late Kokoryov's warehouse on the embankment across the Moscow River. I dined with the Maslovs.

4th. Finished my business and left for St Petersburg.

7th (St Petersburg). Spent a very pleasant day with Lyova, Dora and their delightful children. Yesterday the Chief Procurator of the Senate,

Dobrovolsky, called on the Kuzminskys and me, and promised that my case would be successful in the Senate. This evening I left for Moscow.

12th June. A German baron visited. He has travelled the world and was terribly talkative. I spent the morning with him, then talked to Gruzinsky about the publication of the letters. I sawed dead wood, chopped and mowed. A fine day. This evening Gruzinsky played the piano.

14th. I copied Lev Nikol.'s letters to me, then wrote to Lyova, to a Frenchman about aristocratic families in Europe, to Krapivna about the Circassian guard,* and to Shenshin about books.

17th. My son Andryusha came, I'm always glad to see him, although I disapprove of much of what he does, and grieve for him. The police came after hearing of Konyshev's threats to beat the bailiff to death. So unpleasant! It's raining again. I am writing to the newspapers about our badly behaved visitors.*

25th. My son Ilya arrived last night. A great many visitors today – 11 men on bicycles from St Petersburg, an American from New York, and a husband and wife from Siberia. Then Bulygin came to give advice on the construction of the dam. A lovely hot day! I sketched mushrooms.

27th. Bulgakov and I went to visit Seryozha in Nikolskoe. We travelled from Cherni by cab, and I greatly enjoyed our drive through the fields and country lanes. We spent a quiet family evening chatting together. I love Nikolskoe, and always remember my youth when I go there.

28th. My son Seryozha's birthday – he is 50 already. I congratulated him and gave him 100 golden rubles. Old Countess Zubova was there too, a dear old woman. Varya Nagornova then came with Ada, and their arrival was followed by such a heavy shower that we didn't expect to see my daughter Tanya and her husband – but shortly afterwards they too arrived. We had a very happy day. Bulgakov sang all evening, and Seryozha played the piano beautifully.

29th. The Sukhotins left at 12, followed by Varya. We went for a walk, then visited the orphanage – 30 boys and three teachers. The boys performed a bad play and sang badly for us – earlier they had been playing ball. What sad little city starvelings they are.

12th July. A great many visitors. Later this evening 15 young people came – cadets, young girls and so on. After dinner I went to visit Sasha with Verochka. She has a lovely little place.* I am glad we are now on good terms.

20th. I helped Bulgakov with his work on the library, showed the rooms to 30 waiters from vegetarian canteens in Moscow and read about suicide and spiritualism.

29th. Osman the Circassian guard is wretched. They have refused to allow him and his brother to go home to their native country. The poor old man was sobbing and in a state of despair – I wanted to cry too.

30th. My son Lyova has come, to my great joy. He wants to stay with us for a while.

11th August. I picked flowers, walked to the grave and decorated it, talking loudly to my dead Lyovochka. We haven't been completely separated – I always feel his presence here in Yasnaya. He is *not* happy and at peace, and I pray for his soul. Sasha was here, I'm happy to say, and explained a great deal to me.

24th. Sonya Bibikova brought a priest's daughter here, who I have taken as my companion; she is very sympathetic.

26th. I worked on my *Autobiography*, then played Weber sonatas for a long time. Lyova, Bulgakov and I had a long conversation about war, the social order and so on.

28th. Lev Nik.'s birthday. The Gorbunovs came, and Sasha, Dima Chertkov, Boulanger, all the Yasnaya peasants and various Telyatinki types all went to the grave. The peasants sang 'Eternal Memory' and everyone prostrated themselves three times. I dined with Zvegintseva and Princess Cherkasskaya, who were with an officer I didn't know. I am reading La Bruyère. I have finished a rough draft of my *Autobiography*.

1st September. Some peasant victims of a fire in Telyatinki arrived and I gave them just 10 rubles. This evening I read a woman's interesting memoirs of Guy de Maupassant.

4th (Moscow). Attended to business this morning; took an announcement to the newspapers, paid Levenson 1,000 rubles for the book, petitioned the administrators about Skosyryov, the Zaseka stationmaster.

14th. Worked on my *Autobiography* until almost two in the morning, then read Landau's *Moses.*[*]

15th. Read my *Autobiography* to Bulgakov, Medvedev and Saltanov. A telegram from some Germans about the translation of Lev Nik.'s letters to me. Was visited this morning by six intellectuals.

6th October. Nina Tikhonovna, my new companion, has arrived. She read L.N.'s letters and various articles to me.

16th. Copied and corrected my *Autobiography* all morning, coached the bailiff's little girl, then copied and corrected again till 2 in the morning. I'm pining without my children or any news from them.

18th. Went to the grave with some chrysanthemums and leaves. Had a talk with Taras about the vexing problem of the peasants and how to allot the firewood – to each soul or to each stove. I urged the latter, and this was finally agreed. I pruned some bushes, corrected the proofs of my article on Lev Nik.'s four visits to Optyna Pustyn and copied. Sad and lonely!

4th [November]. Prince Nakashidze came this morning with his 9-year-old nephew, a typical little Georgian, and Dosev, who I received coldly after the letter he wrote while L.N. was alive, about his desire to leave. I finished looking through the *Letters*, then sorted some Georgian newspaper cuttings.

7th. The third anniversary of Lev Nikolaevich's death. I spent the day well. I went to the grave as soon as I got up – there were already various visitors there. Then about a hundred people came to the house, mostly young people. My four sons came, Seryozha, Ilya, Andryusha and Misha, then two ladies, the daughter of N.I. Storozhenko and her friend. Seryozha played the piano, Bulgakov sang, good discussions. Andryusha and Misha have now left.

8th. Everyone left this morning – Seryozha, Ilya and the two ladies. I have hired a new Circassian, after successfully petitioning for our Osman to return to his own country. I did some sewing, and this evening I copied various writers' autographs and dedications to Lev Nik—ch from foreign books.

10th. I did a great deal of typing today, and am still busy with my *Autobiography*. Seryozha took it away to make corrections.

12th. Sasha came and talked to the peasants about their affairs. She had dinner and is staying the night here.

18th. I coached the little girl, and spent the rest of the day copying my *Autobiography* on the typewriter, making corrections as I went along. Solemnly said goodbye to the Circassians, and took visitors around Lev Nik.'s rooms.

23rd (Moscow). Went out on business this morning with Nina; the manager of Levenson's came to visit, and said my book, *Letters to His Wife*, had almost sold out.

3rd December (Yasnaya Polyana). We read Dostoevsky's *The Devils* again after dinner, then sight-read a little of Gluck's *Orpheus* and Mozart's *Don Giovanni*. I sat and discussed books with Bulgakov.

13th. I sent 25 rubles to the priest who performed the funeral service for Lev Nik. We are still reading *The Devils*.

14th. Did a lot of typing – finished copying my *Autobiography*. We read *The Devils*.

17th. We have started reading Dostoevsky's *The Idiot*. Dostoevsky is so coarse; I don't like him.

22nd. I went at last to the grave; the weather was most unpleasant and my soul was desolate. I prayed all the way. Young G.V. Serov came and took away his father's portrait of me for an exhibition. This evening we gilt nuts for the Christmas tree.

23rd. The pre-Christmas commotion is unbearable. This evening we read Gruzinsky's article about Tolstoy's letters, then some Dostoevsky.

30th. I spent the morning alone, but had some delightful letters from various grandchildren. This evening I lit up the Christmas tree for the servants' children. They recited poems and we played the gramophone, and I think everyone had a good time. Sonya Bibikova came, and Nina's sister.

31st. Seryozha, Andryusha and his wife came; Sasha too was here, and we had a nice New Year's party, without much merriment but very amicable. I was grateful to them for not letting me pine on my own. After supper Sasha played – very well too. A sunny day, a brilliant sunset, a quiet moonlit night.

1914

Summer – strike movement reaches its highest point since 1904–6, and violent demonstrations greet President Poincaré of France when he visits St Petersburg. 28th June – Archduke Ferdinand of Austria assassinated in Sarajevo. 28th July – Austria declares war on Serbia and Belgrade bombarded. Tsar Nicholas II orders mobilization. 2nd August – Russia enters war. Wave of patriotism sweeps Russia and there is a lull in strikes and demonstrations. By mid-September some 50,000 Russians killed. Growing discontent at home.

March – legal dispute over Tolstoy's manuscripts finally settled in Sofia's favour. Summer – Yasnaya Polyana empties as peasants conscripted. Sofia, horrified by the war, is dismayed when her son Misha enlists and her daughter Sasha enrols as a nurse at the Turkish front, and finds her ideas becoming closer to her husband's. October – police visit Yasnaya Polyana at night, search it and arrest Tolstoy's former secretary Valentin Bulgakov. Sofia finishes work on My Life.

1st January. The start of another year, and I am still alive. Andryusha and Katya have left. Seryozha played beautifully all evening – Beethoven sonatas mainly.

10th. I copied my letters and finished reading *The Idiot*. I shall now read Chirikov's novel and Yakubovsky's book *Positive Peasant Characters in the Work of Tolstoy*.

1st February. The Chertkovs have been searched by the police.* I am interested in the new change of ministers.

4th. This evening Nina read me Turgenev's *Faust*, which I had forgotten, then we corrected *Tolstoy's Letters to His Wife*. And so it goes every day. It's as if life had frozen. It grieves me that I see so little of my children and grandchildren, but have neither the physical nor spiritual strength for it.

14th. 40 students from Shanyavsky University came to visit the grave and the house. There were some women with them too. I chattered on too long about Sasha and Chertkov. Then I copied out 28 pages of my letters. I have finished reading Turgenev's 'The Calm'.

24th. My son Ilya came, bringing me oranges and candied fruit. He is reading Lev Nik.'s bachelor diaries (up to 1861), which I copied out long ago.

25th. Ilyusha is such pleasant company when he is in good spirits. Someone has suggested he should travel around the cities of Russia giving lectures about his father.*

6th March (St Petersburg). I visited Lyova and Dora and dined with them; the children were adorable. I talked on the telephone with N.A. Dobrovolsky about my case in the Senate concerning the manuscripts. He said: "I simply can't understand why they're dragging it out so long."

10th (St Petersburg). This morning Dora and I went to the Wanderers' Exhibition. It was very weak in subject matter, and technique too; Repin's *The Duel*, or rather *Single Combat*, isn't nearly as good as his earlier works.

11th. I returned to Yasnaya via Tula – a frosty, overcast day. I found Varya Nagornova here with her daughter Ada. My lodgers Bulgakov and Nina are very pleasant. This evening we read aloud 'Lermontov and Tolstoy'.

12th. I wrote a letter to the Tsar, asking for a government post for Andryusha. I find this most difficult and disagreeable, but Andryusha is so ill and anxious I was afraid to refuse him. I have sent him the letter to read through.

18th. Slight frost, everything covered with a light layer of snow. Fine weather, dazzling stars, a bright moon. I coached the little girl, worked hard on my new chapter, and this evening we again read 'Lermontov and Tolstoy'. A letter from Kuzminsky about the favourable outcome of my case in the Senate concerning the manuscripts.

30th. Nina and I started fasting today and went to church. This great mass of peasants is still foreign to me, even though I have lived with them for almost 52 years. There's something wild and incomprehensible about them.

10th April. 25 visitors came to the house and the grave, then all our peasants arrived to invite me to the grave. But alas I was ill!

16th. Nina and I read my daughter Tanya's book about Maria Montessori,* the Italian who practises free educational methods.

10th May. Visited the grave and took flowers. I met three village children there and took them home, where I gave them sweets and played them the gramophone, but they didn't seem to enjoy themselves. I am reading the letters of the Prelate Feofan.

15th (Ascension Day). We didn't count the visitors, but I think there must have been about 150. Nina and I let them in. I copied the inventory of things in Lev Nik.'s rooms and felt so sad!

18th. My son Andryusha came. There was an excursion of 62 young girls here and various other visitors, and I showed them round Lev Nik.'s rooms. Towards 8 this evening my son Lyova came with his two sons Kita and Petya.

31st. I copied, visited the grave and went for a long walk. I was sad to hear my sons have started gambling again. Dora says Lyova has lost about 50 thousand. Poor, pregnant, considerate Dora! Lev Nik. was a thousand times right to give his money to the peasants rather than to his sons. It would only have gone on cards and carousing. It's disgusting and pathetic! And it will be even worse after my death! A hot fine day. Nature is delightful, but my soul is depressed. I didn't sleep all night.

13th June. We all drove to the river for a swim, just like the old days, in two separate trips, with the children and governesses and Lyova's three boys, who drove with their father. It was very hot – 24° in the shade. They've started mowing the old orchard. When we got home I read *Eugene Onegin* to the boys.

19th. I was engrossed all morning in Pushkin's stories; I haven't looked at them for a long time.

2nd July. I read the newspapers and have neither the time nor inclination for any serious reading. They are all full of Rasputin's murder.*

16th. I read the papers with alarm – is it really war?

19th. This ghastly war will lead to great misery in Russia. Everyone is despondent. People torn from their land and families are talking of a strike: "We won't go to war!" they say. From here they've taken the bailiff, seven horses, the coachman and two workers! And Russia is starving! What will happen!

20th. This morning I sat down to copy my letters. I copied up to December 1900, when Lyova's son little Levushka died. Tanya gave birth to a dead baby girl and so on. And I was with them and wept with them all.

21st. I have a heavy weight on my heart. My son Misha has enlisted and has been sent to Bryansk. They've also taken Karin, our bailiff, and our peasants and horses. Tears and terror on all sides – and all in the name of what?

27th. I wandered around Yasnaya Polyana all day with an aching heart, waiting for Andryusha, who is ill. He wrote that Misha would be in Tula on Tuesday and that I should go there and give him 1,000 rubles. They are enlisting him in the *active* regiments, the cavalry – yet another blow for me. Sasha was here, and is going off to be a nurse. We tenderly said goodbye. It's terrible! Here in the country it's sunny, still and warm.

28th. The news is all dreadful: Lyova has sent his family off to Sweden and is leaving with N.S. Guchkov for the Polish front with the Red Cross. Magnificent hot weather, a lot of mushrooms – and on all sides there are groans and tears. A group of 20 women visitors came to see the grave and the house.

29th. So much suffering – yet we continue to live and endure it! I said goodbye today to Misha, who is off to war! I forced myself not to cry, but it was hard! Andryusha is no cause for joy either: he's having difficulties with his wife, he has bad intestines and bronchitis, poor fellow, and is very thin. I am exhausted in body and soul!

1st August. I didn't sleep last night, and this morning I went to church with Nurse.* The church was filled with women – there were almost no men. The deacon shrieked some incomprehensible words, and it was all very sad! My alienation from the people is sad too; I am the *only lady* amidst this peasant population, and the children regard me as something strange and foreign.

5th. This evening I was shocked by the sad news that Sukhotin had had a second stroke. My poor little Tanya.

9th. I received a telegram announcing the death of Sukhotin. I packed hurriedly and prepared to leave for Kochety. My heart was filled with grief and despair, yet I had to see to everything at home before I left. Poor darling Tanya!

10th. I went by coach to Kochety. They have brought Sukhotin's body home from the Abrikosovs'. Tanya is trying to keep cheerful and is organizing everything, but it breaks my heart to see her so thin and anxious. God help her!

11th. Tanya, little Tanya and I all went for a walk, then sat together. The four boys have arrived to bury their father. My Sasha is here too, and Liza Obolenskaya and our Seryozha. There will be a requiem service.

13th. The Kochety house is empty now. Tanya is being very brave and isn't letting herself go, but it's very hard for her, for she loved her sick old man. Her life will be quite different now and it won't be easy. We are all gripped with terror by the events of this ghastly war!

14th. After our walk today Tanya read us her work *Tanya Tolstaya's Childhood*. It's excellent and most movingly written, and we shed a few tears as we listened to her reading it. She and little Tanya are planning to spend the winter with me. How good that will be. I can hardly believe it!

15th. We went for another walk, and again listened to Tanya reading her memoirs. We saw Dorik and Seryozha Sukhotin off to their regiment – Dorik as a volunteer and Seryozha as an officer. The elder Sukhotin boy, Lev, is distraught, and we are all very sad. I have packed and shall leave tomorrow.

22nd. My sister Tanya arrived this morning, and her husband came for dinner. Today is my birthday; I am 70.

7th September. I wandered about aimlessly; I can't do anything with this frightful war on, and my grief and worry for Tanya, my sons and Dora, who is due to give birth any day. I raked up piles of leaves for cattle bedding, gave the day-labourers their receipts and spent the evening doing accounts with Nina.

27th. My sister is distraught because her son Mitya has also volunteered for the war, as an orderly. Incomprehensible hypnotism! We read aloud Makovitsky's memoirs.

30th. I did some typing for my sister. This evening Bulgakov read us his article protesting against the war.* It is very good.

1st October. I showed various visitors around Lev Nik.'s rooms and the drawing room – some officers from the war, two army doctors and a lady. They were touchingly interested in everything.

2nd. My sister Tanya has left. A beautiful still bright day. I went out and wandered around the estate. People have planted apple trees, gathered up brushwood, raked the dead leaves and swept them into four piles. We read the papers. There were 6 visitors today – some officers and army doctors and two women. They looked round the drawing room and Lev Nik.'s rooms.

4th. My daughter Tanya's 50th birthday. I went to Tula with Nina, and saw my nephew Grisha, Sergei Nikolaevich's son. He has received another post. On the way back I met an entire battery of soldiers and officers who had been to Yasnaya Polyana; I am very sorry I didn't see them and receive them personally. I sent Lyova 1,000 rubles.

18th. The American consulate has informed me that my grandson Misha has been taken prisoner in Milevič, in Bohemia.*

21st. I received a letter from my brother-in-law Kuzminsky telling me I had won my case in the Senate and giving me some sad family news: Masha is ill, Mitya is off to war, three more sons are already at war and my grandson is wounded.

26th. I drew pictures and played Mischief with Tanechka. A large number of policemen burst in during the night and arrested Bulgakov for his leaflet against the war.* I was extremely angry and wrote to Dzhunkovsky, Governor of Moscow.*

28th. A sad date – it was four years ago today that Lev Nikolaevich left home.

3rd November. I received a disagreeable telegram from Dzhunkovsky.* These gentlemen make me nervous – they find you guilty when you've done nothing wrong.

7th. The anniversary of Lev Nikolaevich's death. This morning, six members of the Tolstoy Museum came – what pathetic representatives of the Tolstoy Society they were! I was delighted by the arrival of my son Seryozha. Later on all the Yasnaya peasants came and we went to the grave with them and recited 'Our Father' and 'Eternal Memory'. I went with Tanechka; Tanya came too, and my daughter-in-law Sonya with her son Kiryusha, and Seryozha, and it was so good. But the weather and the roads are terrible. It's 2 degrees and there was a fall of wet snow. This evening Sonya sang and Seryozha played the piano.

9th. Once again I spent the day revising *Letters to His Wife* for the second edition, and am reading *Chopin and George Sand*.

13th. I went to Tula with Nina and visited Bulgakov at the police station. He is being very brave but has lost a lot of weight and evidently has no idea what to expect. This evening Tanya read us some verses by Fet.

25th. I had an argument with Tanya about the Church. She repeats her father's words and denounces the Church, forgetting that for more than two decades he was a passionate churchgoer. This evening Andryusha came. He always cheers us up.

27th. Left for Moscow this morning. The train was packed. Austrian prisoners of war at Tula.

28th (Moscow). All morning in the banks. Paid the Stupin warehouse until May 1915. Dined and spent the evening with Seryozha. The roads were mud, travelled by cab.

2nd December. Saw Sasha in Moscow. On the 10th she is leaving with her detachment as a nurse.

4th. Returned to Yasnaya Polyana. It's most unpleasant, the gendarmes are drawing up a statement against Seryozha for saying the captain was wasting his time in the police force.*

11th. Went to Tula with my daughter Tanya and made the Kuzminskys' wing hers for life. Received my pension. Saw Bulgakov at the police station.

12th. Life passes quietly. The war and Bulgakov's foolishness are a great weight on my heart. Makovitsky, who signed his appeal, has also been summoned to Tula by the police.*

19th. I keep myself busy, but cannot apply myself to anything while this war is on. Dreadful sadness in my soul. Of my children I know nothing, and it breaks my heart to see my daughter Tanya looking so ill.

20th. Lyova came for dinner. A lot of talk. It's all war, war, war.

31st. Decorated the Christmas tree as usual. Seryozha came to dinner, and Tanya, Lyova, Andryusha, little Tanya, Antonina Tikhonovna, Dushan and I all saw in the New Year enjoyably together. My nerves are shattered. I want to weep all the time. I'm sad to have no news about Seryozha who promised to come, and I worry about Andryusha, who is ill.

1915

Russia driven out of Serbia. At the front, whole regiments are surrendering and there is open talk of revolution. Russian defeat seems beyond question. At home the economic situation deteriorates, with soaring living costs, declining wages, rampant speculation and administrative chaos. Strikes and demonstrations and women's "food riots" sweep the country. September – Germans advance to gates of Riga, and civilians are ordered to evacuate war zones, and their homes and crops set on fire. Two and a half million registered refugees. Tsar Nicholas assumes supreme command of army.

Summer – Sasha Tolstaya returns briefly to Yasnaya Polyana to recuperate from malaria. 6th June – Taneev dies; Sofia doesn't attend his funeral.

19th January. We're all terribly upset – Dushan has been arrested and imprisoned for signing Bulgakov's appeal.

22nd (Moscow). Went to the State and Merchant banks, then on to the Rumyantsev Museum, where I had a long talk with the keeper of manuscripts, Georgievsky. They are giving me a good room for the manuscripts, but there is a dreadfully steep cast-iron spiral staircase up to it.

23rd. I went to two exhibitions with Nina, the Union and the Wanderers'. Exhibitions are so bad nowadays, not at all what they used to be, there's such a lot of decadent daubing. I saw Chertkov's son Dima in the vegetarian canteen where we were dining.

5th February. I corrected three proof pages of *L.N. Tolstoy's Letters to His Wife*, coached the little girls and added up the income and expenses books. Tanya and Varya Nagornova went to Tula; they weren't allowed into the prison to see either Bulgakov or Dushan.

19th. I often think of poor Dushan. But it's hard for me to protest – my health is poor, I have no energy and my strength has gone. I listened to a reading of Leskov's *No Way Out*.

17th March. My daughter Tanya has returned from Moscow and St Petersburg, where she visited 4 ministers and pleaded for Dushan. He will be tried in a civil court.

3rd April. Everything is so sad, and I can do nothing. A letter from Misha about the death of his son; a letter from Sasha filled with youthful merriment – and she is at war! I simply can't make her out.

6th. Misha has come to say goodbye, for he is off to war again, this time in the staff of the Khan of Nakhichevan. It was painful to part with him yet again, and painful to hear of his son's death.

19th. Today I had visitors from Tula – the teachers and headmistress of the Arsenev High School. Sympathetic people. Some peasants came wanting money for their shop. I visited the grave with the two Tanyas and we decorated it with flowers.

27th. Bad news from the war; they're firing on Liepaja, the Germans have taken five provinces and sunk a private English steamer. I was overwhelmed with such sadness I could do nothing all day but wander about Yasnaya Polyana. I corrected the proofs of the *Letters*.

30th. I showed Lev Nikolaev.'s rooms to a great many visitors, including some revolutionary workers. I went to the grave and planted flowers – violets, daisies and cowslips.

1st May. A lot of visitors – some girls just out of secondary school and a lot of schoolboys and young people. I showed them round Lev Nikolaevich's rooms and told them about him.

10th. Andryusha came with Baranov, and they visited the grave. The public behaved outrageously; I have asked the police to come tomorrow. There were 55 visitors or more.

15th. Nina and I went to Tula and managed to obtain permission from the Police General to visit Dushan and Bulgakov. They were touchingly pleased to see me and asked about everything. Police General Volsky gave us the permit. I sent 700 rubles to my son Andryusha and attended to business in Tula.

7th June. I am deeply shaken by the sad news of Sergei Ivanovich Taneev's death on the 6th.

11th. More visitors. I worked on the index and went out to watch the hay being harvested. Very hot, with the threat of drought. I feel Taneev's death more deeply and painfully than ever. I read about his magnificent, well-attended funeral. He was truly appreciated.

9th July. We sat on the balcony this afternoon sewing respirator cases for the army and drinking tea. I am reading the Gospels all the way through. Every age in life has its own viewpoint.

19th. I am losing interest in life. Bad news from the war. Life here is frightening, with no guards and no dogs.

24th. The house has been plunged in gloom by news of the German capture of Warsaw. I never believed in a Russian victory from the start, and now things are going from bad to worse.

8th August. Dreadful news from the war: Kovno, Novogeorgievsky and many other places have been taken. Riga is being evacuated and there's fighting in the Gulf of Riga.

23rd. My daughter Sasha has returned, cheerful and much thinner, full of experiences and stories.

28th. Lev Nikolaevich's birthday. A wet, overcast morning, then it brightened up. I went to the grave and prayed for the souls of Lev Nik. and the parents who bore him. It's strange how quickly Tolstoy has been forgotten. There was *no one* here today, neither friends nor outsiders.

14th September. I showed some Latvian refugees around Lev Nik.'s rooms. There were more than 40 of them.

17th. I spent my name day happily. Andryusha came with his wife and little daughter, and Sasha with her woman doctor friend, and my grandchildren played and enjoyed themselves all day long.

18th November. I am sewing a blanket for the refugees. Tanya went to Zaseka and came back with a terrible account of their poverty; the children go to school barefoot, many of the women have nothing but thin blouses and short little skirts to wear. I again made notes for *My Life*. It's hard sometimes to relive the old life!

19th. I devoted the day to finishing my notes for 1898. This evening Nina read me a critical article about Sienkiewicz, and the beginning of his novel *Quo Vadis*.*

24th (Moscow). I left for Moscow. Problems with tickets – they had trouble finding me a seat. I travelled with some officers and an army doctor who were home on leave. I am staying at the Slavonic Bazaar on Nikolskaya Street. This evening I went to a quartet recital in memory of Taneev.

2nd December. I left this morning in an excellent compartment, comfortable and spacious. I found both Tanyas in good health and spirits and am overjoyed to be back.

7th. Dushan Petrovich Makovitsky has returned here from prison.*

22nd. My son Lyova arrived early this morning. He curses himself for gambling and living such a disorderly life, but it doesn't make him stop! Yet he has so many good qualities! This evening we read his play.* Gloomy, but clever.

1916

Lull in fighting until March, while arms supply improves. June – new offensive along Austrian front, with some two million Russian deaths and injuries. Mobilization creates havoc in agriculture, industry and transport. December – Rasputin murdered.

February – Andrei Tolstoy dies of pleurisy. Yasnaya Polyana, like other large estates, deteriorates. Ilya Tolstoy leaves his wife and children and emigrates to the United States.

19th January. My son Ilya arrived with two people who want to make a cinematographic film of the story 'What People Live for'.* One appears to be a Jew, the other is a boy of 16. I walked to the grave today and felt a little calmer.

20th. Ilya and the visitors walked around the estate taking photographs for the film. One of them, an actor playing an angel, stood naked in the snow!

11th February. Dreadful news of Andryusha, who is ill with a high fever. The days pass quickly and uneventfully. Bulgakov is leaving for Gusev's tonight with Dushan Petrovich's memoirs. It would have been better to post them.

17th. There are no trains from Tula to Moscow this week, as they're letting a military cargo through. I am planning to leave for Petersburg with Lyova to see Andryusha, and am packing my bags. Andryusha begged Katya to ask me to go there. He is evidently very ill.

18th. Lyova and I left for Petrograd, via Tula. Unimaginably crowded trains. We were given two first-class tickets apparently by mistake, and squeezed ourselves into a compartment with two men who were extremely courteous and obliging. At 8 a.m. we were given our own compartment, and slept until late morning. I stayed with the Kuzminskys, Lyova with his family. Andryusha looks very ill and I am dreadfully worried.

19th. The doctors keep repeating the same senseless words: "It's serious but there's no danger at present." He has pleurisy and a bad liver. His breathing is laboured, he is a greenish-yellow colour, he shrieks and groans continuously, and three or four times a day he is racked by a fierce, agonizing chill.

22nd. I suggested he should receive the Eucharist. He calmly consented, and when the priest came he confessed in a loud voice, repeating the responses and kissing everyone. He grew tired, and towards evening started shivering again.

23rd. Andryusha has been unconscious all day. His breathing is agonizingly laboured.

24th. Andryusha died at 10 minutes past one in the morning. It was on the 23rd that Vanechka died.

26th. A splendid, brilliant funeral. Masses of wreathes, a crowded church. It was like a dream. Seryozha arrived late. We buried him at the Nikolskoe cemetery of the Alexander Nevsky Monastery.

9th March. There has been a strong wind howling all day. Where is my Andryusha now!

23rd. It's very sad that Lyova's family life has broken down, but it's pleasant to have him living here, especially now that Tanya has left for the trial.*

26th. They have written to us from Krapivna ordering us to take in three prisoners of war. I added my signature to those of the other women protesting against the sinking of the *Portugal*.*

27th. I sent for the prisoners of war, four Romanians, who arrived on government horses.

29th. I coloured my children's drawings again, and sit in silence for hours on end, my heart aching for Andryusha.

30th. I heard today that the two Tanechkas won't be coming for another month, and that all the Tolstoyans, apart from Seryozha Popov, have been acquitted.*

16th April. This evening my son Misha arrived, looking well. He is leaving again for this cursed war on the 25th.

10th May. This afternoon I invited a Molokan to tea – an interesting old man who used to visit Lev Nik.

14th. There were a lot of visitors – three officers and 28 common folk from the co-operative society.

23rd. My grandson Andryusha Ilich came. He has two George Crosses from the war.

26th. News of 30,000 soldiers taken prisoner, and a battle in which *all* of our officers were killed.

29th. A vast number of visitors – workers from a metal factory, a great many soldiers with their officer and his wife.

18th June. Sasha's birthday. Where is she now, I wonder? I wrote down some information about the beginning and end of my marriage to Lev Nikolaevich, and became dreadfully agitated.

7th July. Today, 7th July, is a great day – my daughter Sasha returned from the war. She looked cheerful and healthy, thank God, and we listened to her stories all evening.

18th. Sasha has gone off to war again. It was very painful to see her go, worse than before.

24th. Today is the Kuzminskys' 49th wedding anniversary. They've never been very happy together! My sister was telling me only recently that she never truly loved him.

6th August. I had a visit this evening from my grandson Ilya Ilich Tolstoy, who has just finished at the Naval Academy. Such a nice young man.

9th. Spent the day in Tula with Nina and wrote a new will.* It breaks my heart to see the soldiers and hear them singing.

6th September. We had a visit from two Japanese men, a journalist and an artist; they had lunch with us, looked around the house with great interest and asked a great many questions. One of them spoke Russian, the other a little French. Lyova has written a memorandum for the Tsar called 'On Fixed Prices', and wants to give it to him in person.

11th. Today was a happy day. First my two Tanechkas came, then Seryozha arrived with Orlov. Fascinating conversations, then Seryozha played some Indian songs and an Arabian dance on the piano.

22nd October. 33 tourists, final-year students from Malakhovka, came to visit. I showed them Lev Nik.'s rooms, and Tanya gave them tea and something to eat in the wing. Then they all went out to the meadow, played games, sang songs and visited the grave.

3rd November. Lyova has returned with new plans to travel to India and China and give lectures. Ilya has just left for America with the same thing in mind.* I have a lot of grief in store – if I don't die soon.

5th. I am living through my last days with Lyova before his latest mad scheme – a journey through China and India. Today there is to be a Tolstoy evening in Moscow, organized by Tanya in aid of the Tolstoy Museum,* and on the 7th there will be another evening to commemorate Lev Nik.'s death.

6th. I played Schubert's *Tragic Symphony* as a duet with Varya. Lovely. I was interested to read the article about the Tolstoy evening organized by the Tolstoy Society. Tomorrow is the anniversary of his death; it's sad to recall the tragic events of that period.

7th. I visited the grave first thing this morning with some chrysanthemums and primulas. Our visitors today were an old woman and two young Slavs. Every city in Russia is organizing evenings in memory of L.N. Tolstoy.

8th. Varya and I played Mozart's Eighth Symphony as a duet, followed by Haydn's Twelfth. They're both lovely. I read Rolland's *Vie de Tolstoï* and did some newspaper cuttings.

11th. An unbearably sad parting with Lyova today. He has brought so much to our lives – music, ideas and a good, gentle attitude to life. How talented he is, and what a good disposition he has! Yet he is so wretched and unstable.

21st December. I am engrossed in the newspapers. The war, the murder of Rasputin, the chaos in the government – it fascinates and horrifies me.

29th. Visitors to Lev Nikolaevich's rooms all morning. It must be pleasant to feel this deep love for him – especially if one is young. People are always astonished by the simplicity of our life here.

31st. We all saw in the New Year together, and I think everyone enjoyed themselves. But my heart was grieving for my children – Ilya in America, Lyova on his way to Japan, Sasha at war and Misha about to leave any day now. And Andryusha no more! Thank God I still have Seryozha, Tanya and my darling grandchildren. The end of the sad year of 1916!

1917

8th March, Women's Day – women demonstrate in their thousands on streets of newly renamed Petrograd. Strikes, demonstrations and "food riots" become more violent, with buildings set on fire. 16th March – Tsar abdicates, his government is toppled and a new "Provisional" Government of liberal landowners is formed. The Soviet is resurrected and challenges the power of the Provisional Government. Spring – revolutionaries amnestied and many (including Lenin) return to Russia. June – Provisional Government urges on Russian soldiers against Germans; strikes and demonstrations in the towns reach massive proportions. July – unsuccessful attempt by soldiers, sailors and workers to seize power. 25th and 26th October – Bolsheviks take power at the Second All-Russian Congress of Soviets, and declare an end to war with no annexations or indemnities. December – armistice signed with Germany, while Trotsky and others attempt to persuade the German High Command at Brest Litovsk to accept Bolshevik peace terms. France, Britain, Japan and the United States prepare to attack Soviet Russia.

Angry peasants return from front and loot and burn estates near Yasnaya Polyana. Summer – looters driven off by staff brandishing pickaxes, and Sofia Tolstoy applies to the Provisional Government for armed protection. One hundred men dispatched to protect the property, and the Governor of Tula is requested to pay special attention to her needs. Sofia's daughter Tanya moves in with her young daughter (also Tanya, or Tanechka). Sergei Tolstoy gives a series of concerts, which receive good reviews. Tolstoy Museum agrees to bring out new Complete Collected Works, edited by his children Sasha and Sergei Tolstoy, and others.

19th January. Our old nurse, Anna Sukolyonova, died at midnight last night, and the nuns are now reading the psalter over her body. What grief! I lived with her for 35 years, and it was time for her to leave this life – she was 88. I coached my darling Tanechka; I am reading a lot.

21st. We buried Nurse today; the little place by the window where she always sat and greeted me is now empty, and I feel so sad.

23rd. I cannot rid my heart of anxieties about my children, especially Lyova, who is the most unstable and unhappy of them.

2nd February. I paid the workmen's salaries. I feel very sorry for the working people, and would love to feed and clothe them and show them some affection – especially the children.

3rd. Workers at the Tula ordnance factory are on strike. They have to stand in queues to buy food, and when they're late for work they're fined. Where's the justice in that?

17th. Terribly upset by Tanya's account of Lyova's gambling losses in Moscow before he left for Japan. How dreadful! A new weight on my heart.

1st March. An unexpected visit from Seryozha Popov, who was tried with Bulgakov and Dushan Petrovich and has just left prison. A new Provisional Government has been established. Frightful news of people killed in Petrograd when they rioted for bread.

3rd. I read the paper carefully to find out about the change of government and the authority of the new State Duma. Everyone is in a tense and expectant mood.

5th. An important day for Yasnaya Polyana. Workers from the Sudakovo iron foundry arrived with red flags and badges to pay their respects to Tolstoy's house and widow. Bearing portraits of Lev Nik., they tramped through deep snow in a biting wind to the grave. My two Tanyas went too. The workers sang and made speeches about "freedom", and I replied with a short speech about L.N.'s legacy. Then everyone sang 'Eternal Memory' and took photographs.

6th. I sent *Russian Word* my article about the workers' demonstration yesterday.

7th. A little soldier boy was sent here by Sasha to collect four copies of the *Complete Collected Works of L.N. Tolstoy*. The new freedom doesn't make me happy – everything frightens me.

11th. I was shocked to receive a letter from my sister Tanya informing me that her husband had died. He had already embraced death long ago, with his quiet, mild, affectionate attitude to all those around him. My sister wasn't with him – she had gone to a sanatorium.

20th. Dushan Petrovich read us Lev Nik.'s 'Our Revolution'* this evening.

4th April. There were a great many visitors to the house and Lev Nik.'s rooms. A militiaman dictated to me a letter applying for a policeman to protect me. Dushan Petrovich's relatives came to visit. We now have some Slovak prisoners here.

5th. I conscientiously read all the newspapers. Everything is so frightening – the war and the famine; there's menace in the air.

10th. I cannot rid myself of this gnawing anguish. Nothing can awaken my soul now or call it back to life – neither spring, nor my former happiness, music or art. My only pleasure now is having my two Tanyas living with me, but they'll be leaving soon for their home in Ovsyannikovo.

12th. Sasha and Varya Mikhailovna have arrived. Sasha is just the same, thank God, with the same loud, cheerful laugh. I'm delighted she came, but also wish she hadn't, since she'll be here for only two days, and we have waited and worried about her for so long.

15th. Sasha went off to the front again with Varvara Mikhailovna; she was full of energy and high spirits, and I had to force myself not to cry.

18th. Some professional and industrial workers from Sudakovo came to visit with a wreath tied with red ribbon from some soldiers. They carried some magnificent red flags embroidered in gold and silver, and played music which the crowd could understand. It's strange to hear the 'Marseillaise' played here in Russia. They made speeches, then all went off to the grave, and there were more speeches – from a schoolboy, an Italian and a Czech.

19th. 16 soldiers came to see the house and visit the grave. An engineer from Sudakovo called Parshin visited with books for the library.

23rd. Life is dull and pointless and there's little joy in it – apart from my two Tanechkas. The moment I got up today I had to deal with the day-labourers' wages, the widows' pensions, visitors, students, soldiers, officers. The officers were most sympathetic, and said people visited Yasnaya Polyana as Christians visited Jerusalem and Mohammedans Mecca – to pay their respects to a holy place. Terrible news about a peasant murdered by Austrian prisoners.

26th. My son Misha has arrived. He told me a lot of interesting things about the front. The lack of discipline in the troops is terrible, and in general the situation is hopeless.

27th. A mass of visitors. Forty-five schoolboys, five women, four soldiers and several other gentlemen. It has grown warmer and the nightingale is singing. We all had dinner on the veranda together, although everyone brought their own food.

30th. An enormous number of visitors to the house and the grave, all of them soldiers.

30th May. 200 soldiers came on foot to the house, and Ivanov, commander of the regiment, drove up later with his little girl. They were marching to music, and they played very well too, first the 'Marseillaise', and at the grave the Funeral March. There were a lot of discussions – about Lev Nik., the royal family and Chertkov. I invited the commander to dinner, but he declined.

3rd June. I received thanks from Moscow University for donating the *Complete Collected Works* to them, and they praised my edition as "the best".

17th. 400 soldiers arrived this morning with their colonel. They marched into the village last night playing music, and today they came to see us. I showed L.N.'s rooms to more than 62 of them.

18th. More visitors to Lev Nik—ch's rooms – soldiers, Jews, 100 children from Sudakovo and several schoolboys.

25th. I played a Mozart sonata as a duet with my granddaughter Annochka, then we did Beethoven's 1st Symphony and Weber's

'Invitation to the Waltz'. Several guests – ladies, soldiers with their officer and so on. Then the Deputy Minister for Communications, Takhtamyshev, arrived. We gave them tea and berries, and showed them the rooms. The minister had his two sons with him and some friends.

29th. I spent the day with Seryozha and Masha. This evening Seryozha, my sister Tanya, Dushan Petrovich and I all went for a walk; a beautiful sunset, a prisoner was scything the timothy grass. Seryozha's state of mind alarms and grieves me. The raids on the land and property at Nikolskoe are taking a threatening character.

6th July. This evening my sister Tanya and I read the *Early Morning* newspaper. Frightful occurrences in Petrograd: shooting, killing of our own people, looting, rioting. And these bandits are our leaders!* My sister takes it all passionately to heart and follows everything with great interest; I merely suffer deeply.

25th. I have finished a crayon drawing of a thistle (a large burdock). It was very difficult. There is a reference to a thistle in Lev Nik.'s story *Hadji Murat*.

2nd August. Tanya went to Basovo; she is interested in village politics. I am copying letters.

6th. The peasants are all singing in the village, even the two soldiers sent here to defend us. A lot of hateful visitors.

14th. I did a little copying, then at 8 o'clock I went out with my daughter Tanya to buy provisions. We visited eight shops, including four consumers' co-operatives, and found nothing apart from ten lettuces and a loaf of rye bread. Famine looms. Dushan Petrovich's nephew went to Tula, and there too there was nothing to buy. I chattered to Gusev and wish I hadn't.

20th. Reading the papers takes a lot of time and induces a feeling of horror. I read the Gospels every evening.

22nd. Today I am 73 years old. What a terrible anniversary to be alive! Where are my poor children and what are they doing? And what about my countless grandchildren? My heart aches with the tormenting prospect of famine. I was informed today that ten armed mounted soldiers will be arriving tomorrow with two officers.

25th. It's sad that relations with my sister are so bad. She flies into a rage at the slightest thing, and is always losing her temper with me and calling me a holy fool because I appear to take things so calmly. But no one sees what takes place in my soul.

28th. As soon as I got up this morning I went with my granddaughter Tanechka to the grave. We put flowers there and swept it clean and tidied it. Then the ten mounted soldiers arrived with their two commanders.

29th. We read *Communist Ideas*, collected by Posse as a supplement to *Life for All*. Most interesting!

30th. We read the paper avidly this evening, and with great sorrow. Civil war threatens; Kerensky and Kornilov won't yield power. I don't wish to judge them, but this new government has done absolutely nothing for Russia.

1st September. Dreadful rumours on all sides. It's impossible to get bread, all the ministries have collapsed, the best ministers have left, the best generals have been arrested. I fear Kerensky is mentally ill, with delusions of grandeur.

2nd. I was cheered by my son Misha's arrival from the Caucasus, where he wants to take his family for the winter. He was in low spirits and I wept when he left.

5th. I went out to the field and picked nine baskets of potatoes.

11th. Incomprehensible manoeuvres in government circles! Kerensky will evidently soon fall; there are so many intrigues and failures, so much love of power and so little understanding of what the country and the people need!

20th. My son Ilyusha arrived this morning, looking thin, old and wretched. He left this evening, and it was sad having to part so soon.

17th October. An agronomist called Volkov drove here from Tula in a motor car. They brought 12 or 10 soldiers – I can't remember how many – to protect us, and we managed somehow to accommodate them all.* The entire southern part of the Krapivna district has been set on fire.

23rd. There's a rumour that we're about to be raided, and some militiamen have come for the night to keep guard over us. None of us slept – we didn't even take our clothes off.

4th November. Captain Lyzlov and another officer came to say goodbye. The cavalry left today, and tomorrow a hundred light infantrymen will be leaving. Life in the country is becoming more and more frightening, but there's nowhere else to go.

5th. The hundred infantry soldiers left today, thank God. This evening a senior militiaman arrived from Kosaya Gora with an engineer and four other men from there. It turns out they are going to keep guard over everything, the house and the books; they have spent the past three nights here already. This is most reassuring.

7th. Today is the anniversary of Lev Nikolaevich's death – seven years have passed and I am still alive! I visited the grave. There were only four visitors – two peasant intellectuals from a distant district and two Tula men.

16th. My sister and I had the idea of reading something to the village boys, but it's hard to know what. Our peasants came here this evening and held elections to the Committee. None of this is very clear to me. They started talking about an armistice, then read my story about Vanechka.*

23rd. This evening I was notified on the telephone by the chief forester that we will be receiving our food from the Rationing Committee. I read Bulgakov's *Ethics*.

1st December. Butovich came to visit and I showed him round Lev Nik.'s rooms; he is very interested in all forms of visual art.

4th. I am living in a dream and a state of terrible turmoil. Crowds of idle people mill around all day – apart from Tanya and me, of course, who are immersed in worries, mainly about food. The presence of all these useless people prevents me from applying myself to anything. My daughter Sasha has arrived at last with Varvara Mikhailovna. I am so pleased to see them, despite all the difficulties we have had in the past – although even then there was a lot of closeness between us. Sasha and my sister sang beautifully this evening.

18th. Time flies, the war continues, famine looms. Sergeenko helps us to get the things we need – rye, macaroni, beans and rice.*

19th. Endless noise and turmoil… I'm happy to have my two daughters and my granddaughter here – my life depends on it. My heart aches for my absent sons.

26th. Tanya finished reading *Eugene Onegin* today. What a marvellous speech that is of Tatyana's rebuking Onegin! I hadn't read the work for a long time – one should always reread old things.

27th. I sewed handkerchiefs, glued some little boxes and played patience. I yearn for my darling Andryusha and absent Lyova.

28th. Yet more visitors to Lev Nik.'s rooms – the officer of a sappers' regiment called Avenarius, with his comrade and a pretty young girl. There were more soldiers here too – ours – with a guest of theirs.

31st. The last day of a difficult year. This evening Tanya read us 'What People Live for'. We didn't see in the New Year, but everyone had dinner with us – 12 in all. When I was alone in my room my heart ached for my sons. Where are Lyova and Ilya? Are Seryozha and Misha still alive? What of their families? What of Dora and her eight children? My soul grieves for them all.

1918

February – first allied landings in North Russia. Germany resumes invasion. 3rd March – the Bolsheviks finally agree to sign Brest Litovsk peace treaty with Germany, which grants their aggressor a large percentage of Russia's industrial centres and farming land. May – Civil War begins in earnest, when Czech prisoners of war, backed by France and Britain, rise up against the Bolshevik government. This signals a wave of revolts, financed by Britain, France, America and Japan, and led by former tsarist generals and admirals known as White Guards. Anticipating an invasion of Moscow, the Bolsheviks move the capital to Petrograd. Summer – Bolsheviks' fortunes at their lowest ebb. July – Tsar Nicholas II killed by the Bolsheviks. 11th November – war ends.

April – official opening of Yasnaya Polyana Society in Tula, which takes control of the estate. Tanya Sukhotina becomes caretaker of the Yasnaya Polyana Museum. Food is in short supply and life is hard. Tanya knits scarves to sell in the market to support her mother, sister and daughter. May – Bolshevik commissars visit Yasnaya Polyana. November – Tanya Sukhotina replaces secretary of Yasnaya Polyana Society and takes control of the house. Lev Tolstoy leaves Russia with his wife and children to live in Sweden.

1st January. This evening we lit the candles on the Christmas tree and invited 20 children in and gave them all something. After the Christmas tree we had a "democratic ball", and everyone danced – soldiers and prisoners, our servants and maids and the two Tanyas.

4th. Sergeenko went to Tula for kerosene – we sit here with one lamp and a wax candle. For 4 gallons of bad kerosene we now pay 60 rubles.

5th. During the recent storm the roof was damaged and L.N.'s room was flooded with melting snow.

7th. We were shocked to hear that the Constituent Assembly has been dissolved, and Shingarev and Kokoshkin have been murdered by two sailors.* Some peasants came to visit, and Sergeenko and my daughter Tanya talked to them.

14th. I am handing over the management of Yasnaya Polyana to my daughter Tanya, and shall hire a steward. I miss my sons terribly, especially Lyova and Andryusha. Is Lyova still alive, I wonder?!

18th. I spoke on the telephone to the manager of a sugar factory, who is giving us ten pounds. Then I asked Volkov for some iron from the *zemstvo* to mend the roofs, and they agreed to give me seven sheets but refused any more.

21st. Vysokomirny came and introduced some discipline amongst the soldiers;* he is a most agreeable man, also a soldier at present.

23rd. Tanya went to Kolpna for a committee meeting. They are taking our forest from us.

26th. Alarming rumours of a pogrom by the young villagers. Distressing discussions with Tanya about Sergeenko, who has returned from Tula infected with delusions of power and keeps meddling with her instructions. Her unkind attitude to me almost made me weep.

15th February. News that the Germans have seized St Petersburg,* the situation in Russia is desperate. My daughters and I sorted through various manuscripts and documents concerning Lev Nik—ch.

17th. It's a sad life. We are seeing Sasha off to Moscow again, it's particularly hard to part with her this time. I found her a little food to take as she will be arriving at night.

8th March. They have refused me a pension, and have promised me 300 rubles instead of 800.*

21st. I went with Manya to three consumers' co-operatives and two shops, where I found some bad brown macaroni, stale Greek nuts, matches and chicory coffee.

30th. An unexpected joy – my son Misha spoke to me on the telephone and promised to visit tomorrow. I worked hard on *My Life*.

31st. This morning I worked on my memoirs and read the papers. Misha arrived; he is much changed, but he's a splendid fellow – energetic, intelligent and agreeable.

1st April. I spent the day with my beloved Misha, who has now left for Tula. He is cheerful and energetic. Lord help him!

7th. Two agronomists called Volkov and Bogoyavlensky arrived from Tula today to discuss Yasnaya Polyana. They want to repair the garden and set it to rights. The spring brings me little joy; I suffer too much from thoughts of those going hungry in Russia and in our house.

15th. Some of our young peasants came here this evening, saying they wanted to expropriate our land.*

24th. I copied Tanya's letters. Then the whole village arrived and invited me to accompany them to Lev Nik.'s grave. Naturally I went – relations with them are good. Everyone knelt and sang 'Eternal Memory' three times.*

9th May. The religious holiday of Nicholas the Miracle-Worker, which the peasants celebrated in their usual coarse fashion. I had my photograph taken with several visitors – teachers from the railway.

13th. I had a visit from the Tula land committee, all from the common people but not disagreeable.

22nd July. Some commissars and various other gentlemen arrived from Tula – twenty in all – and looked at Lev Nik.'s rooms.

30th. I wandered around the estate all day, my heart heavy with the woes of Russia. An architect-academician came with plans for building a school.

9th August. My son Seryozha came – I was intensely glad to see him. "My dearest eldest children," as Lev Nik. said to Seryozha and Tanya just before his death. This evening Seryozha played the piano and little Tanya beat the drum in time with him. My 55-year-old Seryozha has grown very thin, and this is sad for his mother.

28th. My son Misha arrived this morning, with Sergeenko. I am oppressed by the worry of finding food for everyone – there were twelve of us here for dinner today. Some of our peasants came and invited me to accompany them to the grave again, and we all went and sang 'Eternal Memory' three times.

3rd September. I wrote a new will to include Sasha: she had been cut out for her outrageous behaviour to me after her father's death, but now I have forgiven her.*

13th. Some technicians arrived late this evening to draw up an estimate and a plan for a water pipe.

8th November. Everyone returned from Tula, where they had attended an evening commemorating Lev Nik.'s death. I did a lot of copying, and read a biography of N.A. Nekrasov. What a terrible childhood, and what a monster of a father! And his poor beloved mother!

3rd December. I am mourning the death of my brother Sasha. He had been in poor health for some time.

10th. Sergeenko came and brought an architect to design a model school for the peasants. Nothing will come of it; it's an enormous enterprise.

11th. This evening Sergeenko read us some Ovid and Socrates from the *Circle of Reading*.

21st. My daughter Sasha arrived late this evening with Zosya Stakhovich and my grandson Ilyushok. They are all hungry, but Sasha laughs about everything.

31st. Tanya arranged a surprise New Year's party at my grandson Ilyusha's request. We were all delighted and went to her wing, where we happily saw in the New Year together.

1919

July–August – the Crimea falls to the Whites. September – the Ukraine evacuated as the Whites invade, then the Bolsheviks' fortunes improve. October – Yudenich's White Army beaten back from Petrograd. November – Denikin's White Army in headlong retreat. December – Bolshevik government introduces "militarization of labour".

March – at the request of Sofia Tolstoy and her daughter Tanya, the Yasnaya Polyana Society takes over their portion of the land and uses it as farm. July – Sofia writes a farewell note and distributes her valuables among her loved ones. September – Red Guards quartered in the village of Yasnaya Polyana. October – guards moved to a nearby village after protests from Yasnaya Polyana Society. 1st, 2nd, 3rd November – Sofia Tolstoy catches a chill. 4th November – she dies of pneumonia. Buried beside her daughter Masha in Kochaki cemetery. Shortly afterwards her son Misha emigrates to France.

2nd January. We read *Dead Souls* this evening. I dislike these false-comic characters and situations, but there are some lovely lyrical passages and descriptions of nature. I haven't read it for a long time.

21st. Sergeenko sneaked in and choked me with talk for an hour and a half. What a tiresome man. He said some people have arrived from some sort of committee for the defence of the children of Krapivna, and want to evict everyone but me from the two houses, to build a home for twelve orphans, and I would be given two rooms to live in. I don't believe a word of it, but one feels constantly alarmed.*

26th. I wrote letters, and made copies, to the sales department of Kushneryov and Co., asking them to give me back my book *L.N. Tolstoy's Letters to His Wife*.*

9th February. My sister and I sat together at the large round table in the drawing room, and recalled all the people who had sat at that table in the past. We never thought then that most of them would leave, and it breaks my heart to think that those who are still alive are cold, hungry and at war.

18th. I signed a document handing over the Yasnaya Polyana estate to Kolya Obolensky, my late Masha's husband.

24th. Kolya Obolensky and Sergeenko gave me to understand in a brief conversation that there were disagreements within the Tolstoy Society. As far as I can understand, they want to raise a large loan on the Yasnaya Polyana estate – but who will pay for it no one knows. There is no landlord, no bailiff and no workers.*

28th. My daughter Tanya has gone to Tula for a meeting of the Tolstoy Society this evening. Kolya Obolensky went too.

3rd March. Five Bolsheviks came here with the lawyer Goldenblatt, and for some reason they brought us some white flour, cheese, coffee and tea.

8th. I have recently had a sense of Lev Nik.'s presence, and that he was being quietly affectionate and tender to me. Where is he now? And where are all those I loved who have left? How much longer will I languish on this earth? It is all in God's hands!

8th May. I was visited this evening by two engineers who are building a road to Yasnaya Polyana, and I chatted to one of them who had known Andryusha as a child. His name is Kalita.

25th. A vast number of people came to look round Lev Nik.'s rooms – children, high-school boys, young girls, members of some tribunal.

30th. A mass of visitors this morning. Some young girls sang in a choir and went for a walk, then ate their own lunch in the village – bread, eggs and milk. After we had our dinner they sang again and drank tea with us; then my sister Tanya sang beautifully – first with a small choir, with my little granddaughter Tanechka joining in, then on her own. Everyone was enchanted by her voice. There were more than 200 people here.

8th June. Whit Sunday! Beautiful weather, the lilacs and lilies of the valley are flowering profusely. There are grass snakes and patches of dry moss on the apple trees. Sasha and my granddaughter Annochka arrived from the station, and everyone was delighted to see them. Lots of singing and dancing.

9th. Delightful weather, magnificent lilacs, nightingales, a mass of lilies of the valley. We have everything here, and my beloved eldest children, yet a terrible sadness gnaws at my heart. I have so little love for people, I only love my *own* children and my little Tanechka. Annochka, another granddaughter, has come, and I am happy to see her.

21st. Sasha came this morning, with a pedagogue called Maxin, with whom Tanya had a long talk. We all walked to the Voronka river past the grave, and it was sad to see the old forest devastated by felling.

22nd. We had a great many visitors today and I am exhausted. Another meeting of the Tolstoy Society – all words and no action. More visitors this evening from the Rationing Committee. One of them was nothing but a dreamer.

14th July. Rumours that the White General Denikin is marching on Tula with his troops. Unrest in Tula; people have been marching with white flags and putting them up over the post office building. What will come of it? I wrote a letter to be opened after my death, bidding farewell to my family and begging forgiveness from those I am abandoning.* My grandson Ilya came, and various gentlemen from Tula with splendid horses and carriages to inspect the site for a school.

15th. I felt so unwell these past few days that I thought my death was near. So I summoned my two darling Tanyas, who have been living with me, and the three of us went through my few valuable possessions together. I considered it only fair to give my best things to my daughter and granddaughter. They have lived with me through the most difficult time in my life and have always been such a comfort to me. To my granddaughter I gave my gold watch and chain which Lev Nik. gave me, and a large diamond brooch that was a present from him when we were engaged; to my daughter I gave my mother's bracelet (gold) and a ring with two diamonds and a ruby, a present from Lev Nik. for all my help and labours when he was writing *Anna Karenina*. (This ring was in fact called *Anna Karenina*.)

19th. Rumours that Denikin is marching here with his troops to fight the "Bolsheviks", but whether he will be any better God knows! The Bolsheviks give us everything we need and don't insult us. Sergeenko read to us this evening from his *Tolstoy Almanac*. It was very interesting; I have forgotten so much, and it's good to be reminded of it.

20th. I gave Tanya the will I made in her favour. A worrying letter from my son Seryozha. Where are my sons and their families!!! My soul is heavy.

14th August. Rumours that the Bolsheviks' power is collapsing. Everyone here is rejoicing, but I am grateful to them for their help.

1st September. More rumours that some Red Guards are being stationed in our village to fight Denikin.*

5th. Alarming news this evening that soldiers have been quartered in the peasants' huts with their regimental commander, and that some soldiers have been dispatched from Tula to guard our apple orchard.

6th. They have sent us a large number of soldiers. Some are being lodged in the village to do various jobs of work, and some are guarding the orchard. How terrible to think armed people are living on the land where Tolstoy was born!

12th. Sergeant Dehring came with some aeronautical artillerymen – in a motor car.

29th. After lunch I visited the grave and met one or two people on the way. I sat by the grave for a long time, then wandered about talking silently to my dead Lyovochka – as he was when we loved each other.

7th October. Something sinister and terrible is approaching. A lot of bulls and horses and 4 vans have been driven here from Kursk. Kursk has been routed, and the Jews there were slaughtered.* An agitated Volkov from the Yasnaya Polyana Society dashed in briefly to visit us this evening. He is responsible for sorting out the cattle that were driven over here (for some reason) from Kursk. I have had a bad cough and have been staying at home. I wrote a letter to Davydov in reply to his about 'Polikushka'.* I washed the floors and took the window frames out to the veranda. Rumours that Denikin is in Mtsensk, or very near it.

9th. A great quantity and variety of strangers here to visit Lev Nik—ch's rooms. A certain Levitsky told me some Red Army troops had marched to Tula in the night; he said there would be a battle not far from Tula, and that they were putting up barbed-wire entanglements.

12th. I looked through my memoirs to find some information for Denisenko, who wanted to know about the times when Lev Nik. came into collision with the legal world (refusing to take the oath, the bull that gored the cattleyard worker, and so on). This is a difficult task, but I shall attempt to do it. The weather is brighter and finer but my health is worse – I am terrified I may have paralysis of the throat, like my father. My Tanya is even more precious to me – she has grown prettier recently too.

16th. All the soldiers of the 21st Cavalry Regiment have now left. The younger ones turned out to be good lads, and the older ones were thoroughly decent people.

17th. My daughter Tanya's birthday. I went into her wing to greet her and gave her a little porcelain cup – my mother's last present to me – containing a gold 10-ruble piece. I want to give everything away before my death, which will be very soon now. My choking cough is turning into something like whooping cough – this is my 3rd attack. The weather is overcast and cold, below freezing. It's cold in the house; the winter glazing hasn't been put in and the stoves haven't been mended. We're expecting battles near Yasnaya Polyana.*

19th. There was a meeting to decide how best to defend Yasnaya Polyana against looting.* Nothing has yet been decided. Carts, oxen and people are streaming down the highway to Tula.

III

Appendices

L.N. Tolstoy's Marriage

Our Trip to Ivitsy and Yasnaya Polyana

At the beginning of August 1862, when I was seventeen, Maman told me and my two sisters, to our great joy, that she had decided to drive us three little girls and our brother Volodya to the estate of her father and our grandfather, Alexander Islenev, in an Annensky coach (named after its owner and still in use at the time).

Our grandfather (who appears in Lev Nikolaevich's *Childhood* as "Papa") lived in the Odoevsky district on his estate at Ivitsy, which was all that remained of his large fortune.

The three daughters of his second marriage were young girls at that time, and I was very friendly with the second one.

His estate was some 20 miles from Yasnaya Polyana, where Lev Nikolaevich's sister Maria had been living ever since she returned from Algeria,* and as my mother and she had been close childhood friends and were naturally anxious to see each other again, my mother, who hadn't visited Yasnaya Polyana since she was a child, decided we would call in there on our way. We were in ecstasies at the news, and my younger sister Tanya and I were especially pleased, like all young people eager for change and movement. We cheerfully prepared for the journey. Smart new dresses were made, we packed our bags and waited impatiently to leave.

I don't remember anything about the day we left, and my memories of the journey itself are very vague – just the stopping places, the changing of the horses, the rushed meals and the exhaustion from all the unaccustomed travelling. We went to Tula to visit my mother's sister Nadezhda Karnovich, who was married to the Tula Marshal of the Nobility, and we took a look round Tula, which struck me as a very dull, dirty place. But we were determined not to *miss anything*, and to pay attention to everything on our trip.

After dinner we drove on to Yasnaya Polyana. It was already evening by then, but the weather was magnificent. The highway through Zaseka* was very picturesque, and this wild expanse of nature was a new experience for us city girls.

Maria Nikolaevna and Lev Nikolaevich gave us a noisy and joyful welcome, and their aunt Tatyana Ergolskaya greeted us affably in polite French, while old Natalya Petrovna, her companion, silently stroked my shoulder and winked in a most beguiling way at my sister Tanya, who was then just 15.

They gave us a large vaulted room downstairs,* modestly and even poorly furnished. All round the room there were sofas that were painted white, with hard cushions at the backs and hard seats covered in blue-and-white striped ticking. There was a chaise longue too, similarly made by the local joiner. Set into the vaulted ceiling were iron rings from which gammons, saddles and so on used to hang in the days when the house belonged to Lev Nikolaevich's grandfather, Prince Volkonsky; it was now used as a storeroom.

The days were growing shorter, for it was already the beginning of August. After we had run round the garden, Natalya Petrovna took us to the raspberry bushes. This was the first time we had eaten raspberries straight from the bush, rather than from the little baskets that were brought to our dacha when we were making jam. There weren't many berries left, but I loved the beauty of the red fruit against the green leaves, and enjoyed their fresh taste.

The Night and the Chair

When it began to grow dark, Maman sent me down to unpack the bags and make up the beds. Aunt's maid Dunyasha* and I were getting the beds ready when Lev Nikolaevich suddenly walked in. Dunyasha told him she had made up three beds on the sofas but didn't know where to put a fourth one.

"What about the chair?" said Lev Nikolaevich, moving out a big armchair and pushing a broad square stool against it.

"I'll sleep on the chair," I said.

"Well, I'll make up your bed for you," said Lev Nikolaevich clumsily unfolding a sheet. I felt embarrassed, but there was also something lovely and intimate about making up the beds together.

When it was all ready we went upstairs and found Tanya curled up fast asleep on a little sofa in Aunt's room. Volodya had been put to bed too. Maman was chatting away to Maria Nikolaevna and Aunt about the old days. Liza stared at us inquisitively. I vividly remember every moment of that evening.

In the dining room, with its large French windows, Alexei Stepanovich,* the little cross-eyed butler, was laying the table for supper with the help of the stately, rather beautiful Dunyasha (daughter of old Nikolai,* who appeared in *Childhood*). In the middle of one wall was a door opening into a little sitting room with an antique rosewood clavichord, and the sitting room had French windows leading out to a little balcony, which had the most lovely view. It has given me pleasure all my life, and I love it to this day.

I took a chair and went out to the balcony alone to admire the view. I shall never forget the mood I was in – although I would never be able to describe it. I don't know if it was the effect of nature, real, untamed nature and wide spaces, or a premonition of what would happen a month and a half later when I entered this house as its mistress. Perhaps it was simply a farewell to my girlhood freedom, perhaps it was all these things, I don't know. But there was something so significant about my mood that evening, and I felt such happiness and an extraordinary sense of boundlessness. The others were all going in to supper and Lev Nikolaevich came out to call me.

"No thank you, I don't want anything," I said. "It's so lovely out here."

In the dining room I could hear Tanya showing off, joking and being naughty – everyone spoilt her and she was quite used to it. Lev Nikolaevich went back to the dining room, but returned to the balcony to see me without finishing his supper. I don't remember exactly what we talked about, I just remember him saying: "How simple and serene you are", which pleased me very much.

I had a good sleep in the long chair which Lev Nikolaevich had made up for me. I tossed about a bit at first, for the arms at the side made it rather narrow and uncomfortable, but my heart was singing with joy as I remembered him arranging my bed for me, and I fell asleep with a new feeling of joy in my young soul.

The Picnic at Yasnaya Polyana

I felt full of joy too when I woke next morning. I longed to run everywhere, look at everything, chatter to everyone. How light and airy it was at Yasnaya! Lev Nikolaevich was determined we should enjoy ourselves, and Maria Nikolaevna helped to ensure we did. They harnessed the "*katki*" – a long carriage more like a wagonette – and put Baraban the chestnut in the shafts and Strelka in the traces. Then the bay Belogubka was saddled up with an old-fashioned lady's saddle, a magnificent grey was brought out for Lev Nikolaevich, and we all got ready for our picnic.

More guests arrived – Gromova, the wife of a Tula architect, and Sonechka Bergholz, niece of Yulia Auerbach, the headmistress of Tula high school for girls. Maria Nikolaevna was overjoyed to have her two best friends there – my mother and Gromova – and was in a playful, cheerful mood, laughing, telling jokes and keeping us all amused. Lev Nikolaevich suggested I ride Belogubka, which I was very keen to do.

"But I can't, I don't have a riding habit," I said, looking at my yellow dress with its black velvet buttons and belt.

"It doesn't matter," smiled Lev Nikolaevich. "There are no dachas here, and no one but the forests to see you." And he helped me mount Belogubka.

I was the happiest person in the world as I galloped beside him down the road to Zaseka, our first stopping place. In those days it was all unbroken forest. Later I would drive to those places again and again, yet they never seemed quite the same. Then everything seemed magically beautiful, as it never is in everyday life, only in certain moods of spiritual elation. We rode to a little clearing where there was a haystack. Over the years we would have many picnics in that clearing in Zaseka with Tanya's children and mine, but on that day it was a different clearing, and I saw it with different eyes.

Maria Nikolaevna invited us all to scramble on the haystack and roll down, and it was a cheerful, noisy afternoon.

The following morning we drove off to the village of Krasnoe, which used to belong to my grandfather Islenev.* My grandmother was buried there, and Maman was very keen to visit the place where she was born and had grown up, and to kneel at her mother's grave at the church. They didn't want us to leave Yasnaya, and Maman had to give her solemn word of honour that we would call in on our way back, even if only for a day.

Krasnoe Village

Maria Nikolaevna had lent us a carriage for the journey to Krasnoe, and we hired horses. We didn't spend long there.

I remember the church and the tombstone with its inscription: "Princess Sofia Petrovna Kozlovskaya, born Countess Zavadovskaya." I vividly pictured my grandmother's life: what misery she must have endured with her first husband Kozlovsky, a drunkard, to whom she was married against her will, then with her unlawful second husband, Alexander Islenev, my grandfather, living in this country place, bearing an endless annual succession of children,* and worrying constantly that in the grip of his gambling mania he would lose his entire fortune and be forced to leave the estate – which is exactly what happened to him at the end of his life. The old priest and Fetis the deacon both remembered Sofia Petrovna warmly and spoke of her with great affection. "I committed the sin of marrying them in secret," the old priest told us.

Fetis the deacon, we were told, had died and was in his coffin, and had suddenly come back to life just as they were burying him, and jumped out of his grave and walked home. To this day I can see Fetis's withered little figure, his sparse hair plaited into a grey pigtail at the back of his head. I had never seen a deacon with a pigtail in Moscow, but nothing surprised me any longer. Everything seemed fantastic, full of beauty and magic.

Ivitsy

When the horses had been fed, we left Krasnoe in the same carriage and drove to my grandfather's estate at Ivitsy. We were given a solemn and joyous reception. Grandfather moved rapidly – he seemed to slide across the floor in his soft ankle boots. He kept teasing us, and calling us "the young ladies of Moscow", and he had a habit of pinching our cheeks with his middle and forefinger and winking when he said something funny, then screwing up his humorous little eyes. I can still see his powerful figure, the little black skullcap on his bald head, his large aquiline nose and ruddy clean-shaven face.

Sofia Alexandrovna, his second wife, astounded us by smoking a long pipe, her lower lip sagging; all that remained of her former beauty were her sparkling, expressive black eyes.

Their second daughter, the lovely Olga, cool and imperturbable, took us upstairs to the room they had prepared for us. My bed was behind a cupboard, with just a plain wooden chair instead of a table.

Our arrival created much excitement. A lot of people came over to look at us, and picnics, dances and drives were organized for us.

The day after we arrived in Ivitsy, Lev Nikolaevich suddenly turned up on his grey horse. He had covered 20 miles and was in high spirits. My grandfather, who loved Lev Nikolaevich and the whole Tolstoy family – for he had been friends with his father, Count Nikolai Ilich – was delighted to see him and greeted him warmly.

There were a large number of visitors that day, and the young folk had organized a dance that evening after the day's drive. Some officers and local young landowners came, and a lot of ladies and young girls. They were all perfect strangers and we found them a little odd, but what did we care? We had great fun, that was all that mattered. Various people took turns to play dance tunes on the piano.

"How smart you look! I wish Aunt had seen you in that dress," said Lev Nikolaevich smiling, looking at my white-and-mauve dress with the lilac ribbons fluttering from the shoulders. (This was the current fashion, known as "*suivez-moi*".)

"But why aren't you dancing?" I asked him.

"Oh, I'm too old for that," he said.

Some ladies and old men had been playing cards at two tables, and these were left open after all the visitors had left. The candles were burning down but we didn't go to bed, and Lev Nikolaevich kept us up with his lively talk. Then Maman said it was time for us to go to bed and firmly ordered us upstairs. We dared not disobey. But just as I was going out of the door, Lev Nikolaevich called to me:

"Wait a moment, Sofia Andreevna!"

"What is it?"

"Will you read what I'm going to write?"

"Very well."

"I'm only going to write the initials – you must guess the words."

"How can I do that – it's impossible! Oh well, go on!"

He brushed the games scores off the card table, took a piece of chalk and began writing. We were both very serious and excited. I followed his big red hand, and could feel all my powers of concentration and feeling focus on that bit of chalk and the hand that held it. We said nothing.

What the Chalk Wrote

"Y.y.&.n.f.h.t.v.r.m.o.m.a.&.i.f.h."

"Your youth and need for happiness too vividly remind me of my age and incapacity for happiness," I read out.

My heart was pounding, my temples were throbbing, my face was flushed – I was beyond all sense of time and reality; at that moment I felt capable of anything, of understanding everything, imagining the unimaginable.

"Well, let's go on," said Lev Nikolaevich and began to write once more:

"Y.f.h.t.w.i.a.m.&.y.s.L.Y.&.y.s.T.m.p.m."

"Your family has the wrong idea about me and your sister Liza. You and your sister Tanechka must protect me." I read the initials rapidly, without a second's hesitation.

Lev Nikolaevich wasn't even surprised; it all seemed quite natural somehow. Our elation was such that we soared high above the world and nothing could possibly surprise us.

Then we heard Maman crossly summoning me to bed. We hurriedly said goodnight, extinguished the candles and went out. Behind my cupboard upstairs I lit the stump of a candle, sat down on the floor, put my notebook on the wooden chair and began to write my diary. I wrote down the words to which Lev Nikolaevich had given me the initials, and grew vaguely aware that something of great significance had occurred between us – something we were now unable to stop. But for various reasons I curbed my thoughts and dreams, as though I was locking up everything that had taken place that evening, keeping back things that weren't yet ready to see the light.

When we left Ivitsy we called in at Yasnaya Polyana for the day. But we didn't have such fun this time. Maria Nikolaevna was leaving with us for Moscow, and from there she was going abroad, where she had left her children, and Aunt Tatyana, who adored her, was sad and silent. Maman seemed worried about something too, and Tanya and little Volodya were tired of travelling and longed to get home.

The Journey in the Annensky Coach

We ordered the Annensky coach from Tula, with its two seats at the back, rather like those of a covered cab, and four seats inside. We older girls were sorry to be leaving Yasnaya. We said goodbye to Aunt and her companion Natalya Petrovna, and looked for Lev Nikolaevich to say goodbye to him.

"I'm coming with you," he said cheerfully. "How could I stay in Yasnaya now? It will be so dull and miserable."

I didn't ask myself why I felt so happy, why everything was suddenly shining with joy. I ran off to announce the news to my mother and sisters, and it was decided that Lev Nikolaevich would travel the whole way on one of the outside seats at the back, and my sister Liza and I would take turns on the other; she would sit outside until the first stop, then I would take her place, and so on to Moscow.

We drove and drove... Towards evening I remember I began to get terribly sleepy. I was cold and wrapped myself up, blissfully happy to be sitting next to this old family friend whom I had loved all my life, the beloved author of *Childhood*, who was being so nice to me and whom I now liked even better. He told me wonderful long stories about the Caucasus, of his life there, the beautiful mountains, the wild scenery and his exploits. I loved listening to his steady voice, full of tender emotion and somewhat hoarse, as though coming from somewhere far away. I would nod off to sleep for a moment and wake to the sound of the same voice telling me his lovely poetic Caucasian tales. I felt ashamed of being sleepy, but I was still so young, and although I regretted missing some of his stories I couldn't help dozing off sometimes. We travelled all night. Everyone in the coach was asleep, although occasionally Maman and Maria Nikolaevna would talk together or little Volodya would squeak in his sleep.

At last we were approaching Moscow. At the final staging post it was again my turn to take my place on the back seat with Lev Nikolaevich. When we stopped, Liza came up to me and begged me to let her sit outside.

"Sonya, would you mind letting me sit outside? It's so stuffy in the coach!" she said.

We came out of the station and everyone took their seats. I climbed inside.

"Sofia Andreevna!" cried Lev Nikolaevich. "It's your turn to sit at the back!"

"I know, but I'm cold," I said evasively. And the carriage door slammed shut behind me.

Lev Nikolaevich stood and pondered for a moment, then climbed onto the box.

The next day Maria Nikolaevna went abroad and we left Moscow for our dacha in Pokrovskoe, where my father and brothers were waiting for us.

The Last Days of Girlhood and the Story

My entire life was different now. The surroundings were the same, the people were the same, I was the same – superficially. But I seemed to have lost all sense of who I was – I was still in the grip of those feelings that overwhelmed me at Yasnaya Polyana. My personal "I" was consumed in a limitless sense of space – free, all-powerful and unchecked. Those last days of my girlhood were extraordinarily intense, lit by a dazzling brightness and a sudden awakening of the soul. I have had this same sense of spiritual elation on two other occasions in my life, and it was these rare and extraordinary awakenings of the soul that have done more than anything else to convince me that it has an independent life of its own – that it is immortal, and it is when the body dies and it is liberated that it finds its freedom.

Having driven with us from Yasnaya Polyana to Moscow, Lev Nikolaevich rented rooms in the house of a German shoemaker and moved in there. At that time he was very involved with his school work* and with a magazine called *Yasnaya Polyana*, an educational publication intended for use in peasant schools. It lasted only one year.

Lev Nikolaevich visited us nearly every day in Pokrovskoe. Sometimes he would be driven back by my father, who often went to Moscow in connection with his work as a doctor. I remember Lev Nikolaevich once telling us he had visited the Petrovsky Park and called in at the royal palace, where he handed the aide-de-camp on duty a letter to Tsar Alexander II complaining about the insult he had suffered from the police, who had made a completely unwarranted search of Yasnaya Polyana.*

Lev Nikolaevich and I had long walks and talks together, and he once asked me if I kept a diary. I told him I had kept one for a long time, ever since I was eleven, and that last summer when I was sixteen I had also written a long story.

"Let me read your diaries," Lev Nikolaevich said.

"No, I couldn't do that."

"Well, let me see your story then."

So I gave him the story. The following morning I asked him if he had read it. He replied casually that he had glanced through it. But later I read in his diary the following entry: "She gave me her story to read. What a powerful sense of truth and simplicity!"* He also told me later that he hadn't slept all night, and had been disturbed by my verdict on the main character, Prince Dublitsky, in whom he had recognized himself, and of whom I had written: "The Prince was extraordinarily unattractive in appearance, and was always changing his opinions."

I remember we were once feeling very happy and playful, and I kept repeating: "When I am Tsarina I'll do such and such," or "When I am Tsarina I'll order such and such." Beneath the balcony stood my father's cabriolet, from which the grey horse had been unharnessed. I hopped inside and shouted, "When I am Tsarina I'll drive around in a cabriolet like this!" Lev Nikolaevich immediately stepped into the horse's place, seized the shafts and pulled me along at a brisk trot. "And I'm going to take my Tsarina for a drive!" he said.

"Do stop, please! It's much too heavy for you!" I cried, but I was loving it, and delighted to see how strong he was as he pulled me around.

What heavenly moonlit evenings and nights there were that year! I can still see the little glade at Pokrovskoe bathed in moonlight and the moon reflected in the nearby pond. There was something steely, fresh and bracing about those August nights... "Mad nights!" Lev Nikolaevich would say as we all sat on the balcony or strolled about the garden. There were no romantic scenes or confessions. We had known each other for so long. Our friendship was so simple and easy. And I was not in a hurry to end my free, serene, uncomplicated girlhood. Everything was wonderfully simple, I had no ambitions, no desires for the future.

Lev Nikolaevich kept coming to visit us. Sometimes when he stayed late my parents would make him spend the night with us. Once at the beginning of September we went to see him off, and when it was time to say goodbye my sister Liza asked me to invite him to her name-day party on 5th September. "Why does it have to be the 5th?" he said, and I didn't dare tell him, as I had been told not to mention the name day.

But Lev Nikolaevich promised to come, and to our great joy he kept his word. Things were always so jolly and interesting when he was there.

At first I didn't think his visits had anything to do with me. But gradually I began to realize that my feelings for him were growing serious. I remember I once ran upstairs in a state of great agitation to our bedroom, with its French window overlooking the pond and beyond it the church and all the things I had known and loved all my life (for I was born at Pokrovskoe). And as I stood at the window, my heart pounding, my sister Tanya came in and saw how agitated I was.

"What is it, Sonya?" she asked solicitously.

"*Je crains d'aimer le comte*,"* I said abruptly.

"Really?" Tanya was astonished, for she had had no suspicion of my feelings. She was even a little sad too, for she knew my character. For me "*aimer*" never meant playing with feelings. Both then and later it was something closer to suffering.

In Moscow

In September our whole family moved back to our apartment in Moscow in the Kremlin. As usual Moscow at first felt cramped, dull and stuffy to me after our country dacha, and this had a depressing effect on me. Before we left Pokrovskoe we always used to say goodbye to our favourite places and pay a brief visit to as many of them as possible. But that autumn I was really saying goodbye for the last time to Pokrovskoe, and to my girlhood as well.

In Moscow Lev Nikolaevich started his almost daily visits again. One evening I tiptoed into my mother's bedroom and slipped round the screen to her bed. Whenever we came home from a party or theatre, Maman would always cheerfully ask us, "Well, dear, what happened?" And I would give her a detailed account of everything or act out what I had seen at the theatre. But this time we were both rather glum.

"What is it, Sonya?" Maman asked.

"Well you see, Maman, everyone thinks Lev Nikolaevich will marry someone else, not me, but I'm sure it's me he loves," I said shyly.

For some reason Maman was furious and scolded me roundly.

"She's always thinking people are in love with her!" she raged. "Be off with you and stop thinking a lot of nonsense!"

My mother's response to my candid confession hurt me deeply, and I never mentioned Lev Nikolaevich again. My father was angry too that Lev Nikolaevich should visit us so often without proposing to his eldest daughter, as Russian tradition demanded, and he was cold to him and unkind to me. The atmosphere in our house became strained and awkward, especially for me.

On 14th September, Lev Nikolaevich said he had something very important to tell me, but couldn't manage to say it. It wasn't hard to guess what it was. He spoke to me that evening. I was playing the piano in the drawing room while he leant against the stove crying, "Go on playing! Go on playing!" the moment I stopped. The music prevented others from hearing what he said, and my hands trembled with excitement and my fingers stumbled over the keys as I played for practically the tenth time the same waltz, '*Il Bacio*', which I had learnt by heart to accompany Tanya's singing.

Lev Nikolaevich didn't actually propose then, and I don't remember exactly what he said. The gist of it though was that he loved me and wanted to marry me. It was all hints and allusions. But in his diary he wrote:

12th September 1862. I love her as I never thought it possible to love anyone. I'm mad, I'll shoot myself if it goes on much longer. They had a party. She is enchanting...

13th September. The minute I get up tomorrow I'll go there and tell her everything. Otherwise I'll shoot myself. It's almost 4 a.m. I've written her a letter and will give it to her tomorrow, i.e. today, the 14th. My God, I'm terrified of dying! Help me!

Another day passed, and on Saturday, 16th September, my brother Sasha and his cadet friends arrived. We had tea in the dining room and fed the hungry cadets, and Lev Nikolaevich spent the whole day with us. Then, choosing a moment when no one's eyes were on us, he called me into my mother's room, which was empty at the time, and said: "I wanted to say something to you, but haven't been able to, so here is a letter I've been carrying around in my pocket for several days now. Please read it, and I'll wait here for your answer."

The Proposal

I seized the letter and tore downstairs to the bedroom I shared with my two sisters. This is what the letter said:

Sofia Andreevna, I can bear it no longer. Every day for the past three weeks I've been saying to myself: "Today I'll tell her everything", yet I always leave with the same feelings of sadness, fear and joy in my heart. And every night, as now, I relive what has happened and torture myself – why didn't I speak to you? And if I had, what would I have said? I am taking this letter with me in case it's again impossible for me to speak to you, or my courage fails me. Your family has the wrong idea about me – they imagine I am in love with your sister Liza. They are wrong. I cannot get your story out of my head, because when I read it I clearly realized that, like Prince Dublitsky, I have no business to be dreaming of happiness, that you need an exceptional, poetic kind of love. I am not jealous and shall not be jealous of the man you fall in love with. I thought I could love all of you, like children. At Ivitsy I wrote: "Your presence reminds me too vividly of my old age." But then as now I was lying to myself. Then I might still have been able to tear myself away and return to the monastery of solitary labour and interesting work. But now I can do nothing, for I feel I have created havoc in your household and forfeited the simple straightforward feelings of friendship you once felt for me as a good and honest man. I cannot leave and I dare not stay. You are an honest person. With your hand on your heart and without hurrying (for God's sake don't hurry!) tell me what to do. There's no joy without sorrow. I would have laughed myself sick a month ago if I'd been told one could suffer as I have been suffering, gladly, this past month. Tell me, as an honest person, do you want to be my wife? If you can say yes with your whole heart, boldly, then say yes. Otherwise, if you have the faintest shadow of doubt in your heart, it's best to say no. For God's sake think about it carefully. I am terrified of hearing a "no", but am prepared for it and shall have the strength to endure it. What terrifies me much more is the idea that I shall not be loved as much as I love you!

I didn't read the letter all the way through, I merely skimmed through it to the words: "Do you want to be my wife?" I was on my way upstairs to say yes to Lev Nikolaevich when I ran into my sister Liza in the doorway, who asked me: "Well, what happened?"

"*Le comte m'a fait la proposition,*"* I answered hurriedly. Then my mother came in and realized at once what had happened. Taking me firmly by the shoulders she turned me towards the door and said: "Go to him and give him your answer."

I flew up the stairs on wings, tore past the dining room and drawing room and rushed into my mother's bedroom. Lev Nikolaevich stood in the corner, leaning against the wall, waiting for me. I went to him and he seized both my hands.

"Well, what is the answer?" he asked.

"Yes – of course," I replied.

Within a few moments everyone in the house knew what had happened and was coming in to congratulate us.

My Name Day and Engagement

The next day, 17th September, was my name day. All our Moscow friends and relatives came to congratulate us and were told of our engagement. When the old university professor who came to teach my sisters and me French heard that I and not Liza was going to marry Lev Nikolaevich, he said naively: "*C'est dommage que cela ne fût Mlle Lise; elle a si bien étudié.*"*

But little Katya Obolenskaya threw her arms around me and said: "I'm so glad you're going to marry such a splendid man and writer."

My betrothal lasted only a week, from the 16th to the 23rd September. During this time I was taken round the shops, where I unenthusiastically tried on dresses, underwear and hats. Lev Nikolaevich visited every day, and one day he brought me his diaries. I remember how shattered I was by these diaries, which out of an excess of honesty he made me read before our wedding. It was very wrong of him to do this; I wept when I saw what his past had been.

The week passed like a bad dream. For many people my wedding was a sad event, and Lev Nikolaevich was in a terrible hurry to get it over. Maman said I would have to have at least some essential garments made before the wedding, if not the whole trousseau.

"She's got enough clothes," said Lev Nikolaevich. "She looks very smart too."

She managed to get one or two things hastily made for me, including the dress for my wedding, which was set for 23rd September at 7 in the evening, at the Palace Church in the Kremlin. At our house everyone was rushing about getting ready, and Lev Nikolaevich had a mass of things to see to. He bought a magnificent *dormeuse*,* ordered photographs to be taken of everyone in my family and presented me with a diamond brooch. He also had his own photograph taken, which I had begged him to have fitted into a golden bracelet my father had given me. But I didn't get a great deal of pleasure from the dresses or presents – I wasn't interested, I was too wrapped up in my love for Lev Nikolaevich and the fear of losing him. These fears have never left me; they have remained in my heart throughout my life, although thank God we have kept our love for each other intact throughout 48 years of marriage.

When we discussed our future together, Lev Nikolaevich said I should choose where I would like to live after the wedding. We could stay on with my parents in Moscow for a bit, we could go abroad or we could go straight to Yasnaya Polyana. I said I wanted to go to Yasnaya Polyana, and start a proper family life *at home* straight away. And I could see that he liked this very much.

The Wedding

It was 23rd September at last, the day of the wedding. I didn't see Lev Nikolaevich all day, but he dropped in for a moment. We sat down together on our valises and he started tormenting me, questioning me and doubting my love for him. The thought occurred to me that he wanted to run away, and might have had sudden doubts about the marriage.* I started to cry, and at that moment my mother came in and pounced on him: "Well, you've chosen a fine time to make her cry," she said. "Today is her wedding day, it's hard enough for her as it is and she's got a long journey ahead of her, and look at her crying her eyes out." Lev Nikolaevich looked very penitent, and went off to dine with the Perfilevs, his wedding sponsors, who would bless him and take him to the church. He had asked Timiryazev to be his best man, as his brother Sergei had gone to Yasnaya Polyana to get things ready and would be meeting us there.

From Lev Nikolaevich's side of the family was his aunt Pelageya Yushkova. She was to drive to the church with me and my little brother Volodya, who carried the icon.

Just before seven that evening, my sisters and friends began to dress me. I begged them not to call the hairdresser, as I wanted to do my own hair, and the girls pinned on the flowers and the long tulle veil. The dress was also tulle, and in the current fashion – very open at the neck and shoulders. It was so thin, light and airy, it seemed to envelop me like a cloud. My thin, childish unformed arms and shoulders looked pitifully bony. I was soon ready, and we now had to wait for the best man to come and tell us the bridegroom was in the church. An hour or more passed, and no one came. It flashed through my mind that he had run away – he had been so odd that morning. But then who should appear but cross-eyed little Alexei Stepanovich, his valet, who rushed in looking very agitated and asked us to open the suitcase immediately and get out a clean shirt. In all the preparations for the wedding and the journey they had apparently forgotten to leave one out! Someone had been sent to buy one, but it was Sunday and all the shops were closed. Another age elapsed while they took the shirt back to the bridegroom and he put it on and went to the church. Then began the farewells, the tears and the sobs, and I felt distraught.

"How will we manage without our little Countess!" my old nurse kept saying over and over again. (She always called me that, probably in memory of my grandmother, Countess Sofia Zavadovskaya, after whom I had been named.)

"I'll die of grief without you," my sister Tanya said.

My little brother Petya just gazed at me despairingly with his sad black eyes. Maman avoided me and bustled about preparing the wedding supper. Everyone was plunged in gloom by the impending separation.

Father wasn't well. I went to say goodbye to him in his study, and he seemed deeply moved. They prepared bread and salt, Maman took down the icon of St Sofia the martyr, and with her brother, my uncle Mikhail, standing beside her, she blessed me with it.

We all drove in solemn silence to the Palace Church of the Virgin Birth, which was just a moment away from our apartment in the Kremlin. I was sobbing all the way. The winter garden and the church were magnificently lit up. Lev Nikolaevich met me in the garden, took me by the hand and walked me to the doors of the church, where we were met by the priest. He took both our hands in his and led us to the altar. The palace choir was singing, two priests conducted the service, and everything was very solemn and splendid. All the guests were assembled, and there were a great many strangers, palace employees mostly. They all remarked on my extreme youth and tear-stained eyes.

Lev Nikolaevich has described our wedding beautifully in his account of Levin and Kitty's wedding in his novel *Anna Karenina*. Not only did he paint a brilliantly imaginative picture of the ceremony, he also described the whole psychological process taking place in Levin's heart. As for me, I had already had so much excitement over the past few days that I experienced absolutely nothing as I stood at the altar. I just felt as though something obvious and inevitable was happening, as though it couldn't be otherwise, and there was no point in questioning it.

My best men were my brother Sasha and his friend P.,* a former Guards officer with him.

The ceremony ended, everyone congratulated us, and Lev Nikola-evich and I drove home together, just the two of us. He was being very affectionate to me and seemed happy... At home in the Kremlin they had prepared the usual wedding feast – champagne, fruit, sweets and so on. There were a few guests – just close friends and relatives.

Then I had to change into my travelling dress. Our old chambermaid Varvara, who my father's friend the waggish Doctor Anke had named the "Oyster", was coming with me, and bustled about with Lev Nikolaevich's valet finishing the packing.

The Departure and Send-off

The postilion brought round six mail horses, which were harnessed to the brand new *dormeuse* Lev Nikolaevich had bought, gleaming black trunks were buckled and strapped to the top of the carriage, and Lev Nikolaevich was impatient to be off.

I had an agonizing lump in my throat and was choking with sadness. For the first time I suddenly realized I was actually leaving my family and everyone I had loved in my life *for ever*. But I struggled to control my tears. Then the farewells started. It was frightful! I broke down and sobbed when I said goodbye to my sick father. When I kissed Liza goodbye I stared into her eyes and she too was in tears. Tanya howled like a child, and so did Petya, who had drunk too much champagne in order to dull the sadness and had to be taken to bed. I then went downstairs and made the sign of the cross over my two-year-old little brother Vyacheslav, who was sound asleep, and said goodbye to my nurse, Vera Ivanovna, who sobbed and hugged me, kissing my face and shoulders, then kissing me all over. Stepanida Trifonovna, a reserved old lady who had lived with us for over thirty-five years, politely wished me much happiness.

These were the last moments. I had deliberately kept the final farewell with my mother to the very end, and just before getting into the carriage, I flung myself into her arms and we both sobbed. Those tears of parting expressed our mutual gratitude for all the love and kindness we had given each other, forgiveness for the pain we had unwittingly caused, my sorrow at parting with my beloved mother, and her motherly wish that I should be happy.

At last I managed to tear myself away from her and took my seat in the carriage without looking back. I shall never forget the piercing cry she uttered then; it seemed to have been torn from her heart.

The autumn rain was pouring down, and the puddles reflected the dull glow of the street lights and carriage lamps, which had just been lit. The horses were stamping impatiently and the ones in front with the postilion were straining to be off. Lev Nikolaevich slammed the carriage door shut, his valet Alexei Stepanovich jumped onto the back seat, and old Varvara the "Oyster" got up beside him. The horse's hooves splashed through the puddles, and we were off. I sat crouched in the corner, wretched and exhausted, and wept uncontrollably. Lev Nikolaevich seemed puzzled and dismayed. He had never had a real family and had grown up without a father or mother, and as a man he couldn't understand what I was feeling. He said he could see I didn't love him if it hurt me so much to leave my family. What he didn't realize then was that if I was capable of such passionate love for my family, I would later transfer this love to him and our children. Which is exactly what happened.

We left the city and it became dark and frightening. I had never travelled anywhere in autumn or winter before, and found the darkness and lack of street lights terribly dispiriting. We barely spoke a word until we reached the first stop, Birulevo I think it was. I remember Lev Nikolaevich was particularly gentle and considerate to me. When we arrived at Birulevo, a young couple, titled, in a brand-new *dormeuse* driven by six horses, we were given the royal suite. The rooms were large, bare and cheerless, with red damask upholstery. They brought in the samovar and made tea. I huddled in a corner on the sofa and sat there silently, as if condemned to death.

"Come now, you must be mistress and pour the tea," said Lev Nikolaevich.

I obeyed and we had tea, and I felt terribly bashful and nervous. I simply couldn't bring myself to change to the "thou" form, as he had done, and avoided calling him anything at all; I addressed him by the formal "you" for a long time afterwards too.

Our Arrival at Yasnaya Polyana

The journey from Moscow to Yasnaya Polyana took just under twenty-four hours, and we reached our home the following evening, to my great joy. It felt so strange – I was *at home*, and home was now Yasnaya Polyana.

The first person I saw as I went up the steps of the house where I would spend the next half-century of my life was Aunt Tatyana, holding up the icon of the Blessed Virgin Mary, and Sergei Nikolaevich, my brother-in-law, standing beside her with the bread and salt. I bowed to their feet, made the sign of the cross and kissed first the icon, then Aunt Tatyana. Lev Nikolaevich did likewise. That day was the start of my life in Yasnaya Polyana, where I lived almost uninterruptedly for the first eighteen years of my marriage.

Lev Nikolaevich wrote in his diary: "*25th September 1862*. Unbelievable happiness! Is it possible that this will last all our lives?"

Various Notes for Future Reference, and Remarks Made by L.N. Tolstoy on His Writing

20th November 1873. L.N. has been describing to me the way he got some of the ideas for his novel *Anna Karenina*:

"I was sitting downstairs in my study, examining the white silk embroidery on the sleeve of my dressing gown, and I thought how beautiful it was. And then I wondered how it occurred to people to invent all these designs and decorations and embroideries, and I realized there was a whole world of fashion and ideas and hard work that make up women's lives, and women are so fascinated by all this. And it naturally led my thoughts about the novel to Anna, and suddenly this piece of embroidery on my sleeve suggested a whole chapter to me. Anna is cut off from all the joys of this side of a woman's life, for she is alone, other women spurn her and she has no one to talk to about all the ordinary, everyday things that interest them."

21st November 1876. He came up to me and said: "This bit of writing is so tedious!"

"Why?" I asked.

"Well, you see, I've said Vronsky and Anna were staying in the same hotel room, but that's not possible. In St Petersburg, at least, they'd have had to take rooms on different floors. So as you see, this means all the scenes and conversations will have to take place in two separate places, and all the various visitors will have to see them separately. So it will all have to be altered."

3rd March 1877. Yesterday L.N. went to his table, pointed at his notebook of writing and said: "Oh, how I long to finish this novel (*Anna Karenina*) and start something new. My ideas are quite clear now. If a work is to be really good there must be one fundamental idea in it that one loves. So in *Anna Karenina*, I love the idea of the *family*; in *War and Peace* I loved the idea of the *people*, because of the 1812 war; and now I see very clearly that in my next book I shall love the idea of the Russian people's *powers of expansion*." These powers are demonstrated for Lev Nikolaevich by the constant migration of

Russians to the new lands of South-east Siberia, Southern Russia, the Belaya River region, Tashkent and so on.

One hears a great deal about theses migrants at present. Last summer when we were staying in Samara, the two of us drove out to a Cossack settlement ten miles from the farm where we were staying, and on the way we passed a whole string of carts with several families and numerous children and old men, all looking very cheerful. We stopped and asked them where they were going. "We are travelling from Voronezh to the new lands," they said. "Our people went out to the Amur region some time back, and now they have written telling us to join them there."

Lev Nikolaevich was fascinated by this. And just the other day at the railway station he heard of a hundred or more Tambov peasants leaving to settle in Siberia on their own initiative. They crossed the steppe and finally reached the Irtysh River. There they were told that the land belonged to the Kirghiz people, and they couldn't settle there, so they went on a little further.

This is the idea for his next book, as I understand it anyway, and around this main idea he is gathering new facts and characters, many of which are still quite unclear, even to him.

25th August [1877]. L.N. has gone to Moscow to find a Russian tutor for the children.* His religious faith is becoming firmer with every day that passes. He says his prayers every day now as he did when he was a child, and on every holy day he goes to matins, where all the peasants crowd round him and question him about the war.* On Wednesdays and Fridays he fasts, speaks constantly of the spirit of humility and won't let anyone speak ill of others, stopping them half-jokingly if they do. On 26th July he visited the Optina Pustyn Monastery and was much impressed by the monks' wisdom, culture and way of life.*

Yesterday he said: "My mental valve has been unblocked, but I have a terrible headache." He is very upset about all our reserves in the war with Turkey and the situation at home, and he spent all yesterday morning writing about it. That evening he told me he realized the best way to express his ideas would be in a letter to the Tsar.* By all means let him write it, but it's a risky way to express himself and he mustn't send it.

26th December [1877]. At three in the morning on 6th December, our son Andrei was born. This seemed to release L.N.'s mind from its mental shackles, and a week ago he started writing some new religious, philosophical work in a large bound volume. I haven't read it yet, but today he was saying to my brother Styopa: "The purpose of the work I'm writing is to demonstrate the absolute necessity for religion."*

I like the argument he puts forward in favour of Christianity and against all the socialists and communists, who believe that social laws are higher than Christian laws, so I am going to record it. It goes like this:

"If it hadn't been for the teachings of Christianity, which over the centuries have taken root in us and laid the basis of our entire social life, there would have been no laws of morality and honour, no desire for equality, goodness and a fair distribution of the earth's blessings, which is what people live for."

31st January 1881. Feeling that his knowledge of the Russian language was far from perfect, L.N. decided this summer to set himself the task of studying the language of the people. He had long talks with the pilgrims, holy wanderers and others he met on the highway, and jotted down in his notebook all the popular words, proverbs and ideas he was hearing for the first time. This had some unexpected results.

Until about 1877, his religious feelings were vague, or rather indifferent. He was never an outright unbeliever, but nor was he a very *committed* believer. This caused him terrible anxieties (he actually wrote a religious confession at the beginning of his new work).

But from this close contact with the people, he became deeply impressed by their lucid, unshakeable faith, and terrified by his lack of it, and he resolved wholeheartedly to follow the same path. He started going to church, keeping the fasts, saying his prayers and observing all the laws of the Church. This continued for some time.

But soon he came to see that the source of all this goodness, patience and love that he had witnessed in the people was not the Church and its teachings; as he himself said, having seen the *rays* he followed them to the *light*, and discovered that this was Christianity itself, through the Gospels. He persistently denies any other influence. I shall quote his own words on this: "Christianity lives unconsciously but securely in the spirit and traditions of the people." That is what he says.

Little by little, L.N. saw to his horror what a discrepancy there was between Christianity and the Church. He saw that the Church, hand in hand with the government, had conspired against Christianity. The Church thanks God for the men killed in battle and prays for military victories, yet in the Old Testament it says: "Thou shalt not kill", and in the Gospels: "Love thy neighbour as thyself." The Church demands an oath of allegiance, yet Christ tells us not to take the Lord's name in vain. The Church has given people a lot of rites and rituals which are supposed to assure their salvation, but have been an obstacle to Christianity; its true teachings about God's kingdom on earth have been obscured, because people have been forced to believe that they will be saved by baptism, communion, fasting and the like.

This is L.N.'s current preoccupation. He has begun to study, translate and interpret the Gospels.* He has been working on this for two years now, and it seems to be only half-finished. But his soul is now happy, he says. He has seen the *light* (in his words), and this light has illuminated his whole view of the world. His attitude to people has changed too; according to him, whereas before he had just a small circle of *intimates*, people like *him*, he now has millions of men as his brothers. Before, his wealth and his estate were his *own* – now if a poor man asks him for something he must have it.

He sits at his work every day, surrounded by books, and toils away until dinner-time. His health is deteriorating, he suffers from headaches, his hair is turning grey and he lost a lot of weight over the winter.

He doesn't appear to be as happy as I should wish, and has become quiet, meditative and taciturn. We almost never see those cheerful exuberant moods of his, which used to enchant us all so much. I put this down to excessive overwork and exhaustion. How unlike the old days, when he was writing about the hunt and the ball in *War and Peace*, and looked as joyful and excited as though he himself was joining in the fun. His soul is in a state of calm clarity, but he suffers deeply for all the human misery and poverty he sees around him, for all those in jail, all the hatred, injustice and oppression in the world – and this deeply affects his impressionable soul and undermines his happiness.

Why Anna Karenina Was Called "Anna", and What Suggested the Idea of Her Suicide

We have a neighbour here, a landowner of about 50, neither rich nor educated, called Alexander Bibikov. He had living with him a distant cousin of his late wife, an unmarried woman of about 35 who looked after the house and children and was his mistress. One day Bibikov hired a new governess for his son and niece, a beautiful German woman, with whom he soon fell in love, and to whom before long he proposed marriage. His former mistress, whose name was *Anna Stepanovna*, left the house to visit Tula for the day, saying she was going to see her mother, but she returned from there with a bundle of clothes under her arm (containing nothing but a change of clothes and some underwear), to Yasenki, the nearest railway station, and there she jumped on the tracks and threw herself under a goods train. There was a post-mortem, and Lev Nikolaevich attended, and saw her lying there at the Yasenki barracks, her skull smashed in and her naked body frightfully mutilated. It had the most terrible effect on him. Anna Stepanovna was a tall, plump woman with a typically Russian temperament and appearance. She had dark hair and grey eyes, and although she wasn't beautiful she was very pleasant-looking.*

The Death of Vanechka

A few days before Vanechka's death he astonished me by giving away all his things. He put little labels on everything, addressed in his own hand: "With love to Masha from Vanya", or "To Simeon Nikolaevich our cook, from Vanya" and so on. He took all the little framed pictures off the walls of his nursery and took them to his brother Misha's room; he had always been terribly fond of Misha. Then he asked me for a hammer and nails, and hung up the pictures in his brother's room. He was so fond of Misha that if they had a quarrel and Misha didn't make it up with him immediately, he would be desperately unhappy and would weep bitterly. Whether Misha loved him as much I don't know, but he did call his eldest son after him later.

Shortly before he died, Vanechka was looking out of the window, when he suddenly looked very thoughtful: "Maman, is Alyosha" (Alyosha was my little son who had died) "an angel now?" he asked.

"Why, yes," I told him. "It's said that children who die before they are seven turn into angels."

To which he replied: "Well, I had better die too, before I am seven. It will be my seventh birthday soon, but I may still be an angel yet. And if I don't, dear, dear Maman, please will you let me fast so I won't have any sins?"

Those words of his engraved themselves in my mind. On 20th February, my daughter Masha and Nurse took him to the clinic, where they had made an appointment with Professor Filatov. They all looked so cheerful and excited when they got back, and Vanechka told me with great glee that he had been told he might eat whatever he wanted and could go out walking and even driving. After lunch he took a walk with Sasha, and afterwards he ate a hearty dinner. We had all been through such agony while he was ill, and now the whole house cheered up again. Tanya and Masha, who had no children of their own, lavished all their maternal affection on their little brother.

On the evening of the 20th, Sasha and Vanechka asked their sister Masha to read them the children's version of Dickens's *Great Expectations*, which was called *The Convict's Daughter*. When it was time to go to bed he came to say goodnight to me. I was touched by the sad weary look in his eyes and asked him about the book Masha had been reading to them.

"Oh, don't talk about it, Maman, it's all so sad! You see Estella doesn't marry Pip in the end!"

We went downstairs to the nursery together, and he yawned, then with tears in his eyes he said sadly: "Oh, Maman, it's back again, that, that… temperature."

I took his temperature and it was 38.5°. He said his eyes were aching and I thought it must be an attack of measles. When I realized he was ill again, I burst into tears, and seeing me cry he said: "Don't cry, Maman, don't cry. It's God's will."

Not long before this he had asked me to explain the Lord's Prayer to him, and I explained "Thy Will Be Done" with special feeling. Then he asked me to finish reading a Grimms' story we hadn't finished – the one about the crow as far as I recall. Then Misha came into the nursery, and I went off to my bedroom. I later learnt that Vanechka had said to Misha, "I know I am dying now."

He was very feverish all night, but managed to sleep. Next morning we sent for Doctor Filatov, who said straight away it was scarlet fever. His temperature was 40°, and he had pains in his stomach and violent diarrhoea. (Scarlet fever is often complicated by a distemper of the bowels.)

At 3 in the morning he woke up, looked at me and said: "Forgive me, dear Maman, for keeping you awake."

"I've had my sleep, darling," I said. "We're all taking it in turns to sit with you."

"Whose turn is it next, Tanya's?"

"No dear, it's Masha's."

"Call Masha then, and go to bed."

How lovingly my darling little boy sent me away. He hugged me to him tightly and pressed his dry little lips to mine, tenderly kissing me again and again.

"Is anything hurting you?" I asked him.

"No, nothing's hurting," he said.

"Just miserable?"

"Yes, just miserable."

He never regained consciousness properly after that. The next day his temperature went up to 42°. Filatov wrapped him in blankets soaked with mustard water, and laid him in a warm bath – but it was no good, his little head hung helplessly to one side as if he were dead, then his little hands and feet grew cold. He opened his eyes once more, with a look of pure astonishment, then grew still. It was 11 at night on 23rd February.

My husband Lyovochka led me into Tanya's room and we both sat on the couch together, and I leant my head on his chest and lost consciousness. We were both half-dead with grief.

My daughter Masha and Lyovochka's sister Maria Nikolaevna the nun were with him during the final moments and were praying for him constantly. I was later told that Nurse, maddened with grief, lay on her bed sobbing. Tanya kept running in and out of the nursery.

When Vanechka had been dressed in his little white shirt and his long, fair curly hair had been brushed, Lyovochka and I plucked up the courage to go back to the nursery. He was lying on the couch. I laid an icon on his little chest, and someone lit a wax candle and put it at his head.

Everyone had loved our Vanechka, and before long news of his death had spread to our friends and relatives. They all sent masses of flowers and wreaths and the nursery soon looked like a garden. No one worried about the risk of infection. Dear kind Sapho Martynova, who had four children of her own, came straight away and wept passionately and grieved with us. And we all seemed to cling together in our love for our poor Vanechka. Maria Nikolaevna stayed with us and gave us religious consolation, and Lev Nikolaevich's diary records the cry of his heart: "*26th February*. We have buried Vanechka. It is frightful! No, not frightful, a great spiritual experience. I thank Thee, Father."

On the third day, 25th February, Vanechka's funeral service was held. The lid of his little coffin was hammered down, and at twelve o'clock his father, his brothers and Pavel Biryukov carried it out of the house and set it on our large four-seated sledge. My husband and I sat facing each other and we slowly moved off, accompanied by our friends.

I later described Vanechka's death and funeral in a letter to my sister: "And you know Tanya, all through Vanechka's funeral service I didn't shed a single tear, just held his cold little head between my hands and tried to warm his little cheeks with my lips. I don't know now why I didn't die of quiet. But although I am weeping as I write to you, I shall go on living, and for a long time too I expect, with this sorrow in my heart."

Lyovochka and I silently bore off our beloved youngest child, our brightest hope, to be buried. And as we approached the Pokrovskoe cemetery, near the village of Nikolaevich, where he was to be buried beside his little brother Alyosha, Lyovochka recalled how he used to drive along that road to our dacha in Pokrovskoe after he had first fallen in love with me. He wept and caressed me and spoke so tenderly, and his love meant so much to me.

The Burial

We found crowds of people at the cemetery, both villagers and people who had travelled there to attend the funeral. It was Sunday, and the schoolchildren were walking around the village admiring all the wreaths and flowers.

The little coffin was again lifted from the sledge by Lev Nikolaevich and our sons. Everyone wept to see the father, so old, bent and bowed with grief. Many of our friends came to the funeral, as well as members of our family – Manya Rachinskaya, Sonya Mamonova, Kolya Obolensky, Sapho Martynova, Vera Severtseva, Vera Tolstaya and many more. They all sobbed loudly.

When they lowered the coffin into the grave I again lost consciousness, as if I too were disappearing into the earth. They told me afterwards that Ilyusha had tried to shield me from the dreadful pit, and someone else held my arms. Lyovochka embraced me and held me to him, and I stood there with him for a long time in a stunned state.

I was brought back to my senses by the happy shouts of the village children. I had asked Nurse to hand out sweets and cakes to them, and they were laughing, dropping gingerbread and eating it off the ground. Then I remembered how Vanechka had loved to celebrate and hand out sweets, and I burst into tears for the first time since his death.

Immediately after the funeral, when everyone had left, Kasatkin the artist arrived and made two sketches of the fresh grave. He offered one to me and the other to Tanya, with a most moving, poetic letter expressing his love for Vanechka, who he described as "transparent".

We returned, bereft, to our deserted house, and I remember Lev Nikolaevich sitting down on the sofa in the dining room downstairs (where it had been put for our son Lyova, who had also been ill), and bursting into tears, saying: "I always thought that of all my sons Vanechka would carry on my good work on earth after I died."

And a little later he said almost the same thing: "And I had dreamt of Vanechka carrying on God's work after me. Well, there's nothing to be done now."

The sight of Lyovochka's suffering was even more painful to me than my own. I wrote to my sister Tanya: "Lyovochka has grown bent and old. He wanders sadly about the house, with his eyes full of tears, as though the last ray of sunshine in his old age had been extinguished. Two days after Vanechka's death he sat down and sobbed: 'For the first time in my life I have lost hope.'"

Of all our children Vanechka looked most like him, with the same bright, penetrating eyes, the same earnest, searching mind. Once I was combing his curly hair in front of the mirror and he turned his little face to me and said with a smile: "Maman, I really do look like Papa, don't I!"

After the Funeral

The first night after Vanechka's death I jumped out of bed in terror, hallucinating the most fearful smell. It pursued me for a long time afterwards, even though my husband, who was sleeping with me, assured me there was no smell and I had just imagined it. Then I would suddenly hear Vanechka's dear gentle voice. He and I used to say our prayers together and make the sign of the cross over each other. "Kiss me hard, Maman," he would say. "Put your head beside mine, and breathe on my chest so I can fall asleep with your warm breath on me."

There is no love so strong, so pure or so good as the love of a mother and child. With Vanechka's death the dear little nursery life in our house came to an end. Sasha was inconsolable without her playmate and wandered sadly around on her own. She was wild and unsociable by nature, whereas Vanechka loved people; he loved writing letters and giving presents, he loved organizing treats and celebrations, and how many people loved him!

Even cold Menshikov wrote: "When I saw your little son I was sure he would either die or live to be an even greater genius than his father."

I had many, many wonderful letters from people who wrote to sympathize or remember Vanechka. N.N. Strakhov wrote to Lev Nikolaevich: "He promised much – maybe he would have inherited not only your name but your fame. What a lovely child – words cannot describe him."

The writer Zhirkevich wrote to Lev Nikolaevich: "Without knowing either you or Vanechka, a St Petersburg writer is writing a passionate article about this wonderful little creature who offered us all so much hope. Mothers and fathers everywhere share your grief, and my voice is drowned in a chorus of condolences."

Peshkova-Toliverova, who had published Vanechka's story in her magazine *The Toy*,* wrote: "He stands before me now, a pale modest little boy with enquiring eyes." Our old friend Prince Urusov soothed me with his comforting assurances about the blessed state of Vanechka's soul in paradise. And he believed this so earnestly, for he was a very religious and Orthodox man, that I found his faith infectious.

Many people prayed for Vanechka and for us two, in churches and homes. Many parents sympathized with us, particularly those who had lost children of their own, such as Countess Alexandra (née Kapnist), who had lost her only little girl, Baroness Mengden whose two grown-up sons had died, and others.

I wrote to my sister: "I try to console myself with the thought that my sufferings are necessary if I am to pass into eternity, purify my soul and be united with God and Vanechka, who was all joy and love. 'Thy will be done!' I cry. If this will bring me closer to eternity, so be it. Yet despite these lofty spiritual aspirations, and my sincere and heartfelt desire to submit to God's will, there's no consolation for me in this or anything else."

For some reason Lev Nikolaevich refused to believe in my religious activities. It annoyed him that I kept visiting churches, monasteries and cathedrals. I remember spending nine hours once in the Arkhangelsk Cathedral during Lent, standing up during the services, then sitting on the steps with the pilgrims and old women. There was another educated woman there too, who had just lost her grown-up son, and like me was seeking comfort in prayer in the house of God.

Returning from the Kremlin one day to our house in Moscow in Khamovniki Street, I got soaked in the rain, caught a bad chill and was ill in bed for a long time. Before this Sasha and I had been fasting, and all this was evidently not to Lev Nikolaevich's liking. He wrote in his diary: "*27th March 1895*. Sonya is suffering as much as before, and is incapable of rising to a religious level. The reason is that she has put all her spiritual energies into her animal love for her child."*

Why *animal* love? I have had many children, but my feelings for Vanechka and my love for him were fundamentally spiritual in nature. We lived in spiritual communion with each other, we always understood each other, and despite the difference in our ages we always spoke on a lofty, abstract plane.

But Lev Nikolaevich was very sweet to me then too.* I remember he once asked me if I would go and visit his sister Mashenka on her name day, 25th March, and we both tried to decide what to give her as a present. I remembered she said she would like an alarm clock to wake her up for church services, so we both went out and bought one, and she was delighted with it, and with our visit.

Another time, I remember he invited me out to the market to buy flowers for Palm Saturday, pretending he wanted to buy some books to take to the prison. He thought this would divert me. I bought a lot of artificial white flowers and white lilac which I have kept to this day, which now hangs over the big portrait of Vanechka.

Notes

1862

p. 3, *The whole... accept it*: Before Tolstoy's marriage he gave his fiancée his old diaries to read, as he did not want to conceal anything of his past from her. Reading them made a terrible impression on the eighteen-year-old Sofia Behrs. (See Appendix: 'L.N. Tolstoy's Marriage', pp. 499–516.)

p. 7, *Auntie*: Tatyana Ergolskaya, Tolstoy's aunt and guardian, lived with him at Yasnaya Polyana.

p. 7, *his "people"... live like that*: This entry reveals her attitude towards Tolstoy's "educational activities" with the peasants. In her view, family life should have banished all other interests. Tolstoy wrote in his diary: "All this time I have been busy with nothing but practical matters. But I now find this idleness oppressive. I cannot respect myself. And this makes me dissatisfied with myself and confused in my relations with others. I have decided to finish with my diary, and, I think, with the schools too. I am constantly angry, with my life, and sometimes even with her." But Tolstoy himself always described this time as a very "happy time in my life".

p. 8, *In love... how frightful*: Evidently she had either been rereading or was recalling Tolstoy's reference in his diary, on 13th May 1858, to the Yasnaya Polyana peasant woman Axinya Bazykina: "I am in love, as never before!" Tolstoy portrayed her in his stories 'Idyll' and 'Tikhon and Malanya', and in the long story, 'Devil'.

1863

p. 9, *Never in my life have I felt so wretched with remorse*: She is evidently referring to harsh words spoken by her in a quarrel the day before. Tolstoy refers to it in an entry of 8th January: "This morning it was her dress. She called for me, wanting me to criticize it, which I did – and then there were tears and trite explanations."

p. 10, *Moscow*: On 23rd December 1862, the Tolstoys went to Moscow. They took rooms in the Hotel Chevriet, on Gazetny Street, and stayed there until 8th February 1863. During their visit to Moscow they paid almost daily visits to the Kremlin to see the Behrs.

p. 10, *A.*: Axinya Bazykina (see note to p. 8).

p. 12, *I read his diary and it made me happy*: She was reading Tolstoy's diary from 3rd January to 3rd March 1863. On 23rd February he noted: "I love her more and more."

p. 13, *V.A.*: She was reading his letters to V.V. Arseneva, whom he was planning to marry between 1856 and 1857. In his letters to her he depicted in detail their future family life together and he called himself

Khrapovitsky and her Dembitskaya. This love affair was reflected in the story 'Family Happiness'.

p. 13, *He seems to think... interests him*: At this time Tolstoy was planning to build a distillery with his neighbour, Alexander Bibikov, who owned the estate at Telyatinki. In May 1863 a small distillery started operating, but only existed for eighteen months.

p. 14, *I want to go out... on the estate*: In a letter to her sister of 13th February 1863, she wrote: "We are turning into complete landowners: we buy cattle and poultry, pigs and calves. Come here and I'll show you. We're buying bees from the Islenevs. You can eat the honey, I don't like it."

p. 14, *V.V.*: The identity of "V.V." isn't known.

p. 16, *the baby*: On 28th June 1863, the Tolstoys' son Sergei was born. "I suffered for a whole day, it was terrible," she recalled. "Lyovochka was with me all the time and felt very sorry for me; he was so loving, and his eyes shone with tears, and he kept wiping my forehead with a handkerchief dipped in eau de Cologne. There was another hour of agony, and at two in the morning of 28th June I was delivered of my first-born. Lev Nikolaevich sobbed loudly, clasping my head and kissing me."

p. 16, *He cannot run... restless*: On 18th June 1863, he wrote in his diary: "I am petty and worthless. And I have been so ever since I married the woman I love. I have irrevocably destroyed, in an orgy of farming, the last nine months, which might have been the best but which I have made some of the worst of my life. How frightful and senseless, to link one's happiness with material things – wife, children, health, riches."

p. 17, *why should he be so angry*: Because Sofia Tolstoy was ill, a wet nurse was brought into the house, and this aroused his fury.

p. 17, *And how often... my old self*: Recalling this time later, she wrote: "He was very bitter with me, would go out of the house and leave me alone for days on end, without help, and everything made him angry." Tolstoy himself wrote angrily in his diary that his wife's character was "deteriorating every day". It was only two months later that he felt calm and happy again, immersed in work on his new novel. "It has passed and it's all untrue. I'm happy with her," he wrote. "There's no need to choose. The choice was made long ago. Literature means art, teaching and family."

p. 18, *Comte*: This was what the Behrs family called him before his marriage to Sofia.

p. 18, *Popov*: Nil, Alexandrovich Popov, historian and corresponding member of the Petersburg Academy of Sciences

p. 18, *So he is off to war*: This is the only known reference to his desire to go to war (the war in the Caucasus hadn't yet ended). He evidently didn't pursue it.

p. 19, *Valerian Petrovich*: Valerian Tolstoy, the husband of Tolstoy's sister Maria.

p. 19, *It's my youth*: See entry in Tolstoy's diary for 3rd March 1863: "Today she feels bored and cramped. A madman seeks a whirlwind – but this is youth, not madness. And I fear this mood more than anything in the world."

p. 19, *Alexandrine*: "Alexandrine" was Alexandra Tolstaya, Tolstoy's cousin once removed. He first became friendly with her in 1853; their affectionate correspondence over forty-seven years is exceptionally interesting because of the variety of its content and the openness with which he expressed his views, his literary plans and his emotional upsets. He himself described this correspondence as his best autobiography. Rereading copies of these letters in the last years of his life, he said: "When I look back on my long, dark life, the memory of Alexandrine is always a ray of brightness."

p. 19, *He shouldn't have sent her that letter*: The letter is unknown, but it is plain that he had written very frankly about his family life.

p. 20, *The History of 1812*: Evidently a reference to one of the drafts for the beginning of *War and Peace*.

p. 21, *Alyosha Gorshkoi*: A peasant and guard on the estate.

p. 21, *It hurts me to think of Tanya, she's a thorn in my flesh*: A reference to the love affair between her sister Tanya Behrs and Tolstoy's brother Sergei (Seryozha), which lasted from the summer of 1863 to June 1865.

p. 21, *Seryozha*: Sergei Tolstoy visited Yasnaya Polyana from his estate at Pirogovo; in 1863 he was thirty-seven.

p. 21, *Masha*: When this love affair started, Masha (Maria Shishkina) had already been his common-law wife for fifteen years and they had several children.

1864

p. 22, *Grandmother*: "Grandmother" was what Tolstoy jokingly called Alexandra Tolstaya, even though she was only eleven years older. Their affection was mutual. In 1857 Tolstoy was sincerely enamoured of her, as evidenced by his diary entries for 11th May and 22nd October 1857: "I am so disposed to fall in love that I am appalled. If only Alexandrine were ten years younger. A splendid nature." And: "Alexandrine is a delight, a joy and a consolation. I haven't met one woman to match her."

p. 23, *I keep thinking… all day*: Her mood was induced by his departure to Nikolskoe-Vyazemskoe, stopping off on the way at Pirogovo to see his brother Sergei.

p. 23, *my little girl*: On 4th October 1864, the Tolstoys' daughter Tatyana was born.

p. 23, *It started when he dislocated his arm*: On 26th September 1864, Tolstoy fell off his horse while hunting and dislocated his right arm. The Tula doctors set it unsuccessfully, so on 21st November, he went to Moscow for a consultation with some doctors who, on 28th November, carried out another operation.

1865

p. 24, *Dunyasha*: Evdokia Bannikova (married name Orekhova), a chambermaid at the Tolstoys' house.

p. 25, *A.*: Axinya Bazykina (see note to p. 8).

p. 26, *Dyakov*: Dmitry Dyakov, a landowner and neighbour.

p. 26, *the Zefirots*: "Zefirots" was the family name for Liza and Varya, the daughters of Tolstoy's sister Maria, who stayed at Yasnaya Polyana for much of the time between 1864 and 1866.

p. 26, *His brother's son is dying*: On 15th March 1865 Sergei Tolstoy's two-year-old son Nikolai died; Tolstoy went to the funeral.

p. 27, *his novel*: The first part of *War and Peace*, entitled *The Year 1805*.

p. 28, *The wedding will be in twenty days or so*: The wedding was set for 29th June.

p. 28, *Seryozha has betrayed Tanya. He behaved like a swine*: Sergei Tolstoy abruptly stopped visiting Yasnaya Polyana and explained to Tolstoy in a letter that he couldn't leave Maria Shishkina and their children: "Throughout these ten miserable days I have been lying, believing I was telling the truth, but when I saw I must finally break with Masha I realized this was impossible." Tanya wrote to inform her parents: "Don't be surprised or grieved; I couldn't have done otherwise and would always have had it on my conscience. All may be for the best." Tolstoy described this letter as "wonderful" and her behaviour as "noble" and "splendid".

p. 29, *What a brute... like that*: Tolstoy shared Sofia's feelings about his brother, and wrote to him: "I cannot convey to you the hell in which you have placed not only Tanya but our entire family, including me."

p. 29, *Nurse*: Maria Arbuzova.

1866

p. 30, *We spent 6 weeks in Moscow and returned here on the 7th*: The Tolstoys arrived in Moscow on 21st January 1866. She wanted to "show the children to her parents" and Tolstoy wanted to "revive memories of people and society" (see his letter to "Alexandrine". At first they lived with the Behrs family, but on 3rd February they moved into a separate apartment in Khludov's house on Bolshaya Dmitrovka Street (now 7 Pushkin Street), where they stayed until 6th March.

p. 30, *Lyova and I... P... relations*: She evidently means Mitrofan Polivanov, who she met during this visit to Moscow. "My God, what a scene Lev Nikolaevich made about my somewhat tactless behaviour towards this person," she wrote later. "I was simply being rather affected, as I felt awkward with him, and was insanely frightened of Lev Nikolaevich's jealousy."

p. 30, *Petya*: Pyotr Andreevich Behrs, Sofia's younger brother.

p. 31, *We have a new bailiff here with his wife*: "In the summer of 1866," she recalled, "Lev Nikolaevich hired an impoverished young nobleman and former cadet as his estate-manager. He had a smart, pretty wife, a crop-haired nihilist, who loved to talk and philosophize. I don't remember their surname, but she was called Maria Ivanovna."

p. 32, *the regimental clerk... formality*: Tolstoy involved himself in the case of the soldier Vasily Shibunin, who slapped his company commander's face because of his cruelty and was court-martialled. Tolstoy was a defence witness at the trial, and through Alexandrine he interceded with Tsar Alexander II for Shibunin's pardon. His petition was not successful, and Shibunin was executed on 9th August 1866.

p. 32, *Tanya... very poorly... with the Dyakovs*: In the winter of 1866–67 Tanya Behrs was gravely ill (consumption was suspected). She eventually went abroad with the Dyakov family in April 1867.

p. 33, *I shall always remember... special joy*: 17th September was Sofia Tolstoy's name day. As a surprise, Tolstoy had invited a military band from Yasenki, where a regiment was stationed, and organized a dance; the regimental commander Yunosha visited the Tolstoys that day with his officers.

p. 33, *I now spend most of my time... the first time*: Sofia copied out most of the manuscript of *War and Peace*.

1867

p. 34, *I still find the Englishwoman awkward and gloomy*: The English governess Hannah Tracey arrived at Yasnaya Polyana on 12th November 1866. The cause of their initial awkwardness, according to a letter Sofia wrote to her husband in Moscow, was their "ignorance of each other's languages". Everyone soon grew to love her, however, and her pupil Tanya Tolstaya wrote many years later of the devotion she still felt for her.

p. 34, *Lyovochka has been writing... in his eyes*: In a letter to M. Bashilov dated 8th January 1867, he wrote: "My work is going well and progressing rapidly – so rapidly, in fact, that I have finished three parts in rough (one part – the one for which you are doing the pictures – has been printed, the other two are in manuscript), and have started on the fourth and final one. Unless I am delayed by some unexpected disaster, I expect to be ready with the whole novel by autumn." The novel was not finished by the autumn of 1867 – correcting the original rough version demanded almost three more years of intense labour.

p. 35, *All day... last year*: See first note to p. 33.

1870

p. 38, *I have been weaning Lyova for four days now*: Lev Lvovich Tolstoy was born on 20th May 1869 in Yasnaya Polyana. In the Tolstoys' home he was known as Lyova or Lyolya.

1871

p. 39, *It's not a grief... years to come*: Tanya had married Alexander Kuzminsky, who had been appointed public prosecutor in Kutaisi in the Caucasus. Sofia took her sister's departure very hard.

p. 39, *koumiss*: Fermented mare's milk, believed to have health-giving powers.

p. 39, *For two months... no good at all*: Tolstoy left for Moscow on 9th June 1871, and on 11th June travelled on from there with Sofia's brother Stepan to the village of Karalyk, near Buzuluk, in the province of Samara. He stayed there for six weeks, drinking koumiss, returning to Yasnaya Polyana on 2nd August.

1872

p. 40, *Lyovochka returned from Moscow on 30th March*: Tolstoy left for Moscow on 28th March. Moscow life filled him with such "revulsion for all the idle luxury and all the things men and women acquire so dishonestly" that he decided "never to go there again".

p. 40, *Mitrofan*: Mitrofan Bannikov, the horse-trainer.

p. 40, *We sat up until almost four a.m. getting the proofs of the ABC*: The proofs were sent back to F. Ries's printing house in Moscow, where at the end of December 1871 the manuscript of the *ABC* had been sent for printing.

p. 41, *Varya, and her fiancé, Nagornov*: Nikolai Nagornov married Tolstoy's niece Varya in the summer of 1872.

p. 41, *Masha*: Maria Lvovna Tolstaya, the Tolstoys' year-old daughter.

p. 41, *wrote yesterday... with Ries*: Tolstoy's letter to his lawyer in Moscow to get the original of the *ABC* back from Ries and "stop publication".

1873

p. 42, *Lyovochka has gone to Moscow*: Tolstoy went to Moscow for discussions with M.N. Katkov's printing house about the publication of a third edition of his collected works.

p. 42, *My darling little Petya*: Pyotr Lvovich Tolstoy was born 13th June 1872.

p. 42, *Fyodor Fyodorovich*: Fyodor Fyodorovich Kaufman. Seryozha Tolstoy recalled him as "an ill-educated but decent and kindly man of about thirty-five".

p. 43, *the new Englishwoman*: The governess Emily Tabor arrived at the Tolstoys' on 11th February.

p. 43, *my little Petyushka died of a throat infection*: "His throat swelled up and he couldn't breathe," Tolstoy wrote to his brother Sergei on 10th November. "It was what they call croup." This was the first death in the Tolstoy family for eleven years.

1875

p. 45, *Auntie*: Pelageya Tolstaya, Tolstoy's aunt.

p. 45, *My hope... to be*: In letters to Afanasy Fet and Nikolai Strakhov, which he wrote on 26th October 1875, Tolstoy explained that the cause of this state was his own ill health, the "ill health of his family" and the fact that he had "thrown myself from one piece of work into another, but accomplished practically nothing". Later, in his *Confession*, he wrote: "I began to be afflicted with moments of despair, when life stopped and I no longer knew how I should live or what I should do." These moods of his are connected to his religious quest at the end of the 1870s.

1876

p. 46, *Samara*: On 3rd September, Tolstoy and his nephew Nikolai Tolstoy left Yasnaya Polyana. They arrived at Samara on 7th September, and on the same day Tolstoy travelled by train to Orenburg to buy horses.

p. 46, *Styopa*: Her younger brother Stepan Behrs was staying.

p. 47, *biography... try to do it, though*: On 24th October 1876, Sofia Tolstoy began to write Tolstoy's biography. This work continued, with interruptions, until the end of 1878.

p. 47, *the children... after M. Rey's class*: Ilya Tolstoy remembered Jules Rey as a "crude, stupid man".

1878

p. 49, *Lyovochka attended the liturgy*: Tolstoy was at that time observing all the church rituals punctiliously.

p. 49, *Annie*: Annie was the governess Anna Phillips.

p. 49, *Prince Urusov*: Leonid Urusov was an old friend of the Tolstoy family; from 1876 to 1885 he was vice-governor of Tula.

p. 49, *Alexander Grigorevich*: Alexander Michurin, the music teacher.

p. 50, *Vasily Ivanovich*: Vasily Ivanovich Alexeev, teacher of the older Tolstoy children from 1877 to 1881.

p. 50, *Liza*: Liza, Alexeev's ten-year-old adopted daughter.

p. 51, *The trial... part*: This draft of *The Decembrists* begins with the words: "On 23rd January 1824, at a general meeting of the Department of Religious and Civil Affairs of the State Council, was heard the case of..."

p. 51, *Bibikov has just returned from Samara*: In the autumn of 1871 Tolstoy bought twenty-five acres in the Buzuluka district in the province of Samara. In April 1878 he added to this an adjacent plot of forty acres. Bibikov was manager of Tolstoy's estate from 1878 to 1884.

p. 52, *levashniki*: "Levashniki" – a special cake made by the Yasnaya Polyana cook, M.N. Rumyantsev.

p. 53, *Parasha's*: Parasha, or Praskovia Kryukova, was the daughter of the cook Rumyantsev.

p. 56, *to watch the Tsar travel past*: Alexander II was travelling on the Moscow–Kursk line. Because it was feared an attempt would be made on his life there were three separate royal trains, and it wasn't known in which one the Tsar was travelling.

p. 56, *et le marmiton*: "And the kitchen boy" (French).

p. 56, *dare not*: In English in the original.

1879

p. 57, *the new edition*: The fourth edition of the works of L.N. Tolstoy in eleven volumes, 1880.

p. 57, *Misha*: Mikhail, her tenth child.

1882

p. 59, *We have been in Moscow since 15th September 1881*: In September 1881 the Tolstoys moved to Moscow to be with their eldest son, who was starting at the university. They rented an apartment in Volkonsky's house on Denezhnyi (now Maly Levshinsky) Lane, where they lived during the winter of 1881–82.

p. 59, *Seryozha... next door to us*: Sergei Tolstoy entered the natural sciences department of the university; Tanya Tolstaya was accepted at the School of Art, Sculpture and Architecture. Sixteen-year-old Ilya and thirteen-year-old Lev attended Lev Polivanov's private high school on Prechistenka (now Kropotkin Street).

p. 59, *Our life in Moscow... so unhappy*: On 5th October 1881, Tolstoy noted in his diary: "The past month has been the most agonizing period of my life. Stench, jewels, luxury, poverty. Depravity. Criminals have gathered here to rob people, then assembled soldiers and judges to guard their orgies while they feast." Sofia wrote to her sister Tanya about his state of mind: "Lyovochka has sunk into something far worse than depression – it's a sort of hopeless apathy. He cannot sleep or eat, he often cries – *à la lettre* – and at times I think I shall go mad."

p. 59, *For the first time... is striking four*: Tolstoy's differences with his family became more acute during their visit to Moscow. He described this state in a letter to N.N. Strakhov: "This past winter has been completely fruitless. It appears that people do not in fact need the things I believe in. At times I long to die." Sofia felt equally lonely, without the spiritual unity she was used to with her husband. "You don't tell me what is in your heart and what you are thinking, what makes you happy and what makes you sad, what bores you and what pleases you," she reproached him in a letter of 17th September 1882. To her sister Tanya she wrote that Tolstoy was "very advanced in his views; he leads the crowd and shows people which path they should take", whereas she "*was* the crowd, and went with the common flow"; she saw the light he carried but could "go no faster" for she was "weighed down by the crowd, by home and habit".

p. 60, *Alyosha*: The Tolstoys' ten-month-old son.

p. 60, *Lyovochka has taken Lyova to Moscow*: Tolstoy went to Moscow to supervise building work and repairs on a house he bought in the summer of 1882 in Dolgo-Khamovniki Street (now Lev Tolstoy Street). On 8th October the whole family moved to Moscow, and spent their winters there until 1901.

1883

p. 61, *He continues with his religious writings*: From the end of 1882 to January 1884 Tolstoy worked on a tract entitled 'What I Believe'. The first edition (in 1884) was seized and banned, and it was only in 1906, after the first Russian revolution, that it was published in Russia.

1885

p. 63, *Lyovochka returned yesterday... Urusov*: Tolstoy and Urusov travelled to the Crimean coast for two weeks.

p. 63, *He had... thirty years ago*: Tolstoy was in Sevastopol during the Crimean War, from 7th November 1854 to the middle of November 1855.

1886

p. 65, *Lev Nikolaevich was ill*: At the beginning of August 1886, Tolstoy hurt his leg while working in the fields and it became infected.

p. 65, *So on the one hand... are incapable of doing*: Sergei Tolstoy wrote, apropos of this entry: "One reason for the discord between Lev Nikolaevich and Sofia Andreevna was the undefined nature of the demands he made on her. L.N. demanded that their life should be simplified but gave no limits for this simplification and rarely gave any concrete advice as to what should be done. Questions as to where and how his family should live, what should be done with the estates, how the children should be educated, and so on, remained unanswered."

p. 65, *Lev Nikolaevich is starting on a new play, about peasant life*: From October to November 1886 Tolstoy was writing his play *The Power of Darkness*, inspired by a story related to him by N.V. Davydov. The play was first published by the Intermediary publishing house in February 1887.

p. 65, *Mme Seuron*: Anna Seuron was governess to both Tanya and Masha Tolstaya.

p. 65, *the lives of the philosophers*: L. Diogène, *La Vie des plus illustres philosophes de l'antiquité...* Paris, 1841.

p. 66, *A letter came from Ilya mentioning marriage*: Ilya Tolstoy was in love with Sofia Filosofova, who he married in February 1888. Tolstoy regarded this marriage with "joy and fear".

1887

p. 67, *four students in Petersburg... funeral service*: On 1st March 1887, the police arrested five students for the attempt on Alexander III's life, including Lenin's brother Alexander Ulyanov. They were tried and sentenced to death, and executed on 8th May 1887.

p. 67, *The play is a huge success*: On 3rd February 1887, A.A. Stakhovich wrote to her that he was reading *The Power of Darkness* in St Petersburg and trying to familiarize a large number of influential people with the work in order to exert pressure on the censors. On 27th January he read the play in the presence of Alexander III, who found it a "marvellous piece" and recommended that it be staged at the imperial theatres.

p. 67, *Lyovochka has written a story about the early Christians*: From the end of 1886 until June 1887 Tolstoy was working on and off on a story called 'Walk in the Light While There Is Light. A Tale of the Ancient Christians'. It was first published in Russia in 1893, in an anthology called *The Pathway. A Literary-Scientific Anthology in Aid of the Society for Helping Needy Migrants*.

p. 67, *an article entitled 'On Life and Death'*: This was Tolstoy's first title for his tract *On Life*. He continued working on it throughout 1887.

p. 67, *The new cheap edition has come out*: She is referring to the new cheaply published sixth edition of *The Works of L.N. Tolstoy*, vols. 1–12, Moscow, which appeared in 1887.

p. 68, *Seryozha has gone off to Tula… the peasant bank*: Sergei Tolstoy was then a member of the Tula department of the *zemstvo* peasant bank.

p. 68, *vint*: A card game rather like whist.

p. 68, *Chertkov*: Vladimir Grigorevich Chertkov, friend and fellow thinker of Tolstoy's.

p. 68, *As for Chertkov's work… for that*: Sofia Tolstoy is referring to the Intermediary publishing house, founded by Tolstoy, Chertkov and Biryukov in 1884 to publish literary and popular scientific works for a popular audience. Chertkov wrote to Tolstoy on 25th February 1887, with various questions about the publication of his works by the Intermediary.

p. 68, *Feinerman*: Isaak Feinerman, a young teacher and follower of Tolstoy's, who dreamt of establishing a peasant commune.

p. 68, *Lyovochka is writing… University Psychological Society*: On 14th March 1887, at a meeting of the Moscow Psychological Society, Tolstoy gave a paper on 'The Understanding of Life' – a short résumé of his book *On Life*. In it he criticized prevailing ideas on religion and morality, and formulated his own new world outlook.

p. 68, *vegetarian diet*: Sergei Tolstoy wrote in his memoirs: "He became especially committed to vegetarianism after his acquaintance with the positivist and vegetarian William Fry, who visited him in the autumn of 1885. My sisters Tanya and Masha were also converted at that time to 'food without killing'. My mother thought vegetarianism was harmful and she was wrong: when my father had liver problems it was of undoubted benefit to him. And it never did my sisters any harm."

p. 68, *what a sad… communion*: In a letter of 18th–20th February 1887, Chertkov wrote to Tolstoy: "I am inexpressibly grateful to God for granting me the blessing of being at one with my wife. This always makes me mindful of those for whom this spiritual communion with their wives is not possible and who, it would appear, deserve this happiness far, far more than I."

p. 69, *Ilya has… for drill*: Ilya Tolstoy was serving in the volunteer regiment of the Suma dragoons, stationed in the Khamovniki barracks.

p. 69, *We had a visit… for our play*: At the end of 1886 M.G. Savina, an actress at the Alexandrovsky Theatre, asked Tolstoy's permission to put on a benefit performance of *The Power of Darkness*, and rehearsals started in February. In a letter to Sofia Tolstoy, the director Potekhin wrote that "in order to learn about this type of peasant and the details of their homes and surroundings, and to find the characteristic local costumes for the actors, two specialists were sent off to Yasnaya Polyana."

p. 69, *Grigory*: A servant in the Tolstoys' home.

p. 70, *I miss Ilyusha and am sorry I haven't visited him yet*: The Suma regiment of dragoons was then stationed in the village of Vladykino, near Moscow.

p. 70, *Florinsky's book*: V.M. Florinsky's *Home Medicine. A Medical Guide for Popular Use.*

p. 71, *his article*: Tolstoy's tract *On Life.*

p. 72, *Seryozha was in Samara but hasn't settled anything*: Sergei Tolstoy visited the Tolstoys' Samara estate to put the running of it in order.

p. 73, *The painter Repin*: Ilya Repin (1844–1930), Russia's foremost naturalist painter.

p. 73, *dark ones*: The term "dark ones" had become current in the Tolstoy house, and not only Sofia Tolstoy used it, but Tolstoy too. Sofia Tolstoy called Evgeny Popov an "Oriental" as he was Georgian by birth.

p. 73, *Lev... Yasnaya Polyana*: The last three sentences were added later by Sofia Tolstoy, and a dried flower is attached to the page.

1890

p. 75, *Masha and I... it is*: Masha Tolstaya was very close to her father. Ilya Tolstoy recalled: "She identified closely with her father's loneliness, was the first of us all to renounce her peers, and imperceptibly but determinedly went over to his side."

p. 76, *Thanks to... well pleased*: On 26th November 1890 Tolstoy went to Krapivna to attend a session of the Tula magistrate's court, where four Yasnaya Polyana peasants were being tried for killing when they were drunk a horse-thief from the village, Gavril Balkhin.

Before the trial Tolstoy visited the peasants in jail. The trial he regarded as "shameful comedy". Tolstoy's presence there influenced the sentence. "One was acquitted, and the other three received lenient sentences," Tolstoy wrote to A.V. Alekhin, 2nd December 1890.

The story about the murder of the horse-thief probably served as the basis for the description of the peasant Ivan Mironov's murder in the story 'The Forged Coupon'.

p. 76, *Vanechka*: Ivan, the Tolstoys' two-year-old son.

p. 77, *Then Biryukov came... to rest*: Tolstoy's friend Pavel Biryukov wanted to marry Masha. Sofia was against the marriage.

p. 77, *But what if these things are boots... and mud*: Seryozha Tolstoy writes in his memoirs: "My father's way of life throughout the 1880s, and especially at the beginning of 1884, gradually changed. In Moscow he began to get up early, tidy his own room, saw and chop wood, draw water from the well in the courtyard outside, and drag it to the house in a large tub on a sledge. Then he learnt from a shoemaker how to make boots, and started sewing them in the little room next to his study."

p. 78, *Lyovochka told me... to see me*: Tolstoy noted in his diary, 15th December 1890: "When I went out of the house this morning Ilya Balkhin came to me pleading for a pardon: they have been sent to jail for six weeks. I feel exceedingly depressed, and my heart has been heavy all day. I must leave."

p. 78, *Lyova and I had a talk... of course*: In 1897 Masha Tolstaya married Nikolai Obolensky, and in 1899 Tatyana married Mikhail Sukhotin. The Tolstoys were not in favour of these marriages.

p. 79, *Sasha*: The Tolstoys' six-year-old daughter Alexandra.

p. 79, *article on the Church*: Tolstoy was working on his treatise 'The Kingdom of God Is within Us'. In June 1890 he started on the introduction to his 'Catechism of Non-Resistance'. He wanted "briefly and clearly to express the meaning of Christian non-resistance". The article, 'On Resistance to Evil, the Church and Military Service' grew into a book of social criticism, which was published abroad in 1893. The treatise was banned in Russia and first published there in 1906.

p. 80, *Sonya... had had a son*: A son, Nikolai, was born to Ilya and Sofia Tolstoy on 20th December 1890; he died in 1893.

p. 80, *flattering letter from Fet... unattractive, in fact*: The letter from Fet to Sofia Tolstoy, dated 21st December 1890, begins with the words: "Dear Countess, it is not my fault that I am a poet – you are my shining ideal. Let the matter be tried before the Court of Heaven, and if the word poet means fool I willingly submit to this. It is not a matter of intellect but happiness. And to bear in our heart people dear to us is a great happiness." Sofia Tolstoy's sharp words here about Fet are uncharacteristic: she was always very warmly disposed towards him and visited him in the months of his fatal illness.

p. 81, *U.*: Prince Leonid Urusov, who died in 1885.

p. 81, *The Zinovievs... Mme Giuliani*: Nikolai Zinoviev, Governor of Tula, and his wife and children. Mme Giuliani was a singer.

p. 82, *Sofia Alexeevna*: The mother of Ilya Tolstoy's wife.

1891

p. 85, *Bulygin and Kolechka Gué*: The Tolstoys' friends Mikhail Bulygin, a landowner and neighbour, and the painter Nikolai Gué.

p. 86, *Nikolai Nikolaevich*: Nikolai Gué, son of the painter, arrived at Yasnaya Polyana on 1st January.

p. 86, *Alexei Mitrofanovich*: Alexei Mitrofanovich Novikov, the children's tutor.

p. 87, *Lyovochka... such works*: In the autumn of 1884, he renounced the ownership of his land, property and literary rights, and entrusted Sofia to conduct his affairs and be responsible for all his works published before 1881.

p. 87, *Davydov*: The Tolstoys' friend Nikolai Davydov, president of the Tula, then Moscow circuit court.

p. 88, *Klopsky... dark one*: Ivan Klopsky (or Klobsky) first visited Tolstoy on 1st January 1889, with Fyodor Strakhov. He had lived in Tolstoyan agricultural communities. Gorky refers to him in *My Universities*. Tolstoy wrote to Nikolai Gué: "After you came Klobsky. He has become a very, very good person, you know. I was so glad to see him as he is now."

p. 90, *The Kreutzer Sonata*: She was reading the proofs for vol. 13 of *The Works of L.N. Tolstoy*, which included *The Kreutzer Sonata* and the afterword to *The Kreutzer Sonata*. The volume was compiled without the censors' permission and was banned.

p. 91, *He read me a short story... more of a children's story really*: Lyova Tolstoy's story 'Montecristo' was published in the *Source* no. 4, 1891; the story 'Love' in March 1891, under the pseudonym L. Lvov. Tolstoy wrote to his son about them: "You have, I think, what they call talent, which is very common and of no value – that is, the capacity to see, observe and describe. But there is no evidence of that deep heartfelt need to *express* something. You cling to subjects that are too large, and are beyond your power and experience. Try to take a subject less broad, less obvious, and elaborate it at a more profound level where you might express more simple, childish, youthful feelings and experiences."

p. 91, *J'ai longtemps... espoir*: "I have long tried to be worthy of Tatyana Lvovna, but she has never given me any hope" (French).

p. 92, *Later on Lyovochka read us Schiller's Don Carlos*: Tanya Tolstaya recalls this reading in a letter to Elizaveta Olsufieva of 14th February 1891: "Papa and Maman are both very cheerful and trying to amuse us, Maman with all kinds of things to eat and drink, and Papa with readings from *Don Carlos* – which, by the way, we didn't like."

p. 92, *La Physiologie de l'amour moderne*: By Paul Bourget (Paris, 1891).

p. 92, *Beketov's pamphlet On Man's Present and Future Nourishment*: A.N. Beketov, 'The Present and Future Nourishment of Man', St Petersburg, 1879. Tolstoy advised Chertkov to publish the article in the Intermediary. "This is absolutely necessary," he wrote to him on 16th May 1891.

p. 93, *copied out Lyovochka's Sevastopol diaries*: Tolstoy's diaries for 1854–57. Recalling this work later, she wrote: "I copied out his old diaries so there would be two copies of them. I was filled with the idea that everything that came from Lev Nikolaevich's pen must be preserved, and that there must be two copies."

p. 93, *Masha has opened a school for the riff-raff in "that house"*: In the 1890s Masha and Tanya Tolstaya organized a school in a little stone house near the entrance to the Yasnaya Polyana estate. The school hadn't been officially permitted and was closed on the information of the priest. Lessons continued in "that house", i.e. the left wing of the main house.

p. 93, *He is writing about art and science again*: Tolstoy noted in his diary, on 14th February 1891: "Today, like every other day, I have sat over notebooks of works I have started – on science, art and non-resistance to evil – and I cannot get down to them."

p. 93, *his latest story*: The Kreutzer Sonata.

p. 93, *but his diaries... infuriates him*: Tolstoy noted in his diary on 14th February 1891: "Started rereading my diary, which Sonya is copying out. It was painful. I spoke irritably to her and infected her with my irritation. She lost her temper and said some cruel things. It didn't last longer than an hour. Then I stopped thinking of myself and thought of her instead, and we affectionately made up."

p. 94, *Masha's birthday... twenty years later*: She was evidently referring to the puerperal fever which set in immediately after the birth and continued in an extremely serious form for a month. Her relationship with Masha was complicated and erratic. Masha's desire to serve the simple people sometimes far exceeded her strength, for she wasn't in good health, and provoked her mother's irritation. She didn't always believe in the sincerity of her daughter's intentions, and considered she was "constantly thinking up some new venture which was bound to make her suffer". She didn't encourage her fascination with medicine, which prompted her visits to the hospital. Masha's inclinations and her passionate temperament provoked her mother and she suffered much, always trying to yield to her mother and mollify her.

p. 96, *Borel*: M. Borel was the boys' tutor.

p. 96, *Rovsky Barracks*: A forest lodge, 2 miles from Yasnaya Polyana.

p. 97, *writing... About non-resistance*: The article 'On Non-resistance', which later became the tract, *The Kingdom of God Is within You*. In 1894 it was first brought out in Russian in Berlin.

p. 99, *letter from Countess Alexandra Andreevna Tolstaya... to reply*: Sofia Andreevna wanted an audience with the Tsar about the banned volume 13, and asked Tolstoy's cousin to discover if this would be possible.

p. 99, *I shall bring out... been delayed*: After her return from Moscow, Sofia Tolstoy wrote to Sergei, in a letter of 17th March: "I returned today from Moscow where I had hurried off for a couple of days to find out about the banned Volume Thirteen. It's a bad business: 18,000 copies printed, and it's not known what will happen to them. All the articles in Volume Twelve have been banned. I have arranged that the other twelve volumes will go on sale with a slip of paper inside on which I have written: 'Due to circumstances beyond the Publisher's control, Volume Thirteen cannot be released.'"

p. 100, *I went to Tula... Wanderer's art exhibition*: From the 21st to the 29th of March, the nineteenth Exhibition of Paintings of the Fellowship of Wandering Artists opened in the premises of the Tula Assembly of the Nobility.

p. 102, *Then we resumed... and Vanechka too*: It was L.N. Tolstoy's renunciation of his property that led to its division among members of his family. In a letter to her sister Tanya on 21st April, Sofia wrote: "We have been discussing the division of the property, and still haven't decided how to share it out. There is something sad and improper about the way this division affects Father. Well it's not my business, I didn't plan it." Tolstoy expressed his attitude to this in a letter to Nikolai Gué, dated 17th April 1891: "I am having to sign a document, a deed of settlement, which releases me from the property, and the very signature of it means a retreat from principle. Yet I shall sign it, for if I don't I shall cause them greater anger." Tolstoy signed the deed of settlement on 17th April 1891.

p. 103, *Nikolai Strakhov*: Nikolai Strakhov (1828–95), eminent literary critic and philosopher.

p. 106, *two art exhibitions, the Wanderers' and the Academy*: The nineteenth Exhibition of Paintings of the Fellowship of Wandering Artists, and the Annual Exhibition of the Academy of Arts.

p. 110, *the idea of transforming... by the authorities*: The reference is to Chertkov's Intermediary publishing house.

p. 112, *displeased... meeting with the Tsar... consequences*: Tolstoy wrote in his diary, on 18th April: "Sonya arrived back three days ago. I find it unpleasant that she has been ingratiating herself with the Tsar and complaining to him about people stealing my manuscripts. I couldn't control myself and said some harsh things to her, but it has passed."

p. 113, *We had a wretched letter from Lyova... university*: Lyova Tolstoy was a student for a year at the medical faculty of Moscow University, then transferred to the first year of the philological faculty. In the spring, illness forced him to leave the university. In a letter to his mother dated 26th April, he wrote that he could no longer endure the examination procedures at the university, and couldn't submit to "having a lot of names, figures and Slavonic grammar stuffed down my throat. What will I do then?" he wrote. "Well, first of all, I've never done anything up to now anyway, so at least it will be no worse. Secondly, I have a year of military service. And after that who knows? It's too early to tell."

p. 115, *The censors... Alexeev's book On Drunkenness*: Tolstoy's article 'Why Are People Stupefied?', which contains these phrases, appeared in volume 13, for which Sofia Tolstoy was pleading with the censors. The article had already been published as the preface to P.S. Alexeev's book *On Drunkenness*, Moscow, 1891.

p. 117, *a Jewish sculptor from Paris*: Evidently the sculptor Leopold Bernstamm, about whom A.S. Suvorin wrote to Tolstoy on 21st November 1889: "There is a Russian sculptor in Paris called Bernstamm, a talented man who wrote saying he would like to do a bust of you, and is prepared to leave Paris to visit you. He is held back only by his doubts as to whether you will agree to pose a few times for him." Tolstoy replied: "If you can release me from this sculptor then please do so."

p. 118, *A German... with us*: Richard Deirenfurt had probably been sent by Loewenfeld to take Tolstoy the proofs of his book *Leo Tolstoi. Sein Leben, seine Werke, seine Weltanschauung*, Berlin, 1892. Tolstoy wrote in his diary: "We have had a German visiting. Very tedious."

p. 118, *Timofei Fokanov*: Timofei Fokanov, steward of Tolstoy's estate in Samara.

p. 122, *the pavilion*: The pavilion was what they called the little wooden house with the tiled roof, built in the park at Yasnaya Polyana in 1888. Masha Tolstaya and some local doctors ran a surgery for the peasants in it. It was later used to accommodate guests in the summer months.

p. 122, *started on... book on vegetarianism*: In April 1891 Tolstoy received a book from Chertkov entitled *The Ethics of Diet* by Howard Williams, London, 1883. On 11th April he wrote to Sofia: "I have just been reading a wonderful book, a history of the ancients' attitudes to vegetarianism." As he continued reading this "wonderful and necessary book", he wrote to Chertkov about his desire to write a preface to it, and in a letter to him of 6th May he wrote: "The people at home here have started translating it, and I have been helping." Sofia, Tatyana and Masha Tolstaya all worked on the translation of this book, and others helped to finish it. For the preface Tolstoy visited a slaughterhouse on 7th June. The preface he embarked on then evolved into an article, 'The First Step'. In 1893 the Intermediary brought out a Russian translation of the book, *The Ethics of Diet, or the Moral Basis for a Non-violent Diet for Man, with an Introductory Article by L.N. Tolstoy: 'The First Step'*.

p. 123, *the French exhibition*: The French Trade Fair, with a large art section, opened in Moscow in the spring of 1891.

p. 123, *Lyovochka wrote to me... public property*: In a letter of 11th July, Tolstoy sent his wife the draft of an announcement to the newspapers, written in either his name or hers, renouncing the copyright on all the works he had written since the 1880s, which had appeared in volumes 12 and 13. After a discussion with her, he noted in his diary on 14th July: "She cannot understand, nor can the children, as they go on spending money, that every ruble my books earn that they live on causes me suffering and shame. The shame doesn't matter. But why should they weaken this action of mine, which might have had some power to preach the truth. Well, the truth will do its work without me."

p. 123, *Repin left today... in his belt*: Ilya Repin stayed in Yasnaya Polyana between 26th June and 16th July. In this time he did a bust of Tolstoy and two portraits: a sketch, 'Tolstoy Praying', and 'Tolstoy Working in His Study under the Arches'. According to Sergei Tolstoy, these were less successful than Repin's previous works, because the painter was then under the influence of Impressionism and was "embellishing them with his own imagination".

p. 124, *Ginzburg is sculpting... which isn't so bad*: Sofia Tolstoy later wrote: "If people want to put up a monument to Lev Nikolaevich, not one of the sculptures representing him has managed to convey his true appearance. The best one is the small bust with the folded arms by Trubetskoy."

p. 124, *his letter to various newspapers... works*: In an open letter of 16th September, Tolstoy wrote: "I hereby offer anybody who wants the chance to publish, without payment, in Russia and abroad, in Russian and in translations, and also to put on the stage, all those works which I wrote since 1881, and which were published in 1886, in Volume 12 of my *Complete Collected Works*, and in Volume 13, published in this year of 1891, as well as all my works which are as yet unpublished in Russia, and have been allowed to appear only since the publication of this recent volume."

p. 127, *the story about Lipunyushka*: Tolstoy's story 'Lipinyushka' was taken from an anthology edited by F.A. Khudyakov, *Great Russian Tales*, Moscow, 1861.

p. 128, *woman student... and morality*: "I haven't seen her – she is with Masha at present," Sofia wrote to her daughter Tanya on 29th July. In his diary Tolstoy noted on 31st July: "Larionova was here, a student from Kazan, who I had the pleasure of helping." In a letter to Tolstoy the following day, Larionova wrote: "I didn't manage yesterday to tell you how grateful I was. Thank you! It was the old story: before I came to see you I didn't care whether I lived or died. I was just trying to find a way out of this brutal life – and I didn't succeed. Now I've come to life again! Yesterday I wanted not only to shake your hand passionately and say 'thank you!' – I wanted to weep with love for you."

p. 128, *Two Frenchman have arrived*: The psychologist Charles Richet and writer Octave Gudail visited Tolstoy. On 27th August, Tolstoy noted in his diary: "Of little interest."

p. 131, *a letter arrived from Leskov... for publication*: On 20th June 1891, the writer Nikolai Leskov asked Tolstoy in a letter: "What do you think about this disaster – should we poke our nose in? What is the decent thing to do? Maybe I could be useful in some way, but I have lost faith in all the so-called 'good works' of public charity, and I don't know if one doesn't actually do more harm than good by meddling in something which only results in more idleness. But it's also hard to do nothing. Please tell me what you think one should do." Replying to Leskov, Tolstoy wrote: "You ask me precisely what you can do? My reply to you is to appeal to people's love for one another; not only their love in time of famine, but always and everywhere."

p. 132, *Lyovochka... Pirogovo*: Tolstoy and his daughter left for Pirogovo on 17th September. Between the 18th and the 22nd they visited villages in the Krapivna, Bogoroditsky and Efremovsky districts of Tula province.

p. 132, *Lyovochka went on to visit... a certain woman landowner*: Probably a woman named Burdina.

p. 133, *Lyovochka... and Psychology*: The November issue of the journal in which this article appeared was seized, and the article was sent to the Chief Department of Press Affairs. It was published, greatly abbreviated, in January 1892, under the title, 'Aid to the Hungry'.

p. 134, *I wrote to the Minister of the Court... come of it*: Sofia Tolstoy's request was granted. The money from the performance of Tolstoy's plays went to charity.

p. 134, *some other... sickly fellow*: A.N. Kanevsky worked in Tolstoyan agricultural communes. He had set out on foot for the "Krinitsa" colony in the Caucasus, and on the way visited Yasnaya Polyana. On 24th October 1891, Tolstoy wrote in his diary: "Kanevsky has just left. He is touchingly simple and self-sacrificing. He came from Moscow without a kopeck. I sent him off to his father with 4 rubles. He spent two nights here."

p. 134, *We all had one thing on our mind... the Red Cross*: Lyova Tolstoy couldn't give out in Samara the famine relief measures his father had applied, and was forced to distribute supplies to the peasants individually, which didn't combat starvation as effectively as canteens. Tolstoy was dissatisfied with this decision, and wrote to his son, on 23rd December 1891: "The main thing to realize is that you are not called upon to feed 5,000 or 6,000 or x number of souls, but to distribute the aid that has come into your hands in the best possible way. In all conscience, is this what you are doing?" Sofia Tolstoy quotes unpublished letters from Lyova to his father about conditions of the Samara province: "Why talk of canteens when there isn't so much as a crust of bread? First give us an army of 100 bakers, 10 wagon-loads of supplies and a whole crowd of people." Afterwards Tolstoy regretted he had been so sharp about his son's activities, and told him so in a letter.

1892

p. 136, *They had paraphrased Lyovochka's article... revolutionary*: Tolstoy's article 'On the Famine', was banned by the censors. Tolstoy then sent it to Emilie Dillon, correspondent for the London *Daily Telegraph*. The article was translated by Dillon and published in several issues of the paper between 12th and 30th January, in the form of a series of letters entitled, 'Why Are the Russian Peasants Starving?' The *Moscow Gazette* cited one of these "letters", inaccurately translated back from English, in a lead article entitled 'Count Lev Tolstoy on the Starving Peasants', claiming the "letters" were "open propaganda for the overthrow of the social and economic structure of the entire world". On 23rd January, Sofia sent a 'Letter to the Editors of the *Moscow Gazette*' to refute this, but it wasn't published.

p. 136, *Velichkina*: Vera Velichkina, a doctor and revolutionary. She met Tolstoy in January 1892 and worked with him during the famine. Vera Velichkina, 'The Year of the Famine with Lev Tolstoy', in *Memories of Tolstoy*, Moscow, 1960.

p. 138, *They refused... the Government Herald*: Replying to her on 13th February, Durnovo wrote: "Despite my great desire to grant your request, I find it difficult to agree to the promulgation of the denial you have sent me, since by its very nature it is bound to evoke further denunciations and occasion yet more polemics, which are extremely undesirable in the present social climate."

p. 138, *I wrote... letter today*: Tolstoy's letter, written at her insistence, was not published, and she had 100 copies hectographed and sent to various periodicals, government figures and individuals.

1893

p. 139, *I have just learnt from Chertkov... of all people*: In 1893 Chertkov stored some of Tolstoy's manuscripts with a former fellow soldier in the household cavalry. Sofia wrote: "Knowing he might be searched, he gave Lev Nikolaevich's banned works and manuscripts to his friend Trepov for safekeeping. When he took them back I do not know. This was the beginning of Chertkov's despotic, yet excessively reverential and loving relationship with Lev Nikolaevich." After Chertkov was exiled in 1897, the manuscripts of all Tolstoy's works written after 1880 were sent with Tolstoy's permission to Chertkov's home in England, where they were stored in a special reinforced concrete vault, built near Christchurch, Hampshire. In 1913 these manuscripts were sent to the Academy of

Sciences Library in St Petersburg, and in 1926 they were removed to the Tolstoy Museum in Moscow.

p. 139, *I believe in good and... responsibilities*: Sofia explained this "insane" page in her diary: "I couldn't help it; my overwrought state turned to malevolence and it suddenly seemed to me that the devil had possessed Lev Nikolaevich and frozen his heart.'

1894

p. 140, *he set off for the mushroom... cranberries*: On 2nd and 14th March, she wrote to Tanya and Lyova Tolstoy: "Papa and Dunaev went to the mushroom market by the river. They bought some dried mushrooms for the Pirogovo Tolstoys and some for themselves, then had a little picnic. There were a great many people there, a lot of peasants from other parts, and Papa was absolutely fascinated."

p. 141, *I am preparing Volume 13 for publication*: The ninth edition of Tolstoy's works.

p. 141, *Marcella by Mrs Humphry Ward*: Mrs Humphry Ward, *Marcella*, New York, 1894.

1895

p. 143, *I read Jules Verne's... Castaways*: Tolstoy read these and other novels by Verne to his older children.

p. 144, *some documents... theft at Yasnaya Polyana*: In December 1894 Sofia Tolstoy received a telegram from Yasnaya Polyana to say that thieves had broken into the house through a window, "breaking into trunks and cupboards, opening up everything, throwing things around and stealing clothes, bedding, and overcoats and various other things". Several days later she left for Yasnaya Polyana.

p. 144, *The episode with the photograph still hasn't died down*: At the end of December 1894, Tolstoy was persuaded by Chertkov to have his photograph taken by Mey, with Chertkov, Biryukov, Gorbunov-Posadov, Tregubov and Popov. Tolstoy noted in his diary, on 31st December 1894: "Chertkov was here. There was an unpleasant argument over the portrait. Sonya was as decisive as ever, but rash and spiteful too."

p. 145, *Chicherin... he treasures*: Boris Chicherin, professor of Philosophy at Moscow University, had become friendly with Tolstoy in the winter of 1856–57. In his memoirs Chicherin wrote: "We were soulmates. Even now I cannot read his old letters to me without feeling deeply moved. They breathe youth, sincerity and freshness; they depict him so well in that early period when his talent was just beginning to develop, and they take me back so vividly to those distant times. However, even in those days there was already evidence of that tendency to philosophize which would later prove so fatal to him. His solitary life in the country gave even greater scope to the disease. He was preoccupied by lofty questions of existence, but there was never any basis for their resolution. Instead he gave himself up to his own private train of thought, mixed with large amounts of fantasy."

p. 146, *ariston*: A mechanical musical instrument rather like a musical box.

p. 146, *the petition presented to the new Tsar*: The *zemstvo* representatives of Tver and various other regions sent petitions to Tsar Nicholas II expressing their willingness to participate in the government of Russia. In response, the Tsar gave them an audience and dismissed their wishes as "senseless dreams". Tolstoy responded to this with an article, 'Senseless Dreams'.

p. 147, *Lyovochka... Prince Dmitry Shakhovskoi*: Tolstoy attended a congress called by representatives of the liberal intelligentsia to organize a protest against the Tsar's speech. Those present failed to make any practical decisions. "A complete waste of time," Tolstoy wrote in his diary on 29th January. "All very stupid, and quite obvious the organization was only parading the strength of the individuals present."

p. 151, *this frenzy is an unforgivable, incorrigible vice*: Later recalling her mental state at that time, Sofia wrote: "With time I realized that the real cause of my despair was my premonition of Vanechka's death, which happened at the end of February. I fell into exactly the same despairing state in the summer just before Lev Nikolaevich's death. Such times are beyond our powers of endurance. There are always plenty of opportunities for grief in our life. The question is whether we have the strength to survive them and control ourselves."

p. 151, *Lyova has left for Ogranovich's sanatorium*: Lyova Tolstoy was sent to the hospital for nervous diseases established by Doctor M.P. Ogranovich near Zvenigorod, outside Moscow. On 21st February Tolstoy wrote in his diary: "Yesterday Ogranovich helped me to understand Lyova a little better. He explained that he had some latent form of malaria. And I suddenly began to understand his condition and felt sorry for him, although I still cannot summon up any genuine feeling of love for him."

1897

p. 153, *Masha's wedding... tomorrow*: Maria Tolstaya married Nikolai Obolensky (Kolya) on 2nd June 1897. She wrote to Leonila Annenkova, on 8th May 1897: "Maman was at first opposed to my marriage, since he is very poor and is slightly younger than me. Papa likes my future husband very much, however, and thinks he is the best person I could have chosen. But he pities me and feels wretched for me, although he will never say what's on his mind, never gives me any advice, and just avoids me. I am delighted he likes Kolya, and more importantly, believes in him, but of course the prospect of parting with him is dreadfully painful for me."

p. 153, *Lev Nikolaevich is writing his article about art*: In January 1897, Tolstoy began work on his tract *What Is Art?* Completed in 1898, the first uncensored edition appeared in 1898 in London, translated into English by Aylmer Maude.

p. 153, *Dunaev*: Alexander Dunaev, director of the Moscow Trade Bank and a fellow thinker of Tolstoy's.

p. 155, *I miss Sergei Ivanovich more than anything*: Sofia wrote: "After the death of my little son Vanechka, I was in a state of utter despair, such as one experiences only once in a lifetime. Such grief usually kills one, but if it doesn't, one's heart is incapable of suffering so deeply again. But I survived, and I owe this to fate and to music. Once I had been intoxicated by music and learnt to listen to it, I could no longer live without it, and it was Taneev's music that affected me more powerfully than any other; it was he who first taught me, with his beautiful playing, how to listen to and love music. Sometimes I had only to meet Sergei Ivanovich and hear his calm, soothing voice to feel comforted. I was in a distressed state, and this coincided with my critical period. In the mood I was in at the time, I didn't think very much about Taneev's personality. To all appearances he was not very interesting, quite equable, extremely reticent, and a complete stranger to me to the end."

p. 157, *settled Masha's financial affairs*: In accordance with the division of the property between the Tolstoy children (in 1891), the part belonging to Masha was worth 57,000 rubles. At first she refused this, but after her marriage she decided to accept her share. Her brother Sergei was to pay her this money from the mortgage on the Nikolskoe-Vyazemskoe estate. Before this, however, Sofia had taken the money, assuming that her daughter would later accept her share, and Sergei gave an undertaking to pay the money to his mother. Sofia now had to hand over to Masha the money Sergei had given her, and transfer to her name the remainder of the sum he owed her.

p. 161, *Kholevinskaya... help her*: Maria Kholevinskaya, a *zemstvo* doctor in the Krapivna district of the province of Tula, was arrested in Tula in March 1896 and sent to prison for distributing the banned works of Tolstoy. She was arrested after a search revealed Tanya Tolstaya's visiting card, with the message: "Give Tolstoy's 'What I Believe' to a man you don't know, who is reliable." In April that year, Kholevinskaya was released from prison and exiled to Astrakhan. In a letter to Sofia of 30th May 1897, she said she was in bad health and begged her to "do her utmost to see that the punishment was alleviated". What was "unpleasant" about this letter was that she referred several times to being unjustly punished on account of Tanya's "ill-considered action".

p. 161, *Lev Nikolaevich... Chertkov in England*: Chertkov reproached Tolstoy in a letter of 19th June for not replying to several letters of his. On 20th June Tolstoy sent Chertkov a telegram apologizing for the delay.

p. 163, *Aphrodite*: Pierre Louÿs, Paris, 1896. For Tolstoy's negative opinion of this book, see his *What Is Art?*

p. 163, *Les Demi-vierges*: Marcel Prévost, Paris, 1894

p. 165, *A young man... long time*: Stepan Shidlovsky, a peasant Stundist, living in the village of Kishentsa near Kiev. (The Stundists were an evangelical, communistically inclined sect, living in communes mainly in the South of Russia.) In a letter to P.I. Biryukov, of 14th July, Tolstoy wrote: "New friends have appeared from the province of Kiev. One of them, Shidlovsky, has been staying with us. I liked him very much."

p. 170, *kvas*: A popular mildly alcoholic drink made from fermented bread.

p. 172, *the Englishman Maude*: Aylmer Maude, translator of Tolstoy's works into English and author of a biography.

p. 174, *some factory worker*: Pyotr Bulakhov, a former Old Believer. According to Tolstoy, a man of "Herculean strength, both morally and intellectually".

p. 178, *Boulanger*: Pavel Boulanger, official on the Moscow–Kursk railway and fellow thinker of Tolstoy's.

p. 178, *Chertkov had expressly asked... in English*: Chertkov wrote to Tolstoy: "Recouping the funds spent on publication is directly dependent on the success of the English editions of your writings. And this success is largely dependent on *us* being the *first* to publish your latest works, which means preventing any other translators from acquiring by devious means a Russian transcript, either before us or simultaneously with us. It is most important for us to have a transcript of every new work of yours, if possible three weeks before it is distributed in manuscript form in Russia." On 8th August Tolstoy replied: "There need be no doubt that all my writings will go to you before anyone else, and that you will make arrangements for their translation and publication."

p. 181, *he has decided to write an open letter to be published abroad*: On 29th August 1897, Tolstoy wrote an open letter to the Swedish newspaper *Stokholm Tagblatt* refusing the Nobel Prize. Tolstoy felt the prize should be awarded to the Dukhobors. In October 1897 the paper published his letter. It was published in Russian in the journal *Free Thought*, no. 4, 1899. In referring to Nobel as a "kerosene merchant", Sofia was confusing the Swedish engineer Alfred Nobel with L.E. Nobel, the well-known oil magnate.

p. 182, *his friends have been deported*: Tolstoy's friends and co-thinkers, Biryukov, Tregubov and Chertkov, were exiled for "propaganda and illegal interference in the trial of the sectarians" and for distributing a proclamation, 'Help!', signed by them and Tolstoy, appealing for support for the Dukhobors. Chertkov was deported to England, Biryukov and Tregubov to the province of Courland.

p. 183, *St John... Chertkov*: Arthur St John, formerly an officer in the Indian Army, left the army under Tolstoy's influence and settled in a farming colony in the south of England. In September 1897 he travelled to Russia on Chertkov's instructions to give the Dukhobors money collected by English Quakers. As he wanted to be more closely acquainted with the Dukhobors, he went to the Caucasus, and was arrested there and banished from Russia.

p. 183, *Boulanger is being deported... the Dukhobors*: Pavel Boulanger was deported from Russia for his dealings with the Dukhobors in the Caucasus. In October 1897 Boulanger left for England.

p. 187, *We had a visit from some Molokans*: Molokans, members of the "milk-drinking" sect. On 18th September 1897, some Molokans visited Tolstoy from Samara begging him to use his influence to get their children returned to them. Their first visit to Tolstoy was in May that year. Tolstoy did everything in his power to help them. He wrote two letters to the Tsar and to a large number of influential people and friends. It was only in February 1898 that the children were eventually returned, thanks to the efforts of Tanya Tolstaya, who visited K.P. Pobedonostsev that January.

p. 188, *Lev Nikolaevich's letters to Koni... out of town*: Tolstoy gave the Molokans who visited in May a letter he wrote to the Tsar, as well as letters to A.F. Koni, A.V. Olsufiev, A.S. Taneev, K.O. Khis and A.A. Tolstaya, asking them to help the Molokans. The Molokans destroyed the letters for fear of reprisals.

p. 199, *his application... volunteer in the army*: In 1898 Misha Tolstoy left the Lycée and enlisted.

p. 200, *L.N. has described life in Moscow as "suicide"... not to come*: Sofia Tolstoy wrote to Tolstoy on 25th November: "I thought, Lyovochka, that you would come here with Tanya, but you are evidently delaying your visit for as long as possible. Tanya told me you had even gone so far as to say that living in Moscow would be 'suicide' for you. Since you feel you are only coming here for my sake, this is not suicide, I am killing you. So I am now hastening to write and tell you for God's sake, don't come! This visit, which is such agony for you, will only deprive us both of our peace of mind and freedom. You will feel you are being 'murdered'. Let us not kill one another with demands and reproaches, let us write to one another as friends, and I shall visit you when my nerves are calmer." Tolstoy referred to this in his diary: "An aggrieved letter from Sonya. I shouldn't have said it, but Tanya shouldn't have repeated it."

p. 200, *Safonova*: Varvara Safonova, wife of Vasily Safonov, pianist, conductor and director of the Moscow Conservatoire.

p. 200, *Makovitsky*: Doctor Dushan Petrovich Makovitsky, a Slovak, who had set up a Slovak branch of the Intermediary publishing house in Hungary, made a second visit to Yasnaya Polyana in connection with publishing matters. On that day Tolstoy noted in his diary: "This morning Makovitsky came, a sweet, pure, mild man."

p. 202, *in his diary he writes that I had "acknowledged my crime"*: Tolstoy noted on 7th December: "Yesterday we talked and talked, and I heard something from Sonya that I have never heard before: an acknowledgement of her crime. This was a great joy. No matter what the future holds, it has happened and it is very good."

p. 203, *Qu'est-ce que... jeune*: "How do you manage to stay so young?" (French).

p. 206, *Lev Nikolaevich is totally unperturbed... in God's hands*: Tolstoy wrote in his diary on 21st December: "Received an anonymous letter yesterday threatening to kill me if I didn't mend my ways by 1898. 1898, no later. It's both frightening and good."

1898

p. 208, *Stasov*: Vladimir Stasov, well-known art and music critic.

p. 209, *He is reading all he can find... everything*: In this period Tolstoy was working on his story *Hadji Murat*.

p. 211, *Biryukov is leaving Bauska for England*: Pavel Biryukov, deported in 1897 to Bauska in Latvia for his part in helping the Dukhobors, received permission to go abroad in January.

p. 212, *Molokans... begging for letters of introduction... St Petersburg*: Tolstoy addressed a petition to the Tsar in the name of one of these visiting Molokans – F.I. Samoshkin – and asked Tanya Tolstaya, who was in St Petersburg at the time, to support their campaign.

p. 216, *publish his preface... perfectly*: At the time of writing his article *What Is Art?*, Tolstoy wrote a preface to an article by Edward Carpenter called 'Modern Science', translated by his son Seryozha. Tolstoy confessed that this article "explained" his own "work on art" to him.

p. 223, *Lev Nikolaevich's letter... collecting money for this*: The Dukhobors, having received permission from the Russian government to emigrate, appealed to Tolstoy for help. On 17th March he wrote a letter to the editor of the *St Petersburg Gazette* appealing for public support for the Dukhobors, and also to E.E. Ukhtomsky, the paper's editor. The appeal was not published.

p. 226, *my story*: Her story, 'Song without Words'.

p. 226, *Seryozha about some musical translation... questions*: At Taneev's suggestion, Seryozha Tolstoy was translating from the English Ebenezer Prout's book *Musical Form*, Moscow-Leipzig, 1900.

p. 227, *Lyova has come... sell the house*: After the division of the property between Sofia Tolstoy and the children in 1891, the Tolstoy's Moscow house belonged to Lyova Tolstoy.

p. 228, *In Grinevka... canteens*: Tolstoy stayed in Grinevka from 24th April to 27th May. His son Ilya, who accompanied him on his trips around the region, later wrote that when making these enquiries, "Father always did the hardest work himself – finding out how many mouths there were to feed in each peasant family. He often used to travel round the villages for days at a time, often until late at night." In all, twenty canteens were opened.

p. 230, *asking Tanya for... 10,000 rubles*: Chertkov begged Tanya Sukhotina for a loan in two letters to her from England, dated the 8th and 9th of May. On 14th July Tolstoy informed Anna Chertkova (Chertkov's wife) that his son Lyova Tolstoy had agreed to loan Chertkov the required sum.

p. 234, *those two summers*: S.I. Taneev stayed at Yasnaya Polyana in the summers of 1895 and 1896.

p. 237, *we were obviously in the right*: As a result of this court case the land remained with the Tolstoys.

p. 237, *something L.N. wrote... concerning women... animal*: The exact text of Tolstoy's entry in his notebook, in April 1898, was: "A woman can only be liberated if she is a Christian. A liberated woman who is not a Christian is a wild beast."

p. 240, *Father Sergei... unfinished*: In June 1898 Tolstoy resumed work on his story *Father Sergei*, which he had started in 1890, but after returning to Yasnaya Polyana he did no work on it and it was not published in his lifetime.

p. 241, *He wants to finish Hadji Murat... emigration scheme*: Tolstoy had intended to publish three works which were still unfinished and needed to be revised: *Father Sergei*, 'The Devil' and *Resurrection*. But he then concentrated all his attention on *Resurrection*, on which he worked until the end of 1899.

p. 241, *two Dukhobors... most unpleasant*: Two Dukhobors, P.V. Planidin and S.Z. Postnikov, who arrived at Yasnaya Polyana on 3rd August, had no passports and were hiding from the authorities.

p. 243, *England... the Dukhobors... from Chertkov*: Chertkov was a member of a committee formed by English Quakers in London to help the Dukhobors. At Tolstoy's suggestion two Dukhobors, N.S. Zibarov and I.P. Obrosimov, visited Chertkov in England on 29th August 1898 to clarify the terms of the emigration to Canada and work out how much the journey would cost.

p. 243, *he doesn't marry... be hypocrisy*: The first published edition (1899) of the novel ended with Nekhlyudov's marriage to Katyusha and their departure to London.

p. 249, *Pasternak*: Leonid Pasternak, father of the writer, spent several days at Yasnaya Polyana. He later recalled that he did not want simply to "illustrate certain passages but to do a powerful artistic rendering of the Russian life Tolstoy was describing in his portraits of various layers of society".

p. 253, *Nous jouons gros jeu*: "We are taking a big risk" (French).

p. 253, *Mozart and Salieri, and Orpheus*: On 25th November 1898, the Private Moscow Opera House staged the première of Rimsky-Korsakov's opera *Mozart and Salieri*. The part of Salieri was sung by Chaliapin. Gluck's *Orpheus and Eurydice* was performed on the same night.

p. 259, *arshin and a half*: Forty-two inches.

p. 259, *The Soul of a People*: C. Fielding, *The Soul of a People*. The American writer Ernest Crosby sent Tolstoy this book in November 1898. It was later translated into Russian on Tolstoy's initiative, and published as *The Soul of a People. The Story of the English Officer Fielding and His Life in Burma*.

1899

p. 262, *Andryusha's wedding*: Andrei Tolstoy was about to marry Olga Dieterichs.

p. 263, *Lev Nikolaevich had a visit from Myasoedov... Resurrection*: I.M. Vinogradov, inspector of the Butyrki convict prison in Moscow, was invited by Tolstoy to look over the proofs of *Resurrection* for him. Tolstoy noted down his observations and made use of them in his subsequent work on the novel.

p. 265, *Seryozha... his song... wept*: Sergei Tolstoy's song 'We meet again...' was set to words by A.A. Fet; Tolstoy considered it "sincere".

p. 267, *received a telegram... left for Kiev on Monday morning*: Sofia Tolstoy left for Kiev on 8th February 1899. In reply to a letter from his wife informing him of Tanya Kuzminskaya's almost hopeless condition, Tolstoy wrote, on 11th–12th February: "I know we all die, and there's nothing bad about death, but it is still very painful. I love her very much."

p. 268, *Trubetskoy… horse*: Trubetskoy did several sculptures of Tolstoy on horseback. The Tolstoy Museum contains a bronze sculpture (1904) and a bust (plaster covered in bronze 1900) by Trubetskoy, which Sofia considered the best of all his sculptures.

p. 273, *a novel*: Probably 'Song without Words'.

1900

p. 274, *The Corpse*: Tolstoy worked on his play *The Living Corpse*, originally titled *The Corpse*, from the beginning of January to November 1900. The play remained unfinished and was not published in his lifetime.

p. 275, *They are thinking of starting a journal… the scheme*: Pavel Boulanger had the idea of publishing a weekly, illustrated, literary-political and scientific journal called *Morning*. When they heard about Tolstoy's proposed participation in the scheme, the Chief Department for Press Affairs forbade the journal to be published.

p. 275, *The Ice House*: A.N. Koreshchenko's opera *The Ice House*, libretto by Modest Tchaikovsky, was performed in 1900 in the Bolshoi Theatre.

p. 277, *This Malayan had read… him*: On 19th November 1900, Tolstoy was visited by a Dutchman called Engelberg who had an administrative post on the island of Java and arrived with his friend.

p. 278, *two choral works… 'The Stars'*: S.I. Taneev. Two choral works and one "a cappella" piece for four mixed voices, 'Stars' and 'At the Midnight Hour', words by A.S. Khomyakov; 'Alps' and 'Through the Azure Gloom of Night', words by F.I. Tyutchev.

p. 278, *the lunatic asylum*: Professor S.S. Korsakov's psychiatric clinic.

p. 280, *zhaleiki*: Russian folk wind instrument rather like a fife, made from a young branch of willow, or a reed cane, with a mouthpiece of cow horn or birch bark.

1901

p. 287, *On 24th February… has been excommunicated*: On 24th February 1901, issue no. 8 of the *Church Gazette* published an announcement from the Holy Synod about Tolstoy, dated 20th–22nd February, which said: "The Church does not consider him a member as long as he does not repent and doesn't restore his links with it." On 25th February this document appeared in the newspapers. This was Tolstoy's official excommunication from the Church. The newspaper cutting is pasted into the diary.

p. 287, *I myself wrote… here*: On 26th February 1901, Sofia Tolstoy sent a letter to the Chief Procurator of the Synod, K.P. Pobedonostsev, and the Metropolitans who had signed the excommunication. Learning of its contents, Tolstoy said, "There have been so many books written on the subject that you couldn't fit them into the house – and you want to teach them what to do with your letter." Sofia Tolstoy's letter was printed on 24th March 1901, in a supplement of the *Church Gazette*, along with Metropolitan Antony's reply of 16th March 1901. She pasted a cutting of this letter into her diary, with her own comments in the margin. "There are no limits to my sad indignation," she wrote, "and not because my husband will be spiritually destroyed by this document: this is not men's business, it is God's. The religious life of a human soul is known to none but God, and mercifully it is not answerable to anyone. But as for the Church to which I belong and which I shall never renounce, which was created by Christ to bless in God's name all the significant moments of life – births, weddings, deaths, human joys and griefs – from the point of view of this Church, the Synod's instructions are utterly incomprehensible to me. It provokes not sympathy, but anger, and great love and compassion for Lev Nikolaevich. We are already receiving expressions of this – and there will be no end to them – from all over the world."

p. 288, *upheavals in the university... the poor*: 183 students were drafted into the army for participating in the student uprisings that took place in Kiev University in January 1901. This provoked students in St Petersburg and elsewhere to come out in support of them. On 25th February there was a demonstration of students and workers in Moscow.

p. 288, *None of Lev Nikolaevich's manuscripts... foreign languages*: Her letter was published only in the foreign press and distributed in Russia in hectographed form; the Moscow censorship committee had been sent a circular forbidding papers to publish telegrams and other material "expressing sympathy" with Tolstoy.

p. 288, *Lev Nikolaevich... His Assistants*: Tolstoy's letter was in response to the government's persecution of students who had taken part in the demonstrations, and was also sent to the Grand Dukes and all the Ministers.

p. 288, *my concert in aid of the orphanage... 1,307 rubles*: The concert took place on 7th March 1901. The programme of the concert has been sewn into the Diary.

p. 289, *I received... completely soulless*: Metropolitan Antony wrote to her on 16th March 1901: "It is not the Synod which has acted cruelly in announcing your husband's lapse from the Church, it is he himself who has acted cruelly in renouncing his faith in Jesus Christ, son of the living God, our saviour and expiator. This renunciation should have provoked your grief and anger long ago. And your husband will not of course perish from a scrap of printed paper, but from the fact that he has turned aside from the source of Life Eternal. You receive expressions of sympathy from the entire world. This does not surprise me, but I do not think this is any cause for consolation. There is human glory, and there is the glory of God."

p. 293, *letter from Queen Elizabeth... her little book*: Letter from Queen Elizabeth (pseudonym Carmen Silva) of 16th July. Tolstoy thanked her for her letter, and told her he hadn't received the work she sent.

p. 297, *Doctor Makovitsky*: The Slovak Doctor Dushan Makovitsky had visited Yasnaya Polyana twice before, in 1894 and 1897.

p. 298, *Maxim Gorky*: Gorky was staying at a dacha in Oleiza, about a mile from Gaspra.

1902

p. 301, *Giuseppe Mazzini's On Human Duty*: Tolstoy considered the book "excellent".

p. 303, *Chekhov called*: Anton Chekhov, who was living in Yalta, visited Tolstoy soon after his arrival in the Crimea, and had several meetings with him.

p. 307, *he asked... to it*: Tolstoy was continuing work on 'On Religious Tolerance'.

p. 308, *Count Olsufiev... easy death*: Apropos of the death of A.V. Olsufiev, a friend of the Tolstoy family who died on 9th September 1901 of diabetes, Tolstoy wrote to his brother Sergei, on 6th November 1901: "He was walking about in the morning, talked for 10 minutes, realized he was dying, said goodbye to everyone, gave advice to his children and kept repeating: 'I never thought dying would be so easy.'"

p. 310, *dictated a page of ideas... as he calls it*: Evidently the first version of the Preface to 'Notes for Soldiers' and 'Notes for Officers'. The text was written in Masha Obolenskaya's hand, dated 8th February (unpublished).

p. 311, *my unfinished children's story, 'Skeletons'*: The short story 'Skeleton Dolls', its final title, appeared in: S.A. Tolstoy, *Skeleton Dolls and Other Stories*, Moscow, 1910.

p. 318, *the Wanderers' Exhibition*: Thirtieth exhibition of paintings by the Fellowship of Wandering Artists.

p. 319, *He is dictating ideas... at the moment*: The contents of this dictated text relates to his article 'To the Working People'.

p. 321, *Arguments about the Bashkirs*: This relates to Tolstoy's disagreement with Sofia as to whether some Bashkirs should be invited to Yasnaya Polyana with their koumiss mares; Tolstoy was strongly urged by his doctors to drink koumiss.

p. 322, *saffron milk caps*: A small, yellowish mushroom.

p. 323, *he writes his novel Hadji Murat*: Tolstoy resumed work on *Hadji Murat* on 24th June 1902.

p. 323, *Sergei Ivanovich... musical textbook*: Taneev finished his work *Mobile Counterpoint on Old Notation* in 1908 and published it in 1909.

p. 324, *The priests... him*: Tolstoy observed in his diary: "Leaflet from a priest – very painful. Why do they hate me?"

p. 325, *started on a proclamation to the clergy*: Tolstoy began work on his article 'To the Clergy'.

p. 328, *a legend he has just written, about devils*: The legend 'Destruction and Reconstruction of Hell' on which Tolstoy worked from November 1902 to the end of that year, was thought up as an illustration to his article 'To the Clergy'.

p. 330, *Kropotkin's Notes*: P.A. Kropotkin, *Notes of a Revolutionary*, London, 1902. On Tolstoy's admission, "reading Kropotkin's splendid memoirs" made him consider writing his own memoirs.

1903

p. 332, *Two more Englishmen... will save him*: Tom Ferris and Bert Toy visited Russia to meet Tolstoy and discuss spiritualism with him. They visited Yasnaya Polyana, but their conversation with Tolstoy was a brief one because he was ill.

p. 337, *We had a visit from an old man and his wife... Athanasius*: The peasant A.N. Ageev was sentenced to exile in Siberia, in January 1903, for blasphemy. Tolstoy tried to help him and his family and took an active part in their case. On 29th August 1903, Ageev was sent to Siberia.

1904

p. 339, *three students from the St Petersburg... energy*: A delegation of students from the St Petersburg Mining Institute brought Tolstoy a letter expressing their deep love and admiration. They wanted to discuss the agrarian question and the student revolutionary movement with him.

p. 339, *a rehearsal of Chekhov's The Cherry Orchard*: Rehearsals of *The Cherry Orchard* were going on at the Moscow Public Art Theatre.

p. 341, *the latest news... war with the Japanese*: The Russo-Japanese War started on 27th January 1904, and every day from then on notes appeared in Tolstoy's diary about this "terrible deed", as he called the war.

p. 341, *Lev Nikolaevich told us the story... commenced*: In May 1851, Tolstoy and his elder brother Nikolai left for the Caucasus, where Nikolai was serving. In June Tolstoy took part in a raid as a volunteer, and described this in his story 'The Raid'. On 3rd January 1852, he joined the artillery as a cadet; in January 1854 he was made an ensign and transferred at his own request to the Danubian army, and in November of that year he moved to Sevastopol, where he fought until the end of the siege.

1905

p. 346, *Pavel Biryukov... exile in Switzerland*: Biryukov was deported from Russia in 1897 for giving aid to the Dukhobors. He received permission to return after the manifesto of 11th August 1904. He went to Yasnaya Polyana in December 1904 and stayed there until January 1905.

p. 346, *Lev Nikolaevich is writing an article... zemstvo*: In January 1905 Tolstoy wrote an article entitled 'On the Social Movement in Russia'. It was a reply to innumerable letters begging him to speak out about the *zemstvo*'s agitation for a limitation of the autocracy and the introduction of a representative system of government, and about the massacre of peaceful demonstrators in St Petersburg on 9th January 1905 (Bloody Sunday). The article was published in England by Chertkov in *Free Word*, no. 92, 1905.

p. 346, *Dreadful news from St Petersburg... killed*: Those in Yasnaya Polyana learnt about the events of 9th January 1905 in St Petersburg from the newspapers, and from Pavel Boulanger, who visited shortly afterwards.

1908

p. 349, *There were some very touching presents... signatures*: In a letter to those who had sent him greetings on his birthday, Tolstoy wrote: "I thank all who have written to me, and those dear people who have touched me so much with their presents – the St Petersburg waiters who gave me a lovely inscribed samovar, various workers, and many others."

p. 349, *Some artists sent a lovely album of watercolours*: An album of drawings by Kasatkin, Vasnetsov, Baturin, Pasternak and others (watercolours, pastels and pencil drawings) was sent to Tolstoy by the Moscow Society of Art-Lovers.

p. 349, *numerous portraits of Lev Nikolaevich... of his*: E. Cherchopova sent a satin-stitch embroidery of Tolstoy in the fields. The portrait was sent by the artist Gusikyan.

p. 350, *there was a box... do it himself*: This parcel arrived in Yasnaya Polyana on 1st September 1908. A detachable coupon showed a Moscow address and the surname of the sender, O.A. Markova. Tolstoy replied to O.A. Markova on 3rd September 1908: "You would make me very happy if you would explain to me the reasons for your ill feelings." Later Gusev established that there was no O.A. Markova living at this address.

p. 350, *he had galloped... Caucasus*: Some details of this episode were later used by Tolstoy in his story 'The Prisoner of the Caucasus'.

p. 352, *Eight young revolutionaries... feelings*: This proclamation was issued by the Socialist Revolutionaries in Tula. Four (not eight) Tula printers who were members of the party visited Tolstoy at his invitation.

p. 354, *He has written and published a book about the Apocalypse*: In April 1907 Tolstoy received N.A. Morozov's book *Revelation in Storm and Tempest. A History of the Origins of the Apocalypse*, St Petersburg, 1907, with a dedication: "To Lev Nikolaevich Tolstoy, as a mark of the author's deep esteem, 31st March, N. Morozov".

1909

p. 355, *copying out... completed*: Sofia Tolstoy was copying the rough drafts of his story 'Who Are the Murderers? Pavel Kudryash', on which he worked from December 1908 to February 1909. The work remained unfinished.

p. 355, *Wanda Landowska came today and performed for us*: This was the second time the harpsichordist Wanda Landowska visited Yasnaya Polyana. Tolstoy wrote of her playing: "She plays pleasantly and charmingly, but does not transport one's soul, and I love that experience, however painful."

1910

p. 359, *Chertkov's... mother in Telyatinki*: Chertkov received permission to live in Telyatinki while his mother was staying there. He arrived on 27th June.

p. 360, *Lev Nikolaevich didn't like my letter to Chertkov*: In this letter of 1st July, Sofia explains the reasons for her change of attitude to him: "If you have any feelings for me and Lev Nikolaevich's peace of mind, which will be fully restored if you and I can make friends in the last years of his life, then I beg you, with an aching heart and a readiness to love and appreciate you – give me Lev Nikolaevich's diaries. If you carry out my request then we shall be friends, more so than before. If not, it will be painful for Lev Nikolaevich to see our relations; I am incapable of forcing my feelings in another direction – I have been too shocked by the disappearance of the diaries."

p. 361, *I managed to get Chertkov to write a note... back to L.N.*: In a note to Tolstoy Chertkov wrote: "Dear L.N., in view of your wife's desire that I give her back your diaries, which you gave me to delete the passages you indicated, I shall make haste to finish this work and return the notebooks as soon as I have done so."

p. 362, *I find Sasha's behaviour very painful*: Sasha Tolstaya noted in her diary: "It was decided to extract the passages we didn't want to give Sofia Andreevna, and give her the rest."

p. 362, *She is a "Radstockist"*: E.I. Chertkova was a follower of the English preacher Grenville Radstock: according to his interpretation of the Gospels, man would acquire salvation from sin through faith in the redemption of the human race, brought about by Christ's death.

p. 362, *a fire on Tanya's estate at Ovsyannikovo*: There were suspicions that the fire might have been arson, started by a village youth who had been given shelter by her.

p. 362, *30 letters to her from him*: Apart from one, dated 3rd August 1887, they were all taken from copies kept by Chertkov. He also kept copies that Maria Schmidt had made of 'Investigations into Dogmatic Theology', the final version of the story *Emelyan the Worker* and various other works.

p. 363, *madness and suicide... every angle*: Tolstoy had resumed work on his article 'On Suicide', which had been started in March and was now given the title 'On Madness'.

p. 364, *my grandchildren*: Sofia and Ilya, Andrei Tolstoy's children from his first marriage to Olga Dieterichs, who lived at Telyatinki with her cousin Chertkov.

p. 367, *that letter Chertkov wrote to the newspapers... insensitivity*: On 18th June, shortly after Tolstoy's arrival, the following letter from Chertkov appeared in many major newspapers: "In view of the fact that various announcements have appeared in the press regarding Lev N—ch Tolstoy's visit to my house, I consider it necessary to warn any persons who might wish to visit him here that on those occasions when L.N. leaves Yasnaya

Polyana he is in need of rest and seeks as much privacy as possible. For those who value his health and tranquillity, therefore, the best way to show their good wishes towards him is to refrain from visiting him on these occasions. I am making this announcement with L.N.'s consent, in the full confidence that those who wish him well will respect the feelings that have inspired this appeal, and act in accordance with it."

p. 371, *the letter he gave me this morning*: The letter, written on the morning of 14th July, in which Tolstoy announced his decision: "1) I shall give no one my present diary, and shall keep it with me. 2) I shall take my earlier diaries back from Chertkov and shall keep them myself, probably in the bank." Tolstoy also explained in this letter the reasons for his estrangement from his wife, and suggested "terms for a good and peaceful life". If these were not accepted, he wrote, he would "leave" Yasnaya Polyana.

p. 372, *a house in Rudakovo... Ovsyannikovo*: Sofia Tolstoy was intending to buy the Rudakovo house in place of Tanya's house, where Maria Schmidt had lived, that had burnt down.

p. 373, *several beginnings... important*: Tolstoy started various works in 1910, including 'Three Days in the Country', 'There Are No Guilty People in the World', 'Khodynka' and the article 'On Madness'.

p. 373, *When Lev N. told me he was coming ... not to come*: On this day Tolstoy went himself to see Chertkov. It was his last visit to Telyatinki.

p. 374, *his name derives from the word "devil"*: "Devil" – "chert" in Russian.

p. 376, *22nd July*: On 22nd July Tolstoy signed a will drawn up by his lawyer, Muravyov, according to which all his literary works, published and unpublished, finished and unfinished, all his manuscripts and everything he had ever written would become the "exclusive property of Alexandra Lvovna Tolstaya". Tolstoy was obliged to name someone as his heir, otherwise the will would have been legally invalid. The writer's real wish, that "all his works and all his writings" should not belong "to any private individual" and should be "published and reprinted by anyone who wished", was expressed in an 'Explanatory Note' written by Chertkov as a supplement to the will. Chertkov was granted the right to supervise and publish the writer's manuscripts after his death.

p. 380, *Molochnikov*: V.A. Molochnikov, a follower of Tolstoy's, was twice arrested, in 1908 and 1910, for harbouring and distributing banned works by Tolstoy. He made Tolstoy's acquaintance in 1907 and was in correspondence with him from 1906. Tolstoy treated him very warmly and conducted a wide-ranging correspondence with him (there are known to be more than forty letters).

p. 381, *the Russian Consul to India*: S.V. Chirkin.

p. 385, *Today he wrote... military service*: On that day Tolstoy received five young peasant recruits intending to refuse military service and wrote an appeal for them, 'To the Unknown Ones'.

p. 386, *Christianity and Patriotism... censored*: The treatise 'Christianity and Patriotism' was banned in Russia and distributed illegally. In a letter of 7th August, Stakhovich told Sofia Tolstoy that he had found "dubious" and "indisputably dangerous passages" in all the books she sent him, including in this work.

p. 386, *awaiting trial in St Petersburg... The Construction of Hell*: The trial took place on 20th November. L.L. Tolstoy was acquitted.

p. 387, *I am asking Sasha for my diary... out of it*: At her father's request, she was copying the thoughts contained in the notebook section of his diary.

p. 388, *handed him a scrap of paper... about it*: Tanya wrote to Chertkov on 16th August: "There was nothing but grief and distress when she caught L.N. going into Sasha's room this evening for his diary. And today she wrote him a note about this. Later I asked her not to say any more about it and she agreed, saying she would try to control herself."

p. 388, *skopets*: V. Grigoriev. A member of the *skoptsy* sect that practised castration.

p. 389, *the government... Telyatinki*: On 14th August Chertkov received official notification that the government had lifted the ban against his living anywhere in the province of Tula, and particularly in the village of Telyatinki. This information appeared in many newspapers on 18th August.

p. 390, *Two bulky parcels were posted... Mr Chertkov*: Bulgakov was sent three letters which Tolstoy had received, with his notes and a request for an answer, as well as a letter from Sasha Tolstaya containing a list of books to be sent to the addresses indicated, and one letter for Chertkov.

p. 394, *I sent for the priest... holy water*: Sofia Tolstoy invited a priest called Kudryavtsev to the house to perform a service with holy water exorcizing the spirit of Chertkov. When he heard about this, Tolstoy wrote on 3rd–4th September in his 'Diary for Myself Alone': "She burns his pictures and has a service performed in the house. I must try to remember she is ill."

p. 395, *I wept and sobbed all day... suffering*: Tolstoy noted in his 'Diary for Myself Alone': "She spent the whole of yesterday the 9th in hysterics, ate nothing, wept. She was very pathetic."

p. 395, *Lev Nik... when*: "Painful discussions about my departure. I stood up for my freedom. I shall go when *I* want," Tolstoy noted in his diary.

p. 398, *Malinovsky's Blood Revenge*: Malinovsky's book *Blood Revenge and the Death Sentence*, Tomsk, 1910, sent to Tolstoy by the author with a dedication: "To Lev Nikolaevich Tolstoy, who exposes all violence, and especially the great evil known as capital punishment". Tolstoy found "much good and useful material" in this book.

p. 399, *'On Money'*: The tract 'What Then Must We Do?' She is using one of Tolstoy's working titles for the piece. "I am completely occupied with the article 'What Is to Be Done?', which is all about money," he had written at the beginning of April 1885 to Chertkov.

p. 401, *Chertkov wrote a mean and characteristically unclear letter*: On 6th October Chertkov wrote Tolstoy two letters. In the first he wrote: "I think that both in order to give Sofia Andreevna the opportunity to adopt a more loving attitude to you, and to enable you to derive full benefit from the relief this change will bring, it would be most unwise, while Sofia Andreevna's condition continues to improve, to mention me under any pretext whatsoever." In the second letter Chertkov accepted an invitation to visit Tolstoy at Yasnaya Polyana, on condition that "Sofia Andreevna is not present".

p. 402, *interrupting him... in Nice*: In his 'Diary for Myself Alone' Tolstoy wrote: "I told her everything I thought necessary. She answered back and I lost my temper."

p. 403, *Chertkov has now persuaded Lev N... public property*: It is possible she had read a long letter from Chertkov of 11th August, to which he affixed an excerpt from his diary of 4th December 1908. In this he sets out in detail the story of the drafting of Tolstoy's will, and refers to the mercenary intentions of his family, who, he claimed, would appropriate the rights to his literary inheritance.

p. 403, *the bread... mouths*: She had found Tolstoy's 'Diary for Myself Alone', which he had tried to conceal from her, in which she learnt about the existence of this secret will.

p. 403, *Lev Nik. wrote in his diary... to me*: Entry for 30th July in 'Diary for Myself Alone'.

p. 404, *When I timidly opened the door... hatred*: Tolstoy noted in his diary on that day: "On my desk was a letter from Sofia Andreevna, filled with accusations. When she came in I asked her to leave me in peace. She went out. I had difficulty breathing and my pulse was over 90."

p. 407, *Novikov*: Mikhail Novikov described his meeting with Tolstoy in an article entitled 'My Last Meeting', published in the journals *Unity and the Voice of Tolstoy* and *True Freedom*. Tolstoy told Novikov about his intention to "leave" Yasnaya Polyana. "I want to die in peace, I want to be with God," he told him; "here they're all wondering what I am worth. I shall leave, I shall certainly leave." On 24th October Tolstoy wrote Novikov a letter with a request: "Do you think you could find me a hut in your village, no matter how small, just so long as it's warm and secluded?" Novikov delayed in replying, and spent days and nights pondering how best to dissuade him from leaving Yasnaya Polyana. His letter was eventually brought to Tolstoy at Astapovo when he was dying.

p. 407, *some of our villagers... revolutionary*: "Perevoznikov came too, and Tito's son, a revolutionary," noted Tolstoy. "Tito's son" was M.Y. Polin, who had just left prison for participating in the revolutionary movement. Perevoznikov, a metal-worker and member of a workers' circle, lived with Chertkov.

p. 409, *In his letter to me... like the peasants*: In his farewell letter to his wife, he wrote: "I cannot go on living in the luxury which has always surrounded me here, and am doing what most old men of my age do: leaving this worldly life in order to spend my last days in solitude and silence. Please understand this, I beg you, and do not come to fetch me, even if you discover where I am."

p. 409, *I jumped... alas*: According to Bulgakov, Chertkov's mother told Goldenweiser on 29th October: "Sofia Andreevna has been in a state of great agitation. She has attempted to kill herself by various methods."

p. 409, *They didn't let me in to see Lev Nik*: The only members of Tolstoy's family who were with him were his daughters Tanya and Sasha and his son Sergei. The 'Medical findings on the illness and death of L.N. Tolstoy', dated 9th November and signed by Makovitsky, Nikitin and Berkenheim, gave the following explanation for this: "It was decided at a family council, in accordance with the doctors' proposal, that no other members of his family should be allowed in to see L.N., as there was good reason to believe he would grow extremely agitated at the appearance of any new faces, and this might have dire consequences for his life, which was hanging on a thread."

Daily Diary

1907

p. 415, *her splendid article about the fire... moved*: Tanya's letter to the newspapers of 5th August 1907 about the fire on her estate, and the peasants' attitude to it. Edited by Tolstoy and with a preface by him, it was published in *Voice of Moscow*, no. 188, 14th August 1907. "Tanya's article touches me," wrote Tolstoy after receiving a copy.

1909

p. 417, *a 30-year-old Romanian... The Kreutzer Sonata*: A. Marukhin. Tolstoy's comment on him in his diary was: "an exceedingly interesting man".

p. 417, *some cinematographers from Paris*: Representatives of the French cinematographic firm Pathé received permission to visit Tolstoy and film him. But on 2nd September a telegram was sent on Tolstoy's instructions asking them not to come. They came nonetheless, and filmed his departure from Shchekino station.

1910

p. 418, *officer... scurrilous verses about Lev Nikolaevich*: A retired colonel called Trotsky-Sanyutovich wrote some verses accusing Tolstoy of apostasy towards the Orthodox Church and the government. After talking to Tolstoy he became ashamed of his verses and decided to burn them.

p. 418, *Two real Japanese men*: Harala Tatsuki, director of a high school in Tokyo, and Mitsutaki Hodze, an official at the Ministry of Communications.

p. 418, *I sat down to play the piano... listened happily*: According to Bulgakov's memoirs:

Lev Nikolaevich said as he went out for tea how much he had enjoyed her playing.

She flushed: "You're joking," she said hesitantly.

"Not a bit of it. That adagio in '*Quasi una fantasia*' was so delicate…"

How happy Sofia Andreevna was!

"I deeply regret how badly I play, never more so than when Lev Nikolaevich is listening to me," she said later.

p. 419, *Painful discussion… for me*: Sergei Tolstoy explains this entry thus: "L.N. didn't 'drive' Sofia Andreevna anywhere, he merely said to her, when she complained about the difficulty of running Yasnaya Polyana, that she didn't need to live there and could live anywhere, even in Odoev, a town in Tula province."

p. 419, *the Circassian guard has brought Prokofy in… with him*: Ahmet the Circassian, who guarded the forest and meadows of Yasnaya Polyana, caught the peasant Prokofy Vlasov stealing wood and brought him into the office to be charged; Vlasov was a former student of Tolstoy's, from his first peasant school in Yasnaya Polyana. Tolstoy referred to this episode in his diary: "It has become insufferable here. I have considered leaving."

p. 419, *L. Nik. had gone to Belev… to see his sister Maria Nikolaevna*: Tolstoy set off from Yasnaya Polyana, accompanied by Doctor Makovitsky, his daughter Sasha and Varvara Mikhailovna, to Shchekino station, and from there took a train to Shamordino to see his sister Maria.

p. 419, *Lev Nik. did visit his sister in Shamordino… where*: They left Shamordino early on the morning of 31st October. On arriving at the station of Kozelsk, they boarded a train and travelled south.

p. 419, *Rastorguev, and a young lady fresh from medical school*: Doctor Rastegaev (she has misspelt the name) was accompanied by a medical student called Skorobogatova.

p. 420, *Lev Nik. wired for Chertkov in person*: At Tolstoy's request Sasha sent Chertkov a telegram on 1st November: "Got out yesterday at Astapovo. High fever. Lost consciousness. This morning temperature normal. Chills. Impossible to leave. Expressed desire to see you. Frolova." Wanting to keep his whereabouts a secret, Tolstoy and Sasha used pseudonyms in their correspondence. Tolstoy was "Nikolaev" and Sasha "Frolova".

p. 420, *At 6 o'clock in the morning Lev Nikol. died… Cruel people*: Her daughter Tanya recalled: "Mother went to him, sat at the head of the bed, leant over him and started whispering tender words to him, saying farewell and begging him to forgive her for the wrong she had done him. His only reply was a number of deep sighs."

p. 422, *I wrote to… Taneev*: Sofia Tolstoy wrote to Taneev: "At the end I caused L.N. a lot of distress and grief with my nervous illness and my dislike of Chertkov, who he didn't see on my account, and this is now the chief cause of my unhappiness. I live alone here in this great house, with the same servants and the same furniture as before. Everyone has left apart from Doctor Makovitsky, and he too will soon leave."

1911

p. 427, *my sons Ilya... America to sell Yasnaya Polyana*: Sofia and her youngest son, Vanechka, had been allotted the Yasnaya Polyana property. After Vanechka's death in 1895, the property was left to her and her sons. Immediately after Tolstoy's death the question arose as to the future of Yasnaya Polyana, since his heirs hadn't the means to maintain it. There was a scheme to redeem the property with money collected in "civilized countries", with a view to turning it into an international cultural monument, and selling the rest of the land to Americans for $1.5 million. Sofia's brother-in-law Mikhail Kuzminsky arrived in New York on 1st January, and conducted negotiations with various foreign industrialists. After interviews with Kuzminsky were published in the papers *Stock Exchange Gazette* and *Odessa Leaflet*, it became clear that this plan to sell Russia's national property to foreigners aroused deep indignation, and this was expressed in speeches, articles and letters. At the end of April there was an interview with Tolstoy's sons (Sergei Tolstoy wasn't party to this and refused his share of the inheritance), in which they announced: "We did indeed hold negotiations with American millionaires, but these concerned only the sale of the land, not the property. Our common desire was to sell everything to the nation." Ilya Tolstoy didn't go to America.

p. 428, *The newspapers and lawyers have stood up for my rights*: She is referring to a series of articles sympathetic to her point of view which appeared in several papers.

p. 428, *pages from Lev Nik.'s notebooks... period*: The plan for the novel was familiar to her. But this was evidently her first acquaintance with the texts of the rough versions. "At our recent meeting," wrote A. Ksyunin after visiting Yasnaya Polyana, "Sofia Andreevna told me she had just found some pages written in pencil relating to Tolstoy's planned epic about Peter the Great. L.N. didn't write this work, as he said 'I couldn't recreate the everyday life of the period.'"

p. 428, *my letter to Koni*: Her letter of 4th December 1910 about Tolstoy's flight was published, translated into French, under the title 'Tolstoy's Last Days', *Le Figaro*, 11th February 1923.

p. 429, *Volumes 16, 19 and 20... have been seized*: Vols. 16, 19 and 20 were seized after the censors sent a report to the Moscow Committee on Press Affairs about the instigation of criminal proceedings against the publishers for including "criminal works" in them.

p. 432, *Lyova's letters from America*: L.L. Tolstoy wrote about the problems of organizing an exhibition of his sculptures there.

p. 432, *the Palace of Justice has decided to destroy... edition*: It was announced in the press that the Moscow Palace of Justice had decreed that vols 16, 19 and 20 of the 12th edition should be destroyed because of the articles 'To the Working People', 'The Slavery of Our Time', 'A Great Sin', 'Thou Shalt Not Kill', 'Change Your Mind', 'I Cannot Keep Silent', 'The Law of Violence and the Law of Love', 'To the Tsar and His Assistants' and others, as they were found to contain "blasphemy", "inciting the people to adopt a hostile attitude to the government and an insolent disrespect for the higher authorities".

p. 432, *I went to the Palace of Justice... the new edition*: On this day she wrote to her daughter Tanya: "I visited the Censorship Committee at the Palace of Justice. I demanded, insisted and complained, and was eventually told that at 5 p.m. tomorrow I would be given a list of the banned articles with permission to reprint them; otherwise they would have destroyed 3 volumes."

p. 433, *Visited the censorship inspector... three volumes*: Sofia Tolstoy received permission to republish the last three volumes of the *Collected Works*. "After consideration of S.A. Tolstoy's petition, the Committee For Press Affairs agreed that the articles banned from L.N. Tolstoy's famous three volumes be cut from the published volumes. In the execution of this decree there took place yesterday, 28th April, in S.A. Tolstoy's warehouse, in the presence of representatives of the Censorship Committee, the police and one of the directors of the Kushneryov works, the removal of the seals from the confiscated books. These books will be taken to the printing works where the removal of the forbidden articles will proceed. The printing works are obliged to keep all the cut pages. After the cutting has been completed, officials from the Censorship Committee will take the exact number of cut pages, and the entire mass will either be shredded in the office of the printing works' director, or burnt under the observation of Censorship Committee officials in the stoves of the Kushneryov company."

p. 433, *The Empress has refused me an audience*: Sofia wrote on 3rd May to her sister Tanya: "The Empress has refused me an audience. It is said she hasn't forgotten what was said about me long ago: that I deceived Alexander III by promising not to publish *The Kreutzer Sonata* separately, then bringing it out in a separate edition. In fact it was brought out by some underground publishers."

p. 434, *give the Tsar my letter*: In her letter to the Tsar, dated 10th May, Sofia Tolstoy suggested that Yasnaya Polyana should be bought by the government. "It is our most passionate wish to leave his cradle and grave in the protection of the state," she wrote. "I consider it my last duty to his memory to keep the material and spiritual wealth of the Russian state in its own hands, and to preserve it untouched." She referred also in her letter to the situation with the Tolstoy manuscripts, and explained that it was her desire to "see that everything he wrote stays in Russia and for Russia", to "be kept permanently, free of charge, in some state or scientific safe in Russia".

p. 434, *talked to Guchkov about the sale of the Moscow house*: The purpose of her meeting with N.I. Guchkov, mayor of Moscow, was to propose that the Khamovniki Street house be sold to the town.

p. 435, *an old French book called De l'Amour*: Probably Pascal's *Discours sur les passions de l'amour*.

p. 435, *The plan is for me to move to the Kuzminskys' wing*: The Tolstoys' offer to sell Yasnaya Polyana to the government contained a number of conditions, including the burial of Sofia Tolstoy and her sons beside Tolstoy's grave, and her right to live there for the rest of her life in the so-called "Kuzminskys' wing".

p. 437, *a chapter in Resurrection... published abroad*: Chapter 39 of *Resurrection*, banned by the censors in Russia, was published in the anthology *From the Life of the Clergy*, London, 1902.

p. 438, *an application... Khamovniki Street*: The application was addressed to N.I. Guchkov. Sofia wrote that she agreed to sell the Khamovniki Street house, as well as the furniture in Tolstoy's study and the other rooms.

p. 438, *Does Woman Represent God*: English in original; not attributed.

p. 438, *Lev Nikolaevich's birthday... Lev Nik*: "On this unforgettable day for Russia," wrote the journalist Spiro in his essay, 'The 28th in Yasnaya Polyana', "the anniversary of the birth of the great writer of the Russian land, there gathered at his grave Tula police officers, the Tula police chief, the district police officer, district sergeants, village policemen and approximately a hundred armed mounted police guards. The police from virtually the whole of Tula province were there."

p. 439, *Prince Dolgorukov came to discuss the peasants' library*: Dolgorukov's arrival was occasioned by the decision of the Moscow Society of Literacy to build a reading room named after L.N. Tolstoy beside the Yasnaya Polyana peasant library.

p. 439, *Socrates's last discussion with his pupils*: 'The Death of Socrates. From Plato's Dialogues' in the *Circle of Reading*.

p. 440, *Our wedding anniversary... The Living Corpse*: On this day *The Living Corpse* was published for the first time.

p. 440, *Andryusha... The Living Corpse and the Tolstoy exhibition*: On 24th September *The Living Corpse* opened at the Arts Theatre. Dress rehearsals (on 20th and 21st September) were attended by Sergei, Ilya and Sasha, Tanya and many friends and followers of Tolstoy's. (Andrei Tolstoy was not there.) The solemn opening of the Tolstoy Exhibition took place on 11th October in Moscow, in the building of the Historical Museum.

p. 441, *the album and Skeleton Dolls*: Her album *From the Life of Tolstoy* and her anthology of children's stories.

p. 441, *Spent the morning at the Tolstoy Exhibition... interesting*: Her visit to the exhibition was given wide coverage in the newspapers, which published her replies to journalists' questions about the exhibition.

p. 442, *Arabazhin's book about Lev Nikolaevich*: K. Arabazhin, *L.N. Tolstoy (as Personality, Artist and Thinker). Public Lectures about Russian Writers*, St Petersburg, 1909.

p. 442, *the waltz and the poems*: Tolstoy's musical and poetic works were on display at the exhibition. Having familiarized herself with them, she made a few revisions, on the basis of which an article was written by "S.T." (probably Sergei Tolstoy), which said: "I: *Waltz ascribed to L.N. Tolstoy*. He himself played this waltz several times as his own composition. S.I. Taneev noted it down after hearing L.N. play it. II: *The refrain of a Sevastopol Song*. This is a somewhat variable refrain from an old gypsy song: 'I'm a young gypsy girl, but I'm clever, I can tell fortunes.' L.N. frequently played the accompaniment to this song, or he and another person would play melody and accompaniment arranged for four hands."

p. 442, *Speshnev the notary… Yasyana Polyana*: In the offices of Speshnev Sofia Tolstoy completed a deed of purchase to enable the City to buy the Khamovniki Street house. A commission was set up, headed by the architect A.A. Ostrogradsky, with responsibilities for taking over the house. In her letter to the Tsar, sent on 18th November and delivered by Bogdanov, she wrote: "If the Russian government does not buy Yasnaya Polyana, my sons, some of whom will be left in a greatly impoverished state, will be forced, with much anguish in their hearts, to sell it privately, either in separate plots of as a whole. The hearts of Lev Tolstoy's descendants and of the whole Russian people will grieve if the government does not defend the cradle and the grave of a man who has glorified the name of Russia to the entire world and who is so loved by his people and his country. Do not let Yasnaya Polyana perish by allowing it to be sold into private hands, rather than to the Russian government." The Tsar's response to this letter was: "I consider the purchase of Count Tolstoy's estate by the government entirely impermissible. It is for the Council of Ministers merely to discuss the extent of the pension to be allocated to his widow."

p. 444, *'The Forged Coupon'*: The story on which Tolstoy worked, off and on, from the end of the 1880s to February 1904.

1912

p. 446, *Tolstoy Museum… English guests*: The Tolstoy Museum was visited by members of a British group called the Interparliamentary Alliance.

p. 446, *thanking the Tsar for my pension*: Sofia Tolstoy was "graciously awarded a pension from the State Treasury of 10,000 rubles a year".

p. 447, *A large crowd of strangers unexpectedly arrived… them*: N.A. Sokolov later recalled: "I visited Sofia Andreevna at Yasnaya Polyana in 1912 over Easter. Three of us travelled from St Petersburg to see her. We were received immediately – to our great surprise, for we were quite unexpected, and were shown absolutely everything, to the very last corner of the house, given exhaustive explanations of almost every object, and told a lot about L.N. and S.A.'s life together."

p. 448, *an article about my sister-in-law Maria Nikolaevna*: Almost all the newspapers contained obituaries of Maria Nikolaevna Tolstaya and articles dedicated to the memory of Tolstoy's sister.

p. 448, *Maria Nikolaevna's… funeral*: Maria Nikolaevna Tolstaya's funeral was attended by two members of the Tolstoy family, Ilya and Andrei.

p. 448, *Wrote to Kasso, Minister of Education, about the manuscripts*: "I saw Kasso," she wrote to her sister on 28th April. "He refused to give me the manuscripts and instructed me to complain to the Senate about his refusal. His explanation was that he was afraid to take *sole* responsibility, and that it was the Senate and the judges who should settle the argument." On 12th May she received an official reply from Kasso: "I cannot agree to release the 12 boxes of L.N. Tolstoy's manuscripts, at present in the Historical Museum, in view of the argument that has arisen between you and Alexandra Tolstaya (Sasha) about the rights to the ownership of these manuscripts. Taking copies from the manuscripts and sorting them out may only be permitted with her consent."

p. 449, *Pascal's Pensées*: *Pensées de Pascal*, Paris, 1898 (Sofia Tolstoy's library, with margin notes).

p. 449, *Korotnyov brought an estimate for the forest... sale*: Sasha Tolstaya bought some Yasnaya Polyana land from her brothers to give to the peasants, in accordance with her father's wishes. Sofia acquired for herself the house, the grounds and the garden – about 170 acres in all.

p. 450, *Snegiryov's letter to me*: A letter of 10th April 1911, in which V.F. Snegiryov, a Professor of Medicine, expressed his opinion of Tolstoy's "flight" and shared his impressions of their family life. "There was not an hour, not a minute of your life when you were distracted from him," he wrote. "Your entire being was filled with him and his life. He had much to be grateful to you for."

p. 450, *a strange essay called 'Passion et l'amour'*: *Discours sur les passions de l'amour*, by B. Pascal.

p. 451, *her notes about our genealogy*: Tanya Kuzminskaya's memoirs, *My Life at Home and at Yasnaya Polyana. A History of the Behrs and Islenev Family Lines.*

p. 452, *a cinematographic lampoon about me*: A reference to the film *The Flight of a Great Old Man*, scenario by I. Teneromo, produced by A. Ya. Protazov; the role of Tolstoy was played by V.I. Shaternikov. The preview in St Petersburg was attended by Lyova Tolstoy and Tanya Kuzminskaya, who protested against its screening. Outraged responses to the film, which depicted the last days of Tolstoy's life in a distorted and disrespectful fashion, appeared also in the press. After Sofia's complaint the police department ordered all cinema proprietors to destroy the film.

p. 452, *complaint... Senate*: In this complaint against L.A. Kasso, Minister of Education, which she sent to the Senate, she disputed the actions of the Museum in forbidding her access to the manuscripts, and on the basis of existing civil laws and supplementary documents, she proved her right to them. Her application was discussed by the Senate on 3rd April.

p. 452, *cinematographic lampoon against me... Caucasus*: The film was banned everywhere.

p. 453, *a spiteful note by Chertkov in Speech*: Chertkov published an article called 'The Blessing of Love. L.N. Tolstoy's Attitude to his Fellow Men' with his own "Note", in which he again developed the idea that his "flight" was prompted merely by family circumstances. Stating that Tolstoy's article was written when he was "seriously ill", Chertkov explained that "this illness was the direct consequence of the shock he suffered from those spiritual crises which periodically attacked him in connection with the agonizingly painful conditions of his family life and the circumstances of his life in general". Further on Chertkov sought to prove Tolstoy was "on the point of leaving his family on several occasions" but stayed to "carry his cross".

p. 453, *Rod*: E. Rod, a French writer and author of novels and philosophical works in which Tolstoy was very interested. There are several of his novels, with dedications, in the Yasnaya Polyana library.

p. 453, *Today a young priest... requiem*: This priest, Grigory Lavrentevich Kalinovsky (he told his name to no one but Bulgakov), "announced that he didn't recognize the Synod's prohibition against praying for L.N., as he considered L.N. had brought nothing but good to people".

p. 454, *Pankratov's lying article about the priest's visit*: A. Pankratov's article condemned the funeral service at Tolstoy's grave, on the grounds that this appeared to accept Tolstoy back into the bosom of the Church which he did not recognize and from which he had been excommunicated. She responded with a letter justifying the priest's "selfless" action, since, in her words, Tolstoy "was distinguished by his supreme religious tolerance". The story of the service over Tolstoy's grave was given wide publicity by the press.

p. 454, *the Illustrated Anthology on War and Peace... censors*: On 20th December the Moscow Committee on Press Affairs placed a ban on the book, and the publishers were tried in court. The ban was subsequently lifted and the trial cut short.

1913

p. 455, *the Senate's decision... cowards*: Several newspapers published an announcement that in connection with the Senate's imminent discussion of her complaint to the Minister of Education, L.A. Kasso, the senators had already reviewed the question privately and had come to the conclusion that "The Senate had no right to enter into discussions as to the ownership of the material kept in the Historical Museum", and would only debate the issue of "the legality of the Museum's action in putting a ban on this property, without being granted special legal powers to do so".

p. 456, *numbered L.N.'s letters*: In the first edition of the book *Count L.N. Tolstoy's Letters to his Wife*, Moscow, 1913, she included 656 letters and seven notes.

p. 456, *the buying and selling of Yasnaya Polyana*: "The forest was sold on contract to the merchant Chesnokov," she wrote to her daughter Tanya on 28th February. "I have bought 400 acres of land from my sons – with the estate – for 150 thousand rubles, and have sold my own land to Sasha."

p. 457, *my sons' payment for the trees*: Tolstoy's sons had sold 300 acres of forest for felling.

p. 457, *Sasha's article... manuscripts*: A reference to Alexandra Tolstaya's *Explanation*, in which she invoked Tolstoy's will to reaffirm her exclusive rights to the disputed manuscripts, and urged that the Senate should not support Sofia Tolstoy's complaint.

p. 458, *the Circassian guard*: Osman, the old Circassian who guarded the house at Yasnaya Polyana between 1912 and 1913. He and his brother had been exiled from the Caucasus to Central Russia in their youth for participating in a bloody vendetta. Sofia petitioned for them to return to their native land.

p. 458, *I am writing to the newspapers about our badly behaved visitors*: Her letter in which she referred to the "unbecoming behaviour of the public visiting Yasnaya Polyana and the grave of Count Lev Nikolaevich", and announced she was allowing access to his grave and rooms "only once a week".

p. 459, *Sasha... lovely little place*: Sasha Tolstaya had sold Telyatinki and bought a small farm not far from Yasnaya Polyana called Novaya Polyana.

p. 459, *Landau's Moses*: Dr L.A. Landau, *Moses. An Analysis of His Psychological Life*. (In the series Psychiatric Analysis, issues 1, 2 and 3. Sofia Tolstoy's library.)

1914

p. 463, *The Chertkovs have been searched by the police*: Chertkov was searched when S.M. Belinky, who was living with him, was arrested and charged with distributing 5,000 copies of various works of Tolstoy's.

p. 464, *he should travel... giving lectures about his father*: Ilya Tolstoy visited Moscow, Nizhny Novgorod and various other towns, lecturing on "Personal Memories of My Father".

p. 465, *Tanya's book about Maria Montessori*: Tatyana Sukhotina, *Maria Montessori and the New Education*, Moscow, 1914; Sofia Tolstoy's library, with the dedication: "To dearest Mother, with the author's esteem. Kochety, April 1914".

p. 466, *newspapers... are full of Rasputin's murder*: On 28th June there was an attempt on the life of the Tsar's adviser, Rasputin, but he was not killed.

p. 467, *Nurse*: Anna Sukolyonova, the younger Tolstoy children's nurse.

p. 468, *Bulgakov read us his article protesting against the war*: Bulgakov's article 'On War' appealing to people to refuse to join the army, was distributed in hectographed and manuscript versions.

p. 468, *Misha has been taken prisoner in Milevič, in Bohemia*: M.I. Tolstoy, a cadet of the Tiflis military academy, enlisted in the Intermanland infantry regiment, went to the front and was taken prisoner. He tried twice to escape.

p. 469, *his leaflet against the war*: Bulgakov's appeal *Come to Your Senses, Brothers!* with a call to "love your enemies", was signed by twenty Tolstoyans, fellow thinkers of Bulgakov. Bulgakov also took part in copying and circulating the appeal.

p. 469, *wrote to Dzhunkovsky, Governor of Moscow*: There exists a rough draft of Sofia Tolstoy's letter of 29th October to the Minister of Internal Affairs, Dzhunkovsky: "Yesterday," she wrote, "police appeared in my house, 6 of them, as though to catch a criminal, and arrested and took off to prison Valentin Fyodorovich Bulgakov, who was living with me. The charge is the usual one of spreading harmful thoughts. I feel personally outraged that a police lieutenant-colonel should have demanded that I unlock bookcases belonging to me personally in the room where Bulgakov was staying, then searched them." In her letter she asked that Bulgakov be released on bail "on the recognizance of Sergei Lvovich" and herself, so that "work on the library could be finished."

p. 469, *a disagreeable telegram from Dzhunkovsky*: Dzhunkovsky's telegram of 3rd November read: "Bulgakov properly arrested in your house for circulating criminal appeals to population not to participate in war, and writing to them on your typewriter. Arrest and search could of course have been freely conducted by day, and I offer deep sympathy that you were disturbed at such an hour."

p. 470, *the gendarmes... police force*: Sergei Tolstoy was present during the police search in October, and, enraged by Lieutenant-Colonel Demidov's demand to search Tolstoy's bookcases, he said to him: "I would advise you to change your occupation and find another."

p. 470, *Makovitsky... police*: Makovitsky was arrested too for signing the appeal.

1915

p. 474, *Sienkiewicz... Quo Vadis*: The Polish writer, G. Sienkiewicz, *Kamo gryadeshi (Quo Vadis)*, 1896.

p. 474, *Dushan Petrovich Makovitsky has returned here from prison*: Makovitsky was released on the security of Tanya.

p. 474, *his play*: Probably the play *The Rocket*.

1916

p. 475, *film of the story 'What People Live for'*: The film of Tolstoy's story 'What People Live for' was produced by A.A. Khonzhenkov's film company. Ilya Tolstoy wrote the script, and directed and played the part of the gentleman; the angel was played by A. Vertinksy.

p. 476, *Tanya has left for the trial*: Tanya left for Moscow to appear as a witness in the trial of Bulgakov, Makovitsky and the other Tolstoyans.

p. 476, *I added my signature... Portugal*: She wrote this protest after a German submarine in the Black Sea sank the hospital ship *Portugal*, carrying wounded soldiers and officers.

p. 476, *all the Tolstoyans, apart from Seryozha Popov... acquitted*: From 21st to 28th March the case of the Tolstoyans who had signed Bulgakov's appeal was heard in the Moscow circuit court. Bulgakov, Makovitsky, Tregubov and others were acquitted. S. Popov, who was also accused of "inciting the military ranks to violate their obligations of service", was sentenced to a term in prison.

p. 477, *a new will*: On 9th August her new will was legally ratified by the notary, Kosyakov.

p. 478, *Ilya has just left for America with the same thing in mind*: Ilya Tolstoy left Petersburg for America on 2nd November. On this day he wrote to his mother: "I deeply regret that I was unable to visit Yasnaya to say goodbye before leaving, but I had so much to do, writing and translating my lectures."

p. 478, *a Tolstoy evening in Moscow... Tolstoy Museum*: Tanya helped to organize in the large auditorium of the Polytechnic Museum an evening in the memory of Tolstoy, at which she gave a lecture entitled 'On Popular Education and Tolstoy's Attitude to It'. Three Yasnaya Polyana peasants, coached by her, sang some of Tolstoy's favourite folk songs, and O.A. Ozarovskaya read excerpts from her memoirs *Tanya Tolstaya's Childhood at Yasnaya Polyana*. A third of the money collected was donated to the Society to Aid War Victims. On 7th November there was a musical evening in memory of Tolstoy at the Polytechnic Museum. Tanya wrote to her mother on 8th November: "We had the second Tolstoy concert yesterday. Everything went smoothly, I wouldn't say it was a brilliant success but it was quite satisfactory. A full house both evenings. Stakhovich spoke well yesterday, and actors from the Maly Theatre read *The Fruits of Enlightenment*. My memoirs, as predicted, were appropriate for the children's evening but not for the larger gathering."

Announcements for this evening had been placed in all the Moscow newspapers.

1917

p. 482, *Lev Nik.'s 'Our Revolution'*: The article 'The Meaning of the Russian Revolution' (1906).

p. 484, *the Early Morning newspaper... leaders*: The newspaper carried information about the July events in Petrograd, where the Provisional Government fired on peaceful demonstrations of workers, soldiers and sailors.

p. 486, *They brought 12 or 10 soldiers... all*: Peasants in the province of Tula, dissatisfied with the Provisional Government's agrarian policies, unleashed a great wave of lootings against aristocratic estates. Several young Yasnaya Polyana peasants and some soldiers recently returned from the front incited the people to loot Yasnaya Polyana. Those who disagreed with them informed Sofia Tolstoy. Her daughter Tanya informed the secretary of the commission of enquiry, E.D. Vysokomirny, about the situation, after which the Presidium of the Soviet of Workers' and Soldiers' Deputies dispatched soldiers there immediately to safeguard the estate. "After the October Revolution the protection of the house in Yasnaya Polyana where L.N. Tolstoy lived," announced the Military-Revolutionary Committee of the Commissariat for Internal Affairs, "was made the responsibility of a detachment of Red Guards, and all the property was registered."

p. 486, *my story about Vanechka*: 'Vanechka. A True Episode from His Life', a short story by Sofia Tolstoy included in her anthology *Skeleton Dolls*.

p. 487, *Sergeenko helps us to get the things we need... rice*: "Sergeenko has taken a lot of trouble for us and helped us a great deal," she wrote to Sergei Tolstoy on 12th November. "Thanks to him they are now selling us flour at Kosaya Gora. He raised some interest there in the defence of Yasnaya Polyana, and they are sending us 15 militiamen every night."

1918

p. 488, *Constituent Assembly... sailors*: The Constituent Assembly was dissolved on 6th January on the decision of the Executive Committee of the Bolshevik Party. The ministers Shingarev and Kokoshkin of the overthrown Provisional Government were assassinated by anarchist sailors.

p. 489, *Vysokomirny... soldiers*: Yasnaya Polyana was in an exceptional position compared to other aristocratic estates in Tula province. "The safety of this historic estate is guarded even more carefully at present," wrote Bulgakov. "The Tula political organizations are directly involved in the protection of Yasnaya Polyana, and have assigned a special permanent guard to the estate. The inhabitants are being helped with their provisions. A telephone has been installed there, linking Yasnaya Polyana with Tula and Moscow. The shadow of Lev Nikolaevich guards the estate and keeps it safe."

p. 489, *News that the Germans have seized St Petersburg*: These rumours were caused by the start of an Austro-German offensive against the centre of Russia.

p. 489, *They have refused me a pension... 800*: This decision was changed, and on the orders of the Soviet People's Commissars the pension was continued. The decision (30th March 1918) was taken at a meeting chaired by Lenin.

p. 490, *Some of our young peasants... land*: On 15th to 20th April the provincial meeting of land committees decided "to make L.N. Tolstoy's Yasnaya Polyana estate ineligible for reapportionment amongst the citizens of the adjacent hamlets, and to use it as a historical monument, purely for cultural and educational purposes". The peasants at first agreed with this decision, then decided the land should be taken and used for tillage. Several days later, however, the Yasnaya peasants went back on their decision, and delegates were sent to the estate with an apology.

p. 490, *Then the whole village arrived... times*: "A solemn event took place at Yasnaya Polyana: all the peasants from the village appeared at the estate, met Sofia Andreevna with festive greetings and asked her to accompany them to Lev Nikolaevich's grave. When they got there they all took off their caps, silently knelt on the ground and chanted 'Eternal Memory'. Then, having walked Sofia Andreevna home, they told her there would be no more misunderstandings and went back to the village. As they left they said they had decided to put up a monument to Lev Nikolaevich in the village."

p. 491, *I wrote a new will... her*: Sofia Tolstoy drew up a domestic spiritual will.

1919

p. 492, *Sergeenko sneaked in... alarmed*: Sergeenko's assumptions were without foundation. A children's home was to be built in Telyatinki.

p. 492, *asking them... Letters to His Wife*: Her request was inspired by the Commissariat of Education's decision to take stock of all the books on the market in view of the dearth of books in the country. All the publishing houses had to provide information about the editions sold and in stock. Her request was granted.

p. 493, *they want to raise a large loan... workers*: On 24th February the management committee of the Society appealed to the Soviet of People's Commissars for an extended loan in order to carry out various measures needed to turn Yasnaya Polyana into a state cultural and educational centre. The Soviet government assigned the money to carry out the projected changes.

p. 494, *I wrote a letter to be opened after my death... abandoning*: In this letter, enclosed in an envelope with the inscription "To be opened after my death", she wrote: "The circle of my life is closing, I am slowly dying, and to all those with whom I have lived, recently and in the past, I want to say farewell and forgive me.

"Farewell my dear children who I love so much, especially my daughter Tanya, whom I love more than anyone else on earth – I beg her to forgive me for all the pain I have caused her.

"Sasha too – forgive me for not giving you enough love, and thank you for your kindness to me in recent days.

"Forgive me, sister Tanya, for being unable, despite my unchanging love for you, to comfort you and make things a little easier for you when your life was so lonely and hard. I beg Kolya to forgive me for being unkind to him occasionally. Whatever may have happened, I should have realized how difficult life was, and been more charitable towards him. Forgive me, all you who have helped me throughout my life, and thank you for everything. And for you, my dearest, precious, beloved granddaughter Tanyushka, I have very special feelings. You have made my life so happy. Farewell, my darling! Be happy, I thank you for all your love and tenderness towards me. Do not forget your granny, who loves you so much. S. Tolstoy."

p. 495, *some Red Guards... Denikin*: The White General Denikin's offensive on the southern front, which started in July 1919, and the departure of the Red Army, put the central region of Russia in peril. The troops grouped in the village of Yasnaya Polyana had been quartered for military manoeuvres against the White army that was marching towards Moscow via Kursk and Tula.

p. 495, *Kursk... slaughtered*: The seizure of Kursk by Denikin's army was accompanied by terror and pogroms.

p. 496, *a letter to Davydov... 'Polikushka'*: In reply to a letter from Davydov, she wrote: "I cannot be sure exactly when Lev Nikolaevich had the idea of writing 'Polikushka', as this was before my marriage, but I remember he gave me the story to copy shortly after I had arrived in Yasnaya Polyana. He based the character of Polikushka on a Yasnaya servant."

p. 496, *battles near Yasnaya Polyana*: In October 1919 the Red Army won a series of victories over Denikin's army: Oryol was taken, and Voronezh, and the danger threatening Tula and Yasnaya Polyana was averted.

p. 496, *defend Yasnaya Polyana against looting*: On 13th June 1921, the Presidium of the All-Russian Central Executive Committee passed a resolution about the nationalization of Yasnaya Polyana, and it was declared "national property of the RSFSR". In the years of Soviet power Yasnaya Polyana was converted into a cultural and historical monument of national and international significance.

Appendices

L.N. Tolstoy's Marriage

p. 499, *Yasnaya Polyana… from Algeria*: Maria Tolstaya separated from her husband, Valerian Tolstoy, in 1857, then went abroad and spent the next two winters in Algeria; she returned to Russia from Switzerland in the summer of 1862.

p. 499, *Zaseka*: Zaseka was a huge strip of crown forest adjacent to Yasnaya Polyana, some four miles wide, running through the whole of Tula province. (In the sixteenth and seventeenth centuries the trees in this forest were chopped down to make barricades against the onslaught of the Tartars.)

p. 500, *a large vaulted room downstairs*: The "room under the vaults" had many different functions over the years. From the end of 1862 to 1864 it was Tolstoy's study, where he wrote the beginning of *War and Peace*; between 1864 and the 1880s it was the older children's nursery, then the Tolstoys' sons' room; between 1887 and 1902 it was Tolstoy's study again; and from 1902 onwards the Tolstoys' daughters lived here.

p. 500, *Dunyasha*: See note to p. 24.

p. 500, *Alexei Stepanovich*: Alexei Orekhov.

p. 501, *old Nikolai*: Nikolai Bannikov.

p. 502, *Krasnoe, which used to belong to my grandfather Islenev*: After the death of his first wife Sofia Kozlovskaya (in 1830), Islenev gambled away his Krasnoe estate at cards.

p. 503, *an endless annual succession of children*: Sofia Kozlovskaya had six children by Islenev.

p. 507, *he was very involved with his school work*: Tolstoy was actively involved in pedagogical work throughout 1859 to 1862. Twenty-one schools were opened in the district from the autumn of 1861 on, with him serving as arbitrator. Students banned from the universities were invited by Tolstoy to teach there, and he himself held classes for peasant children at Yasnaya Polyana.

p. 507, *a completely unwarranted search of Yasnaya Polyana*: Between the 6th and 7th of July, while Tolstoy was away in Samara province taking the fermented mare's milk cure, Yasnaya Polyana was searched on the orders of Dolgorukov, Chief of Police. They were looking for a secret printing press, banned works and so on, but found nothing incriminating. When he learnt about the search Tolstoy was extremely angry. "I keep telling myself," he wrote to his cousin Alexandra on 7th August 1862, "what a blessing it was I wasn't there. If I had I would certainly have been arrested – as a murderer."

In his letter to Alexander II (22nd August), Tolstoy wrote that he would like to know "who was to blame for what occurred" so "they could be if not punished, then at least publicly exposed as guilty". The letter was submitted by Tolstoy via S.A. Sheremetev, aide-de-camp to the Tsar. Dolgorukov's explanation for this business completely satisfied the Tsar.

p. 507, *She gave me her story to read... simplicity*: In young Sofia Behrs's story 'Natasha' there were two heroes, Dublitsky and Smirnov, and a heroine called Elena, who had two sisters, the elder called Zinaida and the younger Natalya. The story tells of the pure love between Elena and Smirnov and her attraction for Dublitsky, a man considerably older than she.

p. 508, *Je crains d'aimer le comte:* "I'm afraid I love the Count" (French). On 23rd August 1863, Tolstoy too made his first note in his diary about his feelings for Sofia Behrs: "I am afraid of myself – afraid it may be the desire for love, not love itself. I try to see only her weaknesses, but it won't go away." In a letter to Alexandra Tolstaya he humorously confessed: "Toothless old fool that I am, I have fallen in love."

p. 511, *Le comte m'a fait la proposition:* "The Count has proposed to me" (French).

p. 512, *C'est dommage que... étudié:* "It's a pity it wasn't Mlle Lise; she has studied so well" (French).

p. 512, *dormeuse:* Large sleeping carriage.

p. 513, *he wanted... the marriage:* Compare with this note in Tolstoy's diary: "Doubts about her love, and the thought that she has deceived herself. On the wedding day fear, distrust, the desire to run away."

p. 514, *his friend P.:* Mitrofan Polivanov.

Various Notes for Future Reference

p. 518, *L.N. has gone to Moscow to find a Russian tutor for the children:* In a letter to Fet of 1st–2nd September 1877, he wrote: "I have spent all this time hunting around trying to organize our teaching staff for the winter." In the autumn of 1877 the Tolstoys hired V.I. Alexeev to teach the children. "Vasily Ivanovich was the first teacher we had who genuinely wanted not only to teach us the usual subjects but to give us some sort of moral training too," wrote Sergei Tolstoy.

p. 518, *the war:* The Russo-Turkish War of 1877–78. Tolstoy suffered for the casualties borne by the Russian army in the early months of the war. "This war upsets and grieves me inexpressibly," he wrote to N.M. Nagornov in September 1877.

p. 518, *he visited the Optina Pustyn Monastery... life*: Tolstoy and Strakhov left for the Optyna Monastery on 25th July. On 26th July he talked to Father Ambrosius and the other monks and attended vespers in the monastery.

p. 518, *a letter to the Tsar*: Tolstoy's plan to write to Alexander II about the reasons for Russia's reverses in the war with Turkey, and about the general situation at home, was eventually dropped. Instead he began an article 'On Alexander II's Reign' which was never finished.

p. 519, *demonstrate the absolute necessity for religion*: Tolstoy wrote a dialogue called 'People Talking', then expounded his views on the relationship between faith and reason in the form of an article (under the same title), which remained uncompleted.

p. 520, *He has begun to study, translate and interpret the Gospels*: In March 1880 he started on a work entitled 'Collation and Translation of the Four Gospels', "an investigation of the teachings of Christ based not on interpretation but on what has come down to us from the teachings of Christ, words attributed to him and written in the Gospels; a translation of the four Gospels, brought together here as one". This work continued off and on until the summer of 1881. First edition, vols. 1–3, Geneva, 1892–94.

p. 521, *Bibikov... beautiful German woman... Anna Stepanovna... pleasant-looking*: Pirogova killed herself on 4th January 1872 (information in *Tula Provincial Herald*, 8th January 1872). In April of that year Bibikov married a "beautiful German woman", O.A. Firekel.

The Death of Vanechka

p. 527, *had published Vanechka's story in her magazine The Toy*: Vanechka's story 'The Dachshund Taks Who Was Saved', in the journal *The Toy*, in the section 'For Little Ones', no. 3, 1895. Sofia Tolstoy described how it came to be written: "One day, lying on the ottoman in the drawing room, he said to me: 'Maman, I'm bored, I want to write like Papa. I'll tell you a story and you write it down.' And he proceeded to dictate to me such a clever little story about his childish life."

p. 527, *Sonya is suffering as much as before... child*: She is quoting from two separate diary entries for 17th March: "Sonya is suffering as much as before, and is incapable of rising to a spiritual level. It must be that suffering is necessary for her and is doing its work within her. I feel sorry for her. But I believe it must be thus. It is necessary, so she may feel the hand of God and grow to know and love it." And: "I have thought about it recently. Sonya is suffering terribly. The reason is that she invested all her spiritual energies in her animal love for her little one: she put her soul into the child, in the desire to keep him alive. She wanted to keep herself alive with the child, not to destroy her life for the world or God, but for her child. It's very strange."

p. 528, *Lev Nikolaevich was very sweet to me then too*: In a letter of 27th March [1895], she wrote: "Lyovochka is being very kind to me. He takes me out for walks and has taken me to visit a political prisoner in jail. I find his kindness and affection very comforting, but it grieves me to see him becoming more and more old, bent and thin; he cries all the time, he never smiles and is never cheerful. He is terribly unhappy about Vanechka and cannot see me."

She is here referring to Tolstoy's visit to the Butyrki prison, on 22nd March, to see N. T. Izyumenko, who was deported to Siberia after refusing to do military service.

Index